Venezuela
Handbook

Alan Murphy

Latin America series editor: Ben Box

Footprint Handbooks

*"I was spurred on by an uncertain longing for
what is distant and unknown, for whatever
excited my fantasy: danger at sea, the desire
for adventures, to be transported from a boring
daily life to a marvellous work."*

Alexander von Humboldt, 1801

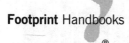

Footprint Handbooks ®

6 Riverside Court, Lower Bristol Road
Bath BA2 3DZ England
T 01225 469141 F 01225 469461
E mail handbooks@footprint.cix.co.uk

ISBN 1 900949 13 X   ISSN 1369-1430
CIP DATA: A catalogue record for this book is
available from the British Library

In North America, published by

PASSPORT BOOKS
NTC/Contemporary Publishing Group

4255 West Touhy Avenue, Lincolnwood
(Chicago), Illinois 60646-1975, USA
T 847 679 5500 F 847 679 2494
E mail NTCPUB2@AOL.COM

ISBN 0-8442-4947-5
Library of Congress Catalog Card
Number: 97-78490
Passport Books and colophon are registered
trademarks of NTC/Contemporary Publishing
Group, Inc.

©Footprint Handbooks Limited
May 1998

® Footprint Handbooks and the Footprint mark
are a registered trademark of Footprint
Handbooks Ltd

**Every effort has been made to ensure that
the facts in this Handbook are accurate.
However travellers should still obtain
advice from consulates, airlines etc about
current travel and visa requirements and
conditions before travelling. The editors
and publishers cannot accept responsibilty
for any loss, injury or inconvenience,
however caused.**

**Maps - the black and white text maps are
not intended to have any political
significance.**

Cover design by Newell and Sorrell;
photography by Robert Harding Picture Library
and South American Pictures.

Production: Design by Mytton Williams;
Typesetting by Jo Morgan, Ann Griffiths
and Alex Nott; Maps by Sebastian Ballard,
Kevin Feeney and Robert Lunn; Proofread by
Rod Gray and David Cotterell.

Printed and bound in Great Britain by
Clays Ltd., Bungay, Suffolk

Venezuela Handbook

South American Handbook, the longest running
guidebook in the English language, has provided
generations of travellers with comprehensive coverage
of the entire continent. This Handbook is in
Footprint's series of guides to the individual countries
of Latin America. Handbooks are now available to
Argentina, Bolivia, Brazil, Chile, Colombia, Cuba,
Ecuador & Galápagos and Peru. These will be followed
by guides to Mexico and Central America.

Contents

5 Rounding up

We try as hard as we can to make each Footprint Handbook as up-to-date and accurate as possible but, of course, things always change. Many people write to us with new information, amendments or simply comments. Please do get in touch. In return we will send you details of our special guidebook offer.

See page 356 for more information

Editors

Alan Murphy

The travel bug takes many forms, but the inspiration for Alan Murphy's first South American adventure came from an unlikely source – a popular children's TV series featuring a small, furry animal from South London named after Venezuela's greatest river. From the moment he first heard the name Orinoco, Alan was bitten. Years later, he abandoned a career in journalism in order to pursue his lifelong dream.

So began his affair with Venezuela. One that is happy, at times stormy and, like all long-distance relationships, one that brings periods of painful absence. It has even survived infidelity, with the publication of *Footprint Handbooks* on Peru, Ecuador and Bolivia. Now at last Alan is reunited with his 'childhood sweetheart'.

Ben Box

A doctorate in medieval Spanish and Portuguese studies provided few job prospects for Ben Box, but a fascination for all things Latin. He switched his attention to contemporary Iberian and Latin American affairs in 1980 when he became a freelance writer. While contributing regularly to national newspapers and learned tomes, he became increasingly involved with the *South American Handbook*, becoming editor in 1989. Since then he has edited the *Mexico & Central American* and the *Caribbean Islands Handbook* with Sarah Cameron. He is also series editor of Footprint's Latin America titles. To seek diversion from a household immersed in Latin America, Ben plays village cricket in summer and is discovering more about his corner of Suffolk with the help of the family's new dog.

The team

Editorial team

For substantial contributions to the text, the Editor would like to thank:

Dr Frances Osborn, resident in Cumaná, and regional correspondent for the *South American Handbook*. Frances rearched and updated the sections on Maracaibo, Puerto Ayaycucho, the state of Falcón, the entire east coast, from Higuerote to the Paría Peninsula and the northern part of the state of Monagas, as well as providing information on scuba diving courses and many maps.

Tom and Raquel Evenou and José Luis Troconis, all of Mérida, who provided updates on the state of Mérida and researched and wrote the sections on climbing and trekking, as well as the other sections in Adventure Tourism relating to the Andes. Tom and Raquel also provided many maps.

Specialist contributors

Peter Pollard – geology and landscape; Nigel Dunstone (University of Durham) – flora and fauna; Cecilia Fajardo-Hill – Venezuelan art; Sarah Cameron – the economy; Gavin Clark – literature; Nigel Gallop – music and dance; Mark Eckstein – responsible tourism; Dr David Snashall – health; Richard Robinson – worldwide radio; Ashley Rawlings – motorcycling; Hallam Murray – cycling; Gilberto Olívar (University of Trujillo) – baseball; Kathy Irwin – yachting and scuba diving.

Venezuela

VENEZUELA HAS a beautiful reputation. Over the past decade and a half it has produced a huge number of Miss World and Miss Universe winners. But Venezuela is not just a pretty face.

This was the first country in South America to be 'discovered' by Columbus. So overwhelmed was he that he described what he saw as "Paradise on Earth". And he wasn't talking about the pulchritude of the native population. He was referring to the country's seductive coastline – the longest in the Caribbean at over 2,500 km. That's an awful lot of dazzling, palm-fringed beaches; not to mention peaceful little fishing villages, colonial towns and hundreds of offshore islands and reefs where you can swim, fish, windsurf, snorkel or scuba dive to your heart's content.

At the heart of the country lie the llanos – or plains – a vast area of flat savannah the size of Italy. Other than the occasional cowboy, you'll scarcely see another human being here. What you will see instead is a greater number and variety of birds than almost anywhere else on Earth. As well as a list of exotic mammals and reptiles longer than anyone's arm.

Once you've enjoyed a close encounter of the animal kind, you should go west, up into the Andean mountains where you can hike, climb, go horseriding, hangliding, paragliding, white water rafting, ride on the longest cableway in the world, explore any number of ancient, timeless villages or simply stand back and gasp in wonder at the breathtaking beauty of it all.

East of the llanos, across the mighty Orinoco river, you enter the Guayana Highlands and step back in time. And I don't mean a few centuries. We're talking many millions of years. For this is the original Lost World: a strange, fascinating place of waterfalls and bizarre tabletop mountains (called locally *tepuy*) whose vertical cliffs rose up from the surrounding land two billion years ago, like islands lost in time. It was one of these mountains – Roraima – which inspired Arthur Conan Doyle and, later, Steven Spielberg, to imagine a land inhabited by dinosaurs. Plunging over the side of another tepuy is the highest waterfall in the world – Angel Falls – with a drop of nearly 1 km; twenty times higher than Niagara Falls.

If you're beginning to think that Venezuela has it all, then you'd be right. What's more, you don't need to spend a fortune to experience all this at first hand. Venezuela is now one of cheapest countries to visit in South America. So what are you waiting for? Just go.

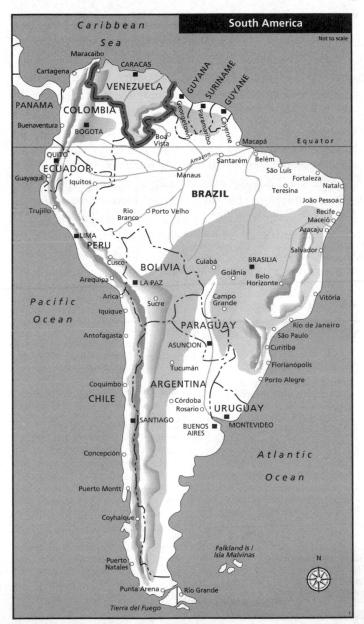

South America

Not to scale

Caribbean Sea

Maracaibo
Cartagena
CARACAS
VENEZUELA
PANAMA
COLOMBIA
Buenaventura
BOGOTÁ
GUYANA
SURINAME
Guyane
Georgetown
Paramaribo
Cayenne
Boa Vista
Macapá
Equator
QUITO
ECUADOR
Guayaquil
Iquitos
Trujillo
Amazon
Santarém
Belém
Manaus
São Luís
Fortaleza
Teresina
Natal
BRAZIL
Rio Branco
Porto Velho
João Pessoa
Recife
Maceió
Aracaju
LIMA
PERU
Cusco
BOLIVIA
Cuiabá
BRASILIA
Salvador
Arequipa
LA PAZ
Goiânia
Belo Horizonte
Arica
Iquique
Sucre
Campo Grande
Vitória
Antofagasta
PARAGUAY
Rio de Janeiro
São Paulo
ASUNCIÓN
Curitiba
Tucumán
Florianópolis
Porto Alegre
Coquimbo
CHILE
ARGENTINA
Córdoba
Rosario
URUGUAY
SANTIAGO
BUENOS AIRES
MONTEVIDEO
Concepción
Pacific Ocean
Atlantic Ocean
Puerto Montt
Coyhaique
Falkland Is / Isla Malvinas
N
Puerto Natales
Punta Arena
Río Grande
Tierra del Fuego

Where to go

Venzuela presents a real problem to those with limited time available. How on earth do you manage to cram at least 6 months' worth of sight-seeing into a few weeks, or even months. Getting around presents no real problems. Almost all of the places you'll want to visit are accessible by road or by air. The real headache comes with deciding what to leave out. For unless you do have unlimited time on your hands, you are, unfortunately, going to miss out on some very nice and very interesting places.

Here, then, follows a region-by-region whistle-stop tour of the main highlights.

PLACES TO VISIT

THE COAST

Venezuela boasts the longest coastline in the Caribbean with numerous picture-postcard palm-fringed beaches of white sand. The best of the beaches, and most accessible, are in the Mochima National Park, which also happens to be one of the best places for snorkelling or scuba diving. Further east, on the Paria Peninsula, are beaches of unrivalled beauty, but these take a while to reach, and once there, it would be a shame to have to leave in a hurry. Only a few hours west of Caracas are some lovely little beaches, which are ideal if you have a few days to spare before flying out. Further west is the very beautiful Morrocoy National Park, which should not be missed. North of Morrocoy is the lovely, historic town of Coro and the Paraguaná Peninsula, but if you're pushed for time and are looking for a classic Caribbean beach, then you could give this a miss.

Offshore lie hundreds of very beautiful islands. Many of these are part of the Mochima and Morrocoy National Parks and can be seen in a few days. The most popular destination in the country is Isla de Margarita, which is full of Miami-style beach resorts with prices to match, and definitely not for budget travellers.

THE ANDES

A visit to Mérida and the Sierra Nevada is a must. Even if you're not planning on doing any hiking or climbing, the trip is worth it for the breathtaking scenery. The city of Mérida is the main centre for exploring the Andes, and offers a huge selection of accommodation, places to eat and nightlife, all at great value. There are numerous tours available from Mérida, from climbing 5,000m-high mountains to visiting remote Andean villages. You could easily spend a couple of weeks in and around Mérida alone, but a week should give you enough time to enjoy some of the main sights and get a flavour of Andean life.

THE LLANOS

If you're visiting in the right season and have the time, this is one of the most memorable trips in Venezuela. The sheer variety and numbers of wildlife on view is truly astounding and will leave the average naturalist trembling with excitement. The cheapest way to see the llanos is as part of a tour from Mérida; these usually last 3 or 4 days and are fantastic value for money. Those with more cash to spare and who prefer a little more comfort can stay at one of the many huge

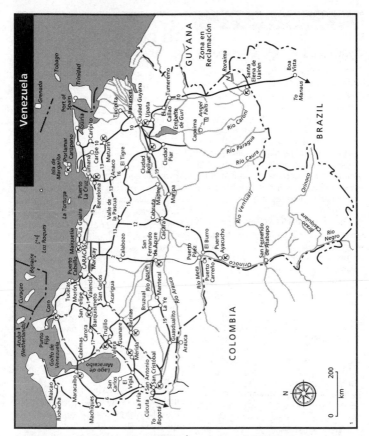

eco-tourism ranches as part of a package from Caracas or your home country with one of the specialized tour companies (see page 355).

SOUTH OF THE ORINOCO

The vast region south of the Orinoco, known as Guayana, contains some of the country's most popular destinations and its most precious jewels. You would need at least 2 weeks to do this justice, and that's not including the Amazon region or the Orinoco delta. Probably the main priority would be a flight over Angel Falls, which ought to be compulsory. Then a day at

Canaima lagoon. If you have more time to spare, a 4-day tour of the many table-top mountains and waterfalls of the stunningly beautiful Gran Sabana is highly recommended. After that, the more physically active could do the amamzing 6-day trek to the top of Mount Roraima, which is thought to be Conan Doyle's original 'Lost World'.

Other highlights in this part of Venezuela include spending a few days in the jungle from Puerto Ayaycucho, in the far southwest of the country, and a trip to the remote wilderness of the vast Orinoco delta.

ADVENTURE TOURISM

MOUNTAINEERING & TREKKING

When we talk of mountaineering and trekking in Venezuela, we are almost exclusively referring to the Andean mountains around Mérida and the excellent national parks. The **Sierra Nevada de Mérida**, in particular, and also the **Sierra de la Culata** offer many and varied possibilities for novices and experienced climbers and trekkers alike. There are, of course, other hiking trails throughout the country; these are detailed in the relevant sections in the main travelling text.

ADVICE AND INFORMATION

Hiking and backpacking should not be approached casually. Even if you only plan to be out a couple of hours you should have comfortable, safe footwear (which can cope with the wet) and a daypack to carry your sweater and waterproof (which must be more than showerproof). At high altitudes the difference in temperature between sun and shade is remarkable and the weather can deteriorate rapidly. The longer trips mentioned in this book require basic backpacking equipment. Essential items are: (list supplied by Andrew Dobbie of Swansea, who adds that it "is in no way finite"): **Clothing**: warm hat (wool or man-made fibre), thermal underwear, T-shirts/shirts, trousers (quick-drying and preferably windproof, never jeans), warm (wool or fleece) jumper/jacket (preferably two), gloves, waterproof jacket and over trousers (preferably Gore-Tex), shorts, walking boots and socks, change of footwear or flip-flops. **Camping Gear**: tent (capable of withstanding high winds), sleeping mat (closed cell – Karrimat – or inflatable – Thermarest), sleeping bag (3-season minimum rating), sleeping bag liner, stove and spare parts, fuel, matches and lighter, cooking and eating utensils, pan scrubber, survival bag. **Food**: very much personal preference but at least two days more supplies than you plan to use; tea, coffee, sugar, dried milk; porridge, dried fruit, honey; soup, pasta, rice, soya

(TVP); fresh fruit and vegetables; bread, cheese, crackers; biscuits, chocolate; salt, pepper, other herbs and spices, cooking oil. **Miscellaneous**: map and compass, torch and spare batteries, pen and notebook, Swiss army knife, sunglasses, sun cream, lip salve and insect repellent, first aid kit, water bottle, toiletries and towel.

When planning treks in the Andes you should be aware of the effects and dangers of acute mountain sickness, and cerebral and pulmonary oedema (see **Health**, page 361). These can be avoided by spending a few days acclimatizing to the altitude before starting your walk, and by climbing slowly. Otherwise there are fewer dangers than in most cities. Hikers have little to fear from the animal kingdom apart from insects (although it's best to avoid actually stepping on a snake), and robbery and assault are very rare. You are much more of a threat to the environment than vice versa. Leave no evidence of your passing; don't litter and don't give gratuitous presents of sweets or money to rural villagers. Respect their system of reciprocity; if they give you hospitality or food, then is the time to reciprocate with presents.

CLIMBING ROUTES

Pico Bolívar
This is Venezuela's highest peak, at 5,007m, and it attracts climbers from all over the world. There are various routes to the summit.

Ruta Weiss: in summer, between December and May, this route can be climbed without much technical difficulty and with rope, harness and climbing helmet (there can be problems with falling rocks). The main problem is the altitude. You should not attempt it alone or without a guide unless you are an experienced climber. From the base to the summit will take about 3½-5 hours. You can camp at the Pico Espejo station, at 4,757m and then descend 700m, or camp at Laguna de Timoncitos (4,600m), which is Bolívar's base camp.

There are other, more difficult, routes for professional climbers. **Ruta Sur Este**:

leave Laguna de Timoncitos very early and ascend through a narrow pass of earth and rocks to the crest of the mountain where you can make out the flank. The crest doesn't present any technical problems; some parts along the way are grade 3. You should reach the summit in 4 hours; up and down should take 7 hours. In the winter months of June-December, the mountain is covered in snow, so you'll need crampons and iceaxe and it becomes a technical climb.

North Flank: this is the most difficult climbing route, as it is across ice. Leaving Pico Espejo very early, you cross the base west of the mountain to the Nido de Aguilas, where the climb begins. You'll need crampons, ice axes, ice screws, helmet and rope. The climb is on a gradient of 60°, and 70° in places. After the glacier you come to a wall of rock, which you must climb to the summit. The descent is via the Ruta Weiss or the normal route. The whole route takes about 8-10 hours.

Pico Humboldt

This is the second highest mountain in Venezuela, at 4,944m. It's visited all year round, with its northeast and west faces being preferred by climbers for their extensive glaciers.

The climb starts from the entrance to the National Park at La Mucuy (2,000m). Take a *por puesto* from Mérida to Tabay, and a jeep from there to La Mucuy (see page 185). From the park entrance it's 4-5 hours up to Laguna Coromoto, a 7 km walk through Andean cloud forest. You can spend the night at Laguna Coromoto (3,200m). The next day you continue for 4-5 hours to Laguna Verde, at 3,800m, through the transition zone between cloud forest and *páramo*. You can camp here. **NB** Don't camp too near any streams, especially during the rainy season, and make sure you have a good tent.

The next day start out very early. The ascent, on the best-known route, on a gradient of 50°, is fairly easy. You need an ice axe, crampons, rope, sunglasses and a helmet (there have been accidents in past years). You can return to Mérida from the basecamp in one day, or you can continue for 6 hours, via Laguna Timoncitos, on a trail up to 4,600-4,800m. You need to be well acclimatized for this route, at the end of which you have the choice of climbing Pico Bolívar by the Ruta Weiss (see above), and from there to Loma Redonda *teleférico* station, via the Cresta del Gallo. We strongly advise a guide for this latter part, as there is no trail in certain places. During the winter months, you should be equipped as for winter climbing in Europe.

Pico El Toro

From the Loma Redonda station it is possible to climb Pico El Toro in 1 day. Views down to Mérida are even better than from Pico Espejo. People with little experience but in good physical condition can attempt it without a guide. Turn right on El Alto de la Cruz pass and traverse and climb gradually up over some fields of loose rocks. Come back the same way or head down for 5-6 hours to Los Nevados.

The following routes are only for experienced rock climbers: La Pared del Abanico (4,900m) is a rock wall 200m from base to top. Setting off from La Laguna de Timoncitos at the base, there are several interesting routes, with degrees of difficulty of 4-5. Of similar difficulty are the series of needles (*agujas*) that form the summit of Pico Bolívar. These are not particularly high, but present a sheer face. Another *aguja*, slightly less difficult (degree of difficulty 3, with some parts 4), is *Aguja la Reina*, which is near Laguna de Timoncitos, and takes 6 hours up and down. **Las Pirámides del Valle** are 25 minutes from Mérida, near the *Hotel Valle Grande*. This is a beautiful site where you can practice 'bouldering', at all levels of difficulty. The views are great, and it's an ideal place for a picnic. Take a *por puesto* heading for El Valle (from Calle 1 y Avenida 19), which drops you off 5 minutes away.

TREKKING ROUTES

Mérida to Barinas

This exceptionally rewarding hike takes you through two states, Mérida and Barinas, starting from Mucuchíes at 3,000m and ending on the southern slopes of the Sierra Nevada at about 400m. This little-known trek is one of the best because of the open *páramo*, magnificent cloud forest on the southern slopes of the Andes and the absence of people. Total walking time for each of the days is about 6-8 hours.

NB This is a rarely-used route and the local people have had little contact with tourists. You will need to show sensitivity towards those you might meet on the way. Also note that after day 2 you may come across snakes on the way, and there are no medical facilities.

Day 1: Early in the morning, take a *por puesto* to Mucuchíes (2,980m). From there try to hitch on the very beautiful secondary road to **Gavidia**: one of the best car trips in the Venezuelan Andes, with the spectacular small canyon and the Gavidia creek. Leaving Gavidia, you take a small road and walk to **Micarache** (3,500m, 1 hour). From here the scenery changes spectacularly from *páramo* to tropical moist forest.

Day 2: Head to **El Carrizal**, through a dense, well-preserved tropical forest, following some small valleys. On the way you cross a wonderful cloud forest with some amazing air bridges. This little paradise is part of the Sierra Nevada National Park. Finally you reach El Carrizal (1,400m), a small Andean village completely cut off from civilization; no road, no electricity, total population of 30 people. Coffee, avocado and oranges abound. You can camp or ask to sleep at a farmhouse.

Day 3: Head for another small village, **Alto La Aguada** (1,000m), crossing some beautiful rivers through sugar cane and coffee plantations and some remnants of cloud forest that are being changed quickly into pastures. From the village you can see all the way to the lowlands and the city of Barinas in the distance.

Day 4: You head for the southern slopes of the Sierra Nevada (400m), in Barinas State. You reach **Canaguá**, a small village where the non-paved road ends its climb uphill. You can try to negotiate a jeep to take you to the main highway (US$40-50 to cover the 22 km of very poor road).

There are several possibilities to cross the entire Andes. These treks are physically demanding and strenuous. Via El Carrizal (see above), via San Juan Bautista or via El Quino are 3 different ways of going down to the llanos. Via Pan de Azúcar takes you down to the Maracaibo basin. All of them are very beautiful and varied hikes taking you through many different climates and vegetations in 4 to 7 days.

Pico Pan de Azúcar

Opposite the Sierra Nevada is a parallel and slightly lower mountain chain called La Culata. Its high *páramos* are Piedras Blancas (4,762m), Tucani (4,400m), Pan de Azúcar (4,747m) and Los Conejos (about 4,200m). Many endangered species live here. The Condor has already vanished and the spectacled Frontino bear 'Tremarctos ornatus' may follow if not protected. The park is also known for its endemic flora, particularly the *'frailejón'* species. These range from small velvety plants to centuries-old trunks with tufted tops whose silhouettes reminded Spaniards of a procession of friars or *frailes*.

This highly recommended trek begins in Mérida with a *por puesto* to **La Culata**, at the end of the paved road. You then continue on foot to the base of the mountain, through valleys full of flowers and *frailejones*. You can camp beside the waterfall which is the source of the Río Mucujún, or at the foot of the mountain, which is about a 4-5 hours' walk from the end of the road. Climbing the mountain presents no technical difficulty, but you'll need to be in pretty good physical shape. The slopes are covered in sand which makes walking quite laborious. The ascent to the summit takes about 3-5 hours.

Once at the top, you can enjoy views across to Lake Maracaibo.

You should take a hat, gloves, a good rain jacket and good camping gear. The mountain can be climbed between June and September. During the winter months the summit is covered in snow. In the afternoons it gets very cloudy; you're advised to take a guide if you plan to spend more than one day here.

El Tisure

You can do this 2 or 3-day hike on your own quite easily. Take an early morning *por puesto* from the terminal in Mérida heading towards Apartaderos and get out at La Mucuchache, about 5 minutes after passing the stone Chapel of San Rafael de Mucuchíes. On your right side you will see a white cross and a small creek coming down. Follow the trail staying in the same valley and you will reach La Ventana pass (4,200m) after 3 to 5 hours. The last hundred metres to reach the pass are pretty tough, zigzaging steeply uphill. Walk down on the other side into the Potrero valley and further down you will get to a house where you can sleep. The chapel of El Tisure is about 20 minutes away from there. You will need 2 to 3 days for the hike; each way is about 5 to 8 hours' walk. Leave early to avoid bad weather and bring a tent, food and warm sleeping bags (see also page 187).

La Laguna de Santo Cristo

From Mucuchíes (2,723m), you walk to **Gavidia** (1 hour) or hitch. There's no transport from here, so you'll have to continue on foot or by mule. It's about a 4-5 hour trek up to the lake, and the route is fairly comfortable. You can camp by the lakeside. Once there, you should spend 2 or 3 hours just walking around and enjoying the magnificent scenery. The best time for this trek is December to April, since at other times there are frequent downpours.

Pico Mucuñuque

This is the highest peak in the Cordillera de Santo Domingo, at 4,672m. It's ideal for those who want to reach a relatively high summit with little difficulty; this mountain presents no technical problems. You start out from Laguna Mucubají and cross the valleys till you reach the foot of the mountain. From here, you can reach the summit in only 4-5 hours. From the summit, on a clear day, you can see right across the Sierra Nevada, to Barinas and north to La Teta de Niquitao.

Pico Espejo

It is a very testing 2-day trek to Pico Espejo, with a strong possibility of altitude sickness as the ascent is more than 2,000m. It is best done early in the morning (before 0830 ideally), before the clouds spoil the view, and from November to June. In summer the summit, with its statue to Nuestra Señora de las Nieves (Our Lady of the Snows, patron saint of mountaineers), is clouded and covered with snow and there is no view. It is a 1-day return to Mérida. **It is not recommended to attempt Pico Espejo alone; better to go with a guide as it is easy to get lost.** The glacier on Pico Bolívar can be seen clearly; so can Picos Humboldt and Bompland, forming the Corona, and to the east, on a clear day, the blue haze of the llanos.

A recommended hike from Pico Espejo, is to the cloud forest at La Mucuy (see **Climbing routes** above), 2-3 days walking at over 4,000m altitude, passing spectacular snow peaks and several lakes. A tent and a warm sleeping bag are essential, as is a good map (local guides may lend theirs to photocopy). Water supply en route is plentiful.

GENERAL INFORMATION

NB Shop around carefully when choosing guides; only use those that are legally registered, have good experience and reliable equipment. Even on the less demanding routes you will be in very remote areas and the mountains you will encounter here make the Matterhorn seem like a sand dune. Don't put your life in the hands of an inexperienced guide just to save a few dollars. Independent guides will have no insurance and often use unsatisfactory equipment.

You will find reputable climbing and trekking companies, and all answers to your questions, in Calle 24 at Plaza Las Heroínas in Mérida: recommended operators are *Bum Bum Tours*; *NatourA*; and *Guamanchi*. All three are in regular radio contact with guides on the mountains (see **Tour companies** in Mérida, page 179). If you don't have your own equipment, make sure you hire gear from a reputable company; *Guamanchi* and *NatourA* are recommended. For repairs of backpacks, clothing, tents, equipment etc, etc, you should see *Expedición Andina*,

Avenida Los Próceres Llanito Arriba, Sector El Caucho No 120, Mérida, T (074) 441710, run by Manuel Rebaque, highly recommended.

Those wishing to enter the National Park should get a permit from Inparques; either at their office in Mérida or their posts at La Mucuy or Laguna de Mucubají (the latter 2 are open Monday-Sunday); it costs US$0.30 per person per night. Younger trekkers need written permission from a representative and copy of that person's ID. They will not give a permit to solo hikers, so make sure you find somebody to go with you. The Inparques office in Mérida also sells a detailed topographical map which shows trails for trekking (this map is also for sale, at twice the price, at most tour agencies). For Inparques office in Caracas, see page 91.

There are specific camping areas in the Sierra Nevada National Park, at the administrative centre at La Mucuy (which is the starting point for Lagunas Verde and Coromoto and Pico Humboldt), where there is drinking water, toilets, a restaurant and car parking; it costs US$1 per tent. There are also camping areas near the Inparques station at Laguna Mucubají. If camping, remember that the area is between 3,500 and 4,200m so acclimatization is necessary as is warm clothing for night-time. (See **Altitude in Health Information**, page 361.) Some treks are very difficult so be sure to check with the tourist office before leaving. Water purification is also recommended.

The best time for climbing or trekking in the Andes is the dry season, from October to May, with clear days and freezing cold nights. The summer runs from December to May; the rains begin in June and continue until October or November, though there's always a chance that the weather will change from one day to the next. During the summer the days are clear and the nights very cold, with minimum temperatures of minus 10-15°C on the high peaks. August is the coldest month on the peaks.

The cheapest place to buy maps of the Sierra Nevada National Park is *La Fotocopiadora Los Andes*, on Calle 24 between Avenidas 6 and 7, beside the Inparques office, Mérida. You can also find copies at *Bum-Bum, Guamanchi, NatourA* or Inparques (at Calle 19, 9-44, between Avenidas 9 and 10, T 529876, open 0830-1230 and 1330-1700.

PARAGLIDING & HANGLIDING

Mérida is situated in a valley surrounded by high mountains. About one third of them are accessible over land or by cable car. Depending on the hour of the day there is always one spot from where you can fly and soar on the thermals. These places are:

La Trampa
A 45-minute drive west from Mérida. Thermal flights and probably the best place for a cross country. It is possible to fly all year round but the best months are from November to May.

La Aguada or Loma Redonda
Take the cablecar and go up to the third or fourth station respectively. Thermal or dereliction flights of some 25 minutes, with an altitude difference of some 2,000m. Excellent views of the city of Mérida. Also good for tandem flights. All year round flying.

Las Gonzales
A 40-minute drive west of Mérida. This is the best site for soaring and tandem flights in the late afternoon, which are best done with an experienced and skilled pilot. The price for tandem flights is around US$60 per flight and includes transport to the respective site. All year flying.

The Flight association is in charge of regulating pilots and prices for more safety. Recommended pilots are Gustavo Kleiss, Antonio Miranda and José García. Remember, no matter how experienced you are, always talk to a local pilot and ask about winds, thermals, sites, cables and landingspots before venturing out.

Courses
Most travel operators and agencies offer paragliding courses of 5 to 8 days. The approximate cost of those is around US$300 and includes a flying license. That

doesn't mean that you are able to fly! Make sure that all security features are taken (radio, parachutes, instructor that speaks your language, insurance etc). A recommended instructor and one of the best and safest pilots is Raul Penso (twice vice-champion of Venezuela); you can contact him through *Bum Bum Tours*. **NB** Beginners must recognize that this is a dangerous sport and conditions in Mérida (lots of wind and thermals) are much better suited to those with experience. Accidents are not uncommon.

RAFTING & KAYAKING

The best time for rafting is during the rainy season from May to November, and sometimes till December. On the southeastern slopes of the Sierra Nevada National Park, some 3 to 5 hours away from Mérida, you'll find unspoiled, virgin rivers flowing down to the flatlands. Here, the water temperature is very agreeable, with a temperature of around 30°C.

Bum Bum Tours offers 1-5 day rafting trips on different rivers of grades 2, 3 and 4 plus. You can even combine rafting or kayaking with their Llanos tour and some treks. They provide all necessary gear according to European safety standards (lifesavers, helmets, ropes etc.) and charge around US$50 per day all inclusive (or US$20-30 extra on their Llanos tour). During the dry season the boats are used for wildlife and fishing tours in the lower Llanos; floating down little siderivers and camping out in the bush. It costs around US$40 per person per day all inclusive; 4-10 days (see also page 217). *NatourA* also offers a rafting and fishing trip on the Río Paguey for US$20 extra on their Llanos tour.

HORSE RIDING

At the main tourist spots such as Pico El Aguila and Laguna Mucubají it is possible to rent the small *criollo* horses for a couple of hours. For those looking for more serious horseriding with healthy Quarter-mixed horses there is Hacienda El Vaho close to Santo Domingo and Finca Yegua Blanca close to Tabay. At both places they keep about 30 horses, offer years of experience and treks of 1 to 10 days to the cloudforest, *páramo*, lakes and the mountains. Expect to pay around US$40 per person per day, all inclusive (contact through *Bum Bum Tours*). It is also possible to rent horses in San José de Acequias (see page 200); ask in the village.

MOUNTAIN BIKING

The popularity of this sport has increased dramatically over the past years. Several operators rent out bikes for one or more days and explain to you where you can go and what to do on your own. Expect to pay US$10-25 for a day's biking (check brakes and gears before setting out); or US$35-70 for organized tours. Jají and its surroundings and the *páramo* are good places for 1 or 2 day options. For longer trips requiring more experience, the Pueblos del Sur offer a good challenge (see also page 200). *Tamanayre, Guamanchi, NatourA* and *Bum Bum Tours* offer bike rental and organized tours from Mérida.

San Juan de Lagunillas San Juan lies southwest from Mérida, in the direction of Ejido, at 1,100m. The first 2 km are on a paved road, then it's an ascent on a dirt track through fields of sugar cane and tomatoes. The next 6 km is a gradual climb on a 20% gradient, with the last 2 km of climbing on clay. At the top of the ascent you can see the route leading to the Pueblos del Sur and also feel the wind that blows; you'll need a good windcheater. Total distance: 30 km, 60% uphill, 30% downhill, 10% level.

Las Gonzales-Tierra Negra Head from Mérida southwards towards Ejido to Las Gonzales (1,400m). From there it's a climb on dirt tracks to Tierra Negra (1,900m), which is also used by paragliders in the afternoon. From Tierra Negra the route follows an ancient unpaved road that leads to the Pueblos del Sur. At the beginning, vegetation is sparse (mostly cactus), and after 6 km bushes and shrubs begin to appear. Total distance: 26 km; time 4-5½ hours; 60% uphill, 30% downhill, 10% level.

Pico El Aguila-Piñango

Take the bus to Pico Aguila. The route starts from there, at 4,000m, to the village of Piñango, at 2,500m. The ride is mainly through *páramo*, until it descends towards Piñango and more verdant countryside. It's a very easy day's ride and ideal preparation for another route which begins at Piñango (see below). Total distance: 45 km, 3-4 hours, 7% uphill, 8% downhill, 85% level, average temperature 5-7°C.

Piñango-Timotes

This is one of the most beautiful mountain biking routes in the Venezuelan Andes, and rarely travelled. On leaving Piñango there is a gradual but continuous ascent of 14 km up to the high *páramo* at 3,600m; then it's a steep descent all the way to Timotes. Total distance: 39 km, 5-7 hours, 32% uphill and level, 68% downhill.

Pico El Aguila-Mérida

This is a steep descent from 4,125m down to 1,650m, along the Transandean Highway, and runs through San Rafael, Mucuchíes and Tabay. Total distance: 68 km, 4-5 hours, 5% uphill, 85% level, 10% downhill.

Canoeing is possible on the road to Jají at La Chorrera de Las Gonzales. You'll need to bring your own equipment as nobody is yet offering it. There are many other nice waterfalls around Mérida; ask at the tour agencies for more information.

FISHING

Venezuela boasts some of the best sports fishing in the world today. Veteran international sports fishermen agree that the waters off the Caribbean coast hold more white and blue Marlin than perhaps anywhere else. Though deep sea fishing has been the focus of the country's international reputation, closer to shore there is other quarry, such as tarpon, barracuda, bonefish, ladyfish, snook, blue fish, kingfish, wahoo, jack crevalle, blue runner and yellowfin tuna. Among the best destinations for fishing trips are:

Macuto (see page 100), which is excellent for blue and white marlin, sailfish, dorado, wahoo and swordfish; there's plentiful accommodation near the marina and a choice of craft ranging from 33 foot Betrams to 45 foot Chris craft.

Río Chico (see page 232) is outstanding for tarpon and snook, either in Tacarigua National Park or offshore for giant tarpon up to 200 lbs.

Los Roques (see page 101) is Venezuela's bonefishing paradise. Small *penero* boats take anglers to the flats where bonefish up to 12 lbs are caught. It's not unusual to catch and release up to 10 fish in an outing.

Lake Camatagua is great for peacock bass fishing.

Fresh water fishing is also excellent in Venezuela. Fishing trips can be made to the Llanos (see under **Rafting** above) and the many lakes in the Sierra Nevada de Mérida offer great fishing for brown trout. The season runs from mid-March to September. As most lakes are within national parks you will need a permit from Inparques.

SCUBA DIVING

As you would expect of a country with the longest coastline in the Caribbean, scuba diving in Venezuela is wonderful, with some of its sites ranking right up there with the better-known and highly acclaimed Bonaire and the Cayman Islands. Venezuela also has the advantage of still being relatively unkown. The coast offers many and varied diving sites and, in addition to the underwater flora and fauna, you can explore sunken shipwrecks from the colonial era.

Large parts of the coastline are protected as marine-based national parks: **Los Roques** is an archipelago of over 300 tiny islands lying north of La Guaïra; **Morrocoy** is in the state of Falcón on the western coast; and **Mochima** lies between Puerto La Cruz and Cumaná on the eastern coast. As well as these national parks, there are hundreds of other potential sites, the best of which are found around the islands.

Note that diving here can be dangerous, if you don't take the correct precautions.

There are only two recompression chambers in Venezuela; one in Maracaibo and the other in La Guaïra. Divers, therefore, should already be quite experienced before they come, or take a course with a qualified instructor. Details of reputable and recommended instructors are given in the relevant sections in the text.

WEST OF CARACAS

Chichiriviche de la Costa is one of the closest dive sites to Caracas, about a 3½ hour drive away (see page 111). The rocky bottom along the sides of the bay gives a good glimpse of marine life such as lobsters and moray eels, while in the shallow bay there are octopus and sea horses. Visibility, though, can be limited by the sediment from the river.

Puerto Cabello lies further west, best approached from Valencia (see page 123). There's some good diving on the outlying islands of **Isla Larga** and **Isla del Sapo**, though the latter is better suited for snorkelling. The seas off Isla Larga are home to a sunken World War Two cargo ship, which is interesting to explore and you can see stingrays, sponges, barracuda, lobsters and crabs, as well as coral. Another good spot accessible from Puerto Cabello is **Los Aves**, which features a great variety of anenomes and a 17th century wreck (for experienced divers only).

Morrocoy National Park is reckoned to be the best place for beginners. The water is very clear, divers can only go down to around 30m, the bottom is sandy and the water temperatures are comfortable enough to render a wetsuit redundant. Because of the clarity of the water, snorkelling is also excellent here. You can spot angel fish, trumpet fish, needlefish and barracuda in water only 3m deep. All details of boat trips and courses available in Morrocoy can be found on page 127. **NB** The park suffered a serious dieback of coral in 1996 and the potential of diving has been greatly reduced. Beginners will still get good value for money, but there is not much on offer for more advanced divers.

EAST OF CARACAS

Near **Higuerote** (see page 230) lie Farallón Centinela and Faralloncito, which are no more than large rocks sticking out of the ocean, but the waters around them contain an impressive variety of flora and fauna. This area is located on the continental shelf, where the ocean bottom gradually drops to over 400m. Here you'll find sharks, grouper and large schools of barracuda and angelfish. Note that there are strong currents around here, and divers should be experienced.

Mochima National Park The islands lying off the coast at Puerto La Cruz and further east towards Cumaná offer some excellent deep-water diving. The currents are strong and the water is cold enough to make full body wetsuits essential. Divers will see the greatest variety of anenomes in the world, as well as dolphins and perhaps even the odd whale. The best time to visit is from July to November, when underwater visibility is at its best. For details of diving instructors and courses available in Mochima, see page 242.

Isla de Margarita There are several good sites around Margarita (see page 269). At **Farallón**, near Pampatar, there is an underwater religious statue and large brain coral, sea fans and large fish, including barracudas, at about 10-15m depth. **La Macura** is a large rock patch with holes in large boulders that are home to colourful parrot fish. **Los Frailes** are 8 small islands northeast of Margarita; they are ideal for current dives and boast a rich underwater life including morays, large barracudas and oysters. **Cubagua**, an island to the southeast of Margarita, has a sunken barge and ferry with cars still inside that have been underwater for over 14 years, and also have abundant fish and fauna. Other sites near Margarita are **La Blanquilla**, and **Los Testigos**, which is only about an hour away and is virgin diving territory.

Diving in Los Roques

The sites around Los Roques (and also **La Orchila**) are among the most difficult for diving, but for experienced divers, they present the very best diving in Venezuela, and are an absolute 'must'. The coral and marine life are abundant and very beautiful, and there are also several underwater caves. For details on travel to Los Roques and accommodation etc, see page 101.

Among the recommended sites in Los Roques are: **Boca del Medio** is an easy dive east of the island chain in clear and shallow waters 10m deep, with a great variety of coral, fauna and flora; **Piedra de la Guasa** is a 10-30m deep underwater cliff, where you can see a wide range of fish, including grouper, snapper, barracuda and horse-eye jack; **Olapa de Bavusqui** are caves where you can see sharks and a great many crustaceans; **Boca de Cote** has spectacular cliffs that drop to 60m with a wide range of fish and coral; **Cayo Sal** is an impressive site with vertical cliffs with caves filled with multi-coloured sponges and black coral formations; **Nordonqui** has a labyrinth of antler coral with a great many fish; **Dos Mosquices** has magnificent reefs and is the site of a biological research station that shelters a turtle breeding centre; **Nordisqui** has formations of coral stones and canals with a few shipwrecks.

Just north of Los Roques is another island, **La Tortuga**, which features a large underwater wall. **La Orchila** is very difficult to reach, since it is a Venezuelan military installation. Since few divers ever visit, the waters are teeming with fish and flora.

NB Because there is no compressor on Los Roques, divers must bring full tanks, unless they can bring their own compressors. This is not a problem for those coming by boat, but commercial airlines flying to Los Roques won't allow divers to board with full tanks.

How to go

WHEN TO GO

One of the main consideration for travellers is the weather. This varies from region to region. The Caribbean coast is very dry and rain is infrequent, especially in the states of Sucre, in the east and Falcón in the northwest. In Caracas, the climate is very agreeable, with the hottest months being July and August, and the coolest January and February.

South of the Orinoco, in the Gran Sabana and Canaima National Park, the dry season is from November to May. If you're planning on trekking to Roraima, the wettest months are July and August. The best time for a tour of the *llanos* is after the end of the May-November rainy season, when the many rivers and channels are still full and the humidity is not so unbearable. The lowlands of Maracaibo are very hot all year round, though the least hot months are July-September.

In the Andes weather conditions assume rather more significance, especially if you're climbing or trekking. See the **Adventure Tourism** section above for a detailed description of seasonal variations in and around Mérida. Generally speaking, the coldest and wettest months are August and September.

Another consideration is national holidays, as hotel and tour prices go up at these times, and many of the better hotels will be booked up. Local festivals are detailed in the general text, and a list of national holidays is given in **Information for travellers** (page 351).

HOW TO GET THERE

Venezuela is one of the easiest and cheapest countires to fly to from Europe and North America. British Airways, Iberia, Air France, Alitalia, KLM and TAP all fly to Caracas. In the US, American Airlines, United, Serivensa and LanChile fly from New York, Miami, Los Angeles, Chicago and Orlando. More details are given in **Information for travellers** (page 334).

Few nationalities require more than a valid passport to visit Venezuela. On entering, you will be given a tourist card, entitling you to 90 days stay in the country. Full details on entry requirements are given in **Information for travellers** (page 329).

PRACTICALITIES

MONEY

The currency is the bolívar, which has been subject to successive devaluations in recent years. Changing US dollars cash or travellers' cheques is not easy; most banks will not do this. The few that do are listed in the main travelling chapters. *Casas de cambio* (exchange houses) are a better bet, though their rates of exchange may not be very good. You're advised to make cash advances with a credit card, as this is the quickest and easiest way to obtain local currency, and the rates are much better. Many banks also have ATMs where you can withdraw money.

COMMUNICATIONS

Communications into and out of Venenzuela are generally good. International calls by phone or fax can be made in all major towns and cities and communication via the Internet is expanding.

The official language is Spanish. In the main tourist centres, people working in the tourism industry usually speak some English, but outside the main centres, tarvelling without some knowledge of Spanish would be a hindrance.

ONCE YOU ARE THERE

The vast majority of Venezuelans are very honest and friendly and will make you feel welcome, but the threat of crime is present in major cities, especially Caracas, which suffers from chronic urban deprivation. You should take the same precautions as you would in any large city in Europe or North America (see also under **Security** in Caracas, on page 89, and **Safety** in **Information for travellers**, on page 339).

People on the coast are generally very friendly, easy-going and gregarious and in Maracaibo people are, let's say, very open. In the *llanos* people are also open and friendly, and famously hospitable. Andean people may not be the friendliest and most open people in the world, but they are always polite and courteous, as well as being extremely honest and hard-working. Wherever you go, though, a smile, a friendly greeting and a few words in Spanish will go a long way to endearing you to the local people, and generally making your trip safer, easier and more enjoyable.

ACCOMMODATION AND EATING OUT

Tourists from Europe and North America, and even from some other South American countries, will find Venezuela good value for money. Though not as cheap as Ecuador or Bolivia, it is certainly a lot cheaper than neighbouring Brazil, and also better value than Argentina or Chile. Accommodation and eating out can be very cheap, if you're prepared to rough it a bit and have a strong stomach, but some parts of the country are relatively expensive. In general Isla de Margarita, Maracaibo and south of the Orinoco are the most expensive parts of the country, and the states of Mérida, Táchira, Lara and Trujillo are the cheapest. Also generally speaking, the more popular a place is, the more you'll have to pay, with the notable exception of Mérida, which is great value for money.

There are hotels and restaurants to suit every budget, and in Caracas there are some very high-class eating establishments of international renown. Away from the main towns, cities and tourist sites, you will have to sacrifice some creature comforts, but not necessarily standards of hygiene. Many of the hotels we recommend are not luxurious but conform to certain basic standards of cleanliness and are popular with travellers, which is often the best sign of an establishment's pedigree.

GETTING AROUND

How you choose to travel will depend on how much time you have available. If you only have a few weeks, then spending hours on a bus is obviously not advisable. Most places you will want to visit can be reached by air, and there are several domestic airlines serving the main tourist destinations and major cities. Air travel is not an expensive way to get around, and there's an air pass, which makes it a very economical proposition (see **Information for travellers**, page 342).

Venezuela has an extensive road network and a million and one bus companies will transport you anywhere at anytime. Bus travel is very cheap due to the fact that petrol (gasoline) costs practically nothing. This makes car hire an attractive option for many travellers with more time on their hands.

The most important things to know about bus travel is that buses (or *por*

puestos, which are like minibuses) always leave as soon as they are full, so it's a good idea to turn up about half an hour before departure time, even though this may mean that you then have to sit for an hour until the bus fills up. Another fact to bear in mind is that many Venezuelan bus drivers appear to be frustrated formula one racing drivers, so it's probably a good idea to try and sleep during the journey and arrive in blissful ignorance. Which brings us to the next important bus travel fact; sleeping is not always possible, due to the freezing temperatures on most long-distance buses. Drivers seem to have an obsessive-compulsive relationship with their air conditioning systems. All you can do is make sure you have enough warm clothing to avoid the dangers of frostbite (if you dare to suggest that the air conditioning is turned down a fraction you may be putting your life at risk). A final point to note is that many bus drivers have an aversion to stopping and picking up passengers with large, heavy-looking backpacks in out-of-the-way places. It might be a good idea to find out where the local people catch the bus, and wait with them. Oh, and another thing, ear plugs are probably a good idea, unless you like listening to kung-fu videos or ear-splitting music.

Full listings of bus times, destinations and prices are given under the relevant towns and cities in the main travelling chapters.

HEALTH

For anyone travelling overseas health is a key consideration. With sensible precautions the visitor to Venezuela should remain as healthy as at home. There are general rules to follow which should keep you in good health when travelling. (These are dealt in the full health section on pages 361-371).

KEEPING HEALTHY IN VENEZUELA

Water in all main towns is heavily chlorinated, so safe to drink, although most people drink bottled water. Medical attention is good and state health care is free (the Clínica Metropolitana in Caracas has been recommended). A doctor's consultation costs about US$10.

Inoculation against typhoid and yellow fever, and protection against malaria, is recommended for the Orinoco and other swampy or forest regions. Malaria tablets may be obtained in Caracas from Hospital Padre Machado (left-hand building as you face it), T 618211, no charge; or Ministerio de Sanidad y Asistencia Social (MSAS), Torre del Silencio (southwest corner of Plaza Caracas), División de Malariología, free, English spoken, yellow fever vaccinations also given, free (also at MSAS, 'La Pastora', Avenida Baralt 36, Caracas); also at Instituto de Malariología, Calle El Degredo y Avenida Roosevelt, T 631-1859/631-0208, open 0900-1200, 1330-1600; metro to Maternidad and taxi, US$4, not easy to find. Chloroquine (anti-malarial) is available, free; alternatively, bring malaria tablets with you. **NB** Protection against mosquito bites is required after an outbreak of dengue fever in 1995.

Some rivers are infected with bilharzia and in some areas there are warning signs; check before bathing. On the coast from Cumaná eastwards precautions against vampire bat bites are warranted since they can be rabies-carriers. Lights over hatches and windows are used by local fishermen to deter bats from entering boats and shore cabins. If bitten seek medical advice. When travelling to the mountainous areas, beware of altitude sickness. It is a good idea to acclimatize for a few days before embarking on mountain treks. Factor 15 sun-tan cream is widely available.

Horizons

GEOLOGY AND LANDSCAPE

Venezuela, 912,000 sq km in size, ranks sixth among the 10 principal republics of South America. It is a little smaller than Bolivia and 20% larger than Chile but exceeds both in population with 22.3 million inhabitants (in 1996). Venezuela has 2,800 km of Caribbean coastline and some 70 islands, although only Margarita is of significance. The country is bounded by Guyana to the east, Brazil to the south and Colombia to the southwest and west. There is an outstanding claim of 150,000 sq km of territory now located in northwest Guyana.

It is entirely within the tropics, stretching from 12N to within 100 km of the equator in the extreme south. Shortly after the Spaniards established their first permanent settlement on the South American continent at Cumaná, they explored the coast to the west and discovered Lake Maracaibo.

Structure

Geologically, Venezuela is South America in miniature. The continent consists of the ancient blocks of the South American Plate in the east, meeting the Pacific Plates to the west which are moving towards each other and thus 'creating' the Andes. Both systems are represented in Venezuela. Within the older continental blocks are three major tectonic basins, the Amazon, the Paraná and the Orinoco. Most of the Orinoco basin is in Venezuela and dominates the centre of the country.

It is to the north of the country, however, where the structure is the most complex. Geologists believe that between 150 and 125 million years ago the land mass known as Pangea broke up and the Americas began to 'float' away from Europe and Africa. It is presumed that prior to this, what is now the Caribbean Sea was an extension of the Mediterranean and in the course of time this expanded to separate the two halves of the Americas. During the Cretaceous period, around 100 million years ago, the Atlantic was undoubtedly connected to the Pacific Ocean, but by the end of the Cretaceous period, the Tertiary mountain building era had begun and the emergence of Central America sealed off the connection.

The continuation northeast from Colombia of the Andes defines much of the northern coastline of Venezuela and the continental shelf to the north includes all the island dependencies. The easterly Andean trend finishes with Trinidad but the arc of the Lesser Antilles continues the structure into the north Caribbean much as in the south, the Andes swing round to meet Antarctica.

In the south of Venezuela, the ancient mass of the South American Plate is known as the Guayana Shield or Highlands, which is one of the largest granite blocks in the world, dating from Pre-Cambrian times and at least 500 million years old.

The Lowlands of Maracaibo

The most westerly geographic region of Venezuela is the natural basin containing the Lago de Maracaibo, the largest lake in South America, covering about

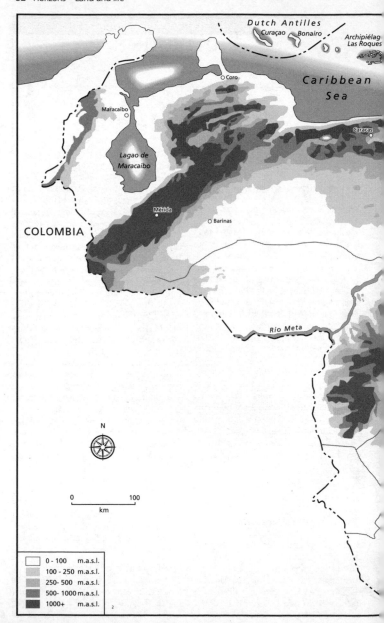

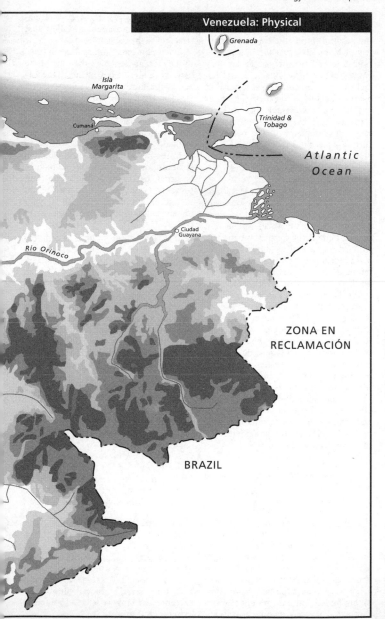

Venezuela: Physical

12,800 sq km. In the south, the water is fresh, fed by the considerable rainfall of this sector. It meets the sea north of the city of Maracaibo, first through a strait from 3 to 11 km wide and 55 km long crossed by the spectacular General Rafael Urdaneta bridge, then across a sand bar into the Gulf of Venezuela. The water has become increasingly brackish toward the north, even though the natural sand bar is only 4m to 10m below the surface suggesting that the high temperatures and low rainfall in this area contributes to the evaporation and hence the salinity of the water.

The main body of Lago de Maracaibo is about 155 km from north to south and 120 km wide and is enclosed on three sides by ranges of the Andes. To the west, the Sierra de Perijá forms the boundary with Colombia, to the south and east the main continuation of the Andes extends towards the coast near Caracas, and to the northeast, subsidiary ranges isolate the state of Falcón and the peninsular of Paraguaná from the rest of the country. In the south many rivers flow down to the lake through the thickest jungles of the country and create swamps on the lake shore. Further north there is a good deal of food cultivation serving the needs of the area, which since 1917, has been dominated by the oil producing fields on both sides of the lake and beneath its surface. Unusually, the oil is found in the Tertiary beds and again in the lower Cretaceous beds beneath, evidence of the long existence of the Maracaibo syncline basin.

The Andes

The Colombian Andes stretch north to the Sierra Nevada de Santa Marta and the Sierra Perijá which ends at the tip of the Peninsular de Guajira on the Caribbean shared by Colombia and Venezuela. From near the border town of Cúcuta, the main range runs northeast as the Sierra Nevada de Mérida with its highest peak, Pico Bolívar, 5,007m well above the permanent snowline. These are truly 'Alpine' type belt mountains, highly folded and metamorphosed with substantial Mesozioc volcanic intrusions.

To the northeast are the Segovia Highlands, a series of ridges and valleys that stretches to the coast at Coro.

The main mountain ranges continue to the east, are less high than the Sierra Nevada de Mérida but extend all the way across the north of the country, with a short break near Puerto La Cruz, to Punta Peñas on the tip of the Península de Paria opposite Trinidad. These mountains have a less violent geological history, and are formed of folded and faulted old rocks from the pre-Cretaceous eras. Although some authorities do not consider them to be strictly part of the Andean chain, their present elevation derives from the recent mountain-building epoch and their topographical connection with the Andes is clear.

In this section, known as the Cordillera de la Costa or the Central Highlands, there are several significant basins such as that enclosing the Lago de Valencia, near Venezuela's third city of the same name. At present, it has no outlet though as recently as 1900, it drained towards the Orinoco to the south. Due to deforestation of the surrounding land and mountains, the lake is now rapidly shrinking through sedimentation and evaporation in spite of receiving the inward flow of several rivers from a catchment area representing 0.5% of the country.

Another smaller basin within the cordillera is the 960m high valley of Caracas, the capital, which is overlooked by the highest mountains in this part of the country rising to Pico Naiguatá, at 2,765m. These Andes are not volcanically active except for hot springs here and there, but earthquakes, occasionally severe, are evidence of the unstable nature of these geologically young mountains.

The Llanos

Inland from the Andes and down to the border with Brazil in the southwest, are the great grasslands of the Río Orinoco, known as the *llanos*, which means 'plains'. This vast area of 570,000 sq km, the size of France or Texas, is indeed almost flat, exceeding 300m above sea level only on its extreme fringes.

About 40% of *los llanos* are in Colombia, the remainder in Venezuela, representing roughly one third of the country. It has been a vast cattle range since the 16th century and is second only to the *pampas* of Argentina for ranching in South America. However, the tropical climate with the more rapid leaching of the soils and the lack of mineral and organic nutrients makes this area less fertile than the plains of Argentina and there is virtually no scope for cereal production in any part of *los llanos* except where a determined effort to improve the land has been made eg the irrigated zone near the Guárico dam.

The Orinoco

Latin America's third largest river system, officially rises on the western slopes of the Sierra Parima, a range of the Guayana Highlands which forms the border with Brazil and flows entirely within Venezuela, 2,150 km to its Atlantic delta in the northeast of the country. Rainfall is heavy in the upper reaches of the river, particularly from May to October, and the water from its many tributaries flows rapidly to La Esmeralda, 50 km below which the river enters a level, marshy area and an interesting geographical anomaly.

It is here that the river divides, with a varying proportion of its waters continuing west as the Orinoco and the remainder southwest as the 'Brazo Casiquiare', a 250 km navigable waterway to the Rio Guainía and thence to the Rio Negro and the Amazon. It was the great explorer Alexander von Humboldt who first established and mapped this link between the Amazon and Orinoco rivers in 1801. It seems likely that this is the early stages of the 'river capture' of the headwaters of the Orinoco by the Amazon.

Below La Esmeralda, there are many significant rivers rising in the Andes which flow across the *llanos* to join the Orinoco. The longest tributary is the Guaviare, whose headwaters rise near Neiva in the Cordillera Oriental of the Colombian Andes, and flows over 1,000 km to join the Orinoco at San Fernando de Atabapo. This source is some 350 km further from

Alexander von Humboldt

the sea than the springs of the Sierra Parima. From San Fernando to Puerto Carreño/Puerto Paéz the river forms the frontier between Colombia and Venezuela by which time it has become navigable all the way to the ocean.

A further 200 km downstream the river makes a great bend to the east and is joined by the Rio Apure in a vast area of perennial swamps which make surface communication very difficult in the wet season. The remainder of the course of the river is through the *llanos* plains and the scattered remnants of low tablelands and outcrops such as those that create the 'narrows' of Ciudad Bolívar. 75 km before the beginning of the delta, the Orinoco is joined by the last major tributary, the Caroní which has a flow of about 5,000m per second and is coloured by the highly mineralized rocks through which it has come from the Guayana Highlands. Its union with the Orinoco is as spectacular as the Negro and the Amazon at Manaus in Brazil.

The Orinoco delta has 2 main channels, one north the other east, the latter the greater called the *boca grande*, and both some 150 km long. There are innumerable other channels and thousands of islands all covered with tropical rain forest. The total discharge of the Orinoco is over 20,000m per second which compares with 22,000m per second for the Paraná/Río de la Plata and 180,000m per second for the Amazon.

The Guayana Highlands

The most remote region of the country is the Guayana Highlands, south of the Orinoco and up to the borders with Brazil and Guyana. This area of ancient crystalline rocks partly covered with stratified alluvium is noted for huge precipitous granite blocks, known as *tepuys,* many of which have their own unique flora, of much interest to the naturalist. The most spectacular of these is Auyán-Tepuy between the Río Caroní and one of its tributaries, the Carrao. It is over 2,500m high towering above the surrounding valleys and includes the Angel Falls, at 979m the highest waterfall in the world. Another notable flat-topped mountain is Mount Roraima, 2,810m at the point where Brazil, Guyana and Venezuela meet and thought for many years to be the highest peak in Brazil. (It is now accepted that Pico de Neblina, 3,014m also on the border with Venezuela but south of the Brazo Casiquiare has that distinction). In all, the Guayana Highlands, which includes the upper Orinoco, represent almost half the country, but much of it remains virtually unexplored.

CLIMATE

As with its physical features, Venezuela has a wide range of differing climates within its territory. The major influences are the tropical latitude, the mountain ranges to the west and south, and the northeast and southeast Trade wind systems.

Temperatures are high in all the low lying territories and the highest average figures for the continent are found in the north of the Maracaibo basin. At altitude, the range of day/night temperatures can be greater than the normal midday range throughout the year though this can be distorted by storms that can happen anywhere. As with all high mountains, extremes of temperature are experienced daily in the Sierra Nevada de Mérida and it goes below freezing every night in the high Andes.

Rainfall patterns are distorted by the mountains east of the country and by the island chain at the east end of the Caribbean (Lesser Antilles). By drawing out the moisture from the prevailing northeast Trades, the immediate coastline of Venezuela has less precipitation than might be expected, but there is progressively more rain with altitude in the Andes backing the coast. This, in turn, reduces the precipitation on the interior plains of the country. Although the Caribbean is famed for its annual supply of hurricanes, they hardly ever touch the Venezuelan coast. The position is quite different in the south, however, where the super moist air brought up by the southeast Trades from the Amazon basin gives plenty of rain to the upper Orinoco area and to the southern part of the *llanos*, especially during the period May-October. Meanwhile, the extreme north tip of the country, the peninsular of Paraguaná, is virtually desert.

For more regional climatic variations, see under the relevant sections in the main travelling text. For more information on weather conditions in the Andes, see under **Mountaineering and Trekking** (page 19).

FLORA AND FAUNA

The neotropical realm is a land of superlatives, it contains the most extensive tropical rainforest in the world; the Amazon has by far the largest volume of any river in the world and the Andes are the longest uninterrupted mountain chain. The fauna and flora are to a large extent determined by the influence of those mountains and the great rivers, particularly the Amazon and Orinoco. In addition to a variety of rain forests there are huge expanses of open terrain, tree-covered savannahs and arid regions. It is this wide range of habitats which makes Venezuela one of the world's regions of

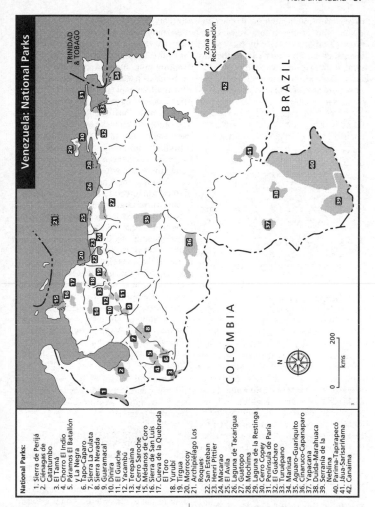

Venezuela: National Parks

National Parks:
1. Sierra de Perijá
2. Ciénagas de Catatumbo
3. El Tamá
4. Chorro El Indio
5. Páramos El Batallón y La Negra
6. Tapo-Caparo
7. Sierra La Culata
8. Sierra Nevada
9. Guaramacal
10. Dinira
11. El Guache
12. Yacambú
13. Terepaima
14. Cerro Saroche
15. Médanos de Coro
16. Sierra de San Luis
17. Cueva de la Quebrada El Toro
18. Yurubí
19. Tirgua
20. Morrocoy
21. Archipiélago Los Roques
22. San Esteban
23. Henri Pittier
24. Macarao
25. El Ávila
26. Laguna de Tacarigua
27. Guatopo
28. Mochima
29. Laguna de la Restinga
30. Cerro Copey
31. Península de Paria
32. El Guácharo
33. Turuépano
34. Mariusa
35. Aguaro-Guariquito
36. Cinaruco-Capanaparo
37. Yapacana
38. Duida-Marahuaca
39. Serranía de la Neblina
40. Parima-Tapirapecó
41. Jaua-Sarisariñama
42. Canaima

high biological diversity. It is estimated that over 60% of Venezuela's landcover remains in its original state – unaffected by agriculture, and with 10% protected as National Parks.

This diversity arises not only from the wide range of habitats available, but also from the history of the continent. South America has essentially been an island for some 70 million years joined only by a narrow isthmus to Central and North America. Land passage played a significant role in the gradual colonization of South America by species from the north. When the land-link closed these colonists evolved to a wide variety of forms free from the competitive pressures that prevailed elsewhere. When the land-bridge was re-established some 4 million years ago a new invasion of species took place from North America, adding to the diversity but also leading to numerous extinctions. Comparative stability has ensued since then and has guaranteed the survival of many primitive groups of mammals such as opossums. Due to the proximity of Venezuela to Central America the fauna shows some interesting biogeographic patterns. Some of the species found here are more common in Central and North America than South America.

Three major biogeographic zones can be distinguished: Caribbean coastal zone; Amazon/Orinoco basin; and the Venezuelan Andes. The Maracaibo basin shows faunal similarities with northern Colombia and Panama in Central America. The fauna assemblage in south-central Venezuela is typical of the upper Amazon basin of Brazil and Peru. The three *cordilleras* of the Andes are an effective barrier to dispersion in the west of the country.

The Caribbean coast

The Caribbean coastal region stretches over 2,500 km and there are many offshore islands – the most spectacular for wildlife are those of the Los Roques archipelago. Parts of the coast have fringing coral reefs and mangrove forests. Mangroves grow along the coast or in the river mouths where they tolerate brackish water. These highly specialized plants excrete salt and are supported on stilt roots which provide a haven for spawning fishes and their fry. Frigate birds, brown pelicans and masked and brown booby are found here along with myriad fishes. The crystal clear seas are excellent for diving. Almost desert conditions are found surrounding lake Maracaibo, and the Gulf of Venezuela is also extremely arid with a few well adapted endemic species of bats, opossums and rodents.

The Llanos

Northeast and north of the river Orinoco and extending almost to the coasts the lowland habitat is characterized by open grasslands, called *llanos*, wherein there are small islands of trees. Poor drainage leads to an alternation between standing water and extreme dessication. This has led to a large area being devoid of trees except for some species of palm, particularly *Mauritia*. Fire has been partly responsible for maintaining this habitat type. The *llanos* provides excellent viewing opportunities for herds of capybara – a sheep-sized rodent – snuffling peccary and wary brocket deer. Above 100m the *llanos* are replaced by predominantly dry forest with marked seasonal rainfall and a pronounced drought. Gallery forest persists only in the regions surrounding permanent rivers and streams.

River systems

The rivers draining the Andes are referred to as white-water (more frequently coffee coloured) because they contain a great deal of sediment. This is in contrast to the rivers that drain the Guayana shield which are referred to as black or clear waters. The forests in the vicinity of the black water rivers are of considerably lower productivity than those of Andean origin. Some of these rivers discharge into the Amazon, others into the Orinoco. The main input to the Orinoco derives from the Andes. The black rivers are quite acid and contain a lot of alkaloids and tannins leached from the leaves of forest trees. The forest trees that grow on these impoverished soils rely on a dense root mat and fungal associations. The low productivity means that they generally have low carrying capacity for animals.

The Amazon basin

The vast river basin of the Amazon is home to an immense variety of species. The environment has largely dictated their lifestyles. Life in or around rivers, lakes, swamps and forest depend on the ability to swim and climb; amphibious and tree-dwelling animals are common. Once the entire Amazon basin was a great inland sea and the river still contains mammals more typical of the coast, eg manatees and freshwater dolphins.

Lianas are plentiful, especially where there are natural clearings resulting from the death of old trees. These woody vines reach the tops of all but the tallest trees, tying them together and competing with them for space and light. Included here are the strangling figs, these start life as epiphytes, their seeds germinating after deposition by birds. Aerial roots develop which quickly grow down to the ground. These later envelop the trunk, killing the host and leaving the hollow 'trunk' of the strangler.

Flooded meadows are frequently found in the still-flowing reaches of the *várzea*. These vast carpets of floating water lilies, water lettuce and water hyacinth are home to the Amazonian manatee, a large herbivorous aquatic mammal which is the fresh-water relative of the marine dugong or sea cow of the Caribbean. Vast numbers of spectacled caiman populate the lakes feeding on the highly productive fish community. *Várzea* is a highly productive seasonally inundated forest found along the banks of the white-water rivers; it is very rich as a consequence of the huge amount of silt and nutrients washed out of the mountains and trapped by the massive buttress-rooted trees. This lake-land swamp forest is flooded for relatively short periods of time. One of the commonest trees of the *várzea*, the Pará rubber tree, is the source of latex.

In the lowland forests, many of the trees are buttress rooted, with flanges extending 3-4m up the trunk of the tree. Among the smaller trees stilt-like prop roots are also common. Frequently flowers are not well developed, and some emerge directly from the branches and even the trunk. This is possibly an adaptation for pollination by the profusion of bats, giving easier access than if they were obscured by leaves. In the canopy epiphytes are common and include bromeliads, orchids, ferns, mosses and lichens. Their nutrition is derived from mineral nutrients in the water and organic debris they collect often in specialized pitcher-like structures. Animals of the canopy have developed striking adaptations to enable them to exist in this green wilderness, for example, the prehensile tails of the opossums and many of the monkeys, and the peculiar development of the claws of the sloth.

The daily temperature varies little during the year with a high of 23-32°C falling slightly to 20-26°C overnight. This lowland region receives some 2m of rainfall per year, most of it falling from November to April. The rest of the year is sufficiently dry, at least in the lowland areas to inhibit the growth of epiphytes and orchids which were so characteristic of the highland areas. For a week or two in the rainy season the rivers flood the forest. The zone immediately surrounding this seasonally flooded forest is referred to as *terre firme* forest.

Many of the bird species which creep around in the understorey are drab coloured eg tinamou and cotingas, but have loud, clear calls. Scuttling around in the understorey are armadillos, rarely seen their presence is demonstrated by burrows. Pock-marked areas may be indicative of the foraging activities of pacas or peccaries, where their populations have not been exploited by over-hunting.

Cloud forests

Mountain rainforests range upwards from about 900m. The forest structure changes, the canopy is lower with more typical spherical crowns, and increased branching. The trunks of the trees are less buttressed and considerably more crooked. The permanent moisture provided by the cloud and fog allows for a prolific growth of epiphytic mosses and ferns. The humidity in the cloud forests stimulates the growth of a vast variety of plants particularly mosses and lichens.

The cloud forests of South America are found in a narrow strip that runs along the eastern slopes of the spine of the Andes from Colombia, through Ecuador and into Peru. It is these dense, often impenetrable, forests clothing the steep slopes that are important in protecting the headwaters of all the streams and rivers that cascade from the Andes to form the mighty Amazon as it begins its slothful 8,000 km journey to the sea. A verdant kingdom of dripping epiphytic mosses, lichens, ferns and orchids which grow in profusion despite the plummeting overnight temperatures.

The high humidity resulting from the 2m of rain that can fall in a year is responsible for the maintenance of the forest and it accumulates in puddles and leaks from the ground in a constant trickle that combines to form a multitude of icy, crystal-clear tumbling streams that cascade over precipitous waterfalls.

The Andes

At higher altitudes, this so-called cloud-forest grades into elfin forest. Here the trees are even lower, branching close to the ground and often misshapen due to pruning by the wind. The treacherous ground layer is made up of a fragile decomposing lattice of broken branches covered by a thin layer of mosses. Fuschias, bromeliads and orchids are common.

Above this, at 2,500m to 3,000m the elfin forest gives way to *páramo* – a vast area of open grasslands with small pockets of cloud forest mainly *Polylepis* in sheltered ravines. Giant groundsels and *Puya* are characteristic plants, and there are tangled thickets of bamboo. Mountain tapir and spectacled bear are the typical mammals of this zone, but are now extremely rare.

History

CONQUEST AND COLONIAL RULE

Venezuela was the first of Spain's New World colonies to be explored. On his third voyage to America, in 1498, Columbus first set foot on the continent, somewhere in the south of the Pária peninsula, then explored the delta region of the Orinoco and the coast of the Pária peninsula. The following year, another expedition headed by Amerigo Vespucci and Alonso de Ojeda, covered the same route, then sailed along the northern coast to Lake Maracaibo. Here, the lakeside dwellings built on stilts in the shallow waters were sarcastically compared to a miniature Venice, giving the country the name 'Little Venice', or Venezuela.

Though the first to be 'discovered', Venezuela was the last to be conquered and developed. The new colony was held in low regard by the Spaniards, due to the considerable environmental barriers to effective colonization and also the lure of other regions such as Mexico and Peru, which were wealthier in both human and material resources.

Spanish missionary under attack by Indians

Colonial society

Venezuelan society during the colonial period was a caste system. Status was determined by colour, position and wealth. At the top of the hierarchy were the whites, who constituted about 15% of the total population. A small minority of royal bureaucrats and Spanish clergy enjoyed the most prestige, but the creoles, the descendents of the conquistadors, owned the land and dominated local politics.

Racial interbreeding was so prevalent from the very beginning of the colonial period that by the end over half the population were *pardos*, of mixed race. Like all non-white groups, the *pardos* were excluded from wealth, political influence or social prestige. They lived mostly in the cities and the *llanos*.

The indigenous peoples occupied the interior of the country, but their numbers were severely reduced by racial interbreeding and labour exploitation. At the end of the 18th century they accounted for less than 10% of the total population. The numbers of blacks increased, following their initial introduction in the early 17th century to work as slaves on the coastal plantations. By the end of the 18th century they made up 20% of the population.

Compared to the Incas, or the Chibchas of neighbouring Colombia, the indigenous people of Venezuela were primitive. The most advanced groups were the farming tribes of the Andes and the northeast coast. Most backward were the nomadic hunting and fishing tribes of Lake Maracaibo and the *llanos*. In the central coastal region were both nomadic and agricultural groups. Many of these tribes were cannibalistic and most of them warlike.

For the first half of the 16th century, Spanish interest was confined to the exploitation of pearls, gold and slaves on the northeast coast and off the adjacent islands, such as Cubagua and Margarita. A few small settlements were founded, such as Cumaná, but these were abandoned as soon as profits dwindled and local indigenous resistance grew too fierce.

In 1528, interest moved to the western part of the country, when Charles V mortgaged the whole colony to the German banking house of Welser. After two decades in hopeless search for El Dorado, the enterprise collapsed and Venezuela returned once more to Spanish control.

During the second half of the 16th century, subjugation of the indigenous peoples proved slow and difficult. Separate wars had to be waged against every scattered tribe and, as a low-priority colony,

Venezuela could not secure royal troops. Geographical obstacles added to these problems. But the Spanish persevered.

By 1545 the only settlement of note was Coro, but by the end of the century there were 20 towns dotted around the Caribbean coast and the Andes, and these regions were effectively occupied by Spanish farmers. Caracas, founded in 1567, was the most prosperous city and province. Conquest was far from complete by the end of the 16th century, however. The *llanos* and Maracaibo basin were still inhabited by nomadic tribes.

The colonial government and administration was characterized by factionalism and decentralization. The colony was, during this period, generally under the rule of more important neighbouring areas, such as the Audiencia of Santo Domingo during the 16th and 17th centuries and, in the 18th century, the Viceroyalty of Bogotá. Neither, however, exercised any real control over the remote government in Caracas. By the same token, Caracas did not exercise much influence over the other 6 provinces. These were ruled by their own *cabildos* (municipal councils) which, throughout the colonial period, successfully resisted any attempts to bring them under the control of a central authority.

The colonial economy

As a relatively isolated colony, Venezuela developed a diversified, self-sufficient economy during the colonial period. The first colonists produced their own staple foods such as maize, beans, wheat and beef. By the end of the 16th century the country began to grow highly valued tropical crops such as tobacco, sugar, cocoa and indigo. And by the early 17th century it was actually exporting cattle hides.

Such potentially lucrative trade, however, was initially exploited not by Spain but by its European competitors, despite being illegal. English and French privateers and smugglers were regularly using Venezuelan ports by the end of the 16th century. At the turn of the century Dutch merchant fleets began exploiting the salt pans on the northeast coast and soon after began supplying black slaves in exchange for cacao and tobacco.

During the 18th century Spain attempted to exert control over Venezuela's trade. To this end they set up a monopoly trading company, the Real Compañía Guipuzcoana (better know as the Caracas Company), in 1728. The Basque company was granted not just economic control but also political power over the country. For half a century the company was successful in limiting foreign competition, developing cacao, cotton and hide production for export, and encouraging domestic manufacturing.

Success, though, came at the expense of the Venezuelan people. Widespread dissatisfaction and resistance forced relaxation of the monopoly in 1781, and a few years later the Caracas Company disappeared. From then until the end of the colonial period, illegal non-Spanish traders prospered once more. The colonists also profited from their new-found commercial freedom.

THE STRUGGLE FOR INDEPENDENCE

Venezuela may have played a minor role during Spanish colonial rule in Latin America, but it was the catalyst for the whole independence movement in South America. The spirit of liberty had long thrived in the *cabildos* and the creoles who dominated these local governing bodies bitterly resisted Spain's efforts to tighten her political grip on the colony in the late 18th century. The antagonism between the creoles and the Spanish colonial officials probably contributed more than anything else to the break with Spain, but the principal cause of the independence movement was the conquest of the Iberian peninsula by Napoleon Bonaparte in 1808-10. The creoles took the opportunity to assume control themselves. In 1810 the creoles of Caracas deposed the Spanish governor, and were followed by the other six provinces, who then set up a governing junta. On 5 July 1811 they declared Venezuela independent and began drawing up a new constitution for the new nation. However, this first move towards independence was not supported by the majority *pardo* class. They viewed with suspicion the transfer of political power to the already dominant creole class. As a result, except in Caracas, the *pardos* fought on the side of the royalists until late into the war.

The initial revolutionary activities were dominated by Francisco de Miranda, the main precursor of the Spanish American

Francisco de Miranda

Bolívar's foreign legions

Although Simón Bolívar's wars of independence were a stirring instance of the New World asserting itself, his success in liberating Venezuela owed much to the presence of troops from Europe. As was the case in the American Revolution, foreigners contributed both military know-how and world prestige to Bolívar's cause.

In his army were Irishmen and Englishmen who had left home because of economic depression, German veterans of the Napoleonic wars, Spaniards who opposed their king, and also French, Italian and Polish officers. Included were the nephews of Joseph Bonaparte, former king of Naples and Spain, and Tadeusz Kosciusko, the champion of Polish independence, as well as the son of Daniel O'Connell, "Libertaor of Ireland". In total, more than 4,000 foreign soldiers joined Bolivar between 1817 and 1819.

independence movement (see page 107). But even this brilliant young creole could not prevent the fall of the first republic, less than 10 months after the declaration of independence, in the face of growing royalist opposition. The patriot demise was hastened by a massive earthquake on 26 March 1812, which razed the patriot cities to the ground but left the royalist strongholds untouched. This was, of course, seized on by the clergy as proof of divine disapproval of the rebellion against the Spanish crown.

With the collapse of the first republic, the leadership of the patriots passed to Simón Bolívar, a young man destined to become the father of Venezuela. He had fled to Colombia after defeat, but returned in 1813 at the head of an invading expedition, declaring a 'war to the death' with the Spanish and their supporters. By August of that year, his victorious army had reached Caracas, where he was proclaimed Libertador of his country.

But complete liberation was still a long way off. The Spanish forces were still strong on the coast and the *pardos* of the *llanos* had not yet been converted to the patriot cause. The royalists had won them over with promises of racial equality and war profits. In less than a year, Bolívar and his patriots were driven from the capital. So the second republic fell in 1814, as suddenly as the first.

In exile once more, Bolívar realized he would need the support of the majority of the *pardos*, as well as foreign help, as Spain

was no longer occupied in Europe. In December 1816 he launched yet another campaign, this time from the northeast. Soon after, the same fierce *llanero* plainsmen who had chased Bolívar from Caracas in 1814, turned on their leader Boves and on Spain. Under a new leader, José Antonio Páez, they raised the flag of freedom in their headquarters, the isolated city of Angostura on the Orinoco river (now appropriately renamed Ciudad Bolívar). Here also, the much sought after European aid began to flow in. By mid-1819 the Liberator was ready to resume the offensive. By August his army had climbed over the Andes and freed Colombia. The way was now clear for the final conquest of Venezuela.

In June 1821 Spanish resitance was decisively broken at the Battle of Carabobo. Venezuela was free, but at a considerable cost. She had suffered more than any other Latin American country. During 11 years of warfare the country had lost one quarter of its population and the economy was left in ruins.

It would be another 9 years before a truly independent status was achieved.

INDEPENDENCE AND AFTER

Immediately after the Battle of Carabobo, Venezuelan and Colombian delegates met at Cucutá to arrange for the joining of their territories into a single nation, an idea which had first been conceived by Bolívar several years previously. This Cucutá Congress proclaimed the formal unification of

Simón Bolívar – Liberator

👣 There isn't a Venezuelan village or town worth its salt that doesn't have a Plaza Bolívar at its centre. Simón Bolívar is so revered in Latin America in general and in Venezuela in particular that streets, currencies and even a country have been named after him.

Bolívar was largely responsible for the liberation from Spanish colonial rule of an area of land of about 5 million sq km and which now comprises modern Venezuela, Colombia, Panama, Ecuador, Peru and Bolivia. Yet this man died virtually alone and penniless, in a room on a Spaniard's farm near Colombia's Caribbean coast on his way to a self-enforced exile in Europe.

Simón Bolívar was born on 24 July 1783. He was by birth part of the *gran cacao*, the richest white land-owning families of colonial Caracas, although he did show a hint of Afro-Caribbean ancestry in his dark complexion. He obviously enjoyed the privileges of the *criollo* class but was acutely aware that neither he nor the poorest of slaves were completely free. In the colonial Venezuela, *criollos* were still barred from public office and trade and it was their cause he initially championed. He was one of the first landowners to propose manumission, if only to gain more widespread backing for independence.

Bolívar was educated privately in Caracas and Europe, where he read the works of Hobbes, Locke and the Enlightenment *philosophes* and he was clearly influenced by the American and French revolutions. On one of his travels to Europe – embarked upon largely to try and relieve the despair he felt following the death of his wife, María Theresa – he met the famous explorer and scientist, Alexander von Humboldt who believed that South America was ripe for independence but lacked the person to bring it about.

For the last 20 years of his life he struggled ceaselessly to remove Spanish rule from South America. On one campaign he marched his army from its base in Angostura through the malarial and yellow-fever-infested swamps and rivers of the *llanos* up into the bitterly cold *páramo* to liberate Colombia.

He was not a tall man, at only 5 feet 6 inches. The Spanish General Pablo Morillo was amazed that the 'little man on a mule' who had come to sign a peace treaty with the Spanish in 1820 after the decisive battle of Boyacá, was Simón Bolívar. As well as being a great soldier and thinker, he was known to swear like a trooper and would enjoy a good ball or fiesta. He was also renowned as being a passionate lover who had a number of stormy relationships, the most important being that with Manuelita Sáenz, an Ecuadorian who saved him from one of several assassination attempts. This side of the liberator is brilliantly depicted in Gabriel Garcia's novel *The General in his Labyrinth*.

Bolívar achieved his goal but failed in his desire to unite Venezuela, Colombia and Ecuador into a single independent nation: 'Gran Colombia'. Many of his former allies, particularly the *llanero* José Antonio Páez and General Francisco de Paula Santander, who later became presidents of Venezuela and Colombia respectively, turned against him. But what finally broke him was the murder of his closest friend and best general, José Antonio Sucre.

In 1830, weary of the bitter rivalries between *caudillos* who had carved up South America for their own ends, Bolívar lamented: "America is ungovernable. Those who serve the revolution, plough the sea. The only thing to do in America is to emigrate." He was trying to do just that when he died of tuberculosis, aged only 47 on his way to take a boat to Europe.

Simón Bolívar on a Bank Note

the two countries and thus formed the new Republic of Gran Colombia. A Constitution was drawn up, Bogotá was to be the new capital and plans were made to incorporate Ecuador, once it was liberated, and Bolívar was elected president.

However, as soon as the Liberator set off on his quest to liberate Ecuador, Peru and Bolivia, the deep-seated separatist tendencies in Venezuela became apparent. They did not want to be subordinate to a central government in Colombia and General Páez, the military commander of Venezuela, did not wish to take orders from Bolívar's second in command, the Colombian, Francisco de Paula Santander. By 1826, the Venezuelan military and creole land owning class united behind Páez, making it clear they would not comply with orders being issued from Bogotá.

Bolívar's attempts to prevent a break up of his beloved Gran Colombia proved fruitless. He assumed dictatorial powers in 1828 but it was already too late. Centralist support was in the minority throughout Venezuela, Colombia and Ecuador. General Páez's strong powerbase could not be challenged. Once Ecuador had withdrawn from the Republic, it collapsed, leading to Bolívar's dissilusionment, resignation, exile and, ultimately, his death, in 1830. So Venezuela was committed to independent nationhood.

Despite the formidable problems that faced the newly emerging nation, the two decades following the break-up of Gran Colombia are seen by historians as a period of political stability and economic progress. Leader of the so-called Conservative Oligarchy during these years was the *llanero* general Páez. He was the country's first President (1831-35) and re-elected for a second term in 1839. Even when not in office he remained the power behind the scenes until 1848.

In the political vacuum of 1830, Páez managed to curb the ambitions of the provincial *caudillos* and forged an alliance with the country's wealthy elite: the owners of the Andean coffee estates, the coastal cacao, sugar, tobacco and cotton plantations, the *llanos* cattle ranches, along with the merchants and leading professionals. A constitution was created reflecting all their interests. Also the special privileges of the church and the army were ended, both were thus rendered subservient to the state.

With stability assured, remarkable progress was made towards reconstructing the war damaged economy, including improved roads and laws to encourage European immigrants to farm unoccupied areas in the north-central highlands. The next major change on the political landscape was the rise of an opposition Liberal Party. This was brought on by a general feeling of antagonism against and within the ruling Conservative Oligarchy and accusations that they were attempting to reconstruct the colonial system of government and not doing enough to end the colonial society and economy. The Liberal opposition was founded in 1840

José Antonio Páez on a Bank Note

by angry non-agrarian Conservatives, whose main spokesman, Antonio Leocadio Guzmán, had been dismissed as minister of the interior for his political intrigues.

A campaign was launched for the emancipation of slaves, extension of the franchise, limitation of punitive interest rates and abolition of capital punishment. Páez's autocratic rule was also condemned. In the face of mounting opposition, the government resorted to force and electoral fraud. But the crisis deepened when the successful conservative candidate in the 1846 elections, General José Tadeo Managas, ousted all his Conservative ministers in 1848 and replaced them with Liberals. Attempts to impeach him failed, as he had already strengthened his position, and he merely intimidated his opponents, including Páez, who was exiled in 1850.

So began a decade of dictatorial rule by Monagas under the banner of Liberal government. The new progressive laws were rendered meaningless by his tyrannical personality. For example, the manumission law of 1854 freed 40,000 slaves, but they were devoid of any political rights and economic opportunities and experienced little change in their social position until Monagas fell from power. The General had no interest in the country's welfare and the economy began to stagnate. He met any sort of political activity with brutality. Such was his obsession with the reins of power that, in 1857, he framed a new constitution which extended the presidential term to 6 years and placed no restrictions on re-election.

The beginnings of federalism

The enraged Liberals joined forces with Conservative opposition and, with the help of army defectors, ended the dictatorship in 1858. This, however, set off a 5 year period of revolutionary uprisings as the Liberals and Conservatives were unable to agree on a coalition government. General Julián Castro was then selected as a compromise president in 1858, but his Conservative leanings soon began to split the coalition administration and a new constitution which ignored Liberal demands completed the schism. Provincial *caudillos* associated with the Liberals, particularly General Juan Falcón in the west, rose against central government and a 5-year Federal War began.

Federalism, created by the Liberal Antonio Guzmán Blanco, son of the Liberal party founder, came to be equated with democracy and economic and social reform and the war threatened to bring about great social upheaval. The desperate Conservatives recalled General Páez, but even his gallant efforts were unable to prevent a final victory for the Federalist forces in 1863, under Generals Juan Falcón and Guzmán Blanco.

Falcón was duly elected president and the new federalist principles were incorporated into a new constitution in 1864. But this led to a period of national disintegration as the constitution brought local tyranny instead of the hoped-for local freedom. The regional *caudillos*, supported by the landowners, who feared social upheaval, set up a new provincial political feudalism which effectively ended the hopes of the masses. The period of political anarchy, national confusion and administrative chaos continued and attempts to curb the power of the local *caudillos* failed because of inept leadership.

THE RISE OF THE MILITARY

Then a new strongman emerged, the Liberal politician-general Guzmán Blanco. He entered Caracas at the head of a victorious army in 1870 to begin 18 years of peace and prosperity. Though an autocratic ruler, he improved agriculture, built roads and railways and undertook the complete downgrading of the Catholic Church. A secularizer as well as a modernizer, he instituted the freedom of religion, transferred the control of education from the Church to the state, made primary eductaion free and compulsory and built many schools.

But if Guzmán Blanco's term marked the fall of the church, it also marked the rise of another power group, the army, which would dominate Venezuelan political and public life for nearly a century.

Antonio Guzmán Blanco

Ironically, it was the generals who brought an end to the era of Guzmán Blanco in 1892 and put General Joaquín Crespo in power for 6 years.

So Venezuela reached the end of the 19th century no closer to achieving the admirable goals for which the Wars of Independence had been fought. The country was still a long way from being a modern democracy.

The Gómez dictatorship

Worse was to come. Venezuela was already suffering from the inordinate political power of the Army but it was yet to face the most brutal, repressive and arbitary military dictatorship in its history, that of Juan Vicente Gómez.

His predecessor, the dictator Cipriano Castro, had built a vast personal fortune but he had no intention of using it to help pay the country's foreign debts. Instead, he decided in 1908 to take a trip to Europe. Castro's trusty lieutenant, Gómez, had been waiting for this moment. In exchange for a promise to pay the country's debts, he was sent US military assistance and the resulting bloodless coup gave Venezuela a new leader.

This cruel tyrant bore such a striking resemblance to another notorious megalomaniac, Joseph Stalin, that one theory was advanced that he he had fathered Stalin by a Russian ballerina who visited Colombia. He had Stalin's peasant cunning to such a degree that Venezuelans called him, among other things, 'The Sorcerer' and believed he had the ability to read people's minds. In fact, Venezuelans became so accustomed to his tricks that they refused to believe the announcement of his death in 1935. It was only after several days that they finally became convinced that the news was true and danced in the streets to celebrate their freedom.

Freedom may have been in short supply during the era of Gómez, but money was not. It was during his tyrrany that the history of the country changed forever with the discovery of vast quantities of oil in Lake Maracaibo. Gómez sold concessions to US and European companies for what seemed to Venezuela large sums of money. In retrospect, the oil companies got much the better deal. Between 1922 and 1926 the Venezuelan treasury received only between 7 and 10% in royalties on all the oil extracted from Venezuelan soil. Since the country did not have the capital or the equipment to drill for the oil, Gómez was forced to make the best bargains he could. The oil revenues allowed him to keep his promise to finish paying off the foreign debt and to line his pockets and those of his favourites.

The long term effect of Gómez' fiscal policies was economic deformation which ruined the countryside. Landowners, realizing they could make more money channeling their capital into the expanding urban sector of the economy, did nothing to improve their farms. Production of coffee and other export crops fell off. And with agriculture depressed, there were fewer jobs for a constantly expanding population and rural workers flocked to the oil fields and the cities in search of employment.

The dictatorship of Gómez and the discovery of oil had thus downgraded the power of the old landowning ruling class by destroying the basis of its power. Gómez also broke the hold of the country's regional bosses – the *caudillos* – and in doing so, initiated the creation of a centralized state.

After Gómez
Another legacy of his despotic rule was a lack of able leaders following his death and a general sense of apathy. Corruption was so endemic that people had abandoned hope of ever creating an honest regime and were reconciled to the fact that the Army was the real ruler of Venezuela. This was underlined by the appointment of another general, Eleazar López Contreras, as Gómez' successor. Though he never attempted the savage repressions which had been the Gómez trademark, Contreras made few concessions to those who demanded liberty.

Credit must be given, however, to López Contreras and his handpicked successor, Colonel Isaias Medina Angarita,

for one important advance. They secured a new agreement from the international oil companies on vastly more favourable terms. This was in part an attempt to avoid a repeat of Mexico's nationalization of its oil industry in 1938 and also due to the outbreak of World War Two. The United States was anxious to ensure the flow of Venezuelan oil while supplies from other parts of the world were threatened by the Axis powers and, in 1943, supported Venezuela in its attempt to increase the country's income from both royalties and taxes, guaranteeing it an amount equal to the profits of the companies. This historic agreement guaranteed the income needed to modernize the economy.

It was during the López Contreras regime that the phrase "to sow the oil" came into popular use. For the first time oil revenues were used to develop other businesses which would replace those revenues when oil ran out, instead of going directly into private pockets. However, neither López Contreras nor Medina seemed interested in tackling the country's growing social problems of poverty and rising unemployment and largely ignored the increasing discontent being voiced by the many political exiles who had returned to Venezuela.

The most famous of these was Rómulo Betancourt, who preached solutions considered too far to the left for that period in South America, such as land distribution, state-sponsored social security, free speech and universal education. At the same time, many other parties took shape, including Rafael Caldera's Christian Democrats, COPEI (Organizing Committee for Independent Electoral Policy), whose revolutionary policies were at first misunderstood because its original support came largely from Roman Catholic circles.

The most significant party to emerge, though, was Betancourt's Acción Democrática. The successor to Medina Angarita was neither strong enough nor liberal enough for Betancourt, so he conspired with a group of young Army officers to seize power in a coup. This succeeded and Betancourt was named as president. Though he ruled by decree at the head of the junta for 2 years, Betancourt did not forget his principles. He passed a law providing for universal suffrage and the election of the president by the people. Acción Democrática comfortably won the elections of 1947 and its candidate, the novelist Rómulo Gallegos, was elected president.

The new government's reforming programme faced strong opposition, however, from the vested interests of the Church, the landed aristocracy and employers. When Gallegos refused to accede to their demands, he and Betancourt were expelled from the country in 1948 by the same Army officers who had helped them to power.

The Pérez Jímenez dictatorship

This was the start of the infamous dictatorship of General Marcos Pérez Jímenez, which lasted until 1958.

Pérez Jímenez came from Táchira, the state which had given the country many of its dictators, including Gómez, whose style of regime he revived, outlawing political parties and repressing any form of opposition. Venezuela's jails were once again filled with union leaders and political activists, and torture and political assassination became commonplace.

Though not as obviously corrupt as Gómez, Pérez Jímenez shared his delusions of grandeur, devoting enormous sums of money to the dramatic modernization of Caracas, turning it into the city we know today. Plans for heavy industry were drawn up on the same lavish scale. While not unreasonable in themselves, these plans were unnecessarily grandiose and plagued by waste. This urban reconstruction provided some jobs but increased social unrest by drawing the unemployed from the country into the city. The rate of inflow continued at a higher rate than the massive futuristic housing developments could be built and the capital's shanty towns mushroomed.

Though the economy seemed to grow as Pérez Jímenez increased oil production

José Antonio Páez

and extended leases to foreign oil companies, economic incompetence and corruption finally took its toll. The government refused to honour its foreign debts and would not cooperate with the country's more progressive business sectors. The regime then suffered a significant setback in 1957 when the Church publicly denounced the dictator. A coup attempt failed but dissatisfaction mounted. The outlawed political parties called a general strike which led to street fighting in the cities. When much of the military revolted the dictator had no choice but to resign and flee the country.

PARTY DEMOCRACY

The flight of Pérez Jímenez marked the end of Venezuela's years of military dictatorship. Acción Democrática (AD) and COPEI re-emerged and the modern Venezuelan two-party system was born on 31 October 1958 when Caldera, Betancourt and other politicians and business leaders signed the Pact of Punto Fijo. This agreement, named after Caldera's residence, stated that the two parties would share power, irrespective of who won the forthcoming elections. It was designed to avoid a repeat of AD's previous short term in office, between 1945 and 1948, when inter-party conflict and social unrest reached such a pitch that the military stepped in to intervene, leading to the dictatorship of Pérez Jímenez.

Both party leaders were determined to establish a partnership strong enough to resist military interventionism and the rapidly growing Communist Party. COPEI was able to offer AD the support of the church and sections of conservative society, and in exchange AD would allow COPEI to participate in government.

The election result gave AD a large majority. Honouring their agreement, AD and COPEI governed together and shared power until 1968, when the two parties changed their relationship to a more adversarial one. A new constitution was created in 1961 which served to reinforce the new political consensus.

A stable democracy has been created since, with regular presidential elections every 5 years. Carlos Andrés Pérez of AD took office in 1974, presiding over a period of rapid development following the first great oil-price rise, and was succeeded in 1979 by Luis Herrera Campins of the COPEI. Dr Jaime Lusinchi of AD was elected president in 1983, to be followed by Carlos Andrés Pérez, who began his second term in 1989.

INSTABILITY AND ECONOMIC CRISIS

Pérez' second term was marked by protests, some violent, against the economic adjustment programme and growing levels of poverty. In 1992 there were two unsuccessful coup attempts by military officers. Among reforms designed to root out corruption, the Supreme Court and Central Bank were given greater independence. Both bodies were instrumental in the decision that Pérez himself be tried on corruption charges in 1993. The president was suspended from office, arrested and, after 2 years of house arrest, was found guilty in May 1996.

An interim president, Senator Ramón José Velázquez, took office until the presidential elections of December 1993, in which Rafael Caldera, now standing as an independent, was re-elected to office. The coalition which supported him did not win a majority in Congress, so Caldera had to forge alliances with all parties to see his policies through. Many of his aims, such as improvement in social conditions, tax reform and the control of inflation, had to be postponed in favour of solving an economic and financial crisis which began in 1994 (see below, **The Economy**).

The stubbornness of the economic difficulties forced Caldera in June 1996 to reverse his policies, which helped him to conclude an agreement with the IMF. Public protest at declining salaries and deteriorating public services included a strike by the medical service in late 1996, early 1997. The government eventually granted doctors a 100% pay rise, followed by 40% for public sector workers. While this threatened efforts to reduce inflation, it also led to agreement with trades unions on issues such as reform of employment regulations and pensions. The very public demolition of the notorious Catia prison in Caracas in March 1997 was a start towards improving conditions in the penal system, generally regarded as violating human rights.

Support for the government's economic reform programme, Agenda Venezuela grew less and less likely as the year wore on and the competing parties began their campaigns for the next election, to be held by December 1998 (proposed reforms included privatization of the aluminium, steel and electricity sectors, reform of the judicial system and the reorganization of public finances). Acción Democrática put up resistance to the proposed structural reforms. AD and COPEI rejected the government's proposal to hold a special session in July to discuss the contract for privatization of the state-owned steel company, Sidor.

As all government reforms require Congressional approval, and Caldera's governing party, Convergencia Nacional (CN) controlled less than 10% of the seats, it needed support from elsewhere.

Its most consistent supporter, Movimiento al Socialismo (MAS), split into two factions and the support of COPEI could not be guaranteed. The only remaining alternative, AD, looked certain to seek major concessions to the government's liberal economic policies in exchange for its support. In addition to the MAS split, the other main left-wing party, Causa R, split in two. This left both parties as secondary players in Congress and ended their pact with COPEI as the 'Triple Alliance', thus returning power to the two traditional parties.

A new figure appeared on the political scene, in the shape of the mayor of Chacao, former Miss Universe, Irene Sáez. She finally registered her party, Intergración Representación Nueva Esperanza (IRENE) on a national level. Despite attacks from rivals, she enjoyed the majority voters' support in the polls throughout 1997 and into 1998. As an independent, Ms Sáez avoided contact with the traditional political parties, but drew support from within all the main parties.

Economy

STRUCUTRE OF PRODUCTION

Venezuela has vast natural resources and is especially rich in energy, possessing 65 billion barrels of proved oil reserves, the largest in the Western Hemisphere. Oil production is concentrated in three major sedimentary basins: the Maracaibo, the eastern and the Apure-Barinas basins. Apart from proved and exploitable reserves there are another 1.2 trillion barrels in potential reserves of very heavy oil in the Orinoco belt. There are 3.6 trillion cu m of natural gas reserves (plus 5 trillion probable) and 500 million tonnes of coal (9 billion estimated) in the provinces of Zulia and Táchira. There is believed to be a hydroelectricity generating potential of 80,000MW; so far the largest project is the 10,300MW Guri dam near Ciudad Guayana.

Venezuela is a founding member of Opec, but consistently exceeds its output quota of 2.35 million b/d in a bid to maximize foreign exchange earnings. It is the largest supplier of oil to the USA. Petróleos de Venezuela (PDVSA), the state oil company, was created out of the nationalization of oil companies in 1976. It was only in 1996 that foreign participation in exploration and production was invited back as the Government realized that it had not the means to increase reserves fast enough to meet demand. Bids for ten exploration areas under profit sharing participation contracts were invited, both offshore and onshore. The Government hopes to have attracted US$65 billion in foreign investment by the year 2005, raising proven reserves by about 40 billion barrels and increasing production to more than 5 million b/d.

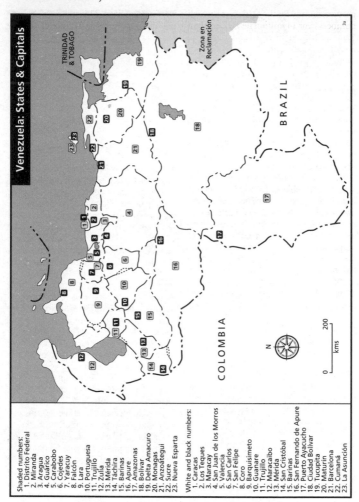

Venezuela: States & Capitals

Shaded numbers:
1. Distrito Federal
2. Miranda
3. Aragua
4. Guárico
5. Carabobo
6. Cojedes
7. Yaracuy
8. Falcón
9. Lara
10. Portuguesa
11. Trujillo
12. Zulia
13. Mérida
14. Táchira
15. Barinas
16. Apure
17. Amazonas
18. Bolívar
19. Delta Amacuro
20. Monagas
21. Anzoátegui
22. Sucre
23. Nueva Esparta

White and black numbers:
1. Caracas
2. Los Teques
3. Maracay
4. San Juan de los Morros
5. Valencia
6. San Carlos
7. San Felipe
8. Coro
9. Barquisimeto
10. Guanare
11. Trujillo
12. Maracaibo
13. Mérida
14. San Cristóbal
15. Barinas
16. San Fernando de Apure
17. Puerto Ayacucho
18. Ciudad Bolívar
19. Tucupita
20. Maturín
21. Barcelona
22. Cumaná
23. La Asunción

The mining sector is buoyant, with important ventures in bauxite, iron ore, ferro-nickel, coal and gold. As a result of cheap energy, the country has been able to build up heavy industry using local raw materials and now has a huge iron and steel industry and is one of the world's largest producers of aluminium. The state steel and aluminium companies were part of a package of 24 state companies to be privatized by 1997, raising up to US$3.5 billion.

Agriculture is relatively unimportant, contributing only 4.6% of gdp, but it employs many more people than the oil industry. The main grain staples are maize and sorghum, while sugar and rice are also important. The main export crop is coffee, with other cash crops being cocoa and cotton. Over 20% of land is used as pasture, mainly for the cattle herd, which numbers over 14 million head. Less than 5% is cultivated for crops and Venezuela is not self-sufficient in foodstuffs, although imports are much less than in the days of the oil price boom.

RECENT TRENDS

Venezuela accumulated huge foreign reserves of over US$20 billion by the mid-1980s from oil wealth, yet the country became unable to service its external debt normally from 1982 because of a bunching of maturities. A US$21 billion debt rescheduling agreement was signed with commercial banks in 1986 but was almost immediately renegotiated because of a collapse in oil prices; oil revenues fell by 44% in 1986. The Government avoided taking adjustment measures and chose instead to spend reserves, until by end-1988 liquid foreign exchange reserves were exhausted. In 1989 the new administration turned to the IMF and World Bank for support for a comprehensive macroeconomic adjustment programme to rebuild reserves, encourage domestic savings and cut the public sector deficit. Previous policies were reversed with the freeing of interest rates and the exchange rate. A debt restructuring package was implemented in 1990 which allowed banks to choose from a menu of options including debt reduction, debt service reduction or new loans.

The initial impact of the reforms was a severe recession and gdp fell by 8.1% in 1989, accompanied by a burst of inflation and higher unemployment. Between 1990 and 1992 the economy rebounded, strengthened by the reforms, a higher level of investment and buoyant oil revenues. The political instability of 1993-94, compounded by lower oil prices, brought renewed recession and inflation. In 1994 the Caldera administration tried to lower the fiscal deficit, but a banking crisis which spread to the rest of the financial system in fact increased the consolidated public sector deficit from 2.7% of gdp in 1993 to 14.4% in 1994 as the state spent heavily on propping up illiquid and undercapitalized banks, which eventually

were nationalized. This increased spending and a loose monetary policy caused heavy capital outflows, a precipitous fall in the exchange rate and higher inflation.

In mid-1994 exchange controls were imposed to prevent further loss of reserves and a fixed rate of Bs170=US$1 was introduced. These controls and a contraction in the economy led to a 30% drop in imports and consequent surpluses in trade of US$8 billion and the current account of US$4 billion, but capital flows remained sharply negative and net international reserves declined by US$1 billion in 1994. Delays in servicing external

Venezuela: fact file	
Geographic	
Land area	912,050 sq km
forested	34.0%
pastures	20.2%
cultivated	4.4%
Demographic	
Population (1996)	22,311,000
annual growth rate (1991-96)	2.2%
urban	84.6%
rural	15.4%
density	24.5 per sq km
Education and Health	
Life expectancy at birth,	
male	70.1 years
female	76.0 years
Infant mortality rate	
per 1,000 live births (1994)	27.7
Calorie intake as %	
of FAO requirement	106%
Population age 25 and over	
with no formal schooling	23.5%
Literate males (over 15)	93.5%
Literate females (over 15)	91.1%
Economic and Employment	
GNP (1994 market prices)	US$59,025mn
GNP per capita	US$2,760
Public external debt (1994)	US$28,039mn
Tourism receipts (1994)	US$486mn
Inflation (annual av 1990-95)	44.3%
Population economically active (1993)	
	7,546,200
Unemployment rate	6.3%
Military forces	79,000
Source *Encyclopaedia Britannica*	

debt and economic uncertainties adversely affected Venezuela's position in international financial markets, leading to credit limitations. The Government was forced to turn to domestic sources of finance and domestic debt rose from 5% of gdp in 1993 to 14% in 1994.

In 1995 arrears in payments to some foreign creditors and domestic bond holders continued to mount and there was constant speculation that despite its political unpopularity, an IMF programme was inevitable. Gasoline prices were raised by 140% from a very low base to US$0.06-0.08 a litre to raise budget revenues, but diesel prices were lowered to avert a rise in public transport costs and avoid riots. No structural economic reforms were implemented, inflation remained higher than interest rates, the bolívar became increasingly overvalued and capital flight persisted. The public sector deficit was about 13% of gdp, financed by debt arrears, debt issues and printing money. Eventually, in December 1995, when the parallel exchange rate (determined by the local market for debt reduction bonds known as Brady bonds) had reached Bs390=US$1, the Government devalued the official rate to Bs290.

1996 was dominated by negotiations with the IMF for a 12-month, US$1.4 billion standby arrangement, which was eventually signed in June, enabling the disbursement of over US$3 billion in related multilateral lending. The economic reform programme included the lifting of exchange controls and the floating of the bolívar in April, tax increases, lifting price controls and raising gasoline prices by up to 500% to reduce the fiscal deficit to 2.2% of gdp in 1996. Opposition was muted, giving the Government confidence to proceed with structural reform, particularly in the public sector.

As a result of the IMF-inspired austerity of 1996, real incomes declined by about 60% and gdp again failed to show positive growth (-1.8% in 1996). On the other hand, the international investment climate improved, renewing confidence in the privatization programme, despite congressional opposition, and giving a massive boost to the bidding for rights to operate in the oil sector. The investment in oil helped stabilize the bolívar in 1996-97 and inspired prospects for gdp growth of at least 4% a year until 2001.

Prospects for the country's ailing economy looked brighter in 1997, with growth of 2.8% in the first half of the year – a faster than expected recovery. The non-oil sector outgrew the oil sector for the first time since 1991. Economic recovery was also helped by the huge public-sector pay awards of around 70% which boosted private consumption. Growth in bank lending also helped, as did a real appreciation of the bolívar which fuelled rapid import growth. On the downside, the appeasement of the public-sector labour force through large pay increases and the increase in consumption meant that the government's inflation target of 25% slipped to between 30 and 35%. Even that achievement looked unlikely as inflation reached 40.5% by the end of July 1997. The failure of the government to impose wage restraint and to stick to its budgetary targets led to a delay in the extension of the IMF standby facility to December 1998.

GOVERNMENT

Form of government
Venezuela has a congressional system headed by the president. It is a federal republic, comprising 72 federal dependencies, 22 states, 2 federal territories and one federal district.

The executive
The president is elected for a non-renewable 5-year term and appoints a Council of Ministers. Rafael Caldera won the presidential election on 5 December 1993 and took office in February 1994. The next presidential elections are due in December 1998.

National legislature
Congress is bicameral (2 legislative houses): a directly elected Chamber of Deputies, with 201 seats, and a 52-member Senate, to which two members are

elected by direct adult suffrage from each state and the federal district, plus others to represent 'minorities'. Former presidents are members of the Senate for life.

Legal system
Supreme Court is at the apex of the court system. Judges and magistrates are elected by both chambers of Congress.

Main political organizations
The current president's party (1998), Convergencia Nacional (CN), which has 19 seats in the Chamber of Deputies and 5 in the Senate; Acción Democrática (AD); Comité de Organización Política Electoral Independiente (COPEI); Movimiento al Socialismo (MAS); La Causa R (LCR).

The current Constitution is dated 23 January 1961. Voting is compulsory for all over 18.

Culture

MUSIC AND DANCE

Venezuelan music is more homogenous than that of some of the other republics. Its highly distinctive sound is based on an instrumental combination of harp, *cuatro* (a small, four stringed guitar) and *maracas*. Many of the rhythms have a very fast, almost headlong pace to them, stimulating both to the senses and to the feet, music here being almost inseparable from dance.

The recipe for Venezuelan music is a classic European/African/Amerindian mix. The country's national dance is the Joropo, a name deriving from the Arab 'Xarop', meaning syrup and which originally meant a country dance. This is a dance for couples with several sequences, such as the Valseao, Zapatiao, Escobillao and Toriao. Closely related to the Joropo are the Corrido, with a ballad content, Galerón (slow for singing or fast for dancing), Pasaje (lyrical, very popular in the *Llanos*) and Golpe, from the State of Lara, to all of which styles the Joropo may be danced in different parts of the country. Note that the little *cuatro* is normally referred to as 'guitarra', while the Spanish guitar is called the 'guitarra grande'.

Some of the dance rhythms have been imported from abroad or are shared with neighbouring countries, such as the urban Merengue (introduced into Caracas in the 1920s), the Jota and Malagueña of Anzoátegui State, the Pasillo (shared with Colombia and Ecuador), the Polo of the Oriente and Isla Margarita and the Bambuco, found in Lara and Táchira states near the border with Colombia.

There is a wealth of dances and musical forms found in particular towns or states

King of salsa

Venezuela is pop culture paradise. Not only have its soap operas taken the world by storm, but it is also a major international centre for Latin music. The hip-swaying rhythms of salsa, merengue, rumba, mambo and calypso can be heard in bars, restaurants, hotels, shops, buses, taxis – everywhere, in fact.

The country's disproportionately young population ensures a large, eager audience and its proximity to the Caribbean islands have placed Venezuela at the fast heart of Latin music. Musicians from Puerto Rico, the Dominican Republic and Central America are drawn to Caracas, where fortunes can still be made. It is also more cost-effective to travel to Venezuela in search of fame and fortune instead of heading for Miami, the world's undisputed capital of Spanish-language music.

If music be the food of love, then salsa is its piquant sauce that gets the taste buds tingling, and Venezuela's master chef is Oscar D'León. This one-time taxi driver has been whetting musical appetites since the 1970s with a string of hits. The all-singing, all-dancing king of salsa is played in *tascas* the length and breadth of the country and is spoken of in revered tones.

at religious festivities. Outstanding among these is the Tamunangue of Lara State, danced in the second fortnight of June to the accompaniment of drums and small guitars and made up of seven individual dances, varying from the 'Batalla', where men battle with sticks, to the 'Bella', a flirtatious dance for couples. Corpus Cristi is the time to visit San Francisco de Yare in Miranda State and see the 80 or so male 'Diablos' of all ages, dressed entirely in red and wearing large horned masks, who dance in the streets to the sound of their own drums and rattles (see also page 97). The Bailes de Tambor take place among the largely black people of the Barlovento coast during the feasts of San Juan and San Pedro and at Christmas. This is a brilliant polyrhythm on huge drums (*cumacos*, *minas* and *curvetas*) held between the legs. Also in Barlovento, but in May, can be heard the Fulias, chant-and-response songs addressed to a venerated saint or cross, to the accompaniment of *cuatro*, *tambora* drum and *maracas*.

Christmas is a great period for music from the Gaitas of Zulia to the ubiquitous Aguinaldos, both in Merengue rhythm, with solo verses responded to by a chorus and varied instrumental accompaniment. Notable in the eastern states are the folk theatre dances of the Pájaro Guarandol (a hunter shoots a large bird that is brought back to life), Carite (from Margarita, using a large model fish), Chiriguare (a monster that is duly despatched) and Burriquita (a hobby horse). More surprising is to find the Calpso, played on steel bands by the black inhabitants of El Callao in the Orinoco region, whose ancestors came from Trinidad and who also perform the Limbo.

Venezuelans enjoy Salsa as much as other Hispanic peoples around the Caribbean, but they are also very keen on their own music, whether rustic 'folk' or urban 'popular'. The virtuoso harpist Juan Vicente Torrealba has performed with his group Los Torrealberos for more than three decades, usually with Mario Suárez as vocal soloist. Another famous singer is Simón Díaz. Outstanding among the folk groups who strive for authenticity are Un Solo Pueblo, Grupo Vera and Grupo Convenezuela. Choral and contrapuntal singing of native music in a more sophisticated style has also been perfected by Quinteto Contrapunto and Serenata Guayanesa.

LITERATURE

The colonial period

Early colonial literature in Venezuela was not as prolific as in Latin American countries with larger urban centres, such as

Mexico City, Lima and Bogotá, though the chronicles of the province did appear, meticulously kept in every American country occupied by the Spanish. One of the earliest known of these is *Historia de la conquista y población de Venezuela* (1723), by José Oviedo y Baños (1671-1738).

Of the other literary forms in the 18th century, *costumbrismo* – baroque sketches of daily life in the new colonies – was perfected by Blas José Terrero (1735-1802) in his 1770 *Teatro de Caracas*. Many forms of poetry also flourished, among them the popular mestizo ballads called *Aguinaldos*, as well as songs and poems in various indigenous languages, though these generally went unrecorded.

Romanticism

The Romantic novel was the first significant phase of Venezuelan literature. Works such as *Venezuela Heroica* (1881), by Eduardo Blanco (1840-1912) and *Biografía de José Félix Ribas* (1859), by Juan Vicente González (1810-1866) were heavily influenced by the writings of Simón Bolívar and served as a consecration of the newly established republic under the hegemony of a ruling class, which saw itself as obliged to civilize a semi-barbaric nation. Romantic literature was a way of spreading this new mentality.

The best representative of Romanticism in Venezuela comes at the end of the 19th century. *Peonía* (1890), by Manuel Romero García (1861-1917) is a first person narrative about a young engineer visiting his uncle at his hacienda. The uncle, Don Pedro, is a cruel and ignorant man engaged in a dispute with his brother, also a landowner but a much more benign character. The narrator is continuously travelling back and forth between Caracas and Don Pedro's farm, where he has fallen for one of his cousins. The characteristic Romantic theme of civilization versus barbarism is apparent, especially when the city-dwelling narrator returns to the hacienda, powerless to intervene as the peasants set fire to his uncle's house. *Peonía* set traditions in Venezuelan literature which would remain for decades, of characters as symbols rather than individuals, struggling against the forces of nature and the social order.

The 20th century

The first third of the 20th century was dominated by the dictatorship of Juan Vicente Gómez. This period marks the culmination of the 19th century Liberal project of an enlightened bourgeois despotism. One of the best novels of this period was written while the author, Rufino Blanco Fombona, was in jail. The 1907 *El Hombre de Hierro* ('Men of Steel'), is a tale of adultery examining the Nietzschean concept of the Superman. Fombona's 1914 *El Hombre de Oro* took the pessimistic view that evil always triumphs over good, with reference to the corrupt politicians and loan sharks who had been successful in contemporary Venezuela.

The influence of European and North American literature spawned the modernist movement among Venezuelan writers. The most important Venezuelan modernist novelist was Manuel Díaz Rodríguez (1871-1927). His first novel *Idolos rotos* ('Broken Idols'), in 1901, is written in the typically modernist refined, sophisticated style with grand themes and symbolic characters.

Reaction to the modernists came soon, in the shape of José Rafael Pocaterra (1888-1955), who generated a new prose style based on Venezuelan slang and dialect, influenced by Russian authors. The tales were of simple urban life, criticizing the dictatorship and police corruption. A new literary from somewhere between the Modernists and Pocaterra was established by Teresa de la Parra (1890-1936), still considered Venezuela's leading woman writer. *Diario de una Señorita que escribió porque se fastidia* ('Diary of a young woman who wrote because she was bored') from 1924, is an early version of the genre popularized today in Britain by *Bridget Jones' Diary*. Parra introduced psychological analysis into Venezuelan fiction for the first time, and was the first writer to bring the female psyche under literary scrutiny.

Rómulo Gallegos

The most internationally well-known of all Venezuelan writers is Rómulo Gallegos (1884-1969), who is famous as much for his political life as for his literary output. His concern for social issues was established in his early fiction, with novels such as *La Rebelión* (1922) and the 1925 *La Trepadora* ('The Climber'). Gallegos defended the cause of mulattos and championed the value of 'mestización' – the mixing of races. His most acclaimed book is *Doña Bárbara* (1929), a novel which was published at a time when civil unrest had led to the formation of the 'Generación de 1928', whose main political wing was the Partido de Acción Democrática. They sought to ally sectors of the bourgeoisie with the awakening peasant and working class movements, with the long-term ideal of instituting full democracy. Gallegos actively participated in this movement and the character of *Doña Bárbara* is identified with the violence of nature, pitted against the civilizing forces emanating from the city, in the guise of the character Santos.

The dictator, Gómez, felt so threatened by the ideas contained in *Doña Bárbara* that Gallegos had to go into exile. In Spain he wrote *Canaima* (1935), which means 'Spirit of Evil'. He was able to return to Venezuela when Gómez died, and after writing a spate of protest novels and working for Acción Democrática, he was elected president of the country in 1947 with 80% of the vote. He only lasted a few months before being ousted by a military coup, forcing him back into exile. He was not to return to Venezuela until democracy was established in 1958, and he stayed there until his death.

Magic realism

Another major novelist sensitive to political issues was Arturo Uslar Pietri (born 1906), who abandoned his early avant-garde style to focus on Venezuela's social problems. He was also forced into exile by the military coup of 1948, returning in 1950. His most famous novel *Las Lanzas Coloradas* ('The Red Lances'), in 1931, depicts the war of independence at the height of the conflict, in the years 1812-14.

He also wrote a mythologized biography of the 16th century tyrant and *conquistador* Lope de Aguirre in 1947 entitled *El Camino de El Dorado*. Some critics cite Uslar Pietri as the first writer to coin the phrase "Magic Realism", describing 'Realismo Mágico' as the 'discovery of mysticism immanent in reality'. A collection of his short stories published in 1978 *Treinta Cuentos* contains many examples of this genre.

Politics and Modernism

By the mid-20th century the literary tradition had been established in Venezuela, influenced by European writers like Proust and Joyce, of detailed introspection, the anti-hero, and the struggle to maintain an inner world with the over-development of mass culture. At this time the literary group 'Sardino' was formed, and Julian Padrón and Miguel Otero Silva introduced Marxist elements into their tales of class struggle in the new oilfields and from all over the country.

The insurrections of the 1960s, inspired by the Cuban Revolution, saw the beginning of guerrilla warfare in Venezuela. Literary supporters were Adriano González León (born 1931) whose *País Portatil* ('Portable Homeland') in 1968, charts the progress of a young guerrilla dodging his way across Caracas to an important meeting. The cityscape mingles with his childhood memories to produce a Joycean interior monologue. Other novels showing support for the armed struggle were *Venezuela Violenta* (1968) by Orlando Araujo (born 1928) and the 1970 *Vela de Armas* ('Deposition of Arms') by Luis Britto García.

Testimonios

The 1970s saw the development in Venezuela of an entirely new literary form, known as 'Testimonio'. Not unlike the 'New Journalism' of the US in the 60s, this style involves incorporating genuine recorded material into a semi-fictional account of a real event. Some of the *Testimonio* novels were about formerly taboo subjects like drug-addiction, for example the 1973 *Pito de Oro* ('The Golden Whistle') by Clara

Posani, in which she uses ghetto argot to depict the seedy world of the capital's criminal underclass. The most notorious of this new crop of novels was *Soy un Delicuente*, published in 1974, by Ramón Antonio Brizuela (1952-73), who was killed at the age of 21 in a shoot-out with the police.

Testimonios are also concerned with more overtly political issues: *Aquí no pasó nada* (1972) by the journalist Angela Zayo (born 1943) uses excerpts from interviews with people involved in the armed struggle. The dramatic subject matter of *Testimonios* has seen many adaptations into TV series and films. Part of the attraction is that they are narrated by the authentic voices of real characters, who, until the 1970s had been consigned to relative anonymity behind the venerated authors of a middle-class elite.

ART

The Colonial period

Painting, silver work, cabinetwork, altarpieces, sculpture and music were developed successfully in Venezuela during the Colonial period; nevertheless much of this art has not survived into the 1990s due to poor conservation, harsh climatic conditions and successive destructions, notably the Earthquake of Caracas (1812), the Wars of Independence (1811-1827 approximately) and later the Federal War (1859-1863). While of the 16th and 17th centuries almost nothing remains, many fine works of the late 18th and early 19th centuries have been preserved. The best examples of Venezuelan colonial art can be found in the Museo de Arte Colonial de Caracas, the Museo Diocesano de Coro, the churches of Nuestra Señora de Altagracia, San Francisco and the Cathedral in Caracas, and also in the towns of Petare, Guanare, Casigua, Piritu and Clarines.

From the mid-17th century to the beginning of the 19th century all types of art works were brought to Venezuela, initially from Spain and Italy and later mostly from Mexico. These imported works became models for future local

artists in all areas. When studying Venezuelan colonial art, it is difficult to separate crafts from high art, as during this period the crafsmen/artists worked indistinctly in different disciplines. Thus we find that one of the most prominent artists of the period, Juan Pedro López (1724-1787) was both a painter and a sculptor. Among his best works are: the sculpture of the *St Joseph and Child* (1777) for the altar of the Cofradía de Animas Benditas and ten pictures for the main altarpiece (1755) of the Caracas Cathedral.

Sculpture

The development of sculpture during this period did not reach the level of other arts. Sculpture stemmed from the Spanish tradition and was devoted almost entirely to religious iconography for churches, convents, and private oratories. Some of the most outstanding sculptors of the period were: Enrique Antonio Hernández Prieto (dates unknown) (*St Peter the Apostle*, 1742, Caracas Cathedral); Juan Pedro López (*Altarpiece of St Joseph*, 1777, Caracas Cathedral); Domingo Gutiérrez (dates unknown) (*Altarpiece of the Holy Child of San Francis*, late 18th century, San Francisco Church, Caracas); José del Rosario Ascanio (1709-1793) (*Child with Statue of Our Lady of the Conception*, 1788, Caracas Cathedral); El Tocuyano (dates unknown) (*Crucifix of San Francisco*, end of XVIII, Church of San Francisco, Caracas); José Francisco Rodríguez (1744-1799) (*Coronation of the Virgin by the Holy Trinity*, 1798, San Francisco Church, Caracas); and José de la Merced Rada (dates unnknown) (*Nazarene of Achaguas*, 1783, Church of Achaguas)

Painting

Painting developed in three main centres: Caracas, El Tocuyo and Mérida. The first paintings appeared in the second half of the 16th century, but no examples have survived. During the 17th century many paintings were imported from Spain and the rest of Europe, constituting the main reference for local painters. Among the most outstanding painters were: El Pintor del Tocuyo (active 1702-?) (*The Virgin of the Rosary*, Museo Lisandro Alvarado, El Tocuyo); Francisco José de Lerma y Villegas (1719-1753) who painted both portraits and religious themes (*The Archangel Michael*, Collection Alfredo Boulton, Caracas); Juan Pedro López (1724-1787) (*Immaculate Conception*, mid-17th century, Caracas Cathedral); Antonio José Landaeta (died 1799) *Immaculate Conception*, 1798, Caracas Cathedral); School of Landaeta (circa 1760-1810) (*Our Lady of Caracas*, 1760, Collection Fundación John Boulton). From this period many interesting works by anonymous artists have also survived.

Until 1810, Venezuelan art was mainly sponsored by the Church.

Independence and after

Venezuela declared its independence from Spanish rule in 1811; nevertheless it was not until 1830 when General José Antonio Páez and General Carlos Soublette came to power, that normality and a more prosperous economy were restored, allowing the arts to flourish again.

Juan Lovera (1778-1841) is the most important painter of the first half of the 19th century. He is the first portrait painter of consequence in Venezuela. Following European Neoclassical precepts and influenced by Romanticism, he executed works such as *19th of April of 1810*, 1835 and *5th of July of 1811*, 1838 (both in the Collection of the Concejo Municipal del Distrito Federal, Caracas).

During the 19th century, European artists travelled to Venezuela and portrayed its landscapes, flora and people. In 1800, the German Baron Alexander von Humboldt visited Caracas; the German painter Ferdinand Bellermann was in Venezuela in 1842; the Englishman Lewis B Adams came in 1836 and painted some important portraits; the Danish landscape painter Fritz Georg came in 1852 together with the French painter Camille Pisarro.

During the Federal War, the arts suffered a new setback. When General Antonio Guzmán Blanco came to power in 1870, culture and particularly painting

flourished. The three most prominent painters for the latter part of the 19th century were: Martín Tovar y Tovar (1827-1902), Cristóbal Rojas (1857-1890) and Arturo Michelena (1863-1898). In the Venezuelan painting of the second half of the 19th century the Spanish influence that had lasted three centuries was displaced by the French School and the taste for Academicism.

Tovar y Tovar initiated the historical genre in Venezuela; his monumental academic paintings include *The Battle of Carabobo*, 1887 (Palacio de Miraflores, Caracas) and *Signing the Declaration of Indepedence*, 1883 (Collection Concejo Municipal de Caracas). Arturo Michelena studied in Paris between 1885 and 1892 and obtained important prizes there. His *Miranda in la Carraca Jail* (Collection National Gallery, Caracas) and '*Vuelvan Caras*', 1890 (Collection Academia Militar de Venezuela, Caracas) are two of his best known paintings. Cristóbal Rojas studied in Paris in 1884 and his work followed the precepts of French Academic painting (*The Tavern* 1887, Collection National Gallery, Caracas). Finally, Antonio Herrera Toro (1857-1914) was one of the most important portrait painters of this period (*Self-Portrait*, 1880, Collection National Gallery, Caracas).

The field of sculpture in the 19th century was also dominated by Academicism. The most famous 19th century sculptor was Eloy Palacios (1847-1919) who studied at the Academy of Fine Arts in Munich. His most important work commissioned by the Government, was *Monument to Carabobo*, 1911, El Paraíso, Caracas. Also amongst the best known sculptors is Rafael de la Cova (dates unknown) whose most famous work is the *Monument to Christopher Columbus in the 'Sad Gulf'*, 1893, which today dominates the Paseo Colón at the entry to Parque los Caobos in Caracas.

20th century

Venezuelan art of the first half of the 20th century was marked by a rapidly increasing sense of modernity and modernization. In 1912 a group of students broke away from the Academy of Fine Arts in Caracas and created the Círculo de Bellas Artes, as they wished to embrace Impressionism and leave behind the rigidity of Academic painting. The Círculo de Bellas Artes which consisted of Manuel Cabré (1890-1984), Antonio Edmundo Monsanto (1890-1947), Armando Reverón (1889-1954), Rafael Monasterios (1884-1961) and Federico Brandt (1879-1932) among others, produced some of Venezuela's best landscape painting.

The Avila Mountain which dominates the north side of Caracas was a favourite subject matter for these painters and it has been popular ever since. Two foreign painters, the Romanian Samys Mützner and the Russian Nicolás Ferdinandov, joined the group and were very influential for their Post-Impressionist styles. Emilio Boggio (1857-1920), a Venezuelan artist who spent many years in France and joined the group later on, was also important. The National Gallery in Caracas, houses a very good collection of works of this period.

Armando Reverón, who by the beginning of the century was painting landscapes in the European Post-Impressionist manner, soon created a unique style that has gained him recognition as one of the most important artists of this century in Latin America. He produced his most important work after moving to Macuto, by the sea. In paintings such as *Macuto en Oro* (Private Collection) Reverón allowed the bright tropical light to dematerialize the landscapes into whites and almost inperceptible browns and yellows. The artist also made lifesize cloth dolls which are some of the most haunting and powerful sculptures of this century in Venezuela. The Armando Reverón Museum has been set up in the artist's former home (El Castillete) in Macuto.

Modern sculpture is accepted to have started with Lorenzo González (1877-1948), Pedro Basalo (1886-1948) and Ernesto Maragall (Barcelona, Spain 1903-1975) as their work moved towards a more Expressionist or idiosyncratic figuration. Maragall's *Ornamental Fountain* in the Parque Los Caobos, Caracas, is one of the outstanding works of this kind. Francisco Narváez (1905-1982) is considered the most important Venezuelan sculptor of the century. He inaugurated a new epoch for monumental sculpture. Narváez moved from a stylized but still figurative stage representing indigenous women and men ('*Las Toninas' Fountain*, O'Leary Square, 1944, El Silencio, Caracas), to organic abstraction in the 1950s (the *Big Volume of Amuay*, 1981, Lagoven Refinery, Paraguaná).

Modernism

Venezuelan Modernism went through many different stages and directions during the 1930s and 1940s: Fauvism, Expressionism, Surrealism, Cubism, Informalism and others. Post 1940s, Venezuela developed an Abstract Geometrical tradition which emerged as a trascendental celebration of Venezuelan modernity and modernization. During the late 1940s a group of artists belonging to the 'Disidentes' Group in Paris focused on abstract geometrical research, among them Alejandro Otero (1921-1990), who produced some of the most important abstract art in Venezuela (Series of *Colorhythmst* 1950s); also Mateo Manaure (1926-), Luis Guevara Moreno (1926-) Carlos González Bongen (1920-), Alirio Oramas (1924-), Omar Careño (1927-) amongst others.

During the late 50s and early 60s Jesús Soto (1923-) and Carlos Cruz Diez (1923-) were precursors of the Kinetic movement and their work had international repercussions, especially in Europe. During the 1980s and 1990s these two artists have been producing very successful monumental works integrated with architecture in Venezuela and abroad. Within the Geometric tradition, Gego (Gertrudis Goldmichdt, 1912-1994) deserves special mention for her series of *Reticuleas* (1967-), irregular and organic metallic modules suspended in the air.

In the 1950s and 60s, figurative art continued to flourish. Héctor Poleo (1918-1989) moved from Social Realism into a more lyrical and personal figuration. One of the leading figurative artists is Jacobo Borges (1931-), who since the 1960s has been producing a higly personal style with political overtones. Also during the 1960s the sculptor Marisol (1930) created pop sculpture based on Assemblage.

Modern architecture

The architect Carlos Raúl Villanueva (1900-1975) was the most important representative of modern architecture in the country from the 1930s to the 1970s. He designed the Ciudad Universitaria de Caracas (1945-63) which is an extremely successful project in the integration of the arts. Villanueva invited national artists such as Jesús Soto, Carlos Cruz Díez, Alejandro Otero, Victor Valera (1927-), and international artists such as Alexander Calder, Henri Laurens, Jean Arp, Sophie Tauber, Fernand Léger and Victor Vasarely to create art works for the different buildings of the Central University of Caracas. Another impressive project is the art work for the Raúl Leoni hydroelectric dam in the Guri area near the Gran Sabana.

The machine rooms of the Guri dam were extensely decorated by Carlos Cruz Díez with *Cromatic Ambientations* – coloured Kinetic compositions – (1977-1986); and Alejandro Otero installed by the dam a 50m tall stainless steel *Solar Tower*, a structure which rotates with the action of the wind.

Post-modernism

During the 1970s, trends such as the Kinetic and Abstract Geometrical continued. Nevertheless, partly as a reaction to the officialition of Kinetic art and as a critical stand towards Venezuelan oil boom society, new trends such as the Conceptual emerged. There was also a beginning of Performances and Happenings. Within the new trends some important artists are: Diego Barboza (1945-), Sigfredo Chacón (1950-), Eugenio Espinoza (1950-), Héctor Fuenmayor (1949-), Claudio Perna (1957-1996), Antonieta Sosa (1940-), Alfred Wenemoser (1954-).

The 1980s saw the emergence of painting reflecting a worldwide context.

Carlos Zerpa (1950-), Eugenio Espinoza (1950-), Antonio Lazo (1943-), Ernesto León (1956-), Miguel Von Dangel (1946-) among others, are some prominent exponents.

Venezuelan art in the 1990s has seen the emergence and establishment of younger generations. Artists have tended towards Installation art, Conceptual art, video, photography and a widespread abandonment of painting as a form of expression. Also, much of the art of the 90s deals directly or indirectly with the economic and social crisis of the country and with representational issues. Some of the most prominent figures of the present are: Alexander Apostol (1969-), Sammy Cucher (Aziz + Cucher) (1958-), José Hernández Díez (1964-), Roberto Obregón (1946-), Meyer Vaisman (1960-) and others.

POPULAR CULTURE

BEAUTY QUEENS

Venezuela has a reputation as a producer of world-class beauty queens. It creates them with almost as much entrepreneurial zeal as it uses to extract its other main export – oil.

Beauty contests may be downplayed in many countries, but Venezuela remains a feminist's nightmare; a thorn in the flesh of political correctness. Whereas beauty competitions elsewhere shift their focus to the personality and intellect of the contestants, in Venezuela it's looks that count. In a big way. Comfort takes a back seat to style not only on the catwalk, but also on the street and in the office. Power dressing the Venezuelan way means the tighter the better. If you see a woman walking down the street on spike heels and a skirt so tight it must have been poured on and left to set, you can bet your bottom bolívar that she's on her way to the office.

If Venezuelan women go to great pains to accentuate their assets, the men are certainly appreciative of their efforts. In this most macho of Latin countries, if you don't hiss, whistle or shout some compliment at a passing *mamita* then you risk having your sexuality seriously called into question. Male travellers take heed. In a country with the worst road accident record in the world, whiplash injury is not confined to car drivers.

It is not surprising, then, that enterprizing Venezuelans have sought to reap profit from such a propensity of pulchritude. A Caracas 'academy' grooms and hones young women as though they were pedigree racehorses. The results have been phenomenal. Venezuela has produced three Miss Worlds and the Miss Universe winner on five occasions. Osmel Sousa, the man who runs the Caracas school and the Miss Venezuela competitions, has turned the country's beauty industry into an assembly line of stunning winners.

But beauty is a cut-throat business. Aspiring Miss Venezuelas are even willing to put themselves under the knife in their search for success. A visit to the plastic surgeon is as much an everyday part of the beauty game as a visit to the gym or the cosmetics counter, bringing a whole new meaning to the term 'operating costs'.

If all this sounds alarmingly like aesthetic fascism, then that's because the potential rewards are great. Beauty opens many doors in Venezuela. Every hopeful model knows that entering the Miss Venezuela contest can be the first step on a glittering career path. More than one *telenovela* star has begun her life on the catwalk. Hollywood actress, María Conchita Alonso, started out as a Miss Venezuela, and perhaps the most famous 'Miss' of all, Irene Sáez, is hotly tipped to be the country's next president.

BASEBALL

Forget football. Though worshipped in every other South American country, the world's most popular game is very much a second-rate sport in Venezuela. Here, baseball is king.

Every town and village has its own baseball stadium, or at least a playing diamond. One of the most common sights in the country is a bunch of kids playing *pelota de goma* – a derivation of the real thing using a clenched fist for a bat and a small rubber ball – in the street, or any available piece of flat ground.

The sport first appeared at the end of the 19th century when Venezuelan expats returned from the United States to promote baseball through a series of matches played in the main cities. As with many other features of Venezuelan life, the history of baseball is linked with the oil industry. The progress of the sport was given a major boost with the discovery of oil in Lake Maracaibo in 1922. US oil companies came to Venezuela and their workers did much to make baseball an integral part of society. Its popularity was then assured with the founding of a professional league in 1945. Teams were formed throughout the country with US support and financial assistance. As the standard of play gradually improved, major league teams in the US started to give promising Venezuelan players an opportunity to compete for places in 'Las Ligas Grandes' (the big leagues).

Baseball - Venezuela's top sport

The first great Venezuelan baseball hero was Alfonso 'Chico' Carrasquel, who played shortstop for the Chicago White Sox in the early 1950s. Carrasquel's fame inspired thousands of imitators, the result of which was a long line of outstanding Venezuelan shortstops. The most famous was Luis Aparicio who replaced Carrasquel in the Chicago team in 1956 and went on to play for the next 22 years.

Many US players now hone their skills in the Venezuelan winter leagues, which run from October to the end of January, before returning home to play in the major leagues during their summer season. Venezuelans also migrate north to compete for places in US teams. Each Venezuelan team, in fact, has a working relationship with a major league counterpart, which provides equipment, coaching and young prospects.

Eight teams compete for two coveted play-off places: Navegantes del Magallanes (from Valencia); Leones del Caracas; Aguilas del Zulia and Pastora de Occidente (from Maracaibo); Tiburones de La Guaira; Cardenales de Occidente (from Barquisimeto); Caribes de Oriente (from Puerto la Cruz); and Tigres de Aragua (from Maracay). The eventual play-off winner goes on to compete with teams from Puerto Rico, Dominican Republic and Mexico in the Serie del Caribe, which takes place in February.

While each of them attracts large crowds and fanatical support, none can compare to the rivalry between Magallanes and Caracas, which borders on a Mafia-style vendetta. It is, quite simply, the biggest sporting spectacle in the country. Though Caracas supporters will probably shoot me for saying this, Magallanes have the largest and most rabid following of any team. This is most likely due to the fact that the team has moved around the country quite a bit in its 70-year history. As one fan put it: "There are three sacred things in Venezuela; the Pope, Acción Democrática and Magallanes".

TELEVISION

Here's the scene: a dewy-eyed and unbelievably beautiful young girl with big hair and immaculate make up lies in a hospital bed making an impassioned plea to her murderous brother not to harm her boyfriend, who has almost killed her in an horrific car crash while under the influence of alcohol. There are tears, histrionics and lots of perfect teeth. Sound familiar? It will if you've ever watched one of Venezuela's numerous TV soap operas, or *telenovelas*, as they call them.

This genre strictly adheres to its own rules and conventions: glamorous stars; completely implausible plots and totally unbelievable conclusions. But people love them. And not just in Venezuela. South America's single most successful *telenovela*, 'Cristal', is a Venezuelan product that interrupted work and social schedules in neighbouring countries. When it was first aired in Spain, it was one of the most popular TV series ever shown, closely followed by Venezuela's second most successful *telenovela*, 'La Dama de Rosa'. Both soaps broke ratings records in Italy. However, their popularity in Europe may have had more to do with post-modern tastes than genuine affection.

This phenomenal success comes despite some formidable obstacles. A Caribbean dialect that can be difficult for other Hispanic people to understand, for one. Also, the use of 'colourful' *Caraqueño* expressions that would normally offend more sensitive southern ears. Despite this, *telenovelas* top the ratings in Peru, Argentina and Ecuador.

Venezuelan soaps are generally more professional than their Mexican counterparts, more scandalous than Argentine equivalents and notorious for their dramatic denouements. Each episode is packed full of scandal, seduction and fashion statements. There's enough glamour in a Venezuelan *telenovela* to make US soaps such as 'Dallas' and 'Dynasty' look positively dowdy and downbeat.

It's not all fluff and flashing teeth, however. Though the *telenovela* usually dramatises the lives of the rich and beautiful, some have taken on more ambitious socio-political themes, touching on issues of poverty, violence and human rights abuses in the *barrios*.

FOOD AND DRINK

It may seem strange for a country whose capital boasts some of the continent's most sophisticated culinary delights, but Venezuela's favourite food is a lump of fried corn or wheat flour about the size of a fist.

Hot gossip

The world of *telenovelas*, salsa and beauty queens has created the monster that is *farándula*. This loosely translates as 'a load of old rubbish' and is used to describe the hype and gossip that surrounds the lives of Venezuela's stars.

Every movement, every sneeze, every waking breath of the country's media stars is documented in minute detail in a hundred glossy magazines and TV chat shows. Venezuela, it seems, is more than a little obsessed with the private lives of its celebrities; and the more sensational and scandalous the better. This may appear trivial to the outsider, but to the dedicated celebrity-watcher the tiniest tidbit of gossip is as essential as the drug-addict's next fix.

When it comes to TV, movies and music, Venezuelans pride themselves not only on being up to the minute with the latest offerings, but also au fait with the ins-and-outs of every performer's personal details. In this crazy world of pop culture, music and acting are virtually one and the same thing. While actors can make it without singing, vocalists must appear in one or two local soap operas, for *telenovela* work is part and parcel of a recording contract. Sometimes TV fame eclipses the music and aspiring singers become better known as leading actors and actresses than musicians. One example is José Luis Rodríguez, better known as "El Puma", whose leading role in the hit soap, *Estefánia*, brought him fame and launched a high-flying singing career. Women have an additional path into the world of *farándula*: the beauty contest. A Miss Venezuela winner is virtually guaranteed an acting or singing career – or both – if she shows even the merest hint of any talent.

The roots of *farándula* as big business go back to the 1980s, when the Venezuelan economy was strong and Caracas was one of the world's most expensive cities. The number of Venezuelans jetting off to Miami for weekend shopping trips caught the eye of entrepreneurs keen to cash in on so much disposable income. Though plagued by economic crisis in recent years, the love of *farándula* continues unabated.

Venezuelans may not enjoy the financial trappings of former times but they can still outspend their Caribbean neighbours. The vast majority of the population owns a TV set and those who don't probably live in areas so remote they wouldn't receive transmission. Even the flimsiest of shanty-towns features a forest of TV antennas sticking up from its roofs. Add to this the fact that 70% of the population is under 18 years old and it comes as no surprise that investors are willing to put money into the country's TV, music and film industries.

The stars of these industries may have to suffer the indignity of having the less savoury aspects of their private lives exposed on TV and in newspaper columns, but the *farándula* provides them with invaluable promotion. As one famous Irishman once said: "If there's one thing worse than being talked about, it's not being talked about."

Yes, the *arepa* is as ubiquitous in Venezuela as fish and chips in Britain or sausages in Germany. The cheap and filling *arepa* is eaten by everyone, everywhere, and it seems, at every hour of the day.

Arepas are sliced open and stuffed with just about anything imaginable (and a few things that aren't!). Among the most popular fillings are: *carne mechada* (shredded beef), *reina pepiada* (chicken with *guacamole*), *ensalada de atún* (tuna salad) or simply *queso amarillo* (yellow cheese). At breakfast they are filled with *perico*, scrambled eggs with tomato and onion. *Arepas* can also be spread with *natilla*, a light cream cheese, or eaten alone as an accompanyment to the national dish, *pabellón criollo*. This features shredded beef spiced with onions, green pepper, tomato, coriander and garlic, rice, fried plantain and *caraotas negras* (black beans). This is part of the staple diet of many working-class people and also a regular on many restaurant menus.

Similar to the *arepa* (but far superior, in my humble opinion) is the *tequeño*. This is made of egg pastry dough, rolled into cigar-shaped pieces, wrapped around strips of cheese and fried (and very yummy, too). These are served as *pasapalos* (hors d'oeuvres) or eaten anytime as a snack. Another culinary ever-present is the *cachapa*, a thick and slightly sweet pancake made with maize. They're eaten at breakfast or as a snack with cheese. And not forgetting the *empanada*, a fried cornmeal turnover filled with cheese, meat or fish (the trout ones in the Andes are to die for), or *cachitos*, which are filled *croissants* (invariably ham and cheese). *Pasticho* is what the Venezuelans call Italian *lasagne*.

Venezuela also boasts fine meat, fish and *mariscos* (shellfish). Beef is produced by the ton in the *llanos* and you can enjoy a steak the size of Belgium for less than the price of a beer in Europe. You can choose between *muchacho* (roast beef), *solomo* (sirloin) and *lomito* (steak). Serious meat eaters can put their arteries at risk with a mighty *parilla*, or mixed grill.

Up in the Andes the lakes and streams are filled with *trucha* (trout), which you would be crazy to miss, and along the Caribbean coast you can dine on *pargo* (red snapper), *dorado* and shellfish like clams or oysters.

Vegetarians can open their eyes again. This section deals with tropical fruit, and Venezuela has a bewildering selection to choose from. There's *lechosa* (papaya the size of a football), mangos, *guayaba* (guava), *guanábana*, *zapote* (sapodilla plum), *níspero* (the fruit of the medlar tree), oranges, pears, breadfruit, melons, pineapples, strawberries, coconuts, *parchita* (passion fruit), *limónes* (lemons) and *aguacate* (avocado). Not surprisingly, then, fruit juices are big business here, and just wonderful. There's *papelón con limón* (lemonade sweetened with raw sugar), or *jugo de caña* (pale green sugar cane juice) and *coco* (coconut, of course), drunk straight from the shell. Anything, in fact, can be made into a mouth-watering *jugo* (juice), *batido* (more fruit and less water than *jugo*) or *merengada* (a milkshake). You'll find every kind of banana here – from the short and stubby *cambur*, to the large *plátano* (which is used for frying). Very tasty are bags of crisply fried, lightly salted banana chips called *tostones*.

At Christmas the Venezuelan love affair with the *arepa* is put on hold, and people's attentions and appetites turn to the *hallaca*, which is not so much made and eaten as lovingly created and worshipped. This icon of the food world is basically a packet of cornmeal dough filled to bursting with chicken, pork and beef, spiced with green pepper, onion, garlic, tomatoes, capers, sugar, cumin, black pepper, parsley, pork fat, olive oil, raisins, pimento-stuffed olives and the kitchen sink (I made that last one up). Each *hallaca* is then wrapped in banana leaves and steamed. The preparation takes days and is the subject of considerable debate among all self-respecting Venenzuelans. But don't forget the most important ingredient of all – love.

A delicious sweet is *huevos chimbos* – egg yolk boiled and bottled in sugar syrup. The Caracas *Daily Journal* (in English) lists many reliable restaurants in Caracas and Maracaibo. You should note that Venezuelans dine late.

Regional specialities

As a large country with many varied zones, Venezuela has its own distinctive regional cooking. On the coast you'll find various *hervidos de pescado* (fish soup), also crayfish, small oysters and prawns. Sometimes there is turtle, though it is a protected species. Turtle may appear on menus in the Península de Paraguaná as *ropa especial*. A favourite is *sancocho*, a rich and delicious fish stew. *Consomé de chipi chipi* is a thin broth with tiny clams, that is reputed to be an aphrodisiac. Around Coro *chivo en coco* (goat in coconut) is a speciality.

Andean cuisine is very different. *Arepas* here are made of wheat, rather than corn. Local potatoes are very sweet and the locally-made cheese is superb. Also good are the cured meats and sausages that are sold at the roadside in many rural villages.

In the Amazon region the staples are *yuca* (yucca or manioc), plantains, corn and beans. *Casabe* (cassava) is a dry, fibrous flatbread that has all the taste of a cornflakes packet. People here also eat fish, turtles, tapirs, monkeys and birds. A local delicacy are deep-fried ants, especially the winged ones known as *culonas* (big bottoms). But don't feel that you have to follow suit.

DRINK

Venezuelan rum is very good; recommended brands are Cacique, Pampero and Santa Teresa. There are four good local beers: Polar (the most popular), Regional (with a strong flavour of hops), Cardenal

I drink therefore I am

Coffee drinking in Venezuela is not just something you do while chatting to friends or waiting for a bus – it's more a way of life. One of the many delights this country has to offer is its magnificent coffee, which ranks among the finest in the world. And it's cheap, too. So cheap, in fact, that connoisseurs will think they've died and gone to coffee heaven.

The country's love affair with coffee began after the Wars of Independence, when political and economic instability coupled with changing tastes in Europe brought about the end of the cacao boom. Venezuela desperately needed a new export commodity and coffee seemed to fit the bill. Demand was growing and the country's climate, terrain and soil combined to make this an ideal crop. Also in 19th century Venezuela the main concentrations of population were precisely in those areas best suited for taking advantage of this new source of income, such as the sub-tropical mountainsides throughout the state of Táchira.

Once the export trade had begun in 1835, the cultivation of the crop expanded rapidly. The effect of this expansion was to incorporate Venezuela's economy more fully than before into those of North America and Europe. Though this export trade brought some prosperity to the country's small and medium-sized landowners and provided work for poor landless peasants, the unregulated World market meant that prices were unstable. When the coffee boom ended around the middle of the 19th century, it left the Venezuelan economy bankrupt and over-dependent on a single commodity.

Now production is mainly for the domestic market, which is why you rarely see it for sale abroad. So, take the opportunity to try Venezuelan coffee when you're here. You can have it *negro* (black), *corto* or *largo* (short or long), *fuerte* or *cargado* (strong), *amargo* or *cerrero* (bitter), *suave* or *claro* (weak), *guarapo* (weak and sweet), *café con leche* (coffee with milk), *marrón* (dark brown), or *marrón claro* (light brown). Don't take too long in deciding, though – you're only delaying the pleasure.

and Nacional (a *lisa* is a glass of keg beer; for a bottle of beer ask for a *tercio*); Brahma beer (lighter than Polar) is imported from Brazil. There are also mineral waters and gin. Now there is a good, local wine in Venezuela. The Polar brewery has joined with Martell (France) and built a winery in Carora. Wines produced are 'Viña Altagracia' and 'Bodegas Pomar'. 'Bodegas Pomar' also produces a sparkling wine in the traditional champagne style. Liqueurs are cheap, try the local *ponche crema*. The coffee is excellent and very cheap. A *pluscafé* is an after-dinner liqueur. Water is free in all restaurants even if no food is bought. Bottled water in *cervecerías* is often from the tap. No deception is intended, bottles are simply used as convenient jugs. Insist on seeing the bottle opened if you want mineral water. *Chicha de arroz* is a sweet drink made of milk, rice starch, sugar and vanilla.

People

Venezuela is seen as the melting pot of South America. Its population includes a large number of people of mixed Spanish and Indian origin; over two-thirds of Venezuelans define themselves as mixed-race. There are some pure Africans and a strong element of African descent. Blacks make up nearly a tenth of the population. They are concentrated mainly along the coast, particularly at the ports, in the villages near Lake Maracaibo, and also in Caracas. Some Afro-Venezuelans are the descendants of the 60,000 slaves imported during the 17th and 18th centuries to work on the cacao plantations. The arrival of 800,000 European immigrants, mostly in the 1950s, has also greatly modified the racial make-up. One in six of all Venezuelans is today foreign born.

It is claimed that racism does not exist in Venezuela's *café con leche* (coffee with milk) culture. One of the country's great thinkers, Arturo Uslar Pietri, wrote: "In Venezuela there are neither whites nor blacks, neither *mestizos* nor Indians. There are only Venezuelans". True, this mixture of Americans, Africans and Europeans has given Venezuela a rich and varied social and cultural life, but this is still a highly unequal society, in which power and wealth remain in the hands of a white elite. Though there is certainly some social mobility today, most black Venezuelans work in poorly paid agricultural or domestic jobs, and the country's indigenous people are among the poorest and most marginalized communities.

THE INDIGENOUS PEOPLES

About 1% of the population (150,000) is indigenous, divided into 27 linguistically

Yanomami Indians

and culturally distinct ethnic groups. Among the best-known are the Yanomami, who live in Amazonas, and the Bari in the Sierra de Perijá, on the northwest border with Colombia. An Indian Reserve gives the Bari effective control of their own land, but this has not prevented infringement from mining, plantation or settlers. The Yanomami, too, have faced such threats from miners and gold prospectors, despite the government setting aside 83,000 sq km of territory for them.

The struggle for land rights is the main issue facing the country's remaining indigenous peoples today. The National Indian Council of Venezuela (CONIVE) claims that 83% of indigenous groups lack title deeds to their own lands. This renders them vulnerable to exploitation from oil companies and cattle barons. Among the groups that do not have title to their territory are the Wayuu (in the Guajira), the Panare and the Piaroa. The largest indigenous group are the Guajira, who number between 200 and 300,000, and live in and around the Sinamaica lagoon north of Maracaibo. They have managed to preserve their language and traditions while also prospering from cattle raising and tourism.

AN URBAN SOCIETY

Venezuela, despite its relative wealth, still faces serious social problems. Many rural dwellers have drifted to the cities, particularly in the decades that followed the discovery of oil. During the dictatorships of Gómez and Pérez Jímenez there was huge social upheaval and demographic change as Venezuela became predominantly an urban nation. People were uprooted from their villages and farms and moved into the huge concrete tower blocks and sprawling suburbs of the reconstructed cities. One result of this exodus is that Venezuelan farmers do not provide all the food the nation needs and imports of foodstuffs are necessary, even for items such as beans and rice.

YOUTH AND EDUCATION

One of the first things that any visitor to Venezuela will notice is the overwhelming youthfulness of its people. Those over the age of, say, 25 will begin to feel like old age pensioners after a few weeks here. The statistics bear out this impression. Over half the population is under the age of 20, and only 3% is over 65.

Such a youthful population presents both problems and opportunities for the country. Taking advantage of this vast resource of 'human capital' depends on investing in education and training and creating a highly qualified workforce for the future. Since the 1980s, however, education has fallen victim to economic reform and austerity measures imposed by successive governments. Drop-out rates at schools have risen alarmingly, and as the whole system creaks under the weight of such a large young population and government cutbacks, the threat of social unrest increases. Poverty is a feature of life for many young Venezuelans, who see little hope for the future. As a result, crime and drug abuse are becoming huge problems in cities, especially in the capital's shanty towns.

Responsible tourism

Much has been written about the adverse impacts of tourism on the environment and local communities. It is usually assumed that this only applies to the more excessive end of the travel industry such as the Spanish Costas and Bali. However it now seems that travellers can have an impact at almost any density and this is especially true in areas 'off the beaten track' where local people may not be used to western conventions and lifestyles, and natural environments may be very sensitive.

Of course, tourism can have a beneficial impact and this is something to which every traveller can contribute. Many National Parks are part funded by receipts from people who travel to see exotic plants and animals, the Galápagos (Ecuador) and Manu (Peru) National Parks are good examples of such sites. Similarly, travellers can promote patronage and protection of valuable archaeological sites and heritages through their interest and entrance fees.

However, where visitor pressure is high and/or poorly regulated, damage can occur. It is also unfortunately true that many of the most popular destinations are in ecologically sensitive areas easily disturbed by extra human pressures. This is particularly significant because the desire to visit sites and communities that are off the beaten track is a driving force for many travellers. Eventually the very features that tourists travel so far to see may become degraded and so we seek out new sites, discarding the old, and leaving someone else to deal with the plight of local communities and the damaged environment.

Fortunately, there are signs of a new awareness of the responsibilities that the travel industry and its clients need to endorse. For example, some tour operators fund local conservation projects and travellers are now more aware of the impact they may have on host cultures and environments. We can all contribute to the success of what is variously described as responsible, green or alternative tourism. All that is required is a little forethought and consideration.

It would be impossible to identify all the possible impacts that might need to be addressed by travellers, but it is worthwhile noting the major areas in which we can all take a more responsible attitude in the countries we visit. These include, changes to natural ecosystems (air, water, land, ecology and wildlife), cultural values (beliefs and behaviour) and the built environment (sites of antiquity and archaeological significance). At an individual level, travellers can reduce their impact if greater consideration is given to their activities. Canoe trips up the headwaters of obscure rivers make for great stories, but how do local communities cope with the sudden invasive interest in their lives? Will the availability of easy tourist money and gauche behaviour affect them for the worse, possibly diluting and trivializing the significance of culture and customs? Similarly, have the environmental implications of increased visitor pressure been considered? Where does the fresh fish that feeds the trip come from? Hand caught by line is fine, but is dynamite fishing really necessary, given the scale of damage and waste that results?

Some of these impacts are caused by factors beyond the direct control of travellers, such as the management and operation of a hotel chain. However, even here it is possible to voice concern about damaging activities and an increasing number of hotels and travel operators are taking 'green concerns' seriously, even if it is only to protect their share of the market.

Environmental Legislation Legislation is increasingly being enacted to control damage to the environment, and in some cases this can have a bearing on travellers. The establishment of National Parks may involve rules and guidelines for visitors and these should always be followed. In addition there may be local or national laws controlling behaviour and use of natural resources (especially wildlife) that are being increasingly enforced. If in doubt, ask. Finally, international legislation, principally the Convention on International Trade in Endangered Species of Wild Fauna and Flora (CITES), may affect travellers.

CITES aims to control the trade in live specimens of endangered plants and animals and also 'recognizable parts or derivatives' of protected species. Sale of Black Coral, Turtle shells, protected Orchids and other wildlife is strictly controlled by signatories of the convention. The full list of protected wildlife varies, so if you feel the need to purchase souvenirs and trinkets derived from wildlife, it would be prudent to check whether they are protected. Venezuela is a signatory of CITES. In addition, most European countries, the USA and Canada are all signatories. Importation of CITES protected species into these countries can lead to heavy fines, confiscation of goods and even imprisonment. Information on the status of legislation and protective measures can be obtained from Traffic International, UK office T (01223) 277427, e-mail: traffic@wcmc.org.uk.

Green Travel Companies and Information The increasing awareness of the environmental impact of travel and tourism has led to a range of advice and information services as well as spawning specialist travel companies who claim to provide 'responsible travel' for clients. This is an expanding field and the veracity of claims needs to be substantiated in some cases. The following organizations and publications can provide useful information for those with an interest in pursuing responsible travel opportunities.

Organizations Green Flag International Aims to work with travel industry and conservation bodies to improve environments at travel destinations and also to promote conservation programmes at resort destinations. It provides a travellers' guide for 'green' tourism as well as advice on destinations, T (UK 01223) 890250. **Tourism Concern** Aims to promote a greater understanding of the impact of tourism on host communities and environments; Stapleton House, 277-281 Holloway Road, London N7 8HN, T (UK 0171) 753-3330, F 753-3331, e-mail: tourconcern@gn.apc.org. **Centre for Responsible Tourism** CRT coordinates a North American network and advises on North American sources of information on responsible tourism. CRT, PO Box 827, San Anselmo, California 94979, USA. **Centre for the Advancement of Responsive Travel** CART has a range of publications available as well as information on alternative holiday destinations. T (UK – 01732) 352757.

Caracas

V ENEZUELA'S CAPITAL is not for the faint-hearted. The term "concrete jungle" could have been coined especially for this fast and frenetic city of 5 million inhabitants. Dizzyingly high  structures of concrete and glass tower over a spider's web of wide, congested freeways where enormous North American gas-guzzling cars belch out clouds of toxic fumes. Concrete plazas are filled with coffee-guzzling *Caraqueños* going about their business while water from a thousand leaking air-conditioning systems pours down like so many man-made waterfalls.

Not surprisingly, many tourists find Caracas less than appealing. The advance publicity in itself is enough to make even the most streetwise urbanite baulk at the prospect of spending any time here. But the city is not without its attractions.

For a start there's the nightlife. The average European or North American clubber would be left gasping at the sheer energy of *Caraqueños* out in pursuit of a good time. Wealthy districts such as Las Mercedes and Altamira are positively throbbing with life as the city's young unwind with a vengeance. For lesser mortals a more sedate alternative lies in the many and varied culinary delights on offer in the city's myriad restaurants. Or you can enjoy some great salsa from the relative safety of your bar stool in one of the Spanish-style *tascas*.

Believe it or not, it is actually possible to escape the hustle and bustle and enjoy a little welcome greenery, for parks there are aplenty. Dominating the northern skyline are the wooded peaks of the Avila National Park, with good walking and camping. Caracas also caters for even the hungriest of cultural appetites with many museums, galleries and theatres.

Caracas lies at a pleasant 960m above sea level in a valley in the Central Highlands, a rift in the thickly forested mountains which runs some 24 km east and west. This is the most important upland area in Venezuela. The mountains rise abruptly from a lush green coast to heights of from 2,000-3,000m.

The valley floor is crammed with high-rise office and apartment blocks, a conspicuous reminder of Venezuela's free-spending years. Equally visible are the city's shanty towns of red brick, plywood and corrugated iron which cling to the hillsides encircling the modern centre. While the massive windfall from increased oil production fuelled massive urban development it also spawned an unprecedented exodus from the countryside.

Caracas' growth since World War Two has been greater than that of any other Latin American capital. Alongside the rural incomers came a wave of immigrants from post-war Europe and the authorities could not keep up with the spiralling demand for housing. The shanty towns, known as *ranchitos*, spread further east and west away from the centre. Some of the older slums have become established working-class suburbs with the gradual arrival of drinking water, electricity and proper roads. The more recent additions, however, remain devoid of even the most basic services.

HISTORY

The original settlement of Santiago de León de Caracas was founded by Diego de Losada on 25 July 1567. The Spanish *conquistador* thought he had found the perfect location. A lush valley, cooled by the soothing breeze and sheltered from the sea by a high verdant wall of mountains. The Río Guaire, which runs the length of the valley, helped determine the location of the city and its crystal clear waters have inspired many a poet to wax lyrical. Today's murky, litter-strewn waters would drive them to despair, however.

Venezuela never figured prominently in Spain's colonial plans and, consequently, the capital's history is unremarkable. In the early 1700s Caracas was still nothing more than a collection of adobe houses with red-tiled roofs. As recently as a century ago it remained an insignificant outpost. But all that changed with the coming of oil. The country's black gold has transformed the city into the high-rise metropolis of the late 20th century. By 1955, the population had soared to 1 million and since then has increased five-fold.

Little remains of colonial Caracas. The past has been flattened to make way for the optimistic modernism of the 1960s. Perhaps the best example of this is the imposing twin tower complex of the Parque Central, built to meet the city's growing housing needs and now a futuristic maze of theatres, galleries and expensive shops.

There is now no single centre to Caracas. The modern city is a broad strip, 10 km from west to east, fragmented by traffic-laden arteries, and contains several centres, which include Plaza Bolívar, Plaza Venezuela, Sabana Grande, Chacaíto, Altamira, La Floresta and Boleíta.

BASICS Caracas has a *population* of nearly 5 million (the city proper 1,825,000). It

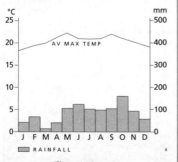

Climate: Caracas

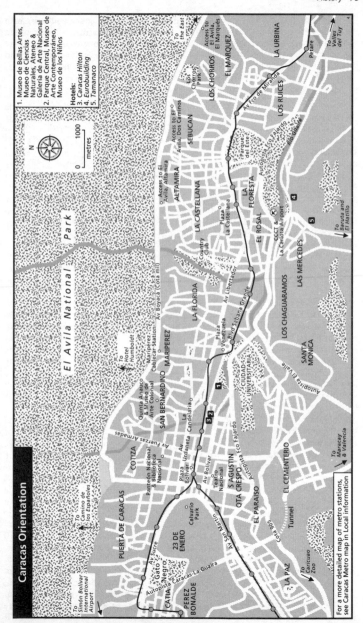

Caracas Orientation

1. Museo de Bellas Artes,
   Museo de Ciencias
   Naturales, Ateneo &
   Galería de Arte Nacional
2. Parque Central, Museo de
   Arte Contemporáneo,
   Museo de los Niños

Hotels:
3. Caracas Hilton
4. Eurobuilding
5. Tamanaco

N

0   1000
metres

El Avila National Park

To Simón Bolívar
International Airport

To Camino de
los Españoles

PUERTA DE CARACAS

COTIZA

SAN BERNARDINO

Quinta Anauco
& Museo de
Arte Colonial

To Hotel
Humboldt

Maripérez
Cable-Car Station

Av Fuerzas Armadas

Panteón Nacional
Biblioteca
Nacional

Plaza
Bolívar

Av Bolívar

Av
Urdaneta

Candelaria

Teatro
Nacional

Av
Sucre

Calvario Park

23 DE ENERO

Av San Martín

Autopista Caracas-La Guaira

CATIA

Av
Gato
Negro

PEREZ BONALDE

QTA CRESPO

S AGUSTIN

Autopista Fco Fajardo

CIUDAD UNIVERSITARIA

EL CEMENTERIO

EL PARAISO

Cota 905

Tunnel

LA PAZ

To Caricuao Zoo

Autopista El Valle

SANTA MONICA

LOS CHAGUARAMOS

To Maracay
& Valencia

LA FLORIDA

Av Boyacá (Cota mill)

Plaza
Venezuela

Blvd Sabana Grande

Av Libertador

LAS MERCEDES

Country
Club

LA CASTELLANA

Plaza
La Castellana

ALTAMIRA

Access to El
Avila, Altamira

Access to El
Avila, Dos Caminos

SEBUCAN

EL ROSAL

CCCT &
La Carlota Airport

To Baruta and
El Hatillo

Access to El°
Avila, Altamira

LA FLORESTA

Parque
del Este

Autopista Fco Fajardo

Rio Guaire

LOS CHORROS

Los Chorros
Park

EL MARQUEZ

Av Fco de Miranda

LOS RUICES

LA URBINA

Access to
El Avila,
El Márques

To the East

Petare

To Valles
del Tuy

For a more detailed map of metro stations,
see Caracas Metro map in Local information

stands at an altitude of 960m, but the southern parts of the city are 160m higher. Temperatures are moderate: a maximum of 32°C in July and August, and an occasional minimum of 9°C in January and February; and it is always cool at night. *Phone code 02.*

GETTING AROUND

A comparatively low pass (1,040m) in the mountains gives Caracas access by a magnificently engineered road from its port, **La Guaira**, and its international and domestic airports nearby at **Maiquetía**. A toll (US$0.05) is charged on this road only when going up.

The modern *autopista* and the winding old road from La Guaira converge at **Catia**, an industrial area in the west. From here, Avenida Sucre runs east to the city centre. Three main routes branch east from Avenida Sucre or its viaduct continuation. **The first route**, Avenida Urdaneta, begins between Palacio Miraflores and the Palacio Blanco, housing presidential offices. It passes the Post Office and Santa Capilla Church, looking like a wedding cake by a Parisian master pastrycook. Turn right here for Plaza Bolívar and the Capitolio Nacional, or carry straight on down the Avenida Urdaneta to San Bernardino. Avenida Urdaneta becomes Avenida Andrés Bello, with a link road to Avenida Libertador which goes to the Country Club and the east. Just below Avenida Libertador is Parque Los Caobos, with the fine mahoganies which give it its popular name.

The second route from the Avenida Sucre viaduct, Avenida Universidad, passes the Biblioteca Nacional (former University), the Capitolio Nacional and San Francisco church (two corners later, on the left, is Bolívar's birthplace), before continuing to the Museo de Bellas Artes and on round Parque Los Caobos. From the Plaza Venezuela intersection at the eastern end of the park, the Avenida Abraham Lincoln leads east through Sabana Grande and continues as the Avenida Francisco Miranda to Altamira, with its fine plaza and obelisk and Parque del Este. Sabana Grande, a modern shopping, hotel and business centre, is closed to vehicular traffic and a popular place to take a stroll or sit at one of its many open-air cafés.

The third route east from Avenida Sucre, and crossing the viaduct, is via El Silencio. From there it runs through the Centro Simón Bolívar, with its twin skyscrapers, underground parking and shopping centre (with an interesting mosaic at the lowest level), and finally along the Avenida Bolívar past Nuevo Circo bullring to Los Caobos. Here it joins the Autopista del Este which passes Ciudad Universitaria and the Sports Stadium. The *autopista* splits at Las Mercedes: del Este goes east past La Carlota airfield, Parque del Este and La Casona, residence of the President to Petare; Autopista Caracas- Baruta goes south past the *Hotel Tamanaco*.

An alternative west-east route is along the Avenida Boyacá from Avenida Baralt in the west, skirting the Cordillera de la Costa, including Monte Avila, and giving fine views along the length of the city. It passes a monument commemorating the battle of Boyacá, and a viaduct over the park in Los Chorros suburb before joining the Autopista del Este to become Route 9 to Barcelona.

The Metro

Getting around Caracas doesn't have to be a lung-destroying, stressful experience. Below the chaos of the city streets runs the clean, shiny and efficient Metro system, which has helped ease the burden placed on an overstretched public transport service. Even if you're not heading anywhere in particular, the cool, air conditioned depths provide some welcome relief. At Plaza Venezuela there's even a giant video screen to keep you entertained. See Metro map on page 92.

PLACES OF INTEREST

The shady **Plaza Bolívar**, with its fine equestrian statue of the Liberator and pleasant colonial cathedral, is still the official centre of the city, though no longer geographically so. It's a pleasant place to sit and relax while waiting for everything to open again after lunch.

The **Capitolio Nacional**, on the Plaza Bolívar, dates from 1873. The Elliptical Salon has some impressive paintings by the Venezuelan artist Martín Tovar y Tovar and a bronze urn containing the 1811 Declaration of Independence. One of the paintings on the ceiling shows a British regiment fighting in the Battle of Carabobo, and the names of the officers appear on the wall. It is open to visitors Tuesday-Sunday, 0900-1200, 1500-1700.

On the east side of the plaza is the present **Cathedral** building, on the site of the original palm-thatch church, built in 1567. The present structure dates from 1674. It has a beautiful façade, gilded altar, the Bolívar family chapel and pictures by Michelena, Murillo and an alleged Rubens 'Resurrection'.

The church of **San Francisco**, one block southwest of Plaza Bolívar on Avenida Universidad y San Francisco, is the oldest church in Caracas, and was rebuilt in 1641. It should be seen for its colonial altars and Murillo's 'San Agustín'. The church of **Santa Teresa**, between La Palma and Santa Teresa, just southeast of the Centro Simón Bolívar, has good interior chapels and a supposedly miraculous portrait of *Nazareno de San Pablo* (there are popular and solemn devotions on Good Friday).

The **Panteón Nacional**, at Plaza Panteón, Avenida Norte y Avenida Panteón, is the country's most sacred shrine and single most important building. For here lie the remains of Simón Bolívar, the Liberator (see page 44). Also here is the tomb of Francisco Miranda (see page 107), who died in a Spanish prison. It has been left open to await the return of his body. Likewise the tomb of Antonio José de Sucre, who was assassinated in Colombia. Every 25 years the President opens Bolívar's casket to verify that the remains are still there. Daniel O'Leary, Bolívar's Irish aide-de camp, is buried alongside. The Panteón is open Tuesday-Sunday, 0900-1200 and 1430-1700. The changing of the guards takes place at 1430 daily.

Modern Caracas

Those who are interested in seeing an example of the more exuberant futuristic visions of Venezuela's most notorious dictators should visit the **Ciudad Universitaria**. This is an enormous and coherent complex in which paintings, sculpture and stained glass are completely integrated with the architecture. The complex is now showing signs of wear, however.

South of the university, reached by Autopista El Valle, is **Paseo de los Próceres**, with its twin monoliths and other monuments to the heroes of independence as well as colourful gardens. Beside the Avenida de los Próceres is the impressive **Círculo Militar**, designed by Pérez Jiménez as a cloverleaf with his initials "MPJ". The pool, lake and theatre are open to the public.

MUSEUMS

Museo de Bellas Artes, at Plaza Morelos in Parque Los Caobos, is the oldest museum in Caracas, and was designed by Carlos Raúl Villanueva. The pictures include an El Greco among works by mainly Venezuelan artists. It is open Tuesday-Friday, 0900-1200, 1500-1730, weekend 1000-1700. Adjacent is the **Galería de Arte Nacional** (T 571-0176), with the same opening hours, which also houses the **Cinemateca Nacional**; open Tuesday-Sunday at 1830 and 2130, and Sunday at 1100 for children's films.

Also in Plaza Morelos in Parque Los Caobos is the **Museo de Ciencias Naturales**, which has archaeological, particularly precolumbian, zoological and botanical exhibits. It is open Tuesday-Friday, 0900-1200, 1500-1730, and weekends 1000-1700.

Well worth a visit is the **Museo de Arte Colonial**, at the Quinta Anauco, Avenida Panteón, in San Bernardino. The Quinta is a delightful house built in 1720, the residence of the Marqués del Toro. Chamber concerts take place most Saturdays at 1800. It is open Tuesday-Saturday, 0900-1200, 1400-1700, and Sunday, 1000-1730. A guided tour in Spanish is available. The beautiful suburb of San Bernardino is full of tropical flowers and whole avenues of

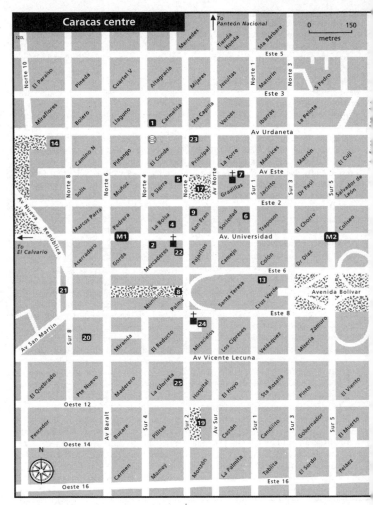

Caracas centre

To Panteón Nacional

0   150
metres

forest trees, smothered in blossom in season. To get there take a *por puesto* from Bellas Artes metro (at the same stop as the metro bus); those bound for San Bernardino go past Quinta Anauco.

Casa Natal del Libertador is a lovely reconstruction of the house where Bolívar was born, on 24 July 1783. It contains interesting pictures and furniture. The first house, of adobe, was destroyed by an earthquake. The second became a stable, and was later pulled down. The house is on Plaza San Jacinto, one block east of the cathedral, and is open Tuesday-Friday, 0900-1200 and 1430-1700; Sundays and holidays, 1000-1700. The **Museo Bolivariano** is alongside the Casa Natal and contains the Liberator's war relics.

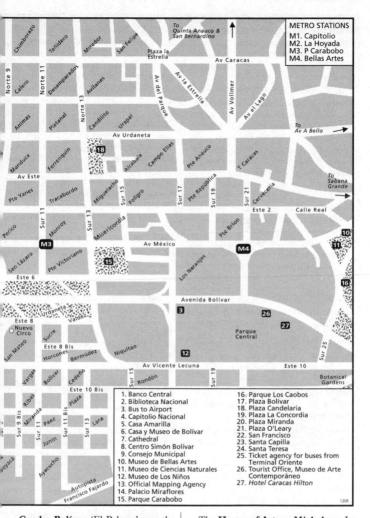

METRO STATIONS
M1. Capitolio
M2. La Hoyada
M3. P Carabobo
M4. Bellas Artes

1. Banco Central
2. Biblioteca Nacional
3. Bus to Airport
4. Capitolio Nacional
5. Casa Amarilla
6. Casa y Museo de Bolívar
7. Cathedral
8. Centro Simón Bolívar
9. Consejo Municipal
10. Museo de Bellas Artes
11. Museo de Ciencias Naturales
12. Museo de Los Niños
13. Official Mapping Agency
14. Palacio Miraflores
15. Parque Carabobo
16. Parque Los Caobos
17. Plaza Bolívar
18. Plaza Candelaria
19. Plaza La Concordia
20. Plaza Miranda
21. Plaza O'Leary
22. San Francisco
23. Santa Capilla
24. Santa Teresa
25. Ticket agency for buses from Terminal Oriente
26. Tourist Office, Museo de Arte Contemporáneo
27. *Hotel Caracas Hilton*

Cuadra Bolívar, 'El Palmar', was the Bolívar family's summer home. It's a beautifully preserved colonial country estate, with walled gardens, stables and Bolívar memorabilia. It's at Bárcenas y Las Piedras, eight blocks south of Plaza Bolívar. Open Tuesday-Saturday, 0900-1300, 1430-1700; Sundays and holidays 0900-1700.

The **House of Arturo Michelena**, La Pastora y Puente Miraflores, four blocks north of Miraflores palace, in the La Pastora section, is a typical 19th century home. It is open 0900-1200 and 1500-1700 (closed Monday and Friday).

Museo de Transporte is at Parque Nacional del Este (to which it is connected by a pedestrian overpass). It includes a large collection of locomotives and old cars, as well as a fascinating series of scale models of Caracas a century ago, although much has been neglected. Open Saturday and Sunday, 0900-1600; admission US$0.10.

In the **Parque Central**, between Avenida Lecuna (east end) and the elevated section of Avenida Bolívar, there are four museums in a complex which includes two octagonal towers (56 floors each) and four large apartment buildings with shopping below. The museums are: **Museo de Arte Contemporáneo**, Cuadra Bolívar, entrance beside *Anauco Hilton*. It has a very good selection of European and Venezuelan painters, a room devoted to Picasso ink and pen drawings, and interesting modern sculptures. Open Tuesday-Sunday 1000-1800; entry free.

Museo de los Niños, next to the east tower, is a highly sophisticated modern science museum, and extremely popular. Allow 2-3 hours for a visit, and book a day or so in advance in school holidays or August. It is open Wednesday-Sunday and holidays, 0900-1200, 1400-1700; otherwise it is for school visits. Entry US$0.75 (adults). Also in the Parque Central complex is **Museo Audiovisual** (open Tuesday-Friday, 0900-1700; entry US$1), which includes a library of Venezuelan television programmes, and a practice TV studio, and **Museo del Teclado** (keyboard instruments).

Casa Amarilla (The Ministry of Foreign Relations), at the northwest corner of Plaza Bolívar, has pictures mostly of national heroes and historical events.

Museo Histórico Fundación John Boulton contains many unique historical items and a library of 19th-century research material and commercial records of the Casa Boulton. The museum was previously in La Guaira (see page 99). It is now at Torre El Chorro, 11th floor, Avenida Universidad y Sur 3, entre El Chorro y Dr Díaz. Open Monday-Friday 0800-1200, 1300-1700; free entry, 2 tours a day by knowledgeable guides. Underground parking is available on presentation of ID.

The Concejo Municipal (City Hall), on Plaza Bolívar, is where the Venezuelan Declaration of Independence was signed, on 5 July 1811. It contains three museums: the **Museo Criollo Santana** is a collection of miniature figures in costumes and poses characteristic of the Creole way of life in turn-of-the-century Caracas, all handmade by Raúl Santana; the **Sala de Arqueología Gaspar Marcano** is an exhibition of ceramics, mostly discovered on the coast; there's also a collection of the paintings of Emilio Boggio, a Venezuelan painter. All three museums are open Tuesday-Friday, 0930-1200, 1500-1800; Saturday and Sunday, 0930-1800. Informative guides are available.

Those with a deeper interest in archaeology might like to contact the *Junta Nacional Protectora y Conservadora del Patrimonio Histórico y Artístico de la Nación*, Palacio de Miraflores, Avenida Urdaneta.

NB Museums and art galleries throughout Venezuela are closed on Monday. Check museum schedules in *El Universal*, *El Nacional* or the *Daily Journal* (which also have details of events for children). Many museums and most religious buildings will refuse entry to anybody wearing shorts.

PARKS AND ZOOS

Jardín Botánico is worth a visit. There are extensive plant collections and a small area of 'natural forest'. Here you can see the world's largest palm tree (*Corypha Sp*) and the Elephant Apple with its huge edible fruit. The gardens are near Plaza Venezuela; the entrance is by Ciudad Universitaria (US$0.30, guide US$1 in English).

Parque Los Caobos is peaceful and has a cafetería in the middle. By the entrance in Avenida México is the cultural centre, Ateneo de Caracas, with a theatre, art gallery, concert room, bookshop and the imposing Teresa Carreño theatre complex.

Parque Nacional del Este (renamed the Parque Rómulo Betancourt in 1989) is a popular place to relax, especially at weekends. There is a boating lake, a

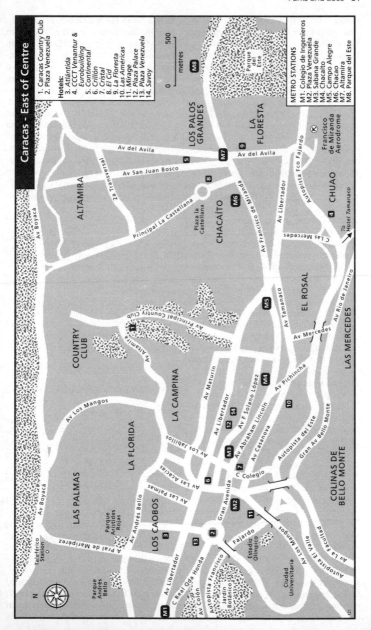

Caracas - East of Centre

Hotels:
1. Caracas Country Club
2. Plaza Venezuela
3. Atlántida
4. CCCT Venantur & Eurobuilding
5. Continental
6. Crillón
7. Cristal
8. El Cid
9. La Floresta
10. Las Américas
11. Mirage
12. Plaza Palace
13. Plaza Venezuela
14. Savoy

METRO STATIONS
M1. Colegio de Ingenieros
M2. Plaza Venezuela
M3. Sabana Grande
M4. Chacaíto
M5. Campo Alegre
M6. Chacao
M7. Altamira
M8. Parque del Este

0   500
metres

replica of Columbus' *Santa María* (being renovated since 1991), the Humboldt Planetarium (weekend shows, US$0.25), a number of different sunken lakes featuring caiman and turtles, monkeys, two frustratingly caged jaguars, many types of water birds and a terrarium (open at weekends, entry US$0.05). The park opens at 0530 for joggers, 0800 for mere mortals, till 1730, it's closed on Monday; entrance is US$0.15. It's reached from Parque del Este metro station.

The heavily-wooded 630 hectares of **Caricuao Zoo** forms part of the Parque Nacional Macuro (15,000 hectares). Originally the territory of the Caciques tribe of Caracas, Caricuao means "*Quebrada del Caribe*". This was the site of a large coffee plantation until 1967, when it was made into a zoo by President Raúl Leoni. The zoo is small, with a limited range of species, some of which are in large cages, others in smaller, less adequate cages, but generally it's well kept (better than Parque el Este). Many of the birds are free, including flamingoes, macaws, parrots and peacocks. Capuchin monkeys also roam free and will steal your food if you're not careful. There's also a small farmyard section for children. The park entrance is beautiful, with many large shady trees and a pond, lots of grassy areas for picnicing and a cafetería. The toilets are clean. It's well recommended for a pleasant day out.

The park is open Tuesday-Sunday 0900-1700, entry US$0.20. It is at the southwest end of the Metro line. To get there take the metro to Caricuao 'Zoológico' (about 20 minutes from Capitolio). Outside the metro station, cross the road towards an *empanada* stand, where there is a metro bus stop. From there, it's a 5-minute walk up Avenida Principal La Hacienda to the entrance.

Parque Nacional El Pinar, founded in 1938, has a 7-hectare zoo, which was newly renovated in 1995. It is larger than Caricuao but it is not nearly as pleasant. It is mostly made up of small concrete enclosures. There is a small cafetería with clean toilets. The park is open Tuesday-Sunday 0900-1745, entry US$0.65. To get there take bus marked 'Paraiso-Montalban' from Avenida Baralt, outside the Capitolio metro station (exit La Pedrera), and ask to be let off at the park entrance on Avenida Páez, on the corner of Avenida Guadalajara. There is a *fuente de soda* "*El Pinar*" on your left and opposite is a Firestone tyre shop. The park entrance is 500m up Avenida Guadalajara on the right.

Also recommended is **Parque Los Chorros**, at the foot of the mountain, which has impressive waterfalls. Entrance is US$0.05. Take a bus marked 'Petare' and 'La Urbina'.

El Calvario, west of El Silencio, with the Arch of Confederation at the entrance, has a good view of Centro Simón Bolívar. It has a small Museo Ornitológico, botanical gardens and a picturesque chapel. But note that muggings have been reported.

A new park, **Parque Vargas**, is planned, similar in concept to the Champs Elysées, and some is already in place. A model of the area is on display in the Galería de Arte Nacional.

EXCURSIONS

El Hatillo has well-preserved colonial style housing, with many art galleries, souvenir shops and restaurants. It has a very popular market which gets really crowded at Christmas. On the plaza is a tearoom serving good cakes. A good Mexican restaurant is *Padrisimo*, one block from the plaza. Nearby is the wealthy residential district of La Lagunita. El Hatillo is 30 minutes from the city centre by car, or take a bus from Avenida Humboldt, two blocks from Plaza Chacaíto.

LOCAL FESTIVALS

3 May: *Velorio de la Cruz de Mayo* is still celebrated with dances and parties in some districts. **18-25 December**: Yuletide masses are held at different churches leading up to Christmas, and traditional creole dishes are served at breakfasts.

LOCAL INFORMATION

● Accommodation

Hotel prices

L1	over US$200	L2	US$151-200
L3	US$101-150	A1	US$81-100
A2	US$61-80	A3	US$46-60
B	US$31-45	C	US$21-30
D	US$12-20	E	US$7-11
F	US$4-6	G	up to US$3

Those marked with an asterisk (*) are bookable through Fairmont International (see hotel reservations below).

Cheap *pensiones* are usually full of long-stay residents and have very few rooms available for travellers. Hotels tend to be particularly full at weekends and in July and August. In the centre all cheap hotels take only short stay customers on Friday afternoons. Better hotels often try to give you a suite instead of a double room. Note also that hotel prices below do not include 12.5% tax. Those marked with an asterisk (*) are bookable through Fairmont International (see **Hotel reservations** below).

Hotels in Chuao/Las Mercedes, which is a business/commercial district southeast of the centre, with no metro station: **L1** *Tamanaco**, Avenida Principal Las Mercedes, PO Box 467, Caracas 1060A, T 792-4522, F 208-7116, a luxury business hotel and the best in Caracas, superb pool, it's difficult to get rooms as it is normally fully booked, price includes service, but not 15% tax, rooms are priced in dollars, courteous staff, good facilities, changes travellers' cheques for guests only (poor rates); **L1** *Eurobuilding*, Centro Ciudad Comercial Tamanaco, T 959-1133, F 993-9285, PO Box 64487, 5-star, modern, has an all-suite wing, well-furnished, air conditioning, includes breakfast, efficient service, large pool, gym, restaurants, many services, weekend rates available; also in CCCT **L3-A1** *CCCT Venantur**, T 959-0611, F 959-6409, smart business hotel with a pool terrace, it's approached through the shopping mall and is not that easy to find; **A2** *Hotel Paseo de las Mercedes*, Las Mercedes, T 991-0444, F 993-0341, almost next door to the *Tamanaco*, good sized rooms, restaurant, bar, small pool on pleasant rear terrace.

Near Altamira metro station, a respectable commercial and residential area, east of the centre: **A3** *Continental*, Avenida San Juan Bosco, T 261-9091, F 261-0131, smart, gardens front and rear and a good private swimming pool; **B-C** *El Cid*, Avenida San Felipe, between 1a and 2a, T 263-2611, F 263-5578, Spanish style interior, large suites with living area, breakfast rooms, kitchenette ensuite, air conditioning, good value for money.

Sabana Grande/Chacaíto, is a varied area with many restaurants and shops; it's convenient for metro stops and is the safest area for cheap hotels: **A2** *Lincoln Suites*, Avenida Francisco Solano, entre San Jerónimo y Los Jabillos, T 761-2727, F 762-5503, top of the range in this area, high quality accommodation and service, no pool; **A2** *Cumberland*, 2da Avenida de las Delicias, T 762-9961, F 762-5549, very good, nice restaurant, taxi service to airport; **A3** *Las Américas*, Calle Los Cerritos, T 951-7387, F 951-1717, a modern tower with a new block attached, tiny roof pool and restaurant, taxi service to airport, good value; **A3** *Tampa**, Avenida Francisco Solano López, T 762-3771, F 762-0112, comfortable but noisy air conditioning, plain interior, interesting bodega-style restaurant.

B *Atlántida*, Avenida La Salle, Los Caobos, two blocks up from Avenida Libertador, T 793-3211, F 781-3696, safe, noisy, air conditioning, restaurant; **B** *Coliseo*, T 762-7916, F 761-7333, Coromoto y Bellomonte, air conditioning, good breakfast, 100m from Sabana Grande metro station, recommended; **B** *Crillon**, Avenida Libertador, esquina Avenida Las Acacias, T 761-4411, F 761-6911, high-rise block with good bar and *Le Chalet* restaurant; **B** *Plaza Palace*, Avenida Los Mangos, Las Delicias, T 762-4821, good; **B-C** *Savoy**, Avenida Francisco Solano y Avenida Las Delicias, T 762-1971, F 762-2792, good food, efficient, secure vehicle park, taxi service to airport.

C-D *El Condor*, Avenida Las Delicias, T 762-9911, comfortable but plain, outstanding restaurant in Spanish bodega style; **C** *Kursaal*, Avenida Casanova y El Colegio, T 762-2922, safe, air conditioning, cheap taxi service to airport; **C** *La Luna**, Avenida Casanova y El Colegio, T 762-5851, recommended.

Las Mercedes

Hotels:
1. Tamanaco

Places to eat:
2. Heladería Italiano
3. Mythos
4. Real Pasta
5. Reggio's Café
6. Café Tiamo
7. Yan's Garden

Sabana Grande

N

0   200
metres

Hotels:
1. Atlántida
2. Coliseo
3. Crillon
4. Cristal
5. Cumberland
6. Escorial
7. Kursaal
8. La Luna
9. La Mirage
10. Lincoln Suites
11. Odeon
12. Plaza Palace
13. Savoy
14. Tampa

Places to eat:
15. Delicatessen Indú
16. Korean Restaurant
17. Vegetarian Restaurant

M Metro Station

D *Broadway*, Avenida Casanova between Calle Guaicapuro and Calle Chacaíto, T 951-1922, near Chacaíto metro, Italian specialities in restaurant, friendly, recommended; **D** *Cristal*, Pasaje Asunción, just off Avenida Abraham Lincoln, near Sabana Grande metro, T 761-9131, with bathroom, air conditioning, TV, hot water, comfortable, safe, good value, disco at weekends, noisy air conditioning, restaurant; **D** *Ritz*, Avenida Las Palmas y Avenida Libertador, near Plaza Venezuela, T 793-7811, air conditioning, safe provided, good beds, quiet, luggage store, restaurant, secure free parking, ask for the cheapest rooms as they're not given first; **D-E** *Escorial*, Calle Colegio, near Plaza Venezuela, T 762-8820, F 762-7505, central, air conditioning, cable TV, secure, mediocre restaurant and bar, receives faxes free and cheap to send, cheap taxi service to airport, excellent service, good value.

E pp *King's Inn*, Calle Oropeza Castillo, Plaza Venezuela, T 782-7534, with bathroom, clean, friendly, TV, air conditioning, recommended; **E** *La Mirage*, Prolongación de Las Acacias, T 793-2733, F 793-0629, with bath, air conditioning, restaurant, reasonable value; **E** *Nuestro*, Calle Colegio near Plaza Venezuela, with bathroom, fan, secure, basic but good value; **E** *Odeon*, Las Acacias y Avenida Casanova, one block south of Plaza Venezuela, T 793-1322, F 781-9380, modern, stores luggage, restaurant serves Colombian food, reported as the best place to stay on Las Acacias. **NB** The Las Acacias/Avenida Casanova area is a red-light district and the majority of hotels are short-stay.

In San Bernardino, a residential area 2 km north of Bellas Artes metro: **A3** *Avila**, Avenida Jorge Washington (T 515128/515173, F 523021), set in park-like gardens and a world away from the bustle of modern Caracas, good service, most of the staff speak English and German, fans, mosquito screens, pool, Metrobus nearby, very good restaurant and poolside bar, phones which accept Visa/Mastercard, recommended.

B *Aventura**, Avenida Sorocaima y Avenida Francisco Fajardo, T 514011, F 519186, big rooms, suites for long lets, small pool in rear courtyard; **D** *Waldorf*, Avenida Industria, T 571-4733, hot water erratic, restaurant, English sometimes spoken, good value, will store luggage; next door is Banco Consolidado for exchange, and a good value Chinese restaurant (the airport tourist office often recommend this hotel).

In the downtown area you'll find most of the cheapest hotels, especially around the Nuevo Circo bus terminal, which is not a safe area (see **Buses** below), along Sur 2 near Santa Teresa, and around Capitolio Metro. In **Parque Central** (near Bellas Artes Metro), an area of tower blocks, concrete walkways and underpasses, is **L1** *Hilton**, Avenida Libertador and Sur 25, T 503-5000, F 503-5003, an ageing luxury hotel, impressive conference facilities, excellent business centre, spectacular city views, especially at night, noisy (from traffic and air conditioning), useful long-term luggage deposit and good breakfast, nice pool, fax service open to non-residents, very helpful, good sushi bar, recommended.

B-C *Plaza Catedral**, Boulevard Plaza Bolívar, next to the Cathedral, T 564-2111, F 564-1797, beautiful location in the colonial part of town, with bathroom, air conditioning, TV, air conditioning, some English spoken, Amex accepted, the roof restaurant (*Les Grisons*) has nice views and serves excellent food at reasonable prices.

D *Avenida*, Calle Sur 4 (near Capitolio Metro), hot water sporadic, air conditioning, safe, recommended; **D** *Hospedaje Fidelina*, Sur 4 No 120, safe, fan, **F** with shared bathroom; **D** *La Neve*, Sur 4, Pilita a Glorieta No 126, near Capitolio Metro, with air conditioning or fan, good, safe, quiet, good restaurant, recommended; **D** *Limón*, Calle Este 10, No 228, near Bellas Artes Metro, safe, parking, often recommended; **D** *Palais*, Sur 4, Pilita a Glorieta, modern, air conditioning, helpful, luggage stored, the restaurant is highly recommended; **D** *Renovación*, on Avenida Este 2, near Los Caobos and Bellas Artes Metro, T 571-0133/571-0744/571-0366, F 577-8910, with bathroom, air conditioning, TV, clean, modern, lots of restaurants nearby; **D-E** *Inter**, Animas a Calero, on the corner of Avenida Urdaneta, near the notorious Nuevo Circo, T 564-0251, helpful, English spoken, very popular, poor restaurant, accepts credit cards.

E *Caroní*, Avenida Baralt, between Muñoz and Piñango, popular, safe but a bit noisy, not very clean, bar, restaurant; **E** *Center Park*, on Avenida Lecuna esquina Sur 3, near Nuevo Circo, with bathroom, fan, TV, clean and friendly; **E** *Guarapiche*, Este 8, Zamuro a Pájaro (diagonal to Palacio de Justicia), T 545-3073, same price for singles, safe, air conditioning, hot water; **E** *Hospedaje Torreiro*, Sur 11, Bolívar a Sucre, next to Lagoven, T 577-2148, nice, helpful, bath, fan, safe, recommended; **E** *Pensión San Gregorio*, Este 12 esquina Arismendi, two and a half blocks from Nuevo Circo, many single rooms, more or less clean, shared or private bath; **E** *Pensión San Marcos*, Este 12, Hoyo a Santa Rosalía, T 545-3723, basic; **E** pp *Río Bravo*, on Avenida Lecuna opposite Parque Central, T 571-0258/571-0102, with bathroom, clean, stores valuables, convenient for the airport shuttle bus.

F *Nueva Lucía*, Sur 9, Arismendi a Pichincha, fan, helpful owner.

Hotel reservations: *Fairmont International*, Torre Capriles, Planta Baja, Plaza Venezuela, Caracas, T 782-8433, F 782-4407, Tx 21232 SNRHO, will book hotel rooms in Caracas and also in 102 hotels in the rest of the country and in other countries, eg Colombia, with no booking fee. They are recommended as helpful. The airport tourist office is very helpful and will book hotel rooms. If you book from abroad, make sure you receive confirmation before beginning your journey. If you arrive by air in the evening without a reservation it is probably a safer bet to get a taxi to Macuto, rather than Caracas, where there are several hotels only 15 minutes drive away. For apartment rental, consult *El*

Universal daily paper, small ads columns. *Residencias Taormina*, Avenida María Teresa Toro, una cuadra Plaza Tiuna delante CANTV, Las Acacias, has good apartments for US$25 per night, and better value for stays of 2 weeks or more.

● **Places to eat**

There is such a profusion of eating places in Caracas that we give the following general advice, with a mention of just a few places currently reported reliable, rather than attempt the impossible task of keeping up to date with all the changes. Guides to eating out in Caracas include *Guía gastronómica de Venezuela*, available in most bookshops, US$5.60.

Don't be shy about asking the price before you order in a bar as beer in one will cost three times as much as in another, and a modest portion of manchego cheese can cost more than a good steak. Food on display in a bar is free with your drink if they offer it as a *pasapalo*, but will be charged for if offered as a *ración*. You can save on the service charge by eating at the bar and not at a table. Restaurants must put up a list of prices on or near the front door, and are prohibited from charging for place settings (*cubiertos*) or bread, butter, condiments etc (*guarnición*). A meal costs between US$4-5 minimum, not including beer, which is an extra US$1 or so (these are 1997/8 prices).

Midday is the most economical time to eat the main meal of the day and about the only opportunity to find fresh vegetables. Particularly good value is the 'menú ejecutivo' or 'cubierto', which is a 3-course meal for US$2-3. Breakfast in your hotel is likely to be less than appetising, consisting of poor bread (or none at all), insipid coffee and orange juice which is half artificial. It is better and cheaper in a *fuente de soda*. Once you have purchased your ticket you will find there is little sense of queuing – shout your order to the staff like the locals. Cheaper still is a *pastelería* or *arepería*.

There is a wide selection of good restaurants around **Avenida Urdaneta** and in the districts of **Altamira, Las Mercedes** (see map) and in **Sabana Grande** (see below). Another good area for eating out is **La Castellana**; especially recommended is *La Estancia*, Avenida Principal La Castellana, esquina Calle Urdaneta, near Altamira Metro, very good beef in traditional style and popular with young Caracas business set; next door is *Primi*, Italian/Creole cuisine, quite chic and friendly, with plenty of vegetarian dishes.

In the downtown area there are plenty of eating places around Plaza Bolívar: *Plaza Mayor*, Torre a Veroes, on the northeast corner of Plaza Bolívar, very good, recommended; *El Paso*, Hospital a Glorieta, Edificio Atlántico, Plaza La Concordia, Chinese, cheap, good. For

seafood try *Las Vegas* near *Hotel Plaza Catedral*. *Casa de Italia*, in the Italia building, next to *Waldorf Hotel*, has the best Italian food for the price, excellent service, view and bar.

Sabana Grande is an area full of cafés, bars and restaurants to suit all tastes and budgets. The main boulevard (Avenida Abraham Lincoln) is lined with tables in the open air. It's the ideal place to sit and relax and watch the world go by. However, it's more expensive to sit here and some waiters may overcharge, so check prices on the displayed list before ordering.

Among the **recommended restaurants in Sabana Grande**: *Tivoli*, on Calle El Colegio between Lincoln and Casanova, good pasta dishes from US$1.70-2.50; *Casiero*, on Fco Solano, and *Urrita*, Fco Solano y Los Mangos, are both very good for national dishes; *Bohío Habanero*, in La Previsora, Cuban food; *La Buca* in *Hotel Kursaal*, international food; *Victor's Pollo*, Avenida Fco Solano y El Bosque (Chacaíto end), has 20 different chicken dishes; *Shorthorn*, Avenida Libertador y El Bosque. On Calle El Cristo, opposite *El Maní es Así* nightclub (see **Entertainment** below) is a good Korean restaurant, about US$10 per head. There is a good selection of Arabic, Chinese and Hindu restaurants on Calle Villa Flor; eg *El Arabito*. All Arabic restaurants have vegetarian options.

Vegetarian: *Buffet Vegetariano*, Avenida Los Jardines; *El Acuarino*, Truco a Caja de Agua; neither are open for dinner. *Almuerzo*, Hoyo a Santa Rosalía, good, cheap; *Comida Arabe*, on Calle Colegio, near *Hotel Kursaal*, excellent. Also *Delicatesen Indú*, on Calle Villa Flor towards the Avenida Casanova end, in Sabana Grande just off Avenida Abraham Lincoln between Sabana Grande and Plaza Venezuela Metro stations, specializes in southern Indian dishes, good quality, small portions. There's also a vegetarian place on Pasaje Asunción, 2 doors down from *Hotel Cristal* (see above), open 1000-1500.

Fast foods: there are countless burger and pizza places, also plenty hot dog stalls for those who really fancy a few days in bed with food poisoning. *Arturo's*, is a chain of clean, modern, chicken-and-chips style restaurants in various locations. *El Coco*, in the Centro Comercial Chacaíto, has very good Venezuelan food at much lower prices than the sidewalk cafés on nearby Sabana Grande. *El Arepazo*, one block south of Chacaíto Metro station, has every kind of arepa filling you could wish for (and more besides). As if you didn't know by now, *arepas* are the favourite snack of most Venezuelans. You can find them absolutely everywhere and they're cheap and filling.

● Airline offices

Avensa, Edificio Atlántida, Avenida Universidad, T 561-3366 (airport 551-5555), Metro La Hoyada; also at Avenida Caura, Torre Humboldt planta alta, Prado del Este, opposite Centro Comercial Congresa, T 907-8000 (take a Metro bus from Altamira). Aerotuy, Avenida Lincoln y Boulevard Sabana Grande, Edificio Gran Sabana, 5th floor, T 761-6247/9782/8043; Air Aruba, Avenida Libertador, Torre Maracaibo, T 719781; Aeropostal, Avenida Principal de La Castellana, Torre Banco Lara, 1st floor, T 264-6422, F 267-8166 (reservations T 800-28466, F 263-4836, 0730-2000).

Air France, Parque Cristal, Torre Este, 2nd floor, Los Palos Grandes, T 283-5855; Alitalia, Edificio Atlantic, 5th floor, Avenida Andrés Bello, Los Palos Grandes, T 800-66666; ALM, Edificio Exa, 8th floor, Avenida Libertador, T 953-7086/6424; American, Centro Plaza, Torre B, T 209-8111; Avianca, Avenida Fco de Miranda, Edificio Roraima, T 953-7254; British Airways, Torre Británica, 11th floor, Altamira, T 261-8006; BWIA, Oficentro Rovica, 1st floor, Boulevard Sabana Grande; Cubana de Aviación, Avenida Rómulo Gallegos con 1a Transveral, Santa Edurijes, Edificio Pascal, Torre 3, 1st floor, oficina 13-B (opposite Torre KLM); Iberia/Aerolíneas Argentinas, Avenida Sur 25, Plaza Morelos, Torre Viasa, 8th floor, Los Caobos, T 576-7969, F 576-9645; also at Avenida San Juan Bosco, Edificio Centro Altamira, 4th floor, Altamira Norte, T 267-8666, F 265-1114/261-3319. KLM, Torre KLM, Avenida Romulo Gallegos, T 285-3333; LIAT, Torre Británica, Mezzanine 2, Avenida JF Sosa, Altamira Sur, T 265-7542; Lufthansa, Avenida Tamanaco, Edificio Bayer, T 951-0044; United, Avenida Fco de Miranda, Edificio Parque Canaima, 8th floor, Los Palos Grandes, T 285-5753; Varig, Avenida Principal de Los Ruices, Centro Emp Los Ruices, 3rd floor, T 238-2111.

● Banks & money changers

(See also the **Currency** section in **Information for travellers**, page 330.)

Citibank will exchange Citicorp travellers' cheques; Banco Unión is good for Visa transactions. For cash advances on Mastercard, go to Credimático for a voucher then to Banco Mercantil for the cash from a side office; you can withdraw up to US$250 a day. Many banks accept Visa cards in their ATMs. For Thomas Cook travellers' cheques try Banco Internacional or Banco Mercantil. To change American Express travellers' cheques, try Banco Consolidado, Avenida San Francisco, Edificio Torre California, 9th floor, Urb Colinas de La California, mornings and afternoons, or any other branchof Banco Consolidado. The Amex rep is Turisol, Centro Comercial Tamanaco, level C-2, Local 53F-07, Chuao suburb, PO Box 62006,

T 959-3050, F 959-2867, they are recommended as helpful and efficient. Stolen or lost travellers' cheques can be replaced, and US$ cash exchanged, at the Amex office in Torre Consolidada, Plaza La Castellana, Avenida Principal La Castellana (nearest Metro is Altamira).

The following **exchange houses** – casas de cambio – have been recommended: Italcambio, they require proof of travellers' cheque purchase, commission 1.70%, open Monday-Friday till 1630, Saturday till 1200. They have offices at: esquina Veroes and Urdaneta; Avenida Casanova (Sabana Grande); Avenida L Roche (Altamira Sur), and Simón Bolívar Airport. They are open on public holidays, but may limit transactions to US$100. Opposite Italcambio (esquina Veroes and Urdaneta) is Visesta CA, which accepts Eurocheques, also for travel arrangements, Walter Kleebinder speaks several languages and is very helpful, T 562-4698/562-5333. La Moneda, Centro Financiero Latino, Urdaneta, 8th floor, and Avenida Fco Solano, one block from Plaza Venezuela Metro, opposite El Molino Rosso restaurant and next to Banco Profesional, open Monday-Friday only; Infesa, Avenida Libertador, between Negrín and Jabillos; Confinanzas, Centro Comercial Paseo Las Mercedes, Local PA-CI, open 0800-1200, 1400-1700, commission of 1% is usually charged on travellers' cheques; MVS Cambios, Avenida Francisco Solano, between Calles El Cristo and Los Manguitos, Edificio Torre Oasis, Sabana Grande, less waiting, good rates. There is also a casa de cambio on Avenida Fco de Solano, esquina Calle El Cristo, open Monday-Friday 0830-1730; and on Boulevard Sabana Grande, two blocks from the Metro, between Calle apamantes and Calle 1 Bello Monte, open office hours.

● Cultural centres

British Council, Edificio Torre la Noria, 6th floor, Las Mercedes; they also offer English classes and have a modest library. Centro Venezolano-Americano, Avenida Las Mercedes, good free library of books in English, and free concerts; also Spanish courses (8 different levels), each lasts 17 days and costs US$50, highly recommended. Asociación Cultural Humboldt (Goethe Institut), Avenida Juan Germán Roscio, San Bernardino, T 527634, library, lectures, films, concerts, Spanish courses.

● Embassies & consulates

Argentine Embassy, Centro Capriles, 2a, Mezz Entrada Este, Plaza Venezuela, T 781-1487, PO Box 569, Caracas 1010-A; Colombian Consulate, Guaicaipuro, Sector Chacaíto, Urb El Rosal, T 951-3631; open Monday-Friday 0800-1400 for visas, you need a photo and US$10, the process can take anything from 10 minutes to 1 day; Ecuadorean Consulate, Centro Empresarial Andrés Bello, 13th floor, Avenida Andrés

Bello, Torre Este, Parque del Este Metro, T 781-6090; **Mexican Embassy** (visa section), Edificio Parque Cristal, Torre Este, 14th floor (Monday-Friday 0900-1300), next to Parque del Este Metro, tourist cards issued on the spot, free; **Brazilian Embassy**, Plaza La Castellana, Avenida Principal La Castellana, nearest Metro Altamira, a visa (valid for 3 months maximum), costs US$13, you need a photo, it takes 24 hours; **Brazilian Consulate**, Edificio 'Centro Gerencial Mohedano', 6th floor, entre Calle Los Chaguaramas y Avenida Mohedano, La Castellano, open Monday-Friday 0830-1230; **Cuban Consulate**, Avenida 3/2, Campo Alegre, behind Clínica Sanatriz, 0900-1300; **Guyanese Embassy**, Edificio Los Frailes, Calle La Guanita, Chuao (same for Jamaican Embassy), T 978-1779, open for visa Monday, Wednesday and Friday, 0830-1200, issued on the same day if you're early, need passport, airline ticket, yellow fever certificate, and 2 photos; **Peruvian Consulate**, Centro Empresarial Andrés Bello, 7th floor, Avenida Andrés Bello, Torre Este, T 781-6168, next to Parque del Este Metro; **Suriname Embassy**, 4a Avenida, between 7a and 8a Transversal, Urb Altamira, T 262-1616; **Trinidadian Embassy**, beside the Suriname Embassy, Quinta Serrana, 4a Avenida, between 7a and 8a Transversal, Altamira, T 261-3748/4772, visa costs US$17, you need 2 photos, it can take up to 1 week.

USA Embassy and Consulate, Calle S con Calle Suapure, Colinas de Valle Arriba (take metro to Chacaíto then taxi for US$3), T 977-2011, F 977-0843, PO Box 62291; **Canadian Embassy**, Edificio Torre Europa, 7th floor, Avenida Francisco de Miranda, corner of Avenida Escuela, two blocks east of Chacaíto Metro, T 951-6166; **Australian Embassy**, 'Yolanda', Avenida Luis Roche, between transversal 6 and 7, Altamira, T 283-3090; **Japanese Embassy**, Avenida San Juan Bosco, between 8th and 9th Transversal, Altamira, T 261-8333.

Austrian Embassy, Torre Las Mercedes, Chuao, T 913863; **British Embassy and Consulate**, Torre Las Mercedes, 3rd floor, Avenida La Estancia, Chuao, T 751-1022/1166/1454/1966, Apartado 1246 for letters, they can issue a new passport in 5 days, best in the morning, call for appointment (T 993-4111), emergency number outside office hours, T (016) 262973; **Danish Embassy**, Avenida Venezuela, esquina Calle Mohedano, Edificio Centuria, 7th floor, El Rosal, near Chacaíto Metro station, T 951-5606; **Finnish Embassy**, Torre C, 14th floor, Centro Plaza, Avenida Fco de Miranda, T 284-5013; **French Embassy**, Edificio Las Frailes, 6th floor, La Guairita; **German Embassy**, Edificio Panavén, 2nd floor, Avenida San Juan Bosco, Altamira, T 267-0181/1205, open Monday-Friday 0900-1300; **Greek Embassy**, Avenida San Gabriel 60, Alta Florida, T 261-7696/262-1590;

Israeli Embassy, Avenida Fco de Miranda, Centro Empresario Miranda, 4th floor, T 239-4511, F 239-4320; **Netherlands Consulate**, Edificio San Juan, 9th floor, San Juan Bosco y Avenida Transversal 2, Altamira, T 266-6522, F 263-0462, send post to Apartado 62286, Caracas 1060a; **Spanish Embassy**, Edificio Banco Unión, Sabana Grande, 1st floor; **Swedish Embassy**, Edificio Panavén, 5th floor, Avenida San Juan Bosco con Tercera Transversal, Altamira; **Swiss Embassy**, Torre Europa, 6th floor, Avenida Fco de Miranda, esquina Avenida Escuela, two blocks east of Chacaíto Metro, T 951-4064.

● **Entertainment**

There are frequent Sunday morning concerts in the Teatro Municipal, 1100. Concerts, ballet, theatre and film festivals take place at the Ateneo de Caracas, Paseo Colón, Plaza Morelos. Also similar events, including foreign artists, at the Complejo Cultural Teresa Carreño (see **Cultural centres** above).

There are numerous **cinemas**, including: *Radiocity*, on Boulevard Sabana Grande, one block from Plaza Venezuela; *Broadway*, Avenida Abraham Lincoln, esquina Avenida Humboldt; also at Plaza Chacaíto, in the carpark under Centro Comercial Chacaíto (go down the ramp next to *Papagayo* restaurant). Normally cinemas have 4 showings a day, usual price is US$3, except the *Lido* in Chacao, which is US$4.20 (half price on Monday). For details of these and other events, see the newspapers, *El Universal*, *El Nacional* and *Daily Journal*, and the Sunday issue of *El Diario de Caracas*.

Nightclubs: Caracas is a lively city by night. Caraqueños dine at home around 2000, and in restaurants from 2100 to 2300, so nightclubs don't usually come to life until after 2300, and then go on to all hours of the morning. *Un Solo Pueblo*, typical Venezuelan music, Tercera Transversal, Altamira (there are many small clubs, restaurants and bars on Plaza Altamira Sur). Opposite is *Café Rajatabla*, in the Ateneo cultural complex, which attracts a young crowd and often has live music; *El Maní es Así*, Calle El Cristo, one block up from Avenida Fco Solano, good for live salsa and dancing, US$6 after 2200 when it starts to liven up, but it's open from 1700. One block east of Nuevo Circo, opposite the filling station, is *Rica Arepa*, an *arepería* which has traditional Venezuelan folk music (free) on Friday, Saturday and Sunday nights. *La Padrona*, Calle Humboldt, Chaguaramas, Brazilian music. Other recent recommendations include: *Pida Pizza*, Sabana Grande; *Weekend*, Las Mercedes; *Palladium*, in CCCT shopping centre, popular, big, and you do not have to be in a couple as in many other places.

There are numerous *tascas* (bars) where you can hear good salsa music and dance (or watch others doing it properly). Two good ones are *Asunción* and *O' Gran Sol*, both on Calle Villa Flor in Sabana Grande, where you can get Spanish and Venezuelan food, both very lively at weekends.

● **Hospitals & medical services**
Hospital de Clínicas, Avenida Panteón y Avenida Alameda, San Bernardino, T 574-2011.

Doctors: Dr Gasser, T 976-2637, recommended by the Swiss Embassy; Dr Jean J Desenne, at the *Instituto Médico La Floresta*, room 106, T 209-6222 (extension 106), in La Floresta district, a few minutes from Altamira Metro station, he charges US$21 per consultation and speaks fluent English and French.

● **Laundry**
Lavandería Austria, Lecuna y Sur 3, self-service or service wash, helpful, reasonably priced; *Lavandería Automática Jescal*, San Agustín, Sur 11, Sucre 106, self-service, cheap, open 0700-2000. *Lavandería Automática*, Sur 17, Este 2, one block from *Hotel Waldorf*, self-service or service wash, open 0800-1600, sometimes later. Also near Capitolio Metro, at Calle Oeste 12, Santa Teresa, entre Calle Sur 2 y Calle Sur 4, open 0730-1830, Monday, Saturday, US$2 per 3 kilos, fast service.

● **Places of worship**
(With times of services in English): **San Ignacio College**, Calle Santa Teresa, La Castellana, Sunday mass 0915. **Protestant**: The United Christian Church, Avenida Arboleda, El Bosque, Sunday 1000; St Mary's Anglican and Episcopal, Calle Chivacoa, San Román, Sunday 1030. **Shalom Temple**, Avenida Jorge Washington, San Bernardino, Saturday 0900 and 1600.

● **Post & telecommunications**
Post Office: the main one is at Urdaneta y Norte 4, close to Plaza Bolívar. You can mail packages abroad from here; it's fast and efficient but not much help with packing boxes (no tape etc). *Lista de correos* costs US$0.30, Monday-Friday 0700-1945, Saturday 0800-1700, Sunday 0800-1200. There's an Ipostel office in Centro Comercial Cediáz, on Avenida Casanova between Calle Villaflor and San Jerónimo, open Monday-Friday office hours, and Saturday till 1200; and also one at the airport. There's an Ipostel box just inside the entrance to the *Lincoln Suites* (see **Accommodation** above) on the Sabana Grande entrance. Collections are every 2 days (apparently).

Telecommunications: are operated by CANTV, on the 1st floor of Centro Plaza on Avenida Fco Miranda, on the corner of Andrés Bello, between Metros Parque del Este and Altamira; open Monday-Saturday 0800-1945, T 284-7932, phone cards are sold here. Public telex at

Centro Simón Bolívar and *nivel* C-I, Centro Ciudad Comercial Tamanaco. There are public phones in the Metro stations and along Boulevard Sabana Grande (Abraham Lincoln).

You can also phone and fax from *Cables Internacionales*, Santa Capilla a Mijares, Edificio San Mauricio, planta baja, open Monday-Saturday 0700-1900, near Capitolio Metro, walk one block east of the main Post Office then half block north; fax to Europe and North America costs US$3 per page, phone to North America US$1.20 per minute, to Europe US$1.80 per minute.

● **Security**
It is advisable not to arrive in Caracas at night and not to walk down narrow streets or in parks after dark. Avoid certain areas such as all suburbs from the El Silencio monument to Propatria, other than the main roads, the area around the *teleférico*, Chapellín near the Country Club, and Petare. Street crime is on the increase, **even armed robbery in daylight**. Never carry your valuables. Even in a crowded place like Sabana Grande, bag slashing and mugging is not uncommon. Car theft is common. The vast majority of Caraqueños are honest and friendly, but you need to take care at all times. For some useful tips, see under **Safety**, in **Information for travellers** (see page 339).

NB also: Police searches are frequent and thorough, especially around Avenida Las Acacias after dark and at airports. Always carry your ID, or preferably a photocopy of your passport. If you have entered overland from Colombia, you can expect thorough investigation. It's better to say you flew in, if you're searched by the police in Caracas.

● **Shopping**
For gems and fine jewellery, visit the *H Stern* shops at the Hotels *Hilton* and *Tamanaco* and at the International Airport; try also *Labady*, Sabana Grande 98, beautifully-made gold jewellery, English spoken. *Pro-Venezuela Exposición y Venta de Arte Popular*, on Gran Avenida, Plaza Venezuela (opposite Torre La Previsora), has a good selection of Venezuelan crafts, no prices, bargain hard. There's a good quality Sunday craft market between Museo de Bellas Artes and Museo de Historia Natural (Bellas Artes Metro). The Indian market on the southwest corner of Plaza Chacaíto has a selection of Venezuelan, Peruvian and Ecuadorean crafts. The **CCCT shopping centre** is worth a visit, as is the Centro Comercial Plaza Las Americanas, mostly for fashion stores and beach wear. Large-size shoes (up to 47) can be found at Catedral Sur 4 y Mercaderes. **Centro Plaza Altamira**, between Metro stations Altamira and Parque del Este, has

shops, cafés, *tascas* and the **Centro Mediterráneo**, with boutiques and cafés and a good quality cinema.

Color Express in the Centro Comercial Chacaíto does good, cheap and quick slide developing.

For **camping and fishing equipment** try *Marvmen*, at 3a Transversal directly north of Altamira Metro, it's expensive but excellent.

Bookshops: English language ones: *English Bookshop*, Concresa, Prados del Este, will exchange nearly new books and stocks the *Caribbean Islands Handbook*; *Lectura*, Centro Comercial Chacaíto; *American Bookshop*, Avenida San Juan Bosco, Edificio Belveder, T 263-5455/267-4134, near Altamira metro, Monday-Friday 0900-1730, Saturday 0900-1400, good selection of second-hand English books; also available in bookstalls in the street. *Audobon Society of Venezuela*, in the basement of Paseo Las Mercedes, T 993-2525, sells guidebooks and gives information, closed on Saturday. *Librería del Este*, Avenida Francisco de Miranda 52, Edificio Galipán, and *Librería Unica*, Centro Capriles, ground floor local 13N, Plaza Venezuela, have foreign language books; *Librería Washington*, La Torre a Veroes No 25, good service. *Novedades* has branches all over the city; *Librería Ecológica*, Plaza Caracas, between Torres Norte and Sur, Centro Simón Bolívar, near CANTV office, for environmental books, also has some maps. A French bookshop is *Librería La France*, Centro Comercial Chacaíto. Italian bookshop, *El Libro Italiano*, Pasaje La Concordia (between Sabana Grande pedestrian street and Avenida Fco Solano López). For German books, *Librería Alemana* (Oscar Todtmann), Centro El Bosque, Avenida Libertador, T 710881, open Tuesday-Saturday, 0900-1230, 1500-1800. *Alcaldía de Caracas*, Puente Brion, Avenida Méjico, used foreign language books.

● **Sports**

Horse-racing takes place every Saturday and Sunday at La Rinconada, which has a magnificent grandstand. Betting is by a tote system. Races start at 1300; admission to the grandstand is US$1.10. Several buses go to La Rinconada. Bull fights take place at Nuevo Circo on the 2nd Sunday in January, and also in February. To hire fishing boats contact Ani Villanueva, T 740862. The most popular sport in Venezuela, by a long way, is baseball. The season runs from October to January. You'd be well advised to catch a game if you're around during these months, in particular the "derby" involving the local *Leones del Caracas* and *Magallanes*, which sends the crowd into a mad, passionate frenzy (see also page 63).

Clubs: there are three country clubs in Caracas, all of which have excellent restaurants. The Country Club in the eastern part has an 18-hole golf course. The Social Centre of the British Commonwealth Association, Quinta Alborada, Avenida 7 with Transversal 9, Altamira, T 261-3060, has a bar and swimming pool, British and Commonwealth visitors only are admitted, entry fee is according to length of stay. The sports club run by the *Tamanaco Hotel* is open to non-guests and suitable for people staying a short time. Radio Club Venezolano is a very welcoming organization of amateur radio operators which is eager to meet amateurs from around the world (address: PO Box 2285, Caracas 1010-A, T 781-4878, 781-8303 – Avenida Lima, Los Caobos; branches around the country).

● **Tour companies & travel agents**

Maso Internacional, Plaza Altamira Sur, Avenida San Juan Bosco, T 313577, reps for Thomas Cook, generally good reports of tours. *Lost World Adventures*, Edificio 3-H, 6th floor, Oficina 62, Avenida Abraham Lincoln, Caracas 1050, T 761-7538, tours to Roraima and Canaima. *Candes Turismo*, Edificio Roraima, Avenida Fco de Miranda, Urb Campo Alegre, Aptdo 61142, T 952-8415, F 953-3176, e-mail: candes@telcel.net.ve, Web: http://www. candesturismo.com.ve, helpful, English, Italian, German spoken; *Orinoco Tours*, Edificio Galerías Bolívar, 7th floor, Avenida Abraham Lincoln, Caracas 1050-A, PO Box 51505, T 761-7712, F 761-6801, German-owned, for flights and tours, very helpful; *Selma Viajes*, Avenida Universidad, Monroy a Misericordia, Edificio Dorado Locales A y B, T 572-0235, run recommended excursions to Canaima; *Paisajes y Turismo SRL*, Avenida Francisco Miranda, Edificio Centro Peru, Piso 5, Oficina 58, T 265-6460/267-4079, F 263-8381, e-mail: paisajesvenezuela@compuserv.com; *Alborada Tours*, 1ra Avenida Sur Altamira, Edif Teatro Altamira, Entrada Oeste, Piso 9, Oficina 91, T 265-2433, F 263-1940.

In the USA: *Lost World Adventures* specialize in tours of Venezuela, ranging from the Caribbean, to the Andes, plus tours of Panama and Ecuador, 1189 Autumn Ridge Drive, Marietta, GA 30066, T (404) 971-8586, (800) 999-0558 outside GA, F (404) 977-3095. *Forum Travel International*, 91 Gregory Lane, Suite 21, Pleasant Hill, CA 94523, T (510) 671-2900, F (510) 671-2993, runs tours to *Las Nieves Eco-Adventure Jungle Lodge*, in the transition zone of savannahs and jungles of the Orinoco, with lots of wildlife, nature tours, canoeing, etc.

In the UK: *Last Frontiers*, Swan House, High Street, Long Crendon, Bucks, HP18 9AF, T 01844-208405, F 01844 201400 (Internet http://www. lastfrontiers.co.uk), run by Edward

Paine (who used to live in Venezuela), organizes tailor-made itineraries to any part of Venezuela, and throughout South America, they also run photographic and painting tours. Also *Geodyssey* run adventure and general tours of Venezuela, including Angel Falls, Mount Roraima, upper Orinoco, Andes treks and specialist tours for birdwatchers, 29 Harberton Road, London N19 3JS, England, T (0171) 281-7788, F (0171) 281-7878.

Tours to Cuba: *Ideal Tours*, Centro Capriles, Plaza Venezuela, T 267-3812, 4 days, 3 nights, US$649, including flight, hotel, half board and city tour. *The Tour Hunters*, T 91-2511, 5 days, 4 nights US$286, 6 days, 5 nights US$340, including everything except flights.

● **Tourist offices**
Corpoturismo, administrative office on floor 35, Torre Oeste, Parque Central (Metro Bellas Artes is closest), T 507-8607/8600; open Monday-Friday 0830-1200, 1400-1630. They are nice and helpful but don't have much information or maps. There is, though, a terrific view of the city from their windows, and they'll record one of their tourist videos if you take along a blank tape. There is also a smaller office at the airport (see below). See page 355 for **Maps** and further recommended reading.

● **Useful addresses**
Inparques: the Instituto Nacional de Parques (Inparques) is part of the Ministerio del Ambiente y Recursos Naturales Renovables (MARNR) which administers Venezuela's national parks. Main offfice is at Avenida Rómulo Gallegos (by north exit of Parque del Este Metro station), T 285-4106/4360/5056, F 285-3070. Regional offices are given under the relevant towns.
Diex: Avenida Baralt, El Silencio, for visa renewal, 2nd floor for new tourist cards, reported as friendly and helpful, Spanish only. **NB** Don't believe anyone who tells you visa extensions are not available and then tries to sell you a 1 year visa.

Touring y Automóvil Club de Venezuela, Torre Phelps, 15th floor, oficina A y C, Plaza Venezuela, T 794-1032/781-7491, ask for the treasurer, Sr Oscar Giménez Landínez, who speaks some English, or Zonaida R Mendoza, Secretary to the Club President.
YMCA: Edificio YMCA, Avenida Guaicaipuro, San Bernardino, T 520291.

● **Transport**
Local Buses: many buses start from Nuevo Circo bus station in the city centre, and are

overcrowded in the rush hours. There's an additional fare after 2100 (the correct fare helps to speed things up). On the longer runs these buses are probably more comfortable for those with luggage than a *por puesto*. Midibuses are known as *carmelitas*. *Por puesto* minibuses run on regular routes. The fares depend on the distance travelled within the city; fares rise for journeys outside. Many *por puesto* services start in Silencio.

Driving: self-drive cars (Hertz, Avis, Volkswagen, Budget, Dollar, ACO) are available at the airport and in town. They are cheaper than guided excursions for less than full loads. A driver's licence from your home country is accepted. A major credit card or cash deposit over US$200 is required. Rates are given in **Information for travellers**, **Motoring** (see page 343). Budget is the only company giving unlimited mileage, if you book and pre-pay outside the country. Auto and personal insurance (US$10-17.50 per day) is strongly advised as you will be lucky to survive 2 or 3 days as a newcomer to Caracas traffic without a dent or a scrape. Cars should be checked carefully as most have some defect or other, and insist on a short test drive.

Garage: *Yota-Box*, 3a Transversal Mis Encantos, Quinta Morava, No 1 15, Chacao, T 313772/331035, owner Gerardo Ayala, recommended, especially for Toyota; *Bel-Cro*, Avenida Intercomunal de Antímano, very good for VWs, also sells new and used parts, very cheap and highly recommended.

Motorcycles: may not be ridden in Caracas between 2300 and 0500. Also see **Motoring** (page 343).

Taxis: are required by law to install and use taxi-meters, but they never use them, if they have not already been removed. Fares must be negotiated in advance. Most city trips are US$1 absolute minimum during the day (most fares US$2). Taxi drivers are authorized to charge an extra 20% on night trips after 1800, on Sunday and all holidays, and US$0.45 for answering telephone calls. After 1800 drivers are selective about where they want to go. Beware of taxi drivers trying to renegotiate fixed rates because your destination is in 'a difficult area'. The sign on the roof of a taxi reads 'Libre'. There are pirates with possibly a taxi sign, but without yellow licence plates/registration-number plate, which are to be avoided. Never tell a taxi driver it is your first visit to Caracas. See yellow pages for radio taxis.

The Metro: operates between 0530 and 2300. It is air conditioned, clean, well-patrolled, safe and more comfortable and quicker than any other form of city transport. There is no smoking, and it's probably best to take rucksacks only during off-peak hours. There are 3 lines: Line 1 runs west to east from Propatria to Palo Verde; Line 2 runs north to south from Capitolio to Las Adjuntas, with a connection to Caricuao Zoológico; and Line 3 runs south from Plaza Venezuela to El Valle, from where there is a metrobus to Los Teques. Tickets cost US$0.20-0.25 per journey; 10-journey tickets (*Multi Abono*), cost US$2 (US$3.60 including Metrobus). Student discounts are available with an ISIC card. Metrobuses connect with the Metro system (US$0.20): get transfer tickets (*boleto integrado*, US$0.20) for services to southern districts (route maps are displayed at stations) – keep your ticket after the exit turnstile. A good selection of maps is available at the shop in La California station.

Air 28 km from Caracas, near the port of La Guaira is **Maiquetía**, for national flights, and **Simón Bolívar** for international flights. They are adjacent to each other, only 5 minutes' walk apart – taxis take a circular route, and charge US$2.25. The airport authorities run a shuttle bus between the two every 10 minutes from

Caracas Metro

Propatria · Pérez Bonalde · Plaza Sucre · Gato Negro · Agua Salud · Caño Amarillo · Capitolio · La Hoyada · Parque Carabobo · Bellas Artes · Colegio de Ingenieros · Plaza Venezuela · Sabana Grande · Chacaíto · Chacao · Altamira · Parque del Este · Los dos Caminos · Los Cortijos · La California · Petare · Palo Verde

El Silencio
Capuchinos
Maternidad
Artigas
La Paz
La Yaguara
Carapita
Antímano
Mamera
Ruiz Pineda
Las Adjuntas
Caricuao
Zoológico

Ciudad Universitaria
Los Símbolos
La Bandera
El Valle

8a

0700. The Tourist Office at the international airport has good maps and is helpful; some English spoken, open 0700-2400, T 551060. The tourist office at the national terminal is open 0700-2100, T 551191. When staffed, both offices are useful, will book hotels and reconfirm flights. They also speak English and offer a better service than Corpoturismo head office. Flight enquiries T (031) 522222; passenger assistance T 552424; police T 552498. Many facilities close on 1 January, including the duty free and money exchanges. Duty free shops close at 2230.

At Simón Bolívar: several *casas de cambio* are open 24 hours (good rates at Italcambio, outside the duty-free area). There's also a Banco Industrial branch and another, less crowded, in the baggage reclaim area. If changing travellers' cheques, you may be asked for your receipt of purchase; commission is 2.5%. There are cash machines for Visa, Amex and Mastercard. There's a pharmacy, bookshops and a basement café, which serves good value meals and snacks, open 0600-2400, but it's hard to find. The cafés and bars on the 1st floor viewing terrace are also good value. There's no official left luggage; ask for Paulo at the mini bar on the 1st floor. Look after your belongings in both terminals. Direct dial phone calls can be made to the USA only, from the AT&T booth in the departure lounge. CANTV have an office at Gates 15 and 24, open 0700-2100, for long-distance, international and fax services, and receipt of faxes.

Always allow plenty of time when going to the airport, whatever means of transport you are using, as the route can be very congested. It can take up to 2 hours in daytime, but only 30 minutes at 0430. Allow at least 2 hours checking-in time before your flight. When several flights arrive close together there are long queues for immigration.

Taxi fares from the airport to Caracas cost on average US$14 minimum, depending on the quality of the taxi, the part of city, or on the number of stars of your hotel. It may save you money to give the name of a cheaper hotel nearby. Fares are supposedly controlled, but it is essential to negotiate with the driver; overcharging is rife. Check the official fares outside the airport terminal. After 2200 and at weekends a surcharge of 20% may be added, and you may be charged up to US$40. Drivers can only surcharge you for luggage (US$0.50 per large bag). Taking a taxi from the city to the airport is cheaper; around US$10-12. If you think the taxi driver is overcharging you, make a complaint to Corpoturismo or tell him you will report him to the Departamento de Protección del Consumidor. A taxi to Macuto should cost US$12. A recommended driver is Jesús A Salas, T (016) 377413/(014) 396213, or contact him at *Posada Hidalgo* in Macuto (see page 100).

The airport shuttle bus, which is blue and white with 'Aeropuerto Internacional' on the side, leaves from the east end of the international terminal (turn left out of the exit). To get to the airport, you need to catch the shuttle bus under the flyover at Bolívar and Avenida Sur 17, 250m from Bellas Artes Metro (see map). This area is poorly lit at night, so it's not advisable to wait here in the dark. A regular service runs from 0400 to 0030, the bus leaves when there are enough passengers, it costs US$1.80. If you're heading for a hotel in Sabana Grande on arrival, ask to be dropped off at Gato Negro Metro station and take the Metro from there to Plaza Venezuela or Sabana Grande. The shuttle bus or *por puesto* to the airport can also be caught at Gato Negro Metro station.

To catch the bus to Macuto, leave the terminal from the upper level, cross the parking lot, pass the exit, climb the steps and cross the 4-lane highway. **NB** Don't, under any circumstances, attempt this at night. If arriving at night, hang around the airport until first light before catching the bus to Macuto.

Long distance buses The chaotic, dirty, Nuevo Circo bus station is in the city centre. The nearest Metro station is La Hoyada. It serves all **western** destinations. Give yourself plenty of time to find the bus you need although there are bus agents who will assist in finding a ticket for your destination. Tickets are sold, at most, 24 hours before departure, sometimes only on the morning of departure. This adds to the chaos at busy periods. Nevertheless, do not be tempted to buy tickets from the touts who wait by buses. Those first on get the best seats so it is advisable to arrive 1 hour before departure. Buses may also leave early. Watch your baggage carefully up until the baggage door is closed (see also **Road Transport**, **Information for travellers**, on page 343).

Buses for all **eastern** destinations leave from Terminal Oriente at Guarenas, which is clean, modern and relatively safe. City buses leave Nuevo Circo bullring for the terminal every 30 minutes, US$0.30. It's usually a 45-minute journey, or 1 hour during rush hour. Alternatively, take a *por puesto* from Petare Metro station. This is an easier option but take care, as this is a dangerous area at night. A taxi to the terminal from the centre costs US$4. To catch a bus from the terminal to the centre (US$0.50), turn left outside the main entrance towards the main parking area where the buses wait. Get off at Bellas Artes or El Silencio. To save the hassle of making an extra trip, you can buy tickets for all eastern destinations in advance from an agency on Avenida Lecuna, opposite INGEVE, between Miracielos y Hospital (see map).

Buses for places close to Caracas leave from the other side of the road from Nuevo Circo bus station, via the underpass (eg Los Teques, Higuerote, Catia La Mar, La Guaira). From La Hoyada Metro, do not go under the bridge, but walk straight down the road for 300m.

On public holidays buses are usually fully booked leaving Caracas and drivers often make long journeys without stopping. Saturday and Sunday morning are also bad for travel into/out of Caracas, especially on longer journeys. Always take identification when booking a long-distance journey. Times and fares of buses are given under destinations. Recommended bus companies are: to Maracaibo, Expresos Los Llanos; to Guayana, Rápidos de Guayana. Aeroexpresos Ejecutivos, Avenida Principal de Bello Campo, Quinta Marluz (between Chacao and Altamira Metro stops), T 266-3601/9011, are recommended for Valencia, Barquisimeto and Puerto La Cruz; reserve 2 days in advance, except for buses leaving on Friday (there is no left luggage). Fares are 3-4 times higher than other companies, but worth it.

Ormeño has buses to Bogotá (US$75), Cali (US$90), Quito (US$130), Guayaquil (US$140), Lima (US$190), Santiago (US$270), Mendoza (US$330) and Buenos Aires (US$340); departures at 1600 on Monday and Friday. They are safe, comfortable and air conditioned, with video and toilet, good meal stops and even stops for showers and change of clothing. The terminal is at Final Avenida San Martín, Sector Oeste, Calle Sucre con Calle Nueva, behind Bloque de Armas, near Metro La Paz.

EL AVILA NATIONAL PARK

The 85,192 hectare **El Avila National Park** forms the northern boundary of Caracas. It runs east from **Catia La Mar** (see page 98) to **La Sabana**, near the eastern border of the Distrito Federal. The green park slopes rise steeply from the central Caribbean coast, providing a dramatic backdrop for a string of little satellite resort towns. Access to the park is easy: through the old Caracas-La Guaira road which crosses the park from north to south on the western side; and in Caracas there are several marked entrances along Cota Mil (Avenida Boyacá) which are designed for hiking.

Amazingly for an area so close to the capital, the park's fauna is said to include red howler monkeys and big cats such as the jaguar and puma. There are also several species of poisonous snake.

A cable railway (*teleférico*) runs up Monte Avila from Avenida Perimetral de Maripérez, giving a stupendous view of the city and the coast. However, this seems to be out of action permanently; it was still closed early 1998. The future of

the *Humboldt Hotel* on the summit (2,159m) has not been decided. It has been refurbished, but not even the ground floor bar/restaurant/disco is open. Camping is possible with permission. A dirt road runs from the La Puerta section of San Bernardino to the summit, and takes 45 minutes in 4WD vehicle. A recommended trip is to ride up in a vehicle and hike back down (note that it is cold at the summit – average temperature 13°C). The *Hotel Tamanaco* offers a jeep with driver for US$50 per person.

HIKING IN EL AVILA

There are three good hikes in the National Park: to Pico Naiguatá, the highest peak at 2,765m; to Pico Oriental, 2,600m; and to the *Hotel Humboldt*, 2,150m. Hikers should go in groups of at least three, from the point of view of both mountain and personal safety. El Avila is not a dangerous place, but the occasional theft has been reported. Always take water and something for the cold at altitude. The unfit should not attempt any of the hikes. You also need to get a park permit from Inparques in Caracas.

Pico Naiguatá

This is a very strenuous hike. Take the metro to La California, then a bus going up Avenida Sanz, and ask to get off at the Centro Comercial El Marqués. From there walk up Avenida Sanz towards Cota Mil (Avenida Boyacá), about four blocks. At the end of Avenida Sanz, underneath the bridge, is the entrance to the Naiguatá trail. In about 40 minutes you reach La Julia *guardaparques* station, where you have to state your destination and pay US$0.25 entrance.

From La Julia the path is straightforward, except at El Eden viewing point. About 1½ hours later you reach Rancho Grande, where the stream is the last watering hole. From Rancho Grande to the ridge is 1 hour through forest and then an hour through sub-páramo. About 500m from the ridge the path divides into lots of smaller ones. Most of these run up to the ridge, but follow the plastic markers. At the ridge, turn right (signposted) to

Naiguatá peak; stay on the ridge path, not the one that runs a little way down. In about 30 minutes you'll reach Los Platos del Diablo, which are large flat rocks stacked on top of one another. In another 30 minutes is the entrance to the Ampiteatro on your left (look for the plastic markers). Once you reach the Ampiteatro, a large flat field on the La Guaira side of the ridge, the cross marking the peak can clearly be seen, up and to the right (10 minutes away).

Pico Oriental

From the Altamira metro station take a bus to 'La entrada de Sabas Nieves', where the *Tarzilandia* restaurant is. From here a dirt road leads up to the Sabas Nieves *guardaparques* station (about 40 minutes). The path to Pico Oriental starts at the back of Sabas Nieves and is extremely easy to follow. In about 1½ hours you reach the "No Te Apures" clearing, where a small path to the left leads down to a little stream, which is the last watering hole. Returning to the main path, you carry up towards the ridge, "La Silla", another 1½ hours away. You are now out of the forest and into the sub-páramo. From here you stay on the same path up to the peak, about another 45 minutes. Most people don't stop at the peak, but continue for another 10 minutes to some large flat rocks for lunch and a spot of sunbathing. There are fantastic views all around, when the peak is not shrouded in mist.

Hotel Humboldt

This relatively easy route takes 3 hours. Take the metro bus from Bellas Artes station to El Avila stop, US$0.25; opposite is a grocery. Turn the corner and walk two blocks up towards the mountain. At the top of the street turn left; almost immediately on your right is the park entrance. **NB** This area is not safe before 0800 or after dark. Plenty of people take this route, starting 0830-0900, giving plenty of time to get up and down safely and in comfort.

About 40 minutes after entering the park is Loma de Vientos *guardaparques* station. An hour further on is Papelon, another small *guardaparques* post. Here

you can either carry straight up on the direct route to the hotel, or you can turn left for a longer, more scenic, less tiring route. Going straight up you will arrive at the hotel in another hour or so. When you reach the top, to the right is the hotel and to the left is a dirt road leading down. If you follow this, in about 15-20 minutes you reach a crossing. Turn left and in about 5 minutes you'll arrive at the *Bodega Galipán*, where lunch is sold (the fruit juices are highly recommended). If you turn left at the Papelon, you'll find yourself going round the mountain. This flat path will take you past a stream where you can get water (15 minutes). Ignore all paths going down the hill to the left and continue until you arrive at a path going upwards and to the right (35 minutes from the stream). Once on this path, which passes an old concrete tank, you need not worry about any diversions, as they all join up with each other. In about an hour you arrive at the same dirt road that goes to/from the hotel. To the right is the hotel, and to the left is *Bodega Galipán*, which can also be reached by 4WD from Caracas or La Guaira (see below).

On the La Guaira side (and best reached from La Guaira) is a Museo Ecológico known as 'El jardín de las piedras'. It is owned by Zoez, a self-styled prophet, and reflects his beliefs. It is open at weekends and is very interesting. Take a picnic, enjoy the designs and views and remember to remove your shoes before entering. It can also be reached from Macuto (see below); 20 minutes by jeep, or 1½-2 hours walk. Ask directions as there are two paths, the first of which goes through a *barrio* which must be avoided.

● **Agencies** *Camel Tours*, La California Sur, Avenida Trieste, Qta Reycara, T Caracas 223261, or 014-255356 (cellular), ask for Roberto Andara (speaks English), who runs day trips to Galipán, a *bodega* on the Hotel Humboldt hike, for US$25 per person (including horseriding and barbecues).

● **Hiking club** *Centro Excursiones de Caracas*, Parcela Zona Verde, Calle Chivacao con Yare, San Ramón, Aptdo postal 50766, Sabana Grande 1050, T 235-3155/985-3210 (Sr Contreras, President), or Sr Barcón (T 573-8515); the club meets every Saturday at 1430 to arrange day and weekend hikes, and is very friendly and welcoming, they also speak some English and German.

SOUTHEAST OF CARACAS

An easy day's outing from Caracas are some very interesting little towns, lying in the Tuy Valley, in the state of Miranda. A road branches south off the main road from Caracas to the east coast (Route 9) and passes through **Santa Lucía, Santa Teresa del Tuy** and **San Francisco de Yare**. Santa Teresa is the gateway to the impressive **Parque Nacional Guatopo**.

The first of the towns, 34 km south of the turn-off, is **Santa Lucía**, famous for its wonderful rococo retable, which dates from 1761. So precious is this retable, that

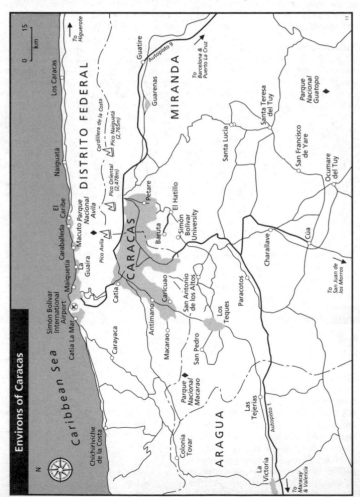

Environs of Caracas

the church was designated a National Monument. The town's lively festival of *San Juan*, is held on 24 June.

10 km further south is the dormitory town of **Santa Teresa del Tuy**, 1½ hours by bus from Nuevo Circo. It's a good alternative to the capital, with cheaper, safe accommodation and a scenic mountain setting.

● **Accommodation** E *Hotel Tahay*, air conditioning, private bath, small, safe; opposite is **F** *Hotel Lamas*, with fan and private bath, small, secure, luggage store, recommended.

GUATOPO NATIONAL PARK

From Santa Teresa a road runs east for 30 km to **Los Alpes**, from where you can explore this beautiful and little frequented **National Park**, which covers 122,464 hectares of lush, tropical forest. The park is a haven for bird watchers and naturalists with an impressive list of fauna and birdlife including the peccary, jaguar, puma, tapir, armadillo, sloth, margay, ocelot, harpy eagle, macaw, helmeted curassow, monkeys and hummingbirds, as well as several varieties of snake, including the venomous fer-de-lance and rattlesnake.

The park is best appreciated on foot, and a whole day can easily be devoted to walking its many good nature trails. There are various convenient places to picnic on the route through the forest, plus swimming area and campsites. A permit must be obtained at Inparques; also take insect repellent.

Those without time or private transport can still enjoy the park by travelling the 56 km paved road south from Los Alpes to **Altagracia de Orituco**, south of the park boundary in the state of Guárico. A bus from Nuevo Circo marked 'El Popular', goes to Altagracia, via Santa Teresa and Los Alpes, allowing you to enjoy the wonderful scenery; US$1.50. Near Altagracia de Orituco, in the National Park, is **Hacienda La Elvira**, an old colonial farm where there is free camping and fresh water from a nearby river. Take jeep from town (US$0.50) and ask to be let off at the turn-off to the Hacienda. From there it's a 45-minute walk.

ROUTES From **Los Alpes** you can continue east to **Caucagua**, on the main road east from Caracas towards **Puerto La Cruz** (see page 230). From **Altagracia de Orituco** you can head west to **San Juan de Los Morros** (see page 223); south to **Chaguaramas** (see page 224); or east to **Barcelona** (see page 234).

SAN FRANCISCO DE YARE

The road southwest from Santa Teresa follows the course of the Río Tuy for 14 km before reaching **San Francisco de Yare** (*population* 18,000), whose church and main plaza are both protected as National Monuments. The town is more famously known, however, as the home of the **Devil Dancers of Yare**, the continent's oldest Devil Dancers' Society. The elaborate celebration is held at Corpus Christi (early

---

The diabolical cost of dancing

Devil Dancing has been performed in South America since the time of the Spanish conquest and is a celebration of good triumphing over evil. The dancers have to promise to participate in the festival over a number of years, and many of them spend considerable sums of money on their elaborate costumes.

The dancers practice all year for their big day, when they don the grotesque *papier-maché* masks and brightly-coloured costumes and dance diabolically for hours on end in order to keep the devil at bay. And for insurance purposes, just in case God won't recognize them in their outrageous outfits, the dancers carry rosary beads and other religious totems.

Devil Dancing in San Francisco de Yare may carry a large financial burden, but it also brings enormous prestige. The chief dancer is worshipped as a kind of pop star or movie idol. When he dies his widow is cared for by the dancers' society and the leadership of the society is often passed down to his sons.

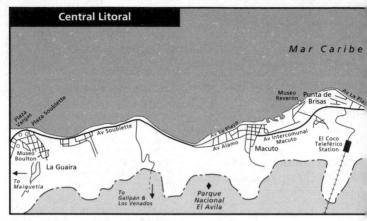

Central Litoral

Mar Caribe

June) and is highly recommended for anyone in the region at this time. (See also the **Music and Dance** section on page 55.)

ROUTES The road runs south from San Francisco de Yare and then turns west, passing after 9 km the turn-off south to the busy, commercial town of **Ocumare del Tuy**. 14 km west of the turn-off the road reaches **Cúa**, where it joins one of the routes south from Caracas to **San Juan de los Morros** (see page 223).

THE CENTRAL LITORAL

The Central Litoral is the name given to the stretch of Caribbean coast directly north of Caracas. A paved road runs east from **Catia La Mar**, past the airport and then through the towns of **Maiquetía**, **La Guaira**, and **Macuto**, ending at **Los Caracas**. Further east the road is unpaved.

CATIA LA MAR

At the bottom of the *autopista* from Caracas to the airport, you can turn west to **Catia La Mar** (*population* 131,400), a resort which is industrial, very littered and polluted, but is also very convenient for Maiquetía airport. A taxi from the airport officially costs US$12, but you can bargain this down to US$4-9. The *Balneario Camuri Chico* has three good beaches, a restaurant, showers, and the water is fairly clean; recommended.

● **Accommodation B** *Aeropuerto*, shower, air conditioning, OK, stores luggage; **C** *Bahía del Mar*, clean, swimming pool, good restaurant; **D** *Catia del Mar*, modern, clean.

MAIQUETIA

The first of the resorts east of the airport is **Maiquetía** (*population* 103,000). Founded in 1670, this was the terminus of the old supply road to Caracas. A pilgrimage is made on foot in February from La Pastora church in Caracas to the Maiquetía parochial church along the old supply route.

● **Accommodation E** *Crillon*, esquina Navarvete, with shower and toilet, basic but adequate; **E** *Granada* (alias Coromoto), up the hill from Plaza Los Maestros, tiled entrance, reasonable. The other hotels cater for short-stay couples.

● **Places to eat** *Avila*, good, near Plaza Los Maestros; also recommended is *Mesón Canarios* and *Cervecería Primera*. Opposite the *Avila* is a good and cheap fish restaurant.

● **Transport Road** You can catch a bus to La Guaira and Maiquetía from Gato Negro Metro. Caracas-La Guaira US$0.40. There are many to Maiquetía, which are also marked Catia. A taxi from Caracas is US$9. If driving, note that the streets in central Maiquetía and La Guaira are extremely narrow. It's best to park along Avenida Soublette rather than try to tour the towns by car. The coastal road east from La Guaira is slow and quite rough, but scenic and interesting, making a worthwhile round trip if you return to Caracas/La Guaira by the paved interior roads.

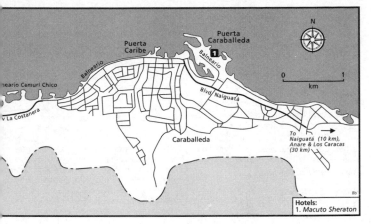

Hotels:
1. Macuto Sheraton

LA GUAIRA

Venezuela's main port (*population* 26,420; *mean temperature* 29°C), is only 45 minutes by road from Caracas, traffic permitting. Dating back to 1567, when it was founded as San Pedro de La Guaira (which translates as "Saint Peter of the Wind"), the town achieved its greatest importance in the 18th century when the Basque Guipuzcoana Company held the royal trading monopoly (see also **Puerto Cabello**, page 123). Many British export-import companies flourished here in the 1800s.

Places of interest The old town, 1 km east of the port, remains intact – though much restoration work is in progress – with delightful colonial houses along steep narrow streets. Several of these streets climb up to the forts of **El Vigía** (the lookout), **La Pólvora** (the Powder Magazine) and the restored **Castillo de San Carlos** (1610), built on the classic star pattern and commanding a fine view of the port and its surroundings. If you're going to the Castillo, aim for Calle León, or take a *por puesto* up and walk down.

You should also see the imposing **Casa Guipuzcoana** (1734), on the coast road (Avenida Soublette), the original HQ of the company. It is now used as government offices, and is also a busy cultural centre, containing the art gallery of the **Ateneo de La Guaira** and the **Litoral** branch of the **Universidad Simón Bolívar**. There are interesting collections scattered throughout the three floors, including regional hammocks, Indian fishing implements, and historic documents. It is open Tuesday-Sunday 0800-1800; the free events are advertised in Caracas newspapers. There are many other mansions and churches, including the **Catedral**, the lovely church of **Ermita Carmen** (open only on weekend afternoons; get the key at the cathedral) and the **Casa José María España**, home of the first 'martyr' in the War of Independence.

The old **Camino Real** continues upwards from the Castillo de San Carlos and can be hiked to Caracas. A second colonial road to Caracas rises from Maiquetía, 2 km further east.

EAST FROM MAIQUETIA/LA GUAIRA

The coast east of Maiquetía-La Guaira has a string of popular seaside resorts and residential districts with a total population of about 75,000. The divided Avenida Soublette sweeps eastwards past the Punta Mulatos market (which serves most of the Litoral) to Macuto, El Caribe, Naiguatá and on to **Los Caracas**. All these places can be reached quite cheaply by most 'Litoral' buses from the west end of Nuevo Circo in Caracas.

MACUTO

5 km east of La Guaira, Macuto was founded in 1740 (*population* 19,370; *phone code* 031). The coastal promenade (Paseo la Playa) is lined with seagrape trees and open-air restaurants. It's a pleasant, if slightly grubby, alternative to Caracas when arriving or before flying out. The beaches tend to be overcrowded at weekends, go in midweek if possible. They are now badly polluted, although less so the further east you go. **NB** Robberies have been reported on the seafront between Macuto and Caraballeda.

Places of interest

From the Plaza de las Palomas (which, as the name suggests, has lots of pigeons) can be seen **La Guzmanía**, the coastal residence of the President, built by Guzmán Blanco, complete with guards in colonial uniforms. Opposite is the **presidential residence** built in 1888 for Joaquín Crespo. The initials J and C can be seen over the entrance (for Joaquín and Jacinta Crespo). The building is now a college but can be visited by arrangement.

The **Castillete de las Quince Letras** is the only building on the beach facing the sea, built by Venezuela's renowned artist, Armando Julio Reverón, whose paintings are on display in the Galería Nacional del Arte in the capital. The museum preserves his daily life, paintings and the life-sized rag dolls he used as models. Open Tuesday-Saturday 0800-1200, 1400-1700, Sunday and holidays 1000-1500.

Local information
● Accommodation

B *Las Quince Letras**, Avenida La Playa, on the eastern side of town, T 461551, F 461432, fully renovated, good restaurant, pool, air conditioning; **B** *Macuto**, Avenida La Playa y Calle 3, Urb Alamo, T 461310, F 461854, air conditioning, hot water, empty midweek, full weekends, 5 minutes walk to the beach, comfortable but poorly maintained, swimming pool, safe parking, good breakfasts, accepts credit cards.

C *Santiago*, Avenida La Playa, T 44214, F 44118, air conditioning, small, bare rooms, large terrace, beautiful view over sea, tiny rooftop pool, noisy bar at night, good restaurant

(*La Choza*), English spoken, accepts credit cards; **C-D** *Posada del Hidalgo*, Paseo del Mar, T 44107, F 45280, good value, helpful, accepts credit cards, safe, noisy, good restaurant/bar on ground floor (separate entrance), taxi service to airport, recommended.

D *Alamo*, Avenida La Playa, T 461263, with fan or air conditioning, good value, bargaining possible, English spoken, accepts credit cards, good restaurant on seafront; **D** *Colonial*, Paseo Macuto 48, T 461462, near the beach, good value, air conditioning, smart, good restaurant and service, accept credit cards; **D** *Diana*, Boulevard Caraballeda, T 461553, 50m from the beach, basic, hot water in some rooms, air conditioning, helpful, noisy on ground floor especially, safe for motorcycles; **D** *Isabel*, Isabel la Católica y Calle 3, 2 minutes from the sea, small, quiet, good; **D** *Pensión Guanchez*, Avenida Alamo Transversal, behind church, T 461253, with ceiling fan, breakfast US$1, excellent set lunch US$3-4, no sign outside, noisy, nice balcony, manager speaks English and Swedish; **D** *Riviera*, Boulevard Caraballeda y Calle San Bartolomé, T 461332, 100m from beach, triples available, helpful, air conditioning, good French food.

E *Alemania*, Paseo Macuto, T 461553, **F** shared bathroom, fans, old building, sparse but clean, veranda overlooking sea, very noisy from disco next door; **E** *Canta Claro*, Boulevard Macuto con Calle Centenario, T 461035, basic, very small, 2 rooms with balcony overlooking Paseo, one with private bath; **E** *Plazamar*, Plaza Las Palomas, Calle 3, near La Guzmanía, T 44291/44271, run by Italians, rooms with up to 6 beds, colour TV, friendly and helpful, pleasant balcony, taxi service to airport, recommended; next door is **E** *Darimar*, T 44798, with bathroom, safe, recommended.

● Places to eat

La Esquina, near *Hotel Alamo*, good. Also on Paseo La Playa are: *El Coral*, next to *Hotel Santiago*, good seafood; *Chifa*, good, huge portions; and *Los Criollos*, cheap, good food.

● Transport

Por puesto from Caracas cost US$2, and take about an hour. A taxi costs US$20. *Por puesto* to the airport, domestic terminal, costs US$1, and takes 15 minutes; or take a Catia La Mar bus (25 minutes), which starts at 0600, and stops on the main highway in front of the airport. The taxi fare from the airport is officially US$12, 30 minutes (plus US$0.50 for a large suitcase or rucksack – beware of overcharging). It costs more to **Caraballeda** (see below). To get a *por puesto* to Caracas at rush hour (weekend afternoons, etc), it's easier to walk back to one of the early stops such as the *Macuto Sheraton*. Most *por puestos* go to El Silencio. There's a recommended tourist transport service with Andrés and Isabelino, T (031) 519146, in an 8-seater van, Spanish only (language, not citizens).

CARABALLEDA

5 km further east along the beachfront from Macuto is the wealthier area of **Caraballeda**, where there is an impressive yacht marina behind the *Macuto Sheraton*.

● **Accommodation L2** *Macuto Sheraton**, on the public beach, Apartado 65 La Guaira, T 944300, F 944317, 3 restaurants, which serve good food and are good value, and all 5-star facilities, sells phone cards for international calls, will store luggage (tip the porter), post office; **L3** *Meliá Caribe**, on the beach just east of the Sheraton, T 945555, 3 good restaurants, pool, disco, noisy, try to get a room on the landside, free tennis, expensive gym; **C** *Fioremar*, near Meliá Caribe and the beach, T 941743, solarium, restaurant, pool; also nearby is **F** pp *Tamacuro*, T 941325, air conditioning, large rooms. There are quite a few aparthotels in the area, which cost up to US$100 a day without meals.

● **Places to eat** Along Avenida Principal are: *Neptuno*, good seafood, recommended; *El Bodegón del Lino*, Spanish-style, recommended; *El Portón del Timotes*, seafood, good service.

EAST TO HIGUEROTE

East of Caraballeda is a series of small resorts, most with their own walled-in public beaches (strong undertows), until the cliff-hugging road arrives at **Naiguatá** (*population* 24,100), an old fishing village in the shadow of the El Avila National Park's highest peak. The village is famous for its Devil Dancers and drummers, which can be seen during the *Fiesta of San Juan*, on 24 June, and *Corpus Christi*, held in early June.

There are lovely views of rocky coast and surf from the corniche road to **Los Caracas**, 54 km from La Guaira, a holiday resort subsidized by the government for low-income workers. For information on accommodation, T 541-6487, Incret (Worker's Training and Recreation Institute).

It is possible to continue on along the Barlovento coast to **Higuerote** and return to Caracas on paved roads via **Caucagua** and **Guatire**, a round trip of about 300 km (see page 230). Beyond Los Caracas you enter into a different world, little changed since people carried cacao and coffee by mule along the dirt road. Today, a 4WD is recommended because of the rivers to be forded. Las Caracas is the last chance to fill up with gas until Carenero, just north of Higuerote.

The road does not hug the coast as before but links many tiny fishing settlements. Near **Osma** (10 km) is the Granja Osmán, which has some cottages for rent (**A** including meals and watersports equipment). In **Todasana** (22 km) is the German-run **D** *Hotel Egua*, with restaurant, fans, modest. The road then passes through **La Sabana**, which has a very popular 2 km sandy beach, and a waterfall on the right side of the road. It then continues through **Chuspa**, with its coconut palm-fringed sandy beach, before reaching **Chirimena** (67 km from Los Caracas), where the highway paving begins again. From here it's a further 14 km to Higuerote.

ISLAS LOS ROQUES

The turquoise and emerald lagoons and dazzling white sands of the **Archipelago de Los Roques** lie roughly 166 km due north of La Guaira and make up one of Venezuela's most stunningly beautiful National Parks (225,153 hectares). Los Roques is basically made up of 42 *cayos* (cays, or reef-formed islands) surrounding a huge lagoon of 400 sq km. Besides the islands which are large enough to have names, are over 300 tiny sand cays, rocks and coral reefs which surface only at low tide. The islands are surrounded by over 12 miles of spectacular coral reef with crystal-clear water and schools of weird and wonderful fish, making it a snorkeller's and skin diver's paradise. There are also long stretches of pristine white beaches, the cleanest in the country, attracting Venezuelan sun-worshippers in their droves on long weekends and at school holidays.

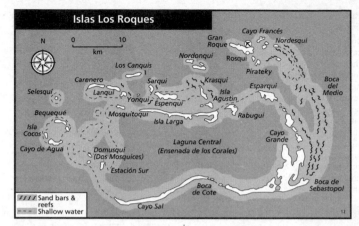

Islas Los Roques

N   0   10
         km

Gran Roque · Cayo Francés · Nordesqui
Nordonqui · Rosqui
Los Canquis · Pirateky
Carenero · Sarqui · Krasqui · Esparqui · Boca del Medio
Selesquí · Lanqui · Yonqui · Isla Agustin
Bequequé · Mosquitoqui · Espenqui · Rabugui
Isla Cocos · Isla Larga · Cayo Grande
Cayo de Agua · Domusqui (Dos Mosques) · Laguna Central (Ensenada de los Corales)
Estación Sur · Boca de Sebastopol
Boca de Cote
Cayo Sal

✓✓✓✓ Sand bars & reefs
- - - Shallow water

Despite their growing popularity as a tourist destination, Los Roques remain tranquil and unspoiled, thanks partly to their remoteness and the relative expense of visiting them. This is one of the least visited diving spots in the Caribbean, with the best sites at Francisqui – Cayo Francés – and Cayo Agua. (See **Diving** section on page 22.) Those who seek solitude can visit midweek, when they'll have the whole place pretty much to themselves. The archipelago's National Park status has also made this one of the Caribbean's largest marine preserves.

Flora and fauna

The islands are a great place for bird watchers, with 92 species recorded, including pelicans, frigates, pink, white and royal seagulls, brown boobies, white herons, scarlet ibises and many more. Among the most populous nesting sites are **Cayo Francés**, where huge gull colonies nest in May, and **Selesqui**, also called Cayo Bobo Negro (Black Booby Cay) which attracts pelicans, boobies and frigates.

The birds share the islands with the sea turtles, which come to lay their eggs on the beaches, while lizards, salamanders and iguanas scamper around. The sparkling waters abound with fish. There are *pargo* (red snapper), *mero* (grouper), *carite* (king mackerel), as well as *rubia*, *corocoro* and *picúa*, which are used in the delicious *sancocho de pescado* (fish soup). The seas attract many commercial fishermen, who come from Venezuela's ports to catch lobster and other seafood. One such delicacy, the queen conch, has almost been fished to extinction, and its sale and consumption are prohibited. This rich marine harvest also attracts sport fishermen from abroad. (See **Fishing** section, on page 22.)

Few plant species can adapt to the extreme conditions on the archipelago. The higher parts of Gran Roque are covered by thorny, cactus-like vegetation. The predominantly arid landscape is broken by mangrove forests near the coast.

Climatic conditions are extreme. The average annual temperature is nearly 29°C, with highs of 33.9°C in July and lows of 23.6°C in January. Days are sunny and nights are cool. There is almost no rain, except between September and January. **NB** You will need strong sunblock as there is no shade.

THE ISLANDS

Gran Roque is the main island and the only inhabited one. The airport is here, as is the national guard, food stores, public phones, medical facilities and accommodation. There is nowhere to change travellers' cheques, but you can use Visa cards in the Aerotuy shop, *Botuto Boutique*. The

Park Headquarters are in the scattered fishing village (*population* 900).

To get to camps or *posadas* on the other cays, you have to fly to Gran Roque and then negotiate with the local fishermen for boats to the other islands. You will need to take your own tent, food and (especially) water. Among the other islands are **Nordisqui**, which is very isolated, and **Madrisqui**, which has many summer houses. **Cayo Francés** is two islands joined by a sandspit, with calm lagoon waters on the south and rolling surf on the north. There is an abandoned house and enough vegetation to provide shaded hammock sites.

Note that many names in the archipelago have changed due to fishermen using phonetic spellings; eg Northeast Cay is now Nordisqui, Sailor's Cay is Selesqui, and Frances Cay is known as Francisqui.

Local information
● **Accommodation**

Prices are slightly higher than the mainland and infrastructure is limited. During the low season, it's not necessary to book in advance. There are lots of *posadas* starting at around US$16 per person, up to around US$200 per person. Most *posadas* include breakfast and dinner.

On Gran Roque: **A2** *Canto de la Ballena*, on the seafront, T 302420, full board, excellent food, relaxed, fans, can pay with travellers' cheques; **A2** *Posada Bora La Mar*, T (02) 238-5408, 4 basic rooms, with bathroom and ceiling fan, run by María Agustín who can put you in touch with local fisherman to take you to other islands at reasonable prices, eg Nordisqui or Isla Larga.

C *Posada Margot*, often has water and electricity problems.

D *Doña Magaly*, Calle Principal, Plaza Bolívar, T (014) 372113, basic, shared bathroom, fans; **D** pp *Posada La Lagunita*, basic but friendly, good food.

There are many other posadas, ranging from **D** pp to **L1**. These include: *Las Palmeras* and *Natura Viva*, both have 15 double or triple rooms with bathroom and fans, are in the middle of the price and are run by Aerotuy T (02) 761-8043, F (02) 762-5254, or T Porlamar (065) 632211. The following are at the lower end of the price range: *Posada de Judith*, 3 comfortable rooms with bathroom, 3 meals; and *La Mecha*, 2 rooms with bathroom, 3 meals and transport to the other cays; both are run by

Judith Campagna de Puig, T (02) 213660, F (014) 263556, who also runs *Campamento Lilo*, where lodging is what nature provides and you eat what you catch, also organizes activities; *Botuto*, 4 double and 2 triple rooms, all with bathroom, run by Frederico Campagna, T (02) 979-4632; *Doña Carmen*, 7 doubles, triples and larger rooms, some with bathroom, run by Sayla Sambrano, T (02) 862-9618; *Gremary*, 11 basic rooms, the oldest *posada* on the island, some with bathroom, lunch and transport extra, run by Gregorio Romero, T (031) 722765/(014) 278614; *Coro Coro*, 3 triple rooms and 1 quadruple, air conditioning, with bathroom, 3 meals, run by Roque's Air, Land and Sea, T (02) 952-2702, F (02) 952-5923.

On the other islands: on **Cayo Francés** there is accommodation at US$30 per person, full board including drinks, good food, friendly staff, nice beach, snorkelling gear, water and light 24 hours, fan, bargaining possible if you stay for several days; also *Campamento Francisqui*, 5 double rooms, price includes all meals, snorkelling gear and transport from Caracas, run by Julio Melian, T (02) 761-4861/9310. There's also a *campamento* on **Cayo Crasqui**, which is fairly expensive, with accommodation in cabin-style tents, price is all-inclusive, run by Sun Chichi Hoteles, T (02) 993-5866, F (02) 916549.

● **Camping**

Campers need a permit from Inparques in Caracas (see page 91). Park entry US$2. **NB** Leave nothing on the ground, the crabs eat everything! Tiny but irritating biting insects in the calmer months can make camping miserable.

● **Sports**

Diving: *Sesto Continente*, on the edge of Gran Roque village, T/F (014) 241853, ask for Jakob, Saul or Hugo, run PADI courses and night dives, mixed reports.

● **Useful addresses**

For more information on the park's wildlife write to La Fundación Científica Los Roques, Apartado No 1, Avenida Carmelitas, Caracas 1010, T 326771.

Tours around the islands: *Eola* is a yacht out of Gran Roque, fully equipped, with cabins, chartered for US$100 per day, all inclusive, highly recommended as a worthwhile way of getting some shade on the treeless beaches. Run by Italians Gianni and Jaqueline, book direct by phone, T (99) 216735. *Guaicamar* is a 75-foot yacht with 3 cabins, air conditioning, bathroom, hot water, and dining room with kitchen, price includes transfer from Gran Roque, 3 meals daily, bar drinks and snacks and use of equipment; contact *Inversiones Navales*, T (02) 352295, F 343279. The *Pelicano Club* has accommodation and organizes excursions, boat trips and dives, recommended.

● **Transport**
Flights to Gran Roque from Maiquetía or Porlamar. Chapi Air from Maiquetía at 0800, returning at 1600, US$110. Aerotuy (T 02-761-6231, F 762-5254) fly from Maiquetía 3 times a day. Their 2-day package (return flight, accommodation, meals, drinks, catamaran excursion with snorkelling and diving equipment) costs from US$300 per person. Aerotuy have several *posadas* of varying comfort (see above); they are reported as very efficient.

A visa is not needed for those arriving by yacht. You should obtain your free tourist card from a Venezuelan Embassy before arrival. Los Roques are not a port of entry, but you can stop for 14 days if the exit clearance from another country lists it on the way to an official port.
NB A week-long package allows you to stay ashore in a *posada* or on board a yacht and to dive daily, but it is much cheaper to travel independently. A 1-day trip is a waste of time.

West from Caracas

A FEW HOURS WEST of the capital is a beautiful stretch of Caribbean coastline, dotted with some lovely colonial villages. The important cities of Valencia and Maracay lie to the south, in the great basin of the Lago de Valencia. A spectacular road runs from Maracay up into the Central Highlands and down to the coast, passing through the bird watchers' paradise of Henri Pittier National Park.

CARACAS TO MARACAY

The Pan-American Highway links Caracas by road with the other capitals of South America. This fast toll motorway runs direct to Valencia with an exit to Maracay (toll US$0.60).

For most of the route to Maracay the Pan-American runs parallel to the old road, known locally as the *Carretera Nacional*. This road forms part of the Transandean Highway, built by the dictator, Juan Vicente Gómez, in 1922 to connect Caracas with the Andean states of Trujillo, Mérida and Táchira. The old road, which for most part follows the Camino Real, built by the Spanish, is renowned for its dangerous bends.

It leaves La Rinconada racecourse to its left and, at Km 11, passes the **Venezuelan Institute of Advanced Scientific Research** (IVIC) which has an excellent Museo de Antropología and the most comprehensive scientific library in South America, which is open to the general public. 2 km further on is **Cristalart**, a glass-blowing factory where visitors are welcome.

The road continues its steady climb into the Teques mountains. Past the turn off to **Carrizal** is the park of **Las Colinas de Carrizal**, with collections of local fish and birds. Just beyond, motorists can look down on the **Cueva de Guaicaipuro** – or **Cueva del Indio** – set in the face of the bare rock cliffs and the

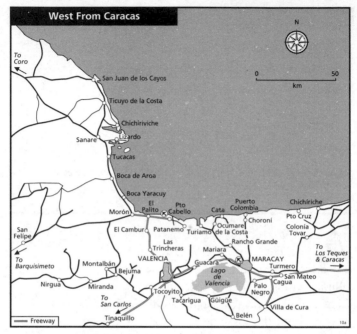

West From Caracas

old Indian gold-mine below it. This was the secret hideaway of the leader of the local Teques Indians (see below) and where he met his end, according to legend.

LOS TEQUES

A 30-minute drive and 25 km from Caracas is **Los Teques** (*population* 164,440; *altitude* 1,180m), founded in 1703 and capital of Miranda state.

Places of interest

The city is a mixture of skyscrapers and colonial buildings around **Plaza Bolívar** and **Plaza Guaicaipuro**, with its bronze statue of the chief of the fierce Carib Indians who inhabited this part of the coastal range. Guaicaipuro was the war leader of a sub-group of the Carib called the Teques. The chief, famed for his heroism, fought off the Spanish invaders, until he was finally tracked down and killed in 1568 by a group led by Don Francisco Infante, who went on to become

the first mayor of Caracas. A few blocks from Plaza Guaicaipuro is **Plaza Miranda**, with its statue of the remarkable man.

There are several pleasant parks in the city and one of the loveliest is **Parque Gustavo Knoop**, named after the director of the German-built Caracas-Valencia railway which ran between the two towns from 1894-1951. The park, popularly known as **Los Coquitos**, is built on the grounds of the former railway station and is open 0800-1800, daily except Monday.

Excursions

A must for all railway-lovers is the trip to **Parque El Encanto** in the mountains nearby. The leisurely 20-minute ride aboard an 1891 German locomotive with antique carriages, starts from the old Los Teques station, 1 km south of the town beside the highway. The station is also the terminus for buses from Caracas. There are 3 trips daily Monday to Friday, and 9 at weekends; the first leaves at 0900, the

Miranda, independence hero

Among the leaders of the Venezuelan independence movement, two stand out above the rest – the Liberator, Simón Bolívar, and Francisco de Miranda. This brilliant military man was an officer in the Spanish Army and fought in the American and French Revolutions – both times on the winning side. Catherine the Great made him an honorary colonel in the Russian Army. He knew Thomas Paine and Alexander Hamilton, Thomas Jefferson, George Washington and John Adams.

Though at first motivated more by hatred of Spain for not recognizing his military genius than by a desire for freedom, once Miranda became committed to the independence movement he was never sidetracked from fighting for freedom for Spanish America. He lived in exile, in London, where he and Bolívar, along with Bernardo O'Higgins, the liberator of Chile, planned to oust the Spaniards from South America, with the help of the English government.

England's main concern was to prevent domination of Europe by Napoleon, but they cooled off when Spain showed interest in coming over to the English side. Miranda then moved to New York and, in 1806, organized an expedition to Venezuela, convinced that his native people would rally to his cause. But Miranda had spent more than 20 years in exile and had lost touch with the realities of his native country. Popular support did not materialize and the Spanish quickly routed his small band. Miranda was lucky to escape to Trinidad, then back to England.

The prospect of success presented itself in 1808, when Napoleon invaded Spain. Two years later, Miranda returned to Venezuela when independence was declared and was given command of the Revolutionary Army. But support for the revolutionaries was limited and internal dissension grew over the form of the constitution and the allocation of top posts. When the Spaniards took the offensive, many of Miranda's troops defected to their side. With defeat staring him in the face, Miranda signed a treaty with the Spanish commander guaranteeing pardon for the rank and file, and free exit from the country for the leaders.

Miranda fled, taking the treasury with him. Bolívar and his associates, however, turned on him, accusing him of selling out their cause for money. They captured Miranda and handed him over to the Spanish troops. He was shipped in chains back to Spain, where he died in jail 4 years later. From then on, Simón Bolívar would become the soul of the independence movement.

last returns at 1800; adults US$1.50, children US$0.75 return.

Beyond the town of **San Pedro**, 5 km northwest of Los Teques, is the small but attractive **Parque Nacional Macarao**. The park is also a short trip away from Caracas, via Antímano, a southwesterly suburb of the capital, and the town of **Macarao**. The 15,000 hectares was declared a National Park in 1973 and stretches from 990m up to the highest point, Pico Ño León, at 2,098m. Another road from Caracas skirts the northern boundary of the park and runs via **El Junquito** to **Colonia Tovar** (see page 108).

Local information
● Accommodation

C *Gran Casino*, Carabobo y Boyacá, central, noisy, disco, has a good restaurant which is open 1100-2300, parking.

D *Alemán*, Plaza Miranda, good food. There are also many motels on the old highway from Caracas.

● Places to eat

Hípico, in the wooded suburb of Club Hípico, their varied menu includes Spanish dishes, open 1100-2300, popular; *Don Blas*, in the shopping centre at the highway interchange for San Antonio, good steaks and fish, open 1130-0100; *Hotel Los Alpes*, at Km 28 on the Panamericana south of city, dining room open 0800-1130, 1200-2200, closed on Monday, the bakery next door has hot chocolate, *empanadas* etc, it makes a good snack stop if you're avoiding Los Teques.

ROUTES The old road continues down into the fertile valleys of Aragua, through the attractive old towns of **Las Tejerías** and **El Consejo** until it reaches **La Victoria**, 24 km beyond Los Teques. Here, you can either join the Caracas-Valencia tollway or continue on the older road to Maracay.

LA VICTORIA

La Victoria (*population* 105,000; *phone code* 044) was founded in 1593 as Nuestra Señora de Guadalupe de La Victoria by Francisco de Loreto and, in 1618, was one of four sites chosen by King Phillip II as settlements for the local indigenous groups. This new Indian town was situated at the crossroads of two important commercial routes; between Caracas and Valencia, and the road to the llanos. The town soon became a commercial centre where recently-arrived slaves were traded for mules.

La Victoria was at the forefront of the movement to abolish slavery and by the second half of the 18th century, most slave labour had, happily, been replaced by freemen. The town was one of the first in the interior to proclaim independence from Spain, in 1810, and agreed to the formation of a local militia made up of the civilian population and its slaves. This militia was under the command of Juan Vicente Bolívar, father of the Liberator.

After the bloody War of Independence, La Victoria was made capital of the newly-created province of Aragua in 1848, but when the dictator Gómez took up residence in Maracay the centre of power shifted and the latter became the state capital in 1917. The town has grown considerably in the past few decades, but despite the surrounding industrial zones the city retains much of its 18th century charm.

On **Plaza Ribas** is a statue to the eponymous hero of the Battle of La Victoria, fought on 12 February 1814. Later the same year Ribas commanded the patriot army at the Battle of Urica. Following their defeat at the hands of the *llanero* forces, Ribas was captured by the Spanish and executed. His head was then boiled in oil and displayed for many years in a cage near Caracas. The statue, however, comes complete with head.

Standing on Plaza Ribas is the impressive **Church of Nuestra Señora de La Victoria**. Built in the second half of the 18th century, the neoclassic church was considered to be one of the most beautiful in Latin America. La Victoria also boasts Venezuela's oldest bullring.

● **Accommodation A2** *Onix*, in the Omni shopping complex, Urbanización Industrial Soco, in older eastern part of city, modern, all facilities, comfortable; **C** *El Recreo*, a converted 1724 sugar hacienda on the highway west of town, restaurant, pool, very pleasant.

NORTH TO COLONIA TOVAR

From La Victoria the well-paved and scenically spectacular but hair-raising Ruta 4 winds its way north up into the mountains to the incongruous German settlement of Colonia Tovar (see below).

This same road, Ruta 4, also leaves Caracas at Antímano and climbs gently west for 19 km to the market town of **El Junquito**, popular with *Caraqueños* at weekends. The town has several short-stay hotels, parking and magnificent views. Roadside stalls sell souvenirs, fruit and barbecued *chorizos* (pork sausages).

The road then winds another 19 km to a paved turnoff, where several roads lead down to the coast (see below). To the south of the road is the **Parque Nacional Macarao** (see page 107). From one point on this road Caracas can be seen to the east and the Caribbean to the north. At the coast turnoff (Km 44) is an arch over the road marking the Aragua state border, and 3½ km beyond is the *Charcutería Tovar*, a good place to stock up on picnic supplies. It is closed all day Monday and Tuesday morning. Nearby is a grass ski slope, where skis can be rented by the hour.

COLONIA TOVAR

The mountain town of **Colonia Tovar** (*population* 4,330; *altitude* 1,890m; *phone code* 033), founded in 1843 by German immigrants, retained its customs and isolation until a paved road reached the settlement in 1963. It is now very touristy, but the blond hair, blue eyes and Schwartzwald-accented German of the inhabitants are still in evidence. *Tovarenses* make tasty bread, blackberry jam and bratwurst, and grow strawberries, coffee, garlic, rhubarb and flowers for the Caracas market.

The steep, winding streets offer great views and traditional architecture (see the Scandinavian-style ceramics) and the townsfolk greet visitors with a dignified hospitality. The local Carnival preserves Black Forest traditions and is unique in Venezuela.

Places of interest

There is a small museum which tells the history of the pioneers who founded Tovar and the nearby offshoot of El Jarillo. The museum is open 1000-1800, weekends and holidays. On the plaza is the L-shaped church of San Martín, a copy of the one in Emmendingen, Germany. Behind the church are three mills, producing coffee, wheat and corn.

Excursions

Colonia Tovar makes an ideal base for walkers and campers as the environs offer numerous hiking possibilities. Ask at any of the hotels for the more popular wooded paths. Note that though the climate is mild by day, at night it can get very cold.

To get to **Codazzi Peak**, the highest point of this part of the coastal mountains, at 2,425m, take the road leading out of the village towards La Victoria. After about 3½ km go right where a cross stands by the road. About 10 minutes later, where the road crosses a stream, look on your left for a path leading through bamboos. The walk to the top takes 30 minutes. The views from the top are breathtaking.

There are also longer 2-3 day hikes down to the coast. Those interested in *petroglifos* (rock paintings) would be well advised to explore the whole area from La Victoria to the Caribbean.

Local information
● Accommodation

Credit cards are widely accepted. All hotels listed below are at least **B** and are normally full at weekends. Room rates include good, German-style food: *Alta-Baviera*, T 51483, 800m above the village on the La Victoria road (Prolongación Calle Codazzi), heated, good view from restaurant terrace; *Bergland*, T 51229, on the same road, some cabins, beautiful views, good cheap breakfasts; *Drei-Tannen*, T 51246, on a private road on the right just before entering the village from the east, 7 rooms, 2 heated apartments, parking, owner Señora Klemperer; *Edelweiss*, T 51139, just past the *Alta Baviera* and the highest hotel in town, superb views, 8 rooms, 3 cabins, parking; *Freiburg*, T 51313, cross the river at the 'El Molino' sign in the village and continue along the hillside until you see signs to the hotel, rooms and cabins, heated, restaurant; **A2** *Kaiserstuhl*, T 51132, Calle Bolívar, in centre of the village, parking, good views, 2 restaurants; *Selva Negra**, T 51072, in the centre near the church, some cabins, heated, children's park, popular restaurant, parking; nearby is **D-E** *Guest House Alicia*, nice; **C** *El Molino*, on Calle Molino next to the historic old mill (which is worth a visit), *cabañas* with use of kitchen, good restaurant, great *jugo de fresas*, wide selection of German dishes, open 0900-1000, 1200-1600, 1800-1900, Monday 0900-1400, highly recommended.

● Places to eat

El Codazzi, in the centre on Calle Codazzi, traditional German and Hungarian dishes, strudel and biscuits, open 1100-1600, closed Monday and Tuesday; *Perolón*, Calle Codazzi, only open weekends and holidays 1100-1900, homemade vegetable soup a speciality; *Café Munstall*, opposite the church, interesting location in oldest house in Colonia Tovar, pastry and coffee at weekends; *La Ballesta*, turn left at the sign before entering Tovar, the restaurant is on 3 tiers with prices to match, snacks and meals weekends and holidays, adjoining rifle and archery ranges, equipment for hire.

Local fruit, vegetables and flowers are sold at *Frutería Bergman*, next to the Lagoven gas station at the eastern entrance to town. Across the street is *Panadería Tovar* for delicious bread. On weekends there are many foodstalls along Avenida Codazzi.

● Transport

Road The 1½-hours drive up from Caracas is easy during the week, but hell on weekends – long traffic jams, difficult to find picnic spots or accommodation, definitely not recommended.

Keep your passport with you in case of military checks. It is generally easy to get a lift if there are no buses. The taxi fare for the round trip from Caracas to Colonia Tovar is about US$20; the driver will wait. **Buses**: leave from Avenida Sur 9 y El Rosario, next to Nuevo Circo, to El Junquito (1 hour, US$0.40), then change for Colonia Tovar (1 hour, US$0.55). *Por puestos* leave more frequently from Plaza Catia or O'Leary; 1 hour, US$1. Alternatively, take a *por puesto* from Plaza Capuchino to El Junquito, then one from there to Colonia Tovar, US$1. If changing *por puesto*, make sure the driver stops at the right place. The last bus back to Caracas is at 1800. To La Victoria there are 4 buses a day, US$1.50.

Black Forest Ghetto

Venezuela's devastating War of Independence left a chronic shortage of farm labour to work the land. In response to the problem, immigration laws were amended to attract farmers from Europe. So, with the financial backing of Don Martín Tovar, a wealthy creole landowner, 392 men, women and children from the Black Forest community of Kaiserstuhl set sail for Venezuela.

Instrumental in the settlement's success were Agustín Codazzi, an Italian geographer, and his map maker Alexander Benitz, a young engraver from Kaiserstuhl. They had already visited Venezuela to scout for possible sites, returning to France to sign up the land-hungry peasants and craftsmen. They also hired the emigrants' ship and bought food and equipment – including a printing press and sawmill. On 11 January 1843, Codazzi and Benitz set sail from Le Havre with the 392 hopeful emigrants.

Things soon went badly wrong. Over 100 lives were lost to smallpox during the long voyage and when the vessel finally reached Venezuelan shores, it was quarantined for 3 weeks, after which they were allowed to land near Choroní. From there, the intrepid settlers dragged all their gear up the mountains and down to Maracay, where they were greeted by the then president, General José Antonio Páez. Then began the long, arduous trek up to present-day Tovar, where they finally arrived, depleted and exhausted, on 8 April.

The colony was self-sufficient, with its own typesetters, carpenters, blacksmith, shoemaker, baker, tailor, barrel-maker, teacher, priest and brewer (who produced the first beer in Venezuela). They set about recreating their Black Forest community in complete isolation, eating traditional food, drinking their own beer, keeping up their customs and traditions and marrying off their blond-haired children to one another. The colonists themselves worsened their isolation by banishing members who married Venezuelans. This led to inbreeding, cultural poverty and an increase in illiteracy.

For almost exactly a century, they survived in their remote mountain home, untouched by the outside world. Then, in 1942, Colonia Tovar became a township, Spanish became the official language and residents were free to marry whom they pleased. Finally, with the opening of a paved road to Caracas in 1963, Tovar's stubborn isolation ended. Curious *Caraqueños* came on weekend trips and Tovar's residents travelled to Caracas to sell their local fruits and beer. With the outside contact, the German language began slowly to disappear. There is still a preponderance of fair-haired, light-skinned residents but their grandchildren have dark hair and Spanish names. The once traditional costumes are now worn for the benefit of visiting tourists rather than a determination to preserve local customs.

Colonia Tovar is said to have been the inspiration for Isabel Allende's fictional backwater, Agua Santa, in her best-selling novel *Eva Luna*, which she wrote while in exile in Venezuela.

COLONIA TOVAR TO THE COAST

The road which leaves Ruta 4, 8 km before Tovar, divides soon after into three paved roads which wind down the mountains through beautiful scenery to Puerto Cruz, Chichiriviche and Puerto Carayaca, running west to east respectively. It is 43 km to **Puerto Cruz**, a tiny harbour with a good beach. Boats can be hired here for a 14 km trip west to the even smaller settlement of **Puerto Maya** (*population* 200), on a beautiful bay and accessible only by boat. The villagers are mostly descended from African slaves.

The second road leads down the valley to the neat little town of **Chichiriviche**, 40 km from Tovar and not to be confused with the more famous resort of the same name in the Parque Nacional Morrocoy (see page 129). Potholes in the last section of the road make a high-clearance vehicle useful. The only accommodation is at **E** *Hotel Restaurant El Montero*, T 862-0436, F (014) 296310, friendly, comfortable, clean, secure, nice restaurant, recommended, best to book in advance at weekends.

A new coastal jeep track now links Chichiriviche with Puerto Cruz to the west, but it's not yet suitable for conventional cars.

The paved coast road begins at Chichiriviche and runs east to Catia La Mar and Maiquetía (see page 98). The first resort is **Oricao** with a lovely palm-rimmed but private beach, then comes **Puerto Carayaca**, where the third paved road down from Tovar reaches the coast. At Puerto Carayaca is **D** *Casa Francisco*, a hotel and restaurant in an attractive setting.

A few kilometres inland are the small towns of Tarma and **Carayaca**, which has the only other gas station in the area apart from Colonia Tovar. From Carayaca, yet another paved road runs from the Tovar-El Junquito road to the coast, at Arrecifes. Many of the coves along this coast are good for swimming and renowned for sport fishing. The vegetation covering the mountainsides is lush and attractive, with many ferns, orchids and bromeliads.

SAN MATEO

Back on the Old Road to Maracay, the next town west after La Victoria is **San Mateo**, famous as the site of the **Ingenio Bolívar**, the old Bolívar family hacienda. The sugar and cacao plantation was home to The Liberator during much of his youth. At the age of 20 he returned here with his Spanish bride, María Teresa, who died only 6 months later from Yellow Fever. The hacienda and museum are a must for anyone interested in Simón Bolívar; they are open daily except Monday, 0800-1200, 1400-1700.

The rich San Mateo Church is also worth a visit. The main treasure of the church is the miraculous image of the Virgen del Belén, painted on a small medallion, which 'appeared' in 1709. The Bolívar family built the left side chapel for the image.

ROUTES Soon after San Mateo, Highway 11 leads off south (45 km) to **San Juan de Los Morros** (see page 223). The new Pan-American highway continues west, avoiding city centres, so all that is seen of Maracay and Valencia are factories.

MARACAY

Maracay (*population* 538,620; *altitude* 445m; *phone code* 043), capital of Aragua State, is a hot, humid, thriving industrial city at the heart of an important agricultural area.

The city was founded on 25 March 1701, and soon became a major centre of tobacco and cacao production. It was the cultivation of indigo, however, which transformed Maracay from a village of thatched houses into an important agricultural and industrial centre.

At the beginning of the 20th century, Maracay gained notoriety as the home of **Juan Vicente Gómez**, one of the worst dictators in a continent renowned for its brutal military leaders. In 1912, Gómez settled permanently in the city, which became the virtual capital of the country until his death in 1935. During his tenure, the essential character of the city did not change much, but his legacy is

Reign of terror

👣 During his 27-year tyranny, Juan Vicente Gómez regarded Venezuela as his own personal estate and he ran it like a tyrannical landowner. He created a machinery of despotism run by an army and police force completely under his control. Their method was, quite simply, terror: dungeons, torture and severe punishment for every offence, including any statement which might be interpreted as challenging the dictator's wisdom or power.

The economic effects of his dictatorship are discussed on page 47, but even more serious was the intellectual and moral vacuum left by Gómez. Practically illiterate himself, the dictator had a deep distrust of learning. Even the university, which in Latin America usually manages to retain some independence under dictatorial regimes, was subjugated during his years in office. In the words of the Venezuelan historian Ramón Díaz Sánchez, Gómez made the country a "region par excellence of order and silence, a walled island completely surrounded by petroleum, without opinions, without feelings, without a window on the future". This most cold and systematic of tyrants, known as *el brujo* (the sorcerer), even moved the great Pablo Neruda to write: "Gómez, Venezuela's quagmire, slowly submerges faces, intellects, in his crater".

considerable and includes the aviation school, the barracks and the bull ring.

In the last few decades Maracay has grown into a city of highrise blocks, factories and residential suburbs. But despite its size, Maracay is still called the 'Ciudad Jardín de Venezuela' – the Garden City – owing to its number of green spaces.

Places of interest

The former hometown of General Gómez still retains some of his more extravagant whims. **Jardín Las Delicias**, with its beautiful zoo (closed on Monday), park and fountain, was built for his revels. It stands on Avenida Las Delicias, en route to Choroní; take an Ocumare bus from the terminal. The **bull ring**, one block west of the **Casa de la Cultura**, is an exact replica of the one at Seville. The pretentious **Gómez mausoleum** on Calle Mariño, built no doubt to remind people of his tyranny rather than in his honour, has a huge triumphal arch.

The heart of the city is **Plaza Girardot**. Its colonial character has been lost to modern apartments, while the streets around the plaza are a bazaar of jewellery, clothing, electrical and shoe shops. On the plaza is the attractive, white **Cathedral**, finished in 1743.

There is an interesting collection of prehispanic artefacts in the museum of the **Instituto de Antropología e Historia** on the south side of the plaza, revealing how densely-populated the shores of Lago de Valencia once were; open Tuesday-Friday 0800-1200, Saturday and Sunday 0900-1300, admission free. At the opposite end of the same building is a poor history museum, with rooms dedicated to Gómez and Bolívar; open Tuesday-Friday 0800-1200, Saturday and Sunday 0900-1300, admission free. At the rear end of the building is the **Biblioteca de Historia** whose walls are lined with portraits of Bolívar. This building was once the headquarters of the state bank and legend has it that Gómez had unrestricted access via a tunnel under the plaza from his house on the north side.

500m east is **Plaza Bolívar**, said to be the largest such-named plaza in Latin America. On one side is the **Palacio del Gobierno**, originally the *Hotel Jardín*, built by Gómez in 1924. Also here are the **Palacio Legislativo** and the modern **opera house**, built in 1973. The plaza is a pleasant place to stroll, with its statues and colonnades.

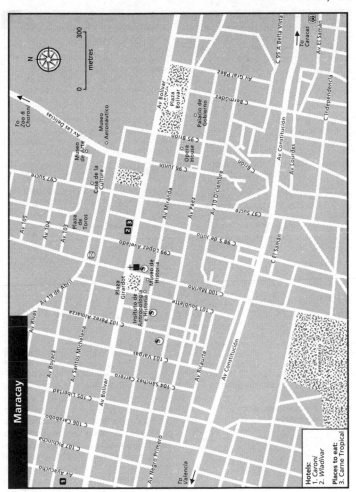

Museums

The **FAV (Fuerza Aérea Venezolana) Museum**, on Avenida Principal in Las Delicias suburb, has displays of Second World War fighters and bombers as well as aircraft from between the wars and more recent jets. The museum has been closed for renovation since 1992.

Local festivals

San José: 16-25 March.

Local information

● **Accommodation**

A3 *Byblos**, Avenida Las Delicias, air conditioning; good restaurant, some English spoken, good value, disco at weekend, recommended; *Italo*, Avenida Las Delicias, T 322166, closer to town, on bus route, 4-star, air conditioning, lovely rooftop pool, safety deposit box; **A3** *Pipo**, Avenida Principal, El Castaño, located in the hills above the city, but there's no public transport, pool, disco, recommended restaurant (*parrillas* a speciality).

C *Princesa Plaza*, Avenida Miranda Este entre Fuerzas Aéreas y Avenida Bermúdez, T 336953, F 337972, one block east of Plaza Bolívar, inexpensive restaurant; **C** *Wladivar*, Avenida Bolívar Este 27, spacious, lots of insects.

D *Caroní*, Ayacucho Norte 197 y Bolívar, air conditioning, hot showers, TV, clean, comfortable, recommended; **D** *La Barraca*, Avenida Bolívar Este 186, air conditioning, safe parking, noisy at weekends, good value; **D** *San Luis*, Carabobo Sur 13, off the main shopping street, clean and friendly.

E *Central*, Avenida Santos Michelena 6, T 452834, clean, safe and central; **E** *Oma*, Calle Libertad 32, entre Avenida Páez y Avenida Miranda, with bath, rooms are run down and rented by the hour.

F pp *Guayana*, on Avenida Bolívar Este opposite *Wladivar*, with bath, clean and friendly but noisy nightclub next door which is open every night except Monday until 0430.

Most budget hotels are located in the streets around Plaza Girardot.

● **Places to eat**
There are many excellent restaurants in the Avenida Las Delicias area, most of which are American style drive-up, fast-food outlets. These include *Vroster*, grills, large portions, popular with locals, good service, recommended; *Carne Tropical*, Avenida Bolívar y 5 de Julio, OK; *Biergarten Park*, on the east side of Plaza Bolívar, a pleasant, covered terrace with bar and restaurant, some German and Italian specialities, cheap and good. Many reliable Chinese restaurants and *loncherías*, *tascas* and inexpensive restaurants can be found in the streets around Plaza Girardot.

● **Banks & money changers**
Banco Consolidado (American Express), Avenida Bolívar y Fuerzas Aéreas, in the basement of Parque Aragua shopping mall, three blocks from the bus terminal. *Cambio* in *Air Mar* travel agency, ground floor of CADA Centro Comercial, Avenida 19 de Abril, Local 20, two blocks north of Plaza Girardot, 2.5% commission.

● **Cultural centres**
Casa de Cultura, two blocks northwest of Plaza Bolívar, art and cultural exhibitions; open Monday-Friday 0800-1500.

● **Tour companies & travel agents**
At the travel agency in Edificio Elizoph, Avenida 19 de Abril Este, Rose-Marie speaks excellent English and is helpful.

● **Transport**
Airport 5 km from the centre.

Buses The bus station is 2 km southeast of the centre. Take a *por puesto* marked 'Terminal' for the bus station and 'Centro' for the town centre (Plaza Girardot). To **Maracaibo** Expresos Los Llanos, US$8; **Valencia**, US$0.50, 1 hour; **Caracas**, US$1.50, 2 hours, *por puesto* US$3; **Barinas**, US$5, 7 hours; for **Choroní** and **Ocumare/Cata** see below; **Ciudad Bolívar**, US$9.50, 10 hours. To **Coro**, US$4.55, 7¾ hours. To **Barquisimeto**, US$3, 3½ hours. Eastern destinations include **Isla de Margarita** served by Expresos Ayacucho, T 349765; there's a daily departure to Margarita at 1400, US$15 (including first class ferry crossing). There are many buses to every part of the country, most leave 0600-0900 and 1800-2300.

HENRI PITTIER NATIONAL PARK

The 107,800 hectare **Henri Pittier National Park** is the oldest in the country, created in 1937 as Rancho Grande National Park. The park was renamed in 1953 to honour Henri Pittier (1857-1952), the remarkable Swiss geographer, botanist, meteorologist and ethnologist who first came to Venezuela in 1913, and who studied and classified more than 30,000 plants.

The park, one of the most important in the country, extends from the north of Maracay to the Caribbean, excluding the coastal towns of Ocumare, Cata and Choroní (see below), and south to the valleys of Aragua and the villages of Vigírima, Mariara and Turmero. The park landscape of steep rugged hills and tumbling mountain streams, rises from sea level in the north to 2,430m at Pico Cenizo, descending to 450m towards the Lago Valencia. The variation in altitude gives great variety of vegetation. There are cactii and thorns along the coast, rising to xerophilous woodland, semi-deciduous woods, then lower and upper cloud forests.

The park is of great interest to biologists and especially birders. 578 species of birds have been recorded, representing 43% of all those found in Venezuela and some 5.4 different species for every square kilometre, one of the highest densities recorded in the world. Included are no less than seven different eagles and eight kites, as well as blood-eared parakeets, white-tipped swifts, swallow tanagers, helmeted curassow, wood quail and, with luck, white-tipped quetzal. For further information

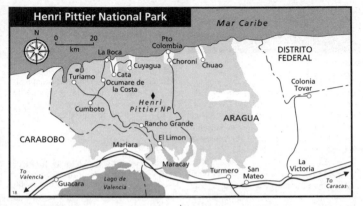

Henri Pittier National Park

refer to *Parque Nacional de Henri Pittier – Lista de Aves*, by Miguel Lentino and Mary Lou Goodwin, 1993. The park's fauna includes many snakes and monkeys, the collared peccary, agouti, otters, puma and tapir.

Climate
The dry season runs from December to March and the rainy season (although still agreeable) is from April-November. You may find conditions in the park very wet, with an average humidity of 92%. If camping, you'll need a good rainproof tent.

Routes into the park
Two paved roads cut through the park. One heads directly north to Choroní (see below). The other road runs to Ocumare de la Costa (see below). This road climbs to the 1,128m high Portachuelo pass, a V-shaped cut in the coastal range between Pico Periquito (Parakeet Peak), which rises 360m above the pass, and Pico Guacamayo (Macaw Peak), 340m higher than Periquito. The road was built by Gómez as an escape route if things grew too hot for him. The pass serves as a natural migratory route for hundreds of thousands of birds and insects flying inland from the sea, or to and from the continent from such far-flung places as Newfoundland.

RANCHO GRANDE
Near the Portachuelo Pass, 12 km from the El Limón Ranger Post at the park entrance, is the Rancho Grande, the uncompleted

palace/hotel Gómez was building when he died. The building is in the shape of a question mark and is now dilapidated. Part of it is occupied by lizards, snakes, bats and insects. Rancho Grande is the favoured base in the park for ornithologists and naturalists as it is close to the migratory routes; September and October are the best months. From the station there are numerous easily followed trails into the forest.

On the 4th floor are the laboratories, museum and offices of the **Estación Biológica Rancho Grande**, a biological research station run by the Institute of Agronomy of the Universidad Central in El Limón, T (043) 450153, situated on the road towards El Limón and Ocumare. When visiting look for Edificio 11 and ask for Iris. You should get your permit to visit Rancho Grande here (though some reports suggest this is not needed in advance) and you'll need a National Parks permit to walk the trails near the station. The park entrance fee is US$0.65 per person.

● **Accommodation** There are plenty beds available for those wishing to stay at the station. It costs US$5 per person per night, including the use of kitchen facilities. Bring a warm sleeping bag (it gets cold at night), candles and food. The nearest supplies are at El Limón, 12 km before Rancho Grande.

● **Transport** A taxi can be hired at Maracay for a day's outing in the park for about US$30 (bargain hard). Buses depart from Maracay Terminal; pay the full fare to Ocumare (US$1.10) or hitch from El Limón Alcabala. The last bus back to Maracay passes around 1730.

THE ARAGUA COAST

OCUMARE

From the Portachuelo Pass the road descends through cloud forest for 23 km until it reaches the next fork; the left hand leads to **Cumboto** and the naval base of **Turiamo**. The right hand road leads to **Ocumare de la Costa**, 13 km beyond the fork. Ocumare (*population* 6,140) is famous as the site of the disastrous landing made by Miranda on 27 April 1806. Ten American volunteers on the expedition were subsequently executed at Puerto Cabello (see page 123). This is also where Simón Bolívar landed on 6 July 1816, and declared the end of the War to the Death policy and freedom for the slaves of Venezuela. This expedition was also unsuccessful, however.

It's a further 3½ km to the sea at **La Boca**, the old town of **Independencia** and the popular beach of **El Playón**.

● **Accommodation & places to eat In Ocumare**: B *Montemar*, D *Casona*, next door, family-run, restaurant, D *Playa Azul*, modest. **In El Playón**: hotel-restaurants *Posada María Luisa*, T (043) 931184; E *La Abuela*, stuffy, nice restaurant and *El Playón*. There are many other restaurants.

● **Buses** From Maracay, 2-2½ hours, US$1.10.

CATA AND CUYAGUA

A few kilometres east is **Bahía de Cata**, once a beautiful beach, but now overdeveloped particularly at the western end. There are basic cabins for rent on the beach, **D**, and a good fish restaurant, run by Pepe. Note that in the low season (May-June) restaurants close at 1530. The smaller beach at **Catita**, at the eastern end of the bay, is reached by fishing boat ferries (10 minutes, US$0.70).

5 km inland is the town of **Cata** (*population* of town and beach 3,120) with its small colonial church of San Francisco. Devil dancers here fulfill an ancient vow by dancing non-stop through the morning of 27 July each year.

The beautifully unspoiled and peaceful beach at **Cuyagua** is 23 km further on at the end of a steep, panoramic road. The waves here are big enough to provide good surfing, but swimming is not advised owing to the dangerous rips. There are devil dancers here, too, on a movable date in July or August.

● **Buses** *Por puesto* to Cata from Ocumare US$0.70; from El Playón US$0.25 from the plaza.

CHORONI

The second road through the Henri Pittier National Park heads north over a more easterly pass (1,830m) to the charming, 300-year-old **Santa Clara de Choroní**, one of the most beautiful colonial towns in Venezuela. The spectacular 45 km road climbs from the flat plains of Maracay steeply up into the cloud forest and then descends through tunnels of bamboo, on tight, twisting bends until it levels out and the Caribbean flavour takes hold.

Choroní was once at the heart of this rich cacao-growing region, with *haciendas* worked by black slaves. In colonial times, Dutch and Spanish ships plied the coast, carrying their cargoes across the Atlantic. The journey, though, was a dangerous one – bloodthirsty English pirates stalked the coast, sometimes coming ashore for raids. That is why towns such as Choroní, Cata and Chuao on this coast were built inland, as protection against the raiders.

The blue Santa Clara de Assisi church on Plaza Bolívar is interesting. The *Fiesta de San Juan* on 31 May is worth seeing.

Choroní is a good base for walking in the park. There are numerous opportunities for exploring the unmarked trails. Many of them originate in picturesque spots such as the river pools ('pozos') of El Lajao (beware of the dangerous whirlpool), and Los Colores, 6 km above Choroní. Agua Fuerte (9 km above Choroní), has an interesting cultural centre, converted from an old hydroelectric power station. From behind the entrance gate rises a trail which soon divides; one branch extends to the heights above the valley. Watch out for snakes when walking in the park. Other recommended 'pozos' are La Virgen, 10 km from Choroní, and La Nevera, 11 km away. 8 km north of Choroní are two waterfalls at a dam, El Dique, where you can bathe. They are easy to find, but ask for directions in Uraca village, where there are drinks on sale.

For more challenging hikes in the area contact Edilberto at the *Robin Hood Restaurant* in Puerto Colombia (see below).

● **Accommodation B** *Hacienda La Aljorra*, breakfast and dinner included, 9 colonial rooms in 62 hectares of wooded hillside, reservations T Caracas (02) 237-7462, F 238-2436; **B** *Posada Pittier*, on the road to Puerto Colombia, 8 small but immaculate rooms, air conditioning, good meals, on Saturday night add US$10, helpful, garden, recommended, T (043) 911028, or Caracas (02) 573-7848, F 577-4410; **B** *La Gran Posada*, 5 km north of Choroní on a steep hillside above the Maracay road, neat, pleasant bar and restaurant, short walks in the park, T (043) 549307, F 545776; **D** *Choroní*, colonial building on the plaza, bed and breakfast, dinners available, basic, attractive, small, shared bath, T (02) 951-7607, F 951-0661.

● **Transport** Buses leave Maracay every 2 hours from around 0630-1700, more at the weekend, US$1.25, 2½ hours. Romerito, 16 km from Choroní in the heart of the park, is reached by the 'Metro-Mar' bus from Puerto Colombia, 6 times a day.

PUERTO COLOMBIA

Just beyond Choroní is the fishing village of **Puerto Colombia** (*phone code* 043). It's a peaceful, laid-back little place with its fleet of brightly-painted wooden boats moored in the river that flows into the sea. Frigate birds wheel overhead and pelicans bob up and down in the tiny harbour, waiting for the day's catch to arrive. The attractive *malecón* is lined with grapenut trees. On weekend nights you can see (and hear) the big *tambores* (hollowed out drums) beating out a pulsating rhythm while dancers' hips gyrate sensually in front of an appreciative and inebriated audience.

Tourists also flock here, to enjoy the dazzling white beach of Playa Grande in a beautiful horseshoe bay fringed by coconut palms and with a spectacular backdrop of lush, green mountains. The beach is 5 minutes' walk from town, across the river and around the headland. At weekends the beach can get crowded and littered. If you're swimming, beware of the strong undertow.

Chocolate money

🐟 The Aragua coast was developed by the Spanish as a major centre of cacao production. The indigenous cacao plant thrived in the warm coastal valleys and the unusually sweet Venezuelan cacao enjoyed an enviable reputation. Trade at first was mostly with the protected market of Mexico but Dutch traders were soon willing to pay even higher prices as they sought to establish their reputation as producers of superior chocolate.

The cacao boom which began in the mid-17th century not only boosted the economic importance of Caracas but also reinforced the wealth and power of a tiny landowning oligarchy. This elite, known as the *gran cacao*, spent lavishly on imported luxury goods from Europe and enjoyed a hectic social whirl of cultural events. At the same time, however, the black slaves, on whose backs the prosperity of the *gran cacao* was built, lived in grinding poverty.

The independence wars and the instability which followed ended the cacao boom as the plantations fell into neglect and slaves were freed. At the same time, tastes were changing in Europe, where coffee was replacing cocoa as the favourite drink.

Cacao is still produced in Chuao, where the entire village is involved in the process. The cacao is then sent to France and Switzerland to be turned into the finest chocolate.

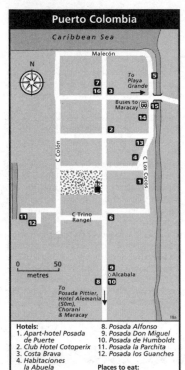

Puerto Colombia

Caribbean Sea

Malecón

N

To Playa Grande

Buses to Maracay

C Colón

C Los Cocos

C Trino Rangel

0   50
metres

To Posada Pittier, Hotel Alemania (50m), Choroní & Maracay

Hotels:
1. Apart-hotel Posada de Puerte
2. Club Hotel Cotoperix
3. Costa Brava
4. Habitaciones la Abuela
5. Habitaciones Playa Grande
6. Hostal Colonial
7. La Montañita

8. Posada Alfonso
9. Posada Don Miguel
10. Posada de Humboldt
11. Posada la Parchita
12. Posada los Guanches

Places to eat:
13. Araguaney
14. El Abuelo
15. Licorería
16. Robin Hood Pizzería

Excursions

Many of the local fishermen will hire their boats for a day trip to one of the several nearby beaches. Although they are not accessible by road they can be popular, especially at weekends. A recommended trip is to the tiny fishing village of **Cepe**, 30 minutes east. Boats cost around US$8.50-12.50 per person, depending on the numbers and usually take 6-10 people. Cepe boasts a beautiful, unspoiled beach. Accommodation is available at **A3** *Posada Puerto Escondido*, T (043) 413614/414614, price includes 3 meals, drinks and boat transfer from Puerto Colombia, 4 clean, spacious rooms, with bath, hot water and

fan, peaceful and homely atmosphere. The owner Freddy Fisher organizes fishing and scuba diving trips, and will also provide a guide and equipment to explore the only bit of coral on this stretch of the Venezuelan coast.

From Puerto Colombia boats go to the colonial village of **Chuao**, famous for its *cacao*, or cocoa. The bay at Chuao is very pleasant with a couple of bars. The village is a 20-minute boat ride, followed by a 5 km walk or jeep trip inland. Boat prices are as above. The most reliable boatman is reported to be Amado. There is a trail which leads to Chuao from Choroní; it's a fairly easy hike, especially if you return by boat. It's also possible to return to Choroní and Puerto Colombia by jeep (US$4), but the trail is often impassable.

The village has a festival 28-29 May, with dancing devils. Also recommended is the *Corpus Christi* festival, celebrated on a Thursday at the end of May or beginning of June and said to be the best in this area.

The usually deserted three beaches of Diario are a 50-minute walk away. Leave Puerto Colombia in the direction of Choroní; after 1½ km you cross a bridge and turn sharp right. Soon after the road becomes a steep concrete track leading to the CANTV station. Go through the gate and when the track bears right, look for the stony path off to the left. It's easy to follow as it runs directly below overhead power lines. Follow this to the double pylon on the ridge from where the small beaches can be seen, down on the other side. The descent is long but gradual and shaded.

Another interesting excursion is to the *Hacienda La Sabaneta*, near Choroní, which has been restored to *cacao* production; contact the *Robin Hood* restaurant.

Local information
● **Accommodation**
L3 *La Posada de Humboldt*, near the checkpoint at the entrance to the village, beautifully reconstructed colonial house, includes all meals (and drinks from 1800-2300!), T (02) 976-2222, cellular (016) 310608.

C *Apart-Hotel Posada del Puerto*, T 911239, fully-equipped apartments for 5-7 people, discounts for longer stays; **C** *Club Hotel Co-toperix*, 16.5% taxes not included, with bath, full or half board also available, OK but a bit overpriced, they have 4 hotels throughout the village, No II is the reception, for reservations T (02) 952-8617/2467/2628; **C** *Posada La Parchita*, with bath, includes breakfast, 5 rooms set around a lovely patio, very nice.

D *Costa Brava*, near the Malecón, T 911057, with bath, cheaper without, basic but clean, friendly, communal sitting area, ceiling fans, laundry facilities, good food, English spoken, family-run, Nora (who also works in the *Robin Hood* restaurant) arranges trips to her home village of Chuao, recommended; **D** *Don Miguel*, near *Posada de Humboldt*, T 911081, with bath, 15 rooms, air conditioning, safe; **D** *Posada Alfonso*, T 911037, German owner, with bath, quiet, hammocks, laundry facilities, recommended; **D** *La Montañita*, T 911132, with bath and fan, nice rooms set around a courtyard on 2 levels, charming owners, packages available, **B** including all meals, recommended; **D-E** *Habitaciones Playa Grande*, above *Tasca Bahía*, with bath and air conditioning, **E** with shared bath and fan, 6 rooms, nice and friendly.

E *Alemania*, 50m beyond the checkpoint at the entrance to the village, T 911157/911036, with bath and fan, restaurant, parking; **E** *Hostal Colonial*, T 911087, or (02) 963-2155, with bath and fan, washing facilities, German owner, good value; **E** *Posada Los Guanches*, off Calle Colón near the plaza, T 911209, **F** pp, costs slightly more at weekends, 9 rooms, with bath, very friendly, clean, recommended.

F-G pp *La Abuela*, basic but clean, fan.

Camping: is possible on the beach, but beware of theft. Water is available from a tap opposite the public payphones near the bridge.

● **Places to eat**
Araguaney, near the bridge to Playa Grande, large portions, good breakfast for US$1, this is the main gringo hangout, always busy in the evenings, changes cash and travellers' cheques at poor rates; on the opposite side beside the bridge is a *licorería* where cash and travellers' cheques can be changed at the same rates, and phonecards can be bought. *Tasca Bahía*, cheap but beware of their salads, rooms for rent (see above – literally); *Robin Hood*, excellent food, pizzas US$3-5, salads US$2, also vegetarian, other dishes US$3-4, highly recommended, the owner organizes 1-day treks into the hinterland, US$10 per person (see **Excursions** above); *El Abuelo*, just before the bridge to Playa Grande, very good food, prices reasonable; *Margo*, on Calle Trino Rangel, good and varied breakfasts, friendly.

● **Transport**
Bus journeys to and from Maracay start and end here. Buses depart from opposite the *licorería* beside the bridge every hour or so from 0500; the last one leaves at 1700.

ROUTES 50 km to the west of Maracay the road reaches Valencia, through low hills thickly planted with citrus, coffee and sugar.

VALENCIA

Valencia (*population* 955,000; *altitude* 480m; *phone code* 041), capital of Carabobo State, is Venezuela's third largest city, the centre of its most developed agricultural region, and the most industrialized.

The city stands on the west bank of the Río Cabriales, which empties into the 352 sq km of Lago de Valencia, the second largest in the country. The lake has no outlet and is consequently polluted. Known as Tacarigua when it was first seen by the Spanish, Lago de Valencia has been shrinking for centuries. It is 40% smaller than it was in the early 18th century and is only 17m at its deepest. When Humboldt took measurements in 1800 it was 56 km long; it is now less than 35 km.

Climate Annual mean temperature 24°C; the valley is hot and humid with an annual rainfall of 914 mm.

HISTORY

The city was founded in 1555 (though some say 1553) by Alonso Arias de Villacinda and named after his hometown in Spain (like its Spanish namesake, Valencia is famous for its oranges). The city has survived a turbulent past to become the main industrial city of central Venezuela. First, it was almost wiped out by the blood-thirsty Basque conquistador, Lope de Aguirre (see page 326). It survived two attacks by Caribe Indians, then the population was decimated by smallpox at the end of the 16th century and, in 1677, the town was sacked by French pirates.

The settlement rose to prominence following the devastation wrought by a terrible earthquake in 1821 on Venezuela's main cities, but only 2 years later, during the War of Independence, it fell to José

Tomás Boves. The Royalist leader certainly earned his *nom de guerre*, "The Butcher". After swearing to respect the lives and property of the defeated Republicans, he and his troops began a frenzied bout of looting and murder. No one escaped the carnage. Even the wounded lying in hospital were slaughtered.

Over 35 major battles were fought around Valencia during the War of Independence. Most important of these was the Battle of Carabobo on 24 June 1821, whose victory ended over 300 years of Spanish rule in Venezuela. Despite these successive poundings, Valencia has been the nation's capital on three occasions and claims to be the first city on the continent to have had electric street lighting. Since World War Two it has continued to grow as an industrial centre.

PLACES OF INTEREST

The **Cathedral** was built in 1580 and then remodelled in 1767 to retain its original style. It stands on the east side of **Plaza Bolívar**, where there are sloths and iguanas in the trees. The statue of the Virgen del Socorro (1550) in the left transept is the most valued treasure. During the Valencia Fair, on the second Sunday in November it is paraded with a richly jewelled crown. The Cathedral is open 0630-1130, 1500-1830 daily, 0630-1200, 1500-1900 Sunday.

Also worth seeing is **El Capitolio**, on Páez, between Díaz Moreno y Montes de Oca; the **Teatro Municipal**, on Colombia y Avenida Carabobo; and the old **Carabobo University** building. The handsome **Plaza de Toros**, at the southern end of Avenida Constitución beyond the ring road, is the second largest in South America after Mexico City. It seats 27,000 spectators and features renowned international matadors during the November Fair. (**NB** Take care around this area.)

At Páez y Boyacá is the magnificent former **residence of General Páez**, the hero of the Battle of Carabobo. It is now a museum where annual painting competitions take place in the Michelena Salon; open Monday-Friday, free admittance.

Equally attractive is the **Casa de Célis** (1766), at Calle 98 y Avenida 104, which houses the Museo de Arte e Historia with precolumbian exhibits; open Tuesday-Saturday 0800-1400. The **Girardot Monument** commemorates Atanacio Girardot, one of Bolívar's warriors.

From the centre Avenida Bolívar extends several kilometres north towards the smart residential area of La Viña. There is a nice country club and a celebrated race track. Construction of a Metro began in late 1994. **NB** Most of the interesting sights are closed on Monday.

Parks and Zoos

There are several pleasant parks. Parques Cristóbal Mendoza, Andrés Eloy Blanco and Metropolitano all have fountains, nicely-tended flower gardens and leisure activities. The landscaped **Parque Humboldt**, six blocks east of the Cathedral, was the terminus of the old railway to Caracas. The station now houses an art gallery and the old passenger cars have become boutiques and restaurants.

There is an **Aquarium**, at the west end of Calle 107, which displays a selection of Latin American aquatic life and features a fresh-water dolphin show at 1600; open Tuesday-Sunday, 0930-1800, admission US$1. There is a small, unremarkable zoo at the snackbar/restaurant behind the aquarium; open Tuesday-Sunday 0900-2400, closed Monday.

EXCURSIONS

One of the largest groups of petroglyphs in Venezuela is to be found in the **Parque Nacional Piedras Pintadas**, 22 km northeast of Valencia. Lines of prehistoric stone slabs, many bearing swirling glyphs, march up the ridges of Cerro Pintado.

The park is reached by turning off the tollway at Guacara (14 km east of Valencia) and driving 6 km north on the road to Vigírima. Turn left at a small blue 'Cadafe Tronconero' sign then a further 3 km. Navy-blue buses run to Vigírima from Valencia at regular intervals (US$1); ask to get off at the 'Cerro Pintado' turn-off.

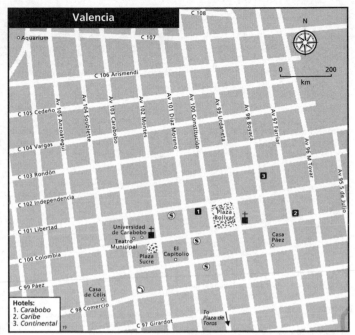

Valencia

Hotels:
1. Carabobo
2. Caribe
3. Continental

Near the southern shore of Lake Valencia, about 34 km east of Valencia, is the regional centre of Güigüe (*population* 44,320). At the nearby village of **La Taimata** other extensive ancient petroglyphs have been discovered. There are more sites along the western shore, and on the rocks by the Río Chirgua, reached by a 10 km paved road from Highway 11 (turn north at La Mona Maraven gas station), 50 km west of Valencia. Leave your vehicle by the cemetery in Chirgua and walk along the east side to the river. A further 5 km past Chirgua, at the **Hacienda Cariaprima**, is the country's only geoglyph, a remarkable 35m-tall humanoid figure carved into a steep mountain slope at the head of the valley. It is above and to the left of the ranch house.

30 km southwest of Valencia, on the highway to San Carlos, is the site of the **Carabobo** battlefield, an impressive historical monument surrounded by splendid gardens. Two battles were fought here: although Bolívar won the first in 1814, his forces were subsequently routed by the *llaneros* of Tomás Boves ('The Butcher') and Bolívar had to flee the country. In 1821, came the famous battle which established Venezuelan independence. On this occasion, Bolívar was greatly assisted by Páez's lancers and by British legionnaires who had joined him at Ciudad Bolívar (they are represented in the bronze bas-reliefs on the monument). The view over the field from the *mirador* where the Liberator directed the battle is impressive. Historical explanations are given on Wednesday, weekends and holidays.

Buses to Carabobo leave from the bottom of Avenida Bolívar Sur y Calle 75, or from Plaza 5 de Julio; 1¼ hours, US$0.25, ask for Parque Carabobo. You should take drinks, as none are available at the park. Those dressed too casually will be denied entrance to the monument.

LOCAL FESTIVALS

In late March is *Valencia Week*; on 15 November, and for one week after, is the *Patrocinales de Nuestra Señora de Perpetuo Socorro*, or Valencia Fair, with bull fights.

LOCAL INFORMATION

● Accommodation

Hotel prices

L1	over US$200	L2	US$151-200
L3	US$101-150	A1	US$81-100
A2	US$61-80	A3	US$46-60
B	US$31-45	C	US$21-30
D	US$12-20	E	US$7-11
F	US$4-6	G	up to US$3

Those marked with an asterisk (*) are bookable through Fairmont International (see under Caracas).

L2 *Intercontinental Valencia**, 5 km north of the centre at Calle Juan Uslar, La Viña, T 211533, F 211033, luxury style resort with pool, garden and all comforts.

A1 pp *Hacienda Guataparo*, 20 minutes from centre, owned by Vestey family, 9,000 hectares of peaceful farm, all meals included, riding and mountain bikes, good birding, must be booked in advance through *Last Frontiers*, UK, T 01844-208405, F 201400; **A2** *Ucaima*, Avenida Boyacá 141, T 227011, F 220461, near the *Intercontinental*, suites, pool, tennis.

C *Canaima*, Avenida Lara con Branger, recommended; **C** *Continental*, Avenida Boyacá 101-70, T 83014, restaurant, good value; **C** *Marconi*, Avenida Bolívar 141-65, T 213445, air conditioning, helpful, safe, laundry, recommended, it's next to a petrol station, good pharmacy and health food store, take a bus or colectivo from the bus station to the stop after 'El Elevado' bridge.

D *Carabobo*, Calle Libertad 100-37, esquina Plaza Bolívar, OK; **D** *Caribe*, T 571157/ 571209, air conditioning, safe, central, popular.

F pp *Colonial*, opposite the Teatro Municipal, a bit dingy, noisy air conditioning, but friendly; **F** *Palermo*, Avenida 97 Farriar, Italian owned, restaurant, quite good.

There are many hotels across the price ranges on Avenida Bolívar, but it is a long avenue, so don't attempt to walk it.

● Places to eat

Fego, Avenida Bolívar 102-75, recommended; *El Bosque*, opposite *Hotel Marconi*, cheap. *La Rinconada*, Plaza Bolívar, recommended, open on Sundays; *Caballo Blanco*, Avenida 97 Farriar, cheap and good food, clean, well-lit, Italian run.

● Banks & money changers

Banco Consolidado (American Express), Avenida Bolívar Norte, Edificio Exterior; *Italcambio*, Avenida Bolívar Norte, Edificio Talia, Local 2, bring original purchase receipt of travellers' cheques, a long way from the centre in Urbanización Los Sauces, get off bus at junction with Calle 132.

● Embassies & consulates

Honorary British Vice-Consul, Corporación Mercantil Venezolana, Calle Silva No 100-70, Edificio Comersa, T 50411/7.

● Laundry

La Fuente, Calle Martín Tovar y Colombia, T 86657, recommended.

● Shopping

Artesanía Típica Edy, Avenida Bolívar Norte, Urbanización La Alegría, opposite Banco República, recommended.

Bookshop: English books are bought and sold between pharmacy and health food store by *Hotel Marconi* on Avenida Bolívar.

● Transport

Air The airport is 6 km southeast of the centre. Avensa/Servivensa flights daily to Caracas, Aruba, Barcelona, Maracaibo, Porlamar, Puerto Ordaz, San Antonio. Aserca flies to Maracaibo, Caracas, Puerto Ordaz, Porlamar and Aruba. Servivensa flies daily to Bogotá and Miami. Aeropostal flies to Maracaibo, Barcelona, Porlamar, San Antonio and Aruba (T 345164, F 346567).

Buses Terminus is 3 km east of centre, and is part of the Big-Low shopping mall with 24-hour restaurants. Entry to the platforms is by *ficha* (token), US$0.05. There's a left luggage store. Minibuses to and from the centre are frequent and cheap, but follow a slow and confusing route at peak times. A taxi costs US$3 to the centre. To **Caracas**, US$1.75, *por puesto* US$3.50, Autoexpresos Ejecutivos (T cellular 014-405010), US$6, 8-9 a day; **Mérida**, 10-12 hours, US$8; to **San Cristóbal**, 10 hours, US$10; **Barquisimeto**, US$3.25, 3 hours; **Maracay**, 1 hour, US$0.50. **Puerto Cabello**, US$0.70, frequent, 1 hour or so; **Tucacas**, US$1.40, or US$3 by frequent *por puesto* service. To **Coro**, US$4.20, 4$\frac{1}{2}$ hours. To **Puerto Ordaz/Ciudad Guayana**, US$12, 13 hours. To **Ciudad Bolívar**, US$8-9, 10 hours.

VALENCIA TO PUERTO CABELLO

The Caracas-Valencia motorway (Ruta 1 to Puerto Cabello) continues across the Cordillera de la Costa through the La Trinchera Pass, reaching the sea near the huge oil refinery of **El Palito**. Turn right here to Puerto Cabello.

18 km from Valencia, the road passes the decaying spa of **Las Trincheras** (*population* 1,350). The explorer/scientist Humboldt stated in 1800 that one of the sulphur springs was the second hottest in the world at 98°C. He boiled his eggs in these waters in less than 4 minutes (spa-spotters should note that the hottest in the world are at Urijimo in Japan). There are three baths (hot, hotter, and third degree burns), a mud bath and a Turkish bath, all in a beautiful setting. Entrance is US$1.50, and the facilities are open 0800-1800 daily.

● **Accommodation B** *Hotel Termales Las Trincheras**, rooms only for guests on cures, minimum 21 days, good restaurant open to the public 1200-1600, 1800-2100, *fuente de soda* 0700-2100. Opposite is **D** *Hotel Turístico*, good. Frequent buses leave from Valencia.

PUERTO CABELLO

This is an industrial city and Venezuela's second most important port, 55 km from Valencia (*population* 137,250; *mean temperature* 28°C; *phone code* 042).

The port sometimes surpasses La Guaira, the busiest in the country, in monthly volume. Its fame as one of the best natural anchorages dates back to the middle of the 16th century, when it was described as the best port in the New World. The origin of the port's name is subject to some doubt. One theory relates to the protection afforded to the waters of the harbour, which were so calm that a ship needed no more than a *cabello* (hair) to be safely moored. It's also been suggested that the name came from an Andrés Cabello, who ran a business trading cacao and wheat for contraband from Curaçao.

The port began life as a smugglers' haven and attracted its fair share of pirates. It was also plagued by yellow fever, cholera and malaria. In the 17th and 18th centuries, it was more of a Dutch trading port than a Spanish settlement, owing to the volume of illegal cacao trade with Curaçao. It was the Basque Guipuzcoana Company who really developed Puerto Cabello in 1730, building their offices and warehouses as well as the impressive fortifications. The fortified city was a Royalist stronghold during the War of Independence. After the Battle of Carabobo, the Royalist troops retreated here and held out for more than 2 years. In fact, Puerto Cabello was the last part of Venezuela to be freed from Spanish authority.

Little of the town's history as a smugglers' port and gateway for the illicit cacao trade with Curaçao is now evident, having given way to today's naval base, shipyard and large container docks.

Places of interest

The **Museo de Historia** is in one of the few remaining colonial houses (1790) on Calle Los Lanceros (No 43), in the tangle of small streets between the Plaza Bolívar and the seafront; open Monday-Friday 0800-1200, 1500-1800, weekends 0800-1200.

The **Fort of San Felipe**, also called the Castillo del Libertador, was built by the Guipuzcoana Company at the entrance to the lagoon in 1732 to protect its commercial operations. The loss of the fort, on 30 June 1812, was a terrible blow to the First Republic. The Republican arsenal had been stored in the fort, and their army, under the leadership of General Miranda, was forced to surrender to the Royalists. Miranda was then imprisoned here before being sent to Spain (for more details see page 107). During the infamous dictatorship of General Gómez, the fort became the main prison for dissidents, until his death in 1935 (see also page 112). It now stands within the naval base. The Navy runs free launches across the channel to the fort.

Also built by the ubiquitous Guipuzcoana Company was the **Fort of Solano**, in 1765. It was the last colonial fort to be built in Venezuela. The isolated ruins, better known as **El Mirador de Solano**, are now in a military zone, but access is unrestricted. The lookout commands a fantastic view of the coast and the perfect lagoon harbour, but take a taxi as it's a long walk up.

El Aguila monument, in the colonial section (El Casco), marks the site where North American mercenaries in the pay of Francisco de Miranda were executed by the Royalists in 1806 during the War of Independence.

Excursions

A recommended hike is on the old, cobbled **Camino Real** to Valencia. The jumping-off point for the trek is the village of San Esteban, 8 km inland from Puerto Cabello.

A paved road runs 18 km east past the picturesque village of **Borburata** (there are pilgrimages here during Holy Week) to **Patanemo**. Both are within the **Parque Nacional San Esteban** (also known as Miguel J Sanz), 44,000 hectares abutting the Henri Pittier Park on the east and stretching almost to Puerto Cabello.

About 30 minutes east on this road is **La Bahía**, a beautiful horseshoe-shaped beach shaded by palms. There's a refreshment stand, changing rooms, toilets and lifeguards, but take your own lunch.

There are two other attractive sandy beaches nearby. **Quizandal** is a *balneario* with restaurant, showers and a drive-in theatre (parking fee). It is near the naval base, but is difficult to find, so take a taxi, US$4 (you may find it hard to get one on the way back). There are five offshore coral islands which can be explored. The best is **Isla Larga**, where sunken ships make one for ideal snorkelling. To get there, take one of the *lanchas* from Quizandal; US$2, 15 minutes, 0700-1600. Buy tickets at weekends at the wharf, on weekdays you'll need to seek out individual boatmen; and take your own shade. (See also Scuba diving, page 22.)

Bahía de Patanemo is a little resort tucked away in the trees.

● Accommodation **C** *La Churuata*, family-run hotel, without bath, English, French, Spanish, Italian spoken, pool, horses, excellent food and drink, local excursions, highly recommended but very small rooms.

Note that all these beaches are very crowded and noisy at weekends.

NB The beach to the west of Puerto Cabello is not so attractive. Do not go beyond the bathing area as the beach is notorious for armed robbery.

Local festivals

Shrove Tuesday, carnival festivities.

Local information
● Accommodation

B *Balneario Caribe*, Urbina Palma Sol, on beach front, T (052) 71395, cold showers.

C *Cumboto*, on the beach in the old Hacienda Cumboto, air conditioning, pool, open-air restaurant, was being renovated (mid 1997).

D *Miramar*, at El Palito, T 3853, with its own beach.

● Places to eat

Marisquería Romar, Edificio Sabatino, below Ondas del Mar radio station, Avenida Bolívar, Rancho Grande, seafood, recommended; *Briceñoven*, Paseo Malecón, one and a half blocks from Plaza El Aguila, good criollo cuisine; *Mar y Sol*, Calle El Mercado 6-110, facing the sea, local favourite for seafood.

● Tourist offices

On the main plaza, helpful, friendly, no English spoken, few maps or brochures.

● Transport

Air The airport is west on the highway. To Maiquetía 30 minutes, Coro 40 minutes, one daily non-stop; Maracaibo 80 minutes, 2 daily (LAV). Taxis to the old town, US$4. There's a Hertz agency at the airport.

Trains To and from Barquisimeto twice daily (see under **Barquisimeto Transport**, page 147, for details).

MORON

24 km west of Puerto Cabello, at the junction of the Pan-American Highway and the road to Tucacas, is **Morón** (*population* 56,450). The town is notable for its massive, ugly petrochemical complex and the bizarre **Monument to the Mosquito**. This is a large dead mosquito lying at the foot of an obelisk and commemorates the eradication of malaria, which had been a major killer in Venezuela, in the early 1960s.

Quite near Morón is the lovely beach of **Palma Sola**, 16 km long and deserted save at Easter time when Venezuelans camp out there in crowds. The water can be dangerous but the sands and palms are superb. There are hotels, many closed in the off-season.

From Morón a road goes north to **Tucacas**, 30 minutes away (see page 129). This road continues to **Coro** (see page 131). Another road heads west from Morón, up into the hills to **San Felipe** in Yaracuy state (see page 148).

The Northwest

THE NORTHWESTERN CORNER  of Venezuela comprises the state of Falcón and contains some of the country's most popular attractions as well as some lesser-known delights. The Morrocoy National Park offers sparkling white beaches, clear turquoise waters and wildlife in abundance. In Los Médanos de Coro National Park, would-be Lawrence of Arabias can strut their stuff on board camels over the massive sand dunes that stretch north on a narrow spit from Coro. This gem of colonial architecture is worth a visit in itself and is gateway to the remote, barren and windswept Paraguaná Peninsula. South from Coro the very beautiful Sierra de San Luis offers some fantastic treks.

Falcón comprises more than one quarter of Venezuela's entire coastline. While the coast is lined with beautiful beaches backed by arid scrub and cactus, inland lie mountains of lush forests, sugarcane and coffee plantations. Being so close to Maracaibo Lake, much of the state's economic development is based on oil and some of the country's largest oil refineries are located on the Paraguaná Peninsula.

MORON TO TUCACAS

From Morón the Falcón-Zulia highway, Route 3, parallels the entire coast of Falcón, all the way round to Coro and beyond to Maracaibo (see page 157). The first section heads north for 38 km to **Tucacas**, the southern access point for the **Morrocoy National Park**.

On the way to Tucacas Route 3 runs past **Boca Yaracuy**, on the Carabobo-Yaracuy-

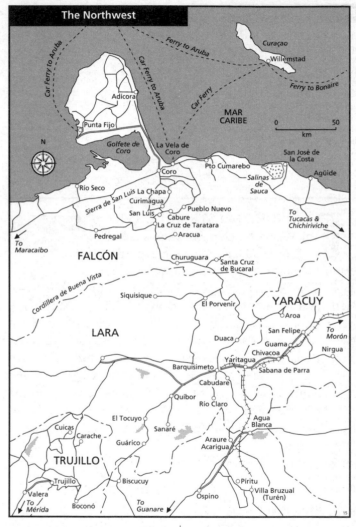

Falcón state boundary. From here, if you're lucky, or persistent, or preferably both, you just might be able to arrange with local fishermen to take you up the Río Yaracuy, where you'll enter an untouched tropical paradise of Morpho butterflies, parrots and macaws, ibises, herons, alligators and monkeys. Unfortunately, this part of the region is so untouched that we have no information on how to go about getting there, or how much you should expect to pay. Would-be explorers take note.

The road continues to follow the coast into Falcón to the Morrocoy National Park.

PARQUE NACIONAL MORROCOY

The **National Park of Morrocoy** comprises hundreds of coral reefs, palm-studded islets, secluded beaches and calm, shallow turquoise waters for water-skiing, snorkelling, and scuba-diving. The park's 32,090 hectares is mostly covered by water and lies between Tucacas to the south and Chiriviche to the north, in the Golfo Triste. The water is so shallow in parts of the park that, with appropriate footwear, it is possible to walk between some of the islands! This is not only one of most outstandingly beautiful parts of the Venezuelan coast, it is also ecologically important, consisting as it does of numerous cays (coral islands), coral reefs and mangroves.

Adjoining the park to the north is the vast **Cuare Wildlife Sanctuary**, one of the most important nesting areas in the country. Created in 1972 to protect a mind-boggling abundance of marine birdlife, the Sanctuary is home to 79% of Venezuela's aquatic birds and 66% of its migratory birds. Here you'll see huge colonies of frigate birds, brown boobies, pelicans, flamingos, egrets, scarlet ibis and herons, as well as hawks, hummingbirds, the barred tinamou, the limpkin and the great kiskadee. As one of the country's great poets once said, this is where "the birds of Venezuela and other countries meet to rest their wandering, love each other, discuss their right to the highest branch and to found a family".

Most of the flamingos are in and around the estuary next to Chichiriviche, which is too shallow for boats but you can walk there or take a taxi. The birds are best watched in the early morning or late afternoon.

AROUND THE PARK

From Tucacas

At the southern end of the park is **Tucacas**. The sheltered waters in the lagoon here, coupled with the excellent beaches, make this the perfect base for water-sport enthusiasts to enjoy water-skiing, snorkelling, swimming or sailing. Among the many beaches which can be reached from Tucacas are **Playuela**, which is very beautiful and better for snorkelling, though you need to beware of mosquitoes in the mangrove swamps. **Boca Seca** is more exposed to the open sea than the other islands and thus has fewer mosquitoes; it has a small café which is closed on Mondays. Also good is **Paiclás**, which has a restaurant and ecological toilets.

● **Boat trips** From Tucacas: prices per boat depend on the distance: US$17 return to Paiclás; US$24 return to Boca Seca; US$36 return to Cayo Sombrero (maximum 7 persons per boat). The ticket office is to the left of the car entrance to the Park. Recommended boatmen are Orlando and Pepe.

From Chichiriviche

Chichiriviche is at the northern end of the park and is the embarkation point to visit the most northerly *cayos*: **Borracho**, **Sal**, **Los Muertos**, **Peraza** and **Pelón**.

Cayo Borracho is one of the nicest islands, while Cayo Sal also has a good beach, but no palm trees for shade. Cayo Peraza is worth a visit, but not recommended for camping as there are few visitors and the litter attracts lots of rats (also watch out for stingrays which bask in the shallows in the early morning). The largest, cleanest and most popular of the islands is **Cayo Sombrero**, which can also be reached easily from Tucacas. It's very busy at weekends but has some deserted beaches, with trees to sling a hammock. It also has a restaurant and ecological toilets.

● **Boat trips** From Chichiriviche: prices per boat vary according to distance: from US$7.50 to Cayo Muerto, up to US$28 to Cayo Sombrero. There are 2 *embarcaderos* (ports); one is close to the centre and the other at Playa Sur. The latter has a ticket system which is supposed to guarantee that you will be picked up on time for the return trip. There are 2 basic trips from Chichiriviche: tour a) is a 3-4 hour trip which goes through the Golfo de Cuare to the Cueva de Los Indios, where you can see petroglyphs and La Piedra de la Virgen, also to the mangroves to see scarlet ibises (if you go early in the morning or at dusk), and then an hour long stop at one of the closer islands, the trip costs US$42 per boat; tour b) is a 5-6 hour trip to the Tucacas side of the park and includes Isla de los Pájaros, Las Juanes (a natural swimming pool with a

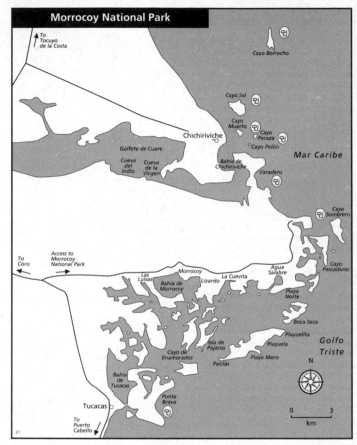

Morrocoy National Park

sandy bottom) and Cayo Sombrero, it costs US$63 per boat (maximum 8 persons per boat). These tours are good, if a little expensive, but bargaining is possible. **NB** Playa Sur is not safe after dark; muggings have been reported.

● **Camping in the park** You can camp on the islands but there are very few facilities and no fresh water. Also note that at weekends and holidays it is very crowded and litter-strewn; you need to beware of rats. To camp you must first make a reservation with Inparques (T 800-8487). There is a fee of US$2.10 per person per night. **NB** No alcohol is permitted.

Camping gas is available in Tucacas or Puerto Cabello.

The procedure is as follows: 1) phone Inparques to make your reservation at least 8 working days in advance. You need to stipulate the number of people, number of nights and which islands you wish to visit. You will then be given a code number. 2) Then deposit the total cost of your stay in the *Banco Industrial de Venezuela* (Cuenta Corriente No. 17-101170-3), or *Banco Unión* (Cuenta Fondo de Actividad Líquidos (FAL) No. 807801595-1) in Tucacas or Chichiriviche, under the name Programa Especial Parque Nacional Morrocoy. 3) Phone Inparques again. This time give them both your code number and the number on the bank deposit slip. This will confirm your reservation (you have 48 hours from the first phone call to complete steps 2 and

3). **NB** If you decide to cancel, Inparques still keeps your money. If you wish to postpone, you must inform Inparques 72 hours before the date confirmed. The alternative, of course, is to stay in a hotel!

● **Inparques office** In Tucacas, at Final Avenida Libertador, opposite Comando de la Guardia Nacional, T 830069.

TUCACAS

Tucacas (*population* 15,100, *phone code* 042), 30 minutes from Morón, is a hot, busy, dirty and expensive town, where bananas and other fruit are loaded for Curaçao and Aruba. Lots of new building is in progress in the town, and the only attraction is its position as a base from which to visit the various islands and beaches within the park.

Local information
● **Accommodation**
The only accommodation within the park is **A1** pp *Villa Mangrovia* on the Lizardo Spit between Tucacas and Chichiriviche, 3 rooms, excellent food and service, charming owner, book through Last Frontiers, or Journey Latin America, both in the UK (see **Useful addresses**, page 355).

A2 *Posada Baliju*, price includes full board and trips to the islands.

B *Manaure*, Avenida Silva, one block up from *Posada del Mar* (see below), T 830286, air conditioning, hot water, good restaurant, pool.

C *Apart-hotel Posada del Mar*, on Avenida Silva (parallel to Avenida Principal), turn right after *Las Palmas* (see below), T 830524, air conditioning, hot water, TV, cooking facilities; **C** *Gaeta*, two blocks down from the main road, air conditioning, TV, 10% discount for cash; **C** *Punta Brava*, next to the *embarcadero*.

D *La Suerte* on the main street, air conditioning, **E** with fan, small shop; **D** *Posada Jonathan*, turn right just past *Las Palmas*, air conditioning, **E** with fan.

E *Las Palmas*, next door to *La Suerte*, with shower, fan, basic, fan, kitchen and laundry facilities, helpful, cheap boat trips to islands, recommended; opposite is **E** *La Esperanza*, fan, with bathroom, fridge, safe lockers, clean, German owner arranges trips to islands and is helpful; round the corner is **E** *Oti Daly Mar*.

Cheap accommodation is difficult to find, especially in high season and at weekends, hotels are generally more expensive than elsewhere in Venezuela.

● **Places to eat**
La Entrada, between *Marisquería Bodegón del Mar* and *Lotería Cayo Sombrero*, good and substantial cheap meals for around US$2, open weekday lunchtime only.

● **Banks & money changers**
Banco Unión, one block down from the main road, cash advance on credit cards only. **NB** In Falcón generally it is practically impossible to change dollars cash or travellers' cheques. Travellers are strongly advised to carry Visa, Mastercard, or Amex, if possible. Hotels and Travel Agents will change money but at very low rates. Furthermore, do not count on travel agencies in Tucacas having enough cash to change money.

● **Sports**
Scuba diving: the most highly recommended place in Tucacas for diving trips, information or equipment hire is *Submatur*, Calle Ayacucho 6, T 830082, F 831051, the owner is Mike Osborn who speaks Spanish and English, 4 day PADI course US$330, 1 day trip with 2 dives costs US$65 (US$45 with your own gear); Mike also rents rooms (**E**, with fan and cooking facilities) and arranges tours to the Cuare Wildlife Sanctuary. The *Hotel Baliju* also runs PADI courses (US$325), but we have no information on the quality.

● **Tour companies & travel agents**
Guilica, two blocks up from *Hotel La Esperanza* on Avenida Principal, T 830939, runs tours to the islands, Puerto Cabello, also bird watching; *Valadero Tours*, on the left just around corner from *Hotel La Esperanza*, runs tours to the islands and other parts of the country (Mérida, Canaima, Puerto Ayacucho etc), they also have a fax service and will reconfirm flights. **Bicycles** can be hired in town.

● **Transport**
To get to Tucacas, take a *por puesto* or bus (frequent) direct from Valencia, US$3, bus US$1.40; alternatively, take a bus for Mirimire and get off at the entrance to town, US$1.50, 1½ hours; from Coro, US$3.

CHICHIRIVICHE

Several kilometres beyond Tucacas, towards Coro, is **Sanare**, which is the turn-off to the popular beach resort of **Chichiriviche** (*population* 4,700, *phone code* 042). Though a friendly and not unpleasant town, it's an expensive place and can be filthy and crowded at holidays and long weekends.

Local information

● **Accommodation**

B *La Garza*, attractive, pool, restaurant, price is for full board, cheaper without, comfortable, popular, they have a post box in the lobby which is open to the public and collected daily, changes cash, recommended; **B** *Náutico*, T 99-35866, includes breakfast, dinner and a trip to the nearest islands, good meals, fan, popular; **B** *Parador Manaure*, T 86121, F 86569, apartments for 5, small pool, fully-equipped kitchen (except utensils); **B** *Villa Marina*, T 86503, aparthotel, good, safe, pool, recommended.

C *La Puerta*, out of town, near the Playa Sur port, nice bar and restaurant, helpful owners, recommended.

D *Capri*, near the central port, with shower, fan or air conditioning, pleasant, Italian owned, good restaurant and supermarket; **D** *Residencial Linda*, one block from the central port, with or without bathroom, modern, Italian owners, helpful, use of kitchen, recommended; **D** *Villa Gregoria*, Calle Mariño, one block north of the bus stop behind the large water tank, fan, laundry facilities, has hammocks, Spanish-run, nice breeze on the 1st floor rooms and terrace, highly recommended.

E *Centro*, above a *panadería* (good) and opposite *Hotel Capri*, air conditioning, cheaper with fan, tiny rooms, shared bathroom, not very clean; **E** *Posada La Perrera*, Calle Riera, near centre, 150m from the bus stop, quiet, fan, laundry facilities, patio, hammocks, luggage stored, Italian owner, tours arranged, friendly, very good; **E** *Residencial Delia*, Calle Mariño 30, one block from *Villa Gregoria*, T 86089, includes breakfast, 4 double rooms, shared bathroom, organizes tours.

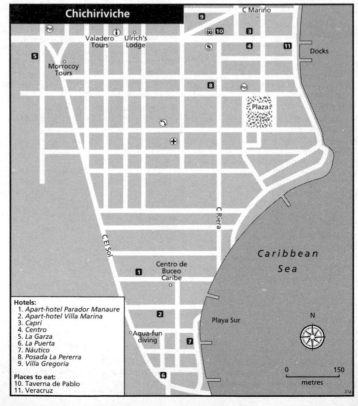

Chichiriviche

Caribbean Sea

Valadero Tours
Ulrich's Lodge
Morrocoy Tours
Docks
Plaza
C Mariño
C Riera
C El Sol
Centro de Buceo Caribe
Playa Sur
Aqua-fun diving

Hotels:
1. *Apart-hotel Parador Manaure*
2. *Apart-hotel Villa Marina*
3. *Capri*
4. *Centro*
5. *La Garza*
6. *La Puerta*
7. *Náutico*
8. *Posada La Perrera*
9. *Villa Gregoria*

Places to eat:
10. *Taverna de Pablo*
11. *Veracruz*

N

0   150
metres

● **Places to eat**
Veracruz, at the top of the main street overlooking the beach, good fish; *Taverna de Pablo*, opposite Banco Industrial, good pizzas and seafood etc.

● **Banks & money changers**
Banco Industrial, opposite the bus terminal on the main street, this is **the only bank in the state of Falcón which changes dollars cash**, it's open weekdays 0930-1530. Otherwise, *Valadero Tours* (see below) and *Hotel La Garza* may change cash and travellers' cheques, but at very poor rates, and if they have enough dollars at the time.

● **Sports**
Scuba diving: *Centro de Buceo Caribe*, Playa Sur, runs PADI courses for US$360, 1 day trip for US$65 (for divers with a *carnet*), they also rent equipment (also rooms for rent, **D**, with cooking facilities); *Aqua-Fun Diving*, Casa El Monte, Calle El Sol, Virgen del Valle, T 86265, run by Pierre and Monika who speak German, English, French and Spanish, high quality dive equipment, PADI courses from beginner (US$340) to advanced (US$240) levels, excursions for divers with certification card (US$40-65 per person, US$30-55 with your own equipment), can also be booked through *Valadero Tours* (see below), they also have 2 double rooms to rent, **D**, including breakfast, with fan.

● **Tour companies & travel agents**
Valadero Tours, two blocks from Banco Industrial on the opposite side, tours to the islands cost US$16-19 per person, they also run tours to other parts of the country (Mérida, Canaima etc), have a fax service and will reconfirm your flights. *Morrocoy Tours*, behind the gas station near the *Hotel La Garza*, island tours for US$13-15 per person, including drinks; they also operate from *Ulrich's Lodge* restaurant on the main street towards the port.

● **Transport**
Buses To **Puerto Cabello**, frequent *por puestos*, 2 hours, US$2; to **Barquisimeto**, 3 hours; to **Valera**, 9 hours. Direct buses leave from **Valencia**, or take a bus from Morón to Coro and get out at the turn-off (1½ hours, US$1), then hitch, or wave down the next bus from Valencia.

ROUTES It is 177 km from Tucacas to Coro. Beyond the Sanare turn-off to Chichiriviche, Route 3 turns inland and heads northwest, before reaching the coast again at **Puerto Cumarebo**, 40 km east of Coro. It then passes the old colonial port of **La Vela de Coro** (see **Excursions** below) and, 15 km further on, reaches Coro.

CORO

Coro (*population* 131,420; *mean temperature* 28°C; *phone code* 068) is capital of the State of Falcón. This old city is clean and well kept and a good place to relax for a few days. The colonial heart of the city lies between the Church of San Francisco on the corner of Avenida Miranda and the Church of San Clemente and is lovely with many beautiful buildings and shaded plazas.

As well as beautiful colonial architecture, Coro has other attractions close at hand. The amazing Médanos (sand dunes) lie a few kilometres to the north, and serve as the gateway to the windswept and interesting Paraguaná Peninsula, while to the south are the easily accessible tropical forests of the San Luis mountains.

HISTORY

Founded in 1527, Coro was one of the first Spanish settlements in South America. It was a comparatively peaceful place at first, thanks to the Governor's just treatment of the indigenous Arawak people. But Coro's harmonious beginning was short-lived. In 1527 Emperor Charles V created the province of Venezuela and leased it to the German banking firm of Welser, in order to pay off the huge debts which had been accrued to finance his excessive vanity.

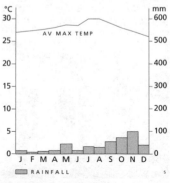

Climate: Coro

The new Governor, Alfinger, immediately showed no interest in peaceful coexistence with the natives. Coro was seen as nothing more than a base from which the Germans attempted to bully, ravage, rape and murder their way to a share of the fantastic riches already found in Mexico and Peru. After 20 years of increasingly frantic and ill-fated searching, Venezuela was returned to the Spanish, by which time Coro was in a state of near-terminal decline, despite having been capital of the colonial province.

The city continued to deteriorate through the 17th century, but was saved by the flourishing contraband trade between the mainland and the Dutch islands of Curaçao and Bonaire. This new-found and much-needed prosperity led to the regeneration of Coro throughout the 18th century.

Today, Coro boasts the finest examples of colonial architecture in the country and was decreed a National Monument, thus ensuring its continued preservation for future generations of Venezuelans and foreign visitors.

PLACES OF INTEREST

Coro's compactness means that it can easily be explored on foot. The **Cathedral** was begun in 1583 and not finished until over 50 years later. It is one of the two oldest churches in Venezuela (the other is in La Asunción, on Isla de Margarita) and among the oldest in the Americas. It was tastelessly remodelled in 1928, but then declared a National Monument in 1957

Colonial architecture in Coro

and restored to its original impressive simplicity. It is one of the few churches in Coro which is open other than for services.

San Clemente church was built in the second half of the 18th century in the shape of a cross with arms pointing to the cardinal points, one of only three churches in the country to be constructed on such a plan. It is currently undergoing renovation. The wooden cross in the **Plaza de San Clemente** in front of the church is said to mark the site of the first mass said in Venezuela and is believed to be the country's oldest such monument.

There are several interesting colonial houses in Coro, most of which are along the first two blocks of Calle Zamora, east of the plaza. **Los Arcaya**, on Zamora y Federación, is one of the best examples of 18th century architecture (see the Museo de Cerámica below). **Los Senior**, at Talavera y Hernández, is where Bolívar stayed in 1827.

Las Ventanas de Hierro, at Zamora y Colón, was built in 1764/65 by Don José Garcés de la Colina.

It is now a museum of period furniture, owned by the Zárraga and Tellería families; open Tuesday-Saturday 0900-1200 and 1500-1800, Sunday 0900-1300, entry US$0.20. Opposite Las Ventanas de Hierro is the **Casa del Tesoro**, which is now an art gallery displaying the work of local contemporary artists; it is open Monday-Saturday 0900-1800 and Sunday 0900-1500, entry is free.

The **Jewish cemetery** is on Calle 23 de Enero esquina Calle Zamora, four or five blocks up from the colonial part of town. It is the oldest still in use on the continent and was declared a National Monument in 1970. Many Jews fled Spain at the end of the 15th century in the face of the Inquisition. Despite laws prohibiting them coming to the New World, they settled in the Dutch territory of Curaçao, later moving to the mainland. A strong commercial community of Dutch and Portuguese Jews began to form in Coro, and many of the families have been prominent in the economic advancement of the state of Falcón and the country as a whole.

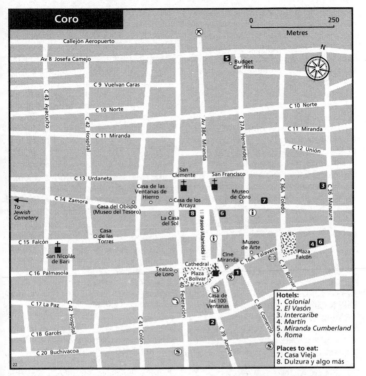

Coro

0   250
Metres

N

Callejón Aeropuerto

Av 8 Josefa Camejo

C 9 Vuelvan Caras

C 43 Ayacucho
C 42 Hospital

C 10 Norte

C 11 Miranda

5 Budget
Car Hire

C 10 Norte

C 11 Miranda

C 12 Unión

Av 38C Miranda
C 31A Hernández

San
Clemente
C 13 Urdaneta   San Francisco

Casa de las
Ventanas de   Museo
C 14 Zamora   Hierro   de Coro   **7**
Casa del Obispo   Casa de los
(Museo del Tesoro) Arcaya   **6**
To   La Casa   **8**
Jewish   del Sol
Cemetery   Casa
C 15 Falcón   o de las
Torres   Museo
San Nicolás   de Arte   **4 6**
de Bari   Cine   Plaza
C 16 Palmasola   Cathedral Miranda C 16A Talavera Falcón
Teatro   Plaza   **1**
de Loro   Bolívar   **S**
C 42 Hospital

C 364 Toledo
C 38 Manaure
C 31 Bolívar
C 37 Comercio

Casa de
C 17 La Paz   las 100
Ventanas

C 18 Garcés

C 40 Federación
C 41 Colón
C 39 Ampíes
C 38 Comercio

2

C 20 Buchivacoa   **S**

S

Hotels:
1. Colonial
2. El Vasón
3. Intercaribe
4. Martín
5. Miranda Cumberland
6. Roma

Places to eat:
7. Casa Vieja
8. Dulzura y algo más

MUSEUMS

The **Museo de Coro 'Lucas Guillermo Castillo'** (or Museo Diocesana) is housed in a lovely old monastery and is worth visiting. It has a good collection of church relics, 18th and 19th century furniture and a small, but varied 20th century art exhibition. There are good guided tours available (in Spanish). It is on Calle Zamora, opposite the Plaza San Clemente; open Tuesday-Saturday 0900-1200 and 1500-1800, Sunday 0900-1400, entry US$0.20.

The **Museo de Cerámica** is housed in Los Arcaya (see above). It's a small exhibition, but very interesting and with lots of information (in Spanish) including the mythology of ceramics, their medicinal uses and ceramics from different countries, etc. The garden (or inner courtyard) is

beautiful, with many old trees and cactii, and makes the perfect place to sit and relax. The museum is open Tuesday-Saturday 0900-1200 and 1500-1800, Sunday 0900-1300, entry US$0.10.

The **Museo de Arte** is similar to the Casa del Tesoro. It's at Calle 16A Talvera, between Plaza Bolívar and Cathedral, and is open Tuesday-Saturday 0900-1230, 1500-1630, Sunday 0900-1600; entry is free. There's a daily collection from the post box in the entrance.

EXCURSIONS

15 km east of Coro is the city's port, **La Vela de Coro**, from where you can take a launch or ferry to the islands of Aruba, Bonaire and Curaçao (see **Sea transport** below). This was the most important port

in Falcón, until the coming of oil and the development of the refinery ports on the peninsula, and makes for an interesting side trip. This was where Francisco de Miranda landed, in 1806, on his first abortive attempt to free Venezuela from colonial rule (see page 107).

Near La Vela, along the Morón road, rocking chairs of all sizes are made from cactus wood. On the road to La Vela, near the turn-off, is the **Jardín Botánico Xerofito Dr León Croisart**, which has plants from Africa, Australia, etc, and is very interesting. It is open Monday-Friday 1430-1730, Saturday 1000-1500, Sunday 0830-1200, free entry, guided tours in Spanish. To get there, take a La Vela bus from the corner of Calle Falcón, opposite Banco Coro, and ask to be let off at Pasarela del Jardín Botánico – the bridge over the road.

LOCAL FESTIVALS

26 July, Coro Week; **9-12 October**, state fair; **24-25 December**, *Tambor Coriano* and *Parranda de San Benito* (Coro, La Vela and Puerto Cumarebo). **In August** there's a Yachting Regatta, from Curaçao to La Vela, with competitors from USA, Holland and the Caribbean; ask at Capitanía (Port Captain's office) for information.

LOCAL INFORMATION

● **Accommodation**

Hotel prices

L1	over US$200	L2	US$151-200
L3	US$101-150	A1	US$81-100
A2	US$61-80	A3	US$46-60
B	US$31-45	C	US$21-30
D	US$12-20	E	US$7-11
F	US$4-6	G	up to US$3

Those marked with an asterisk (*) are bookable through Fairmont International (see under Caracas).

It can be difficult to find a good, cheap hotel.
A3 *Miranda Cumberland**, Avenida Josefa Camejo, opposite the old airport, T 523011, beautiful hotel, restaurant, swimming pool.

D *Arenas*, opposite the bus terminal, cold water, air conditioning, pool, restaurant; **D** *Federal*, out of town on Avenida Los Médanos esquina Avenida Manaure, air conditioning, fridge, good restaurant, 15-20 minutes walk from the centre of town; **D** *Intercaribe*, T 511811, Avenida Manaure entre Zamora y Urdaneta, air conditioning, expensive restaurant, pool, recommended.

E *Coro*, on Avenida Independencia, half block from Avenida Los Médanos, air conditioning, helpful, accepts credit cards; **E** *Posada Alemania*, Avenida Cementos, German owner, price includes a good breakfast and use of the kitchen, clean, rents snorkelling gear; **E** *Roma*, near Plaza Falcón, small rooms, fan, old beds, very basic, plumbing problems, no windows (unless you count a big hole in the wall as a window), otherwise OK; next door is **E** *Martín*, very clean, friendly owner organizes guided trips to Los Médanos and Sierra de San Luis; **E** pp *Zamora*, nearby on Calle Zamora, two blocks from Avenida Manaure, T 516005, with bathroom, cold water but no shortages, huge rooms with table and chairs, air conditioning, colour TV, good value, recommended; **E-F** pp *Colonial*, beside the cathedral, with bathroom, air conditioning, OK value.

F *Capri*, near Plaza Bolívar, very basic, large selection of rooms, with fans, poor maintenance and water supply.

Camping About 30 km west of Coro at *La Cumara* is nice campsite, where there's a good beach and dunes; US$1.20 per person.

● **Places to eat**

Mersi, off Calle Zamora, one block down from *Hotel Venezia*, good pizzas; *Cervecería Alhambra*, Calle Zamora, good, cheap; next door is *Casa Vieja*, good food served in a shaded courtyard, lovely atmosphere, reasonable prices, recommended; *Chupulún*, Avenida Manaure esquina Calle Monzón, recommended for lunch and homemade *chicha*; *El Bogovante*, Avenida Los Médanos, cheap and reasonable; *Rica Pizza*, in the same building, is also recommended; *Makokas Café*, on the boulevard between Plaza Falcón and Cathedral, recommended for breakfast; on the same street is *Heladería Brudrimar*, which is good for a quiet beer in the evening; *El Vasón*, on Calle Garcés, one block down from the CANTV building, good and filling meals for US$2, very basic, no atmosphere and lots of mosquitoes, recommended if you're really hard up; *Dulzura y algo más*, on the corner of the Alameda boulevard, recommended for ice cream and typical sweets.

● **Banks & money changers**

Banco Unión, Avenida Manaure esquina Avenida Romulo Gallegos, gives cash on Visa or Mastercard. **Banco Venezuela**, Plaza Talavera, for Visa. Otherwise you'll need to try the hotels and travel agents: eg *Hotel Sahara*, Calle 20, one block from Avenida Manaure; or *Kuriana Travel Agents* (see below).

● **Post & telecommunications**
Telephone: CANTV is in the very fine '100 Windows House'. International calls can be made from the Centro de Monedas, on Plaza Sucre, opposite the jail.

● **Tour companies & travel agents**
Kuriana Travel, Calle Zamora, opposite the Cathedral, Edificio Avila, 2nd floor, oficina 2B, T 522058, F 513035, ask for Mercedes Medina, who has an excellent campsite nearby (*Llano Largo*), highly recommended, they specialize in eco-tourism, with an English-speaking guide; they also run tours to the Paraguaná Peninsula, Sierra San Luis and to Los Médanos (in the evenings).

● **Tourist offices**
On Paseo Alameda, English spoken, helpful. The office at the airport will help to find a hotel.

● **Transport**
Local Car hire: Budget Car Hire, next to the *Hotel Miranda Cumberland*, on Avenida Josefa Camejo; prices from US$52-77 per day, open Monday-Friday 0800-1800, Saturday and Sunday 0900-1600.

Air The airport is 10 minutes' walk from the centre. There's a good restaurant on the 1st floor, but no money changing facilities. Flights to Caracas and Barquisimeto. Ask at the airport for details of private flights to Curaçao, eg, *Aero Caribe*, US$70 one way (see also under air travel from **Punta Fijo**, on page 136).

Buses To/from **Caracas** US$7.25, 10 hours; **Maracaibo**, US$4, 4½ hours, *por puesto* US$8; **Tucacas**, US$3, 3 hours; to **Adícora**, bus goes via Cerro Santa Ana and Pueblo Nuevo, 2 hours, *por puesto* goes via the coast, 1 hour. Buses to the terminal go up Calle Falcón (US$0.10), a taxi costs US$1.20. Expreso Occidente has its own terminal, on Avenida Manaure between Calle Libertad and Calle Monzón, T 512356, daily bus to San Cristóbal at 1900, 12 hours, US$10.25; also to Caracas, Maracaibo, Valencia and Punta Fijo.

Sea The port of La Vela de Coro is called Muaco, and is 3 km east of the town. Several small launches make trips to Curaçao weekly. Contact Oscar Guerrero at Oficina de Migración, La Vela, T 068-78922; or Nelson García (T 522553), owner of *Carmen Reynely* and Douglas Zavala (T 78268), of *Trinidad II*, neither speaks English. A newly-restored ferry runs to Curaçao and Aruba (room for cars). The coaster *Don Andrés* makes a weekly run to Bonaire. Captains can be contacted through the maritime agency, two blocks from the Plaza Bolívar.

LOS MEDANOS DE CORO

Unique in the whole of Venezuela are the massive sand dunes, **Los Médanos de Coro**, which form a **National Park**. The dunes, some of them up to 30m high, cover a vast area of 80 sq km along the coast east of Coro and the eastern side of the **Istmo de Médanos**, the long narrow neck which connects the 'head' of the Paraguaná Peninsula to the 'shoulders' of the mainland. The illusion one has of being suddenly in the middle of the Sahara Desert is further enhanced by the sight of camels bearing nervous-looking tourists across this sea of sand. The whole area is constantly buffeted by winds which not only change the shape of the dunes, but also make visitors aware of how Coro got its name (Coro means 'wind' in the original Arawak language).

We have received mixed reports on the safety of the dunes, but most people agree that it is safer than it once was. The place is continually guarded by police and there should be no problems, as long as you stay close to the entrance and don't start wandering off across the dunes. At the entrance is a kiosk which sells fruit juices, burgers, sandwiches etc; it is open till 2400. To get there, take a bus marked 'Carabobo' from Avenida Falcón. It goes past the road leading to the Médanos on Avenida Independencia, where there is a large sign that reads 'Santa Ana de Coro'. From there you can walk the remaining 500m to the entrance, or, if you're feeling lazy, a taxi will take you; or an old man with a horse-drawn cart, 'Arturo's Coche'. **NB** The best time to visit the dunes is late afternoon, when it's much cooler and you don't feel like you're on a training exercise with the French Foreign Legion.

ROUTES West of Coro, the Falcón-Zulia highway, Route 3, continues through fairly uninteresting countryside, all the way to Maracaibo, 219 km from Coro.

PARAGUANA PENINSULA

Paraguaná is connected to the mainland by the most tenuous of links, the **Istmo de Médanos**, a 25 km sandbar that runs north from Coro. This is the largest peninsula in

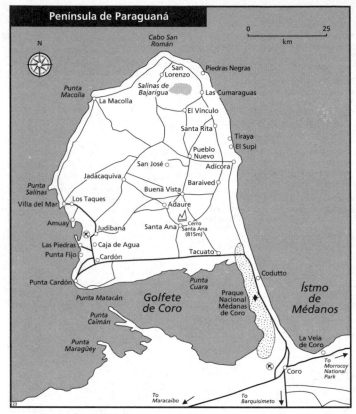

Península de Paraguaná

the country, with 300 km of coastline. The western side of the peninsula is industrialized, with oil refineries at **Cardón** and **Amuay** connected by pipeline to the Lago de Maracaibo oilfields. The eastern side, meanwhile, is relatively unspoiled, and relentlessly battered by the wind. The interior is mostly cactus-covered desert, except for the forested slopes of **Cerro Santa Ana**, the highest point on the peninsula.

PUNTA FIJO

The main town is **Punta Fijo** (*population* 89,500; *phone code* 069), is a busy, unkempt and unappealing place, with little to offer

the tourist. 5 km from Punta Fijo is the residential area of **Judibana**, which is a much nicer place to stay, if you're prepared to pay that little bit extra, with shopping centre, cinema and restaurants.

The beaches around **Los Taques** are at least 30 minutes north of Punta Fijo. Many of them are accessible by car, but attract few visitors. There's good camping but no shade or facilities.

Parks and zoos
A very interesting zoo with exclusively Venezuelan species, many of which you will never see in the wild, is at **Comunidad Cardón Maraven**, on Avenida 6 (T 403485/54222). It is open Tuesday-

Friday 1400-1800, Saturday and Sunday 1000-1800; entry US$0.20. There's a *fuente de soda*, which is open weekends only. To get there, take a *por puesto* from Avenida Brasil entre Calle Arismendi y Falcón in Punta Fijo. Opposite the zoo the **Museo de Historia Natural de Paraguaná** is due to open.

Local information
● Accommodation
C *Concord Suites*, Avenida Jacinto Lara next to the Franco Italiano supermarket, with bathroom, air conditioning, TV, fridge, phone, large clean and airy rooms, restaurant, games room, sitting room, accepts credit cards, changes US dollars cash, friendly.

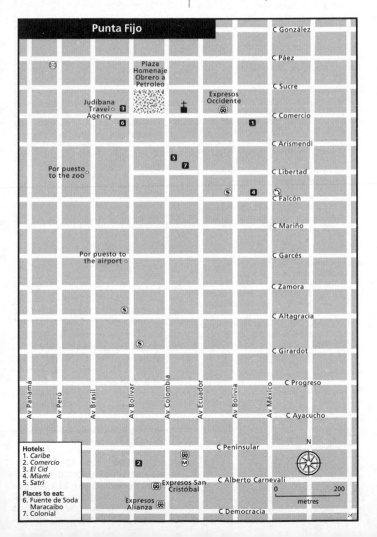

Punta Fijo

C González
C Páez
C Sucre
C Comercio
C Arismendi
C Libertad
C Falcón
C Mariño
C Garcés
C Zamora
C Altagracia
C Girardot
C Progreso
C Ayacucho
C Peninsular
C Alberto Carnevali
C Democracia

Plaza Homenaje Obrero a Petroleo

Judibana Travel Agency

Expresos Occidente

Por puesto to the zoo

Por puesto to the airport

Av Panamá
Av Perú
Av Brasil
Av Bolívar
Av Colombia
Av Ecuador
Av Bolivia
Av Mexico

Expresos San Cristóbal
Expresos Alianza

N

0   200
metres

Hotels:
1. *Caribe*
2. *Comercio*
3. *El Cid*
4. *Miami*
5. *Satri*

Places to eat:
6. Fuente de Soda Maracaibo
7. Colonial

D *Caribe*, Calle Comercio 21-112, with bathroom, air conditioning, TV, restaurant, accepts Visa and Mastercard; **D** *Satri*, Avenida Colombia 78-15, between Calle Libertad and Arismendi, T 468419, F 464175, with bathroom, air conditioning, TV, phone, central, changes US dollars cash (at the same rates as *Fukayama*, see below).

E *Comercio*, Avenida Bolívar con Calle Carnevali, just around the corner from the bus terminal, T 465430, with bathroom, air conditioning, TV, fridge, clean, highly recommended, good *panadería* opposite; **E** *Miami*, Calle Falcón between Avenidas México y Bolivia, just down from CANTV, air conditioning, recommended.

In Judibana: C *El Jardín*, on Avenida Mariscal y Calle Falcón, 200m from the roundabout, near the airport, T 461727, with bathroom, air conditioning, TV, fridge, adequate rooms, pool, games room, restaurant, accepts credit cards, changes US dollars cash; **C** *Luigi*, on Calle 10 next to Banco Venezuela, one block from the cinema, T 460970, with bathroom, air conditioning, TV, fridge, pleasant, good restaurant, changes US dollars cash, accepts credit cards.

● **Places to eat**
Colonial, Calle Libertad entre Colombia y Ecuador, nice place, good cheap meals (including goat), popular with locals, recommended; *Fuente de Soda Maracaibo*, on the corner of the plaza.

● **Banks & money changers**
Banco Provincial, Avenida Bolívar y Calle Zamora, is the only place in Punta Fijo to get cash on Visa or Mastercard; **Banco Consolidado**, Calle Falcón y Avenida Bolívar, changes Amex travellers' cheques; **Banco Mercantil**, Avenida Bolívar with Calle Girardot, only changes Citicorp travellers' cheques (up to US$300). **Casa Fukayama**, Avenida Bolívar entre Calle Altagracia y Girardot, changes US dollars cash at a lower rate than the official one (but still better than many places).

● **Embassies & consulates**
Dutch Consul in Judibana at Urb. La Laguna, Calle Mucubají 38, Roque Hernández, T 407211, open weekdays 1600-1700.

● **Post & telecommunications**
CANTV: at Calle Falcón with Avenida México, international calls can be made at some of the pay phones outside; ask at the desk for information.

Post office: on Calle Páez with Avenida Panamá, T 458843; post is collected only every 10 days or so, so probably not worth the trek down there.

● **Tour companies & travel agents**
Judibana, on Calle Comercio, next to *Hotel El Cid*, friendly, run tours around the peninsula and to the Sierra San Luis, a bit expensive, they also change dollars (at lower rates than *Hotel Satri* or *Casa Fukayama*) and will let you make international phone calls at the official rate per minute. Their main office is in Judibana, in the Centro Comercial, on Avenida Mariscal (opposite Cada supermarket).

● **Transport**
Air The airport is at **Las Piedras**. To get there, take a *por puesto* from Calle Garcés y Avenida Bolívar. A taxi from Punta Fijo costs US$3.50, and from Coro US$29. Avensa (T 461893), Avensa and Acerca (T 475596) fly to Aruba; Avensa fly to Curaçao.

Buses The terminal is on Calle Peninsular entre Colombia y Ecuador. *Por puestos* go to Pueblo Nuevo, Adícora, Coro, Valencia and Maracaibo. Long distance buses: Expresos Occidente (recommended), on Calle Comercio entre Ecuador y Bolivia (near *Hotel Caribe*), go to Maracay, Barquisimeto, Caracas and Maracaibo; Expresos San Cristóbal, Calle Carnevali just behind *Hotel Comercio*, go to Mérida, Barinas and Caracas; Expresos Alianza, on Avenida Colombia between Carnevali and Democracia (just up from Expresos San Cristóbal), go to Valencia, Coro, Maracay, Puerto La Cruz, Maracaibo, Mérida, El Vigía, San Cristóbal, Barquisimeto, Guanare, Acarigua, Barinas and Caracas.

ADICORA

Adícora (*population* 4,500, *phone code* 069) is a quiet, sleepy little resort on the east side of the peninsula. Compared to Morrocoy National Park, the beaches here are not great. There isn't a palm tree in sight, which makes them look a bit desolate, and then, of course, there's the wind. It's very refreshing at first, but after a few days of relentless gales, it can wear you down. Adícora is, however, a good base for exploring the peninsula and an absolute must for windsurfers.

Windsurfing in Adícora has won worldwide renown. The wind is constant and the permanent on-shore breeze makes conditions very safe. Furthermore, Adícora has been relatively untouched by the hand of tourism and sailing is blissfully uncrowded. There are three windsurfing schools in town, some of which also arrange local tours (see below).

Local information

● **Accommodation**

D *Posada Familia Kitzburger*, on the boulevard next to the beach, fan, German owners, good restaurant, friendly, clean, recommended; D *Posada La Caratoña*, on Calle Comercio, one block from the beach and three blocks from *Posada Kitzburger*, clean and friendly but full of mozzies, the owner, Sr Alvaro will organize trips around the peninsula for US$42 per car (5 maximum).

E *Hotel Montecano*, T 88174, Italian-owned, meals, has up-to-date information on bus times, recommended.

NB Do **not**, under any circumstances, rent a beach house in Adícora. Robbery from these is rife and the house cannot be left alone even for 5 minutes without being looted.

● **Places to eat**

Rancho Cacique, opposite *Posada Kitzburger*, good food, slightly cheaper than the restaurant in *Kitzburger*.

● **Windsurfing schools & tour companies**

Windsurfing Place, run by Canadian couple Carlos and Victoria, is on Playa Sur. Carlos gives lessons to beginners; 3 hours per day at around US$7 per hour. He also rents equipment; US$35 per day, or US$250 per week. All his gear is up-to-date and renewed annually. You can also store equipment here, on a short-term or long-term basis. Carlos and Vicotria also have a couple of rooms for rent next to their house; D including breakfast, cooking and washing facilities, T (014) 680660, F (068) 519747, or (02) 914094.

Windsurfing Adícora, run by Alex, a German who also speaks English, is at the last house on the spit overlooking Playa Sur. Alex teaches beginners; 3 hours per day at US$7 per hour, or free with hire of equipment – and also hires out equipment, US$30 per day, or US$150 per week, plus deposit. He can also rent out tents, hammocks, mosquito nets, sunchairs etc, as well as organize Spanish classes. Transport to the airport costs US$20. Alex also has a couple of rooms for rent; D including breakfast, cooking and washing facilities. He will let you sling a hammock in his house (E). Alex also runs tours around the peninsula, taking in Laguna Boca de Caño, the salt mines, Cabo San Román and Los Médanos Blancos (see **Around the peninsula** below). After lunch in Pueblo Nuevo, you then go to the Montecaño Nature Reserve for a 1-hour walk around. The tour costs US$19 per person, and is recommended for those wishing to get a general idea of the peninsula. Alex will also take you up Cerro Santa Ana for around US$10 per person, which is also recommended.

Moustacho Vacations, on the sea front, just down from *Posada Familia Kitzburger*, or next to Alex's house on Playa Sur, T 88271, F 88054. They offer classes and hire of equipment: 1st week is US$210, 2nd week US$170, 3rd week US$140; kayaks for US$2 per hour, or US$10 per day. Also rent out bicycles, canoes, sunchairs etc, and offer Spanish classes. They organize trips around the peninsula (see below), and further afield to Coro, Sierra de San Luis and other parts of the country. They also have accommodation; **B-C** fully-equipped rooms or apartments.

● **Transport**

Buses From Coro, Linea Pueblo Nuevo buses take 50 minutes to Adícora along the autopista, several daily from 0630-1830, US$0.70. There's also a bus which leaves Coro at 1030 and takes 2½ hours. To Punta Fijo, at 0630, 1000, 1200, 1500, 1630 and 1830. **NB** These times are subject to change.

AROUND THE PENINSULA

Cerro Santa Ana

At 830m, this is the only hill on the peninsula. Santa Ana, formed by igneous metamorphic rocks, has three peaks and commands spectacular views over the whole peninsula, and, on a clear day, across to the islands of Aruba and Curaçao.

The best entrance is at **El Moruy**. Take the bus from Adícora to Pueblo Nuevo (0730-0800), then change to one going to Punta Fijo, and ask to be dropped off at the entrance to Santa Ana. From the plaza (where there is a church), walk back to signpost for 'Pueblo Nuevo, Autopista and Santa Ana' and take the dirt road going past a deserted white building '*Restaurant Parador Turística*'; 20m further to the left is *Restaurant La Hija*. Walk 1 km through scrubby vegetation and a small *barrio* (watch out for dogs) to the Inparques office, which is closed Monday-Friday but gets quite busy at weekends. You should register here before beginning the climb.

The hill has four distinct vegetation zones: a semi-arid zone dominated by cactus and small thorny trees; then a deciduous dry forest zone; and further up it's cloud forest; right at the top is a bare patch of grassland (and a very strong wind). It's a steep 2-3 hour climb, depending on your level of fitness and includes some scrambling at the top. Also the path is difficult to follow in places, but the views are spectacular and well worth the effort. The best time to do the climb is at weekends, unless you go with a guide. During the week the place is deserted and, although no robberies have been reported, it's better to be safe than sorry!

Laguna Boca de Caño

Also known as Laguna Tiraya, this is a nature reserve north of Adícora, inland from **El Supi**, along a dirt track normally fit for all vehicles. Bird life here is abundant, particularly flamingos. It is the only mangrove zone on the east side of the peninsula. The reserve is run by a project called Bioma (information from their office at: Avenida Arévalo Gonzales y Calle Páez 10, Pueblo Nuevo, T/F 069-81048). They also run other protected nature reserves on the peninsula.

The salt mines (salinas)

The salt mines are just past the Laguna Boca de Caño. The water has a pinkish tinge, owing to the effect of the salt. They are usually deserted, except at certain times of the year when the salt is collected. At these times, the area around the mines becomes crowded with temporary shelters (*ranchos*) where the workers live during the collection period. They work at night to escape the heat of the day, carting the salt in wheelbarrows from the pans to the roadside, where it forms huge mounds which are then transported away by truck. In the distance you can make out the now abandoned *Hotel Caribe*, built as a tourist complex by the government in the 1980s, and now a very impressive-looking white elephant.

Reserva Montecaño

This reserve used to be run by Bioma, but is apparently due to be taken over by Inparques. It lies in the centre of the peninsula, close to Pueblo Nuevo, and is about 200-300m above sea level. The vegetation is typical of the peninsula; cactus, low scrubby trees and bushes. Bird life is abundant and relatively easy to spot, and there are good views of the peninsula. There is

a short, easy walk through the reserve up to an old, abandoned radio station, and then back down to the entrance. This is recommended for those not fit enough to climb Cerro Santa Ana.

Cabo San Román

At the northernmost part of the peninsula, the Cabo San Román forms a rocky promontory, made up of old corals. The road effectively disappears, and you have to make your way round the Cabo as best you can. The water level used to be much higher, but has now dropped considerably leaving the corals exposed. From here you can see across to the oil fields and the island of Aruba. Past the Cabo is a fisherman's cove. All this part of the coast is largely deserted and there is still apparently a healthy trade in contraband between here and Aruba, especially rum (from Venezuela) and whisky (from Aruba).

Los Médanos Blancos

This is a small group of white sand dunes at the end of what road there is after Cabo San Roman. It's a wild and desolate place, where the sand and old gnarled trees give it a distinctly African look. It's very beautiful, though, and really makes you feel that you are slap bang in the middle of nowhere (which is exactly where you are). The beach is littered with shells of varying types, sizes and colours. **NB** The northern part of the peninsula is a very remote place and there have been reports of armed robbery of vehicles.

SIERRA DE SAN LUIS

South of Coro, Route 4 runs across the Falcón-Lara state boundary and on to Barquisimeto (see page 144). On the way, the road passes over the **Sierra de San Luis**, which includes the **Parque Nacional Juan Calle Falcón**. The Sierra de San Luis is a mountainous region that rises up to 1,500m. The whole of the Sierra is built on limestone and houses one of the largest subterranean lakes in all of South America. As a result of its geology, the Sierra is riddled with caves, underground rivers and chasms. The vegetation is varied,

A deep, dark secret

Probably one of the most famous *ahitones* in the Sierra, and one of the deepest, is the Ahitón de los Lamentos, east of the village of San Luis. If you listen at the edge of its steep walls you can hear the wind murmuring at the bottom, like a low cry, or *'lamento'*, which has inspired stories about its source.

It is said that this *ahitón* was not formed by natural means, but instead was excavated at the command of the Spanish landowner, Don Juan de las Colinas, in colonial times. Don Juan was the richest landowner in the region, but lived in constant fear of robbery from pirates and thieves. As his wealth increased, so did his fear of being robbed.

Finally, he could take no more, and ordered his slaves to excavate the *ahitón* in order to hide his wealth from potential thieves. Once completed, Don Juan put all his treasure into a huge trunk and threw it over the edge into the deep pit, together with all the slaves, to ensure that there would be no one alive who knew of his secret. Today, according to local legend, the sound you can hear coming from the bottom of the *ahitón* is not the wind, but the long lament of the slaves sacrificed by Don Juan.

ranging from semi-arid scrub in the lowlands to exuberant rainforest in the higher parts. The main source of income for the inhabitants is the production of coffee and oranges, for which the Sierra is famous. This area is a paradise for nature lovers and highly recommended for hiking and bird watching, with many various options (detailed below). This is also a relatively accessible region, compared to other rainforest zones in Venezuela, and due to the many paths that run through it, can be explored on foot (with a guide) at little expense.

CURIMAGUA

The small, quiet and picturesque village of **Curimagua** is the best access point for visiting the park. As well as the accommodation listed below, there's also a supermarket, pharmacy and a few restaurants (which are not always open). Jeeps to Curimagua leave from Coro bus terminal (US$1.50).

- **Accommodation C-D** *Apolo*, 50m up the road from *Falconese*, T (068) 517634, with bathroom, hot water, TV room, games room, accepts Visa and Mastercard, sometimes runs tours around the Sierra for US$7-10 per person (depending on the tour), which is cheaper than the *Falconese* but you don't see as much; **C-D** *Falconese*, on the main road just outside the village, with bathroom, hot water, TV room,

games room, restaurant, accepts Visa and Mastercard, changes dollars cash but at very low rates, run by German, Hans Westdorf who organizes tours around the Sierra, a 5-hour tour taking in several points of interest costs US$95 per jeep (maximum 12 persons); **D** *Finca El Monte*, 10 km from the village (ask the driver to let you off here), it's a genuine *Finca* run by a lovely Swiss couple, Ernesto and Ursula, it produces mostly coffee and oranges on an ecological basis, no pesticides are used and everything is done as organically as possible, with bathroom, hot water, clean basic rooms, breakfast US$2, lunch and supper US$4-4.50, highly recommended, Ernesto takes tours round the park (US$63 per car load, 4 maximum) and to the Paraguaná Peninsula (US$84 per car load), also recommended is to walk the 'Spanish road' (see below) past the Acarite Caves to Cabure, where you'll be picked up in the car and driven to the Cataratas de Hueque and then back to *El Monte* (US$42 per car), other walking tours can be organized from the *Finca* using local guides (US$6-8 per day); **D** *El Trapichito*, 5 km outside Curimagua (the jeep from Coro will drop you at the entrance, from there walk 300m, then take a left at the fork and walk another 200m to the hotel), with bathroom, hot water, clean and basic rooms, friendly, similar meal prices as *El Monte*, there are a couple of other restaurants in El Trapichito, but they're usually only open at weekends.

CABURE

The lovely colonial town of **Cabure** is the capital of the Sierra. It has a supermarket, *panadería* (with public phone), pharmacy, restaurants and bars. Jeeps to Cabure also leave from Coro bus terminal (US$2.15).

● **Accommodation D** *Camino Viejo*, in town behind the old cemetery, T (069) 4043346, with bathroom, hot water, air conditioning, fridge, TV, also *cabañas* (without private bathroom but with cooking facilities), restaurant, pool (US$1 per day for non-guests), clean and pleasant but noisy; **E** *El Duende*, 20 minutes uphill from the town, at the end of the old Spanish road (see below), T (068) 611079, (069) 483626, a beautiful old *posada*, basic but clean rooms, with bathroom, cold water only but they provide soap, toothpaste, shampoo and towel, restaurant with good and reasonably priced food, very friendly and relaxing, highly recommended; **E** *La Montaña*, in town at the bottom of the turn-off to *El Duende*, with bathroom, hot water, air conditioning, restaurant, games room, also rents out rooms by the hour, so quite noisy at times, sometimes runs tours to the Cataratas de Hueque.

Between Curimagua and Cabure, just off Route 4, is the beautiful village of **San Luis** with its interesting church, reached by taxi from Coro. Ask for the Cueva de Pereguey to the south and the falls nearby.

Accommodation is not easy to find here, but try renting a room with Señora Jovita, who lives near the liquor store (there is a sign outside 'se vende comida').

EXCURSIONS IN THE SIERRA DE SAN LUIS

Sima de Guarataro

Roughly halfway between Curimagua and San Luis is the Sima de Guarataro. Simas, or 'Ahitones' as they are called in the Sierra, are vertical caves formed by the slow trickle of rainwater through weak points in the limestone rock. Eventually the rock caves in, forming potholes. The Ahitón de Guarataro is a pothole 305m deep and 12m broad at its widest point, and possibly the largest one in the Sierra. Along its 305m length there are several pools of water, a small subterranean river and a 6m waterfall. In the same area there are other structures formed by the collapse of the limestone known as 'sumeridos'. These capture the rainwater which drains eventually into the subterranean lakes underneath the mountains.

Las Cataratas de Hueque

This huge set of waterfalls is 30 minutes from Cabure. Unfortunately, the setting has been spoiled by overuse. The place is very quiet during the week, but at weekends it gets overcrowded and noisy, with kiosks selling food and drinks. Five minutes walk up from the falls is a nice pool for bathing.

The easiest way to get there is to take a tour from Curimagua, though this is also more expensive. If you want to go it alone, take a *por puesto* going from Cabure to Coro and ask to be dropped off at the entrance (US$0.50), or you can hitch from Cabure to the entrance. In both cases, it's more or less a 2 km walk to the falls. A taxi costs about US$5, but you'll still have to find your own way back. At weekends this is no problem, but can be difficult through the week.

Cerro Galicia

At 1,500m, this is the highest point of the Sierra de San Luis. Unfortunately, however, the magnificent view towards Coro and the coast of Falcón has been ruined by the presence of several TV and radio antennae, which, apart from spoiling the view, also produce an annoying humming noise, which shatters the peace and quiet.

A better alternative for those who don't mind walking, or lots of mud, is a 1½ hour walk from behind *Finca El Monte* up to the top of a hill, where the view is truly spectacular. The walk is not difficult, except for the last 5m or so, which involves a scramble through, under and over some trees up to a large rock (slippery in the wet). From the top you can enjoy in peace and splendid isolation the fantastic view across the Sierra to the semi-desert of Coro. **NB** You **must** go with a guide, as there are several trails which criss-cross each other, and it's easy to get lost (or impossible not to!). Guides only cost around US$4 and can be contacted at the *Finca El Monte*.

THE SPANISH ROAD

This is a fantastic walk through orange groves and rainforest. It takes you right through the Sierra, from Curimagua down to Cabure. It can be done as part of a 1-day guided tour (see **Curimagua Accommodation** above), or in a group, without a guide, as a way of getting from Curimagua to Cabure. The trail is about 3 hours long, not counting a stop off at the **Cueva de Acarite**, and is easy to follow. **NB** Take water as there is none en route.

The route starts at *Finca El Monte*. From there, go right along the main road. After 7-10 minutes, you reach a blue house next to a dirt road going downhill on your left. Opposite is another house and, 20m down the track, a white house on the right. Turn left down the road and after about 40 minutes, you reach a point where the road (now going uphill) has been concreted over. At the end of the concrete (approximately 200m), take the side track to the right which goes along and downhill. 5 minutes later you come to a fork; go left and in 2 minutes you reach the Spanish Road (at this point a dirt road). Turn right and walk along through a small collection of houses, and in 15 minutes you get to the last house. 5-6 minutes later is the old Spanish bridge, made of stone, but so overgrown it's easy to walk right over it without noticing it. 200-300m further along on your right is a small track which leads to 'El Nacimiento', a small cave, usually full of water. Back on the main road, 150m ahead, is another path on your right (50m ahead you can see a small roadside hut with a Virgin Mary in it).

This path is the entrance to the **Acarite Cave**, which is a worthwhile diversion. The path goes up and along into the forest for about 10-15 minutes and stops at the cave entrance. The cave is very impressive. The entrance is a large archway with lots of stalagtites and stalagmites, some of which have joined to form huge columns. The cave has partly been explored by cavers who have found massive galleries in its interior.

Once back on the main path again, follow the trail up and down through the valley. Much of the original cobblestone road is still in place and Morpho butterflies fly up from under your feet as you walk along. In 1 hour you reach the top of the trail, marked by three crosses on a rock. The views of the valley of Cabure below are superb. From here it's downhill all the way, at first through tropical forest and then through well-kept gardens with flowering shrubs, as you get closer to an inhabited area. In about 30 minutes, you reach a small stream; 10 minutes further on there is a sharp bend in the road where it widens, with a huge tree in the corner and benches to sit on. 50m later you reach the *Posada El Duende* on the left (see **Cabure Accommodation**).

Zarragoza

Another interesting side trip from Curimagua or Cabure, is to the small coffee processing works at Zarragoza, west of San Luis, reached by a side road running west off the road between Curimagua and San Luis.

San Luis is one of the oldest centres of coffee production in Venezuela. The coffee made here used to be renowned throughout the world for its high quality, the result of the variety ('*café criollo*') and the method of processing (*lavado*, or washed). However, the quality of the coffee has declined, owing to the introduction of more productive, but lesser quality varieties, and the use of faster methods of processing the beans. In an attempt to rescue the '*café criollo*', a civil association, Pecaza (Pequeños Cafecultores de Zarragoza) has been founded to promote the production of high quality coffee. The processing works at Zarragoza, which processes the coffee in the traditional *lavado* method, is helping to ensure a high quality coffee product.

Lara and Yaracuy

T HESE TWO STATES, lying between Coro to the north, the Andes and the llanos to the south, tend to be overlooked by most tourists on their way to or from more popular destinations. But nestled in these tropical valleys are towns and villages that haven't changed much in centuries. Many villages specialize in their own handicrafts, and Barquisimeto, the largest city in the region, is renowned for its folk music. The great advantage of this region is that there are many beautiful, unspoiled places to visit and it's much cheaper than other parts of Venezuela.

CORO TO BARQUISIMETO

The 275 km drive from Coro south to Barquisimeto takes around 4-5 hours. Just over the Falcón state boundary, at **El Porvenir,** a road heads west off Ruta 4 for 42 km to the lovely, unspoiled colonial town of **Siquisique**. Ruta 4 continues south, through the colonial village of **Bobare** to Barquisimeto.

An alternative route leaves Ruta 4 at **Santa Inés** and heads through the town of **Duaca,** set among rolling hills northeast of Barquisimeto. Some of the stores in town sell the perfumes, bath oils, soaps, powders and potions used in the rites of the cult of María Lionza (see page 148).

BARQUISIMETO

Barquisimeto, capital of Lara State, is Venezuela's fourth largest city and stands on one of the many Andean alluvial fans (*population* 723,000; *altitude* 565m; *phone code* 051; *mean temperature* 25°C). The climate, dry and hot, is not uncomfortable.

Barquisimeto is the commercial and communications centre for the central and western part of Venezuela and is easily reached from other major cities such as Maracaibo, Punta Fijo and Valencia. It was founded in 1552, on a different site. Not long after, in 1561, it was burned to the ground by the notorious Lope de

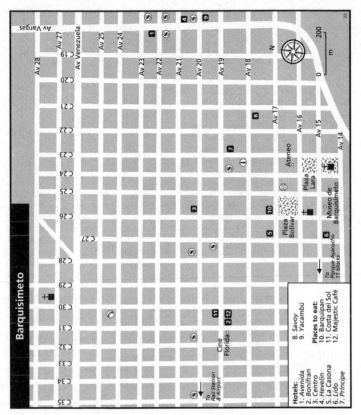

Av Vargas
Av 28 · Av 27 · Av 19 · Av Venezuela · Av 25 · Av 24 · Av 23 · Av 22 · Av 21 · Av 20 · Av 19 · Av 18 · Av 17 · Av 16 · Av 15 · Av 14

N

0 — 200 m

C 19 · C 20 · C 21 · C 22 · C 23 · C 24 · C 25 · C 26 · C 27 · C 28 · C 29 · C 30 · C 31 · C 32 · C 33 · C 34 · C 35

Barquisimeto

Ateneo
Plaza Lara
Museo de Barquisimeto
Plaza Bolívar

To Parque Ayacucho 11 blocks

Cine Floridao

To Rail Station & Airport

Hotels:
1. Avenida
2. Bonifran
3. Centro
4. Hevelin
5. La Casona
6. Lido
7. Príncipe

8. Savoy
9. Yacambú

Places to eat:
10. Barquipan
11. Costa del Sol
12. Majestic Café

Aguirre. But the Basque tyrant paid for his indiscretion and was duly captured and executed, on 27 October that same year (see also page 326). The next site, the Valley of Women, between the Turbio and Claro rivers, was abandoned due to the excessive dust during the dry season. The third and final move, in 1563, was to its present location, by the Río Turbio.

The people of Barquisimeto are open, lively, practical and exceptionally musical. It is said that every native of the city is expected to play at least one musical instrument, which accounts for its unofficial title of 'musical capital of Venezuela'. Aside from making sweet music, the townsfolk make their own instruments, as well as weaving blankets and making pots.

Despite its arid climate, Lara produces a large variety of fruit and vegetables: pineapples, tomatoes, onions, sugar cane and most of the country's sisal are all grown locally and sold in Barquisimeto.

The city was largely destroyed by an earthquake in 1812, so little of the original colonial architecture remains. The few remaining old buildings are perched above the Río Turbio, interspersed with modern construction. The centre, though, is well worth exploring, as many fascinating corners have been preserved and a law prohibiting demolition of older buildings means that more are being restored. Barquisimeto is a nice place to spend a few days visiting the area and it's very easy to find your way around.

PLACES OF INTEREST

Some old buildings can be found around the lovely, peaceful **Plaza Jacinto Lara**. The **San Francisco church** faces the plaza. On the opposite side, at Carrera 17 y Calle 23, is the small **Anteneo de Barquisimeto** which has a small room of contemporary local art in an 18th century house; open Monday-Friday, 0830-1200, 1500-1830, Saturday 0900-1200, it also has a restaurant (open 0830-1830) and occasional evening concerts, admission free. Nearby is the **Centro de Historia Larense**, a study centre which has small temporary exhibitions. The **Cathedral**, at Calle 30 y Carrera 26 (Venezuela), is an innovative modern structure of reinforced concrete and glass.

At the heart of the old city is the tranquil, shaded **Plaza Bolívar**, with towering palms, a heroic statue of the Liberator and an assortment of ancient and modern buildings. Most attractive is the white-painted **Iglesia Concepción**, on the south side. Also on the plaza, the **Palacio Municipal**, Carrera 17 y Calle 25, is an attractive modern building.

Museums

The **Museo de Barquisimeto**, at Avenida 15 between Calle 25 and 26, has several nice displays detailing the town's history, as well as contemporary art. Renovations are currently going on (in mid-1997). It is open Tuesday-Friday 0900-1700, Saturday-Sunday 1000-1700, admission free.

Parks and zoos

On Carrera 15 (Avenida Francisco de Miranda) between Calle 41-43 is **Parque Ayacucho**, with lush vegetation, paths, fountains and a bronze statue of Mariscal Sucre. The **Concha Acústica** park is a block east of Plaza Lara.

Parque del Este, or **Parque José María Ochoa Pile**, between Avenida Libertador and Avenida Los Leones, is a green space for joggers and cyclists. The local Inparques office is here; it's not a lot of use, but

you can get a permit here for Yacambú or Terepaima National Parks. To get there take No 12 bus from Avenida 17.

Parque Zoológico Botánico 'Miguel Romero Antoni' is on Avenida Los Abogados y Calle 13. The zoo is large and pleasant with a decent selection of animals, including African and Australian varieties as well as native ones. Some of the cages are very creative but others are less than adequate. The zoo is open Tuesday-Sunday 0900-1730, US$0.55. To get there take a No 6 bus from Avenida 21.

LOCAL FESTIVALS

Fiesta de La Zaragoza is held on the morning of 28 December, when colourfully clad participants and children pass through the streets accompanied by music and dancing. *La Divina Pastora* takes place in early January. Huge crowds are attracted to this procession, when an image of the Virgin Mary is carried from the shrine at Santa Rosa village into the city. Also in January is the *Festival of the Golden Voice*, a competition to find the best male and female singing voices in Venezuela.

LOCAL INFORMATION

● Accommodation

Hotel prices			
L1	over US$200	**L2**	US$151-200
L3	US$101-150	**A1**	US$81-100
A2	US$61-80	**A3**	US$46-60
B	US$31-45	**C**	US$21-30
D	US$12-20	**E**	US$7-11
F	US$4-6	**G**	up to US$3
Those marked with an asterisk (*) are bookable through Fairmont International (see under Caracas).			

L3 *Hilton**, Urbanización Nueva Segovia, Carrera 5 entre 5 y 6, T 536022, F 544365, excellent restaurant, pool, air conditioning, TV, accepts credit cards, exchanges cash dollars at poor rates, good value.

B *Hostería Obelisco**, Avenida Panamericana, T 410311, F 422133, motel-style, pool, air conditioning, TV, restaurant, accepts credit cards, always full.

C *Bonifran*, Carrera 19 y Calle 31, T 321314, F 317509, a few blocks from the centre, air conditioning, TV, accepts credit cards; **C** *Príncipe*, Avenida 18 entre Calle 22 y Calle 23,

T 312111, F 311731, pool, restaurant, air conditioning, TV, accepts credit cards, recommended; **C-D** *Gran Hotel Barquisimeto**, on Calle 59, one block from Avenida Pedro León Torres (not a nice area), T 420511, F 420354, restaurant, air conditioning, TV, pool is open to non-residents for US$1.70.

D *Hevelin*, Avenida Vargas entre Calle 20 y 21, T 523986, hot water, air conditioning, TV, good value, recommended; **D** *Motel El Parador*, on Avenida Intercommunal near El Obelisco, a huge roundabout in the northern suburbs, hot water, TV, air conditioning, restaurant, accepts credit cards, excellent, their pool is open to non-residents at weekends for US$3.20; **D** *Yacambú*, Avenida Vargas, between Calle 19 and 20, T 513022, F 522474, pool, air conditioning, TV, restaurant, accepts credit cards.

E *La Casona*, Avenida 17 con Calle 27 near Plaza Bolívar, T 315311, air conditioning, hot water, parking, restaurant, recommended; **E** *Lido*, Avenida 15 between Calle 26 and 27, hot water, rooms with fan or air conditioning, TV (which may or may not work); **E** *Savoy*, Avenida 18 entre Calle 21 y 22, T 315134, hot water, air conditioning, TV, some rooms have a fridge, OK; **E-F** *Avenida*, Avenida Vargas, No 21-124, 2nd floor, with fan or air conditioning, TV.

F pp *Centro*, Avenida 20, between Calle 25 and 26, T 314524, with bath, air conditioning, a bit tatty but better value than the budget hotels near the bus terminals. There are many small cheap hotels near the bus terminal, but it's not a nice area. Opposite the terminal is **E** *Yaguara*, T 453956, basic, air conditioning, TV.

● **Places to eat**
Barquipan, Calle 26 entre Carreras 17 y 18, good breakfasts, snacks; there's a vegetarian restaurant opposite on Calle 26 esquina Avenida 18; and the *Fuente de Soda* next door is open 1100-1500 for good cheap lunches; *Sabor Vegetariano*, on Calle 24 entre Avenida 20 y 21, next to *El Rincón Griego* restaurant, for vegetarian snacks and other natural products; *Majestic*, Avenida 19 con Calle 30, very smart breakfast café with good vegetarian options, recommended; opposite is the very ornate *Costa del Sol*.

● **Banks & money changers**
The best bet for Visa and Mastercard transactions are **Banco Provincial**, at Avenida 20 entre Calle 31 y 32 and Calle 23 entre Avenidas 18 y 19 (opposite *Hotel Principe*), and **Banco de Lara**, at Avenida 20 entre Calle 27 y 28. **Banco Unión**, Avenida Vargas entre Calle 21 y 22, will also advance cash on Visa and Mastercard. **Capital Express**, Avenida Los Leones, Centro Comercial Paseo, next to Calle 90 (take bus No 5 from Avenida 19), changes US$ cash at low

rates; also **Turisol**, Avenida Vargas entre Calle 20 y 21, next to *Hotel Hevelin*, for Amex.

● **Entertainment**
Cinema: *Florida*, at Avenida 19 con Calle 31.

● **Hospitals & medical services**
Health clinic: *Clínica Rozetti*, efficient and not expensive.

● **Post & telecommunications**
Post Office: Ipostel at Avenida 17 con Calle 25. **Telephone**: CANTV at Calle 30 entre Avenidas 24 y 25.

● **Tour companies & travel agents**
In general, tourism in Lara is very disorganized. There are very few tours on offer to sites of interest, and those that do exist tend to be improvised. Nonetheless, the public transport system is good and it's possible to get to many places under your own steam.

Turisol (address above under **Banks & money changers**), is the only travel agents that offer individualized local day trips, minimum of 4 people, US$30 per person; *Danesa Tours*, Avenida 20 entre Calle 28 y 29, T/F 327227, they can put you in touch with a local guide, Sr Jesus Franceschi, who organizes day trips. The *Avensa*, *Aeropostal* and *Iberoamericana* agencies are at Avenida 18 con Calle 23.

● **Tourist offices**
Corpoturismo Edo Fundalara, on Avenida Libertador; has a library if you want to look up tourist possibilities in Lara. Take a 12 bus to get there.

● **Useful addresses**
Inparques: opposite CC Las Trinitarias, Avenida Los Leones (al lado 3ra Brigada Ejército), T 541448.

● **Transport**
Local Car hire: (Volkswagen best), Avenida Pedro León Torres y Calle 56, also at the airport.

Air Jacinto Lara international airport is 8 km southwest of the centre, 10 minutes, US$3 by taxi. Local buses stop outside, US$0.12. Avensa flies daily to Miami via Maracaibo and to Caracas (also Servivensa and Aserca), Maracaibo, San Antonio, Coro, Porlamar (Margarita) and Valencia. Aeropostal flies to Caracas, Maracaibo, Barcelona, Porlamar, San Antonio, Port of Spain and Barbados (T 421390/425076, F 424317).

Trains To Puerto Cabello, 175 km, 2¾ hours, twice a day in each direction. Tickets are sold 2 hours before departure; note that the timetable is unreliable. There are many extra trains at carnival time, but they're always full. It's a bumpy ride on a bad track but a worthwhile experience nonetheless. Daily trains run from Yaritagua en route to/from Acarigua for Puerto Cabello.

Buses The terminal is on the edge of the city at Carrera 25 and Calle 44; not a very salubrious area. A 13 bus takes you to the corner of Plaza Bolívar in the centre of town and then up Avenida Vargas; bus route 12 also goes to the centre. From the centre, take a *ruta* 15 bus or Lara 1.

To **Mérida**, 3 to 4 a day, at 1020 and several between 2000 and 0200, 8 hours via Agua Viva and El Vigía, US$7; to **Acarigua** (see page 219), 1 hour, US$1.75. To **Valera**, US$2.80 (with 1a de Octubre); *por puesto*, 3½ hours, US$5. To **Tucacas** every 2 hours, 9 hours. To **Coro** every 2 hours, 7 hours, US$5. To **Caracas**, US$4-5, 6 hours (all buses to Barquisimeto stop at Santa Paula service station soon after the turnoff to Barquisimeto from Valencia; this is a highly recommended toilet stop).

EAST FROM BARQUISIMETO

ROUTES The Barquisimeto-Valencia freeway heads east across the state boundary into Yaracuy, passing through **Yaritagua**, 20 km from Barquisimeto. Just before **Sabana de Parra**, on the south side of the freeway, is a statue of José Antonio Páez, one of Venezuela's independence heroes (see page 43).

CHIVACOA

About 60 km east of Barquisimeto is **Chivacoa** (*population* 40,400), set amidst sugar-cane plantations. The town would be of no particular interest to the tourist were it not for the fact that, on the mountain to the south are the most sacred centres of the mysterious María Lionza cult.

Many thousands of devotees congregate around this sacred mountain to be instructed in the ways of the cult under the guidance of a medium. These spiritual guides are believed to have the power of healing and reading the future and fall into a trance-like state when performing their initiation rites.

The faithful first proceed to the riverside shrine of **Quivallo** where candles are burned, cigars smoked and signs read from the ashes before images of María Lionza and Simón Bolívar, among others. After bathing in the river, they move on to the *portales*, or gates. These are trees, caves, streams and rocks at the foot of the mountain, where the spirits of nature and those of powerful people are worshipped and called upon to help in the lives of the believers.

Various forms of magic are practised at the gates, which include smoking more cigars, the laying on of hands, burning coloured candles and the use of essences and perfumes to attract good influences. Often, devotees make the 3-hour climb to the top of the mountain, where the spirits are said to become more powerful. All the way up are more shrines, where offerings of alcohol, perfumes, fruit, candles, flowers and, of course, cigars, are made.

Celebrations are held here mostly at weekends and holidays. The most important day is 12 October, *Día de la Raza*. Anyone interested in witnessing this spectacle should note that devotees are very, very serious about their sacred place and do not take too kindly to inquisitive 'outsiders'.

More orthodox forms of religion are also practised in Chivacoa. There is a Catholic festival, *La Inmaculada Concepción*, from 8-14 December.

ROUTES A few kilometres east of Chivacoa, the road forks. Route 11 heads due east through **Nirgua** to Valencia (see page 119). The other branch, Route 1, turns northeast to **San Felipe**.

SAN FELIPE

The modern, attractive city of **San Felipe** (*population* 30,750; *altitude* 550m; *phone code* 054) is capital of Yaracuy State. It is about 4 hours from Caracas and stands on the Barquisimeto-Puerto Cabello rail line.

The city was founded on 6 November 1729 as San Felipe El Fuerte, the regional administrative centre for the all-powerful Guipuzcoana (or Caracas) Company. It soon became the commercial hub for the company's cacao trade in what was one of Venezuela's richest regions. After the demise of cacao, San Felipe remained the region's commercial centre, until the city was razed to the ground by the terrible earthquake of 26 March 1812, the worst in the country's history. A new city was built to the north of the old site.

The site of the original town is now occupied by **Parque El Fuerte**, a beautifully-landscaped park which includes many of the old ruins.

Who is María Lionza?

The cult of María Lionza has survived fierce opposition from the clergy, the Spanish colonial rulers and successive Republican governments and continues to attract many followers.

This eclectic mix of indigenous nature worship, African voodoo and Christian rituals is not based on moral rules – there is no concept of right and wrong. Indeed, the only taboos are the theft of anything belonging to the cult and the needless killing of animals. This is probably just as well, for those who do break these few rules face the unappealing prospect of being kept in a huge glass cavern beneath a river bed, watched over by giant snakes.

The purpose of this cult is practical and straightforward – to help people achieve their needs. Any favours asked must be repaid with offerings or services. The origins of this popular myth, however, are not so clear. According to the faithful, María Lionza – also known as 'Queen' and 'Our Mother' – is a female deity, daughter of an Indian princess and a Spanish *conquistador*. She lives in a place called Villanueva, in a sumptuous golden palace deep in the tropical forests of Lara, surrounded by wild animals and her many subordinate spirits.

Among these 'assistants' are the various Don Juans, commanders of certain forces such as wind and water, the doorkeeper, Francisquito, and La Niña María, messenger and retriever of lost objects. Besides these, there are local spirits known as *duendes* (elves). Unlike the serene María Lionza, these are cruel and vengeful spirits who are not to be crossed.

The actual identity of María Lionza herself is also something of a mystery. She is described as a beautiful woman riding through the forest on her tapir; an image which can be seen in the statue on the Francisco Fajardo freeway, between Plaza Venezuela and the Central University in Caracas. However, this bears little resemblance to the effigies of her for sale in Chivacoa and throughout Venezuela which show a pale-skinned young woman wearing a crown.

Above the present city is the small, delightful **Parque Leonor Bernabó**, which is part of the **Yurubí National Park**. The beautiful 7-hectare park makes for a pleasant walk and affords great views down the Yurubí River and across the Yaracuy valley. The entrance to the park is on Avenida Los Baños.

Local festivals are held on 2 April, *día patronal*; 3 May, *Velorio de la Cruz de Mayo*; and 23 June, *San Juan*.

● **Accommodation** *Turístico Río Yurubí*, at the end of Avenida Los Baños at the city's edge, pleasant, safe, good but expensive restaurant, **D** *Hostería Colonial**, on Avenida La Paz, pool. There are others in the **D** and **E** range along Avenida 6A.

ROUTES A well-paved and scenic road runs from San Felipe down to the coast at **Morón** (see page 124). From there, you can continue east to **Puerto Cabello** (see page 123) or head north for **Morrocoy National Park** (see page 127).

SAN FELIPE TO AROA

Another road runs to the former gold and copper mining town of **Aroa**, 77 km away. The road turns north off Route 1, 8 km east of San Felipe and crosses the densely forested mountains of **Yurubí National Park** before dropping down to the cane fields of the Río Aroa valley and then detouring west. Aroa can also be reached from **Duaca**, north of Barquisimeto (see page 144).

SOUTH FROM BARQUISIMETO

A pleasant excursion from Barquisimeto by bus or car is to **Río Claro**, about 28 km south, 'where the Andes begin'. You follow a lush river valley through the mountains. There are banana plantations in the area

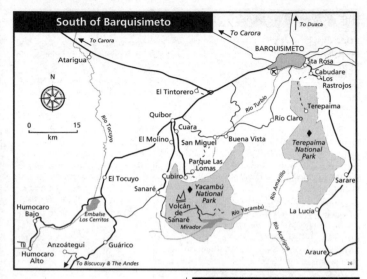

South of Barquisimeto

[Map showing the region south of Barquisimeto, including Atarigua, El Tintorero, Quíbor, Cuara, El Molino, San Miguel, Buena Vista, Parque Las Lomas, El Tocuyo, Sanaré, Cubiro, Yacambú National Park, Volcán de Sanaré, Mirador, Terepaima National Park, Sarare, La Lucía, Araure, Humocaro Bajo, Humocaro Alto, Anzoátegui, Guárico, Embalse Los Cerritos, with rivers Río Tocuyo, Río Turbio, Río Claro, Río Amarillo, Río Yacambú, Río Acarigua. Roads to Carora, Duaca, Biscucuy & The Andes. Scale 0–15 km.]

and many dirt trails you can follow on horseback or in a 4WD vehicle. From Río Claro a scenic dry season gravel road goes to Buena Vista and on to Quíbor, passing through attractive little villages.

TEREPAIMA NATIONAL PARK

The 18,650 hectare **Terepaima National Park** lies due south of Barquisimeto. The park has an uneven relief with altitudes ranging between 300m and 1,775m. Two thirds of the park is made up of savannah and old fields but from 1,100m there is dense cloudforest. The park's fauna includes the ocelot, puma, agouti, tamandua, capuchin monkey and rattlesnake.

The park can be reached from **Cabudare**, from where a rough road leads up to the village of **Terepaima**, lying within the northern section of the park. Your best bet, though, is to approach the park from **Sarare**, about 30 minutes south of Barquisimeto. Once in Sarare, ask for the **Parque Recreacional Sarare Las Mayitas**, where there are fast food shops and several paths.

ROUTES South of Sarare Route 4 reaches the city of **Acarigua**, lying at the edge of the vast plains of the Llanos (see page 219).

SOUTHWEST FROM BARQUISIMETO

The **Quíbor Valley** runs southwest from Barquisimeto towards the northern fringes of the Andes. This valley was originally inhabited by various communities. When the Spanish invaded the natives suffered a long process of intercultural integration, at best, or, in the worst cases, decimations. This almost wiped out the indigenous population and culture.

Descendants of the original peoples still inhabit this area and produce handicrafts using the same tools as their ancestors and techniques passed down from generation to generation by word of mouth. Different villages specialize in different handicrafts: in Tintorero they make hammocks and rugs; in Guadaloupe they work with wood; in Quebrada Seca (Guaca) with stone; and the distinctive pottery from Quíbor is known throughout the country.

TINTORERO

At the Km 25 signpost, a road turns right to **Tintorero**, a little community of dyers and weavers. The name actually means 'dyer'. It's a quiet, unassuming place, quite spread out. There is a Casa de la Cultura in the village centre with a good display of the pottery, woodcarvings and hammocks made here and in other villages in the area.

Here, and all over the village, are family-run factories and shops selling hammocks which are of excellent quality and good value. They are made of 80% cotton and 20% wool, which gives them a very soft feel. Also made from local wool are blankets, in bright coloured stripes or plaids. These serve well as colourful rugs and are also very good value. An International Craft Fair is held annually, usually in June or July.

Buses to Quíbor depart regularly from the terminal in Barquisimeto, and can also be caught from the Avenida Pedro León Torres. Ask to be dropped off at the Tintorero turnoff, from where you can either wait for a taxi or hitch.

QUIBOR

About 34 km southwest of Barquisimeto is the busy agricultural centre of **Quíbor** (*population* 53,525; *altitude* 700m; *phone code* 053). Despite dating back to early colonial times, this is no picturesque tourist town. Having said that, the Plaza Bolívar is pleasant and shaded and you can enjoy a *chicha de maíz* or *arroz*, a refreshing local drink. There are also some interesting pottery workshops to look around.

Probably the main attraction is the **Centro Antropológico de Quíbor**, two blocks down from the Plaza Bolívar. The centre's museum features exhibits from a prehispanic Indian cemetery found at the southwest corner of the plaza by accident in 1967. The museum is reputed to be one of the best in the country and should be open in early 1998 following renovations.

Huge copies of the archaeological pieces stand on the *paseo* in front of the **Iglesia de Nuestra Señora de Altagracia** which fronts the plaza. Many shops in town sell reproductions of these unique Quíbor ceramics. In the northern part of town is the fortress-like **La Ermita** church, built as a shrine for the highly-venerated Virgin of Altagracia. On 18 January is a festival held in honour of *Nuestra Señora de Altagracia*, and on 12 June is the festival of *San Antonio de Padua*.

- **Accommodation & places to eat D** *Hostería El Valle de Quíbor*, on Avenida 5 con Calle 7, T 42601, F 42603, hot water, air conditioning, TV, credit cards accepted, restaurant, pool; **F** *El Gran Duque*, on Avenida Florencio Jiménez (ask to be let off the bus at the Ceibita petrol station), fan or air conditioning, good and very cheap food in the restaurant below, excellent fruit juices, highly recommended. *Comedor Naturista*, is three blocks up from Plaza Bolívar on Avenida 7.

- **Banks & money changers** Banco de Lara, on Avenida Florencio Jiménez just before it divides into Avenidas 6 and 7, for Visa and Mastercard; also **Banco de Venezuela**, on Avenida 6 between Calles 8 and 9.

ROUTES Three roads run south from Quíbor: to El Tocuyo, Sanaré and Cubiro. On the road to Cubiro there is a large weekend craft market; a huge 3-legged pot marks the entrance.

CUBIRO

About 18 km from Quíbor on a beautiful road is the attractive, friendly town of **Cubiro** (*population* 4,780; *altitude* 1,560m; *phone code* 053). The town is set high on a mountain with superb views all around and is an ideal base for walking. As a major agricultural town, there are lots of farmers' tracks covering the hills, and these offer numerous walking opportunities. Cubiro is also very popular with people from Barquisimeto as the climate is much cooler.

The town was founded by Don Diego de Lozada, who had previously founded a little place called Caracas. His remains lie in the church, in full armour. The *Festival de Los Sueños* is held in October, when writers and poets gather for spiritual peace. Ask Lucy or Juan Torres at *Las Rosas Delicias* for information.

The biggest tourist attraction in Cubiro is **Las Lomas**, a range of rolling hills above the town which are very popular at weekends when the hills are alive with the sound of Venezuelans. You can hire horses for short guided circuits around the hill, and there are loads of kiosks selling fast food and handicrafts. During the week, the hills are deserted, making this a pleasant spot for a stroll and a picnic – though it can get a little windy.

Below Cubiro is **El Parque Higuerón**, a small wood with paths, benches and the usual stuff. It's now abandoned because the road is not passable by car.

To get to the wood, walk down the hill out of Cubiro past the post office. Almost immediately there is a fork. Go straight down; do not follow the road round to the left. After about 10 minutes you'll reach a stream; follow the path round to the right and keep walking down for another 10 minutes until you reach the park entrance. There's not much to do here but it makes for a nice walk, and the return trip will help work up a healthy appetite.

● **Accommodation** D *Centro Turístico Cubiro*, T/F 48155, with bath, hot water, restaurant, public phone (international calls can be made from here), accepts credit cards, also arranges tours by car for large groups of 10-12 people (to Las Lomas or Río Caraó) and walking tours, eg to Volcán El Humo, all tours require at 1 week's notice; **D** *Diego Lozada*, beautiful colonial building, large rooms, clean, hot water, superb views; **D** *La Flor Serrana*, T 48194, hot water, restaurant, sitting room with TV; **E** *El Paramito*, on the main street, two blocks from Plaza Bolívar, T 48085, hot water, clean, friendly, some rooms with TV; **E** *Residencias Milagro*, one block down from Plaza Bolívar, T 48123, hot water, TV, friendly, clean, lovely view, best value in town.

● **Places to eat** *Nacer Cubireño*, one block from Plaza Bolívar on the main street, excellent *criollo* food, very reasonable prices, nice atmosphere, highly recommended; the *arepería* opposite the plaza sells good *empanadas* and coffee for breakfast. **NB** Everything shuts early in Cubiro.

● **Post & telecommunications** Post office is on the corner of Plaza Bolívar; collections are on Tuesday and Thursday. They also have a fax machine.

● **Tour companies & travel agents** Although this area has plenty of potential for tourism, there is little organization. This means that everything is cheap, but you will have to be prepared to improvise. Sr Carlos Pacheco will organize tours to Las Lomas, to the river and the caves at Caraó, and to the villages around Quíbor. Sr Pacheco is friendly, helpful and speaks Spanish only; he also works as the local ambulance driver so will need several days' notice before taking a tour. He can be contacted at the Medicatura on Calle Urapal, two blocks down

from the main street, or at his home two blocks down from the *Hotel Diego Lozada* (T 48080), outside is a small pink kiosk called "*Mi Pulpería*". Also see *Hotel Centro Turístico Cubiro* above for guided tours and walks.

● **Transport** Direct buses leave from the terminal in Barquisimeto. Buses also leave from the Plaza Bolívar in Quíbor, though it's better to get a jeep from Avenida Florencio Jiménez, one block down from *Hotel El Duque*.

SANARE

22 km south of Quíbor, and 56 km from Barquisimeto, is **Sanaré** (*altitude* 1,360m; *phone code* 053), on the edge of the **Yacambú National Park** (see below). The town is quite a large, lively agricultural trading centre with all services, except a post office. The colonial part (known as El Cerrito), near the Plaza Bolívar, has been renovated and is very pleasant to wander around. In El Cerrito look for the **Casa la Providencia**, a house built in 1902, which is now a museum with a large garden and craft shop; open weekends 1000-1600.

● **Accommodation** **D-E** *Los Sauces*, out of town, 5 minutes' walk from the edge of El Cerrito heading towards Yacambú, T 490853, hot water, restaurant, disco; **D-E** *Parador Turística El Cerrito*, in El Cerrito district, 5 minutes' walk from Plaza Bolívar, walk up the hill past the Banco de Lara, T 49016, beautiful colonial hotel, the friendly manager speaks English and organizes tours to local sites and Yacambú, has a good, reasonably priced restaurant, credit cards accepted, highly recommended; **D-E** *Taburiente*, on Avenida Francisco de Miranda near Plaza Bolívar, T 490148, hot water, clean, secure, some rooms with TV, restaurant, *panadería* downstairs, good value.

● **Places to eat** *Cantaro de Miel*, one block down from Plaza Bolívar on Avenida 4, vegetarian snacks, *arepas*, pizzas, sandwiches, cakes etc, sells "the best *quesillo* in Venezuela", highly recommended.

● **Banks & money changers** Banco de Lara, two blocks from Plaza Bolívar at the entrance to El Cerrito, cash on Visa and Mastercard; **Banco Consolidado**, one block from the plaza, may change cash.

● **Post & telecommunications** CANTV is four blocks down from Plaza Bolívar on Avenida 4 (Simón Bolívar) between Calle 12 and 13. Phone cards on sale here, but no international calls. These can sometimes be made from *Restaurant Yacambú Sancocho*, on the Sabana

Grande road close to El Cerrito, or from *Hotel El Cerrito*.

● **Transport** Buses to Sanaré leave from the terminal in Barquisimeto and from Plaza Bolívar in Quíbor.

YACAMBU NATIONAL PARK

Sanaré is the main access point for **Yacambú National Park**, created in 1962 to protect 14,850 hectares of the Sierra de Portuguesa. The entrance to the park is 8 km from the *Hotel Los Sauces* (see above).

The park forms part of the lower mountain range of the Andes and is densely covered with beautiful tropical moist forest from around 500m up to 2,280m. It protects the headwaters of major rivers, such as the Yacambú, which drains into the Quíbor and is an important supplier of water for Barquisimeto. The birdlife in the park is said to be among the best in the country north of the Orinoco and includes tanagers, parakeets and hummingbirds.

The major attractions in Yacambú are the **Laguna El Blanquito**, the **Reservoir** and nearby the **Angostura Canyon**. The Laguna is basically a picnic spot – very pretty but not a lot to do except eat and sleep. About 2 km before El Blanquito is an Inparques camp, where there are cabins for large groups of more than 12. Permission to stay in one of the cabins or to camp in the park must be sought from the Inparques office in Barquisimeto (see page 147). Unfortunately, if you do not have a car, none of these places is very easy to reach. It's easier to visit through the week when the Hidrocapital workers leave Sanaré to work at the reservoir. The best place to catch a lift is around the corner from the Banco Consolidado along the road to Sabana Grande. You may also be able to take a *por puesto* from here during the week.

One of the best things you can do in Yacambú is the 2-3 hour hike up the Fumerola. From the hamlet of Bojo, you walk up through tropical forest to the Fumerola, which is actually a sleeping volcano. Guides for this route can be contacted via the *Hotel El Cerrito*.

EL TOCUYO

From Sanaré a road curves south and west to **El Tocuyo** (*population* 44,000; *altitude* 615m; *phone code* 053). A road also runs 28 km directly southwest from Quíbor to El Tocuyo.

Founded in 1545 as Nuestra Señora de la Pura y Limpia Concepción, this is one of the oldest towns in all of South America. It was a place of great importance to the Spanish, who set out from here to found the major cities of Venezuela. El Tocuyo was even the country's capital, from 1547 to 1577, when it was moved to Caracas. This is also the place where sugar cane was first grown in Venezuela, and remains one of the few places in the world where it can be grown all year round. A significant percentage of the country's sugar cane still comes from El Tocuyo.

Today, though, there is nothing to show for the town's proud past. In 1950, it was almost destroyed by an earthquake. All that remains are the ruins of two of its churches, **Santo Domingo** and **Belén**, and an 18th century convent on Plaza Bolívar, now the **Casa de la Cultura**. The modern town is spacious, clean and pleasant, but with little to offer the tourist. The **Museo Arqueológico J M Cruxent**, in the government building on the west side of the main plaza, is worth visiting, as is the beautiful pink and white **Iglesia de La Inmaculada Concepción**, a reconstruction of the 18th century original.

A good time to be here is on 13 June, during the festival of the patron saint, *San Antonio de Padua*. Country people come from all around to perform a complex set of dances known as the *Tamunangue*. This is considered one of the most stunning dances in the Americas.

● **Accommodation D** *Colonial*, just off the Plaza Bolívar, T 632495, beautiful colonial-style hotel, with bath, air conditioning, some rooms with TV, with moderately priced restaurant, pool, amazing value, tourist agency on ground floor, highly recommended; **E** *Nazaret*, on Avenida Fraternidad, T 62434, some rooms without bath or air conditioning.

● **Transport** Direct buses go to El Tocuyo from Barquisimeto or Quíbor.

ROUTES Several kilometres south of El Tocuyo the road forks: the main road continues south through **Guárico** and then southwest to **Biscucuy**, in the foothills of the Andes (see page 199); another road turns off to the west to the attractive village of **Humocaro Bajo**, 40 km from El Tocuyo.

HUMOCARO ALTO

8 km further on is Humocaro Alto, gorgeous little village nestling in the mountains at 1,094m, only an hour from El Tocuyo. This is an important horticultural area and there's also a factory making local butter and cheese. At the entrance to the village is a Closed Trappist Nunnery. The nuns are not normally allowed contact with the outside world, but they sell jams and other preserves and coffee to visitors. They also run a rest house, attended by two nuns who are allowed out.

● **Accommodation & transport** There is one posada, **E**, next to the Plaza Bolívar; a large, unnamed pink and white colonial building run by Gabriel and María Colmenares, a very friendly couple. Rooms are clean and some have hot water; there is no restaurant as such but they offer delicious homecooked meals using local produce.

● **Transport** Buses and por puestos go to Humocaro Alto from El Tocuyo terminal; also direct from Barquisimeto.

Walking tours can be arranged from the posada (see above) into the mountains. Guides are necessary as there are no good maps or signposts in the area. It's also a good idea to get permission from Inparques in Caracas (see page 91) if you plan to do any serious hiking, as this area is close to the **Dinira National Park**, which forms part of the Andes.

There are plenty of walks closer to the village. The **Cascada El Obispo** is along a paved road, about 2 km from the village. To get there, leave from the Plaza Bolívar, two blocks down from the road coming into the village. On the corner is a white and blue building 'Pool Las Canarias'. Go left here down the hill and stay on this road until you reach the falls. You can also ask at the posada for directions to **Cueva El Zumbador**, **Cueva de Na Diega** and **Cerro El Peñon**.

A good 2-day hike is to **Buenos Aires**, where there is a fauna and flora refuge. It's 6 hours from Humocaro Alto. There is an Inparques office and campsite; permission is needed to camp. Camping is also possible close to Humocaro Alto; ask at the posada for details.

WEST FROM BARQUISIMETO

CARORA

75 km past Barquisimeto the Lara-Zulia motorway to Maracaibo forks off to the right, through the cattle farming centre of **Carora** (population 82,500; phone code 052). The town has a nice colonial centre with a very pleasant Plaza Bolívar. It is possible to visit the Bodega Pomar Winery on the Lara-Zulia road, 1 km out of town. Call beforehand to organize your trip, T (052) 212191, F 341014.

The small village of **Altagracia** where the grapes are grown, is nearby. Cross the bridge next to Plaza Bolívar and it is about 20 km away. In the village there are some highly recommended restaurants serving typical fare (including iguana).

Another point of interest, south of Carora, is the **Cascada del Vino**, a waterfall that looks like red wine when the sun shines on it. It's not easy to find as there is no public transport and 4WD is necessary. Follow the road from Carora east to Barquisimeto and after 10 km turn right (south) to Agua Viva and Trujillo. Continue on this main road for 60 km before turning left (east) to the village of **San Pedro**. Take the steep, badly-maintained road until you arrive in the village itself. You can reach this point in a normal car, but thereafter you follow a badly-potholed gravel road, which is slippery when wet, to the village of **Barbacoas**, about 25 km from San Pedro. At the Inparques office (a white house), turn left, drive down the steep road for 1-2 km to a parking spot. You need to be there by 1500, otherwise the sun will have disappeared. There are good picnic facilities, but bring all provisions as there are no shops nearby.

● **Accommodation In Carora**: Madre Vieja and Katuka are the best hotels, each with a good restaurant and good value. In Madre Vieja you can sit outside, under a very old vine.

The Lowlands of Maracaibo

F OR MOST VENEZUELANS, this part of their country can be summed up in three letters – oil. For others, it can be summed up in four letters – heat. Both are certainly true. This is the main oil producing region as well as being one of the hottest places in all of Latin America. At times you could swear that the vast quantities of oil produced here are being used to fuel some giant blast furnace that reduces everyone to a little puddle of perspiration.

Not too many tourists find their way here. Those that do are usually on their way to Colombia via the border crossing on the Guajira Peninsula to the north. If you've got the time, though, and can handle the heat, the state of Zulia is worth a detour. Maracaibo is the only town or city in Venezuela where you'll see indigenous people in traditional dress going about their everyday business. Just north of the regional capital is a lagoon where you can see the same houses built on stilts that inspired the first Spanish invaders to christen it "Little Venice". In the southwest is the Catatumbo delta, a huge swamp brimming with wildlife and one of the most fascinating trips in the whole country.

The state of Zulia produces wealth in abundance for the rest of the country. Not just through oil but also milk, meat and plantains. This economic muscle has helped shape the people of Maracaibo, or *Maracuchos* as they are called. *Maracuchos* are legendary throughout Venezuela for being tough, proud, loud and brash. You won't need to be told someone is from Maracaibo – you'll just know. They'll be short and stocky, talk endlessly about how wonderful everything is in their hometown

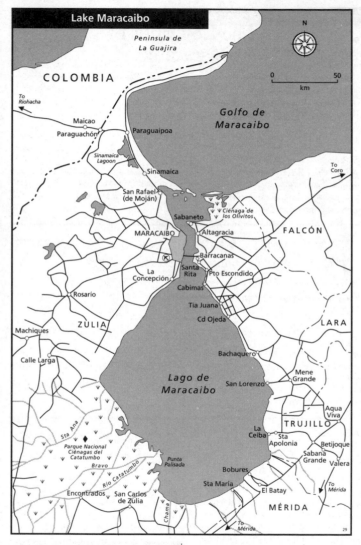

Lake Maracaibo

Peninsula de La Guajira

COLOMBIA

To Riohacha

Maicao

Paraguachón

Paraguaipoa

Sinamaica Lagoon

Sinamaica

San Rafael (de Moján)

Sabaneto

Golfo de Maracaibo

Ciénaga de los Olivitos

MARACAIBO

Altagracia

FALCÓN

To Coro

Barracanas

La Concepción

Santa Rita

Pto Escondido

Cabimas

Tia Juana

Cd Ojeda

Rosario

ZULIA

Machiques

Calle Larga

Bachaquero

Mene Grande

San Lorenzo

LARA

Aqua Viva

Lago de Maracaibo

Sta Ana

Parque Nacional Ciénagas del Catatumbo

Bravo

Río Catatumbo

Punta Palisada

Encontrados

San Carlos de Zulia

La Ceiba

Sta Apolonia

TRUJILLO

Betijoque

Sabana Grande

Valera

Bobures

Sta María

El Batay

Chama

MÉRIDA

To Mérida

To Mérida

0   50 km

N

29

and no doubt be cracking some politically incorrect joke. *Maracuchos* tend to be well liked in Caracas for their unique sense of humour, but less so by more sensitive people in the Andes, who tend to be the butt of many of their jokes. You may come to love them or hate them, but you certainly can't ignore *Maracuchos*.

Climate

The Lowlands of Maracaibo, lying in the encircling arms of the mountains, are

The oil boom

🦶 Lake Maracaibo is not only the largest lake in South America, it is also the richest lake in the world. But it took a long time for the lake's oil wealth to be fully realized.

At the beginning of the 20th century the Venezuelan economy was backward and insignificant. Although the country was the world's second largest exporter of coffee after Brazil, it had little income from other sources and almost no industry. There were no large cities and the vast majority of people lived in rural poverty. Within 40 years, though, spectacular prosperity came to Venezuela, transforming it from one of Latin America's poorest countries to by far its richest.

The entire history of the country was completely transformed one day in December 1922. Oil had already been found at Mene Grande, near the eastern shore of the lake, in 1914, but production was small – only 8,000 barrels a day from 9 wells. But it all changed when Los Barrosos No 2 well, near the village of Santa Rosa, on the northeast coast, blew out, gushing out 100,000 barrels of oil in the first day!

The 1922 oil find triggered a huge expansion in the country's exports. In 1920-21 Venezuela exported 100,000 barrels, which amounted to less than one ninth of coffee exports. By 1935-6 that figure had risen to almost 23 million barrels, worth 20 times more than coffee earnings. From the mid-1920s until the Second World War, Venezuela was the world's second largest oil producer after the USA, and its biggest exporter. Today, Venezuela continues to be the largest exporter of oil to the US, ahead of Saudi Arabia. Investment plans for the next 10 years would see Venezuela producing 7 million barrels a day.

more or less windless and extremely humid. Rainfall decreases steadily from the foothills of the Sierra Nevada to the coast. The hottest months are July, August and September, but there is usually a sea breeze from 1500 until morning. The mean temperature of 28°C and average humidity of 78% are most felt at sea level.

LAGO DE MARACAIBO

The semi-salt Lago de Maracaibo is the largest lake in South America. It is about 12,800 sq km, 155 km long and in places over 120 km wide. It is joined to the sea by a waterway, 3 to 11 km wide and 55 km long, at the mouth of which is the bar of Maracaibo.

Once dependent on fishing and the transport of coffee across the lake from the Sierra, the discovery of one of the world's greatest oilfields brought prosperity to the towns which line the lake's shores and turned the lake into a forest of oil derricks which cover its waters and shore swamps.

The 1922 oil find transformed the Lake Maracaibo area. 60 years ago this was a trackless wilderness, unpopulated except for the village of Lagunillas, built out over the lake on stilts. Most of the region around the lake was dense, virgin jungle and people travelled on foot or by mule. In the early days of oil exploration most of the travel from one camp to another was done by boat. Now, the new oil towns along the northeastern shore are connected by a fast, sleek highway. Perhaps the greatest symbol of the new-found prosperity is the spectacular General Rafael Urdaneta bridge, which spans the lake at its neck. Built in 1963, this is one of the most beautiful bridges in the world. It is also the longest pre-stressed concrete bridge in the world, at 8 km long.

MARACAIBO

Venezuela's second largest city (*population* 1,218,800; *phone code* 061), on the north-western shore of Lago de Maracaibo, is capital of the State of Zulia. This is Venezuela's oil boomtown: 70% of the nation's output comes from the Lake area.

Arriving over the stunning General Urdaneta bridge, Maracaibo can seem like it's in a different country. The first view of the city is mightily impressive, with the tower blocks on the lakeside reminiscent of the Manhattan skyline. Maracaibo is a modern commercial city with wide, clean streets and, apart from the intense heat, it's a pleasant place to walk around, especially around Plaza Bolívar.

Maracuchos have a reputation for idleness (among other things), but after a few days spent in this searing heat, all you'll want to do is sit in the shade with a cold drink. Activity grinds to a halt in the city around midday as temperatures soar. Don't expect to find anything open between noon and around 1500.

HISTORY

When Lake Maracaibo was first seen by Alonso de Ojeda and Amerigo Vespucci in 1499, there was nothing to suggest the great prosperity that would later come to this area. All they saw were the houses along the shore built on stilts and connected by little bridges and walkways which reminded them of a certain European city.

In 1569, Alonso Pacheco founded a settlement here which was destroyed by the Indians. It was refounded in 1574 by Pedro Maldonado and named Nueva Zamora de la Laguna de Maracaibo, which stuck for the next 200 years. During the 16th and 17th centuries the city suffered repeated sacking and pillaging by pirates, until the San Carlos fort was built in 1683 to protect it from such attacks.

The city came to prominence during the latter stages of the War for Independence, when a decisive naval battle was fought on Lake Maracaibo on 24 July 1823. Despite the fact that Bolívar was busy liberating Peru, the Republicans mounted a successful campaign against the despotic Spanish General Morales, who had taken control of the area, under the command of Admiral José Padilla and General Manuel Manrique. It was this victory that sealed the independence of Venezuela and virtually ended the long and bloody War of Independence.

Maracaibo was, for many years, isolated from the rest of the country due to its position on the west side of the lake. It was closer geographically and commercially to the Dutch Antilles and during the 17th and 18th centuries was involved in a flourishing trade with the islands. This led to a strong Dutch influence in the city's architecture, which can still be seen today in the few remaining older sections. Right up until the end of World War One, Maracaibo was still a sleepy town of only 75,000, but it all changed dramatically with the discovery of oil.

PLACES OF INTEREST

The traditional city centre is **Plaza Bolívar**, at the east end of which stands the **Cathedral**. Also on the plaza is the **Casa de Gobierno**, the **Asamblea Legislativa** and the **Casa de la Capitulación**. The latter, also called **Casa Morales**, is the only residential colonial building left in the city and is a national monument. Here, on 3 August 1823, the Capitulation was signed by the defeated Spanish after the naval battle of Lake Maracaibo. It has an extensive library dedicated to the Liberator (copies are available of Tovar y Tovar paintings of Bolívar's life and times). Tours of the Casa are free, it's open

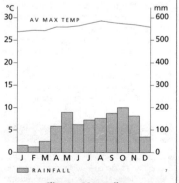

Climate: Maracaibo

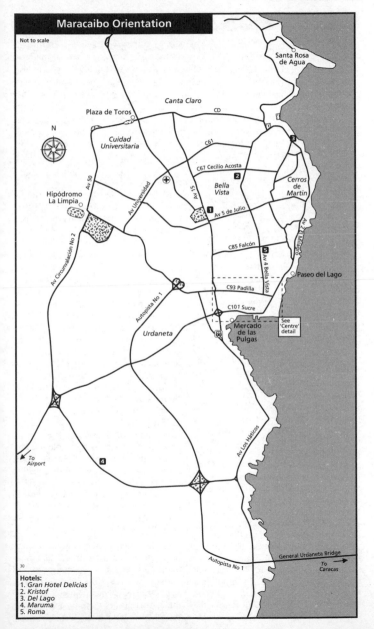

Maracaibo Orientation

Not to scale

N

Santa Rosa de Agua

Canta Claro

CD

Plaza de Toros

Cuidad Universitaria

C61

C67 Cecilio Acosta

Bella Vista

Cerros de Martin

Hipódromo La Limpia

Av 50

Av Universidad

Av 15

Av 5 de Julio

C85 Falcón

Av 4 Bella Vista

Av 2 El Milagro

Paseo del Lago

Av Circunvalación No 2

C93 Padilla

C101 Sucre

See 'Centre' detail

Autopista No 1

Urdaneta

Mercado de las Pulgas

Av Los Háticos

To Airport

General Urdaneta Bridge

To Caracas

Autopista No 1

30

Hotels:
1. *Gran Hotel Delicias*
2. *Kristof*
3. *Del Lago*
4. *Maruma*
5. *Roma*

A Christmas hit

If you've been in Venezuela between October and the end of December, you will be familiar with the *gaita*, a type of music synonymous with Maracaibo. The word translates as bagpipes, but this folk music has nothing to do with the famous Scottish instrument. The Venezuelan version is a series of improvised rhyming verses sung to a fast-paced rhythm played on *maracas*, four-stringed guitars called *cuatros* and *furrucos*.

The origin of the *gaita* is a matter of conjecture. Some say it was brought to Maracaibo by Spanish priests. There is also debate as to whether the original *gaitas* were political, religious or for propaganda purposes. Then, as now, the lyrics are primarily political and often satirical, but since *gaita* is sung during the Christmas season, religious themes are common.

Whatever the true source and purpose of this music, the popularity of *gaita* has spread from its Maracaibo base to become part and parcel of a Venezuelan Christmas. In the run up to the festive period there is no town or village, *tasca*, restaurant, hotel lobby, shop, house, bus, *por puesto*, taxi, riverboat, cow shed, dog kennel or mousehole where you can escape from it.

Monday-Friday, 0800-1600. Next door is the 19th century **Teatro Baralt**.

Running west of Plaza Bolívar, between Calle 95 and 96 and Avenida 4 (Bella Vista) and 10, is the **Paseo de las Ciencias**. This 1970s development levelled all the old buildings in the city's oldest neighbourhood, **El Saladillo**, said to be the home of *gaita*. The only original building left standing is the **Iglesia de Santa Bárbara**. Now the paseo is an attractive and lively place where *Maracuchos* come in their droves to stroll, play or just hang out together. **Calle Carabobo**, one block north of the Paseo de las Ciencias, is a very good example of a colonial Maracaibo street and a pleasant place to enjoy a stroll.

One block south of the Paseo is **Plaza Baralt** on Avenida 6, leading to Calle 100 and the old waterfront market **Mercado de las Pulgas**, The Flea Market. The **Centro de Arte de Maracaibo Lía Bermúdez** is housed in the 19th century Mercado de las Pulgas building, where the work of national artists is displayed. The building is air conditioned and a good place to escape the midday heat. The museum also has a good historical display of photographs of Maracaibo and makes a good starting place for a walking tour of the city centre.

The new part of the city round **Bella Vista** and towards the University is in vivid contrast with the **old town** near the docks. The latter, with narrow streets and brightly-painted, multi-coloured colonial style adobe houses, is hardly changed from the last century, although many buildings are in an advanced state of decay. The buildings facing **Parque Urdaneta**, three blocks north of Paseo de las Ciencias, have been well-restored.

Also well-preserved is the church of **Santa Lucía** and the streets around it. This charming old residential area, called **El Empedrado** is made up of narrow streets and little Maracaibo-style houses painted in a blaze of bright colours. This district also claims to be the origin of the *gaita*. It is a short ride, or long walk, north from the old centre. Near Santa Lucía, in the **Galería de Arte Brindhaven**, you can see more of the work of Jesús Soto (see below). He is often in residence here; entry is free.

4 km north of Parque la Marina is the picturesque old waterfront district of **Santa Rosa de Agua**. The houses are still built on (*palafitos*) stilts out over the lake, as are the many good fish restaurants in the district. To get there take a *por puesto* (US$0.20) from Avenida Las Delicias.

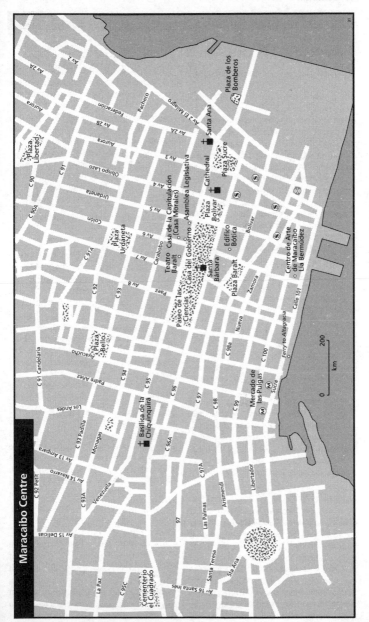

Maracaibo Centre

Plaza de los Bomberos

Santa Ana

Cathedral

Plaza Sucre

Av 2A
Av 2
Av 2A
Pacheco
Av 2 El Milagro
Santa Ana
Av 3
Av 4
Av 5

Plaza Libertad

C 91
C 90
C 90A
C 91A
C 92
C 93

Aurora
Federación
Aurora
Obispo Lazo
Urdaneta
Colón

Plaza Bolívar

Asamblea Legislativa

Casa de la Capitulación
(Casa Morales)

Edificio Bótica

Centro de Arte de Maracaibo
Lía Bermúdez

Teatro Baralt
Casa del Gobierno

Av 6
Av 7
Av 8

Paez

Santa Bárbara

Plaza Urdaneta

Plaza Baralt

Paseo de las Ciencias

Bolívar
Zamora
Nueva
Calle 101

Plaza Bello

Ayacucho

C 94
C 95

Padre Añez

Ferry to Altagracia

Mercado de las Pulgas

Sucre

C 98a
C 100
C 99
C 98
C 97
C 96

C 91 Candelaria
Los Andes

Basílica de la Chiquinquirá

C 96A
C 97A

0   200
km

C 93 Padilla
Monagas

Av 13 Ampara

Venezuela

C 92 Petit
Av 14 Navarro
C 93A

Libertador
Arismendi
Las Palmas

Cementerio el Cuadrado

Av 15 Delicias

La Paz
C 95C
C 95C

97

Santa Teresa
Sta Ana
Av 16 Santa Inés

PARKS AND ZOOS

Parque La Marina, formerly the Plaza del Maestro, is a small park on the shores of the lake containing sculptures by the Venezuelan artist, Jesús Soto. These depict scenes from the Battle of the lake in 1823 which consolidated the country's independence. The park also contains a 70m high tower, with good views over the lake and part of the city. The elevator to the top costs US$0.40 and there is a *fuente de soda* at the top selling snacks, soft drinks and beer; open Monday-Friday 1530-2100. Weekends 1100-2300. To get there, take a *por puesto* marked 'Milagro', or a bus marked 'Norte' and ask to be dropped off at the entrance. Opposite the entrance is the **Mercado de los Guajiros** (see **shopping** below).

Paseo de Maracaibo, or del Lago, is a lakeside park built in the late 1970s, near the *Hotel del Lago*. It offers walks along the shores of the Lake at its narrowest point, spectacular views of the Rafael Urdaneta bridge and of oil tankers sailing to the Caribbean. There are also places to sit and watch life go by. The park attracts a wide variety of birds. To get there, take a Milagro bus northbound from the Mercado de los Guajiros (see above), and ask the driver to let you off at the entrance, which is well-marked.

10 km from the city, on the road to La Canadá, is **El Parque Sur de Maracaibo**. The 90 hectares of parkland includes a 40 hectare zoo, housing animals from Venezuela and around the world. There's also a café, toilets and kids' playground; open at weekends and holidays, 0900-1700.

EXCURSIONS

Next to Lake Peonías is a public park which contains the **Simón Bolívar Planetarium**. There is one showing per week, on Sundays at 1400. The park also has a café and small swimming pool which is open at weekends only. There is also a hygiene museum, with models and diagrams of the human body, which is more of educational value than interest. The park is 15 minutes from the city. An El Mojan bus (see below)

goes past the entrance; catch it at the terminal or from Avenida Las Delicias between Calle 76 and 77.

LOCAL FESTIVALS

1-6 January, festivals featuring *gaitas* are held at **Cabimas** (see page 167) on the east shore of the lake; **5 October**, *Virgen del Rosario*; **18 November**, is the culmination of a week of festivities in honour of the patron saint of Zulia, *Nuestra Señora de Chiquinquirá*, also known as *La Chinita*, the many events include processions and bullfights, this is the main regional religious festival; **15 May**, *San Isidro*, held at Lagunillas, with processions and games.

LOCAL INFORMATION

● **Accommodation**

Hotel prices

L1	over US$200	**L2**	US$151-200
L3	US$101-150	**A1**	US$81-100
A2	US$61-80	**A3**	US$46-60
B	US$31-45	**C**	US$21-30
D	US$12-20	**E**	US$7-11
F	US$4-6	**G**	up to US$3

Those marked with an asterisk (*) are bookable through Fairmont International (see under Caracas).

It is difficult to obtain rooms without making reservations well in advance.

L3-A2 *Hotel del Lago Intercontinental**, El Milagro, Avenida 2, T 924022, F 914551, T 924180 for reservations, PO Box 90, 5-star services but plastic atmosphere, pool open to non-residents.

A1 *Maruma Internacional**, Circunvalación No 2, T 972911, F 981258, has old and new sections, hot water, air conditioning reasonable restaurant.

A2 *Kristoff**, Avenida 8 entre Calle 68 y 69, T 972911, F 980796, air conditioning, TV, fridge, accepts credit cards, nice pool open to non-residents US$6, disco, laundry service, restaurant, changes dollars cash at terrible rates.

B *Gran Hotel Delicias**, Avenida 15 (Las Delicias) esquina Calle 70, T 976111, F 973035, air conditioning, TV, recommended restaurant, good value, pool, disco, accepts credit cards, changes dollars cash at poor rates.

D *Doral*, Calle 75 y Avenida 14A, T 981792, air conditioning, helpful, recommended.

E *Almería*, Avenida 3H No 74-78 (next door to the *Delfín Maracaibo* restaurant), T 914424, air conditioning, with bath, hot water, TV; **E** *Astor*, on the south side of Plaza de la República, Bella Vista, T 914510, air conditioning, TV on request, popular; **E** *Europa*, Calle 93 y Avenida 4, air conditioning, run down but OK; **E** *Falcón*, Avenida 4, No 84-158, T 220967, air conditioning, laundry facilities; **E** *Novedades*, Calle 78 (also known as Dr Portillo) No 9-43, Bella Vista, T 75766, air conditioning, shower, safe, small rooms, safe parking, basic; **E** *Roma I*, Calle 86, 3F-76, Bella Vista, T 220868, air conditioning, with or without TV, restaurant, laundry service; **E** *San Martín*, Avenida 3Y (San Martín) con Calle 80, T 915097, air conditioning, TV, restaurant next door, accepts credit cards.

● **Places to eat**
Note that most restaurants are closed on Sunday. *Pizzería Napoletana*, Calle 77 near Avenida 4, excellent, closed on Tuesday; *Mi Vaquita*, Avenida 3H con Calle 76, one block from Plaza de la República, Texan steak house, best meat in town, popular with locals, good atmosphere, recommended. There are several good restaurants around the Plaza de la República, on Calle 77 (5 de Julio) and Avenida 31 (Bella Vista), such as *Chips*, at Avenida 31 opposite Centro Comercial Salto Angel, its regional fast food includes *tequeños* and *patacones* and is recommended.

El Carite, Calle 78, No 8-35, T 71878, excellent selection of fish and seafood, delicious and moderately-priced; *La Habana*, Avenida Bella Vista (Avenida 4) near Calle 76, good salads and milkshakes, open 24 hours; *La Friulana*, Calle 95 con Avenida 3, good cheap meals, repeatedly recommended, closes at 1900; *San José*, Avenida 3Y (San Martín), 82-29, good; *El Gaucho*, Plaza Banderas, Argentine-style, good; *Larga Vida*, Avenida 13A between Calle 75 and Calle 76, health food store; *Bambi*, Avenida 4, 78-70, Italian run with good capuccino, pastries, cheap and recommended; one block away, near Calle 76, is *Panadería Bella Vista*, recommended for *quesillo* and *tiramisu*.

There are many good clubs and restaurants on Calle 72, eg *Malanga Café*, with outdoor patio and live music most nights; *Pizza Pizza*, for good pizza and other Italian foods. On Calle Carabobo (see above), *Zaguán* serves traditional regional cooking at reasonable prices. There are many good fish restaurants in the Santa Rosa de Agua district (see **Places of interest** above).

● **Banks & money changers**
Banco Mercantil, on the corner of Plaza de la República, gives cash advance on Visa and Mastercard; also at **Banco Unión**, Avenida 4 y Calle 78. The best place for dollars cash and travellers'

cheques is *Casa de Cambio de Maracaibo*, Calle 78 con Avenida 9B; *Turisol*, Avenida 4 (Bella Vista) con Calle 67 (Calle Acosta), Amex representative; **Citibank**, Avenida 15 (Las Delicias) con Calle 77 (5 de Julio), for Citicorp travellers' cheques. All banks close at 1630, and will change money in the mornings only. The *Cambio* at the bus terminal will change Colombian pesos into bolívares at a poor rate. Note that all Thomas Cook transactions have to be verified in Caracas.

● **Embassies & consulates**
Colombia, Avenida 3Y (San Martín) 70-16 near Avenida 4 (Bella Vista), T 921483, F 921729, 10 km from the centre of town, take a bus or *por puesto* (Bellavista) out of town on Avenida 4 to Calle 70; open Monday-Friday, 0700-1300 prompt, 60-day visa in 5 hours, no questions and no tickets required (better than Caracas). **Denmark**, Avenida 15, No 88-78, Las Delicias, Apartado 301, T 591579, F 595763, open 0800-1200, 1400-1800. **France**, Avenida 3F y C70, T 912921, F 77671. **Germany**, C77 No 3C-24, Edificio Los Cerros, 9th floor, T 912406, F 912506. **Netherlands**, Avenida 3C y C67, El Lago, Unicentro Virginia, office 6, 2nd floor, T/F 922885. **Italy**, Avenida 3H No 69-79, T 72182, F 919903. **Norway**, Km 1 Carretera a Perijá, Sector Plaza Las Banderas-Los Haticos, T 616044, F 616555. **Spain**, Avenida Sabaneta y Calle El Prado No 9B-55, T 213445. **Sweden**, Avenida 15 Las Delicias No 88-78, T 595843, F 595763. **Switzerland**, Avenida 9B No 75-95, T 77710, F 71167. **UK**, Avenida 9B No 66-146, T 73745, F 82794.

● **Hospitals & medical services**
Doctors: *Dr García*, Hospital Coromoto, Avenida 3C and Calle 72, T 912222, speaks English, as does *Dr Carlos Febres*, a dentist, Avenida 8, No 84-129, weekdays 0900-1200, 1500-1800, T 221504.

● **Laundry**
Lavandería Laza, Calle 72 near Avenida 3H, Bella Vista, recommended.

● **Places of worship**
Anglican Church: Christ Church, Avenida 8 (Santa Rita) con Calle 74.

● **Post & telecommunications**
Post Office: Avenida Libertador y Avenida 3. **Telecommunications**: Servicio de Telecomunicaciones de Venezuela, Calle 99, esquina Avenida 3, payphones for local calls only, CANTV, Calle 76 near Avenida 3E, Bella Vista, open weekdays 0700-2330. If the offices are closed, phone cards are available at the desk of the nearby *Hotel Astor*, on the south side of Plaza de la República, where international calls can also be made.

● **Security**

The old part of the city is not safe after 1700 and even requires care in daylight.

● **Shopping**

Fin de Siglo is a chain of department stores which sell records, tapes and posters of local sights. The huge new *Mercado de las Pulgas* is on the south side of Calle 100 entre Avenida 10 y 14, it sells mostly clothes, shoes, and general household goods. *Centro Comercial Costa Verde*, Avenida 4 (antes Bella Vista), is a good new shopping complex. *El Mercado de las Guajiras*, is an open market at Calle 96 y Avenida 2, opposite Parque la Marina (see above), which has a few crafts, some pottery, hammocks, etc. Most of the shops on Calle Carabobo sell regional crafts, eg *La Salita*.

Maracaibo is a good place to buy *artesanía*, particularly those of the Guajiro Indians.

Bookshops: *Librería Universal*, Avenida 5 de Julio y Avenida 4, maps, stationery and Caracas newspapers but has a poor selection of books; *Librería Cultural*, Avenida 5 de Julio, best Spanish language bookstore in town; *Librería Italiana*, Avenida 5 de Julio, Edificio Centro América, for postcards and foreign publications. There's a good bookshop in the Arrivals lounge of the airport (see below). Staff at the public library, on Avenida 2, are helpful to tourists.

Photography: *Foto Bella Vista*, Avenida Bella Vista, Calle 78, recommended service.

● **Tourist offices**

Corpozulia, the government tourist agency, is at Edificio Corpozulia on Avenida 4 (Bella Vista) between Calle 83 and 84, T 920836, F 920663, have information on tourist sites and are friendly and helpful.

● **Tour companies & travel agents**

Turisol, are the only reliable agents who organize local tours; they are very helpful and accept credit cards. They will take you to Sinamaica and Caiman El Chico (a popular beach resort next to Sinamaica) for US$50 per car per day (maximum 4 people); they also run individual tours throughout Venezuela and will hire buses for large groups of up to 50.

Navetur, Propela Clubin Puntica de Piedra on Avenida Norte, 300m from Parque de la Marina, T 415021/415047, run excursions to Isla San Carlos at the weekends and holidays, they leave Maracaibo at 0900 and San Carlos at 1600, take your own food and drink; same day return costs US$4.50, next day return US$6.50. They also offer charters for large groups to the Petrochemical installations.

● **Transport**

Local *Por puestos* go up and down Avenida 4 from the old centre to Bella Vista. Ruta 6 goes up and down Calle 67 (Cecilia Acosta). The San Jacinto bus goes along Avenida 15 (Las Delicias). Buses from Las Delicias also go to the centre and the terminal. From Calle 76 to the centre you can take a *por puesto* marked 'Las Veritas' or a bus marked 'Ziruma'. Look for the name of the route on the roof, or on the front window, on the passenger's side. A ride from downtown to Avenida 5 de Julio in a 'Bella Vista' *por puesto* costs US$0.20. **Taxis**: US$1.50-2. *Luquis Taxis* will do city tours for US$6.50 per hour. You'll find them on Avenida 14A entre Calle 76 y 77, near *Hotel Doral*, T 971556.

Air La Chinita airport is 25 km southwest of the city centre. The terminal has international and national lounges; shops include a bookshop which sells a city map; *casa de cambio* open 0600-1800 daily, no commission; Banco Venezolano; car hire offices outside. Taxis charge between US$5-6, but there are no *por puestos*. There are frequent flights with Aserca, Avensa, Servivensa and Aeropostal to Maiquetía, Valencia, Barquisimeto, Las Piedras, Mérida, San Antonio (be early to guarantee a seat), Barcelona, Porlamar and Puerto Ordaz. International flights from Maracaibo to Curaçao and Aruba with Servivensa, to Miami with Servivensa and to Aruba, Barbados, Curaçao, Manaus, Port of Spain, St Maarten and Santo Domingo with Aeropostal (T 526986, F 527664).

Buses The bus terminal is a 15-minute walk from the centre, 1 km south of the old town. Ask for buses into town, as local services are confusing. There are several fast and comfortable buses daily to: **Valencia**, US$7.75 with Expresos del Lago; **San Cristóbal**, US$6.50, 6-8 hours, *por puesto*, US$19; **Barquisimeto**, 5½ hours, US$5; **Coro**, US$4, 4 hours; **Caracas**, US$12, 10-13 hours, *por puesto* US$24; **Mérida**, 2300, US$7, 5-7 hours, or *por puesto*, US$10, 6½ hours.

NORTH OF MARACAIBO

There is a variety of excursions which can be made from Maracaibo. Most of the interesting ones are to the north of the city, towards the Colombian border.

About 1 hour north is the little fishing port of **El Moján**, on the Río Limón estuary. Take a bus (US$0.40) from the terminal in Maracaibo or Avenida Las Delicias between Calle 76 and 77. You'll find yourself riding with the Guajira Indians as they return to their homes on the peninsula.

Near the bus terminal in El Moján is a jetty from where launches go to the **Isla San Carlos** (US$1.20 each way). On the island is the restored **Castillo San Carlos**, built in the late 17th century to protect the entrance to Lake Maracaibo from pirate attacks. There are guided tours of the fort (US$0.40); a small museum, San Carlos de la Barra, houses permanent exhibitions of the castle's history and has a gift shop. As well as the Castillo there are beaches where you can swim, sand dunes and mangroves to explore. The last launch back to El Moján leaves between 1600 and 1700, so be ready to leave the island by 1530. Near San Carlos is **Toas Island**, with excellent fishing, deserted beaches and beautiful scenery. **NB** San Carlos island was closed to visitors due to a large oil spillage in early 1997; check on conditions.

SINAMAICA LAGOON

The attractive Sinamaica lagoon is an intricate system of canals, characterized by mangrove swamps and home to the Zulian ethnic group of Añú-Parajuana. Several thousand of these people live on the lake in houses built on *palafitos* (stilts), much as they did when Alonso de Ojeda and Amerigo Vespucci first saw them in 1499 and named this the Gulf of Venezuela (Little Venice). The roofs of the houses are covered in *estera*, which is a type of reed similar to papyrus that grows on the lagoon – these are also used for walls, window shutters and to sit and sleep on. The manufacture of *estera* is one of the local industries of the Añú-Parajuana; another being the extraction of coconut oil.

From El Moján, *por puestos* go to the village of **Sinamaica** (US$0.80), or take a taxi (US$3). From there transport can be taken to the small port of **Puerto Cuervito** at the lagoon (US$0.50). You can hire a boat; US$17 per boat for 1½ hours on the lake. Close by is **El Barro**, a village built on stilts on the lagoon. Near El Barro on the lagoon is the *Parador Turística*, a *fuente de soda* and craft shop built on stilts using traditional materials. An hour further up the river is another traditional settlement, **La Boquita** (*population* 2,500).

Palafitos on Laguna Sinamaica

There are also excursions by boat from Maracaibo to the Sinamaica lagoon, ask for *el libro de reclamaciones* which should give the maximum official price. Sinamaica has an agricultural show on 15-21 August.

SINAMAICA TO THE COLOMBIAN BORDER

Beyond Sinamaica, a paved road (Route 6) leads north to **Paraguaipoa** and then turns west to the border with Colombia.

This part of the country is home to the Guajira Indians, the largest indigenous group in Venezuela and the only Indians you'll see in the cities dressed in traditional clothing. Many of them still live nomadic lifestyles on the barren **Guajira Peninsula**. They pack up their reed houses and carry them by mule, following the seasonal water supply on the peninsula. Theirs is a matriarchal society where the women do all the work, tending sheep and goats, selling slippers and raising very little on the dry, hot, scrubby Guajira Peninsula. In contrast, the men do nothing, save for a little hunting and fishing to supplement the family diet of meat and dairy products. The Guajiro dance, the *Chichamaya*, is the only one in the country where the woman takes the initiative.

Guajira women wear long, brightly-coloured tent-shaped dresses called *mantas* and sandals with big wool pom-poms (which they make and sell for US$2, as against the US$7-10 in the tourist shops). Some women you see are in black; all the women of a tribe wear black to mourn the death of their chief. Guajira women also paint their faces; red, yellow and black in the case of young girls reaching puberty. The men dress as they always have done, nude except for a short loincloth. When travelling, they wear a large loincloth, shirt and straw hat.

The Guajira have their own language, customs and laws. They have little to do with non-Indian affairs and are not required to carry *cédulas*, or identification cards. And since they do not recognize borders, they are free to move between Venezuela and neighbouring Colombia without passports or official interference.

Paraguaipoa, 95 km north of Maracaibo, is the only notable town on the Venezuelan side of the Guajira Peninsula. There is an interesting Guajira market at **Los Filudos**, 2 km beyond Paraguaipoa. Here you can buy the local tent-dress (manta) for about US$5-10, depending on the quality, but much cheaper than in Maracaibo. You can also buy the *chinchorro*, a locally-made hammock. This is no tourist market, however. It is where the Guajira come from remote parts of the arid peninsula to buy their supplies in their brightly-painted and decorated trucks and jeeps.

NB The Guajira peninsula is not a place to travel alone. If going in your own transport, check on safety before setting out. Remember, it is very hot, there is little shade, very little water and it is easy to get lost.

CROSSING INTO COLOMBIA VIA MACAO

The border opens at 0800; though buses from Maracaibo pass through from 0630. Note that Venezuela is 1 hour ahead of Colombia. Ask for 90 days on entering Colombia. Formalities are said to be straightforward in Colombia but slow on the Venezuelan side. Latest reports suggest that an exit tax of US$5 must be paid at the border. Bus passengers from Maracaibo to Maicao have to pay the exit tax at a booth in Maracaibo bus terminal, and the receipt must be shown at the border.

● **Entering Venezuela**
To enter Venezuela by land a visa is essential despite what may be said by Venezuelan Consulates. Only 72-hour transit visas are issued at this border; *tarjetas de turismo* must be obtained from DIEX in Maracaibo – not an easy task. Get a visa in advance. You can expect vigorous searches at the border and en route to Maracaibo.

● **Colombian consulate**
See under Maracaibo, above.

● **Buses**
Maracaibo-Maicao, with Expreso Maicao or Expreso Gran Colombia, US$3.50, 3 hours, from 0500-1600, leaves when full; *Colectivos* US$5 per person, 6 in car.

● **Security**
NB This is a particularly sensitive section of the Venezuela/Colombia border and has a reputation as a lawless place. The journey on either side of the border is described as tense and worrying. There is also a risk of ambush by bandits/guerrillas. The Colombian town of **Macao** is full of Venezuelan contraband and at the centre of the narcotics trade; it is not a safe place to hang around, especially after 1700.

● **Into Colombia**
A paved road runs from Macao to the port of Riohacha, which has accommodation, banks and a Venezuelan Consulate (reports are that it is easier to get a visa in Baranquilla). Buses to Riohacha, US$1.35.

NORTHEAST COAST OF LAKE MARACAIBO

From the port of Maracaibo, you can take a ferry to **Altagracia**, directly opposite on the eastern side of the neck of Lake Maracaibo. Also known as *Los Puertos*, The Ports, Altagracia still has many old colonial houses.

The first ferry leaves at 0645, the trip takes only 25 minutes, US$0.40. You can return the same way or take a minibus (US$0.55), travelling through exotic scenery for almost an hour and crossing the General Urdaneta bridge.

CIENAGA DE LOS OLIVITOS

About 20 km from Altagracia, in the municipalities of Miranda and Almirante Padilla, is the **Ciénaga de los Olivitos**. The 26,000 hectares of sand dunes, beaches, lakes, mangroves and salt mines was declared a fauna and fishing reserve in 1986. It is important as a resting and feeding area for migratory birds, especially flamingos and other species in danger of extinction, such as sea turtles, the coastal alligator and manatee.

Unfortunately, getting to the Ciénaga is not all that easy. The area is not very accessible and there are no organized tours available. Corpozulia are apparently trying to promote the area for low-grade eco-tourism and may have more information by the time you read this (see under **Tourist offices** in Maracaibo, page 164). It may also be worth trying the travel agency, *Turisol* (see under **Travel agents** in Maracaibo).

ROUTES From the eastern end of the General Urdaneta bridge, a road runs northeast to **Coro**, in the state of Falcón (see page 131).

SOUTHEAST FROM MARACAIBO

Two roads head southeast: Route 17 bypasses the towns along the lake shore then turns east to **Carora** and **Barquisimeto** (see page 154); Route 3 follows the lake, passing through a succession of new oil towns.

First is **Cabimas**, with **A2** *Cabimas Internacional*★, T 45692, luxury, pool, discotheque. Next come **Tía Juana**, **Ciudad Ojeda** and **Lagunillas**, where there is accommodation in **D** *Hotel Lagunillas*★, T 21423, pool. The road continues through **Bachaquero** to **Mene Grande**, which lies 30 km inland from the lake and was the first oilfield in Venezuela. South of Mene Grande the road enters the state of Trujillo, where it joins the Pan-American Highway at **Agua Viva**. Here the road forks. The southern route climbs up to **Valera** (see page 193) and from there to the Sierra Nevada de Mérida.

The southwestern route is the Pan-American Highway which is asphalted and runs along the foot of the Andes through rolling country planted with sugar or bananas, or park-like cattle land. At **Sabana de Mendoza**, 24 km south of Agua Viva, there is accommodation in the *Hotel Panamérica* (good,

with air conditioning). Just beyond, at **Sabana Grande**, a road branches east to **Betijoque** and on to Valera.

The Pan-American Highway goes straight on, with plenty of restaurants, hotels and filling-stations, especially at **Caja Seca**. It eventually reaches **El Vigía** (see page 168), from where you can head north along the western shore of the lake back to Maracaibo.

SOUTHWEST FROM MARACAIBO

The road southwest from Maracaibo, the fast Route 6, passes through long stretches of empty countryside and carries little traffic. West of Lake Maracaibo still has the feel of an emerging frontier territory. These are the former lands of the **Motilones** Indians, who, until 1960, refused to have dealings either with white men or other Indians. The Motilones defended their ancestral lands fiercely against cattle ranchers and oil explorers. Gradually, the persistent ranchers gained a foothold, along with Capuchín missionaries, both using very different methods. Most of the Motilones lands have been lost to the settlers over the past few decades and today most of the remaining Indians have retreated into the valleys of the **Serranía de Perijá** (also known as the **Sierra de Motilones**) which runs along the border with Colombia. A large part of the Sierra is taken up by the **Parque Nacional Sierra de Perijá**, 295,288 hectares of wild and dense cloud forest.

MACHIQUES

Machiques (*population* 43,200) is the only town of any size west of Lake Maracaibo and is at the centre of a major milk-producing area. The town celebrates the *Fiesta de San José* on 19 March, and the *Feria de Virgen del Carmen*, with agricultural shows, on 14-18 July.

● **Accommodation D** *Motel Tukuko*, good; **E** *Hotel Italo Zuliano*.

A road leads southwest from Machiques for 51 km to the mission settlement of **Los Angeles del Tocuco**. It's a very beautiful journey with lots of birds and other animals to be seen. Visitors are welcome at the mission but it helps to take a present, such as dried milk. There's a simple, family-runshop-cum-restaurant which sells filling food; also accommodation, **F**. To get there take a *por puesto* from Machiques, US$0.80, 1¼ hours.

ROUTES   Route 6 continues south through lush fields of sugar cane, crossing a number of major rivers that feed Lake Maracaibo: Río Negro, Río Tucuco, Río Santa Ana and the Río Catatumbo. A road turns east off the main highway to **Casigua**. From there it runs northeast to **Encontrados**, then east to **San Carlos del Zulia** and **Santa Bárbara**, a milk, meat and plantain producing centre, with an important annual cattle show.

PARQUE NACIONAL CIENAGAS DEL CATATUMBO

Between the rivers Santa Ana and Catatumbo is a vast area of swampland inhabited by the Motilones Indians. The 269,400 hectares, also called Ciénaga Juan Manuel, Aguas Blancas y Aguas Negras, was decreed as a reserve in 1991 to protect the vegetation. The lands of the Catatumbo delta are very fertile and of vital importance for Lake Maracaibo. The area is a major bird sanctuary, with a huge number of aquatic birds such as the Great Egret, Blue Heron and Jabiru among others. The park is also home to a great variety of mammals including capybara and raccoons and river dolphins can be seen in the channels which cross it. The Catatumbo delta is famed for its almost nightly display of lightning for which

there is, as yet, no accepted explanation and which caused it to be known in the old days as 'The Lighthouse of Maracaibo'.

On the fringes of the park, 3 hours drive from Mérida, is the old port of **Encontrados**, once of great economic importance but now very much off the beaten track. There are no tourist facilities in the park, but accommodation should be possible to find in the neighbouring villages. The easiest way to visit the park, and one that is highly recommended, is on a 2-3 day tour from Mérida (for details see under **Travel agents** in Mérida, page 179).

SOUTH TO EL VIGIA

From **San Carlos/Santa Bárbara**, the commercial hub of the south lake area, a road runs south for 56 km to **El Vigía** (*population* 70,290; *phone code* 075) standing on the Río Chama, which flows into the lake from the high Andes near Mérida. Flights diverted from Mérida often land at El Vigía, which is now connected to the state capital by a new tunnel, taking only 1 hour by por puesto (US$3).

● **Accommodation In El Vigía: E** *La Suiza*, Avenida 15, opposite the bus terminal, recommended.

ROUTES   From El Vigía, the Pan-American Highway continues westwards fairly flat until **La Fría** to join Ruta 6 from south Maracaibo. From La Fría the Highway runs south to **San Cristóbal** (see page 204). Another road from El Vigía heads due south up into the Andes to meet the Transandean Highway, where you can turn east to **Mérida** (see page 171) or west to **Tovar**.

The Andes

THE VENEZUELAN ANDES run southwest from the state of Trujillo all the way to the Colombian frontier and comprise the main mountain ranges of the **Sierra Nevada de Mérida**, the **Sierra de La Culata** and the **Sierra de Santo Domingo**. At the heart of the region is Mérida, the highest state in the country, known as *El techo de Venezuela* – the roof of Venezuela. This region is far removed from the golden beaches and tropical jungles of glossy tourist brochures, yet Mérida and the Sierra Nevada acts as a magnet for both foreign travellers and Venezuelan vacationers. People come here to hike and climb in the National Parks, fish in the rivers and lakes or just soak up the unique atmosphere of rural Andean life and enjoy the breathtaking scenery.

Bisecting this rugged mountain landscape is the Transandean Highway, passing through a series of neat little rural towns of red-tiled roofs. The road snakes its way past fields and terraces of maize, wheat and potatoes, farmed by the hardy, industrious and deeply religious Andean people. Some of these fields rise up on

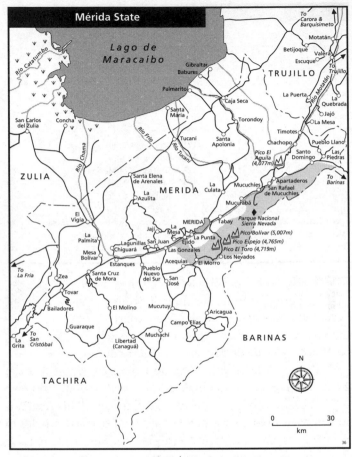

Mérida State

Lago de Maracaibo

To Carora & Barquisimeto

Motatán

Betijoque

Valera

Rio Catatumbo

Gibraltar

Babures

Escuque

To Trujillo

Palmarito

TRUJILLO

La Puerta

La Quebrada

Caja Seca

Santa Maria

Jajó

La Mesa

San Carlos del Zulia

Concha

Tucaní

Torondoy

Timotes

Pueblo Llano

Chachopo

Santo Domingo

Las Piedras

Rio Frio

Santa Apolonia

Pico El Aguila (4,077m)

Rio Chama

Santa Elena de Arenales

ZULIA

La Azulita

La Culata

MERIDA

Mucuchíes

Apartaderos

San Rafael de Mucuchíes

To Barinas

Mucurubá

El Vigia

Jaji

La Mesa

MERIDA

Tabay

Parque Nacional Sierra Nevada

La Palmita

Lagunillas San Juan

La Punta

Pico Bolívar (5,007m)

Chiguará

Las Gonzales

Pico Espejo (4,765m)

Mesa Bolívar

Estanques

Acequias

Pico El Toro (4,719m)

El Morro

Los Nevados

Santa Cruz de Mora

Pueblo Nuevo del Sur

San José

Zea

Tovar

El Molino

Mucutuy

Aricagua

Bailadores

Guaraque

Campo Elias

BARINAS

La Grita

To San Cristóbal

Libertad (Canaguá)

Muchachí

TACHIRA

N

0   30
km

36

precipitous gradients to the very edge of the *páramo*, seemingly defying gravity. This is the only part of the country where snow lies permanently on mountain peaks. The highest of these, Pico Bolívar, is 5,007m (although a recent measurement has indicated that it is 9m lower than the original estimate).

Mérida is also a convenient stopping-point on the way to or from Colombia and a good place to escape the heat of Maracaibo, the northwest coast or the Llanos to the east.

BASICS The three main population centres are Mérida, Valera and San Cristóbal. The inhabitants are concentrated mainly in the valleys and basins at between 800 and 1,300m above sea level. The basins are intensively cultivated and two crops of the staple food, maize, can be harvested annually up to an elevation of about 2,000m. There are two distinct rainy and dry seasons in the year (see below).

MERIDA

The capital of Mérida State, founded in 1558, is one of Venezuela's top tourist destinations. The city stands on an alluvial terrace – a kind of giant shelf – 15 km long and 2½ km wide, guarded by the higher peaks of the Venezuelan Andes and within sight of Pico Bolívar. But this is no cold, breathless Andean outpost. Mérida lies in a lush valley of trees draped in Spanish Moss and flowering plants and its relatively low altitude means that it enjoys a pleasantly mild climate.

Though a few colonial buildings remain, the city is no architectural beauty. This is compensated, though, by a dramatic backdrop of five of the highest peaks in the Sierra Nevada. Known locally as *Las Cinco Aguilas Blancas* (The Five White Eagles), they are: La Corona (which consists of Pico Humboldt and Bonpland), El Toro, La Concha, El León and La Columna (which comprises Pico Bolívar and Espejo). Not that visitors come here to admire colonial buildings, anyway. They are here to climb mountains, ride horses, hike, mountain bike, paraglide, go on any number of tours, meet other travellers, drink, dance, learn Spanish and, not least, take a ride on the highest cablecar in the world.

Just simply hanging around in Mérida is enjoyable in itself. There's a lively buzz about the place, created not only by large numbers of tourists but also by the incredibly high student population. Over 35,000 young people from around South America and the Caribbean come here to study at the city's Universidad de los Andes (see below).

BASICS *Population* 222,700 (including students); *Altitude* 1,640m; *Phone code* 074. *Mean temperature* 19°C; in January-February, the coldest months, and August-September, it rains almost every late afternoon. In August and September it often rains throughout the night, too. Mérida is 173 km from Valera; 674 km from Caracas.

ROUTES There are several routes into and out of Mérida: south from Maracaibo, via **El Vigía** (see page 168); by a spectacular road west from **Barinas** (see page 220); northeast from **San Cristóbal** (see page 204); and southwest from **Valera** (see page 193).

HISTORY

Unlikely as it may sound, Mérida should not have been founded when it was. Captain Juan Rodríguez Suárez had been sent into the Sierra Nevada to search for gold and subdue any Indians he encountered en route, but instead he decided to found a town. In those days towns could only be legally founded by Royal Decree, so Rodríguez Suárez found himself in deep trouble. He was branded a criminal, arrested and returned to Bogotá to face trial.

Once found guilty, he was sentenced to be dragged behind his horse through the streets of Bogotá until dead, then his body quartered and each part displayed on a pike at each of the main roads entering the city. Luckily for the accused, he was helped to escape and flee to Venezuela, where he was granted the first ever political asylum in the New World.

Like many other Venezuelan towns and cities, the present site of Mérida was not its first – not even its second. The site of present-day Mérida was established by none other than Juan Maldonado y Ordoñez, the man who arrested Rodríguez Suárez, and the city was given the rather grand title of *La Ciudad de Santiago de los Caballeros de Mérida*. Quite a mouthful but also quite apt, for *caballeros* means

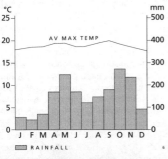

°C / mm

AV MAX TEMP

RAINFALL

Climate: Mérida

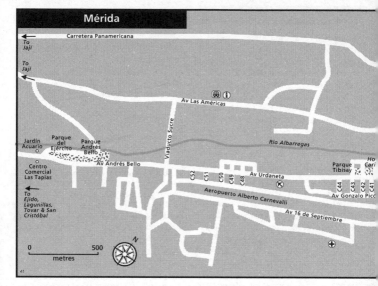

Carretera Panamericana

To Jají

To Jají

Av Las Américas

Río Albarregas

Jardín Acuario

Parque del Ejército

Parque Andrés Bello

Parque Tibisay

Centro Comercial Las Tapias

Av Andrés Bello

Viaducto Sucre

C52 C51 C50 C49 C48

Av Urdaneta

C44 C43 C42 C41

To Ejido, Lagunillas, Tovar & San Cristóbal

Aeropuerto Alberto Carnevalli

Av Gonzalo Picó

Av 16 de Septiembre

0   500
metres

gentlemen and, compared to the more raucous citizens of many other Venezuelan cities, Mérideños can seem reserved and polite.

These well-mannered Andean folk were the first in the country to hail Simón Bolívar as *El Libertador*, on 23 May 1813, when he returned from Colombia to try once more to liberate his homeland. Mérida was virtually left intact during the bloody War of Independence and saw an increase in population as refugees fled from other parts of the country to relative safety. It has continued to grow, especially in the last few decades, to the point where it seems to be in danger of falling over the edge of the steep cliffs of the Chama valley.

PLACES OF INTEREST

The Plaza Bolívar lies at the heart of the city and is pleasant and shaded. Surrounding it are the **Cathedral**, started in 1803 but not finished until 1958; the **Archbishop's Palace**, which houses a small collection of colonial paintings; and the **Government Palace**. Just off the plaza, on Avenida 3, is the original building of the

University of the Andes, founded in 1785 and the second oldest in the country.

Not to be missed on any visit to Mérida is the most amazing ice cream shop in the world, the **Heladería Coromoto**, at Avenida 3 y Calle 29, opposite Plaza El Llano (T 523525), which opens Tuesday to Sundae (sorry, Sunday), 1400-2200, and is closed Mondays (see below).

PARKS AND ZOOS

Mérida is known for its many parks and statues. There are no fewer than 33 parks, though some are little more than traffic roundabouts. **Parque de las Cinco Repúblicas**, on Calle 13, between Avenidas 4 and 5, beside the barracks, had the first monument in the world to Bolívar (erected in 1842 and replaced in 1988) and contains soil from each of the five countries he liberated. Three of the peaks known as the Five White Eagles – Bolívar, Toro (4,755m), and León (4,740m) can be clearly seen from here. The others, Humboldt (4,942m) and Bonpland (4,882m) are out of view. Note that photography is strictly prohibited.

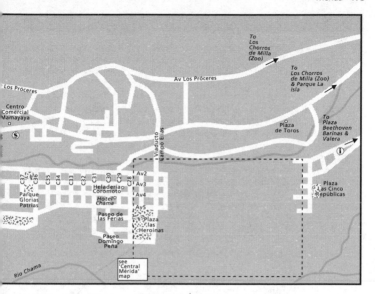

The **Parque Los Chorros de Milla** is some distance from the centre of town but a firm favourite with locals. Legend has it that the park's waterfalls were produced by the tears of an Indian princess, Tibisay. On hearing of the death of her lover by Spanish conquistadors, she cried herself to death. A statue of the heartbroken princess stands at the entrance to the park. Also in the park is a zoo (with some cages less than adequate) and plenty of handicraft shops nearby. The park is closed on Monday. To get there take a *buseta* (US$0.35); on the way, there is a new chapel, built on the site where the Pope said mass in 1985.

Jardín Acuario, beside the aquarium on Avenida Andrés Bello, is an exhibition centre, mainly devoted to the way of life and the crafts of the Andean *campesinos*. Entry is US$0.10; open Tuesday-Sunday 0800-1200, 1400-2000; *busetas* leave from Avenida 4 y Calle 25, passing by the airport (US$0.10).

The **Parque La Isla** contains orchids, basketball and tennis courts, an amphitheatre and fountains. In the **Plaza Beethoven**, a different melody from Beethoven's works is chimed every hour (when the clock's working). *Por puestos* and *busetas*, run along Avenida 5, marked 'Santa María' or 'Chorro de Milla'; US$0.15.

Museums

Museo de Arte Colonial is on Avenida 4, between Calle 17 and Calle 18, three blocks from the Plaza Bolívar. It's open Tuesday-Friday, 0900-1200, 1500-1800; Saturday 1500-1800, and Sunday, 1000-1200, 1500-1800. More interesting is the small **Museo Arqueológico**, on Avenida 3, Edificio del Rectorado de la Universidad de los Andes, just off Plaza Bolívar, which shows precolombian exhibits from the Andean region and has good explanations of prehispanic history, in Spanish. Open Tuesday-Friday 0800-1200 and 1400-1800, weekends 1500-1900. Nearby, on the plaza, is **Casa de la Cultura Juan Féliz Sánchez**, which has displays of local handicrafts; open daily 0900-2000, free entry.

Museo de Arte Moderno is in the Centro Cultural Don Tulio Febres Cordero, between Calle 21 and 22 and Avenidas 2 and 3, diagonally opposite

Spoiled for choice

Fancy a spaghetti and trout sundae? What about a garlic and ginger split, or black beans and rice? If you happen to come across the *Heladería Coromoto* in Mérida then these are only a tiny fraction of the 641 ice cream flavours from which you can choose.

The Portuguese-born owner, Manuel Da Silva Oliveira, concocts these fabulous flavours using only natural ingredients and his wild culinary imagination knows no limits. Among the exotic and eccentric ices that tourists love to lick are Miss Universe, Polar Malta, *South American Handbook* (though most would argue that it cannot be licked) and, appropriately, Guinness, for Manuel's tasty tally has earned him a coveted place in the *Guinness Book of Records*.

It all began many years ago when a friend suggested that Manuel might try selling ice cream, to which he replied that he knew nothing about it. All that changed soon after when Manuel experimented with avocado flavour, and 50 kilos of the stuff later, he had perfected the recipe. Things mushroomed from there. Now, there are so many to choose from that an entire wall is taken up with the list of flavours, though in any one day only around 150 of the most popular are actually on offer.

Plaza Bolívar. Also check here for cultural events.

Roger Manrique has an impressive butterfly collection (more than 10,000) and is also knowledgeable about Andean wildlife; T 660962 for directions.

LOCAL FESTIVALS

For 2 weeks leading up to Christmas there are daily song contests between local students on Plaza Bolívar, 1700-2200. *Feria del Sol* is held on the week preceding Ash Wednesday, in early February, which is also the peak bullfighting season. On 1-2 January is *Paradura del Niño*; on 15 May, *San Isidro*.

LOCAL INFORMATION

● Accommodation

Hotel prices

L1	over US$200	L2	US$151-200
L3	US$101-150	A1	US$81-100
A2	US$61-80	A3	US$46-60
B	US$31-45	C	US$21-30
D	US$12-20	E	US$7-11
F	US$4-6	G	up to US$3

Those marked with an asterisk (*) are bookable through Fairmont International (see under Caracas).

NB It is difficult to find hotel rooms during the school holidays and the *Feria del Sol*. During the week of 4 December hotels will only let for the whole week. Also note that it's recommended to book higher grade hotels in advance.

B *Belensate*, on the outskirst of town in a small park, T 663722, F 661255, pool, spacious rooms, nice open bar area, Italian and English spoken, recommended; **B** *Chama*, Avenida 4 con Calle 29, T 521011/521224, F 521157, pleasant, restaurant, *Candilejas* disco, guarded car parking, recommended; **B** *El Tisure*, Avenida 4 between Calle 17 and 18, T 521744, F 526061, modern colonial-style building, 34 rooms, very nice but not always hot water, danger of flooding when it rains; **B** *Park Hotel**, Parque Glorias Patrias, T 637014, F 634582, car hire, noisy, good service, good restaurant, recommended; **B** *Pedregosa**, Avenida Panamericana, T 663181, F 664295, on the edge of town, laid out like an Andean village with guests' cottages, pool, restaurant, their *Tops* disco is open later than others, recommended, particularly for families with children, safe, armed guards, National car hire office, horse riding, rowing boats and bicycle rental nearby; **B** pp *Posada La Sevillana*, at the end of the Pedregosa valley, about a 30-minute drive from the centre of town, run by Ilse Gudrun Gasser, 12 colonial-style rooms around central courtyard, price includes breakfast and supper, peaceful, good walking up to the *páramo*, book through Frontino Tours T (074) 520955.

C *Caribay**, Avenida 2 (Lora) Prolongación, T 636451, F 637141, excellent restaurant; **C** *Gran Balcón*, Paseo de las Ferias, T 524056, a few minutes' walk from the *teleférico*, safe; **C** *Mintoy*, Calle 25 (Ayacucho), No 8-130, T 520340, F 526005, 10% discount for cash,

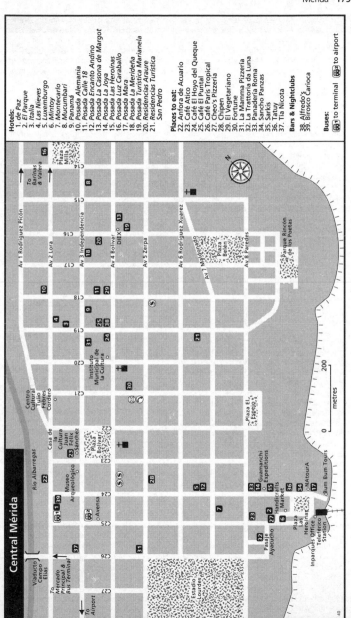

Central Mérida

Hotels:
1. de Paz
2. El Parque
3. Italia
4. Las Nieves
5. Luxemburgo
6. Mintoy
7. Montecarlo
8. Mucumbari
9. Panamá
10. Posada Alemania
11. Posada Calle 18
12. Posada Encanto Andino
13. Posada La Casona de Margot
14. Posada La Joya
15. Posada Las Heroínas
16. Posada Luz Caraballo
17. Posada Mara
18. Posada La Merideña
19. Posada Turística Marianela
20. Residencias Araure
21. Residencias Turística San Pedro

Places to eat:
22. Ánfora de Acuario
23. Café Ático
24. Café El Hoyo del Queque
25. Café El Puntal
26. Café Paris Tropical
27. Cheo's Pizzería
28. Chipen
29. El Vegetariano
30. Fortune
31. La Mamma Pizzería
32. La Trattoria da Luna
33. Panadería Roma
34. Sancho Panzas
35. Sarkis
36. Tatuy
37. Tía Nicota

Bars & Nightclubs
38. Alfredo's
39. Birosco Carioca

Buses:
B1 to terminal   B2 to airport

comfortably furnished, poor breakfast, good value, parking, suites with separate sitting area (sleeps 5), noisy at night from Plaza Las Heroínas nearby, recommended; **C** *Prado Río**, Cruz Verde 1, T 520633, F 525192, good views from the garden, pool, rooms in the main building or individual cabins, recommended.

D *Hispano Turístico*, Avenida 3 Independencia No 27-51, T 528019, comfortable; **D** *La Casona de Margot*, Avenida 4 entre Calle 15 y Calle 16, T/F 523312, with bathroom, hot water, owners both speak English and organize trips, friendly, barbecues in back garden, parking, recommended; **D** *Oviedo*, Avenida 3 No 34-37, T 636944, excellent restaurant.

E *Alemania*, Avenida 2 y Calle 18, T 524067, **F** without bathroom, family atmosphere, nice patio, busy, German owner runs excursions, recommended; **E** *De Paz*, Avenida 2 entre Calle 24 y Calle 25, T 523666, with bathroom, good value, recommended; **E** pp *Dorado*, Avenida 5 No 16-25, entre Calle 16 y 17, T 525187/520731, with bathroom, hot water, restaurant; **E** *Glorias Patrias*, Plaza Glorias Patrias, Avenida 2, No 35-64, T 638113, with bathroom, clean, stores luggage, laundry facilities, very friendly, nice views from the back rooms, recommended; **E** *Las Nieves*, Avenida 2 y Calle 19, hot water, cooking facilities, TV, good, recommended; **E** *Luxemburgo*, Calle 24, between Avenidas 6-7, T 526865, with bathroom, cold water, rooms are available in their annex guesthouse when the hotel is full, safe, recommended; **E** *Montecarlo*, Avenida 7 between Calle 24 and Calle 25, T 526688, safe, parking, hot water, restaurant, ask for a back room with mountain view, recommended; **E** *Posada Doña Pumpa*, Avenida 5 y Calle 14, good showers, spacious rooms, cable TV, quiet, very comfortable, friendly and helpful, owned by English-speaking Juan Carlos Mendoza; **E** *Posada Encanto Andino*, Calle 24 No 6-53, entre Avenidas 6 y 7, T/F 526929, cheaper without bathroom, fully-equipped kitchen, communal sitting area, cable TV, very friendly and helpful, highly recommended; **E** *Posada La Merideña*, Avenida 3 No 16-39 entre Calle 16 y 17, T 525738, F 520647, with bathroom, hot water, inner rooms noisy, washing machine; **E** *Posada Luz Caraballo*, Avenida 2 No 13-80, opposite La Plaza de Milla, T 525441, excellent cheap restaurant, good bar, 40 rooms with bathroom, hot water, colonial style old building, recommended; **E** *Posada Turística Marianela*, Calle 16 entre Avenida 4 y 5, T 526907, hot showers, breakfast available, terrace, laundry and kitchen, owner Marianela speaks English and is helpful, often full.

F *Italia*, Calle 19 between Avenidas 2 and 3, with bathroom, **G** pp in smaller rooms without bathroom, hot water, laundry facilities, front rooms are noisy, post box, has its own travel agency next door, speak English and French, changes dollars, mixed reports but generally recommended as good value; **F** pp *Panamá*, Avenida 3 entre 18 y 19, hot water, with bathroom, popular with students and backpackers, changes dollars and travellers' cheques; **F** pp *Posada Calle 18*, Calle 18 entre Avenidas 3 y 4, rooms for 3 or 4, shared bath, hot water 24 hours a day, cooking facilities, laundry, salsa lessons (not included), nice and clean, friendly, recommended; **F** pp *Posada Mucumbari*, Avenida 3 entre Calle 14 y 15, T 526015, German, French and English spoken, shared bathroom, hot water 24 hours, nice and very clean, laundry, breakfast and snack bar, has its own travel agency *Cacao Expediciones*, highly recommended; **F** *Residencial de Rafael Cuevas*, Avenida 8 entre Calle 20 y 21, No 20-49, helpful, recommended; **F** pp *Residencias San Pedro*, Calle 19, No 6-36, entre Avenidas 6 y 7, T 522735, family run, fully equipped, cheaper without bathroom, hot water, laundry facilities, kitchen, luggage store, highly recommended; **F-G** pp *Posada El Rincón de las Poetas*, Pasaje María Simona No 8-106, Avenida 8 entre Calle 16 y 17, T 523598/524413, shared bathrooms, small and cosy, family atmosphere, washing and cooking facilities, quiet, German spoken.

G pp *Posada Las Heroínas*, Calle 24, No 8-95, Plaza Las Heroínas, T 522665, owners Raquel and Tom Evenou, shared bathrooms, hot water, helpful, popular, safe, stores luggage, use of kitchen, laundry, good atmosphere, parking facilities, highly recommended (see also *Bum Bum Tours* below).

Also on Plaza Las Heroínas: **E** *El Parque*, T 521938, with or without TV; **E** *Planeta Mérida*, opposite Guamanchi Expeditions, basic rooms with or without bath, good; **E-F** *Posada Mara*, with bathroom, pleasant, clean, friendly, will store luggage; **F** *Posada La Joya*, Calle 24 No 8-51, shared bathroom, hot water, Italian owner speaks some English, very helpful, secure, stores luggage, TV, kitchen facilities, great value, recommended, also has mountain huts for rent.

For longer stays: **G** pp *Residencias Araure*, Calle 16 No 3-32, entre Avenidas 3 y 4, T 525103, popular with language students.

Houses for rent: *Finca La Trinitaria*, a beautiful farm with a 3-bedroom colonial house, 10 minutes from the centre of town towards the Hechicera, sleeps 6 in comfort, self-catering, well-furnished and equipped, US$50 per night, contact Ian and Mary Woodward, T/F (074) 440760, e-mail: woodward@ing.ula.ve.

Camping *Gasolina blanca* is sold in *Mérida Gas*, Avenida 4 No 29-47, beside *Hotel Chama*.

● **Places to eat**
Chipen, Avenida 5 entre Calle 24 y Calle 23, good for meat, try their *chateaubriand* – yummy! Even better *chateaubriand* at *Los Pinos*, Avenida Urdaneta just above the airport, "probably the best restaurant in town"; *Tatuy*, Calle 24, No 8-197, Plaza Las Heroínas, good food, try filled trout with seafood; *Zaguán de Milla*, Avenida 2, Calle 13/Calle 14, pizzas cooked over wood-fired stove, very good service; *Chino*, Avenida Los Chorros de Milla, a few hundred metres before the zoo (but don't let that put you off), 15 minutes by bus, excellent Chinese; *Fortune*, Calle 21 entre Avenida 2 y 3, good Chinese food, English and German spoken; *La Taberna de Eugenio*, off Avenida 5 below the viaduct, expensive but recommended; *La Mamma*, Avenida 3 and Calle 19, good pizza, pasta and set lunches, excellent salad bar, popular in the evening, live music at weekends, very cheap local wine; *El Sabor de los Quesos*, Calle 13, Avenida 1-2, very good and cheap pizzeria; *Sancho Panzas*, Plaza Las Heroínas, excellent, cheap, good variety with good service, recommended; *Mesón La Cibeles*, Calle 25 y Avenida 3, good food, well-priced, open until late; *D'Angelos Pizzería*, Edificio El Coronel, Paseo Las Ferias, excellent; *Cheo's Pizzería*, three separate pizza restaurants on Plaza Las Heroínas serving the best pizzas in town; *Café Ático*, Calle 25 near Plaza Las Heroínas, excellent set lunch for US$1.70, highly recommended, get there by 1200. Many places offer student set lunches for US$1-1.50; eg *Juan Arepa*, Calle 20 No 4-35, open 1100-2100; and *Los Corales*, Avenida 4 y Calle 16.

El Puntal, Calle 19, entre Avenidas 3 y 4, part of Centro Comercial La Glorieta, good cakes and coffee, Arabian food, falafel recommended; *Sarkis*, Calle 26 y Avenida 5, Arabic, vegetarian, falafel etc, recommended; *El Palacio*, Calle 23 entre Avenida 4 y 5, good *batidos*, cheap set meal, friendly Lebanese owner speaks French; *Café París Tropical*, on Boulevard de los Pintores, near Plaza Bolívar, good service, cheap, highly recommended for sandwiches and fruit drinks, very popular but closes at 1800; *Café Gala*, in Centro Comercial at Avenida 2 y Calle 26, good coffee, cakes, breakfasts, dinner, excellent salads, reasonable prices, German and US magazines, Finnish owner; *Tía Nicota*, Avenida 3 entre Calle 25 y 26, Galería 1890, recommended for coffee, pancakes, pies; *Romana*, Avenida 5 y Calle 19, set lunch for US$1.25, also Italian food; *Panadería Roma*, Avenida 8 y Calle 24, recommended

for breakfast; *Café Makedonia*, Centro Comercial San Antonio on Avenida Andrés Bello, offers authentic Macedonian food from 1600 onwards. The best and cheapest breakfasts are available on the 3rd floor of the Mercado Principal.

Those who love *arepas* (and who doesn't) should try *Arepería Andina*, Avenida 5 entre Calle 21 y 22, lots of fillings, US$0.40 each. Fast food junkies should try the very popular burger and hot dog stand on Avenida 4 y Calle 30, conveniently opposite the *licorería*; while caffeine addicts would be advised not to miss *Café 1001*, Avenida 3, below Plaza Bolívar, T 527325, which has 30 types of coffee, US$0.20-75.

Vegetarian restaurants: *Madhkarma*, Avenida 4 con Calle 14, excellent Indian food, set lunch for US$1.50, also à la carte; *Fonda Vegetariana*, Calle 29 y Avenida 4, recommended; *Anfora de Acuario*, Avenida 2, Calle 24 and Calle 23, good set lunches; *El Vegetariano*, Avenida 4 y Calle 18, set lunch US$1.40, good service, recommended; *El Rincon de la Sabila*, Avenida 4 entre Calle 18 y 19, at the entrance to Alfredo's, sells excellent *empanadas* (US$0.30), also cakes, drinks, falafel and natural medicines.

● **Banks & money changers**
Note that most banks will not change cash dollars. Some shops advertise that they change dollars, or you could try travel agencies. Cash is generally less welcome than travellers' cheques and rates are poor.

Banco Unión, Avenida 4, Calle 23 y 24, cash advance on Visa and Mastercard; **Corp Banca**, Avenida Las Américas, one block up from the Mercado Principal, this is the only bank for Amex travellers' cheques and charges no commission, cash withdrawal with Amex card and may change cash dollars if you insist; **Banco Mercantil**, Avenida 5 y Calle 15, ATM takes Cirrus, with lower commission than Visa, they also change Thomas Cook travellers' cheques. Italcambio, at the airport, is often the quickest place to change cash or travellers' cheques. Open daily and doesn't close for lunch.

● **Embassies & consulates**
Colombian, in Centro Comercial San Antonio, Avenida Andrés Bello y Calle 25, T 662059, open 0800-1400, visas take 10 minutes. **British**, Professor Robert Kirby, Honorary Vice-Consul, Pedregosa Media, Conjunto Residencial Las Ardillas 2a, Transversal Calle Las Dantas, Parcela 20-A, T/F 712479, he can replace stolen passports, which are sent from Caracas and cost US$30 plus US$9.50 postage, this takes a few weeks, he can be difficult to get hold of as he works at the University.

● **Entertainment**

Cinemas: the best is *Cinemax Viaducto*, in Centro Comercial Viaducto, 2nd floor, at the first viaduct on Avenida Las Américas, 4 screens showing films in the original language with Spanish subtitles. Also good is *Multicine Tibisay*, on Avenida La Universidad after the Charlie Chaplin statue heading out of town, 2 screens with films dubbed into Spanish; also showing dubbed films in the cinema on the 3rd floor of Centro Comercial Las Tapias.

Bars & Nightclubs: *La Basura*, Comercial Alto Chama on the road to Parroquía; *Tops*, in *Hotel Pedregosa* (see above), is very popular, small cover chargel; *La Cucaracha*, in Centro Comercial Las Tapias (a taxi there costs US$2), open till 0600; *Birosca Carioca*, Avenida 2 y Calle 24, popular, with live music; *Universidad de la Caña* (UDLL), Avenida 4 y Calle 18, studenty crowd. There is usually no cover charge for nightclubs but always take your passport or a copy. The best-known bar is *Alfredo's*, Calle 19 y Avenida 4, very popular with locals and travellers, a good meeting place.

● **Hospitals & medical services**

Doctor: *Dra María Yuraima C de Kirby* at *Clínica Médica*, Calle 22 (opposite the Cultural Centre), T 521859, speaks English and is recommended. *Centro Clínico*, Calle Tulipán, off Avenida Urdaneta, opposite the airport, good for all kinds of specialists, best in the afternoon.

● **Language schools**

Iowa Institute, Avenida 4 y Calle 18, T 526404, run by Cathy Jensen de Sánchez, US$85 for 20 hours, US$150 for 25 hours, recommended, Website: http://www.ing.ula.ve/~iowainst/; e-mail: iowainst@ing.ula.ve., also contact Christy Mantle, 615 Antelope Creek Road, Wheatland, Wyoming 82201, T/F 307-322-5799. *Insituto Latinoamericano de Idiomas*, CC Mamayeya, 4th floor, oficina C-5-38, Avenida Las Américas, T/F 447808, director is Carmen Hortensia Montilla P, skilled teachers and good atmosphere, accommodation in private homes, recommended. Contact Marinés Asprino, Conjunto Residencial Andrés Bello, Torre Calle, 5th floor, Apartado 6-1, T 711209 for private lessons and cheap accommodation recommended. Other recommended private tutors are: *María Eugenia Olívar*, Avenida 2 con Calle 19, Edificio Chiquinquirá No 19-11 Apartado 3, T 520845, US$4 per hour; *Nora Garcé*, Apartado 9, Edificio Tevere, Avenida 5 No 16-72, CC 17; *Carolina Tenías*, ask for her in *Alfredo's* or F 215358/528504. Many tutors place ads in *posadas* and bars.

● **Laundry**

Lavandería Estudiante, Avenida 2, near Plaza de Milla, quick service; also laundry service at Calle 15 entre Avenidas 4 y 5, with café.

● **Post & telecommunications**

Post: Ipostel, Calle 21 entre Avenidas 4 y 5, 0800-1900 daily; There's also a Post Office at the bus terminal, 0800-1200, 1400-1700, weekdays only. A good courier service is *MRW*, at Avenida 8 CC 26, T 525666. Western Union is part of *Zoom International Services*, T 639965.

Telephone, fax & e-mail: CANTV, Calle 21 y Avenida 4, Monday-Saturday 0800-1930. E-mail service at the computer shop in Centro Comercial Canta Claro on Avenida Las Américas, opposite the bus terminal; you can open an account here to send e-mail through Telcel, US$6 per month for a minimum of 6 months. A recommended fax and computer service is at *Las Flores*, Centro Comercial Las Pirámides local 12, Avenida 2 CC 18, T/F 528504, very friendly, a bit more expensive than CANTV but worth it; they'll even call your hotel to let you know there's a fax waiting.

● **Security**

Mérida may seem a safe place, but theft and robbery does occur. You should avoid the Pueblo Nuevo area by the river at the foot of the stairs leading down from Avenida 2, as well as Avenida 2 itself and Viaducto Miranda. Also it's best not to leave *Alfredo's* or *Birosca Carioca* at night drunk and alone.

The police are reported as unhelpful if you need to register a theft report for insurance purposes or to get a new passport. A better bet is to go to the *Cuerpo Técnico de Policia Judicial* (PTJ), who will provide a *constancia* reporting the crime and listing the losses. Their office is on Avenida Las Américas, just below the Mercado Principal. It's open daily but they won't issue a *constancia* on a Sunday. To get there, take any bus marked 'Terminal Sur' or 'Mercado' leaving from Calle 25. You can also get a *constancia* from the *Prefectura Civil del Municipio Libertador*, but it can take all day and it is only valid for a limited period of time. Their office is at Avenida 4 No 21-69, just off Plaza Bolívar; opening hours are variable.

● **Shopping**

There's a small handicraft market on Plaza Las Heroínas, opposite the *teleférico*, which has an interesting selection of shops and a good café. The market on Calle 26 near Avenida T Febres Cordero has expensive but beautiful and unusual jewellery. The **Mercado Principal**, on Avenida las Americas (buses for bus station pass by), is a huge building containing many small shops. It's good for souvenirs as well as fruit and vegetables (bargaining possible), and the top floor restaurant serves *comida típica*. A good record shop is *Discoteca Internacional*, Avenida 3, Edificio Trujillo. The up-market Centro Comercial *Las Tapias* has shops, a disco, a multiplex cinema (see above), it's 1½ km southwest of the airport on Avenida Andrés Bello, opposite the Jardín Acuario. Less salubrious but cheaper is the Centro Comercial *Viaducto*, Avenida Las Américas at Viaducto 26.

Bookshops: *Libros Usados*, J Santos, Avenida 6, 21-43, very good prices, including some second-hand English, German and French books. *Librería Universidad*, Avenida 3 Calle 29/30, superb. Next to the *Centro Cultural Juan Félix Sánchez* is *Librería Kuai-Mare*, which is good for cultural and educational stuff.

Films: 1-day service, *CA*, Calle 23 between 5 y 6, T 527981. *Kodak*, on Plaza Bolívar, recommended for good colours on prints, US$0.33 each, 1-hour service, slides developed in 2-3 days, good selection of films; *Profot*, Avenida 3, Calle 25, best for Fuji film, good colour quality for prints.

Hairdressers: *Jesgret Alta Peluquería*, Paseo Artesanal, La Glorieta, Calle 19, opposite the Tabay *por puesto* stop, run by José Gregorio, good, US$1.20 for a haircut.

● **Tour companies & travel agents**

Bum Bum Tours, Calle 24, No 8-301, T/F 525879, e-mail: raquele@bolivar.funmrd. gov.ve; owned by Tom and Raquel (and Janik) from *Posada Las Heroínas*, English, French and German spoken, tours with great guides, fair prices, very helpful and hospitable, highly recommended for Los Nevados, trekking and climbing in the Sierra Nevada, horse riding, mountain biking, river rafting and sandboarding; they also offer a book exchange and sell the best jam in the world; English-speaking guide Alan Highton is highly recommended for the tours of the Llanos and the Río Catatumbo.

NAtourA, Calle 24, No 8-237 (beside the teleférico), T/F 524075/524216, e-mail: natoura@tel-cel.net.ve, website: http://www. natoura.com; open Monday-Sunday 0830-1900, highly recommended for tours on foot or by car, climbing, trekking, hang-gliding, horse riding, mountain biking, fishing, birdwatching, 4WD hire with guide and driver, equipment hire, and trips in Barinas state, small, friendly company run by José Luis Troconis and Renate Reiners, English, French, German and Italian spoken.

Guamanchi Tours (owned by John Peña), Calle 24, No 8-39, T/F 522080, e-mail: geca@bolivar.funmrd.gov.ve; website: http://www.ftech.

net/~geca, recommended for hiking, paragliding, horse riding, biking, equipment hire, exchange, information, mountain climbing, tours to the Llanos, Amazonas and Angel Falls. *Montaña Adventure*, Edificio Las Américas, ground floor, Avenida Las Américas, Mérida, T/F 661448, Apartado Postal 645, also at the airport; ask for Gustavo García-Quintana, who is an excellent guide, especially in the Andes, he offers climbing holidays, horseriding, birdwatching, hang-gliding, mountain biking, trout fishing, trips elsewhere in Venezuela, English-speaking guides.

For jeep tours in the Sierra Nevada and elsewhere, the following are recommended: Ponciano Dugarte Sánchez, T 665096/528416, Spanish only spoken; Lucio, T 528416, and Nicolas Saavedra, T 712618.

For more detailed information on tours and activities on offer, and for equipment hire, repair etc see under **Climbing & trekking** in the **Adventure Tourism** section on page 16.

● **Tourist offices**
Centro de Información Turística Norte, between Avenidas Próceres and Universidad (next to the Charlie Chaplin Statue), T 441076, low season 0800-1200, 1400-1800, high season 0800-1800, closed Sunday, supply a useful map of the state and town. Also at the airport, in the waiting lounge, T 639330, they are very informative, and operate the same low season hours, 0730-1330 in high season; in the bus terminal, T 633952, same hours as Centro Norte, have a free map of the city. **Centro de Información Acuario**, Avenida Andrés Bello, T 633117, low season 0800-1200, 1400-1800, high season 0830-1830.

Inparques (National Parks) office is at Calle 19 entre Avenida 5 y 6, T 528785, and at the ground station for the *teleférico* (for permits). Both offices sell a mediocre map of the Sierra Nevada national park for US$1.50.

● **Useful addresses**
Immigration Office: DIEX, Avenida 4 y Calle 16; they cannot issue a new *ingreso de tarjeta*, you need to go to Caracas.

● **Transport**
Local Car hire: there are several companies at the airport, including *Mérida Rent a Car*, T 630722, ask for José Félix Rangel; or *Dávila Tours*, Avenida Los Próceres opposite Urbanización la Trinidad, T 660711, or at the airport T 634510. **Taxis**: in town about US$1; from the bus terminal to the centre of town US$1.50. A

recommended company is **Línea Tibisay**, outside the Park Hotel, T 637930. A tour of local sites by taxi costs around US$25 per day per car.

Air The airport is on the main highway; a *por puesto* into town costs US$0.10, taxi US$1.50. *Por puestos* to the airport leave from Calle 25 entre Avenidas 3 y 4, marked 'Avenida Urdaneta', check with the driver that he's going past the airport. There is a *casa de cambio* (see **Banks & money changers** above) and a good little restaurant and bar. Airport tax is US$1. Watch out for unofficial tour guides touting for business.

Daily flights: to **Caracas** (1 hour direct), at least 7 flights a day with Avensa, Servivensa, Air Venezuela and LAI; **San Antonio**, 1 flight daily (25 minutes); **Maracaibo**, 4 daily with Air Venezuela, Bárbara and Oriental de Aviación; to **Cumaná**, 1 daily except Saturday with Air Venezuela. Air Venezuela also fly to **Maturín**, daily except Saturday and Sunday; and daily to **Porlamar**. Also to/from Aruba. In the rainy season, especially on afternoon flights, flights may be diverted to San Antonio, 3-5 hours away by road, or El Vigía, 1 hour away. It is advised to check in the day before your flight with Avensa or Servivensa; this will secure your seat and save a lot of time, as check in and baggage queues are separate. The Avensa office is at Calle 25, Avenida 3-4, T 522244, open Monday-Friday 0800-1200, 1500-1800. See also **Information for travellers**, page 334. An airpass for Colombia is available at NatourA (see above), costing US$45 per flight and valid for 3 months.

Buses The bus terminal is about 3 km from the centre of town on the west side of the valley, connected by a frequent minibus service from Calle 25 entre Avenidas 2 y 3. There's a good tourist information office, which will book hotels and has free maps. To call a taxi ring the bell on the left just outside the entrance as you leave. A small exit tax of US$0.10 is charged at the information desk; make sure you pay as officials check buses before departure. On interstate buses, it is essential to book in advance. For buses within the state you pay on board. Those hitchhiking east from Mérida should take a minibus to Tabay (US$0.45) and try from there.

Bus companies: Expresos Occidente, daily direct to Caracas at 0830, US$12.50, 12 hours; via Valencia and Maracay at 0800, US$11; to Coro/Punto Fijo at 0700, US$11, 12-14 hours. **Expresos San Cristóbal** (T 631881), daily direct to Caracas at 1930, 12 hours, via Valencia and Maracay at 1700, 2030; to Maracaibo, at 1930, 8 hours, US$5-7. **Expresos Mérida** (T 633430/639918), to Caracas hourly from 1800, some direct, others via Valencia and Maracay (US$9, 10-11 hours); also to Barquisimeto (US$7, 8 hours), Maracaibo and Punto Fijo. **Transportes Barinas** (T 634651), 4 daily to Barinas via Santo Domingo, US$2.50, 5 hours;

3 to Valera, US$2.60, 5 hours. **Expresos Unidos** (T 631592), to San Cristóbal (US$5, 6 hours), direct to San Antonio at 0300. **Expresos Los Llanos** (T 655927), to Caracas at 1900; to San Fernando, via Valencia and San Juan, at 2045, 18 hours, US$17.70.

Local *por puestos* leave from the upper level of the terminal to: Jají (US$0.85, 1 hour), Chiguará, Apartaderos (US$2.50), Mucuchíes (US$0.75, 1½ hours), Barinas (US$4, 4 hours), Maracaibo (US$10), Barquisimeto, Caracas, El Vigía (1 hour, US$3), San Cristóbal (US$7), Valera (US$5.45, 4 hours).

SIERRA NEVADA NATIONAL PARK

In the heart of the Venezuelan Andes is the 276,446 hectares of the **Sierra Nevada National Park**, the second National Park created in the country, in 1952. The park contains the highest peaks in Venezuela: **Pico Bolívar** (5,007m), **Pico Humboldt** (4,920m), **Bonpland** (4,942m), **La Concha** (4,920m), **El Toro** (4,755m) and **El León** (4,740m).

The park covers a vast area south of the Mérida to **Santo Domingo** road, across the Andes and down to the fringes of the huge plains of the Llanos. Most of the park lies within the state of Barinas, but it is best approached from the Mérida side. It protects the mountain ranges of the Sierra Nevada de Mérida and Serranía de Santo Domingo. This landscape of deep, narrow valleys and glacial lakes is exceptionally beautiful and ideal for excursions and mountain sports (see the **Adventure Tourism** section on page 16).

With altitudes ranging from 600m up to 5,000m, the park's flora and fauna is rich and varied, from tropical wet forests on the foothills up to the high *páramo*, where you can see the legendary *frailejón* plant (see page 190). The park is the last refuge of two of Venezuela's most threatened species, the condor and spectacled bear. It is also home to the puma, jaguar, fox, red howler monkey, squirrel, opossum, brocket deer, Andean paca, raccoon and porcupine. Among the long list of birds on view are the speckled teal, black and chestnut eagle, Andean snipe, white-capped parrot, bearded helmet crest and yellow-billed toucanet.

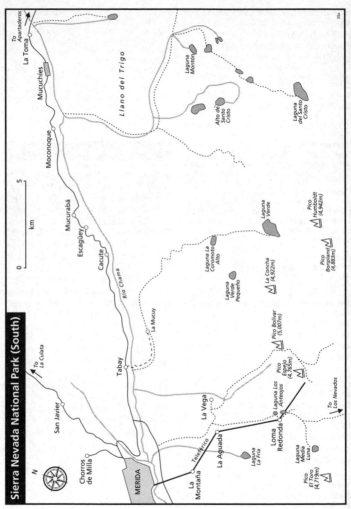

Sierra Nevada National Park (South)

The two most popular routes into the Sierra Nevada National Park are: via the *teleférico* or by jeep to **Los Nevados** (see below); and via the entrance at **Laguna Mucubají** (see page 189).

Park information

Because this is a national park, you need a permit to hike or climb in the Sierra Nevada and camp overnight. It must be obtained from the Inparques (National Parks) office in Mérida (see above). Permits are not given to single hikers; a minimum of 2 people is required. The exception is the hike to Los Nevados. A permit costs US$0.20 per person per day; have your passport available and return the permit after your hike.

For all the information on weather conditions, mountain guides, equipment hire and routes see the **Adventure Tourism** section at the beginning of the book, page 16. For details on how to avoid, or deal with, the effects of altitude see **Health in Latin America**, on page 361.

MERIDA TO LOS NEVADOS

One of the most popular excursions from Mérida is to the tiny village of **Los Nevados**, which lies along the southern border of the National Park, at 2,711m. The most commonly-used transport there is cable car (*teleférico*), though jeeps also make the trip (see below).

Via the teleférico

The world's highest (4,765m) and longest (12½ km) cable car – known as the *teleférico* – runs all the way from Mérida to **Pico Espejo** in four stages. It leaves from the **Barinitas** station on Plaza Las Heroínas and goes to **La Montaña** station, at 2,442m. From there it continues up to **La Aguada** station, at 3,452m, then **Loma Redonda**, at 4,045m, and finally on to the final station, **Pico Espejo**, at a breathtaking 4,765m. This magnificent feat of engineering was built by the French in 1958, but in November 1991 a cable snapped on the final section, killing two workers. Since then it has been running only to the penultimate station, Loma Redonda, but plans are afoot to open the last section by mid to late 1998. **NB** At the time of writing, questions were being raised regarding levels of safety and maintenance on the sections that are open. Seek advice from tour companies in Mérida.

A one way or return trip costs US$15.65; it's about an hour from the Barinitas ground station up to Pico Espejo. In the high season it runs daily and during the low season it is closed Monday and Tuesday. During holiday periods it's a good idea to book in advance as queuing can take several hours.

By jeep

An alternative to the *teleférico* is to take a jeep as far as Los Nevados. Jeeps depart for Los Nevados at 0700 from Plaza Las Heroínas in Mérida. They return from Los Nevados to Mérida in the late afternoon. The journey takes 4-6 hours and costs US$20-25 per person. **NB** The jeep trail is treacherous; do not attempt it on your own. Check first with recommended tour companies in Mérida; they have experienced drivers who know the route well.

LOMA REDONDA TO LOS NEVADOS

The most popular hike around Merida is the 14 km hike from the Loma Redonda station to Los Nevados. The 5-7 hour hike is not difficult and the views are breathtaking. The paths are clear, wide and marked so there's little chance of getting lost. Be prepared for cold rain in the afternoon, and start very early. Mules can be hired at Loma Redonda for US$4 but are not necessary (better to use them on the way back as the going is a lot harder).

From Loma Redonda walk up to the Alto de La Cruz pass at 4,200m. Then it's downhill for 12 km. There is one turn to the left about half way down, take it and you get to Los Nevados.

LOS NEVADOS

This 'typical Andean village' is very picturesque, but is in danger of becoming more of an Andean theme village, as everyone tries to cash in on the tourist boom. There are about 8 or 9 *posadas* all charging US$5-12 per person for the night, with dinner and breakfast included.

● **Accommodation** The following have been recommended: **E** pp *Posada Bella Vista*, behind the church, run by the Sánchez family, price includes breakfast and dinner, great views, even some hot water; **F** pp *Posada del Buen Jesús*, run by the *casa del montañista*, pioneers of climbing in the Sierra Nevada, good value; **F** pp *Florencia*; **F** pp; *Posada Guamanchi*, owned by travel agency of same name in Mérida, solar power, great views. For delicious wheat arepas ask Josephina whose house is just behind the plaza. She also hires mules and *arrieros*.

You can hike back the same way you came or take a mule back up to the station; all the *posadas* will arrange food and mules.

LOMA REDONDA TO MERIDA

You can walk down from **Loma Redonda** to **La Aguada** station (3,452m) in about 2 hours on a rough path. You need hiking boots and should walk slowly; take water. This is not recommended for children or the elderly. *Posadas* at La Aguada charge US$4 for dinner, bed and breakfast. At La Aguada station you can see the *frailejón* plant and throughout the area there is a great variety and quantity of flora.

From La Aguada you can walk to the main road to Mérida in 3-5 hours and catch a *por puesto* to town. It is a 30-minute walk from La Aguada to Los Calderones' farm, where there is accommodation and horses for hire. From La Aguada to the next station down, **La Montaña** (2,442m), it's a lovely 2½ hours walk descending from *páramo*, through cloud forest and passing waterfalls. From La Montaña, the penultimate station on the way down, it's a 2½-3½ hour walk to Mérida.

LOS NEVADOS TO EL MORRO

An alternative to returning to Loma Redonda is to continue to the village of **El Morro**, which actually lies outside the National Park boundary. The 24 km walk from Los Nevados to El Morro takes 7-9 hours and is very steep in parts, particularly the last few kilometres. It's worth hiring a mule for your backpack. Make sure you take your own food and drink as there's only one *bodega* selling cold drinks en route (about halfway). In El Morro Sr Oliver Ruiz provides information on the history of the church and Indian cemetery.

● **Accommodation In El Morro**: *Posada Abel Gámez*, run by Adriana Dugarte, meals, recommended; *Posada Doña Chepa*, is on the right as you enter the village from Los Nevados, very friendly and welcoming, good meals, highly recommended; **F** pp *Posada El Oregano*, including meals, basic, friendly, good food, recommended; **G** *Hospedaje Nerios*, meals, recommended. Also *Posada Casa Vieja*, on the plaza, run by Henry, a park warden who knows the area very well, recommended. There are no restaurants in the village but several stores sell basic provisions.

Those with less stamina and more money can hire a 4WD in Los Nevados to return to Mérida via El Morro and **Ejido**. The jeeps charge US$50 per vehicle for the 4-6 hour drive back to Mérida. From El Morro it's 47 km to Mérida on a mostly paved road; jeeps do this route daily.

Instead of returning to Mérida from El Morro, you can carry on to **Acequias** and the **Pueblos del Sur** (see page 200). From there a road joins the Transandean Highway west of **Ejido**, thus completing the circuit.

MERIDA TO APARTADEROS

The Sierra Nevada National Park continues northeast from Mérida. Its northern border follows the Río Chama valley as it climbs dramatically from Mérida up to Apartaderos, rising 1,850m in only 62 km. The road also shadows the Río Chama, passing through some lovely little Andean towns and villages on the 2 hour journey. This is the heart of the cultivated highlands, with the fields extending right up to the edge of the *páramo*.

Even the most precipitous slopes are farmed, using stone terraces called *andenes*. These stones, pulled from the soil to make the land tillable, were also piled up into walls and enclosures. Some of the walls near Apartaderos (see below) date back to the Timoto-Cuica Indians and are still called *poyos*, their original name. The apparent rural idyll, however, belies the poverty and harsh life of the Andean people, which is why the road is always lined with children selling fruit and vegetables, flowers, souvenirs and the famous *mucuchíes* puppies.

Between Mérida and Apartaderos most of the towns are roughly 14 km apart from each other. This is because they began as overnight mule stops, and this was the average distance that could be covered in a day across such steep terrain. Another feature of this stretch of road is the number of place names with the prefix *mucu*, which means 'place of' in the local indigenous tongue. Many hotels, restaurants and *artesanía* shops have sprung up along the main highway to take advantage of the passing tourist trade, for this is an area definitely worth a few days of exploring.

THE MUCUJUN VALLEY

The road east from Mérida winds its way through lush tropical forest draped in Spanish Moss down to the Río Mucujún. Before it crosses the river, a side road branches north up the beautiful Mucujún valley to **San Javier** and **El Valle**, ending at **La Culata**. Thereafter a stony track leads up to the head of the valley and beyond, crossing the watersheds. You can go around the locked gate marked 'propiedad privada' after about 1 km.

● **Accommodation & places to eat In the valley**: **D** *Valle Grande*, T 443011, 10 km from Mérida, in a lovely setting, expensive restaurant. Further on up this road is **B** *La Culata*, T (074) 523915/526128, Cellular (014) 740340, F 638802, 24 km from Mérida, a rather gaudy, up-market retreat in a magnificent setting. There are lots of snack stops and marmalade/preserves shops along the way to La Culata; at the start of the road is *Catalina Delicatessen* (see also below).

● **Transport** It's an easy trip by *buseta* from Calle 19, entre Avenidas 1 y 2; US$0.30, 30 minutes. Ask for La Culata as some *busetas* stop short.

SIERRA DE LA CULATA NATIONAL PARK

The town of La Culata is the main access point for the **Sierra de La Culata** which lies within the bounds of the eponymous 200,400 hectare National Park. The park runs almost parallel to the Sierra Nevada de Mérida, rising from 400m up to the highest point, the **Páramo de Piedras Blancas** (White Rocks), at 4,737m, so named because of the movable soils which resemble white rocks. The park's vegetation incorporates subtropical cloudforest, mountain cloudforest and Andean *páramo*.

The route into the park follows the Mucujún Valley through very beautiful mountain scenery, and is a bit like entering some huge natural temple. There are marked trails throughout the park, leading up to the highest points. For more detailed information on routes, weather conditions, guides and equipment see the **Adventure Tourism** section (page 16). For guided excursions into the park, in particular the highly recommended 3-day trip to Pico Pan de Azucar, or hire of equipment, see **Tour companies** in Mérida (page 179).

TABAY

10 km east of Mérida on the main highway is **Tabay**, best known for its **Aguas Calientes** (or Termales). To get there, you turn left just before the cemetery at the end of the town and walk up for some 30 to 45 minutes. At first you'll be walking on a small path, then you join the road again. Keep on walking uphill and about 300m above the place where you got to the road, turn right and walk for less than 5 minutes. There are two small pools in a stream, warm and lukewarm. You need to pay US$1, and don't forget your swimsuit and towel. New cabins have been built and should be open by early 1998.

● **Accommodation** 1½ km from the plaza on the Mérida road is **D-E** *La Casona de Tabay*, T (074) 830089, a beautiful colonial-style hotel, surrounded by mountains, comfortable, home cooking, family-run, highly recommended, take a *por puesto* from the town, the hotel is well signposted; **D-E** *Posada Turística Tabay*, Avenida Bolívar y Calle Santos, on the main plaza, T (074) 830025, F 830121, nice; **G** pp *Posada de la Mano Poderosa*, dormitory rooms, lovely, quiet, hot showers, good food, great value, get off at La Plazuela then walk for 15 minutes towards Vivero Tutti Flor.

● **Places to eat** *El Morichal*, 50m from plaza, good, cheap.

● **Transport** A regular *por puesto* service runs from Mérida, Calle 19 entre Avenidas 3 y 4 (30 minutes). Gasoline is available in Tabay.

Excursions from Tabay

From the Plaza Bolívar in Tabay a jeep can be taken for the 25 minute ride up to the cloud forest at **La Mucuy**. It's a beautiful 6-hour walk from here up to **Laguna Coromoto**. At the park entrance is a *dormitorio* for groups of up to 20; US$1 per person, book through Inparques in Mérida. You can also camp here.

This is where serious hikers and climbers start their ascent of **Pico Humboldt** and **Pico Bolívar**. The climb takes 4 to 6 days. For either peak, or the travesia, you need to be in very good physical condition, be well prepared and fully

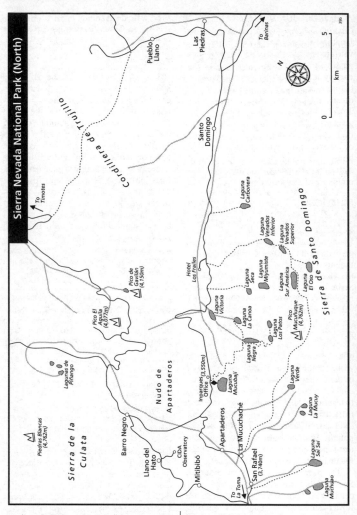

equipped. Remember that just a couple of kilometers walking will take you from tropical surroundings to Arctic conditions. For both peaks a guide is recommended; see **Tour companies** in Mérida (page 179) and the **Adventure Tourism** section (page 16).

7 km east of Tabay is **Los Aleros**, a reconstruction of a 1930s town. It's a kind of Andean Disneyland, where the staff wear authentic rustic costume and even the drunks are for real – they're paid by the government! In front of the bus stop is the colonial style restaurant *El Caney*, which is cheap and serves good steak, trout and *arepas andinas*. It is highly recommended, but gets busy at weekends. Entry to Los Aleros is US$5.

A few kilometres before **Cacute** is *Catalina Delicatessen*, which sells fantastic jams and chutneys, with hundreds of flavours to taste; open at 0800. The road then passes through the little villages of **Escagüey** and **Mucurubá**. A few kilometres before Mucurubá a sign on the right indicates the turnoff to *Posada San Ramón*, T 014-740220 (cellular), great kitchen, good meals, nice relaxing courtyard. Further east is **Moconoque**, which consists of a few houses and a trout farm. The house at the entrance to the farm is where Bolívar stayed when he travelled through on his way to Colombia.

MUCUCHÍES

6 km beyond Moconoque is **Mucuchíes** (*population* 9,175; *altitude* 2,980m). Founded in 1596, this long, narrow town gives its name to a local breed of dog. The famous Mucuchíes dogs are derived from the Great Pyrenees dogs imported from Spain to be used as sheep dogs. The unbearably cute puppies are sold by the roadside throughout this part of the Andes. But remember, a dog is for life not just for the holidays.

As if to prove this point, in the town's attractive Plaza Bolívar, sharing a plinth with the ubiquitous Liberator, is a statue of the Indian boy, Tinajaca, and his Mucuchíes dog, Nevado (Snowy). According to legend, the boy and the dog were given to Bolívar when he stopped off here in 1813 during one of his liberation campaigns. Both remained devoted to him until their deaths on the same day at the Battle of Boyacá.

The patron saint of Mucuchíes is San Benito. His festival, on 29 December, is celebrated by participants wearing flower-decorated hats and firing blunderbusses continuously.

● **Accommodation A3** *Castillo de San Ignacio*, a massive and wonderfully incongruous fairy tale castle on the main highway at the north end of town which offers 5-star facilities and services, recommended; **D** *Centro Campesino El Convite*, on Calle Bolívar at the south end of town, T (074) 81163, this is actually a training centre for local farmers to promote sustained development and teach improved methods,

they offer lodging and meals for the farmers, but tourists can also stay here, if they have room, it's quiet and the atmosphere is pleasant, rooms are for 4 sharing with bathroom, the restaurant serves local food, laundry service, **E** in low season; **E** *Los Andes*, an elegant old house on Calle Independencia, the main road through town, T (074) 81151, it has 5 cosy rooms, hot water, shared bathrooms, the excellent restaurant serves delicious trout and closes at 2030, this lovely little hotel can't be recommended highly enough. There are a few other *posadas* in town.

SAN RAFAEL DE MUCUCHÍES

The road from Mucuchíes leads up to **San Rafael de Mucuchíes**, said to be the highest village in Venezuela at 3,140m. Many people stop here on their way to or from Mérida to visit a curious little chapel, pieced together from thousands of stones. It was built by the remarkable Juan Félix Sánchez and his wife Epifania Gil, and completed in 1984, when he was 83 years old. Juan Félix died in 1997 and is now buried in his own chapel.

Below San Rafael is an old flour mill which is still in operation.

Páramo El Tisure

An increasingly popular trip is to El Tisure to visit the original chapel built by Juan Félix Sánchez and Epifania Gil. You can spend the night in their old house, which

The Church of Juan Félix Sánchez
in San Rafael

The architect of the Andes

The chapel in San Rafael is actually a replica of the original, built in the remote Páramo El Tisure by Juan Félix Sánchez and his wife. They also built a simple stone house and lived here for many years, following the death of Juan Félix' mother almost 50 years ago. Only when he became too frail to manage the gruelling trip across the mountains to San Rafael by mule every week did they move to a house in the village.

Known as 'The Architect of the Andes', Juan Félix was revered in Venezuela as a saint. He was even paid a visit by the Pope, when he came to Venezuela in 1985. Despite such impressive credentials, Juan Félix and his wife remained as humble as their little house beside the chapel.

is still looked after by a caretaker. Accommodation is free but you need to take your own food and bedding.

To get to El Tisure take an early morning *por puesto* from the terminal in Mérida to Apartaderos and get out in **La Mucuchaché** (US$1.20, 2 hours), about 5 minutes after passing the stone chapel of San Rafael de Mucuchíes. On your right side you'll see a white cross and a small creek coming down. Follow the trail staying in the same valley and in 3-5 hours you'll reach **La Ventana** pass, at 4,200m. The last hundred metres up to the pass are pretty tough as the path zigzags up a very steep incline. Continue down on the other side into the **Potrero valley** and further down you'll see the house. The chapel of El Tisure is about 20 minutes further on from there. You'll need a minimum of 2 to 3 days to visit El Tisure from Mérida and the walk each way is about 5 to 8 hours. Leave early to avoid bad weather and bring a tent, food and warm sleeping bags.

Alpine influence in the Andes

An alternative to walking is to hire mules or horses in San Rafael for the 6 hour trip. Just look for the signs offering horses or mules for hire.

● **Accommodation & places to eat In San Rafael: E** *Posada El Rosal*, hot water, good. There are a few other *posadas* in the village; eg at Calle Bolívar 3. Further up the street from *El Rosal* Mme Crys Fauvelle Vestrini, a French artist, will provide meals if you book in advance. There are several other restaurants as well.

APARTADEROS

The road continues climbing for a further 12½ km to **Apartaderos** (*population* 2,000; *altitude* 3,473m), which is really just a collection of hotels, Alpine-style chalets and souvenir shops, with little farmsteads scattered across the surrounding countryside. The 'town' stands at the junction of Route 7 to **Timotes** and **Valera** (see page 193) and the road over the Sierra Nevada to **Barinas** (see page 220). The shops and hotels serve the tourist traffic between Mérida, Laguna Mucubají and Santo Domingo. This traffic is particularly busy at weekends and during holidays and at these times the locals are out in force, attempting to supplement their meagre income by selling local produce. It would take a hard heart indeed to refuse one of the round-faced children, cheeks burnt red by the sun, especially when proffering the fat, squirming bundles of fluff they call *mucuchíes* puppies.

Those hard-hearted enough to say 'no' can always opt for the tastier alternative of the fine local cold cured hams, which can be found hanging in the roadside *charcuterías* (delicatessens) throughout the region. The flavour and texture of the ham is similar to Spanish *jamón serrano* and Italian *prosciutto*. Another local speciality well worth trying are the smoked sausages. Those of a vegetarian disposition should not despair, for the *charcuterías* also stock the local white cheese, *queso del páramo*, also available smoked as *queso ahomado*. Other local delicacies include *mantecada*, a sweet bread, *miche*, an anise liqueur mixed with hot spiced milk to make the local drink *calentadito*, and, my own personal favourite, *arepas* made from wheat, which are far superior to the cornmeal ones (though don't try saying this to any lowland Venezuelans or you'll end up in the next filling).

● **Accommodation** B *Parque Turístico*, an attractive modern chalet-style building, heating, very hot showers, helpful owner, the restaurant is expensive but recommended; B *Hotel y Restaurant Mifafi*, good food, beautiful, but no heating; E *Posada Viejo Apartaderos*, with bathroom, clean, friendly, good value, good restaurant with reasonable prices. There are several places to eat, eg *Posada Molineras*.

● **Buses** To Mérida US$1.20. If you're heading to Barinas or Valera, it's best to catch a bus from Mérida as drivers are unlikely to stop.

An old colonial trail, **El Camino Real**, can be walked from Apartaderos to Mucuchíes, taking about 3-4 hours. The path sometimes joins the main road, and passes through small villages. It's very easy to get lost on the trail and asking directions can sometimes lead to even more confusion.

About 1 km before the Barinas-Transandean Highway junction, the road loops around a small hill topped with a statue of **La Loca Luz Caraballo**. This woman, immortalized in a poem by Andrés Eloy Blanco, was driven crazy by grief at the tragic loss of her five sons and wandered the *páramo* until she died.

APARTADEROS TO SANTO DOMINGO

From Apartaderos the road winds up to the junction, where it branches left (north) to **Timotes** and **Valera**, and right (east) to **Santo Domingo**.

SIERRA NEVADA NATIONAL PARK (NORTH)

A few kilometres past the junction, on the road to Santo Domingo, is the entrance to the northern section of the **Sierra Nevada National Park**. The southern part can be approached from Mérida (for details on this and for more park information see page 181).

At the turn-off to the park is a motel, **E**, a shop selling local *artesanía* and a restaurant which serves great coffee and wonderful *arepas*. Buses heading for Mérida from the north or east make a meal stop here. One of the more bizarre experiences is to wake up here, having boarded the bus in the hot tropical lowlands, and stumble out into the freezing cold and dense mountain mist, wondering where on earth you are.

Laguna Mucubají

Near the entrance to the park is Laguna Mucubají, the largest of over 200 glacial lakes in the state of Mérida. The lake sits at 3,600m in the starkly beautiful *páramo*, against the backdrop of the Santo Domingo range. Most of the time, though, the mountains are obscured by the ever-present fog that hangs over the *páramo*, especially during the June to October rainy season. Despite the bleak terrain, birdlife is abundant around the lake and includes the bearded helmetcrest hummingbird.

On the shores of the lake is a free campsite, but be prepared for near-freezing temperatures at night. There's also a visitors' centre, with an interesting interactive explanation of the park's flora and fauna, as well as a coffee shop and bookshop with good maps.

To camp or hike in the park, you'll need a permit from the Inparques office at the entrance. The staff are very helpful.

Hikes from Laguna Mucubají

A recommended 2-3 hour hike from Mucubají is to the enchanting **Laguna Negra**, fed by the snows of **Pico Mucuñuque**, whose glacial waters ultimately flow into the mighty Orinoco. It's best to set off early before the mist descends. Fishing is permitted at the lake and you can camp at the

Park life

🐾 The high *páramos* of the Venezuelan Andes are characterized more than anything else by the legendary *frailejón* (*fraile* means friar). This prolific plant, easily recognized by its curious felt-like leaves of pale grey-green, blooms with yellow flowers from September to December. It can grow up to 2m tall on thick, wood-like stems, giving the mountainsides the appearance of massive football terraces populated by spiky-haired punk rockers.

The *frailejón* not only adorns the *páramo* with its yellow bloom, but some of the 45 species found in Venezuela give off a delicate fragrance. And it doesn't just look and smell good. The leaves can be used for anything from wrapping butter to stuffing mattresses.

far end, where a very steep trail leads up through the forest for 1½ hours to the very beautiful **Laguna Los Patos**. A recent landslide, however, has obscured the trail.

Horses can be hired at Laguna Mucubají; US$5 per person including guide. Guides (not absolutely necessary) can also be found at Laguna Mucubají or at the hotels in Santo Domingo (see below).

● **Transport** Take a bus or *por puesto* from Mérida bound for Barinas and get off at the park entrance; 2 hours, US$2. Most agencies in Mérida offer day tours to the *páramo* including a visit to the lakes; US$25-45 per person. A cheaper option is to rent a taxi for the day, which costs around US$50 for up to 4 people.

Between Laguna Mucubají and Santo Domingo is the former 17th century monastery, **A3** *Hotel Los Frailes★*, at 3,700m, the rooms in this unique hotel are heated and some feature ornate four-poster beds, the restaurant has international menus and expensive wines, but service is reported as poor, the bar is very cosy and appealing with a log fire. Book ahead through Hoturvensa, T (02) 9078054/

9078153, but don't pay in advance as money will not be reimbursed in case of transport problems.

On the other side of the river is the cheaper alternative, **C** *Hotel Paso Real*.

SANTO DOMINGO

The Mérida-Barinas road begins to wind its way down from the *páramo*. Several kilometres beyond the turn-off to *Hotel Los Frailes* it reaches the town of **Santo Domingo** (*population* 3,200; *altitude* 2,180m), perched on a *mesa* above the river of the same name. This is a good place for fishing and for buying handicrafts. If you're heading up from the intense heat of the Llanos you may want to prepare for the cold chill of the Andes by purchasing a *ruana*, a distinctive local woollen poncho, red on one side and blue on the other.

4 km before the town is the **El Baho** trout farm, where visitors can see the various stages of development from the incubator to the restaurant table.

● **Accommodation & places to eat** **B** *Cabañas Halcón de Oro*, individual cabins with fireplaces; cheap rooms are available for rent next door, opposite the *Panadería Santo Domingo*. The beautiful **C** *Moruco★*, T (073) 88155, F 88225, is a little further out, in a lovely setting at 2,300m, good value, food very good, bar expensive, reservations can be made through the *Hotel Río Prado* in Mérida; **D** *La Trucha Azul*, has rooms with open fireplace, but is expensive for what it offers; **D** *Santo Domingo*, 20 minutes from the town centre, log cabins for up to 4 people, log fireplace, games room with pool, table tennis, hot water, excellent restaurant with a good selection of wines but not very good value overall. *Restaurant Brisas de la Sierra* is recommended.

Hotel Los Frailes, Mérida

- **Tourist offices** On the right, leaving town, a 10-minute walk from the centre.
- **Buses** Buses or busetas pass through in either direction at approximately 2-hour intervals through the day. To **Mérida**, 2½ hours, US$2.35 by *por puesto*; to **Barinas**, 1½ hours, US$2.50.

BEYOND SANTO DOMINGO

Several kilometres further on, a road turns off the highway to the left, leading up to **Pueblo Llano**, where there is accommodation in **E** *La Gruta*, good, cheap restaurant, recommended; and *El Campesino*, for good pizza. From Pueblo Llano you can hike across the **Páramo Estrella** to **Timotes** (see below) or head north to **Tuñame** in the state of Trujillo (see page 192).

Before Pueblo Llano, about 2 km from the Mérida-Barinas highway, a road branches off to the village of **Las Piedras**. Nearby, in **Parque Las Piedras** there is a good campsite with shelters, barbecue facilities and good views across the valley. Ask the bus driver to stop at the turn-off and walk from there.

APARTADEROS TO VALERA

The Transandean Highway branches left at Apartaderos and takes you up over the **Pico El Aguila** and down through **Timotes** to **Valera**. From Valera you can continue northwest to **Maracaibo** (see page 157) or northeast to **Barquisimeto** (see page 144).

CIDA ASTROPHYSICAL INSTITUTE

Only 3 km from the Apartaderos turnoff, a narrow paved road (signposted) turns west off the highway at the small one-room schoolhouse 'Escuela Estatal 121'. The road winds its way up through **Llano del Hato**, at 3,510m, the highest place in Venezuela served by road, and on to the 3-domed CIDA *Astrophysical Institute* at 3,600m. On a clear day, the views from the road, across to the Lake Mucubají plateau, are among the most spectacular in all of Venezuela. In fact, the side trip is worth it just for this alone. A further treat lies in store for cyclists, who can freewheel from the institute back down to the village plaza.

It's just over 2 km from the village up to the institute. CIDA's four telescopes and modern facilities are open to visitors daily, 1000-2230, during school holidays, Easter Week, and in August and December. At other times it is open Saturday 1000-2230, Sunday 1000-1630; US$1.75 entry. To confirm opening times, T (074) 712780.

From the village of Llano del Hato a good paved road descends for 7 km to meet the Mérida highway at La Toma, just above Mucuchíes. This route offers fantastic views across to the valleys of Mucuchaché, Michuras and Laguna Verde as well as offering a fascinating close-up of prehispanic terraces and irrigation systems, adobe houses and ox-ploughed fields (*poyos*).

PICO EL AGUILA

The Transandean Highway, meanwhile, continues past the turnoff to Llano del Hato and climbs through the increasingly wild, barren and rugged beauty of the *páramo* up to the windy pass of **Pico El Aguila** (4,007m), the highest roadpass in Venezuela. On a clear day the views are superb and it's not uncommon to see condors flying around. It's best to pass this way early in the morning, as the pass is frequently submerged in low cloud. Fittingly enough, a local expression for dying is *pasar el páramo*, to pass over the *páramo*.

This is the way Bolívar came in 1813 when crossing the Andes from Colombia on his way to liberate Caracas. To commemorate this feat a bronze statue of the '*aguila*' stands on the peak (though the eagle is actually a condor). In the months from May to October snowfall can occur up here and Venezuelans go crazy seeing and touching snow for the first time in their lives.

At the pass is the tourist restaurant *Páramo Aguila*, which is reasonably priced and, more importantly, has an open fire. There are also foodstalls, souvenir sellers and horses for hire. Across from the statue is a small chapel, which looks directly down onto the *Hotel Los Frailes* (see page

190) and across to the watershed of the Chama, Mototán and Santo Domingo rivers.

Those keen on fishing should check out the paved road which leads from the left of the restaurant for 2 km up through crowds of tall *frailejones* to a CANTV microwave tower at 4,118m. Beyond the tower a dirt road turns off from the paved road and goes down towards the remote **Piñango Lakes**, noted for their large trout. The lakes are a further hour's walk from the road. The paved road continues to the tiny village of **Piñango**, at 2,480m, offering great views of high altitude lakes and even as far as Lake Maracaibo. In the village the Aranjo family provides food and lodging and hires horses. From Piñango a rough track leads southeast to join the Transandean Highway just north of Timotes.

The road from Pico El Aguila to Mérida is perfect for cyclists; downhill all the way until Km 718, before Mérida, with lots of *posadas*, hostels and campsites en route. For more details and for a description of the mountain biking route from Pico El Aguila-Piñango-Timotes, see **Adventure Tourism**, page 21.

ROUTES   The road from Pico El Aguila drops a dramatic 2,000m in only 52 km, down through the tiny community of **La Venta**, the village of **Chachopo**, and on past terraced fields before finally reaching **Timotes** in an hour and a half.

TIMOTES

The pleasant town of **Timotes** (*population* 10,550), stands at 2,016m surrounded by lush, forested hills just before the state boundary with Trujillo. The town is named after the Indian tribe which occupied the area for many centuries before the Spanish invasion. It is notable for its unusual church on the Plaza Bolívar and its festival of *San Benito*, held in December in honour of the Black Saint and featuring the traditional maypole dances, the *Giros de San Benito*.

● **Accommodation & transport   C** *Las Truchas*, very nice, good food; **D** *Carabay*, family run, good rooms, excellent restaurant; **E** *Posada Caribe*, good value, restaurant. Bus from Valera, US$1.50.

EXCURSIONS FROM TIMOTES

Just north of Timotes, across the state border into Trujillo, a road branches right (east) to **La Mesa de Esnujaque**, situated at 1,743m on a mesa high above the Río Motatán. Surprisingly for such a small, remote town, there is plentiful accommodation. This is because it's a popular highland resort for *maracuchos* and only a 3-hour drive from Maracaibo.

A dirt road climbs from the town for 5 km up to **Juan Martín** and a further 10 km (3-4 hours driving) up to the *páramo*, where there are two strikingly beautiful lakes, **Laguna de La Estrella** (3,410m) and **Laguna El Chorro** (3,310m). Visit these early in the morning as they are covered by cloud by midday.

● **Accommodation   In La Mesa: B** *Tibisay*; **D** *Miraflores*, with bathroom, hot water, beautiful garden, restaurant, good value.

The charming, unspoiled village of **Jajó** is only 10 km from the Transandean Highway and can be reached from Timotes, or from **Valera** and **Trujillo** (see page 196). From Timotes, turn left off the road which branches off the Transandean Highway to La Mesa. Founded in 1611, Jajó stands at 1,796m among terraced fields and eucalyptus trees and has a real off-the-beaten-track feel. There is accommodation in the village.

From Jajó a jeep track continues to the tiny, remote settlement of **Tuñame**. From there you can hike along a rough track across the *páramo* to **Las Mesitas** and from there down to **Niquitao** (see page 199). Alternatively, another track forks right (south) down to **Pueblo Llano** and from there to **Santo Domingo** (see page 190).

TIMOTES TO VALERA

The highway winds its way down to the fertile valley of the Río Momboy. On the way it bypasses the neat little town of **La Puerta**, where there is accommodation in the rambling, old **C** *Hotel Guadalupe*; as well as **D** *Chiquinquirá*, and **E** *Los Andes*, both on Avenida Bolívar.

The highway continues through the Momboy Valley past fields of sugar cane

Footprint Handbooks

...step inside
a world other travel
guides miss

**Win a 7 night Cuban Highlights Tour
for two courtesy of Hayes and Jarvis**

We want to hear your ideas for further
improvements as well as a few details about
yourself so that we can better serve your needs
as a traveller.

Well established as one of the UK's leading
long haul tour operators Hayes and Jarvis
prides itself on providing good quality, reliable
arrangements at sensible prices for the discerning
traveller. Every reader who sends in the completed
questionnaire will be entered in the Footprint
Prize Draw.

Mr ☐   Mrs ☐   Miss ☐   Ms ☐   Age..........

First name..

Surname...

Permanent Address..

....

....

Postcode/Zip...

Country...

Email...

Occupation...

Title of Handbook..

**Which two destinations would you most
like to visit in the next two years?**

....

....

How did you hear about us?
Recommended ☐   Bookshop   ☐
Used before   ☐   Media/press article ☐
Library   ☐   Internet   ☐

There is a complete list of Footprint
Handbooks at the back of this book.
**Which other countries would you like
to see us cover?**

....

Offer ends 31 May 1999. Prize winners will be
notified by 30 June 1999 and holidays are subject
to availability. Hayes and Jarvis may offer an
alternative tour if the prize is no longer featured
at time of travel.

If you do not wish to receive information from
other reputable businesses, please tick box ☐

for 8 km to the old town of **Mendoza**, birthplace of Colonel Antonio Nicolás Briceño. It was Colonel Briceño who first put into practice the policy of 'War to the Death' which was formally proclaimed later by Bolívar in Trujillo (see page 195).

From Mendoza it's a further 6 km to Valera, through rich sugar-cane country. All around this area you'll find traditional sugar-cane processing factories, called *trapiches*, which are very interesting to visit. The techniques used are little changed from colonial times in the production of *panela*, a solid brown brick which is used locally instead of the more conventional form of sugar to sweeten food and drinks.

VALERA

The hot, commercial centre of **Valera** (*population* 119,400; *altitude* 547m; *phone code* 071) was a bit of a late developer, founded as late as 1820, and only really started to grow with the completion of the Transandean Highway in 1925. It is now the largest and most important town in the State of Trujillo.

Valera is, strangely enough, known as the 'City of the Seven Hills', despite the fact that it's fairly flat. Maybe, though,

the name comes from its strong Italian influence. Even the most fanatical of pizza lovers will find enough restaurants to satisfy their tastes. Other than good Italian food, however, there's little of real interest for those on a tight schedule. If you've time on your hands, it's a pleasant place to stop and explore the hidden delights of the state of Trujillo, and you'll also experience some of the friendliest, wittiest and most welcoming people in the entire country.

Local festivals
The town hosts an agricultural and industrial fair in August.

Local information
● Accommodation
As a commercial centre rather than a tourist one, accommodation tends to focus on the top end, and there are few budget options.

B *Camino Real*, Avenida Independencia, near the bus terminal, T 53795, F 51704, air conditioning, TV, restaurant, bar, parking, high standard of facilities and service; **B-C** *Valera**, Avenida Maya, four blocks from the bus terminal, T 57511, F 57937, including taxes, air conditioning, hot water, TV, restaurant, parking.

D *Albergue Turístico*, Avenida Independencia, near the bus terminal, T 56997; **D** *El Palacio*, Avenida 10 con Calle 12, T 52923/57708.

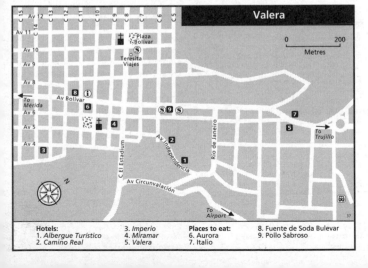

Valera

Hotels:
1. *Albergue Turístico*
2. *Camino Real*
3. *Imperio*
4. *Miramar*
5. *Valera*

Places to eat:
6. Aurora
7. Italio
8. Fuente de Soda Bulevar
9. Pollo Sabroso

E pp *Miramar*, Calle 9 No 5-38, T 316293, with bath, restaurant, clean; **E** *Mocoties*, Avenida 9 entre Calle 7 y 8, with bathroom, looks more or less OK, strange owner; **E-F** pp *Cristol 2*, Calle 11 y Avenida 9, with bathroom, "a bit prison-like but OK for one night"; **E-F** pp *Napoli*, Avenida 9 entre Calle 11 y 12, shared bath.

● **Places to eat**

There are lots of Italian restaurants, eg *Aurora*, Avenida Bolívar between Calle 9 and 10, good, lunch for under US$2, open 0700-0100; *Italio* opposite *Hotel Valera*, recommended; *Fuente de Soda Bulevar*, Avenida Bolívar between Calle 11 and 12, good breakfast and juices; *Pekin*, Calle 6 y Avenida Bolívar, good Chinese. On the corner of Avenida Bolívar and Calle 7 is *Centro Comercial Iglio* which has a nice café upstairs with terrace seating. Opposite Banco Consolidado (see below) is *Pollo Sabroso*, a large, modern, fast food type outlet.

● **Banks & money changers**

Banco Consolidado, Avenida Bolívar con Calle 5, changes Amex travellers' cheques, no commission. There's an ATM for Visa and Mastercard at Banco Unión nearby. **Banco de Venezuela**, Calle 7 con Avenida 10, cash on Visa and Mastercard, very efficient and helpful.

● **Tour companies & travel agents**

Teresita Viajes, Calle 8 entre Avenidas 9 y 10, T 55997, for booking flights.

● **Tourist offices**

Avenida Bolívar entre Calle 10 y 11, very friendly and helpful.

● **Transport**

Air La Cejita airport is 7 km to the north of town, on the road to Trujillo. Flights to Caracas, via Barquisimeto, daily with LAI at 0630, US$48, book well in advance (see above).

Buses The terminal is on the edge of town. To **Boconó**, regular *por puestos*, US$2.25, 3 hours; to **Trujillo**, regular *por puestos*, 30 minutes, US$0.45; to **Caracas**, 9 hours, US$7.50, at 0930, 2030, 2100 and 2145 via Valencia and Maracay, direct at 2230 with Expresos Mérida (T 56334); to **Mérida**, 4 daily with Transporte Barinas at 0800, 1000, 1300 and 1500, US$2.60, 4½ hours; *por puestos* to Mérida, 3 hours, US$5.20, leave when full; to **Maracaibo**, *micros* every 30 minutes with Expresos Valera from 0400 until 1730, 4 hours, US$3.85; to **Barquisimeto**, at 0700, 1100, 1500 and 1730 with 1ro de Octubre, US$2.75; to **San Cristóbal**, at 0300 and 0600-1800, US$6.75; to **Valencia**, as for Caracas, also at 0900 and 1300 with 1ro de Octubre, US$5.30.

EXCURSIONS FROM VALERA

There are thermal baths at **Motatán** (240m). The hot, sulphurous waters are piped into the town's *Hotel Hidrotermales San Rafael*. Non-guests can also use the facilities. To get there take the Valera-Agua Viva road north for 11 km then turn left at the large sign for the hotel, which is 4 km further on.

15 km west of Valera is the little town of **Isnotú**, the birthplace of Dr José Gregorio Hernández, regarded by many in Venezuela as a saint and a remarkable medical doctor who is credited with being the founder of Bacteriology in the country. He was knocked down by a car and died on 29 June 1919, while on his way to administer medicine to a sick patient. He devoted his life to caring for the sick and the poor of the Andes and his effigy can be seen throughout Venezuela, wearing the trademark hat, suit and tie and carrying his doctor's bag. Many thousands make the pilgrimage to the modest memorial chapel in the town, not only to honour this humble man but also in the hope that his spiritual intervention can help cure illness or unhappiness.

3 km west of Isnotú is the little town of **Betijoque**, unremarkable in itself but commanding amazing views of Lake Maracaibo to the northwest. 11 km beyond Betijoque the road joins the Panamerican Highway, just south of **Sabana de Mendoza**. From there you can continue on the Panamerican Highway southwest to **El Vigía** (see page 168), or head northeast to join the road north from Valera at **Agua Viva** (see below).

ROUTES From Valera the Transandean Highway continues north for 23 km then it forks right (east) until it meets the road east from **Trujillo** and then heads south to **Boconó** (see below), from where it continues down to the Llanos at **Guanare** (see page 219). The other branch heads north to **Agua Viva** (see page 167), where it meets the Panamerican Highway running northeast to **Barquisimeto** (see page 144).

TRUJILLO

An excellent new paved highway covers the 35 km from Valera to the state capital, **Trujillo** (*population* 44,460; *altitude* 805m; *phone code* 072). Founded in 1557 by Captain Diego García de Paredes, and named after his birthplace, Trujillo was moved so many times that it became known as the 'Portable City'. Seven different locations were tried until the present one was finally chosen in 1572.

Trujillo is a lovely, old historic town with many restored colonial houses. The old centre basically consists of two streets running uphill for several blocks until they meet. The town is enclosed on both sides by lush, steep-sided hills and offers great views across the valley of the Río Castán. Towering above is the huge Virgen de La Paz monument, which seems to stand guard over the town below.

The state of Trujillo is not a major tourist destination and the eponymous capital has an off-the-beaten-track feel to it. It's a quiet, sleepy and very friendly place with an extremely pleasant sub-tropical climate. A local friend described it – very fittingly – as a Venezuelan version of Gabriel García Márquez' fictional town of Macondo. The town and state are not without their attractions, however, and are definitely worth exploring for a few days. Trujillo is a better option than Valera if you do wish to get to know this hidden corner of Venezuela.

Places of interest

The heart of town is the **Plaza Bolívar**, whose cathedral was built in 1662, though the present structure was completely restored in 1968-70.

The interesting **Centro de Historia de Trujillo**, on Avenida Independencia, is a restored colonial house and museum. It was here that Bolívar signed the famous proclamation of 'War to the Death', under which all enemies of the patriot cause were summarily executed. Among the various pieces of period furniture in the museum is the bed in which the Liberator slept and the table on which the proclamation was actually signed.

La Virgen de la Paz, Trujillo

The 47m high monument to the **Virgen de la Paz** stands at 1,608m high above the town and was built in 1983. The views from the top are fantastic – you can even see as far as Lake Maracaibo – but go early before the cloud descends. It's open 0900-1700, and entry is US$0.75, there's a small café and gift shop.

To get there take one of the jeeps which leave when full from opposite *Hotel Trujillo*; 20 minutes, US$0.55 per person one way. You can also walk up to the monument, which takes about 2½ hours. Take a *por puesto* on Avenida Independencia with a blue or yellow flag and get off well beyond the *Hotel Trujillo* where the road begins to curve to the left. Take the turning on the right by the CANTV public phone and you should see a yellow sign with red lettering which reads "Red de Emergencia". The path begins between this sign and an old house with a tin roof. It's about a 2 hour very steep walk uphill through sub-tropical forest, coffee and sugar plantations.

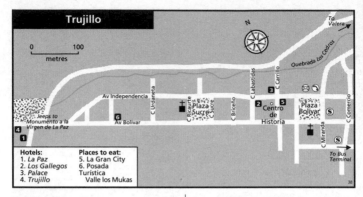

Hotels:
1. La Paz
2. Los Gallegos
3. Palace
4. Trujillo

Places to eat:
5. La Gran City
6. Posada Turística Valle los Mukas

Local information

● Accommodation

C *Trujillo*, 1 km uphill from Plaza Bolívar on Avenida Independencia, opposite Parque de Los Ilustres (to get there see above), T 33952, with bathroom, air conditioning, rooms with balcony and good views, pool, restaurant, bar, international phone calls.

D *La Paz*, just behind *Hotel Trujillo*, T 34864, spacious apartments for rent with bathroom, hot water, TV and lounge.

E *Los Gallegos*, Avenida Independencia 5-65, T/F 33193, with bathroom, hot water, fan, very friendly, clean and comfortable, highly recommended; **E** *Palace*, on Avenida Independencia near the plaza, crumbling old building, basic rooms set around a courtyard, friendly, cold water. Due open soon is *Posada Turística Valle Los Mukas*, on Avenida Bolívar just before it meets Avenida Independencia, in a converted colonial house, looks very attractive, their restaurant is already open.

● Places to eat

Tasca Restaurant La Gran City, Avenida Independencia, good and friendly service, US$4-5 main dish; *Café D'Adria*, next to *Hotel Los Gallegos*, good lunches and breakfast; *Restaurant Conticinio*, on Avenida Isaias Medina Angarita (take the same bus as for San Lázaro and get off at Plaza Medina Angarita), good for Sabaneta-style charcoal-broiled chicken with *mojo* sauce (US$2.50), a local speciality, great views across the valley.

In the suburb of **San Jacinto**, perched high above the plaza, is *Bar Mirandoy*, one of the most famous bars in the state, if not the country, as the place where José Ramón Barrios wrote his Trujillo Waltz. It is frequented by artists, poets and writers and often referred to in local songs. It also serves food

at reasonable prices. To get there take a *por puesto* from Plaza Bolívar and walk uphill from the plaza in San Jacinto.

● Banks & money changers

Banco Provincial, on Plaza Bolívar, cash advance with Visa and Mastercard; **Banco de Venezuela**, one block down from the cathedral, has ATM machine for cash withdrawals. It's probably a better bet to use the banks in Valera.

● Transport

The bus terminal is on the other side of the Río Castán; take a *por puesto* from the centre of town. Buses to **Caracas**, 9 hours, US$7.50, at 2000, 2100 and 2130; to **Barinas** and **Mérida**, at 0700; to **Boconó**, *por puestos* at 0830, 1000, 1130, 1300, 1400, 1530 and 1630, US$1.50. *Por puestos* leave for **Valera** every half hour from the terminal. When arriving from Valera, get off in the main plaza, otherwise you'll end up at the terminal.

EXCURSIONS FROM TRUJILLO

Just outside Trujillo, on the road to Valera, is the perfectly restored colonial village of **La Plazuela**. Here you'll find the headquarters of the state tourist office, where you can pick up a free map and guide to the sites of interest. Next door is a small café which serves excellent home-made cakes. On the tiny plaza is **D** *Posada San Benito*, 6 rooms with bathroom, hot water, fan, restaurant. Next door Sra Carmen sells beer and soft drinks.

It's a pleasant 30-40 minute walk from here to a working *trapiche*, where you can see the local *panela* being produced (see also page 193).

A recommended side trip is to the beautiful colonial village of **San Lázaro**, a peaceful little place which straddles the Río Tiny and is kept meticulously clean by the local populace. Accommodation is available in **F** *Posada Turística de San Lázaro*, a nice, clean, comfortable place, with bathroom, cold water only, restaurant. Buses to San Lázaro leave frequently from the terminal in Trujillo. It's a lovely 45-minute ride through beautiful, lush countryside and coffee plantations.

5 km beyond San Lázaro is the smaller but equally attractive village of **Santiago**, where the Spanish had to settle in order to keep the peace, as San Lázaro was already populated.

ROUTES From Santiago an unpaved road heads south to **La Quebrada** (a 1½-hour drive). From there a paved road continues northwest to **La Quebrada de Las Cuevas**, where it branches right (north) to **Valera** (see page 193) and left (south), following the course of the Río Matatán, to a point where another road branches left to **Jajó** (see page 192).

TRUJILLO TO BOCONO

The spectacular 93 km paved road from Trujillo to Boconó winds its way like a coiled spring into the mountains, from the warm lush valleys up into damp, dense cloud forest. Along the way it bypasses several enchanting little mountain villages, seemingly untouched by the hand of 20th century 'progress' and almost never visited by foreign tourists. In fact, so unused are people here to foreigners that they may stop and stare.

The road passes through **Pampán** and **Flor de Patria** before it reaches the turn-off on the left for **Santa Ana**, 38 km from Trujillo. On a clear day, the peaceful little colonial town, at 1,600m, commands beautiful views. It was here, on 27 November 1820, that Bolívar and Don Pablo Morillo, the General of the Spanish forces, met to renounce the War to the Death policy and sign a 6-month armistice, so allowing the patriots a breathing space in which to consolidate their positions. A monument in the little plaza near the entrance to the town commemorates their meeting. There is accommodation in the hotel, **D-E** (not signposted) at the top of the hill where you enter the town. It is owned by a friendly elderly couple who also have a coffee business and is very clean, with use of the kitchen included.

23 km further on is the turn-off for the remote farming *pueblo* of **Burbusay**. It is 5 km from here to the village itself.

27 km before Boconó, 3 km off the main road, is the little town of **San Miguel de Boconó**, at 1,600m in a beautiful, lush valley. Founded in 1597, the town is dominated by its massive church, one of the most remarkable colonial religious buildings in the entire country, which was completed in 1760. Even those who are usually less than excited at the prospect of visiting colonial churches cannot fail to be overawed at the magnificent and beautiful simplicity of the exterior. Inside are the finest polychrome colonial retables in all of Venezuela. The town is also renowned for its festival of the *Romerías de los Pastores y Payasos* (Procession of shepherds and clowns) *de San Miguel*, held on the 4-7 January.

Accommodation is available in San Miguel at the homely **E** *Hostería San Miguel*, including breakfast. 2 km beyond the turn-off on the road to Boconó is **E** *Los Valles*, cabañas with nice views.

BOCONO

Boconó (*population* 39,220; *altitude* 1,225m) is a rural provincial town famed for its crafts. It's also the commercial centre of one of the most intensively cultivated regions of the country. The town follows the contours of the valley sides, with its streets running steeply from the Río Boconó up to the Plaza Bolívar and beyond.

Boconó was settled in 1560 by Don Diego García de Paredes as one of Trujillo's many potential sites. When this city was moved yet again in 1563, many of the citizens refused to leave, renaming their new town after the river on whose banks it was built. It remained an isolated country town, until the road from Trujillo was completed in 1935, and even today there's an air of this isolation about the place.

Places of interest

Those who do make it here most likely come to buy the superb local *artesanía*. There are several places where you can buy, or just see them being produced. At the **Casa Artesanal**, on the right of the main road into town from Trujillo, just before the bridge, you can see demonstrations of weaving techniques.

At the bottom of the road directly opposite is the **Centro de Acopio Artesanal Tiscachic**. Alternatively, if you're coming from town, turn right immediately after crossing the bridge and walk 300-400m. The centre works with the local *campesinos* to promote local crafts and has

Artesanía from Boconó

a wide selection at good prices. There's also a museum, a livestock market, fruit and vegetable market and a *comedor popular* where you can queue up with the *campesinos* for a US$0.70 lunch.

Another recommended place to visit is the pottery workshop of the **Briceño family** on the outskirts of town. Here you can see the method used to produce the fine local pottery.

Excursions

Southeast of Boconó is the **Guaramacal National Park**, in the Páramo El Rosario. The 21,491 hectare park runs from 1,600m up to heights of 2,500m and among the species of fauna are the spectacled bear, puma, brocket deer, paca, three-toed sloth and raccoon. Birdlife includes the helmeted curassow and yellow-headed parrot. Facilities are scarce, but one of the lagoons, **Laguna Los Cedros**, offers camping and picnic facilities. To get there, take the road northeast out of town towards Campo Elías for 3 km till you see a sign on the right for the lagoon. This rough road continues through the park to the little town of **La Vega de Guaramacal**.

Local information

● **Accommodation**

E-F pp *Colonial*, on Plaza Bolívar, with bathroom, hot water, restaurant, basic, small rooms.

F pp *Venezia*, half block uphill from the plaza, T 522778, with bathroom, hot water, restaurant; **F** pp *Italia*, one block downhill from the plaza on Calle Jauregui, with bathroom, cold water, basic but clean, cheap meals in restaurant.

● **Places to eat**

There are not too many places to eat other than in the hotels. One good place is *Restaurant-Tasca El Río*, on the left by the bridge as you enter town from Trujillo, US$4-5 per main dish.

● **Banks & money changers**

Banco Unión, near the main plaza, has an ATM; also **Banco de Venezuela**, on Calle Sucre, one block below the plaza.

● **Post & telecommunications**

Ipostel and public telephones are both on Calle Sucre.

● **Transport**

Por Puestos leave frequently to Trujillo and Valera from Calle Páez 2-27, T 522566. Buses also leave from here to Maracaibo.

A matter of taste

🦶 Among the many handicrafts for sale in Boconó are the little round boxes carved from horn which are used to carry *chimó*. This is a mixture of tobacco, ash and *urao* crystals chewed by many Andean men and also used for medicinal purposes. There are two strengths – *bravo* (strong) *and manso* (tame) – which are sold throughout the Andes. Anyone curious enough to try it, however, should be warned: it tastes like a mixture of cow dung, asphalt and the sweat from a Sumo wrestler's jockstrap.

NIQUITAO

A road runs southwest from Boconó through **Tostós** and a further 26 km to the lovely little town of **Niquitao**, 1 hour away by public transport. Founded in 1625 (*population* 4,400; *altitude* 1,917m), Niquitao is still relatively unspoilt and retains much of its original colonial architecture. It sits in a beautiful and intensively cultivated valley. Among the local specialities are the blackberry wine and *leche de burra*, a mixture of milk, sugar, eggs, spirit and spices.

Among the town's many festivals is Holy Week, when paper is rolled out in the streets for children to create a giant painted mural.

● **Accommodation & places to eat** D *Posada Turística de Niquitao*, T (072) 53111/31448; and D *Na Delia*, T (072) 52113/52522, on a hill 500m out of town, both have restaurants; F pp *Posada Don Jérez*, on the corner of Plaza Bolívar, has a few rooms and serves simple local food; also F pp *Posada Guirigay*. On the plaza is *La Estancia*, T 52499/52888, a Tasca-restaurant and bar with excellent pizzas, owner Golfredo Pérez is helpful, kind and knows the area well. For a family atmosphere and good cooking try *Posada Mama Chepi*.

A recommended excursion from Niquitao is to the **Teta de Niquitao**, a 4,007m peak which can be reached by jeep in 2 hours, or on horseback or by mule. It's a tough climb to the top but the scenery is superb. A good guide is Jhonny Olivo; ask for him at the video games shop on the plaza.

Another trip is to the waterfalls and pools known as Las Pailas, and a nearby lake: Robert Fama (San Francisco, CA) writes, "For a full day's hike, walk from the plaza uphill past the municipal building. The paved road becomes a rough track. Continue for about 30 minutes until the track crosses a small river. After the river, take a right fork and follow the river uphill and over a bluff. Here are 3 or 4 beautiful swimming holes and the perfect picnic spots. The main falls are another 30 minutes further upstream. A very scenic walk."

Southwest of Niquitao, a partly-paved road climbs up to **Las Mesitas**. It's a rough trip, and a cold one, and you'll need to camp as there's no accommodation in the village. On the way is a monument commemorating the Battle of Niquitao, fought on 2 July 1813, during the Wars of Independence, which saw the first example of Bolívar's 'War to the Death' policy.

From Las Mesitas you can continue up a steep hill towards **Tuñame** (see page 199). From there, turn left on a good gravel road (no signs), cross the pass and descend to **Pueblo Llano** (see page 191).

BOCONO TO THE LLANOS

A road heads northeast from Boconó, passing the turn-off for **Laguna Los Cedros** (see above) and then **Mosquey**, 10 km from Boconó, where there is accommodation at *Estancia de Mosquey*, family run, great views, good beds, good restaurant, pool, recommended. The road then crosses the state boundary into Portuguesa state at **Campo Elías**, before turning east to the town of **Biscucuy** (*population* 27,000). From here you can continue down to **Guanare** in the Llanos (see page 219). It's a 3½-hour trip by bus and costs US$2.

From Biscucuy you can also head north on the Transandean Highway through **Guárico**, **El Tocuyo** and **Quíbor** to reach **Barquisimeto** (see page 144).

SOUTHWEST OF MERIDA

ROUTES The Transandean Highway runs southwest from Mérida, through the towns of **Tovar**, **Bailadores** and **La Grita** before reaching **San Cristóbal**, capital of Táchira state. From there you can continue west into Colombia or head east towards the *Llanos*.

JAJI

An interesting detour from the main Transandean Highway is to head west from Mérida to **Jají**, 43 km away. The village (*population* 1,500; *altitude* 1,781m) is a complete reconstruction of the colonial original. The lovely main plaza and adjoining streets are mainly given over to *artesanías* from all over the continent. The town is obviously tourist-oriented and gets very busy during the high season, but out of season, there are few visitors. There is good walking in the surrounding hills.

● **Accommodation & places to eat** E *Aldea Vieja*, near the plaza, with bathroom, hot water, large well-furnished rooms with balconies and great views, very friendly, free coffee in the morning, restaurant, recommended; **F** *Hospedaje Familiar*, good, friendly, nice roof terrace. *El Bosque*, good local food, US$7 for 2 including drinks, excellent *parrilladas*, bar, open 1600-2230, limited menu but recommended; a cheaper option is *La Montaña*, recommended.

● **Transport** *Busetas* leave Terminal Sur hourly, 50 minutes, US$0.60. The road passes forested mountains, cliffs and waterfalls; sit on the left for the best views.

The road continues for 62 km – narrow, but mostly paved – beyond Jají, to reach **La Azulita**. A recommended excursion from La Azulita is to **La Cueva del Pirata** (Pirate's Cave). Accommodation is available in town at **E** *Posada Colono de Molinillos*, on the plaza, basic but good; and **D-E** *Posada La Azulita*, also on the plaza, recommended.

ROUTES The road continues beyond La Azulita down to join the Panamerican Highway, just west of **Capazón** and east of **El Vigía** (see page 168). There are several gas stations on the way.

Off the road to Jají, 20 minutes from Mérida, is *Venezuela de Anteayer*, where regional culture is recreated in a series of displays, including typical music and food, US$8. To get there take a *por puesto* from Calle 26, Mérida.

MERIDA TO BAILADORES

At **Ejido**, just west of Mérida, a road branches right to the village of **La Mesa de Ejido**, where you can stay at **D** *Posada Turística Papá Miguel*, recommended, good food. **Mesa de Los Indios** is a small village beyond Ejido, near which there are fantastic hot springs where cold rain water from the mountains meets hot spring water.

PUEBLOS DEL SUR

From Ejido another road runs south to **El Morro**, a little village high in the Sierra, which can also be reached from **Los Nevados** (see page 184). In Los Nevados you can arrange a jeep to take you beyond El Morro to Acequias (see below). It's a gruelling 8-hour trip, and impossible in the wet season. It costs a minimum of around US$60 per person, but bargain hard. It is dangerous to attempt it on your own. Alternatively you can walk from El Morro to Acequias in a day.

Between El Morro and the village of **San Pedro** you cross a deep river valley, then climb up the next mountain on a very steep, hair-raising road. Beyond San Pedro you can see the ruins of San Antonio Mucuño, better known as **Pueblo Viejo**. In former times this was the most important village in the area, but it had to move twice in the 17th and 19th centuries due to earthquakes. The modern village is called **Acequias**. You can stay overnight at **E** *Posada Mama Emilia*, an old house with a nice patio, rooms with bathroom. If their restaurant is closed, ask at the little shop; they will prepare basic meals. There is no public transport back to Mérida from Acequias, but you can hire a jeep.

It's a 2-hour walk to the ruins. Take water and allow plenty of time to enjoy the impressive setting and the magnificent views of the peaks of the Sierra Nevada.

From Acequias it's a 5-6 hour walk through *páramo* and then a beautiful valley to **San José**, the first of the **Pueblos del Sur**.

● **Accommodation** In San José: **E-F** *Posada San José*, at the entrance to the village, it's basic with a small restaurant. At the other end of the village by the river is **E-F** *Posada Mochabá*, run by Martin Sosa, it consists of 2 double cabins and 1 room for 4 with hot shower, very relaxing with a family atmosphere, you can cook together or Martin will prepare organic meals, highly recommended. Martin will also arrange trips by 4WD, horse or on foot to the lakes nearby. You can even fish for trout in front of your own cabin! Haydee Ruiz rents a cottage, T (074) 792-2222.

● **Transport** Road From San José a good road runs back to Mérida, via **Las Gonzales** on the Transandean Highway. Regular jeeps and *por puestos* do this trip in 2½ hours. To get to San José from Mérida take a bus from Avenida 2 to El Ejido, 30 minutes, then a *por puesto* from the main plaza, 2 hours, US$1.50.

It's possible to visit the other **Pueblos del Sur** but this involves a lot of driving and there's little public transport. You can continue to **Mucutuy**, where there are 2 *posadas*, and on to **Mucuchachí, Canagua, El Molino** and from there to **Estanques**, back on the Transandean Highway (see below).

AROUND LAGUNILLAS

Another road from Las Gonzales goes northwest to **San Juan de Lagunillas**, believed to be the first site of Mérida (*population* 15,900). It has a striking church and is noted for its craftwork especially weaving. Fiestas are held here from Christmas to Candlemas (2 February); *San Isidro* is held over 3 weeks in May (with 14 and 15 the highpoint); and in July.

From San Juan, or from further along Route 7 (Transandean Highway), **Lagunillas** can be reached. The **Laguna de Urao** (1,079m) is the source of the *urao* crystals which are mixed with tobacco to make *chimó* (see also page 199). On the edge of Lagunillas is **Jamu**, a reconstructed indigenous village, named after an indigenous tribe, where demonstrations of weaving and other skills are given. Entry to the village is US$1.20.

ROUTES From Lagunillas the road continues northwest until it forks; north to La Azulita (see page 200), and west to **Chiguará** and **Estanques** (see below).

PUEBLO NUEVO

Soon after the second turn-off for Lagunillas, a turning on the left leads to **Pueblo Nuevo**, a pretty colonial village (*altitude* 2,050m). The well-paved road climbs up steeply, giving impressive views all around. The whole village has very lively celebrations starting 10 days before Christmas when "everyone runs around the cobblestone streets, setting off firecrackers, firing blunderbusses into the air, playing violins and getting extremely drunk", but is otherwise quiet. There are also pleasant walks in the hills.

● **Accommodation & places to eat** **F** *Posada Doña Eva*, is on the southeast corner of the main plaza in a restored 300-years-old building, basic but with a family atmosphere, delicious and cheap vegetarian meals served to order, highly recommended. For good, cheap food try *Comedor Doña Rosa*.

● **Transport** From **Mérida** to Pueblo Nuevo, taxi-jeeps leave from Avenida 2 near the new cultural centre, US$1.50.

ESTANQUES AND CHIGUARA

30 minutes beyond Lagunillas lies **Estanques** (442m). The little church has a stupendous gold colonial altar, but is seldom open except on Christmas Day.

A few kilometres north of Estanques is the quiet colonial village of **Chiguará**, where there are beautiful mineral springs and good walking. At **El Pedregal** there are botanical gardens and a good view over the town. Giant cacti in the area are said to be 300-years-old.

In the **Valle de Mocotíes**, by the *Alcabala La Victoria*, is the Museo del Inmigrante in a reconstructed coffee *finca*. It is open daily 0800-1800 and also has a *cafetería*.

● **Accommodation & transport** In Chiguará: **E** *Posada Colonial Cantarranos*, has a pool fed by mineral springs, clean, owner Fanny speaks some English and is very helpful; **E** *Posada Los Rurales*, at the entrance to the village. *Buseta* to Mérida, US$0.90.

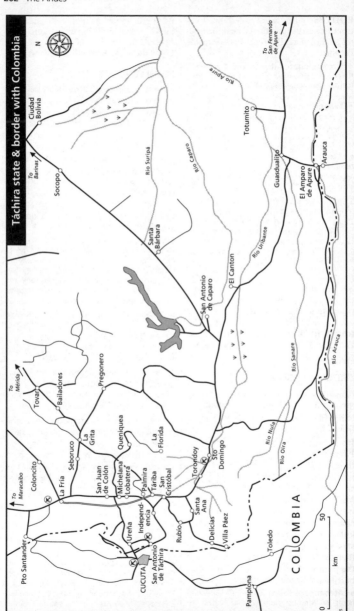

Táchira state & border with Colombia

ROUTES At **Puente Victoria**, a few kilometres west of Estanques a road branches off right (north) to **El Vigía** on the Panamerican Highway (see page 168). The Transandean Highway meanwhile, leaves the dry Chama valley and runs through lush tropical vegetation to Tovar.

TOVAR

96 km beyond Mérida is **Tovar** (*population* 30,000; *phone code* 075), a nice little town with pleasant excursions.

● **Accommodation & places to eat** D *Hostería Sabaneta*, private bathroom; E *Valle del Mocotíes*, opposite the bus terminal; F *Pensión Ideal*, basic, laundry facilities; F pp *El Parque Carabobo*, on Parque Carabobo, T 730137, with bathroom, very clean and friendly, laundry facilities, very good value; F *Hospedaje Tovar*. *Restaurant Kek Duna*, Hungarian owner speaks 6 languages and serves interesting food.

● **Transport** To Bailadores, US$0.75; to La Grita 0900 and 1530 via the old route (see below); to Mérida, 1¼ hours, US$1.50.

ROUTES From Tovar you can rejoin the Panamericana via **Zea**, a pleasant village to the north.

BAILADORES

15 km from Tovar is the peaceful little agricultural town of **Bailadores** (*population* 10,330; *altitude* 1,750m; *phone code* 075). The name is short for *indios bailadores* (dancing Indians) and was used by the Spanish to describe the local people in battle. The town also celebrates its fiesta from Christmas to Candlemas.

It's a beautiful walk to the waterfall in **Parque Páez**, 3 km from the highway on the eastern fringes of town. The waterfall is called *La Cascada de la India que Murió de Amor* (the Waterfall of the Indian Maiden who Died of Love). Legend has it that Princess Carú, daughter of a local chief, carried the dead body of her lover, killed in battle by the Spaniards, to this spot and cried herself to death. Her tears then formed the waterfall. On the way to the park you can treat yourself to strawberries and cream at La Capellería.

● **Accommodation** C *La Cascada*, a modern hotel, Wilfredo plays electric organ in the bar on Saturday night, and at Mass on Sunday in the beautiful church, and is entertaining on both occasions; also E *Hospedaje Villa*.

● **Transport** To La Grita, US$1.80; San Cristóbal, US$3.60, *por puesto*, US$1.50, bus.

BAILADORES TO SAN CRISTOBAL

This 135 km stretch of Transandean Highway takes about 3 hours to drive and is well worth it for the views alone. The road climbs steeply from Bailadores up to 2,800m, where it forks. The paved road, Route 31, bears left. 10 km beyond the fork, at the sign for Portachuelo Pass, another road branches left to **Pregonero**. It's about another hour on Route 31, through numerous bends and switchbacks, to **La Grita**. 7 km before La Grita is the turn-off to C *Hotel de Montaña*, T (077) 82401/2, with bathroom, recommended.

The right fork, the original Transandean Highway, is unpaved but by far the more scenic route. It climbs up to the very wild and beautiful **Páramo de La Negra**, at 3,050m, before dropping down to La Grita. This road is highly recommended in the dry season and there is virtually no traffic.

LA GRITA

The pleasant town of **La Grita** (*altitude* 1,440m; *phone code* 077) sits in a fertile valley and enjoys a lovely warm climate. Though founded in 1572, the Spaniards first appeared in the valley in 1558. The local Caricuana Indians greeted them with a great cry (*grita*) and so the town was given its name.

The town comes to life on Sunday when farmers from all around come to town for the market, where they sell their produce and handicrafts. The town's festival is on 6 August.

● **Accommodation** E *La Casona*, Carrera 2A, No 6-69; E *Capri*, Carrera 3, good value; good pizza restaurant next door.

ROUTES 5 km west of La Grita, at **La Quinta**, the excellent Transandean Highway, Route 7, turns left (south) to San Cristóbal, passing over the beautiful **Páramo Zumbador**. It is 70 km from La Grita to San Cristóbal. The road to **La Fría** (see page 207) continues west from La Quinta. From La Grita to La Fría is 37 km.

PARAMOS BATALLON Y LA NEGRA NATIONAL PARK

This 65,000 hectare park is situated on the border of Mérida and Táchira states and offers typical Andean scenery of mountains and glacial lakes as well as a wide variety of flora and fauna, including, if you're lucky, a sight of the rare Andean, or spectacled, bear.

The park is best approached from La Grita. Take a bus from there to **Las Porqueras**, from where you can start a 1-4 day trek through beautiful countryside with great views of **El Pulpito** (3,942m). There are some very nice towns in the area, such as the old village of **El Cobre** and **Mesa de Aura**, a typical Andean village with some good restaurants. Near El Cobre, on the way from San Cristóbal, there is accommodation in wooden cabins beside a river at *Finca de la Huérfana*, which also provides excellent homemade food and various excursions with professional guides, as well as mountain biking and meditation, the owner speaks English. (Thanks to Yiftah Shalev and Eran Shayshon, Jerusalem, Israel for the above information.)

SAN CRISTOBAL

The capital of Táchira State stands on a plateau on the east bank of the Río Torbes, 55 km from the Colombian border (*population* 290,900; *phone code* 076; *altitude* 830m; *average temperature* 22°C). The city is on three levels, running north to south; a level area along the Río Torbes (which flows south into the Orinoco basin), and two terraces, one of them 200m above the river, and 5°C cooler. Its streets run steeply up and downhill, rather like San Francisco (California).

San Cristóbal is a busy modern city, but pleasant nevertheless. There are plenty of quiet little plazas where you can escape the noise and activity. Though it can be quite hot and humid, the climate is by no means oppressive. It serves as the ideal base from which to explore one of the most interesting and least known parts of Venezuela.

The city was founded in 1561 by the same Juan de Maldonado who first founded Mérida. It has only really grown in recent years, with the completion of the Transandean and Panamerican Highways, linking it with the rest of the country. Before then, it and the rest of Táchira had closer ties to Colombia, which is not surprising as it's twice as far to Caracas as it is to Bogotá.

Places of interest

The city's colonial heritage is still in evidence, most notably around the **Plaza Juan de Maldonado**, the traditional heart of the city. The Cathedral, finished in 1908, had its towers and façade rebuilt in colonial style for the 400th anniversary of the foundation. Also interesting is **Plaza Sucre** and the new **Plaza Libertad**, from where you get a great view of the city.

Museums

The **Museo del Táchira** is on Avenida Universidad, T 565764.

Local festivals

The *International Fair of San Sebastián*, held on 7-30 January, is one of the largest and most impressive festivals in Venezuela. Many of the streets are decorated and closed to traffic for the dancing and parades. Many sports events take place and the bullfighting is second to none, featuring some of the world's top matadors. Accommodation in the whole state is booked solid for months in advance.

Local information
● Accommodation

Hotel prices			
L1	over US$200	**L2**	US$151-200
L3	US$101-150	**A1**	US$81-100
A2	US$61-80	**A3**	US$46-60
B	US$31-45	**C**	US$21-30
D	US$12-20	**E**	US$7-11
F	US$4-6	**G**	up to US$3

Those marked with an asterisk (*) are bookable through Fairmont International (see under Caracas).

B *Círculo Militar De Ferias El Tamá**, Avenida 19 de Abril, overlooking the town, 5-star, 112 rooms, safe, spacious, good pool and gymnasium, recommended.

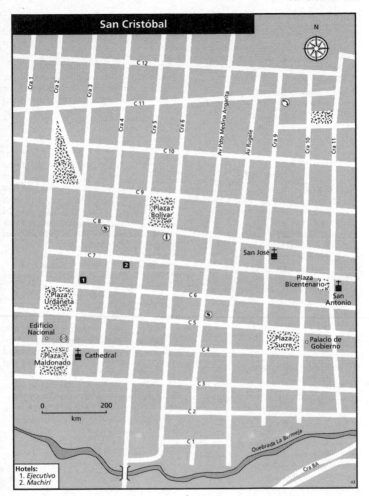

C *Korinu*, Cra 6 con Calle 5, T 449866, shower, restaurant, recommended.

D *El Rey*, Avenida Ferrero Tamayo, T 432703/430561, F 463704, 40 rooms, good showers, fridge, quiet, recommended; D *Machirí*, Calle 7 No 4-30, hot water, central.

E *Ejecutivo*, Calle 6, No 3-45, old and basic but clean and central; E *Tropicana*, next to the bus terminal, with bath, basic; E *Río*, outside the bus station, big rooms, hot shower; E *Unisa*, also near the bus terminal, OK.

There are several cheap hotels on Avenida 6A, just off the central plaza, and around Avenidas 5-7, Calle 4-8, all **E-F** category.

Camping *El Petroleo* is 15 km from the city on the old road to Rubio, ask for Hacienda Santa Teresa, the owner is Carlos Eduardo Cruz, it's a very good site, on a coffee and sugarcane farm, good atmosphere, helpful, English spoken US$2 per day.

● **Places to eat**
Fuente de Soda La Bohème, Avenida García de Hevia y 7 Avenida, Centro Cívico, expensive,

breakfasts all day; *El Rancho de Esteban*, 500m from *Hotel El Rey*, open air with fine view over city, special barbecue dishes, highly recommended; *Pietro*, Calle 14 y Carrera 20, pizzería. There's a pleasant café in Casa Francesa, near the Cathedral, which serves good *merengadas* at reasonable prices.

● **Banks & money changers**
Banco Consolidado (American Express), 5a Avenida, Edificio Torre E.

● **Embassies & consulates**
German, Edificio Torovega, Carrera 8, La Concordia, T 448866.

● **Entertainment**
Mario's Disco Pub, on Plaza Los Mangos; *Atena's Café*, Calle 22, Pasaje Acueducto near Plaza Los Mangos; *American Pub*, Calle El Pinar; *Discoteca Insomnia*, in *Hotel Dinástica* on Avenida 7; *Pietro*, Calle 14 y Cra 20, pizzería-pub with live music on Tuesday.

Cinemas: at Avenida 5 y Calle 19 and Cra 20 entre Calle 13 y 14; both have 3 screens, half price on Monday.

● **Post & telecommunications**
Post Office: in the Palacio Municipal, next to the Cathedral. CANTV: on Carrera 23, Calle 10 y Pasaje Acueducto.

● **Shopping**
Bookshops: English language books can be found in some bookshops on Avenida 7 and at Plaza Los Mangos.

● **Sports**
There is bungee jumping and pendulo jumping from the Puente Libertador at weekends and holidays.

Camping equipment can be found in various shops in the centre, on Avenidas 5-7.

● **Tour companies & travel agents**
There are very few guides in the city. *Ortega Edwards* at *Everest Club* specializes in mountain climbing and offers other tours, T 401050, he speaks 4 languages. For more information try Inparques or Cotatur.

● **Tourist offices**
Cotatur, Pabellones de Exposición, Avenida España, Pueblo Nuevo, very helpful, good city map and hotel list. Inparques, Parque Metropolitano, Avenida 19 de Abril, T 465216. Touring y Automóvil Club, Avenida Libertador Calle y Avenida Principal Las Lomas, Edificio Olga, T 442542/664/675, ask for Sr Hernán Sojo González.

● **Transport**
Local Car hire: Budget, Avenida 19 de Abril cc El Parque. Taxi: to Cúcuta, US$11 to San Antonio, US$5 to wait at border, then US$6 to Cúcuta.

Air There is no airport at San Cristóbal, the nearest is 40 km away at Santo Domingo, the city's official airport. From Santo Domingo take a taxi to San Cristóbal, US$11, or walk 30 minutes to the highway and catch a bus (1 hour, US$0.30). Equally close is the airport at San Antonio. There are daily flights with Aeropostal to **Caracas** and **Porlamar**. Aeropostal also flies to: **Maturín** (daily except Saturday), **Barcelona** (daily except Saturday), **Maracaibo** (daily except Saturday), **Puerto Ordaz** (daily except Saturday), **Aruba** (Monday, Friday and Sunday), **Curaçao** (Tuesday, Wednesday and Thursday) and **Manaus** (Thursday and Sunday). Check all flight details in advance, as they are subject to change (Aeropostal, T/F (076) 559896). Servivensa flights on the Caracas-Bogotá-Guayaquil route stop at Santo Domingo.

Buses The bus station is 2 km south of the centre. It is well-equipped and the information booth has city maps and some hotel information. To **Maracaibo**, 6-8 hours, US$6.50, *por puesto*, US$19. To **Mérida**, US$5, 6 hours, US$7 by *por puesto*. To/from **Bailadores** US$1.50. To **Caracas**, US$12.50, 15 hours (Expresos Occidente), executive service US$13.50. To **Valencia**, US$10. To **San Antonio**, 2½ hours by bus, US$2; or by *por puesto*, which continues to **Cúcuta**, stopping at Immigration in both countries, runs every 20 minutes.

EXCURSIONS FROM SAN CRISTOBAL

11 km north of San Cristóbal on the Panamerican Highway is the busy little town of **Táriba**. Those who like markets will especially enjoy the town's lively and colourful Monday morning farmer's and livestock markets, where you can soak up the local atmosphere and enjoy many of the region's typical dishes. The town's **Virgen de Táriba** church is also worth visiting.

A highly recommended side trip is 19 km southwest to **Rubio**, the third largest town in the state. The town gets its name from its founder, Don Gervasio Rubio, who was the first to grow coffee in the region. Rubio is known as *La Ciudad Pontalica* (The City of Bridges) and it's easy to see why if you take a visit to the old part of town, where many old colonial buildings remain. The town is also home to some of the most beautiful churches in the country. 1 hour's walk from Rubio is **Pozo Azul**, where there are lots of interesting caves.

The 10,800 hectare **Chorro del Indio National Park** runs northeast from San Cristóbal and is best approached from **San José de Bolívar**. To get there, turn right (east) off the road to La Grita. The park is named after the **Chorro del Indio** waterfall, which lies just 11 km east of San Cristóbal.

Among the many interesting villages worth visiting around San Cristóbal are **Independencia** and **Libertad**, next door to each other on a road running northwest, where you can see the local woodcarvers at work. A few kilometres east is the turn-off to **Peribeca**, a tiny village in a picturesque setting. In the colourful plaza you can buy typical local delicacies and *artesanía*.

EL TAMA NATIONAL PARK

Near the border with Colombia is this 139,000 hectare National Park, the largest in the region. Facilities are limited, but there are a few possibilities for travelling around the park.

From San Cristóbal, take a bus west to **La Petrólia**, which is a nice park. This is where oil was first found in Venezuela, in 1894. A monument and museum mark the site, and there's a visitor centre and camping ground. La Petrólia is the starting point for a trip to **Río Chiquito**, a typical agricultural Andean village in a forested valley. From there you can walk up to **El Cruz**, which takes about an hour, or continue to **San Vicente**, from where there are several options for hiking. To get to La Petrólia, Río Chiquito or San Vicente, take a San Vicente bus from San Cristóbal (4 a day).

La Línea is a high mountainous area in the park (3,000-3,500m). The main attractions are: the Río Tǎchira; the Guácharros Caves (where you can see these blind birds which live in the caves); and La Ventana, a natural 'window' atop a mountain, through which you can enjoy fantastic views. To reach La Línea take a bus from San Cristóbal to **Delicias** (2½ hours), and from there take a bus to **Betania** (1 hour), at the foot of the mountains. This is the base for the trek around

the area, which can take 4-9 hours, depending on conditions. Make sure you get a permit, and more information, from the Inparques office in San Cristóbal. You can spend 3 or 4 days exploring this area. (Thanks to Yiftah Shalev and Eran Shayshon, Jerusalem, Israel for the above information.)

SAN CRISTOBAL TO LA FRIA

The 68 km of road north from San Cristóbal to La Fría takes less than 2 hours to drive and passes through some very stunning scenery. On the way, just before **San Juan de Colón**, is the turn-off left to **San Pedro del Río**, a well preserved colonial village, where you can stay at **D** *Posada Valparaíso*, T 077-911032, beautiful garden, recommended.

From San Pedro the road continues west to **Ureña**, on the Colombian border, from where you can head south to **San Antonio** (see below). The town hosts a festival on 3-12 December. 7 km before Ureña are the natural hot springs of **Aguas Calientes**, where you can stay at **B** *Hotel Aguas Calientes**, private thermal bath, swimming pool. Note that crossing the border at Ureña is not permitted.

From San Juan de Colón, the road drops gradually to **La Fría** (*population* 26,000). This hot and humid part of the country suffered greatly from a type of malaria which caused prolonged chills, hence the name.

● **Accommodation E** *Turística*, on the main plaza, family-run, basic but clean, recommended; **E** *Miramar*, Calle 6-50, near Plaza Bolívar, T (077) 41790.

ROUTES From La Fría Ruta 6 heads north to **Maracaibo** (see page 167). The Panamerican Highway runs northeast through fairly flat countryside to **El Vigía** (see page 168).

SAN ANTONIO DEL TACHIRA

From San Cristóbal a good road runs for 56 km over the mountains, with beautiful Andean views, to San Antonio del Tǎchira. The frontier town (*population* 42,630; *phone code* 076; *altitude* 438m) is connected by an international bridge with Cúcuta on the

San Antonio del Táchira

Buses:
1. Expresos Mérida
2. Expresos Los Llanos
3. Expresos San Cristóbal
4. Por Puestos to San Cristóbal

Hotels:
1. Colonial
2. Frontera
3. Neverí
4. Terepaima

Colombian side. It's about 16 km to Cúcuta, from where you can continue by road or air to Bogotá.

San Antonio has an attractive colonial cathedral and some pleasant parks, but is by no means tourist-oriented. As a busy border town, with all the attendant 'problems', it's best to pass through quickly.

Local festivals
The town hosts a festival on 13-20 May.

Local information
● **Accommodation**
D *Neveri*, Calle 3, No 3-11, esquina Carrera 3, air conditioning, TV, safe, parking nearby.

E *Colonial*, Carrera 11, No 2-51, T 78018, with bathroom, basic, restaurant; **E** *Lorena*, Carrera 6, No 6-57, fan; **E** *Terepaima*, Carrera 8, No 1-37, safe, good meals, recommended.

F *Frontera*, Calle 2 y Carrera 9, No 8-70, T 77366, pleasant, good value. There are many other hotels near the town centre.

● **Places to eat**
Refugio de Julio, Carrera 10, good value pizzas; *La Giralda de Sevilla*, next door to *Hotel Neveri* (above), very good, open on Sunday evenings, unlike everywhere else.

● **Banks & money changers**
Visa at **Banco Unión**, and Amex at **Banco Consolidado**, both on the main plaza. Travellers' cheques are difficult to change. *Casas de cambio* near the international bridge will not all change travellers' cheques and some will only change Colombian pesos, not even US dollars cash. The exchange rate for changing bolívares to pesos is the same in San Antonio as in Cúcuta.

● **Transport**
Air The airport has exchange facilities (mainly for Colombian pesos). Taxis run to DIEX (emigration) in town, and on to Cúcuta airport, US$8.50. *Por puesto* to airport, US$0.20. Internal flights: Aeropostal, Aserca, Avensa and Servivensa fly to Caracas, Porlamar, Barquisimeto, Maracaibo and Valencia (Aeropostal, T 713955, F 710502). Avensa and Servivensa also fly to Bogotá and Medellín daily.

Buses To Caracas US$13.50, at 1600 and 1800, 12 hours.

FRONTIER WITH COLOMBIA

● **Venezuelan immigration**
DIEX, Carrera 9 y Avenida 1 de Mayo, San Antonio.
To get a Venezuelan exit stamp here, buy a stamp from opposite DIEX (US$2), then take it back to DIEX for your exit stamp.

Entering Venezuela There is no point in buying a bus ticket to San Cristóbal before going through formalities. Go to DIEX first. Resist any demands to pay extra "because your visa is incorrect". **NB** Venezuelan time is 1 hour ahead of Colombian.

● **Venezuelan customs**
Customs is often closed at weekends; at such times it is not possible to cross from Cúcuta. There is a customs post 5 km after San Antonio. Be prepared for strip searches and for further searches between San Cristóbal and Mérida.

● **Crossing by private vehicle**
Car documents are checked at DIEX. You must have a visa and a *carnet de passages*. See the **Motoring** section in **Information for travellers** (page 343), for details on exit formalities. Once in Venezuela, you may find that police are ignorant of requirements for foreign cars.

● **Colombian consulate**
10 Centro Cívico San Antonio, 2nd floor, open 0800-1400. It's better to go to Mérida for visas.

● **Transport**
Air It is cheaper, though slower, to fly Caracas-San Antonio, take a taxi to Cúcuta, then take an internal Colombian flight, than to fly direct Caracas-Colombia. The airport transfer at San Antonio is well-organized and taxi drivers make the 25-minute trip with all the necessary stops. Air tickets out of Cúcuta can be reserved in advance in a Venezuelan travel agency. You can fly San Antonio-Bogotá as part of a Colombian airpass, which can be bought in Mérida (see page 181).

Road San Antonio to the border bridge by bus, US$0.80, in bolívares or pesos. Bus to **Cúcuta**, US$7.20. On any form of transport that crosses the border, make sure that the driver knows that you need to stop to obtain stamps. *Por puesto* drivers may refuse to wait. Taxi drivers will stop at all the right offices.
    NB Just to visit Cúcuta, no documents are needed.

● **Entering Colombia**
You must obtain both a Venezuelan exit stamp and a Colombian entry stamp at the border. Without the former you will be sent back; without the latter you will have problems with police checks, at banks and leaving the country. You may also be fined. Exit and entry formalities are handled at the DAS office in the white house before the international bridge on the Colombian side. For air travellers, formalities can also be undertaken at Cúcuta airport.
    Cúcuta is a sizeable city with plenty and varied accommodation and several banks offering good rates of exchange. **Venezuelan consulate**: Avenida 0, Calle 8, Cúcuta, T 713983/712107. For visa requirements to enter Venezuela see **Information for travellers** (page 329).
    NB Cúcuta bus terminal is notorious as being overrun with thieves and conmen. You should take great care. For San Cristóbal, only pay the driver of the vehicle, not at the offices upstairs in the bus station. The new Berlinas de Fonce terminal is reported as much safer.

The Llanos

THE VAST *llanos*, or plains, of Venezuela lie at the very heart of the country – spiritually and geographically. These flat grasslands cover an area of 300,000 square kilometres between the Andes and the Orinoco Delta, almost a third of the entire country. This is Venezuela's Wild West. A mythologized land of hardy *llanero* cowboys driving massive herds of cattle across ranches the size of small European countries. It is also fast becoming one of Venezuela's most prized tourist attractions: a nature paradise full of capybara, caiman, monkeys, anacondas, river dolphins, big cats and a variety of birdlife unmatched anywhere in the world.

Though rich in wildlife, the *llanos* contains only around 10% of Venezuela's human population. People here are outnumbered by cattle. About 5 million of the country's 6.4 million cattle, many of them the Zebu type from Brazil and India, are in the *llanos*. The vast flatland is only varied here and there by *mesas*, or slight upthrusts of the land. It is veined by numerous slow running rivers which are forested along their banks. During the wet season, which runs from May to November, torrential rain falls, flooding the rivers and turning the whole area into a giant inland sea. When the whole plain is under water, the *llaneros* (plainsmen) drive their cattle into the hills or through the flood from one *mesa* to another.

The dry season accounts for the rest of the year, during which not a drop of rain falls and the plain is parched by a relentless sun. The savannah grasses become uneatable, so the *llaneros* herd the cattle down to the damper region of the Apure and Orinoco. Finally they drive them into the valley of Valencia to be fattened.

South of these cattle lands stretch the forests through which flow the Orinoco and its tributaries.

As you'd expect with such an underpopulated region, most of the *llanos* is wilderness. There are very few towns, the largest being Barinas, capital of Barinas state, and San Fernando de Apure, capital of Apure state. The few roads that cross the region are generally poor, particularly after the rainy season, when bridges may be down. Until recently, this was the most undeveloped and neglected region in the country. Now, though, the government is investing in rice and cotton production in some parts to complement the cattle ranching.

The plains can be divided into two distinct zones. The high plains are farthest from the Orinoco and closer to the northern and Andean mountain ranges and feature *mesas* and hills. They can be further divided into the eastern plains (Anzoátegui and Monagas states) and the central plains (Guárico and Cojedes states).

The low plains are closer to the Orinoco and almost completely flat, which brings about flooding for several months each year. The low plains can also be subdivided into the western plains (Portuguesa and Barinas states) and southern plains (Apure state). The monotony of the flat lowlands is broken occasionally by small forests, known as *matas*, of the ubiquitous *moriche* palms.

Criss-crossing the plains are numerous rivers. Some are fast-flowing and originate in the surrounding mountains but the majority originate in the plains or in the *morichales*, which are dense growths of *moriche* palms. They all form part of the gigantic Orinoco basin. Lining the banks of the rivers are the **gallery forests**, which are teeming with birds and monkeys. The *llanos* are also bisected by many *caños*, branches of one river or the union of two rivers, which flow only during the rainy

season. In the dry season the plains are dotted with *lagunas* (lagoons) and *préstamos*, which are artificial lagoons, created by the extraction of earth to build road embankments. These *lagunas* and *préstamos* serve as a life-saving haven for the wildlife and as watering holes for cattle.

CLIMATE

The climate of the *llanos* can be divided into a wet and a dry season, as mentioned above. The dry season is called summer and the rainy season is the winter. The average temperature throughout the year is 27°C. During the rainy season the stifling heat and high humidity create a suffocating atmosphere. In the 'summer' the climate is more bearable, the sky clears and winds blow in from the northeast.

WILDLIFE OF THE LLANOS

A visit to the *llanos* is an absolute must, not just for keen birdwatchers, but for anyone remotely interested in seeing animals in their natural habitats. The magnificent fecundity of fauna can be found in the woodlands, the savannah, the lagoons and marshes and along the rivers and *caños*.

Collared anteater

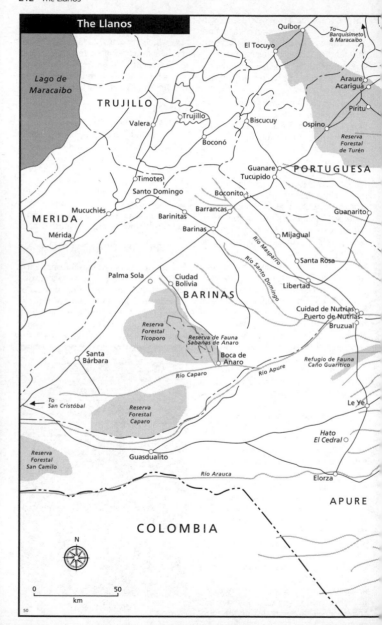

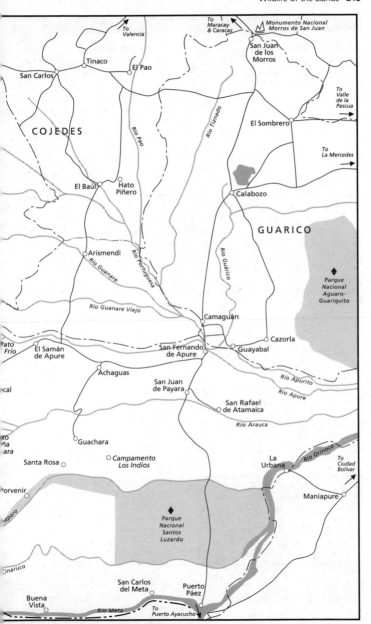

Killer fish

🦶 The much-maligned piranha has a fearsome reputation as a flesh-eating monster who will tear any unsuspecting tourist to shreds within seconds of setting foot in a tropical river. But is this infamous fish really so bad? Or is it merely the unfortunate victim of some bad publicity?

There are over 30 types of piranha in South America but only one or two types are flesh eaters. Some feed on other fish and some are even vegetarians. The red-bellied piranhas, though, are real flesh eaters. These 20 cm long fish with razor-sharp teeth hunt in packs or schools in the many rivers that intersect the *llanos* floodplains.

They breed early in the wet season, when both sexes turn a dark shade and the female is swollen with eggs. Then begins the courtship ritual, which can last several nights, as the female takes her time in deciding on her potential partner's suitability as a father. Once her mind is made up they mate and the female takes off, leaving the male to guard the eggs.

Although as many as 4,000 come from a single batch of eggs, only a handful survive the first few months. Their greatest test comes in the dry season when there is a danger of becoming isolated from the main rivers and food becomes scarce. The weaker piranhas then become victims as they fall prey to the stronger ones in a frenzy of cannibalism. Birds also join in, feeding on the dying fish. The fabled killer now has no defence against the elements. Those that are too large to be swallowed by the storks are picked off by vultures. Caiman also feed on dying piranhas, attracted by the birds. Piranhas are their favourite snack.

But when the rains come the savannah is turned into a huge inland sea and the tables are turned. The piranhas prey on the great white egrets, which nest in the trees, attracted by the young egrets' constant pleading for food. In their desperate attempts to find more food than their parents can supply the clumsy chicks leave the nest and fall in the rivers where they are grabbed by the piranhas.

In the lagoons and marshes you'll see numerous ducks, herons, the metre-and-a-half tall jábiru storks and great flocks of scarlet ibis, a stunning contrast to the whites and blacks of egrets, hawks and buzzards. In the winter you can witness one of the most spectacular sights of the

Puma

plains, when massive numbers of cormorants, herons, ibis and storks gather at the same nesting sites to reproduce.

Along the waterways you'll see kingfishers skimming the surface in search of lunch, cormorants sunning themselves on the riverbank, while noisy hoatzins sit in the branches of trees digesting their last meal. Occasionally an osprey will suddenly plunge into the water to spike its prey. Along the shorelines of the *caños* are huge numbers of spectacled caiman, or *babas*, basking in the sun. If you're lucky (or unlucky), you'll catch a glimpse of an anaconda, the largest snake in the world at up to 12m in length.

The gallery forests which line the many meandering rivers are home to fruit-eating birds such as macaws, curassow, the troupial (Venezuela's national bird) and cacique with its long hanging nests. These birds share their home with reptiles such as the fer-de-lance, iguana and boa constrictor. Providing the vocal backdrop are many songbirds and the incredibly noisy howler monkey, the largest primate in Venezuela whose screams can be heard miles away. Its smaller, and quieter, cousin, the capuchin can be seen skipping from tree to tree in large troops.

With so much life around, and potential food, the *llanos* are also home to hawks, eagles, falcons and vultures. By night the plains play host to a wide range of nocturnal beasts, among them the giant anteater, savannah fox, jaguar, puma, ocelot and *onza*, or mountain cat, while the blood-sucking vampire bat seeks out its sleeping prey.

PEOPLE OF THE LLANOS

The *llanos* is frontier territory, far removed from the bustle of modern Caracas or Venezuela's other urban centres. This wild and untamed land has been much eulogized over the years in words and song, and still today many Venezuelans will talk of this part of their country, and the people who inhabit it, in dewy-eyed wonder.

Only men of steel and muscle survived in this inhospitable land. This is the *llanero* – Venezuela's equivalent of the Argentine *gaucho*. He is a romantic and mysterious cowboy who typifies the national traits of bravery, independence, individuality, generosity and hospitality. He is the ultimate macho figure, whose close proximity to nature is in stark contrast to the Europeanized city-dweller. In the words of novelist Rómulo Gallegos, the *llanero* was "indomitable and long-suffering, indolent and tireless; impulsive and wary in combat, undisciplined and loyal with his superior, a realist and a weaver of fantasies, humble afoot and proud on horseback." His famous novel *Doña Bárbara* remains the best-known example of the *llanos* cult (see **literature** section on page 56).

The *llanos* were first settled in the mid-16th century, near present-day Calabozo, following a number of expeditions across the vast plains in search of the mythical

Llanos cowboys

Capybara (Chigüire)

One of the most common sights in the lowlands is the capybara, or *chigüire*, a large aquatic rodent that looks like a cross between a guinea pig and a hippopotamus. It is the largest of all the rodents at over 1m long and weighing over 50 kilos. They live in large groups along the river banks, where they graze on the lush grasses. It comes out onto dry land to rest and bask in the sun, but at the first hint of danger the whole troop dashes into the water. Its greatest enemies are the jaguar and puma. They are rather vocal for rodents often emitting a series of strange clicks, squeaks and grunts.

golden city of El Dorado. Later, Catholic missionaries came to convert the many diverse indigenous groups. In fact, nearly all the towns in the region began as mission settlements.

The *llaneros* were the product of the racial mix of Spanish frontiersmen and local Indians, as well as escaped black slaves. During the Wars of Independence, they were a formidable fighting force. Their leader, José Tomás Boves (The 'Butcher'), played on the *llaneros*' animosity against the wealthy Creoles to gain their support for the royalist side. Following Boves' death, the next leader, José Antonio Páez, won them over to Bolívar's patriot cause, but only after promising them social and economic reforms and the reward of lands confiscated from royalist supporters.

The *llaneros* were the backbone of the Liberator's army but they gained very little from their contribution to the country's independence. The reforms were quickly forgotten by the new Creole rulers and the distribution of land proved unworkable. Wealthy Creole officers bought up the smaller pieces of land, thus creating a new landowning class. Many of the owners of today's huge *hatos* (cattle ranches) are descended from these Creoles.

During the rest of the 19th century, the massive growth of the beef industry brought with it the arrival of transport links and fences, imposing limits on the freedom of the *llaneros*. It was at this time when the customs and traditions of the true Venezuelan cowboy began to die out, that writers and intellectuals began to romanticize him.

Though their lifestyle has been compromised by the advances of the 20th century, the *llanero* still works on the ranches, using traditional skills to round up and brand cattle, and they still sing their melancholic *llanero* ballads of romance, hard-drinking and breaking in wild horses. (See **Music and Dance**, on page 55.) Visitors to the *llanos* will still experience the strong 'Wild

West' atmosphere and the famous generous hospitality.

TOURS TO THE LLANOS

It is possible for independent travellers to explore the *llanos* but not altogether practical and virtually impossible during the May-November wet season. Though a lot of wildlife can be seen from the road, towns are few and far between and you'll miss the best of it. Those with their own transport have the option of stopping more often and will see more wildlife close up. Given the famed *llanos* hospitality, accommodation is never a problem as you can pretty much sling your hammock anywhere, or even spend the night on a farm. However, because of the immense distances involved, driving deeper into the *llanos* can mean several gruelling days of travel across relentlessly flat landscape. This is recommended, therefore, only for the most committed motorist.

A much better option is to visit the *llanos* as part of a tour and with an experienced wildlife guide. This way, you can explore the many rivers and *caños* by boat and see the best of the wildlife. This also cuts down the amount of time spent travelling by road.

The best time to visit the *llanos* is probably around the end of the wet season, when the rains are beginning to subside, the air feels less humid, but the water level on the floodplains is still high enough to allow you to get around the *caños* by boat. But whatever the time of year, if you have a week to spare you should definitely include this in your itinerary.

STAYING AT A TOURIST RANCH

The most popular means of visiting the *llanos* is to stay at one of the many cattle ranches, or *hatos*, which offer packages for tourists. These cost from US$50-150 per person per day, and include meals, accommodation, excursions by jeep, boat or horseback and guide. In the evenings, entertainment is also provided, in the shape of traditional *llanero* music and dancing. Though considerably more expensive than tours offered by some tour companies

in Mérida (see below), staying at a ranch is more comfortable and gives an insight into the working life and culture of the *llanero*. The *hatos* are mostly run on an eco-friendly basis and hunting is prohibited.

While it is possible that the owners may accommodate you if turning up unannounced, you should make reservations in advance through a local agency, either in Caracas or San Fernando de Apure. In addition to those listed below, are *Epsilon*, T 752-4592, and *Turven*, T 951-1032, F 951-1176, both in Caracas. They can also be booked through specialist tour companies in Europe and North America (see **Useful addresses** on page 355). Stays are for a minimum of 2 days and discounts are often given for longer periods.

The following *hatos* have been recommended as providing comfortable accommodation and a full range of services and facilities.

● **Hato Piñero** is a cattle ranch of 80,000 hectares which has been converted into a privately-owned nature reserve and Biological Research Station. It costs US$140 per person per day, fully inclusive, US$240 per person including return overland transport from Caracas, US$560 by chartered plane. All rooms with private bathroom, dining room and sitting room, free drinks, bi-lingual nature guide for excellent bird- and animal-watching trips. Contact address: Hato Piñero, Edificio General de Seguros, 6th floor, Oficina 6B, Avenida La Estancia, Chuao, Caracas 1060, T (2) 916965/916854/916576, F 916776. It is near El Baúl (turn off Tinaco-El Sombrero road at El Cantón). There is no public transport to the ranch but ask the police in El Baúl for a ride with the Hato Piñero workers. The last part of the road is very bad. From Caracas the direct route is 6 hours. An expensive alternative is to use the airstrip.

● **Reserva Privada de Flora y Fauna Mataclara** provides lodging with full board, horse riding, fishing and animal watching trips; it costs US$50 per person per day. It is located on the road to El Baúl at Km 93, next to the Hato Piñero turn off. Contact address: Prof Antonio González-Fernández, Universidad de Los Llanos 'Unellez', Mesa de Caracas, Guanare 3323, Estado de Portuguesa, F 057-68130.

● **Hato Turístico El Cedral** is a beautiful ranch of 50,000 hectares, 3 hours by road from Barinas, 4 hours from San Fernando. It can also be reached by light aircraft. Accommodation in air conditioned bungalows, with private bathrooms, small pool, bar, excellent bi-lingual guides, good entertainment. They charge about US$150 per person per night including 3 meals, 2 tours per day, or US$45 for a daytime visit. Visits can be arranged only through Turismo Aventura, Caracas, T 02-951-1143.

● **Hato Doña Bárbara** is named after the heroine of Romulo Gallegos' eponymous novel. It's a 95,000 hectare working ranch where you can see the traditional *llanero* skills in practice, including the unique rhyming couplets which are sung to relax the cows while they're being milked by hand. Accommodation consists of 20 simple but comfortable rooms with bathroom. It costs about US$150 per person per night including 3 meals, 2 tours per day, or US$45 for a daytime visit. Book through the *Doña Bárbara* travel agency, which occupies the ground floor and Mezzanine of *Hotel La Torraca*, Paseo Libertador, Apartado 55, San Fernando de Apure, T (047) 25003, F 27902.

● **Hato El Frío** offers similar facilities and services to those above and charges about the same price. It is near the town of Mantecal (see below) on the road west from San Fernando.

TOURS FROM MERIDA

Taking a tour to the *llanos* need not be expensive. Several tour companies in Mérida offer 3-4 day tours for around US$20-25 per person per day, including road transport, guide, boat trips, meals and accommodation. Some tours even include horse riding and, for a small additional cost, white-water rafting. Check exactly what is offered before booking a tour. For a list of recommended agencies in Mérida offering tours to the *llanos* see under **Tour companies & travel agents**, page 179.

A typical 4-day tour of the *llanos* takes in the spectacular road from Santo Domingo down to Barinas, via Barinitas (see **Routes to the Llanos** below). From Barinas you head deeper into the vast savannah lands, stopping frequently to see huge flocks of migratory birds, caiman and capybara, monkeys, macaws, toucans and iguanas, perhaps even an anaconda. I once saw a puma run across the road right in front of us. Accommodation is rustic, sleeping in hammocks under rough thatch shelters, but it all adds to the feeling of being close to nature. Food is good and plentiful,

including the delicious local fish and huge, tender *llanos* steaks.

As mentioned above, some tours include white-water rafting. When the water is too low for white water, you can just float along a slow-moving river, admiring the passing scenery. One of the highlights is the trip by motorized canoe through the maze of *caños*, where you can get really close to the birds and animals, including the river dolphins which sometimes follow the boats. You can even enjoy a spot of piranha fishing. Another highlight is the breathtaking *llanos* sunset, which has to be seen to be believed.

ROUTES TO THE LLANOS

The main points of entry into the *llanos* are the two main cities of Barinas and San Fernando de Apure. They can be reached from most of Venezuela's main cities: south from **Caracas, Valencia** and **Barquisimeto**; east from **Mérida** and **San Cristóbal**; west from **Ciudad Bolívar**; or north from **Puerto Ayacucho**.

VALENCIA TO BARINAS

An excellent paved road (Ruta 5) runs from Valencia to the western *llanos* of Barinas. It runs past the site of the famous **Battle of Carabobo** (see **Excursions from Valencia**, page 120), then enters the state of Cojedes and heads south to the **Tinaca** junction, where another road (Ruta 13) heads left (east) to meet Ruta 2 running south from **San Juan de Los Morros** towards **Calabozo** (see page 224).

21 km east of Tinaca on Ruta 13 is the turn-off to the unremarkable town of **El Pao**. 17 km beyond the turn-off on Ruta 13 is another turn-off (Ruta 8) which heads south through **El Baúl** (see **Hato Piñero**, page 217) and deep into the *llanos* before joining the main **San Fernando de Apure-Barinas** Highway at **Apurito** (see page 227). The road to El Baúl is in fairly good condition, but is difficult in the rainy season. South from El Baúl it is passable only in a 4WD vehicle and completely impassable during the rainy season.

Ruta 5, meanwhile, continues 17 km west from Tinaca to **San Carlos**.

SAN CARLOS

San Carlos de Austria (*population* 71,650; *phone code* 058), as it is known in full, is capital of Cojedes State. It's a handsome, prosperous-looking town set in rich cattle ranching and agricultural country. Rice, cotton and tobacco are all grown around here. The town boasts some fine 18th century architecture, including 3 colonial churches. It hosts festivals on 18 January and on 2-5 November, the *San Carlos Borromeo*.

● **Accommodation & places to eat C** *Central*, safe, air conditioning, good bar and restaurant, secure parking; **E** pp *Motel San Carlos*, Avenida Carabobo, air conditioning, bathroom, OK for a stopover.

ROUTES Ruta 5 continues west from San Carlos for 37 km to the Araure-Acarigua by-pass, which meets Ruta 4 running south from **Barquisimeto** (see page 149).

ARAURE-ACARIGUA

The city of **Acarigua** (*phone code* 055) has grown rapidly in the last few decades to become the largest city in Portuguesa state. It has also merged with neighbouring **Araure** to become virtually one city. In the process it has also swallowed up the little town of **Curpa**, birthplace of General José Antonio Páez, the great *llanero* hero of the Wars of Independence and first President of the Republic (see **History** section on page 43). This is a thriving agricultural centre, with little of interest for tourists. One of the main local festivals is the *Virgen de la Corteza* held in Acarigua on 11 February, with bull-baiting and dancing.

● **Accommodation In Acarigua**: **C** *Motel Payara**, on the road to Guanare, pool, air conditioning; **C** *Hotel Parigua*, Calle 31, air conditioning, secure parking; **E** *Motel Rancho Grande*, safe, very mediocre restaurant attached; *Campeste*, near the bus terminal.

ROUTES The Arure-Acarigua by-pass rejoins Ruta 5 at **Ospino**, 36 km to the southwest. The highway continues towards **Guanare** along the edge of the Andean foothills through fields of sugar cane and pastureland.

GUANARE

The capital of the state of Portuguesa (*population* 32,500; *phone code* 057) is a prosperous agricultural centre. The town is more famously known, though, as the country's spiritual capital and a national place of pilgrimage. For here is the much venerated Sanctuary of the Virgin of Coromoto, the Patron Saint of Venezuela. The huge gilded sanctuary is housed in the neoclassic **Basílica de La Virgen de Coromoto**, built in 1788-90 and beautifully restored in 1949, which stands proudly on the Plaza Bolívar. The image of the Virgin was moved to its present site in 1654. The original site of the apparition lies several kilometres south of Guanare, just off Ruta 5 near the town of **Tucupido**.

Pilgrimages to the Sanctuary of Coromoto are made on 2 January, the traditional Day of the Virgin, and 8 September, the day of the apparition. Another celebration in Guanare is Candlemas on 1 February.

The Virgin and Coromoto

It was in 1651 that the Virgin first appeared to the Cospes Indians, near Guanare, and told them to be baptized so that they could go to heaven. The Indian chief, Coromoto, refused though he did hedge his bets by getting other members of the tribe baptized. When the Virgin reappeared to tell him a second time, Coromoto grew furious and told her to leave. When she approached him he threatened her and then made a grab at her. But she vanished leaving in his hand a likeness of herself on the inner surface of a split stone now on display in the church in Guanare (another version has her image on a parchment, which is also on display). For years, little attention was paid to the image, and it was only in 1942 that this Virgin was declared the Patron of Venezuela by his Holiness Pope Pius XII.

• **Accommodation & places to eat** C *Italia*, Carrera 5, No 19-60, air conditioning, bar and restaurant, parking; C *Motel Portuguesa*, on the northern outskirts of town (beware of the dangerous intersection), air conditioning, cold water, good restaurant, pool, small zoo with tiny cages for animals; D *Colina*, near the river at the bottom of town, motel-style, comfortable, restaurant; E *Colonial*, Avenida Miranda; E *Vega del Río**, with restaurant; E *Venezia*, with shower, recommended. On the main road to Acarigua is *Motel Sultana*, air conditioning, safe, reasonable bar and restaurant adjacent. A popular restaurant is *El Paisano*. Others include *Restaurant Don Quixote*, near *Hotel Italia*, good atmosphere but expensive; and *Turística La Casa Vieja*, good food, good value, lots of old photos of the area.

ROUTES A road from Guanare runs northwest up into the hills to **Biscucuy**, where it joins Ruta 7 west to **Boconó** and from there on to **Trujillo** and **Valera** (see page 199).

The El Llano Highway (Ruta 5) runs southwest from Guanare towards Barinas. After 38 km is a turn-off to the left (east) which leads to the towns of **Ciudad de Nutrias** and **Bruzual**, standing on opposite sides of the Río Apure (see page 228). From the turn-off it's a further 41 km to Barinas.

MERIDA TO BARINAS

From Mérida, the Transandean Highway forks at **Apartaderos** and the right branch heads through **Santo Domingo** (see page 190), across the state border into Barinas and down to the state capital. This is one of the most spectacular roads in the country, which descends dramatically from over 2,000m down through increasingly lush, tropical vegetation till it reaches **Barinitas**. Though small by anyone's standards, Barinitas is still the second largest town in Barinas state. 'Little Barinas' gets its name from the fact that this was big brother's penultimate move, before finally coming to rest at its present site. From here, it's a further 27 km through coffee and cacao country to the state capital.

BARINAS

Seated along the banks of the Río Santo Domingo, **Barinas** (*population* 192,000; *phone code* 073), is the hot and sticky capital of the cattle-raising and oil-rich State of Barinas and the only city of note in the province.

Founded in 1567, Barinas was second only to Caracas in terms of wealth and importance throughout the colonial period. Though the city declined somewhat in significance after independence, it remains commercially important. Agriculture and ranching are the city's economic mainstays. While the timber industry has moved on after having stripped the area of most of its valuable tropical woods, it has been replaced by the petroleum industry, now actively drilling in the eastern section of the state.

For those not arriving with business interests, there's little to see or do here. The city, like most others in the country, is laid out in a grid pattern emanating from the Plaza Bolívar. The most important streets are the Avenida Marqués del Pumar and Medina Jiménez. Along these parallel thoroughfares you'll find the majority of the city's banks, exchange houses, hotels and restaurants, as well as commercial enterprises.

At present there is little in the way of tourism infrastructure in Barinas. Visitors wishing to spend time at a *hato* or explore the *llanero* culture would be better off in the neighbouring Apure State. Similarly, those wishing to hike through the Sierra Nevada National Park (most of which is in Barinas State) will find easier access from Mérida.

Places of interest

On the west of the plaza is the restored **Palacio del Marqués**, the one-time residence of the city's most famous aristocrat, the Marqués de las Riberas de Boconó y Masparro. Too large to be kept as a residence now, it houses several municipal offices as well as the police station.

This is one of the few colonial buildings still standing. Another is the **Casa de la Cultura**, on the north side of the

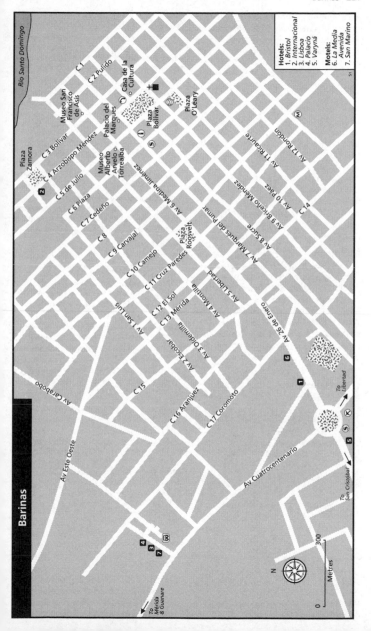

Barinas

Río Santo Domingo

C 1
C 2 Pulido

Museo San
Francisco
de Asís

C 3 Bolívar

Plaza
Zamora

C 4 Arzobispo Méndez

C 5 de Julio

C 6 Plaza

C 7 Cedeño

C 8

C 9 Carvajal

C 10 Camejo

C 11 Cruz Paredes

C 12 El Sol

C 13 Mérida

C 15

C 16 Aranjuez

C 17 Coromoto

Casa de la
Cultura

Palacio del
Marqués

Museo
Alberto
Arvelo
Torrealba

Plaza
Bolívar

Plaza
O'Leary

Plaza
Roosvelt

Av 6 Medina Jiménez

Av 1 San Luis

Av 2 Escobar

Av 3 Olleminia

Av 4 Montana

Av 5 Libertad

Av 7 Marqués del Pumar

Av 8 Sucre

Av 9 Briceño Méndez

Av 10 Páez

Av 11 Ricaurte

Av 12 Rondón

C 14

Av 26 de Enero

Av Carabobo

Av Este Oeste

Av Cuatrocentenario

To liberdad

To San Cristóbal

To Mérida
& Guanare

N

Métres

0   300

Hotels:
1. Bristol
2. Internacional
3. Lisboa
4. Palacio
5. Varyná

Motels:
6. La Media
Avenida
7. San Marino

S1

plaza. Originally built as a city hall-cum-prison, it is now a well-run cultural centre. Its use as a prison ended only in 1966 and is notable as the site of a famous 1850 escape by the *caudillo* José Antonio Páez, who succeeded in freeing 115 other prisoners at the same time!

To the east of the plaza is the **Cathedral**, built between 1760 and 1780. The interior has been renovated, although the original art has been replaced in the process. To the south of the plaza sits the beautifully restored **Escuela de Música**, a mid-19th century building originally commissioned as a Masonic Lodge.

Just outside the city, along Avenida 23 de Enero, is the shady **Parque Universitario** which has a botanical garden and a zoo. It is open Monday to Friday and admission is free.

Museums

The **Museo San Francisco de Asís**, on Avenida Medina Jiménez, two blocks northwest of Plaza Bolívar, has a collection of antique religious art. It's open weekdays only; entry US$1. The **Museo Alberto Arvelo Torrealba**, at the corner of Calle 5 de Julio and Avenida Medina Jiménez, one block west of the plaza, houses exhibits on *llanero* culture. Open Tuesday to Sunday, 0900-1200 and 1500-1800; entry US$1.25.

Local information
● Accommodation

Hotel prices

L1	over US$200	L2	US$151-200
L3	US$101-150	A1	US$81-100
A2	US$61-80	A3	US$46-60
B	US$31-45	C	US$21-30
D	US$12-20	E	US$7-11
F	US$4-6	G	up to US$3

Those marked with an asterisk (*) are bookable through Fairmont International (see under Caracas).

On Avenida 23 de Enero, near the airport are: **C** *Bristol**, air conditioning, safe, good, recommended, nondescript restaurant; and **C** *Varyná*, air conditioning, recommended.

D *Internacional*, Calle Arzobispo Méndez on Plaza Zamora, T 22343, air conditioning, safe, good restaurant.

E *Motel La Media Avenida*, also on Avenida 23 de Enero near the airport, T 22278, cold showers, bar, restaurant, parking, recommended.

Opposite the bus terminal are: **E** *Palacio*, air conditioning, good value; **F** pp *Lisboa*, basic, fan; **E-F** pp *Motel San Marino*, with bath, air conditioning, small rooms, not too clean.

● Places to eat

Adán y Eva, Avenida Sucre, *criollo* restaurant, good; *Don Enrique*, opposite *Hotel Palacio*, good, cheap. There's also a good patisserie opposite the bus terminal. *Yoanna*, Avenida 7, 16-47, corner of Márques del Pumar, Arab owner, excellent; *Franko Café*, on Plaza Sucre, bar/restaurant, good, music; *El Estribo*, Calle Apure entre Avenida Garguera y Andrés Varela, roast and barbecued local meat, good, open 1100-2400.

● Banks & money changers

Banco Italo or Banco Unión, for Mastercard or Visa cash withdrawals. Banco de Barinas accepts Thomas Cook travellers' cheques.

● Tourist offices

On Avenida Marqués del Pumar, less than a block southwest of Plaza Bolívar; open Monday to Friday, 0830-1200 and 1430-1730, helpful, but no English spoken, local maps are available here, and at the three kiosks (at the airport, the bus terminal and in Parque Los Mangos).

● Transport

Air The city's airport is served twice daily by Avensa flights to/from Caracas. The tourist office here is friendly and has a free town map and hotel list.

Buses The bus terminal is 2 km west of the main plaza, on the edge of the town. A taxi to/from the centre costs US$1. To **Mérida**, 5 a day with Transportes Barinas, US$2.50, 5-7 hours, a spectacular ride through the mountains (sit on the right going up for the best views); *por puesto*, US$4.15, 4 hours. To **Valera** at 0730, US$3.15, 7 hours. To **Santo Domingo**, 2½ hours, US$1.40. To **Caracas**, US$6.70, 8-9 hours, several companies go direct or via **Maracay** and **Valencia**, regularly 0730-2300. To **San Cristóbal**, several daily, US$3.75, 5 hours. To **San Fernando de Apure**, US$8.15, 9 hours with Expresos Los Llanos at 0900 and 2300. The same company also goes to **Maracaibo** (at 2000 and 2200, US$7.80, 8 hours), **San Antonio** (at 2330) and **Puerto La Cruz** (at 0730 and 1445, US$14.25, 16 hours).

SOUTH OF BARINAS

The El Llano Highway (Route 5) runs southwest from Barinas along the eastern edge of the Andes to **San Cristóbal** (see page 204). Running throughout this area is a network of prehispanic raised causeways, called *calzadas*. There are also a number of artificial mounds (*montículos*), some of which measure up to 90m in diameter. Though the exact purpose or construction date is not yet known, it is thought they were used as island village sites during the rainy season. One can be seen near the **La Acequia** bridge, on Route 5, before **Palma Sola**. There are also some 17 km south of **Ciudad Bolivia**, on the **Mijagual-Boca de Anaro** road. The colonial mission churches at Palma Sola and Ciudad Bolivia were both built on huge mounds.

ROUTES Motorists travelling east from Mérida to Ciudad Bolívar can either head east from Barinas across the *llanos* to San Fernando de Apure; or they can head north via San Carlos, Tinaco, El Sombrero, Valle de la Pascua and El Tigre. The latter route requires no ferry crossings and has more places with accommodation.

CARACAS TO SAN FERNANDO DE APURE

There are two main routes from Caracas south to the *llanos*. One heads due south through **Cúa** while the other turns south off the Pan-American Highway to Maracay, just beyond **San Mateo** (see page 111), near the town of Cagua. Both routes converge at **San Juan de Los Morros**, the northern gateway to the vast plains.

VIA CUA

The former route (Route 15) branches left (east) off the Panamerican just south of Caracas. It bypasses **Charallave** and then **Cúa**, 40 km south, from where another road runs east through **Ocumare del Tuy** to meet Route 9, the main highway east from Caracas to Barcelona, at **Caucagua** (see page 230). There is accommodation in Cúa at **E** *Hotel Cúa*, with bathroom, air conditioning.

38 km south of Cúa Route 15 meets Route 11, where you head right (west) for 37 km to San Juan de Los Morros, via **San Sebastián**. From here you can also head east on Route 11 and then south to **El Sombrero**, at the junction with Route 13

from **San Carlos** to **Valle de la Pascua** (see page 224).

The road to El Sombrero is via **Camatagua** (*population* 8,050), 2 km off the highway. There are 2 hotels in town. 7 km from town is a very good campsite by a hydroelectric dam and lake; US$0.30 per person, safe, drinking water, pit latrines, 'cabañas'. The turn-off is 1 km before town.

VIA VILLA DE CURA

This route leaves the Pan-American Highway near **Cagua** (*population* 92,000), 16 km east of Maracay. 21 km south of the turn-off is the town of **Villa de Cura**. Founded in 1717 by the paternal great grand-father of the Liberator, Villa de Cura has twice been the capital of Aragua State. The town gets its name from the indigenous word for avocado (*cura*) which is common to many towns in Aragua.

A good road leads 21 km southeast to San Juan de los Morros. On the last section you'll be able to see the famous *Morros*.

SAN JUAN DE LOS MORROS

The capital of the state of Guárico (*population* 78,500; *phone code* 046) gets its name from the terracotta-coloured, sugar-loaf mountains which rise spectacularly out of the surrounding hills. These are actually remnants of ancient coral reefs which were squeezed into position with the formation of the coastal range. The highest *Morro* is *El Morro del Faro* (1,060m), so-called because the former dictator Gómez had a huge beacon built on top in order to orient cowboys driving their herds from the *llanos* to market. The *Morros* have become popular with mountain climbers, and several routes have been opened.

Morros de San Juan

The town was never formerly founded, but it grew to prominence when its hot springs came to the attention of President Guzmán Blanco. The dictator Gómez then had a road built from Villa de Cura to ease access. The *balneario* has since been renovated and improved by a succession of dictators. Today, the hot (35°C), sulphurous waters can still be visited.

● **Accommodation D** *Gran Hotel Los Morros*, on the road towards Villa de Cura; **D** *Excelsior*, on Calle Marino.

SOUTH FROM SAN JUAN

51 km south of San Juan, just past **Ortiz**, Route 2 meets Route 13, which runs west to **San Carlos**, and east to **El Sombrero**, a place best passed through quickly.

● **Accommodation, places to eat & transport In El Sombrero: E-F** *Brasilia*, near the plaza, with bathroom, good fans, colour TV, safe parking, recommended. There's very good food at *Restaurante Mary*, Calle Descanso 2, US$2-3 per person, good and varied menu. Buses leave from the intersection 5 minutes' walk from town across the bridge. If you're waiting at the *Estación* restaurant look out for buses going to Ciudad Bolívar as they leave from across the road and will leave without you. To Ciudad Bolívar, at 1700, 7 hours, US$2.90.

90 km east of El Sombrero is **Chaguaramas**, with accommodation in the motel at the west end of town: **E**, bathroom, air conditioning, check for scorpions in shoes and snakes in bedside tables. There's a good restaurant across the highway.

From Chaguaramas Route 12 turns south to the Orinoco. It passes through **Las Mercedes**, where there is accommodation: **E** *Gran Hotel Las Mercedes*, noisy air conditioning, mosquitoes, poor restaurant, safe parking. The badly potholed road runs through flat cattle land for 179 km to **Cabruta** (*population* 4,300), on the banks of the Río Orinoco. On the opposite bank is the town of **Caicara del Orinoco** (see page 283). From here you can either head southwest to **Puerto Ayacucho** in the Amazonas region (see page 322), or east to **Ciudad Bolívar** (see page 284).

● **Accommodation & transport In Cabruta**: there is a small hotel, infested with rats and cockroaches. A daily bus goes to Caracas, US$6.75.

Back on Route 13, 28 km east of Chaguaramas, is **Valle de la Pascua** (*population* 75,200).

● **Accommodation In Valle de la Pascua**: **E** *Hotel Venezuela*, on Plaza Bolívar; **E** *San Marcos*, on the main road towards El Socorro; **E** *Gran Hotel Monte Carlo*, opposite the bus station, suites available, air conditioning, shower, locked car park.

There are two options east from Valle de Pascua. Route 13 heads east and slightly north through **Tucupido** (30 km), **Zaraza** (54 km) and **Aragua de Barcelona** (47 km) to meet the main highway from the coast to **Ciudad Bolívar**, just north of **Anaco** (see page 242), in the state of Anozoátegui.

Another road, Route 15, meanwhile, heads southeast towards **El Tigre** (see page 242). The first 38 km to **El Socorro** is okay, but beyond El Socorro the road to El Tigre is in poor shape, especially for cyclists. 53 km beyond El Socorro is **Santa María de Ipire**, a pretty, old village with narrow streets, but no hotel. 4 km east is a restaurant and petrol station which may provide accommodation. In **Pariaguán**, 83 km further on towards El Tigre, there is accommodation in **E** *Hotel Modin*, opposite the bus terminal, bathroom, air conditioning, small and filthy.

CALABOZO

The main route from San Juan de los Morros to San Fernando de Apure continues beyond the crossroads south of Ortiz through increasingly flat grasslands to **Calabozo** (*population* 91,000; *phone code* 046), 132 km south of San Juan. On the left, as you approach the town you'll see the massive Guárico dam, which has excellent fishing.

Calabozo was first settled by Capuchin Missionaries as a stopping point on the way further south to convert the Indians of the Orinoco. The neoclassic **Cathedral**, built in 1754-1790, is one of Venezuela's finest examples of baroque religious architecture. The town also boasts many other interesting colonial buildings and is worth a brief visit, if you're passing through.

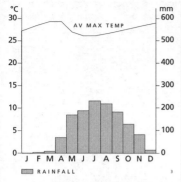

Climate: Calabozo

● **Accommodation & places to eat** D *Motel Tiuna*, Avenida via San Fernando, air conditioning, good restaurant, safe car park, good value, recommended. *El Castañuelo* is a restaurant on the main road junction, it is elegant, serves good food and is popular.

CALABOZO TO SAN FERNANDO

The main road south to San Fernando (132 km) drives deep into the heart of the vast *llanos*, through a landscape that's flat as a pool table. On the way you pass great flocks of birds and see caiman basking on sandbanks and around the many tiny lagoons, especially around **Camaguán**, just before San Fernando.

An alternative route from Calabozo turns southeast to **Paso del Caballo** (81 km). This road goes on to **Cazorla** (85 km). On the swamps you can see egrets, parrots, alligators and monkeys (and hear howlers). At Cazorla the road then turns west to **Guayabal**, passing through **Puerto Miranda** on the Río Apure. It's 64 km to Guayabal and a further 21 km to San Fernando.

APURE STATE

At 76,501 sq km, Apure is the country's third largest state, behind the enormous states of Amazonas and Bolívar. Its namesake, the Río Apure, forms its northern border with the states of Táchira, Barinas and Guárico, while the mighty Orinoco demarcates its eastern border with Bolívar State, and the Río Meta forms its border with Amazonas and much of its southern boundary with Colombia.

With roughly 500,000 inhabitants, Apure is one of Venezuela's least populated states. Much of the population is based in the capital city, San Fernando de Apure. Additional settlements are few and far between, the other main ones being **Achaguas** (see page 227) and **Guasdualito** (see page 228). Most of the land is taken by the *hatos*, enormous autonomous cattle-raising ranches that can stretch for hundreds of kilometres. Many of these ranches are foreign-owned and have opened their lands to the potentially-lucrative business of eco-tourism. Apure is home to a number of well-known *hatos* which now offer accommodation and excursions for tourists (see page 217).

The Apure landscape is relentlessly flat, the climate oppressively hot (especially in the wet season) and the road system negligible. Not surprisingly, then, it doesn't attract too many visitors. But the state is home to an abundance of wildlife, particularly along its rivers, that thrives in an undisturbed habitat. Two indigenous tribes, the Yaruro and Guajibo, inhabit the forests along the Meta and Orinoco rivers. The distinct Apure culture is perhaps the most isolated in all of Venezuela, which only enhances its image as a far away place. Even the name 'Apure' in the native dialect means 'farther away'.

SAN FERNANDO DE APURE

San Fernando is the hot and sticky capital of the state of Apure (*population* 115,000; *phone code* 047). As the only city in the entire eastern *llanos*, it is a fast-growing trade and transport hub for the region. Originally settled as a missionary town in the 17th century because of its convenient location on the Río Apure, its rich farmlands now attract many new arrivals. San Fernando's status as a provincial capital and business centre gives it unrivalled stature in the region, especially as no other sizeable settlements exist for hundreds of kilometres.

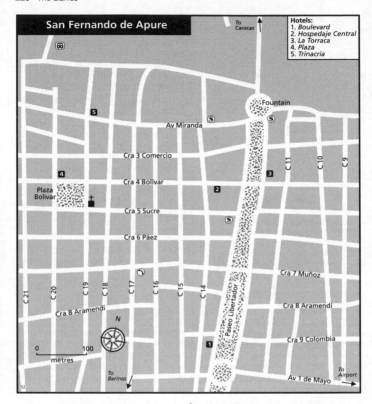

San Fernando de Apure

To Caracas

Hotels:
1. *Boulevard*
2. *Hospedaje Central*
3. *La Torraca*
4. *Plaza*
5. *Trinacria*

Fountain

Av Miranda

Cra 3 Comercio

Cra 4 Bolívar

Plaza Bolívar

Cra 5 Sucre

Cra 6 Páez

Cra 7 Muñoz

Cra 8 Aramendi

Cra 8 Aramendi

Cra 9 Colombia

C 21 C 20 C 19 C 18 C 17 C 16 C 15 C 14

C 11 C 10 C 9

Paseo Libertador

0   100
metres

N

To Barinas

To Airport

Av 1 de Mayo

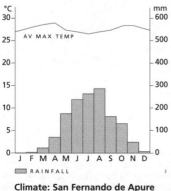

Climate: San Fernando de Apure

There is little to see or do in San Fernando and, unless you're using it as a base from which to visit one of the *hatos*, a stay of a few hours is enough. Like every other town or city, there's a pleasant Plaza Bolívar, next to which is the cathedral and, surprisingly, a century-old Masonic temple. Unlike most cities, however, the main thoroughfare does not run off the plaza, but instead is six blocks east. This is Paseo Libertador, which is also known as Avenida Miranda as it approaches the river. At the northern end is a fountain depicting some alligators and also a statue of Pedro Camejo ('El Negro Primero'), a black lancer who gained honour (and death) at the Battle of Camejo. At the southern end of the paseo is a monument to the town's ancestors who fought with Bolívar in the Wars of Independence.

The only other point of interest in town is the **Palacio Barbarito**, just off the paseo at the northern end. It is a relic of the city's heyday in the last century as a river trading town and boasts ornate Italianate features. Once stunning, it is now sadly run-down and completely incongruous. There is a small pottery museum upstairs. Admission to the building and museum is free.

Local information
● **Accommodation**

Most hotels are within one block of the intersection of Paseo Libertador and Avenida Miranda.

C *Gran Hotel Plaza*, on the Plaza Bolívar, T 21504, air conditioning, accepts Visa and Mastercard, good.

D pp *Trinacria*, on Avenida Miranda, near the bus station, T 23578, huge rooms, air conditioning, no breakfast.

E pp *El Río*, on Paseo Libertador near the bus terminal, T 23454, with bathroom, air conditioning, good value; **E** pp *La Torraca*, Avenida Boulevard y Paseo Libertador, T 22777, excellent rooms, air conditioning, plush bathroom, balcony overlooking centre of town, recommended (on the ground floor is the *Doña Barbara Agency* which also functions as a *de facto* tourist office).

F pp *Boulevard*, Paseo Libertador, with bath, air conditioning; **F** *Maracay*, Sucre 88, fan, a little run down, lots of bugs.

G pp *Hospedaje Central*, Calle Bolívar 98, T 24120, with bathroom, colonial-style, basic but friendly.

● **Places to eat**

Mister Pollo, Avenida Carabobo, good value chicken; *Punto Criollo*, Avenida Miranda, good value; *Europa*, opposite *Hotel La Torraca*, cheap, excellent, creole Italian and other international food, good service, occasional evening cabaret, recommended; *Gran Imperio Romano*, small, popular, two blocks along Avenida Boulevard from *Europa*, good and cheap. The *Comedor* in the building beside CANTV has a good *menú*, Monday-Friday, 1100-1200.

● **Banks & money changers**

Most of the banks are along Paseo Libertador, such as **Banco Unión**, at Libertador and Carretera 5, cash advance on Mastercard and Visa. One block away from the main street, on Avenida Miranda, is **Banco Consolidado** for American Express.

● **Transport**

Air San Fernando has the only municipal airport in the region. There are daily Avensa flights to **Caracas**, and to **Puerto Ayacucho**. It's best to arrive early at the airport. It's a 30-minute journey.

Buses The terminal is modern and clean, and not far from the centre. A taxi costs US$1.20. To **Caracas**, 3 daily, US$6.50, 7-8 hours; to **Maracay**, 10 daily, 6½ hours, US$4.20; to **Barinas**, 6 daily (also during the night), 9 hours (take food and drink), though the road is paved it's a rough ride, US$8.15; to **Puerto Ayacucho**, 3 daily, US$9, 8 hours; to **Calabozo**, 1½ hours, US$1.80. To **Ciudad Bolívar**, take a bus to Calabozo, and a *por puesto* from there to El Sombrero (US$1.10), where you can catch a bus to Ciudad Bolívar (see page 224). **NB** The roads north to Calabozo and west to Barinas can be very difficult during the rainy season.

River From San Fernando you can travel east to **Ciudad Bolívar** by taking a boat (which is expensive and unreliable and not possible in the dry season) from opposite the airport to **Caicara del Orinoco** (see page 283).

SAN FERNANDO TO BARINAS

From San Fernando you can drive 468 km west towards Barinas, through the heart of the *llanos*. The road more or less parallels the Río Apure for the first part of the trip as it passes through **Achaguas**, **Apurito** and **El Samán de Apure**, from where it turns south towards **La Ye** (see below).

The road is paved all the way to Barinas and beyond, but some sections are badly potholed, particularly the stretch between **Mantecal** and **Bruzual**, which is in terrible condition. The poor driving conditions are more than compensated by the incredible variety of fauna and birdlife that can be seen from the road (preferably through binoculars), especially in the early morning. In the dry season caiman and capybara can be seen on the sandy riverbanks and in the myriad lagoons dotted across the plains. In the wet season you'll see them cross the road. You can also see iguanas, deer, *arrau* (Orinoco turtles) and vast numbers of white and blue herons, scarlet ibis, ducks, storks and Orinoco geese.

MANTECAL

Mantecal is a cattle-ranching town, 220 km west of San Fernando and 13 km east of the La Ye junction (see below). Stepping off the bus here is like walking onto the set of a low-budget western movie, especially in the wet season when everyone is knee-deep in mud. Stetson hats, jeans and cowboy boots are *de rigeur* and all that's missing is the saloon with swing doors and a full-scale gunfight. Despite the Wild West connotations, though, the legendary *llanos* hospitality is very much in evidence. The town hosts a *Fiesta* on 23-26 February.

There are no tours on offer here but take a taxi to **Modelo Mantecal**, an eco-tourism area where caiman and capybaras can be seen. To view the waterbirds from the road be there before sunrise. A rough track runs south from Mantecal to the *Hato Doña Bárbara* (see page 218).

● **Accommodation** E *Hotel El Pescador*, air conditioning, restaurant, OK; F *Hospedaje Centro Llano*, fan, shared shower, basic but good value. There are two other hotels and many places to eat, such as *Gardenia*, which is excellent, cheap, and very friendly.

● **Buses** To/from San Fernando de Apure, 4-5 hours, US$2.70; to Barinas, 4 hours, US$3.60.

ROUTES 13 km west of Mantecal is **La Ye** crossroads. From here, you can head south to *Hato El Cedral* (see page 217). Another road heads west for 192 km before it reaches **Guasdualito**, from where you can turn south to the Colombian border at **El Amparo de Apure**. The main highway continues west for 121 km until it meets Route 5, the Llano Highway from Barinas to San Cristóbal (see page 222). It's a good idea to take spare gasoline on the road to Guasdualito.

The road to **Barinas** turns north at La Ye and heads 60 km to **Bruzual**.

BRUZUAL

The little town of Bruzual (*population* 4,800) sits on the south bank of the mighty Río Apure, opposite **Puerto de Nutrias**. The town is periodically flooded in the wet season when the Apure bursts its banks. The main plaza can be under 2m of water and people have to get around by canoe.

● **Accommodation** There are a few primitive hotels: E *Los Llaneros*, restaurant, dirty bathroom; E-F *Golpe Criollo*, on the plaza, with bathroom, air conditioning, good beds, safe parking, cheap and OK restaurant, unfriendly, basic rooms full of insects.

● **Transport Road** To Mantecal, US$1.50. Note that there are not many buses on Sunday, though one leaves at 1000.

ROUTES The road to Barinas heads across the bridge and through **Ciudad de Nutrias**, from where it runs 134 km further north to the junction with Route 5 at the Barinas-Portuguesa border, near the Río Boconó (see page 220). A shorter route turns off this road at **Dolores**, 38 km north of Bruzual, and runs 95 km directly to Barinas.

SAN FERNANDO TO PUERTO AYACUCHO

206 km due south of San Fernando is the trading outpost of **Puerto Páez** (*population* 2,600) at the confluence of the Meta and Orinoco rivers. Here there are crossings to **Puerto Carreño** in Colombia (see page 228), and to **El Burro**, west of the **Caicara-Puerto Ayacucho** road (see page 228). A road is being built from San Fernando to Puerto Páez. The first 134 km is paved, then from the Río Capanaparo it is dirt, deeply rutted and passable only in the dry season by 4WD vehicles or buses. There are 3 buses daily from San Fernando to Puerto Páez in the dry season, and 4 ferry crossings. If this road is closed, to get to Puerto Ayacucho from San Fernando involves a 15-hour (minimum) detour via the Caicara ferry.

Between the Capanaparo and Cinaruco rivers is the **Parque Nacional Cinaruco-Capanaparo**, also known as **Santos Luzardo**. The park is scarcely a decade old and comprises nearly 6,000 sq km of pristine sub-tropical ecosystem where you can see over 300 species of birds, as well as everything from the ubiquitous capybara to caiman, fresh-water dolphins and even the elusive jaguar. The park has no infrastructure or guides. Access is by the unfinished San Fernando-Puerto Páez road, which will run right through the park when it's completed.

The Northeast

THE NORTHEAST COAST of Venezuela, from Caracas all the way to the Paría Peninsula, holds some of the country's most beautiful scenery. It was here that Columbus first set foot on South  American soil. So overwhelmed was he by what he saw that he was moved to describe it as "paradise on earth".

An awful lot of tourists have passed this way since then, but the sights which greet them are still every bit as heavenly. This is very much the Venezuela of glossy tourist brochures. Dazzlingly white, palm-fringed beaches and crystal-clear turquoise waters backed by steep jungle slopes, deserted offshore islands, tiny fishing villages, old colonial ports and that unique Caribbean flavour help to make this one of the most visited parts of the country. At the far eastern tip you can make the crossing to the island of Trinidad, or take the more straightforward alternative and visit Isla de Margarita, Venezuela's very own Miami beach.

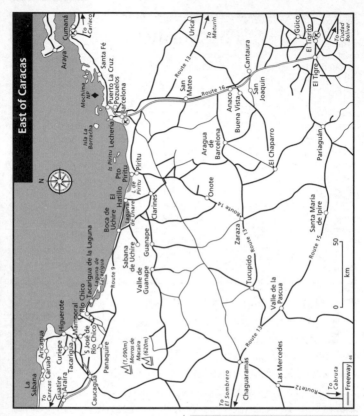

East of Caracas

BASICS The eastern part of the North-Eastern Highlands, with summits rising to 2,000m, has abundant rainfall in its tropical forest. The western part, which is comparatively dry, has most of the inhabitants and the two main cities, Cumaná and Barcelona.

ROUTES Route 9, the main coastal highway east from Caracas, passes through **Guarenas** and **Guatire**, before turning southeast to **Caucagua** (35 km). From here you can head east to **Higuerote**, **Río Chico** and **Laguna de Tacarigua** on the Barlovento Coast (see below); west to **Guatopo National Park** and the towns of the **Tuy Valley** (see page 96); or continue on Route 9 to **Barcelona** (see page 234).

THE BARLOVENTO COAST

Barlovento is the name given to the great bay which sweeps southeast from **Cabo Cordera** to the Miranda state border at **Boca de Uchire**. It covers the entire coast of Miranda and includes the resorts of **Higuerote** and **Río Chico** and **Laguna de Tacarigua National Park**. The name Barlovento derives from the moist trade winds that blow directly onto the shore, giving year-round rainfall, numerous rivers and canals and, untypically for the normally arid east coast, a verdant landscape.

HIGUEROTE

It is 44 km northeast from the Caucagua

crossroads to **Higuerote** (*population* 13,700; *phone code* 034), the most westerly of the resorts on the Barlovento coast. It's not a particularly attractive town but is surrounded by some fine sandy beaches and currently the focus of large-scale tourist projects. Despite this, it remains quite tranquil but is expensive, especially during the festival of the *Tambores de San Juan*, on 23-26 June, which feature the famous African drums. (See also **Music and Dance**, on page 55).

The wild and beautiful partly-paved coastal road east from **Los Caracas** (see page 101) also goes to Higuerote, via **Chirimena** (see below).

● **Accommodation** D *Barlovento*, on the littered beachfront northeast of Jardín Higuerote condos, colonial style, bare rooms, fan, safe, small pool, restaurant; **D** *Mar-Sol*, on Avenida 1, opposite Plaza Bolívar, just around the corner from the *Terminal San Isidro*, T 21030, air conditioning, private bathroom, open-air restaurant open 0730-2300, *tasca*, parking, credit cards accepted; **D** *Posada El Palmar*, on Avenida 2 on the seafront, next to the National Guard, hot water, private bathroom, air conditioning, TV, open-air restaurant, accepts credit cards; **E** *Cabañas Brisas Marinas*, Avenida Serrano at Plaza Bertorelli, huts for 3-4 people, simple restaurant 0800-2200 serving local specialities, good.

● **Transport** To **Caracas**, buses leave from the end of Calle 12, opposite the beach and 50m from the Malecón; to **Laguna de Tacarigua**, buses leave from 50m south of the CANTV antenna.

AROUND HIGUEROTE

The nearby village of **Caruao**, rebuilt in old style, is friendly, with a good beach and one hotel. Ask for Josefa, who cooks delicious seafood. The sports club has a wild beach party each Saturday afternoon. Near Caruao is the Pozo del Cura, a waterfall and pool, with good swimming.

Another interesting side trip is to the village of **Curiepe**, the folklore capital of Barlovento. The famous local drumbeats can be heard in May during the *Velorios de Cruz de Mayo*, on the 23-24 June for *San Juan*, and on 27-29 June for *San Pedro*. Those who are around at these times can count themselves lucky if they witness this spectacle.

North of Higuerote are a number of nice beaches. **Chirimena** (see also page 101) is about an hour away by *por puesto*; these leave from the *Terminal San Isidro*, opposite *Restaurant A Portado Vento*.

Other beaches closer to Higuerote are **Buche** (the closest and cheapest), **Totumo**, **Punto Francés** and **Caracolito**. You can reach them from the *Nuevo Terminal* at **Carenero** boat terminal, a 10 minute bus ride from Higuerote. You can

Slave to the Rhythym

This fertile humid lowland was one of the country's main centres of cacao production. The very first cacao plantation was in the valley of Curiepe, just west of Higuerote. Some of the best chocolate in the world came from Barlovento cacao, and the plantation owners became so wealthy that the word cacao was, for many years, synonymous with wealth. Indeed, the word *a 'gran cacao'* was the name given to a wealthy man, whether or not his money came from cacao.

The losers in the cocoa business were the many black slaves. This part of Venezuela was called the "Slave Coast" and the African influence is very strong here. The *gran cacao* found the local indigenous people completely unmanageable, so they bought slaves from Africa to work their plantations. Though slavery was abolished in 1823 by Bolívar, the slaves stayed in the area and continued to work on the plantations. It was not until 1854 that they were officially freed by then President Monagas.

Today, the Bantu, Yoruba and Mandingo influences are still very much in evidence through the dances and, especially, the African drums, for which Barlovento is famous.

camp at all the beaches mentioned above, though there is a *posada* at Chirimena.

RIO CHICO

14 km before Higuerote on the road from Caucagua is **Tacarigua de Mamporal**, where you turn-off to the **Laguna de Ta-carigua National Park** (see below). The road passes a tunnel of vegetation (almost 3 km long), cocoa plantations, and the town of **San José de Río Chico** before reaching **Río Chico** (*population* 14,900; *phone code* 034), 30 km from the turn-off.

In the town are the derelict remains of the old station on the disused 54 km French-built 1889 railway from El Guapo to Carenero, as well as many of the colonial homes of the cacao families. Río Chico is a lot nicer than Higuerote and the nearby beaches are popular with *Caraqueños*.

A road runs 4 km north from the town to the coast, where many of the canals snaking from the olive-green Laguna de Tacarigua have been incorporated into private subdivisions, with modest hotels and bridges to the sandy beaches. Off this road is the *Caballerizas Dos Estrellas*, a paso fino stud farm. The owner, Sr Pérez Mata, is happy to show visitors around.

● **Accommodation & places to eat** E *Hotel Italia*, on Calle Miranda, three blocks from the baseball stadium, T 74248, air conditioning or fan, bath, excellent; F *Posada Loritos Enanos*, on Calle Páez con Calle Comercio, one and a half blocks from the stadium, fan, shared bathroom. *Pizzería Río Chico*, one block from Plaza Bolívar behind the church, takeaways, open till midnight on weekends. You can find excellent natural fruit ice cream at several kiosks on Calle Miranda.

● **Transport** Buses to Tacarigua de Mamporal, El Guapo and Higuerote leave from the stop behind the baseball stadium. To get to **Caracas** you have to catch a bus from San José de Río Chico.

TACARIGUA DE LA LAGUNA

A road from Río Chico runs a further 8 km east along the coast to the fishing village of **Tacarigua de la Laguna** (*phone code* 034), on the west bank of the outlet to the lagoon. The village is the main access point for trips on the lagoon. *Por puesto* from Río Chico, US$0.30.

● **Accommodation & places to eat** E *Casa de Ivan Pastuch*, 200m from the Inparques *muelle*, in the house with 2 mango trees outside, quiet, fan, use of cooker and fridge, German spoken, recommended. About 3 km before the village on the road is **C** *Villa del Río*, apart-hotel, price is for 1-7 persons, bathroom, kitchen facilities, fan, connected with *Remigios Tours*, transfer to and from Tacarigua for US$20. You can eat delicious lebranche fish at the *Bar-Restaurant Poleo Lebranche Asado*, also ask here for details of the unmotorized ferry which crosses the lagoon. On the Caribbean side of the eastern sandspit is a beach resort, **B-C** *Club Miami*, price includes breakfast and dinner, to get there take a boat from the *Ciudad Tablita Muelle* (see below), US$7 there and back.

LAGUNA DE TACARIGUA NATIONAL PARK

The 18,400 hectare national park encompasses a coastal lagoon, 30 km long and 6 km wide between the Ríos Cúpira and El Guapo. The lagoon is an important ecological preserve, with mangroves, good fishing and many water birds, including flamingos, frigates, pelicans, cormorants, egrets and scarlet ibises.

Tours of the lagoon

For trips on the lagoon, and for transport to *Club Miami*, your best bet is to go to the *Muelle Ciudad Tablita*, which is on the right of *Casa de Ivan Pastuch* (see above). Boats also leave from the Inparques *muelle*, but overcharging is common here. You need a permit from the Inparques office at the *muelle* for trips on the lagoon, US$0.50. If you want to take photos, you'll need permission from Inparques in Caracas, so it's better not to say anything and hide the camera. The best time to see the birdlife is 1700-1930. All the agencies run evening tours.

Most of the agencies (see below) have offices in the Sector Belén in Tacarigua. Prices are fixed between the tour operators at US$9 for two, so there's no chance of bargaining. Boats can be hired to anywhere in the park and to *Club Miami*. The beaches beyond *Club Miami* are unspoilt and relaxing, but mosquitoes are a problem after sunset.

● **Tour companies & travel agents** *Remigios Tours*, Calle Principal con 4a transversal, Sector Belén, T 711142, run evening tours on the lagoon which last about 1½ hours, US$18 for 2 persons, discount for larger groups, also offer sports fishing and day tours; *Viajes Canario*, on Calle Principal two blocks from the entrance to the Inparques *muelle*, offer tours on the lagoon and a boat taxi to *Club Miami*; *Viajes Tederor*, Calle Ciudad Tablita, tours of the lagoon (US$9 for 2; US$11 for 3). A recommended guide is Sr Teodoro Rivas (T 711012), who charges about US$7 per person for a 3-hour tour of the lagoon. Ask for Ivan Korovainchenko, a recommended guide who lives near the Inparques office; he runs 2-3 day tours to Isla La Tortuga, 80 km northeast of Tacarigua (see page 281), he charges US$20 per person per day, with food and water and fishing, take a tent, sunblock and repellent, he also runs trips through tropical forest from El Guapo.

ROUTES Route 9, the main Caracas-Barcelona highway, can be joined 25 km south of Río Chico at **El Guapo** ('The Handsome One'), an unlikely name for a decidedly unattractive town. There's accommodation at **E** *Wilfred*, on Calle San Felipe, just off the main road into town, T (034) 810131, with bathroom, air conditioning, TV, restaurant. From El Guapo you can head west back to Caracas, or continue east towards Barcelona.

BOCA DE URICHE

From El Guapo Route 9 runs east for 64 km till it hits the coast at **Boca de Uchire** (*population* 4,500; *phone code* 081). This small, unremarkable and neglected-looking coastal town stands on the northwestern shore of **Laguna de Unare** and is a popular holiday resort with *Caraqueños*. It's surrounded by many vacation homes which continue all the way along the narrow sandbar that runs east to the little fishing village of **El Hatillo**, sealing off the lagoon at its northeastern point.

From Boca de Uchire you can see the **Morro de Unare** (517m), a rugged hill which juts out into the olive-green waters of the lagoon.

● **Accommodation & places to eat C-D** *Pitisay*, right on the beach 3 km from town on the road east to El Hatillo, T/F 51185, doubles only, very nice, restaurant, bar, run by Klaus and Carmen, who will organize trips anywhere in the country, full board for US$245 per week; **D** *Shangri-La*, 5 km out of town on the road going east, T (02) 284-5868, F 24789, use of

cooker and fridge, you need to bring your own food, cooking utensils and bedsheets, can pay with Visa, Mastercard or Amex in Caracas, but cash only in Boca de Uchire; **E** *Boca de Uchire*, on the main road at the entrance to town, air conditioning, private bath, good restaurant behind. There are 2 restaurants in town; *Landuriña*, which serves Spanish dishes, and *Puerta Oriente*, for *criollo* food.

● **Transport & services** CANTV is at the northwest corner of Plaza Bolívar, with four public telephones which accept international calls. Buses to Caracas leave from the terminal on Avenida Principal, every 3 hours or so.

ROUTES From Boca de Uchire the main coastal highway turns inland to **Clarines**. Alternatively, you can head east on the paved road that runs along the sandbar between the Caribbean and the lagoon to **El Hatillo** and then south for 24 km to meet Route 9 at Clarines.

CLARINES

Clarines (*population* 9,000) is a quiet, attractive little town with one of the best-restored colonial churches in Venezuela, dating from 1760. The town's *Fiestas Patronales* take place on 14-15 June, with religious festivities and street processions to honour the patron saint, San Antonio de Padua. Apparently, local women pray to him in order to attract a man. Another festival is held on 16 July, to honour the Virgin with dance and music. *Quesos Clarines* at the entrance to town has 15 different types of local cheeses, and you can look around the factory; open Monday-Friday, 0900-1200 and 1500-1800.

● **Accommodation** There are comfortable cabañas, restaurant, snack bar, pool and sports facilities at the *Parador Turístico Clarines* at the western entrance to the town.

PIRITU AND PUERTO PIRITU

16 km further east are the twin towns of **Píritu** and **Puerto Píritu** (combined *population* 18,000; *phone code* 081), about half way between Caracas and Cumaná. Worth seeing in Píritu is the imposing 18th century Franciscan church of Nuestra Señora de la Concepción.

3 km north of Píritu, on the coast, is the delightful, unspoiled colonial town of Puerto Píritu. It has long stretches of

lovely beaches with shade provided, but the waves are strong. On the west side of town is the **Laguna de Píritu**, a small mangrove lagoon populated by various water birds, including egrets and ibises. It's a very pleasant place for a relaxing stroll.

Excursions

From Puerto Píritu you can visit the **Isletas Píritu**, which lie just offshore. The water here is crystal clear and calm, and there's good scuba diving on the north side of the isletas, as well as sulphurous 'cosmetic' mud, which is sold by pharmacists for skin cleansing. You need to take sunblock, shade and food and drink. (See below for details of trips.)

El Viejo Píritu is a tiny village, built in 19th century style. It includes a large open-air restaurant, museum, shop, billiards and games room, craft shop and other bits and bobs. It's very much like Los Aleros in Mérida (see page 186). All the staff are dressed in authentic garb. It should be open in early 1998. It's a 10-minute drive from Puerto Píritu. If you're driving, take the first entrance on the right at Pueblo Viejo; otherwise, take a taxi from El Tejar.

Local information
● **Accommodation in Puerto Píritu**

C *Balneario Casacoima*, on Calle Unare one block up from the beach almost opposite *Neptuno* restaurant, T 411511/13, T/F 411970, air conditioning, TV, some rooms with hot water, accepts credit cards, restaurant, pool open to public; **C** *Bella Mar*, Calle Bolívar, air conditioning, pool, restaurant, parking; **C** *Casagrande*, on Avenida Peñalver, about six blocks up from Plaza Bolívar on the main road out of town, T 411650, cold water only, air conditioning, TV, fridge, restaurant, laundry, *tasca*, accepts Visa and Mastercard; **C** *Posada Coromotana*, on Calle las Flores y Calle Arismendi, three blocks from the plaza and one block from the beach, T 412963/413796, a lovely colonial *posada* run by Alfredo and Rosa Viginia Alcantara who also live here, ceiling fan, cold water, beautiful rooms done out in wood and clay, breakfast US$5 extra, they also organize boat trips to the Isletas Píritu (see above) for US$6-7 per person including soft drinks, highly recommended; **C-D** *La Posada de Alexis*, 10 minutes walk from El Tejar gas station, and a long way from the town centre and beach,

T 413754/410469, air conditioning, TV, cold water only, pool, restaurant.

E *Posada Beach*, on Calle Bermúdez con Calle La Colina, one block west of the plaza and two blocks from Laguna de Píritu, T (014) 811951, cold water, air conditioning, organize tours to the Isletas (US$12 per person).

There are several hotels on the main road at El Tejar (see below); eg **E** *La Posada*, on top of a small hill overlooking the main road, T 411316, with bathroom and fan, safe and quiet, 30 minutes walk from Puerto Píritu.

● **Places to eat**

Sol y Brisas, on the beachside boulevard, near *Balneario Casacoima* on the opposite side, expensive but good quality, especially the seafood. One block west of Plaza Bolívar along Calle Anzoátegui, just around the corner from *Posada Beach* is an Arabic restaurant, in a white building with a blue door. *La Dulcita*, on Avenida Peñalver, five blocks up from Plaza Bolívar, recommended for local sweets and well worth the walk!

There's a market opposite the lagoon, which is open in the mornings and sells just about everything. Try the shrimp *empanandas* for breakfast – Mama!

● **Transport**

To get to Puerto Píritu from Caracas: take a Cumaná or Puerto La Cruz bus and ask to get off at the El Tejar gas station, on the outskirts of town. From there, take a taxi or *por puesto* to the beach. From Cumaná or Puerto La Cruz: take a Caracas bus (but they'll charge you the full fare), or hop from Cumaná to Puerto La Cruz to Barcelona to Puerto Píritu by *por puesto*; except the Puerto La Cruz-Barcelona section where you need to take the intercomunal bus from Avenida 5 de Julio in Puerto La Cruz, which takes you to the terminal at Barcelona. (See page 241). It's 47 km from Píritu to Barcelona.

BARCELONA

Barcelona (*population* 266,750; mean temperature 27°C; *phone code* 081), capital of Anzoátegui State, straddles the Río Neverí, 5 km from the sea. The city was founded in 1671 by Catalans and named after the capital of their home province in Spain. Barcelona boasts a rich heritage and the narrow streets and colonial buildings of its old centre make a pleasant tour, even if they are a bit run down. Those who prefer a quiet life and an early night would be better off staying here rather than the noisy neighbour, Puerto La Cruz.

Places of interest

In the main **Plaza Boyacá** stands a statue of General Anzoátegui, hero of the Battle of Boyacá, and after whom the state is named. Until 1671, the plaza was actually a lagoon and favourite fishing spot of the local Cumanagoto Indians. Also on the plaza are the **Palacio de Gobierno** and **San Cristóbal Cathedral**. The Cathedral – started in 1748 and rebuilt in 1773 after an earthquake in 1766 – contains the embalmed remains of the Italian martyr, San Celestino; it is open 0600-1200, 1500-1930.

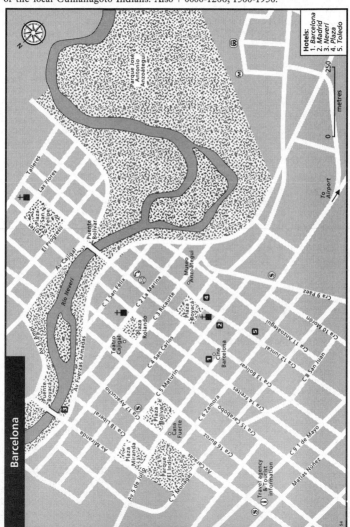

Barcelona

Hotels:
1. Barcelona
2. Madrid
3. Neverí
4. Plaza
5. Toledo

Several blocks north, on Avenida 5 de Julio, are **Plaza Bolívar** (with the obligatory statue) and **Plaza Miranda**. Facing Plaza Bolívar are the ruins of the **Casa Fuerte**, a national monument, where 1,600 of Bolívar's followers were massacred by Royalist troops in 1817. Details of this bloody episode and other historic epics can be found next door in the **public library**, which is open weekdays only. **Teatro Cajigal**, facing the small Plaza at Carrera 15 with Calle 3a, is a replica of the Teatro Municipal in Caracas.

Next to the bus and *por puesto* station on Avenida San Carlos, over 1 km south of Plaza Boyacá, is the **Mercado Libre**, where you can buy food and just about anything else that takes your fancy. For a pleasant stroll, you can try the overgrown park which follows both banks of the Río Neverí right through the city.

Museums

Museo de la Tradición on Calle Juncal, is in the oldest surviving building in Barcelona, built in 1671. In colonial times a slave auction was held here every Sunday. Now, it houses a wide collection of indigenous and Spanish religious art. It's open Monday-Friday 0800-1200, 1400-1700, weekends 0900-1500.

Local information
● **Accommodation**
D *Barcelona**, Avenida 5 de Julio con Calle Bolívar, one block from the cathedral, T 771065, F 771076, some rooms have hot water, air conditioning, TV, parking, 6th floor restaurant (good fish); **D** *Neverí*, Avenida Fuerzas Armadas con Avenida Miranda (by the bridge), T 772376, with bathroom, air conditioning, TV, good restaurant *Castillo del Oriente*, accepts Visa, Amex and Mastercard; **D** *Venus*, Avenida Intercomunal y Lecherías, on the road to Puerto La Cruz at the flyover near the Vista Mar shopping centre, about 10-15 minutes by car from the centre, T 774202, hot water, air conditioning, TV, laundry service.

E *Madrid*, just behind the cathedral, with restaurant, fans, unfriendly owner; **E** *Toledo*, on Calle Juncal, one block from Avenida 5 de Julio, with bathroom, basic but good value.

F *Plaza*, on Calle Juncal opposite the cathedral, in a colonial building, rooms with bathroom, air conditioning and TV also available, recommended.

● **Places to eat**
There is a wide variety of restaurants in town, including *Lucky*, Avenida Miranda No 4-26, north of Plaza Bolívar, Chinese, recommended.

● **Tourist offices**
Carrera 13, No 3-7, just off Plaza Boyacá; open weekdays only.

● **Tour companies & travel agents**
Venezuela, is an agency at Avenida Caracas con Calle 9a Altos de Belén, four and a half blocks up from Avenida 5 de Julio, next to Banco Federal and opposite Banco Italo Venezolano.

● **Transport**
Air The airport is 3 km to the south of town and also serves Puerto La Cruz. Avensa, Servivensa, Aserca, Aeropostal and Laser all operate from Barcelona. There are many daily flights to Maiquetía, a daily flight to Porlamar, Puerto Ordaz, San Tomé, Valencia, San Antonio, and Maracaibo, and a flight to Maturín daily except Saturday. Aeropostal: T 774965/ 770315, F 771735 (Barcelona); T 685426/ 687642, F 673265 (Puerto La Cruz). At the airport are Oficambio exchange facilities (no travellers' cheques), artesanía shops, a small museum, car rental agencies, and a Corpoturismo booth which stays open late for some incoming flights. It has a few handouts and is friendly, but cannot book hotels. A city map can be scrounged from National Car Rental. A taxi to the airport from the bus terminal is US$2.25. A taxi to Puerto La Cruz costs US$5-6.

Buses The Terminal de Pasajeros next to the Mercado Libre is used mostly by *por puestos*, with regular departures to Valle la Pascua, Anaco, El Tigre, Maturín, Cumaná, Boca de Uchire, Valle Guanape and other nearby destinations. Buses leave from here to: **Caracas**, 5 hours, 11 daily, US$5; **San Félix** (Ciudad Guayana); **Ciudad Bolívar**, 6 daily; **Maturín**, 2 daily. Buses to **Puerto La Cruz** take 40 minutes, they run every few minutes from another terminal, along Avenida 5 de Julio, past Plaza Bolívar. **NB** Take care around the bus terminals.

Sea The port for Barcelona and Puerto La Cruz is **Guanta** (see below, under Puerto La Cruz, Boats). Vessels from La Guaira call here.

BARCELONA TO PUERTO LA CRUZ

Barcelona has been surpassed touristically and commercially by Puerto La Cruz, 12 km away by a four-lane highway (Avenida Intercomunal) that skirts the pleasant residential resort of **Lechería**. To get to Lechería take a minibus (US$0.15), then walk, or take a *por puesto* to the beach, where there are several good restaurants.

Off the highway is the 10,000-seater Polideportivo sports stadium, with a covered gymnasium, velodrome, basket-ball courts and two swimming pools. Most of the facilities are available to the public without charge (open daylight hours daily).

Soon after Barcelona is **El Morro Tourist Complex**, with hotels, cultural centres and condos with access from the street or from a new system of canals. Among the resort/marinas are *Maremares* (see **Accommodation** below) and *Bahía Redonda* (see **Entertainment** below). There's also the Plaza Mayor, a large shopping centre done out in pastel shades next to one of the canals. It's pretty but very expensive, like the rest of the complex.

Based at the Marina Amérigo Vespucio is *Horisub*, the company which manages the docks. They run diving courses, arrange fishing trips and boat tours, and are friendly and speak English. The Marina El Morro is frequented by Venezuelans and less expensive. This is the country's yachting centre; a great place to meet other yachting people and perhaps even find a ride on a boat. Look out for special events in the marinas.

A very circuitous inland road goes around the tourist complex to Puerto La Cruz. Alternatively, a passenger ferry crosses the main channel to the Amérigo Vespucio Marina, US$0.05. To get there, take an 'Intercomunal' bus from Avenida 5 de Julio in Puerto La Cruz and ask to get off at the Vista Mar shopping centre. From there, walk one block towards Puerto La Cruz and go left. Plaza Mayor is a further two blocks down on your right.

PUERTO LA CRUZ

Puerto La Cruz (*population* 220,000; *phone code* 081) began life as a collection of thatched shelters, built by fishermen from Margarita who came to fish the huge grounds around the Chimana Islands. It has since grown out of all recognition to become the principal commercial centre of Eastern Venezuela and a major petroleum town, refining and exporting oil

from the interior. Puerto La Cruz is better known, though, as one of the east coast's main tourist destinations. It's a noisy 24-hour party town of hotels, restaurants, bars, cafés and sweaty nightclubs packed with tourists hell-bent on having a seriously good time.

The older part of town is a traffic-choked grid with a seafront avenue, the Paseo Colón, extending to the eastern extremity of the broad sweep of Bahía de Pozuelas. The wide avenues of the modern city have also spread west along the bay as far as the prominent El Morro headland beneath which lies **Lechería** (see above).

The pulsating heart of the city is the **Paseo Colón**. By day, the vibe is more relaxed: waterfront cafés serve coffee and fruit juices to unhurried customers content with the wonderful views of the bay and the islands of Mochima National Park (see below); street vendors hawk their wares and shoeshine boys try to persuade you to have your sandals polished for a third time. Things begin to liven up towards evening as people leave work and converge on the *paseo* to meet up with friends.

Now the outdoor cafés fill up with locals. Fast food outlets and vendors do a roaring trade in *empanadas*, *schwarmas*, burgers, hot dogs, ice cream, soft drinks and beers. The *paseo* also fills with strolling, chatting groups, people sitting on benches, stopping for a drink, or admiring the local *artesanía* (silver, glass pieces, paintings, puppets, carvings and all kinds of leather goods and jewellery). This is the perfect time to take an evening stroll. You can savour that unique Caribbean flavour and enjoy the first cool caresses of the delicious sea breeze.

Tourist facilities are generally good, if a bit on the expensive side, and all types of water sports are well catered for. Note that the sea in the bay may look inviting, but you cannot swim in it because of sewage pollution (a warning sign to this effect is posted).

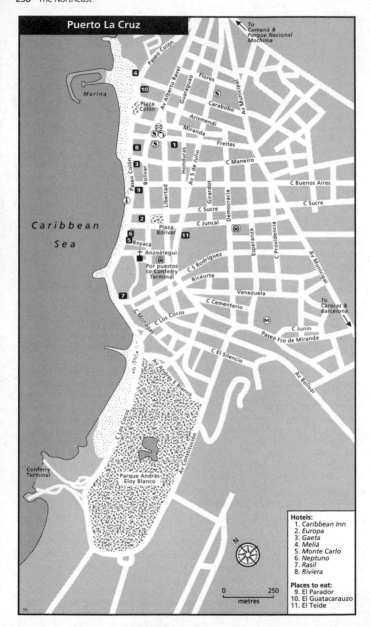

Puerto La Cruz

To Cumaná &
Parque Nacional
Mochima

Marina

Plaza
Colón

Paseo Colón

Av Alberto Ravel

Guaraguao

Flores

Carabobo

Arismendi

Miranda

Freites

Honduras

Av 5 de Julio

C Maneiro

C Buenos Aires

C Sucre

Girardot

Democracia

Esperanza

C Providencia

Av Municipal

Caribbean
Sea

Bolívar

Libertad

C Sucre

C Juncal

Plaza
Bolívar

Boyacá

Anzoátegui

Por puestos
to Conferry
Terminal

C S Rodríguez

Ricaurte

Venezuela

C Cementerio

To
Caracas &
Barcelona

C Junín

Paseo Fco de Miranda

Av Bolívar

C Monagas

C Los Cocos

C El Silencio

Av Andrés E Blanco

C Los Cocos

Av Constitución

Conferry
Terminal

Parque Andrés
Eloy Blanco

N

0   250
metres

Hotels:
1. *Caribbean Inn*
2. *Europa*
3. *Gaeta*
4. *Meliá*
5. *Monte Carlo*
6. *Neptuno*
7. *Rasil*
8. *Riviera*

Places to eat:
9. *El Parador*
10. *El Guatacarauzo*
11. *El Teide*

EXCURSIONS

The main attractions of Puerto La Cruz lie offshore on the many islands of the beautiful **Mochima National Park** and in the surrounding waters, which offer excellent snorkelling, fishing and swimming. Several small jetties reached from the central part of Paseo Colón offer trips to the westerly islands, such as Islas Chimanas and Las Borrachas. The islands to the east are best reached from the port at **Guanta**. To get to Guanta take a taxi from town, or take a *por puesto* from Calle Freites between Avenida 5 de Julio and Calle Democracia, and ask to be dropped off at the Urbanización Pamatacualito. For details of boat trips to the islands see **Boats** below, and also **Mochima National Park** (page 243). **NB** Boat trips to the islands are cheaper from **Santa Fe** (see page 246) or **Mochima** (see page 247).

La Sirena is a park with a beautiful waterfall and pool near the village of **Chorrerón**. There is a park guard but nowhere to buy food and drink. You can take public transport. The *por puesto* to **Guanta** goes past the park, but then you have to walk for 3-4 km through a dangerous *barrio*. It's safer to take a taxi all the way to the park and arrange to be picked up later.

LOCAL FESTIVALS

3 May: *Santa Cruz*. **8 September**: *Virgen del Valle*, during which boats cruise the harbour, clad in palms and balloons, and there's an afternoon party on Isla del Faro, with lots of salsa and beer.

LOCAL INFORMATION

● Accommodation

Hotel prices

L1	over US$200	L2	US$151-200
L3	US$101-150	A1	US$81-100
A2	US$61-80	A3	US$46-60
B	US$31-45	C	US$21-30
D	US$12-20	E	US$7-11
F	US$4-6	G	up to US$3
Those marked with an asterisk (*) are bookable through Fairmont International (see under Caracas).			

The newer, up-market hotels are at Lechería and El Morro. The middle grade and budget hotels and nightlife are concentrated in central Puerto La Cruz, though it's not easy to find a cheap hotel.

L2 Meliá*, on Paseo Colón, at the eastern edge of the centre, T 6536111, F 653117, the best hotel in the centre of town, 5-star, with all services and facilities, 2 poolside restaurants, car rental, taxi to airport, 2 travel agencies, American Airlines office, all credit cards accepted.

A1 Maremares, on Avenida Amérigo Vespucio in El Morro (see above), T 811011, F 813028, 5-star, fully-serviced resort of the Golden Rainbow group with a vast lake-style pool, 9-hole golf course and marina; **A3-B Rasil**, Paseo Colón with Calle Rodríguez, T 672422, F 673121, rooms, suites and bungalows, air conditioning, TV, 3 restaurants, bar, pool, gym, money exchange, car rental and other facilities, accepts all credit cards, convenient for ferries and buses, highly recommended.

B Cristal Park, Calle Buenos Aires between Calle Libertad and Honduras, T 670744, F 653105, air conditioning, TV, fridge, laundry service, accepts Visa and Mastercard, changes money at a better rate than *casas de cambio*; **B Gaeta**, on Paseo Colón with Calle Maneiro, T 650411, very modern, set back slightly from the sea front, air conditioning, TV, fridge, phone, safe box, good location, restaurant, scooter rentals, cash exchange, travel agent, credit cards accepted; **B Senador**, Miranda y Bolívar, air conditioning, TV, back rooms quieter, phone, restaurant with good view, parking, accepts major credit cards.

C Caribbean Inn, Calle Freites between Calle Libertad and Calle Honduras, T 674292, F 672857, big rooms, very well kept with quiet air conditioning, small pool, very good service, recommended; **C La Marina**, Andrés Eloy Blanco, near the ferry terminal, air conditioning, good views, expensive waterside restaurant, parking for those using the Margarita ferry, recommended; **C Riviera**, Paseo Colón 33, T/F 691337, noisy air conditioning, some rooms have balcony, phone, bar, watersports, very good location, poor breakfast; **C Sorrento**, Avenida 5 de Julio with Calle Freites, T 686745, F 688550, air conditioning, cable TV; **C-D Aparthotel Cristián del Valle**, Maneiro 15, T 650925/8, large rooms with air conditioning, TV, hot water, kitchen, some cheaper rooms (**D**) are available without kitchen, clean, the Trinidadian owner speaks English, very friendly and efficient staff, rooms on the top floor are quieter, usually full, accepts Visa, Mastercard and Amex, recommended; **C-D Neptuno**, on Paseo Colón at Calle Juncal, T 653261, F 655790, hot water, air conditioning, TV, excellent restaurant *Terraza* on the top floor, recommended.

D *Comercio*, on Calle Maneiro with Libertad, one block from Paseo Colón, T 651429, cold water only, air conditioning, TV, public phones, accepts Visa and Mastercard, recommended; **D** *Europa*, Calle Sucre, esquina Plaza Bolívar, T 688157, air conditioning, cold water, TV, laundry service; **D** *Luna y Sol*, on Calle Ricaurte half block from Paseo Colón, T (016) 806856, hot water, TV, air conditioning, safe, quiet, laundry around the corner; **D** *Nacional Inn*, Miranda 44A, esquina Avenida 5 de Julio, T 685252, basic, air conditioning (**E** with fan), water problems, clean, friendly, laundry opposite, space to sit out on the roof, recommended; **D** *Puerto La Cruz*, Avenida 5 de Julio, phone, recommended; **D-E** *Monte Carlo*, on Paseo Colón between Calle Juncal and Boyacá, cold water only, TV, shower and air conditioning unreliable.

E *Pippo*, on Calle Freites with Municipal, two blocks up from Avenida 5 de Julio, T 688810, cold water, modern, good value, some rooms with TV, very noisy.

● **Places to eat**
On Paseo Colón: *El Parador*, 2nd floor, excellent food and service; *Da Luigi*, Italian, good; *El Espignon*, very good dinner in the open air, romantic; *Big Garden*, delicious seafood; *Casa Nápoli*, cheap, recommended; *Reale*, No 69, pizzería, good for breakfast; *Ristorante O Sole Mio*, cheap, excellent, wide variety; *Pastelería Fornos* for breakfast; *Las Cabañas*, very good value and service; *El Guatacarauzo*, near Pizza Hut, live music, the waiters wear silly hats and play practical jokes, good atmosphere (if you like that sort of thing), good value.

La Taberna del Guácharo, on Calle Carabobo, at the eastern end of Paseo Colón, tacky interior with plastic guáchara statues but excellent cheap Venezuelan cuisine, good service, not as tourist-orientated as the restaurants along the sea front, recommended; *El Teide*, Avenida 5 de Julio 153, near Plaza Bolívar, good and cheap local food, closes at 2000; *El Farao*, at the eastern corner of the main bus station, gaudy interior, fair service, excellent, authentic, spicy Arab food. Between Paseo Colón and *Hotel Europa* is *Tostadas El Paseo*, excellent arepas, highly recommended.

Vegetarian: *Nature*, Constitución 70, lunch and dinner, self-service buffet, tasteless, mostly corn-based dishes; *Celeri*, on Avenida Municipal, one block from Calle Guamaché, open weekdays 1130-1530, recommended. Also try *La Colmena*, next to *Hotel Riviera*; and *La Granela*, on Calle Miranda with Honduras. Vegetarian snacks are available on the corner of Paseo Colón with Calle Sucre.

You should try the delicious *Shwarmas* (roast meat in pitta bread) which are sold at the many street stands on Paseo Colón; a recommended one is *Buen Gusto* opposite Burger King.

● **Airline offices**
Avensa, Avenida Municipal y Pepsi, and at Barcelona airport; **Alitalia** and **American Airlines** have offices in *Hotel Meliá*; **Dominicana**, Independencia 124, Chapurín Central.

● **Banks & money changers**
Banco Consolidado, Avenida 5 de Julio, Local No 43, for Amex. Other banks: **Banco Mercantil**, on Calle bolívar behind CANTV; **Banco Unión**, Calle Libertad y Bolívar. The Amex representative is **Turisol**, T 662161/669910. **NB** No banks will change money.

Casas de cambio: **Oficambio**, Calle Maneiro y Libertad, also in the shopping centre at *Hotel Rasil*, no commission on travellers' cheques, best rates in town, open 0800-1200, 1400-1730 Monday-Friday; *Venezuela*, in *Hotel Riviera* on Paseo Colón, open Monday-Friday 0800-1200 and 1430-1830; *Asecambio*, in *Hotel Gaeta*, good rates, open Monday-Saturday 0800-1200 and 1400-1800.

● **Entertainment**
For good 1970s salsa (the best) don't miss a night at *Casa Latina*, opposite *Hotel Meliá*; *Los Zulianos*, live folk music on Friday, Saturday and Sunday nights, good atmosphere, no cover charge, recommended; *Gamblers*, a nightclub on Paseo Colón, near Burger King, excellent music, free entry; *Christophers*, a Canadian owned bar, Calle La Marina, one block from Paseo Colón, an informal cellar-type watering hole open from 1600 till late, happy hour 1730-1830; *Bitter Coral*, the bar/restaurant in the *Bahía Redonda* resort/marina often has live music, with a happy hour before, dinner reservations are needed when the marina is full (June to December).

● **Post & telecommunications**
Post Office & telecommunications: CANTV and Ipostel are next to each other on Freites y Bolívar, one block from Paseo Colón. CANTV office will hold faxes, F 651266. There's also a shop with postal service next to *Hotel Riviera*.

● **Shopping**
Street vendors sell paintings, jewellery, leather, hammocks, etc on Paseo Colón in the evenings. These are cheaper than in the souvenir shops on the Paseo and along Avenida 5 de Julio.

● **Sports**
Diving: several companies run diving courses and trips and rent equipment. Most of these can be found along Paseo Colón. They tend to be quite a bit more expensive than comparable

courses on offer in Santa Fe and Mochima. We have received favourable reports on the following: *Explosub*, at *Hotel Meliá*, T 653611/ 650574, T/F 673256 (ext 3347), PO Box 4784, they are efficient, helpful and will dive with 1 person, Carlos is the dive leader, good, comfortable boat, they charge US$75 for 2 dives, US$220 for 3 days/6 dives, US$80 for night dive, plus 15% for credit cards, trips depart at 0900; *Lolo's Dive Centre*, based at the Marina at the port of Guanta (see **Excursions** above), T 683052, F 682885 (or contact Eddy Revelant T 014-801543/806700 cellnet, 24 hours), very experienced, English spoken, they will collect you from your hotel and provide lunch, charge US$60 for 2 dives, 2-3 persons minimum, they also run a 4-day PADI course for US$300. Hotels and travel agents also organize trips. The nearest recompression chamber is on Isla Margarita.

For more details on diving in Mochima National Park see the introductory section on **Scuba diving** (page 22).

● **Tour companies & travel agents**
There are several travel agents in town, some of which claim to have 'exclusive' rights to the Isla La Tortuga and other tours. Take no notice of this and shop around. The travel agency in *Hotel Meliá* is recommended for arranging and confirming flights. *Expresur* in *Hotel Gaeta* have competitive prices for tours to Mochima, Delta Amacuro and the Gran Sabana (roughly US$50-70 per person per day). Also recommended as being helpful and reliable are *Expedition Tours*, Paseo Colón 27, by the roundabout, speak English, Italian and German. For flights to Anfel Falls and elsewhere, call Steve Patterson, T 653371.

NB Do **not** buy tours from wandering salesmen not affiliated to a registered agency or tour company. If in doubt, go to Coranztur (see below).

● **Tourist offices**
Coranztur is the government-run tourist agency. They have an office on Paseo Colón opposite *Hotel Diana*, T 688170, French, English, Italian and Dutch spoken, very helpful and friendly, open daily 0800-2100.

● **Transport**
Air Puerto La Cruz uses the airport at nearby Barcelona airport (for flight details see page 236).

Buses The bus and *por puesto* terminal is at Avenida Juncal and Calle Democracía. A new bus terminal has been built to the east of town, which is clean and safe but not easy to reach and there's no accommodation nearby; best to take a taxi. To Caracas, 5 hours, US$5-8, various companies depart regularly night and day from

the new terminal; among those recommended are Expresos Los Llanos (T 671373, air conditioning, movies), Sol de Margarita (*por puesto*, departs 1550, 4 hours, US$17.50), Autoexpresos Ejecutivos (4 a day, US$12.65, T 678855, depart from Terminal Bello Campo next to the ferry terminal, also have buses to Maracay, Valencia, Barquisimeto and Maturín). To **Mérida**, US$22.35, 16 hours. To Ciudad Bolívar US$5, US$2.50 student discount, but often full since the service starts at Cumaná; alternatively, take a *por puesto* to **El Tigre** (US$4.25) and a *por puesto* from there to Ciudad Bolívar (US$3.50). To Cumaná, US$3 (Expresos Guyanesa are recommended), *por puesto* US$6, 1½ hours, you'll have to fight to get on any bus which arrives. To Barcelona, US$1, 40 minutes. To Carúpano, US$3, 5 hours. There are also services to San Félix, Ciudad Bolívar, Río Caribe, Maracay, Valencia, Acarigua, Barinas, San Cristóbal, Güiria. *Por puestos* cover the nearest destinations and charge a little over double; eg to Playa Colorado is US$1.20, and to Santa Fe about US$1.10. Along Avenida 5 de Julio runs a bus marked 'Intercomunal', which links Puerto La Cruz with Barcelona and intervening points, including the entry to Lechería; the connecting *por puesto* stop is one block further along the Avenida Principal of Lechería, on the left side (see also page 237). This bus also passes within a few kilometres of Barcelona airport. Another Barcelona bus is marked 'Ruta Alternativa' and uses the inland highway via the Puerto La Cruz Golf and Country Club and Universidad de Oriente (both 5 km southwest of city), US$0.12.

Boats The offshore islands of Mochima National Park can be visited from the waterfront in Puerto La Cruz or from the port at Guanta (see **Mochima National Park**, page 243). *Windward Lines*, which sails to Margarita and Trinidad, operates from Marina Puerto La Cruz, next to the *Hotel Melia*. For details on this and on **Ferries to Margarita**, see under **Isla de Margarita** (page 280).

PUERTO LA CRUZ TO CIUDAD BOLIVAR

From Puerto La Cruz a toll road (Route 16) goes inland, skirting Barcelona. At **La Encrucijada** (Km 52), a road forks left (east) to Santa Bárbara and **Maturín** (see page 264). 38 km further south, at **El Crucero**, a road branches right (west), passing through **Aragua de Barcelona**, **Zaraza** and **Tucupido**, before meeting Route 15 west from **El Tigre** (see below). The main highway south from Barcelona parallels Route 16, to a point 17 km beyond **Anaco**, near **Cantuara**, where it joins Route 16 and continues south to **El Tigre** (see below).

ANACO

10 km south of **El Crucero** Route 16 and the main highway pass on either side of **Anaco** (*population* 60,000). It has an airport and is a base for oil-well service contracting companies. Beyond Anaco a branch road leads to the oilfields of San Joaquín.

● **Accommodation**   **D** *Motel Canaima*, Avenida Aeropuerto, good; nearby, on the same street is **E** *Dragón Oriental*; **E** *Mand's Club*, Avenida Venezuela, restaurant, bar, a bit noisy; **E** *Muñiz*, on Sucre, basic; **E** *Viento Fresco*, some fans, dark rooms, poor security.

EL TIGRE

The two main roads join up near the market town of **Cantaura**, and continue south as Route 16 to **El Tigre** (*population* 105,000), a busy city on the edge of the Guanipa Plateau. The town is surrounded by numerous oilfields and large peanut plantations.

10 km east of El Tigre is its neighbour and 'little brother', **El Tigrito**, which is also called **San José de Guanipa** (*population* 48,220). Both are well-served by highways to all parts of the country.

The local airport is at **San Tomé**, 5 km from El Tigrito. A regular bus runs to/from El Tigre; US$3.50. In San Tomé, the eastern headquarters of Menevén, the former Mene Grande oil company, the public relations office (on Calle Guico) is happy to arrange tours to the nearby oil wells.

● **Accommodation & places to eat**   **In El Tigre**: **C** *Internacional Gran Hotel*, Avenida Intercomunal, pool, nightclub, the best hotel in town but not central; **D** *Tamanaco*, Avenida España, opposite the bus terminal, air conditioning, good, with a highly recommended restaurant; **D** *Orinoco*, Guayana, best of the cheaper places, cafetería. On Avenida España: **E** *Caribe*; **E** *La Fuente* (near the main plaza); **E** *Arichuna* and **E** *Santa Cruz*, which is clean and basic. Also on Avenidaw España is a Chilean restaurant which serves excellent Chilean food and salads. **In El Tigrito**: **D** *Rancho Grande*, acceptable. Services are better in El Tigre. **Warning** Pickpockets work the city buses, usually in pairs.

ROUTES   From El Tigre, Highway 15 leads west to Caracas (550 km). 222 km west, at **Valle de Pascua** (see page 224), it meets Route 13 running west from just north of **Anaco** (see above).

Route 16 continues south, straight and flat, 130 km across the *llanos*, to the Angostura bridge which crosses the mighty Orinoco River to **Ciudad Bolívar** (see page 284), 298 km from Puerto La Cruz.

PUERTO LA CRUZ TO CUMANA

Starting east from Puerto La Cruz is the Costa Azul, a seemingly endless series of beaches backed by some of Venezuela's most beautiful scenery. Offshore lie the islands of the **Mochima National Park**. Highway 9 follows the shore for much of the 85 km to Cumaná. It's a memorable coastal drive with stunning views across to the islands and down into many sandy coves tucked away snugly into a series of bays protected by rocky headlands. If driving, you'll need to take extra care on the stretch of road between Playa Colorada and Cumaná, which is as treacherous as it is dramatic.

Warning At holiday times this part of the Venezuelan coast gets very busy and becomes littered and polluted, especially on the islands. Robbery is a problem, particularly at Santa Fe and Playa Colorada. If you take extra care, however, you should be no more at risk than in other parts of the country. *Posada* owners in Santa Fe take very good care of their guests. Camping on the islands is reported as unsafe; robbery and rape have occurred. It is only advisable to go to islands with guards (during the day) and where people live.

LOS ALTOS

17 km east of Puerto La Cruz, at **El Chaparro**, is the turn-off to **Los Altos de Santa Fe**, a small village at 900m with spectacular views of the Mochima Park coastline. It is also a craft centre (pottery, metalwork, woodcarving and papermaking).

● **Accommodation**   **C** *Casa Quini*, at the end of the village on Calle El Baño, 2 double rooms, hot water, very pleasant, price includes breakfast and a short tour, lunch and dinner are also available with an emphasis on healthy Venezuelan food, tours are to the craft shops in the village and to the owner's coffee and cacao plantations, where you can see the chocolate and coffee making process, tours cost US$10 per person for non-guests; **D-E** *Posada El Paraíso*, cheaper without TV, no hot water, fan, accepts Amex for bills of over US$45, the restaurant-tasca is closed on Tuesdays.

● **Places to eat** *Los Flores*, run by Boris (Russian) and Yoki (Dutch), they serve Indonesian, Russian, Dutch and Venezuelan dishes for US$5-8, recommended, Boris also has a small art gallery which exhibits mostly watercolours of Mochima.

● **Shopping** Recommended for pottery is *Humberto Adrianza*; the entrance to the house and shop is along into Los Altos, opposite the entrance to the school, next to the La Tobar building, the house is a large red building at the end of a long drive, the shop is on the right as you enter the drive. *Cerámica Los Altos*, run by Gorgio Gariga, is also along the main road into the village, T (014) 143504, and is also recommended. There's also *Taller Bogar*, for homemade paper, and *Gouri Metales Artísticos*, both opposite *Terra Aventura*.

● **Transport** Take a jeep from the bus terminal in Puerto La Cruz, 30 minutes, US$1.30.

EXCURSIONS FROM LOS ALTOS

There are some spectacular waterfalls and rapids, especially in the wet season, and lovely bathing pools, on the **Río Neverí**, which flows from the reservoir at **Turimiquiri**, above Santa Fe, to Puerto La Cruz (see also page 246). There is a wonderful walk along the banks of the river, from **El Rincón** (on the outskirts of Puerto La Cruz, 30 minutes up from the hospital) to the road that leads to the reservoir at Turimiquiri. The largest waterfall, **El Salto de La Toma**, is about 20 minutes along the road from El Rincón. Here the river, which is 30m wide, falls 20m into a narrow gorge only 5m wide. Another delightful spot is a crystal-clear pool and waterfall, amidst virgin forest, 30 minutes' walk up from La Toma.

This area is not geared up for tourism and it is not advisable to wander around on your own, as there may be thieves lurking. Also the entrance and exit of the walk are fairly inaccessible. There is no public transport, and it is not safe to leave your car on the road. You are strongly advised to take one of the inexpensive guided tours on offer (see below). The river is also good for canoeing, especially beginners. There are 35 rapids – grade 1 and 2 – along an 8 km stretch. For canoeing or rafting trips on the river see below.

● **Tour guides** Marlene Lamas knows this area well and can take you on several recommended walks: for example to the **Mirador La Silleta**, an hour away, where you get the best views of the coast (take your bathing suit for a swim in the small pool close by); or to **El Naranjo**, a series of waterfalls about 1¾ hours away. She also does jeep trips to Salto La Toma, and runs a coffee plantation, which she will show you round. Marlene lives at 'Aldebaran' in the village and offers traditional *criollo* food, T (081) 664932, or via Humberto Adrianza, T (016) 817352. Pedro Mazzglia also does hiking tours; contact him via Gorgio Gariga (see above). Jim and Linda Chaser offer day tours to Los Altos from Puerto La Cruz for US$20 per person, T (016) 802879. Rodolfo Plaza and Bernardo García run canoeing and rafting tours along the river; they are very experienced and highly recommended, and charge US$30 per person, including transport, equipment and guides. To contact Rodolfo, see under **Mochima** (page 248), or contact him through Bernardo, T (02) 985-3344/1474 (work).

MOCHIMA NATIONAL PARK

The entire coast from the El Morro headland at Barcelona to Cumaná is incorporated into the 94,935 hectares of the Mochima National Park. The park encompasses the islands of Chimanas, Mono, Picuda Grande, Caracas, Venado and Borracha, among others, as well as the numerous beautiful beaches, gulfs and inlets between Santa Fe and Cumaná and the mountainous hinterland as far as the Río Neverí.

THE ISLANDS

Many of the islands offer excellent fishing, snorkelling and diving. Most of them are uninhabited and some have lovely beaches, while others are surrounded by coral reefs. **Las Borrachas, Chimana Grande, El Faro, Monos** and **Islas Caracas** are all recommended for their impressive coral and colourful, exotic marine life.

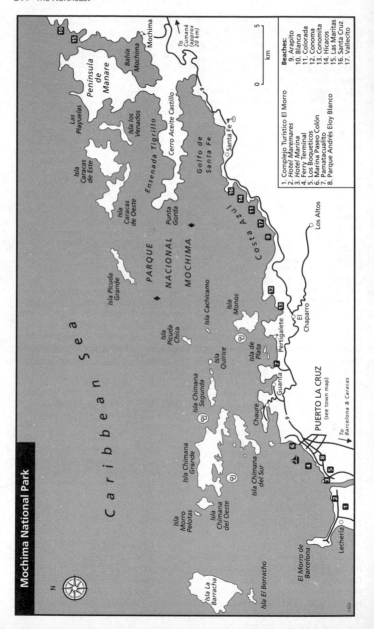

Mochima National Park

Beaches:
9. Arapito
10. Blanca
11. Colorada
12. Conoma
13. Conomita
14. Hicacos
15. Las Maritas
16. Santa Cruz
17. Vallecito

1. Complejo Turístico El Morro
2. *Hotel Maremares*
3. *Hotel Marina*
4. Ferry Terminal
5. Los Boqueticos
6. Marina Paseo Colón
7. Pamatacualito
8. Parque Andrés Eloy Blanco

0 — 5 km

N

Caribbean Sea

Isla La Barracha

Isla El Borracho

Isla Morro Pelotas

Isla Chimana del Oeste

Isla Chimana Grande

Isla Chimana Segunda

Isla Chimana del Sur

Isla Picuda Grande

Isla Picuda Chica

Isla Quirice

Isla Cachicamo

Isla de Plata

Isla Monos

PARQUE NACIONAL MOCHIMA

Las Playuelas

Península de Manare

Bahía Mochima

Isla Caracas de Este

Isla los Venados

Isla Caracas de Oeste

Ensenada Tigrillo

Cerro Aceite Castillo

Punta Gorda

Golfo de Santa Fe

Santa Fe

To Cumaná (approx 20 km)

Mochima

Los Altos

Costa Azul

El Chaparro

Pertigalete

Guanta

Chaure

Lechería

El Morro de Barcelona

PUERTO LA CRUZ
(see town map)

To Barcelona & Caracas

El Faro is also a good place to see iguanas, and to watch them steal your lunch if you're not careful. This island is a bit greener than the others, and you can climb up to the top of the lighthouse for a great view. Another recommended island is **Isla de Plata**, with its dazzling white beach and crystal clear water which is ideal for snorkelling. The palm-fringed 'paradise-like' beaches of **Conoma** and **Conomita** are actually on the mainland, but can only be reached by boat.

Take a hat and sunscreen when visiting the islands. Note that they are very popular and consequently are badly littered; so don't add to it! All have restaurants, snack bars and thatched shelters for hire. It's a good idea to take your own lunch as the restaurants are expensive; eg US$12 for fish. **NB** It's cheaper to visit the more easterly islands from Santa Fe and Mochima than from Puerto La Cruz or Guanta.

Getting there

The westerly Islas Chimanas, La Borracha and El Borracho are all easily reached from various points along the Paseo Colón in Puerto La Cruz. The more easterly islands of Isla de Plata, Monos, Picuda Grande and Chica and the beaches of Conoma and Conomita are best reached from the port of **Guanta**, east of Puerto La Cruz (to get there, see page 239).

There are three companies in Puerto La Cruz that will take you to the islands: *Transtupuerto*, on Paseo Colón opposite *Hotel Diana*, T 667138, owned by Sra Carmen Garrido, will take you to the closest islands around Puerto La Cruz for US$5, a day tour around several islands with stops costs US$18-26, including transport, snorkelling equipment and soft drinks; *Transporte Turístico Virgen del Valle*, offers similar deals (US$6 extra for food); *Transtupaco*, next to *Hotel Meliá*, don't run tours, but act as a taxi to the islands.

Alternatively, you can reach the islands with the *Embarcadero de Peñeros*, on Paseo Colón, behind the *Tejas Restaurant*. Departures from 0900-1000, return at 1600-1630; US$3.50 per person. The tourist office in Puerto La Cruz provides tour operators for day trips to various islands

for swimming or snorkelling. A 6-hour trip to four islands costs US$15 per person, including drinks.

THE COAST

Beyond the beaches of Conoma and Conomita, is **Playa Arapito**, where there is a restaurant. Parking costs US$0.35. You can hire boats here to take you to **La Piscina**, a beautiful coral reef near some small islands, for good snorkelling and lots of dolphins. Expect to pay US$8-10 per boat.

● **Accommodation** Just along from the entrance to Playa Arapito is a *posada*, **D**, run by Sr Marcel, with cooking facilities, contact him via Sra Monica at Playa Colorada (see below).

PLAYA COLORADA

Only 5 minutes east of Arapito is the popular beach of **Playa Colorada** (Km 32) with beautiful red sands and palm trees. It gets very crowded on weekends but is quiet through the week and well worth a visit. The hotels and *posadas* are all up the hill, about 5 minutes from the beach, in a wealthy-looking residential area full of big houses owned by foreigners. There's a whole host of small bars and restaurants right on the beach.

Boats also leave from here to La Piscina, as well as to **Isla Arapo** and **Isla Arapito**. It costs US$10-12 per boat, or US$50 per day; the boatmen will pick you up later then take you to a restaurant.

● **Accommodation At Playa Colorada**: **B** *Colorada Bungalos Hotel Club*, delightful mini-apartments with ceiling fan, fridge, cooker, garden and pool; **B-C** *Villas Turísticas Playa Colorada*, Avenida Principal, T (016) 6816365, comfortable air conditioned rooms with TV, also air conditioned trailers for 4 people, **D**, with cooker and fridge, also pool and good restaurant, accepts Visa, Apartado 61355, Caracas 1060-A, T (02) 952-1393; **D** *Bed and Breakfast Jali*, Quinta Jali, Calle Marchant, Playa Colorada, T (016) 6818113, run by Lynn and Jack Allard, air conditioning, shared bathroom, hot water, very quiet, smaller rooms are also available, **E**, free transport to surrounding beaches, family atmosphere, English and French spoken, washing facilities, German books, price includes a good American breakfast, dinner is also served on request, highly recommended; they have another house four blocks away, with washing facilities and which is also recommended. Opposite *Jali* is **D** *Villa Nirvana*, run by Sra Rita who is Swiss, T (081) 651266, rooms to rent with fan, also mini-apartments with kitchen for 2-4 people, **D**.

Sra Monica, who is French, has 2 rooms for rent, **D**, on Avenida Principal, 3 minutes' walk from the beach, T (016) 6816465, air conditioning and use of kitchen facilities. Doña Rosa lets out a house or apartment, **D**, while Seniorca, who runs a beach bar, hires tents at US$8 per night. Camping is permitted for a small fee (but there is no fresh water). For good food try *Daniel's Barraca*, at the east end of the beach.

● **Transport** To get to Playa Colorada, take a Linea Santa Fe *por puesto* from the the corner of the terminal in Puerto La Cruz, US$0.80.

Nearby is **Playa Vallecito**, with camping for US$1.50 per tent. There's a security guard, car parking for US$0.80 and a bar with good food and bottled water on sale. There are also plenty of palm trees for hammock-slinging. At **Playa Los Hicacos** is a beach club for the Universidad del Oriente in Cumaná and a lovely coral reef. At **Playa Santa Cruz**, 30 km east of Puerto La Cruz, you can buy fresh seafood from the fishermen's huts.

SANTA FE

40 km from Puerto La Cruz, in Sucre state, is the fishing village of **Santa Fe** (*phone code* 093). It's larger and noisier than Mochima further east, and a lot livelier, but nevertheless a good place to relax. The dark red beach has been cleaned and now looks really good. Almost all the *posadas* are situated on the beach, as is the golf course. Another attraction is the fact that there's a greater variety of organized and resonably-priced tours to the islands than most other places on the coast. There's a weekly market on Saturdays.

NB Because of it's popularity and proximity to the main road, robbery is more of a danger here than some of the smaller beaches (see **Warning** on page 242).

Excursions

About 10 minutes away by car, on the road to **Tumiriquire** reservoir (see also **Excursions from Los Altos**, page 243) is a river with the beautiful, 20m-high **Salto de San Pedro** waterfall, which is great for bathing.

There's also a small cave behind the fall. To get there, take a taxi from the entrance to Santa Fe for around US$2-3. You'll need to organize the return trip in advance as hitching a ride is difficult. Alternatively, ask Alfonso to take you (see **Tour companies** below). This is much easier because he'll either wait for you or pick you up at an arranged time; he's also more reliable than most of the taxi drivers.

Jeep, boat or diving tours are all available from Santa Fe. Francisco is recommended for boat trips; you'll find him a few houses to the west of the *Hotel Cochaima*. Fishermen offer similar trips but their prices are much higher. It may be a better idea to hire your own boat for half the price, or hitch down the road to Colorada. Ask for Thomas, he has a boat and will take you wherever. (See also **Tours** below).

Local information
● **Accommodation**
All hotels listed have private bathrooms unless otherwise indicated.

D *El Café*, the first hotel you get to on Playa Cochaima, fans, spotlessly clean, run tours to the river, waterfalls and islands, also fishing trips, minimum 4 persons, US$5-10 per person; **D** *Siete Delfines*, on the beach near the market, T (016) 6385668, T/F 314166, e-mail:dolphins@telcel.net.ve, Website: http//www.emergente.com.ve/sietedelfines, price includes breakfast, **E** without, rooms with private bathroom, fan, laundry service, café, bar, pool table, cable TV on the terrace (where you can cook), excellent food available in the restaurant, great atmosphere, you can make international collect calls from the public phone on the beach, closed circuit TV for security, warmly recommended, the owner Ricardo offers several tours, watersports and diving courses (see below); **D** *Posada El Jardin*, also on Playa Cochaima, T/F 210073, with continental breakfast, cheaper without bath, US$2 reduction for singles, kitchen, garden, run by Diego Rubio and his Swiss wife, Cristina, who speaks English, French and German, airport transfer and tours, recommended; **D** *Café El Mar*, on Playa Cochaima, owner Matthias (German), air conditioning, rooms OK but toilets a bit smelly, restaurant, bar, very good food.

E *Cochaima*, next to the restaurant of the same name right on the beach, run by Sra Margot, fans in rooms, friendly, popular, meals available, safe (Sra Margot will look after your valuables), recommended; **E** *La Sierra Inn*, just along from

El Café, T (014) 933116, run by Sr José Vivas, fan, also run tours (see below), very warmly recommended.

You can also rent rooms in several private houses: Sr Julio Cesar ('El Portugés'), **E**, the last house on the beach, a bit further down from *Restaurant Cochaima*, sign 'Rooms for Rent', fan, some rooms without private bathroom, very friendly, you can cook in his kitchen and use the fridge, very helpful, recommended; *Salón de Juegos Chomena* has 1 basic, cheap room for real budget travellers, the owner changes travellers' cheques. Also rooms for rent on 2 floors at **D-E** *Casa de Nany*, behind *La Sierra Inn*. Ask at *La Sierra* about the *Escapada*, a 3-bedroom house with its own private beach.

● **Tour companies & travel agents**

Tours: Ricardo at the *Siete Delfines* runs IDEA scuba diving courses for US$250, US$100 for a resort course and US$60 per day (2 dives) for experienced divers; he also offers windsurfing in season (December), horseriding, tours to the islands (US$4 to Isla Arapo, US$10 to Playa Blanca, including lunch) and hires out beach games. José Vivas at the *Sierra Inn* runs tours to the islands, from US$4 per person including transport and snorkelling equipment, departing at 0930, returning at 1500; also tours around the National Park and fishing trips. *Alfonso Tours*, based at the *Cochaima* hotel, as well as local tours (see **Excursions** above) Alfonso runs 7-day tours to Roraima (see page 317) for US$250 per person, and 6-day tours of the Gran Sabana for US$210 per person. These are probably the best value tours on offer; Alfonso has spent many years in the Gran Sabana and knows the area very well. He can also be contacted in Maracay, T (043) 459982 (Thursday or Friday).

Other tour companies include: *Pauji Expeditions*, Calle Principal, T 210067; *Tierra Sacra Expeditions*, Playa Cochaima, T 210667, run by Miguel Gasco, tours of Gran Sabana (see also under Ciudad Bolívar **Tour companies** on page 284).

● **Transport**

To **Cumaná**, *por puesto* at 0600, US$1; they leave Cumaná from one block down from the Redoma del Indio along Avenida Perimetral. It is sometimes difficult to get the bus from Puerto La Cruz to stop at Santa Fe, so a *por puesto* may be a better bet from the terminal, US$1.10, 1 hour. A taxi costs around US$13-14, including wait. Gasoline is available in Santa Fe.

MOCHIMA

The picturesque little fishing village of **Mochima** lies beyond Santa Fe, 4 km off the Puerto La Cruz-Cumaná main road

(hitching is difficult). The town is very quiet and peaceful and only comes to life at weekends. The beach at Mochima is not worthwhile and the sea is not too clean near the town, but there's an *embarcadero* from where you can get boats at very reasonable prices to take you to the islands and other, nicer, beaches (see below). There are also more opportunities for walking and canoeing tours, if you need a break from the beach.

Excursions

Boats to the islands and nearby beaches cost from US$8.50-11.50 per boat, depending on the distance. A 6-hour tour of 4 islands for swimming and snorkelling costs US$15 per person (including drinks), and can be arranged by the tourist office. Saturday and Sunday at 1000 is rush hour, when the *pineros* take all the weekend visitors to the islands. A couple of recommended local trips are to **Playa Marita** and **Playa Blanca**, where there is excellent snorkelling (take your own equipment). Several huts at the beaches serve fresh fish, but it's probably better to bring your own water and food, just to be on the safe side.

There are numerous walks around Mochima; ask Rodolfo for information (see **Scuba diving** below). A good, short walk (30 minutes) goes up behind the village to a river (which is dried out in the dry season but full in the wet). At the entrance to the village where the road divides, take a left (looking towards the mountains) along a dirt road. This goes past a white house, then a 2-storey mustard house. The road continues, passing two dried-up rivers (the second one twice) and then narrows to a track. After about 10-15 minutes you come to an open space which has been cleared for planting. Follow the track round to your left and go up for another 10 minutes or so till you reach the stream.

There are also caves to explore, one of which you have to swim underwater for 2m to get to. Again, Rodolfo knows about them and will take you there if you ask.

Local information

● Accommodation

All have private bathrooms, unless otherwise stated.

D *Servicios Turísticos Gaby*, at the end of the road next to the sea, with its own pier, air conditioning or fan, breakfast available, a "lovely place", they'll also take guests to the islands for US$3-4 per person.

E *Posada Beatriz*, fan, TV in salon, use of cooker, fridge, friendly, run by Sr Juan Remez; **E** *Puerto Viejo*, opposite the *embarcadero*, small apartment for 2, fan, fridge, **D** with cooker, fridge and a house (for 4, with cooker and fridge). Also opposite the *embarcadero* is **D** *Posada de los Buzos*, run by Rodolfo Plaza (see **Scuba diving** below); and Sr Cesar Bareto, who rents double rooms with fan, and a house (for 4, with cooker and fridge). Sras Cellita Día, Mama Inés and Doña María also let out rooms, **E**; as does Sr Padriño, **F**, basic but safe, he will store luggage when you go to the nearby beaches by boat, the house has no sign but it is just a few houses before *Servicios Turísticos Gaby*. There are also houses to rent with kitchens and fans from US$12 per day depending on length of stay.

● Places to eat

El Mochimero, just along from the *embarcadero*, excellent food, highly recommended (try the *empanadas* with ice cold coconut milk), open daily. Also open during the week is *El Guyacán*. *Don Quijote*, Avenida Bermúdez, very good. Sra Argelia, in the third house along from the entrance to the village, sells the best *arepas* in town.

● Sports

Scuba diving: Rodolfo Plaza runs a diving school and hires equipment. It's best to contact him in Caracas, as he's only in Mochima at weekends; Los Palos Grandes, Avenida Andrés Bello between 3rd and 4th transversal, T (014) 216020, T/F (02) 963-6736. He offers a basic CEMA course, and 1-day resort courses for those who want an idea of what diving is like (US$80, food not included). Rodolfo also runs canoeing tours nearby (US$30 per person, 2 minimum), as well as walking tours around the area and to other parts of the country; he comes highly recommended. Francisco García (2 doors down from Rodolfo), runs a diving school offering PADI courses, and shop, T 932991.

● Transport

From **Cumaná**: take a bus from the centre going to the Redoma del Indio (eg San Luis, Hospital Brasil, or Cooperativa Cumaná), then walk back along Avenida Arismendi (via centro) one block to a small green plaza. Jeeps leave from here to Mochima, and they're easily recognized. Don't believe taxi drivers who'll tell you that the jeeps are not running on any particular day for any particular reason! Jeeps run daily to and from Mochima until around 1800 (1500-1600 on Sundays). There's also a bus to Cumaná at 1400 (US$0.80). Buses do not travel between Santa Fe and Mochima; take a *por puesto*, bargain hard on the price, US$10-12 is reasonable.

CUMANA

Cumaná (*population* 250,300; *phone code* 093; *average temperature* 27°C) capital of Sucre state, straddles both banks of the Río Manzanares. Not only is Cumaná the main commercial centre for the state – with an economy based on coffee, sugar, cacao, fishing and salt from the mines on the Araya Peninsula – it is also a thriving tourist town. Aside from boasting nice beaches and sites of historic interest, it also serves as a convenient base from which to visit Isla de Margarita, the Araya peninsula, Monagas and the Orinoco Delta.

HISTORY

Cumaná is the oldest Hispanic city on the South American mainland. The first Spaniards to come here were Franciscan missionaries, sent to convert the local indigenous population in 1506. Their work suffered a severe setback, however, when settlers from the nearby island of Cubagua came to Cumaná to 'recruit' more slaves to replace the ones who had died during the exploitation of the rich pearl beds. The

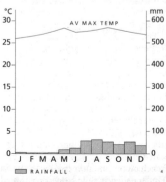

Climate: Cumaná

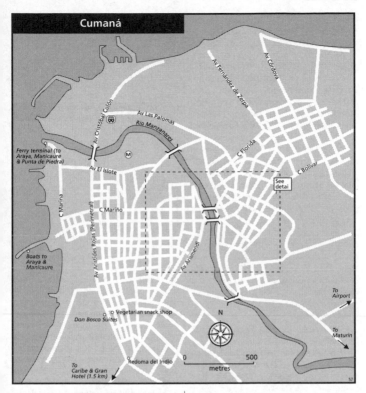

Cumaná

Ferry terminal (to Araya, Manicaure à Punta de Piedra)

Av Cristobal Colón

Av Las Palomas

Río Manzanares

Av Fernández de Zerpa

Av Córdova

C Florida

C Bolívar

Av El Islote

M

Boats to Araya & Manicaure

C Marina

C Mariño

Av Arístides Rojas (Perimetral)

Av Arismendi

See detail

To Airport

To Maturin

N

Vegetarian snack shop

Don Bosco Suites

Redoma del Indio

0   500
metres

To Caribe & Gran Hotel (1.5 km)

natives, not surprisingly, took exception to this and retaliated by attacking the mission settlements. Thus was the city of Cumaná founded, in 1521, as a base from which the Spanish could exact revenge.

This set the tone and the ensuing years were ones of bloody conflict and terrible atrocities carried out by both sides, during which the town was destroyed and rebuilt several times. Its present name is the original indigenous one (dating from 1569) and for the first 100 years Cumaná was largely made up of converted natives. The town and its people continued to suffer over the following centuries: repeated attacks from English, Dutch and French pirates and slave traders; the Wars of Independence; and a succession of devastating earthquakes, the first in 1530, the

most recent in 1997, and most devastating in 1929.

Not surprisingly, then, only a few historic sites remain, but Cumaná remains a charming place with its mixture of old and new. The older sections flow around the base of the hill dominated by the Castillo de San Antonio. The streets around the Gobernación and Plaza Bolívar are narrow and partly pedestrianized and more relaxing than the busy surrounding streets. They also have several budget hotels and eating places. **NB** The port area, 1½ km from the centre, is not safe at night.

PLACES OF INTEREST

An enjoyable walk is along the treelined banks of the Río Manzanares (but beware mosquitoes), and through **Parque Ayacucho** and **Parque Guaiqueri** (on the west bank of the river). There are markets on both sides, which sell food and craftwork.

The impressive **Castillo de San Antonio de la Eminencia** dominates the town and affords great views of the Araya Peninsula and coast. It was built in 1686 as a defence against pirates, with 16 mounted cannon, drawbridge and dungeons from which there are said to be underground tunnels leading to the Santa Inés church. General José Antonio Páez, the first president of the new Republic, was held captive here with his son from 1849-50 (see page 43). The fort was completely destroyed by an earthquake in 1853, rebuilt and then razed once more by the devastating earthquake of 1929, which also reduced most of the coast to rubble. It was restored in 1975. The **Castillo de Santa María de la Cabeza**, built in 1669, is a rectangular fortress with a panoramic view of San Antonio and the elegant homes below.

The **Convento de San Francisco**, the original Capuchin mission of 1514, was the first school on the continent; its remains are on the Plaza Badaracco Bermúdez facing the beach. The **Church of Santa Inés** (1637) was the base of the early Franciscan missionaries. Like the rest of the city, it has been rebuilt and repaired on five occasions between 1637 and 1929 due to earthquakes. A tiny 400-year-old statue of the Vírgen de Candelaria is in the garden.

On Plaza Bolívar is **La Gobernación** around a courtyard lined by cannon from Santa María de la Cabeza, noted for its gargoyles and other colonial features.

In the suburb of **Chaima** a bronze monument marks the 450th anniversary of the city's founding. It depicts in bas-relief the notoriously bloody encounters between Spaniards and natives. A Capuchin friar and a Cumanagoto Indian top the 16m column. To get there take a 'Brasil/Terminal' bus near Plaza Ayacucho (US$0.30).

MUSEUMS

The **Museo Gran Mariscal de Ayacucho** in the old Consejo Municipal in Parque Ayacucho commemorates the 150th anniversary of the battle of Ayacucho. It contains mainly portraits, relics and letters of Bolívar and José Antonio Sucre. Sucre was born in Cumaná in 1795, became Bolívar's first lieutenant, then President of Peru in 1826, before being assassinated in Colombia in 1828. The museum is open Tuesday-Friday 0845-1130 and 1545-1830; free guided tours are available.

The maritime museum, **Museo del Mar**, has good exhibits of tropical marine life. It's at the old airport, on Avenida Universidad with Avenida Industrial; open Tuesday-Sunday 0830-1130, 1500-1800, US$0.60. To get there, take a San Luis minibus from outside the cathedral.

The home of **Andrés Eloy Blanco** (1896-1955), one of Venezuela's greatest poets and politicians (see **Literature** section on page 56), is on Plaza Bolívar. It has been nicely restored to its turn-of-the-century elegance and turned into a museum, with photographs, poetry recordings, political notes and personal effects of the owner. It is open Monday-Friday 0800-1200 and 1600-2000, Saturday and Sunday 0900-1200 and 1600-2000; free entry.

Museo de Arqueología e Historia del Estado Sucre, is in the house of Dr Luis Daniel Beauperthuy (1807-71). In 1854 he discovered the mosquito which acted as the vector of Yellow Fever. Dr Beauperthuy lived in the house from 1839 until his death. It is at Calle Sucre, opposite Santa Inés Church and open Monday-Friday 0830-1100 and 1430-1730. Nearby on Calle Sucre is **La Casa de Ramos Sucre**, another Venezuelan poet (1890-1930); open Monday-Friday 0830-1100 and 1430-1730.

BEACHES

Los Uveros on the **Ensenada de Manzanillo** is the largest public beach in Venezuela. There are two restaurants and camping is allowed on the 3 km long clean, sandy stretch just west of the airport. **San**

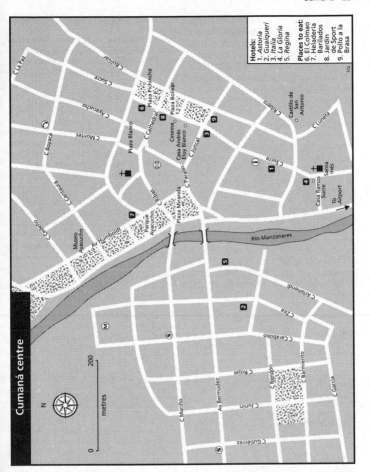

Cumaná centre

N
metres
0   200

Hotels:
1. Astoria
2. Guaiqueri
3. Italia
4. La Gloria
5. Regina

Places to eat:
6. El Colmao
7. Heladería
8. Barilados
   Jardín
9. Pollo a la
   Brasa

Luis beach is a short local bus ride away, and is also recommended, but the water is dirtier than Los Uveros.

EXCURSIONS

A paved road runs south, down the Río Manzanares for 56 km to **Cumanacoa** (*population* 18,750), a traditional Creole town in a rich agricultural area. At the Casa de Cultura, Calle Motedano 20, authentic folk music is performed by 'Los Carrizas Precolombinos', a band of local musicians and members of the Turimiquire tribe. Near the town is the Cuchivano grotto from which flares a jet of natural gas.

● **Accommodation In Cumanacoa**: rooms for rent at an unsigned place on the first road after the church heading south; **F**, clean, friendly, with bathroom (ask at the hairdresser). There's only one other hotel, **E**.

On the road to Cumanacoa, 22 km from Cumaná, is **Río Brito**. To get there, take a bus or *por puesto* from Plaza Miranda. Ask to be let off at the *Entrada a Río Brito*, by a small shop just before a road sign 'Barrancas'. From the entrance walk past a *conuco* and over a bridge which crosses the Río Manzanares. From there it's a pretty 40 minute walk through old *conucos* and past mango trees. At the first fork it's quicker to go right to Pozo Azul, but it's much nicer to go left and meet the river further up. 30 minutes from the Pozo Azul fork you reach a clearing with five massive mango trees. The righthand path goes to the river, which is easily crossed in the dry season when the water is low. From there take a left and 100m further up is a good bathing place. Alternatively, take the lefthand path without crossing the river and walk along it until you find a place which takes your fancy.

This makes for a very pleasant day out, and it's popular with locals, especially at weekends. Take all your food and drink. It's probably safer to go in a group; and you should beware of sudden rises in the river level in the wet season which can easily sweep you downriver.

LOCAL FESTIVALS

22 January: *Santa Inés*, a pre-Lenten carnival throughout the state of Sucre. **2 November**: *Santos y Fideles Difuntos*, at El Tacal.

LOCAL INFORMATION

● **Accommodation**

Hotel prices

L1	over US$200	**L2**	US$151-200
L3	US$101-150	**A1**	US$81-100
A2	US$61-80	**A3**	US$46-60
B	US$31-45	**C**	US$21-30
D	US$12-20	**E**	US$7-11
F	US$4-6	**G**	up to US$3

Those marked with an asterisk (*) are bookable through Fairmont International (see under Caracas).

All the hotels below have private bathrooms unless stated otherwise.

A2-A3 *Los Bordones*, at the end of Avenida Universidad, T 513111, F 515377, 8 km from the bus station, beautifully situated on a good beach with excellent restaurant, swimming pool, air conditioning, casino, bar, accepts major credit cards, prices depend on the view (sea or mountain), recommended.

B-C *Gran Hotel**, on Avenida Universidad close to the beach at San Luis, between *Hotel Cumanagoto* (which was still undergoing renovations in mid-1997) and the town centre, T 515867, F 512677, air conditioning, TV, hot water, pool, restaurant, clean, friendly, accepts major credit cards, recommended.

C *Caribe*, on Avenida Universidad right on San Luis beach, T 514548, air conditioning, TV, fridge, also basic cabins for 4-5 persons, **D**, with air conditioning, TV, cooker and fridge, English spoken, also organizes tours to Mochima and Guacharo Cave for US$35 per person including transport, drinks and lunch, highly recommended; **C** *Mariño*, Calle Mariño y Junín, T 320751, air conditioning, near the centre, but not very clean; **C** *Turismo Guaiqueri*, Avenida Bermúdez 26, T 310821, comfortable, air conditioning; **C-D** *Minerva**, on Avenida Colón, near Avenida Perimetral on the northern edge of town (little to do in this area), take a 'Brasil-Terminal' bus which passes the hotel, T 662712, F 662701, air conditioning, TV, restaurant, modern.

D *Don Bosco Suites*, 19 de Abril with Avenida Perimetral (near the Redoma del Indio), T 310969, air conditioning, TV, fridge, no hot water but recommended; **D** *Regina*, on Calle Arismendi with Avenida Bermúdez, T 311073, hot water, air conditioning, TV, restaurant, room service, safe box for valuables, good views from the upper rooms, very helpful, good value; **D** *La Savoia*, on Avenida Perimetral, two blocks from *Don Bosco*, T 314379, air conditioning, clean, accepts major credit cards.

E *Astoria*, Calle Sucre, T 662708, with cold shower, air conditioning, TV room outside; **E-F** *Italia*, Calle Sucre, esquina Plaza Bolívar, T 663678, with fan or air conditioning, safe but not very clean.

F *Hospedaje La Gloria*, Sucre 31, opposite Santa Inés church, with fan or air conditioning, basic, helpful. Other cheap hotels can be found on Calle Sucre and around Plaza Ayacucho.

● **Places to eat**

El Colmao on Plaza Pichincha, Calle Sucre, T 663251, very good fish, charming service, not expensive; *Sand Hills* and *Los Montones*, near the *Hotel Caribe* on San Luis beach, recommended. On Calle Sucre are: *Italia*, cheap and good; *Pucheff*, good pizza. *Ali Baba*, Avenida Bermúdez near the corner with Calle Castellón, excellent, cheap, middle eastern food, recommended; *Jardín de Sport*, Plaza Bolívar, outdoor café, good food, good atmosphere, recommended. All central restaurants close Sunday lunchtime. There are many good restaurants on Avenida Perimetral in the area near *La Savoia Hotel*. Try *El Mercadito*, at the Redoma del Indio, where all the locals eat, excellent and cheap fish soup and stew, open for lunch only. There's a good vegetarian restaurant on Avenida Bermúdez, which does good and varied lunches to order.

● **Banks & money changers**
Cash advance on Visa and Mastercard at: **Banco Provincial**, Avenida Bermúdez, three blocks from Plaza Estudiante; **Banco Mercantil**, Avenida Bermúdez y Calle Gutierrez; **Banco Caribe**, Calle Mariño y Calle Junín; **Banco Unión**, Calle Mariño y Calle Carabobo. Exchange at **Oficambio**, Calle Mariño, Edificio Funcal, one block from Plaza Estudiante, changes cash and travellers' cheques at official rates, open Monday-Friday 0800-1130 and 1415-1730, Saturday 0830-1130.

● **Entertainment**
Cinemas: on Plaza Bolívar, next to *Jardín de Sport*.

● **Post & telecommunications**
Ipostel: next to the cathedral on Calle Paraiso. CANTV: on Calle Montes y Calle Boyacá, two blocks from Plaza Blanco.

● **Tour companies & travel agents**
Ya-wer Tours, Sucre 65, T 313134, organizes launches to Araya Peninsula and nearby beaches and scuba diving; *Ancar*, Calle Bolívar 29, T 663821/22; *Interamericana*, Avenida Perimetral, Edificio Sesta, planta baja, T 313308; *Totem Tours*, Calle Sucre, Centro Comercial Cumaná, T 661843; *Joanna Tours*, Avenida Perimetral, Edificio Miramar, T 663833.

● **Tourist offices**
The tourist office is near the church of Santa Inés. Ask to see their photos of the surrounding area. They're very helpful and speak English, but their information is not always accurate.

● **Transport**
Air The airport is 10 km east of the centre. A taxi costs US$2.50. Flights to Caracas and Porlamar with Servivensa (T 312484).

Buses The terminal is 3 km northwest of the centre on Avenida Las Palomas, just before the junction with the peripheral road (T 662218). Local buses into the centre US$0.10, taxi US$1.50. *Por puesto* to **Puerto La Cruz**, US$6, bus US$3, 1½ hours. To **Güiria**, US$3.60, 1230, *por puesto* US$7.20, 5 hours (beware of overcharging), often stop in Carúpano. To **Caripe**, at 0730 and 1230, 4 hours, get there early and buy your ticket on the bus, US$2.50. To **Caracas**, US$7 and upwards depending on the company (7-8 hours), frequent service but not all advertised buses run, many cancellations. Many daily buses to **Ciudad Guayana** and

Ciudad Bolívar (US$6 with Expresos Guayanesa, T 66218, 6 hours). Other destinations include: Maracay, Valencia, Carúpano (US$3), Cumanacoa, Maturín, Barcelona and San Félix.
Sea For Ferries to **Isla de Margarita**, see page 269; to **Araya**, see below.

ARAYA PENINSULA

The long, thin arm of the Araya Peninsula stretches west out into the Caribbean to a point north of Cumaná. The peninsula is characterized by desert landscapes and pink salt lakes. The main settlement, Araya, is reached by ferry from Cumaná or by road via Cariaco.

ARAYA

The town of **Araya** (*population* 21,000 including Manicuare; *phone code* 093) has an airport and ferry dock and is an easy day trip away from Cumaná.

The major point of interest in the town is the mightily impressive **Castillo de Santiago** (or Fuerte Araya), built by Spain in 1625 to protect the peninsula's salt mines. The authorities spent 3 years constructing the fortress, bringing all materials, food and water in by sea. Very little remains apart from the ruins of its walls, passageways and cistern. Entry is free, but the only facilities are a refreshment stand and a picnic area. Today the mines are exploited by a Government-owned corporation and annual production has almost reached 500,000 tonnes. Ask permission for a visit from Ensal (Empresa Nacional de Salinas). Their office is near the pier at Puerto Sucre.

Windsurfing in Araya is reported as excellent for those with experience. There's a strong offshore wind, so it's not a good place for beginners. The best time is from December to June and the wind gets up to 95 km per hour around March and April. For any information on windsurfing in Araya you should see Sergio Martín (see below), who is a keen windsurfer and very helpful.

● **Accommodation & places to eat**
D *Araya*, a long way from the dock, mainly used by the Salt Company for its visitors, air conditioning, hot water, with private bathroom, TV

Expensive tastes

Salt was a very precious commodity in 16th century Europe and much in demand. Until refrigeration came into widespread use, salt was indispensable for preserving food, especially fish, which was the main source of protein for northern European peoples.

A measure of its importance is the word 'salary', which derives from the Latin word for salt, *sal*. In Roman times, soldiers were actually paid in the stuff – hence the expression "a man worth his salt". Cakes of salt were also used as money in parts of Africa, China and Tibet until this century.

Not surprisingly, then, the discovery of the rich Araya salt beds by the Spanish in 1499 was viewed with more than a little interest by the salt-starved Dutch. For over 50 years, they pretty much helped themselves from the unpopulated and unprotected peninsula, until the Spanish finally decided to do something about it and embarked on the construction of the Castillo de Santiago, the greatest fortress built in the country and the costliest project ever undertaken in the Americas during their colonial rule.

in lounge, restaurant, tasca, accepts Visa credit cards, runs tours to the salt mines (free for large groups; groups of 4 or less pay US$5 for the jeep), also tours around the peninsula; **D-E** *Posada Araya Wind*, near the fort, just up from the *Parador Turística Eugenia* restaurant, T 71442, fans, some rooms with private bathroom, everything is scrupulously clean, good restaurant, owned and run by Sergio Martín (see above), recommended; **E** *Posada Helen*, next to the *Araya Wind*, T 71101, fans, private bathroom; **F** *Hospedaje San José*, on Avenida Principal going into town, just up from the tourist office, it is very basic and best avoided. Private houses also have rooms available. The state-owned company, Ensal, has an air conditioned guesthouse and dining room open to the public and runs 2-hour tours of its saltworks (up to 1400). Bars on the beach near the dock serve meals and a *panadería* at the end of the main street going uphill from the dock serves good breakfasts.

CUMANA TO ARAYA BY BOAT

A boat to Araya departs every hour from Cumaná; ½ hour, US$0.60. To get to the ferry terminal in Cumaná, take a Conferry bus from the *parado del centro* in town, just up from the CANTV building where the phone boxes are. Avoid the walk from Avenida Perimetral to the ferry, as it can be dangerous, especially at night (three Conferry buses take you straight to the ferry). An alternative to taking a ferry direct to Araya, is to take a *tapaito* (passenger ferry) to **Manicaure**, a small village on the peninsula, and from there take a *camioneta* to Araya. Frances Osborn (our correspondent in Cumaná) writes: "It's really pot luck which is quicker, but I prefer the *tapaito*. There's usually less of a wait for it to fill up, the crossing's quicker and the 15-minute ride to Araya gives you an idea of the Araya landscape, and a good view of the castle and salt works."

Getting a return ferry from Araya can be haphazard and difficult at weekends, as there are more cars than spaces. Return ferries from Araya leave from the main wharf at the end of Avenida Bermúdez. There are several passenger launches a day, some with upper seating decks.

CUMANA TO CARUPANO

The Araya Peninsula can also be reached by road from Cumaná. The main coastal highway, Route 9, runs east through **Cariaco**, **Carúpano** and all the way to **Güiria** on the Paría Peninsula.

The coastal route from Cumaná east along the Gulf of Cariaco is beautiful, running past a succession of attractive beaches and small villages. At **Villa Frontado** a road runs south for 52 km to **Caripe** (see page 266). Even the larger places along this stretch of coast – **Marigüitar** and **San Antonio del Golfo** – are very quiet and have little accommodation to offer. One particularly good place to stay, though, is *Balneario Cachamaure*, 44 km from Cumaná, between Mariguitar and San Antonio de Golfo; the cabins, **D**, are situated on a beautiful beach with all facilities (including barbecue equipment, US$2) and shaded by coconut palms.

Further east on the main road is **Cerezal**, famed for its basket-making and other *artesanía*. 15 mintues beyond Cerezal is **Cariaco** (*population* 25,350; 84 km from Cumaná), hometown of the great independence hero, José Francisco Bermúdez. Here, Route 9 winds inland over the Paría Ridge to Carúpano, a further 51 km northeast of Cariaco.

A paved road runs west out to Araya, 95 km away at the very western tip of the peninsula. The views of the rugged Caribbean coastline are dramatic as the road heads north and then turns west past the turn-off to the fishing village of **Chacopata** (see page 257).

An alternative road between Cariaco and Carúpano runs due north for 17 km, before reaching the coast at **Saucedo**, an attractive fishing village on a clean stretch of white sands. The road then heads east along the Caribbean for 38 km, passing **La Esmeralda** and **Guaca**, where clams packed with peppers are sold. North of Guaca is **Playa Escondido**, a deep calm bay surrounded by sand dunes. The beaches on this coast are covered with shells, which make swimming a less attractive proposition, but an exception is near the **Balneario Costa Azul**, 4 km east of Guaca. At the end of the road which runs west behind the village is a long, deserted beach of white sand on the **Bahía de Güiria** (not to be confused with the town on the Paría Peninsula).

CARUPANO

The colonial town of **Carúpano** (*population* 87,600; *phone code* 094), which dates back to 1647, sits between the Ríos Revilla and Candoroso. Its beach is wide and desolate but the waterfront boulevard, Avenida Bermúdez, is landscaped and attractive. The town's wealth was built on the local cocoa plantations, and today 70% of Venezuela's cocoa is still shipped from Carúpano. Here in 1816, Bolívar managed simultaneously to further the causes of emancipation and freedom from colonial rule by freeing the black slaves who worked on the wealthy cocoa plantations in exchange for their support for the Republican side in the Wars of Independence.

Excursions

Corpomedina (see **Tour companies** below) run excursions from Carúpano, Playa Medina and Pui Puy from between US$45 and US$65, depending on where you set out from and the number of people. They go to Hato Río de Agua, a buffalo farm; Agua Santa, a 'tourist' cocoa plantation, where cocoa is only produced for the tourists, but you can see how it's all done; also to El Pilar Botanical Garden, which is actually more of a garden centre.

Playa Medina is one of the nicest beaches on the entire east coast and subject to many a tourist brochure cliché. As well as a magnificent beach, there are also hot springs, a waterfall and water slide. The cabins at the beach must be booked through *Corpomedina*; price includes 3 meals and transport from Carúpano (transport is extra for groups of more than 5), with fan, fridge and cooker. Transport only costs US$72 per jeep (4 people) there

Playa Medina, Sucre

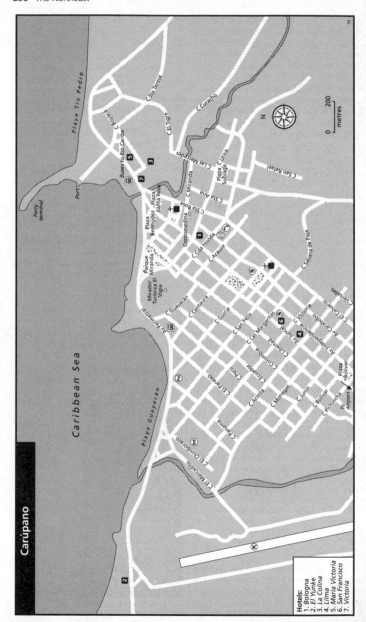

Carúpano

Hotels:
1. Bologna
2. El Yunke
3. La Colina
4. Lilma
5. María Victoria
6. San Francisco
7. Victoria

and back. Alternatively, take a taxi from the bus terminal in Carúpano. Taxis 'linea' charge a fixed rate US$50 one way; private taxis may offer a lower price if you bargain and look poor. You can also reach Playa Medina and Playa Pui Puy from Río Caribe (see below).

Beach cabins at **Pui Puy** cost US$32 for two, US$48 for four; they are basic with private bathroom. You can also camp here for a nominal fee.

Local festivals

Carúpano is famous throughout Venezuela as the last place still celebrating a traditional pre-Lenten Carnival in **February**, reputed to be the liveliest and most colourful festival in the whole country. It involves days of dancing in fabulous costumes, rum drinking, completely masked women in black (*negritas*) and much else besides! You'll need to book accommodation well in advance at this time. Other festivals include: **3 May**, *Velorios de la Cruz* (street dances); **15 August**, *Asunción de la Virgen*.

Local information
● Accommodation

C *Lilma*, Avenida Independencia 161, T 311341, air conditioning, TV, hot water, good restaurant, tasca, cinema, accepts credit cards; **C** *Posada La Colina*, behind *Hotel Victoria*, F 322915, 17 double rooms with air conditioning, TV, hot water, breakfast included, 2 restaurants, accepts credit cards, part of the Corpomedina group; **C** *Victoria**, Avenida Perimetral, air conditioning, TV, hot water, has seen better days but still good value, pool, restaurant, post box; **C-D** *El Yunque*, at the Yunque roundabout on Avenida Perimetral (about 2 km from the centre), T 313683/314310, air conditioning, TV, hot water, good seafood restaurant, casino, games room, cafeteria, laundry service; **C-D** *Posada Nena*, at Playa Copey, one block from the beach, T 317624, F 317297, roof fans, hot water, pool and games room, clean, friendly, good restaurant, comfortable, garden, public phones, German/Venezuelan owners, highly recommended, organize day tours to Playa Medina, Playa Pui Puy, Cueva del Guácharo, Aguas Calientes, jungle waterfalls, Mochima and the north coast of Pária, US$45 per person for 2 people, discounts for larger groups.

D *Bologna*, Avenida Independencia, excellent, cheap restaurant, air conditioning, cheaper rooms with fan only, intermittent water, owner speaks German, recommended; **D** *Casa Blanca*, at Playa Copey, 7 km west of Carúpano (to get there, ask buses approaching from the west to stop; or take a taxi from town), T 316896, 6 rooms with fan and private bathroom, hot water, clean, friendly, family atmosphere, very helpful, safe, very relaxing, restaurant serves excellent Spanish food cooked by the owner, who also speaks German, the nearby private beach is illuminated at night, motorbike parking, discounts for longer stays, highly recommended; **D** *María Victoria*, Avenida Perimetral (100m from *Hotel Victoria*), T 311073, safe, some rooms with air conditioning, basic, no hot water; **D** *San Francisco*, Avenida Juncal 87A with Calle Las Margeritas, T 311074, F 315176, good restaurant, tasca, parking, credit cards accepted.

● Places to eat

La Brasa Dorada, Avenida 5 Libertad, recommended; *El Kiosko*, Paseo Boulevard, by the seafront, OK; *Pizza Haití*, on Avenida Independencia, wide choice, good.

● Tour companies & travel agents

Corpomedina (*Encuentro viaje y turismo*), in the 'Casa del Cable' (the first telecommunications centre in Venezuela), on the south of Plaza Santa Rosa, T 315241/312283, F 312067, they are responsible for renting the beach huts at Playa Medina, Playa Pui Puy and Hato Río de Agua, as well as organizing various local trips (see **Excursions** above). *Pária Intertur*, Avenida Independencia 12, T 320542, run by Claudio and María Eugenia Ceglia, or contact Louisa Weston, T (016) 6345753 (01604-405802 in the UK), they run 8-day tours of the Pária Peninsula for US$640 all inclusive, or US$80 per day. *Evasión*, on Avenida Independencia, opposite *Hotel Lilma*, T 319577, day tours to Finca Vuelto Larga (see **Excursions** above) and other local sites. The travel agent next to *Hotel Lilma* on Avenida Independencia sells tickets for *Windward* to Trinidad (see page 261).

● Transport

Buses To Caracas, US$8, 8 hours, with Responsable de Venezuela; to Cumaná, US$3, 2 hours, *por puesto* US$6. Bus to **Güiria** US$2.50, 3 hours, *por puestos* (US$4) are quicker and depart when full, both leave from the bus terminal. Bus to **Puerto La Cruz**, US$4.70, 5 hours. No buses leave direct from Carúpano to **Caripe**: go first to Maturín or Cumaná; a taxi Carúpano-Caripe costs US$35.

Ferries Passenger-only ferries (*tapaitos*) leave from the village of Chacopata, west of Saucedo on the Araya peninsula.

Araya Peninsula, to **Isla del Margarita**; 1 hour approximately, US$8 one way. To get to Chacopata from Carúpano: leave the bus terminal and 50m down the road towards Cumaná is a covered bus stop where buses for Chacopata pass by; 1-1½ hours, US$3. Alternatively, you can get to Chacopata from Cariaco; jeeps leave from the plaza (*por puesto* Cumaná-Cariaco US$3).

PARIA PENINSULA

East of Carúpano, the Paría Peninsula reaches out to the most easterly point on Venezuela's Caribbean coast, forming the Gulf of Paría, with Trinidad to the east and the vast Orinoco Delta (Delta Amacuro) bordering it to the south.

Highway 9 continues a further 160 km east along the Peninsula to Güiria. The coast is left behind until Irapa, as the main highway climbs over the central spine through luxuriant forests of bamboo and Spanish moss to the village of **El Pilar** (33 km, *population* 17,000), where there are a number of hot springs (El Hervidero and Cueva del Pato) and the river bathing resort of **Sabacual**.

FINCA VUELTA LARGA

East of El Pilar, and 40 minutes from Carúpano, is **Guaraúnos**, near **Tunapuy**, on the road to Irapa and Güiria. Here is the **Finca Vuelta Larga** (not part of the *Corpomedina* group), the base of Klaus Müller, who has worked with indigenous communities and in conservation for 25 years. You can find him at Calle Bolívar 8 (T 094-69052).

Finca Vuelta Larga is a buffalo farm, but also produces fish, and is run on an ecological basis, with no insecticides and no burning of land. The result is a dramatic difference between Klaus's land and the surrounding countryside. The former has far more trees and, consequently, a greater diversity of birdlife and fauna. Klaus is also undertaking experiments with organic farming techniques for marshland conditions and promoting the use of traditional Warao weaving for furniture. The intention is that weaving should be developed for the production of functional objects instead of purely decorative 'tourist' items. Furthermore, Klaus hopes that, as a result of his efforts,

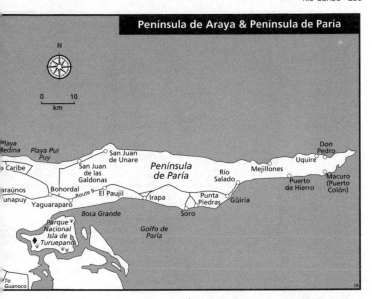

Península de Araya & Península de Paría

more appropriate means of land use will be found, producing food without destruction, and even improvement. His land, in fact, acts as a buffer zone for the flood marsh and mangroves of the **Turuepano National Park** to the south and east.

To get to the Finca, take a *por puesto* going to El Pilar and ask to get off at 'La Casa de Klaus'.

Tourists on a standard 2-day visit will see the Finca, and be taken on a walk along a river surrounded by gallery forest. There is also another walk on the Paría ridge, with spectacular views of the north coast and of the mangroves in the south. For those who stay longer trips can be organized to Cerro El Humo, a trek over the mountains to the north coast, a walk to Guanoco and the Asphalt Lake, Cueva del Guácharo and the mangroves of the Turuepano National Park. Both Cerro El Humo and the farm itself are wonderful for birding; Cerro El Humo even has endemic species. Daniel, Klaus's son, is an excellent bird watcher and speaks English and Spanish. There are also special packages for students wanting to work on the farm and scientists wishing to do research. Tours with Klaus cost US$60 per person per day for 4WD, food and lodging; the money is ploughed back into the local community.

ROUTES A second road which joins the Route 9 highway beyond El Pilar follows the coast east of Carúpano to the fishing village of **El Morro de Puerto Santo** (15 km), on a sandspit between the coast and a rocky offshore island, then heads on to Río Caribe.

RIO CARIBE

The little fishing town of **Río Caribe** (*population* 25,100; *phone code* 094) is an attractive and peaceful place to spend a few days. It's only 15 minutes east of Carúpano, and a very convenient jumping-off point for Playas Medina and Pui Puy. The old pastel-hued houses in town testify to the former prosperity of the place when it was the chief cacao-exporting port.

NB There are two Plaza Bolívars in Río Caribe: one is opposite the pier and the other is about seven blocks further up, opposite the church, from where buses leave for Caracas and Maturín.

Excursions

There are several sandy beaches on either side of the town. The best ones, Playas Medina and Pui Puy, lie to the east.

To get to **Playa Medina** and **Playa Pui Puy**: take a taxi from Río Caribe with *Linea San Miguel*; at Calle Rivero cc Calle Mariño, seven blocks up and one along to the left from Plaza Bolívar, T 61107. They leave for the beaches in the morning until around 1000, and bring people back in the afternoon from around 1500. It costs about US$30-35 per car there and back to Playa Medina, and US$35-40 to Pui Puy. It is also possible to bargain with local fishermen to take you, but it works out more expensive than a taxi.

There is also a *camioneta* (1 hour, US$0.50) which leaves for Guyana from the Río Caribe exit, opposite the petrol station. This drops you off at the entrance to both beaches (La Entrada), but from there it's a long, hot walk; 1½ hours to Medina and further still to Pui Puy.

Local information
● **Accommodation**

A3 *Hotel Playa Medina*, T 094-315241/ 312283, reserve in advance, includes full board and drinks, cottages on the beach with a small snackbar restaurant and toilets open to the public, changing facilities, car parking (US$1), well worth a visit.

B *Posada Caribana*, Avenida Bermúdez, excellent and cheap restaurant; in the process of opening another *posada* between Medina and Pui Puy.

C *Mar Caribe*, on the corner of the main boulevard, next to the pier, T 61494, air conditioning, TV, hot water, including breakfast, pool, restaurant, good coffee and cocktails, accepts credit cards; **C-D** *Evelin*, on Avenida Bermúdez, two blocks from Plaza Bolívar, T 61759, air conditioning, TV, hot water, restaurant; **C-D** *La Posada de Arlet*, to get there go up five blocks from Plaza Bolívar (next to the sea), take a right at the end of Avenida Bermúdez and it's two blocks further along, a white 2-storey house with brown edgings, T/F 61290, price includes breakfast, fans, spotlessly clean, very friendly, English and German spoken, small bar, space to sit around, laundry service, recommended, also arrange tours (see below).

E *Casa de Sra Adelina*, on the right as you enter town, sign reads "Se Alquilan Habitaciones", T 61670, fans, private bathroom, basic but clean and friendly, use of cooker and fridge.

Posada Turística San Miguel, is three blocks up from the church and two blocks left, on the corner where the road fords the river, T 61894, it looks pleasant from the outside. There are also private, unsigned pensions in town, but you'll need to ask for them.

● **Tour companies & travel agents**

Tours: a variety of tours are offered by *La Posada de Arlet* (see above). To Playas Medina and Pui Puy by boat for US$25 per person, including lunch, US$2 extra for drinks; also trips to Los Caños del Río Aji, a 3-hour boat trip along the river and mangroves with lots of animals and birds to see, US$60 per person (not including food); also to Caripe, Cueva del Guácharo, Caribbean islands and the Río Orinoco for US$60 per person, with English, French, Italian and Spanish-speaking guides. They also rent mountain bikes. Ask for Sra Ivette.

● **Transport**

Bus direct to Río Caribe from Caracas with Cruceros Oriente Sur; depart Terminal del Oriente in Caracas at 0730-0800 (check times as they change frequently); from Maturín with Expresos Maturín. Buses leave Río Caribe from the Plaza Bolívar opposite the church, seven blocks up from the pier.

ROUTES A paved road runs southeast from Río Caribe across the mountains to meet Route 9 at **Bohordal**; 55 km from Carúpano and 32 km from Río Caribe. It then parallels the southern coast of the peninsula to Irapa and Güiria.

SAN JUAN DE LAS GALDONAS

A few kilometres beyond Bohordal, at **Río Seco**, on the road east towards Irapa, is the turn-off to **San Juan de las Galdonas**, on the north of the Pariá Peninsula, along the coast from Playas Medina and Pui Puy (but not connected by road). This delightful little village is straight out of a picture postcard, with endless beaches of dazzling white sand stretching as far as the eye can see, backed by palm trees and facing the crystal-clear waters of the Caribbean.

There are no banks or money changing facilities in the village. There are a few basic shops and a pharmacy.

● **Accommodation D** *Posada Las Tres Carabelas*, mosquito nets, TV, restaurant, bar, wonderful view of the bay, recommended, run by a retired Spanish professor who is trying to develop tourism in the area and is in the process of building two other *posadas*, one in Mejillones at the far eastern end of the peninsula, and the other in the hills above San Juan. He'll also take you to other beaches along this stretch of coast, such as Santa Isabel and can arrange diving, horseriding and bike rental (ask for Philippe Dutriaux); opposite is **E** *Posada San Juan*, which is nothing like as nice, with stifling rooms and a restaurant.

● **Tour companies & travel agents** An excellent tour agency *Aventura Turismo Descanso*, run by Santiago and Monica Roch, organize tours all over the Pariá Peninsula; costing from US$37-83 per person, depending on the trip. Trekking trips around the peninsula cost US$184 for 3 days and 2 nights, US$243 for 4 days and 3 nights, all inclusive, sleeping in hammocks at basic *campamentos*, minimum of 6 persons. Tours are very well organized; all boats have a full first-aid kit, including anti-snake bite serum, and are in constant communication with each other and the mainland. Insurance is also included in the price. Trips may start from Carúpano, at no extra cost. All drinks are free on board the boats, which are covered to protect tourists from the sun. All guides are highly experienced and speak English. This is probably the safest and most comfortable way to see the Pariá Peninsula, and is highly recommended. Santiago and Monica live in the last house on the beach, or you can find them in the bright yellow house on Calle Comercio parallel to the beach; T (016) 694-0113/622-1682, F (016) 694-0113.

● **Transport** To get to San Juan isn't easy. A jeep leaves from Plaza Santa Rosa in Carúpano at 1100, arriving in San Juan between 1300 and 1400, depending on road conditions. Otherwise, the only cheap alternative is to hitch from the turn-off to San Juan at Río Seco, on the Bohordal-Irapa road. It is also possible to negotiate with a fisherman at Playa Medina or Río Caribe; expect to pay around US$50-70 per boat.

IRAPA

Route 9 continues to **Irapa** (*population* 11,500; *phone code* 094), 117 km from Carúpano. It's a quiet and pleasant fishing town surrounded by a grove of coconut palms, but the beach is muddy and covered in broken glass. If that doesn't put you off, though, there are beach huts and a restaurant. It is said to be here that Papillon came ashore after his last escape from Devil's Island in 1945 (see also page 309). Across the Gulf of Pariá are the swamps of the Orinoco Delta, and Irapa is probably one of the cheapest places from which to arrange a trip into the mangroves (see

Accommodation below). The town hosts a *fiesta* on 19 March.

The climate is dry and very hot but the coast east of Irapa is a string of coves, palms and rich vegetation, which so impressed Columbus that he named the region 'Los Jardines'.

● **Accommodation & places to eat C** *Tierra de Gracia*, on Calle Bermúdez with Calle Piar, two blocks from Plaza Bolívar and one block from the beach, T 97863/97756, price includes full board, drinks, and a trip to the mangroves or a walk through a local cocoa plantation to a waterfall, rooms with air conditioning, private bathroom, open-air tasca/restaurant, the owner Sr Domencio also organizes trips to Playa Medina and Pui Puy, Macuro etc, for US$100 per day per group, he also has two yachts for local cruises; **D** *Marjoli*, T 97315, air conditioning, with bathroom, TV, tasca, restaurant; **E** *Posada de Chuchu*, on Calle Carabobo with Calle Piar, two blocks from the church on Plaza Bolívar going left looking towards the sea, T 97810, private bathroom, fans, basic; **F** *Licorería Bacco*, on Calle Bolívar opposite *Expresos Camargui* and CANTV, shared bathroom, very basic and to be avoided unless you're really desperate. A recommended restaurant serving excellent creole food is *Posada de Hilario*, from Calle Bolívar (facing the sea) turn right at *Muebleria Balia*, just past Banco Mercantil, the restaurant is two blocks down from there. There's also a food market near sea front in the mornings and enough shops for supplies.

● **Post & telecommunications** Ipostel: on Calle Mariño, just behind Banco Mercantil. CANTV: on Calle Bolívar.

● **Transport** The bus terminal is five blocks from the sea. Several companies leave to **Caracas**, mostly in the evening, but check times in advance as they change constantly. To **San Félix**, with Expresos Maturín at 0630. Cruceros Oriente Sur go to Carúpano, Río Caribe and Cumaná. *Por puestos* leave for Güiria (check times) from Calle Mariño towards the exit from town.

GUIRIA

The well-surfaced Route 9 highway finally ends its 737 km journey along the coast from Carcacas, 42 km east of Irapa at **Güiria** (*population* 20,200; *phone code* 094). This important fishing port is a peaceful place and there's not a whole lot to do here. There is no organized tourism as yet, and the nearby beach is badly littered and not at all nice. In saying that, however, it's a friendly place which comes alive every 2 weeks when the *Windward* sails (see below). The town holds a fishing festival, *Feria de la Pesca*, on 14 July. If driving, there are fuel supplies for the return journey. A bus runs to the nearby Balneario beach (US$0.10), where there's a good restaurant with cheap, cold beer. It's easy to hitchhike back to town.

Local information
● Accommodation

NB There are water restrictions at night in some places.

C *El Digno*, Avenida Miranda via Las Salinas, on the way out of town towards the beach, T 81982, F 820759, best hotel in Güiria, air conditioning, TV, hot water, restaurant, executive salon, you can arrange expensive trips from here to Pedernales, Macuro and Trinidad for US$400 per boat (maximum 30 persons).

D *El Milagro*, opposite the church, one block from the Plaza Bolívar, air conditioning, TV, restaurant/tasca; **D** *Gran Puerta*, on Calle Pagallos, two blocks from the top righthand corner of Plaza Bolívar (looking away from the sea), T 81343, air conditioning, TV, restaurant/tasca, good, accepts credit cards; **D-C** *La Posada de Chuchu*, on Calle Bideau, two blocks from Plaza Bolívar, T 81266, air conditioning, TV, hot water, accepts credit cards, restaurant, recommended; **D-C** *Playa Paraíso*, next to the dirty and noisy beach on the road to Las Salinas, 10 minutes out of town, T 820350, F 820451, air conditioning, TV, hot water, some rooms with fridge, pool, restaurant, public phone outside, laundry service, run boat trips to Macuro (see below), Uquire, Don Pedro, Pedernales and Trinidad, US$200 per boat per day (maximum 12 persons), or US$92 per boat per day (maximum 6 persons).

E *Miramar*, at the end of Calle Turipiari heading towards the sea, almost opposite Banco República, T 820732, fan, **D** with air conditioning, bar/restaurant.

F *Plaza*, on the corner of Plaza Bolívar next to Guardia Nacional, T 820022, with fan, **E** with air conditioning, restaurant (not always open), basic; **F** *Fortuna*, very basic, not recommended.

● Places to eat

There's not a lot of choice. *El Milagro*, on the corner of Plaza Bolívar, serves Spanish food and is OK; *Rincon Güireño*, on the corner of Plaza Sucre (where the buses leave from), is recommended for breakfast; it also rents rooms, **D-E**, air conditioning, T 820773. There's also an Arab-run restaurant on the main plaza, with good *falafel* and *humus*. Everwhere is closed on

Sunday, except for the kiosks on the edge of Plaza Bolívar which sell hot dogs and Arabic food.

● Banks & money changers

Banco Orinoco changes Amex and Citicorp travellers' cheques, good rates, no commission, US$300 limit. **Banco Unión**, on Calle Bolívar, cash advances on Visa and Mastercard.

● Post & telecommunications

International phone calls can be made from *Acosta Asociados*, on Calle Bolívar. Ipostel was closed at time of writing (late 1997).

● Transport

Air The airport is undergoing renovation (mid-1997), so there are no flights.

Buses Departures from Plaza Sucre at the top end of Calle Bolívar. *Expresos Maturín* go to Caripito, San Felix (at 0500, US$6.50), Maturín (US$3.50, 6 hours), Cumaná (6 hours), Puerto La Cruz and Caracas (at 0600-0700); *Camargui* go to Caracas and Puerto La Cruz; *Expresos Los Llanos* are recommended and go to Caracas and all intermediate stops. There are several buses daily to Cumaná and Caracas, most leaving between 1600 and 1800. **NB** *Expresos Los Llanos*, *Rodovia de Venezuela* and *Cruceros Oriente Sur* are generally recommended for journeys to eastern parts of the country. Long trousers and long-sleeved shirts are obligatory (vest tops are not permitted). It is also advisable to take a blanket with you as the air conditioning is fierce.

● Boats

To **Pedernales**, leave early in the morning (not daily) from the pier one and a half blocks down from *Hotel Miramar*. Be prepared to bargain the price. Take protection against the sun and plastic sheeting in case of rough seas. To **Macuro**, boats leave daily around 1100, from the Playita (down towards the harbour, to the left of Plaza Bolívar facing the sea). The boat owned by the *Alcaldía* costs US$2 per person; fishermen charge US$4 per person.

TRAVEL TO TRINIDAD

The *Windward* sails every 2 weeks on a Wednesday at 1100; it calls in at Trinidad, San Vicente, Barbados and Santa Lucia. A 1-week cruise costs US$180. To Trinidad only costs US$80 return; the boat will pick you up on its way back. It arrives in Trinidad on Tuesday at around 2130. Tickets are valid for 6 months and can be bought at *Acosta Asociados CA*, Calle Bolívar 31, T 81699/820964, F 81112 (English spoken), or from *Las Novedades* bookshop next door. On alternate weeks the ship goes to Margarita (same fares; travellers' cheques may be changed on board at good rates).

Cruises can also be arranged from Trinidad: *Windward Lines Ltd* (Global Steamship Agencies Ltd), Mariner's Club, Wrightson Road, PO Box 966, Port of Spain, Trinidad, T 624-2279, F 809-627-5091.

Immigration, etc Visa arrangements cannot be made from Güiria. Most countries do not need a visa for Trinidad, but it's worth checking (British passport holders definitely do not need a visa). The maximum stay is 14 days. For trips of longer than 14 days, visas must be arranged from Caracas. Remember to get an exit stamp here, if leaving Venezuela. Officially, to enter Trinidad and Tobago you need a ticket to your home country, but often a return to Venezuela will suffice. Extending permission to stay in Trinidad is possible. Returning to Venezuela this way poses no problems.

MACURO (PUERTO COLON)

Two hours by boat from Güiria is **Macuro** (*population* 1,500), now officially called **Puerto Colón**, a very small, abandoned-looking, unattractive, though friendly, town on the tip of the Peninsula. The beach here is not an attractive proposition and the sea is polluted, but Macuro is a great place from which to organize cheap excursions to the other side of the peninsula (see below).

Macuro is surrounded on its landward sides by dense jungle, and is accessible only by boat, passing deserted, palm-fringed beaches.

It was in one of these coves – perhaps Yacúa, there is no record – that Spaniards of Columbus' crew made the first recorded European landing on the continent on 5 August 1498, before taking formal possession in the estuary at Güiria the next day. This was actually the only place on the South American mainland where Christopher Columbus set foot and, convinced it was another island, named it 'Isla de Gracia'. The local people like to believe the landing took place at Macuro, hence the town's official new name. A big party is held here every year on 12 October to mark the official 'discovery' of America.

● **Accommodation** E-F *Posada Beatriz*, on the corner of Calle Mariño and Carabobo (a cream house with blue door), basic but clean, fan, private bath, friendly; **F** *Posada Marlo*, on Calle Mariño, just over the small bridge (a green house with blue bars on the windows), fan, shared bathroom. You can also camp or sling your hammock somewhere.

● **Places to eat** Restaurants are only open at weekends. Across from Plaza Colón is *Tasca-Restaurant Colón*. At the end of Calle Mariño is Bar-restaurant *Frente al Mar*. Good food can be had from Sra Mercado, on Calle Carabobo, just around the corner from *Posada Beatriz* (a blue house with a brown door); give her about an hour's notice for meals.

● **Services** There are a couple of small shops selling basic goods, and a small pharmacy. Shops open after 1600. To find the public phones, turn right at the church.

● **Transport** The boat to Güiria leaves at 0500, but it's best to arrive a bit earlier (US$2-4 per person).

EXCURSIONS FROM MACURO

On the north side of the Pariá Peninsula the coastline is stunningly beautiful, with crystal-clear water and dense jungle right down to the shore. Excursions can be made to **Uquire** and **Don Pedro**, two little hamlets on the north coast. Of the two, Uquire is the more developed (marginally) and transport is easier. There are places to hang a hammock; ask the Inparques guard, Nestor Mata, or pitch a tent. There is also at least one place that will cook food for you. A *posada* is being built, but no opening date as yet (early 1997). A recommended walk is from Macuro to Don Pedro (6 hours) and from there to Uquire (2 hours); then take a boat back from Uquire (see **Tours** below).

NB The northern coast of the Pariá Peninsula, east of **Unare**, lies within the bounds of the **Parque Nacional Península de Pariá**, which covers 37,500 hectares. This means you will need an Inparques permit if you plan to visit this area. Permits are easily obtained at the main park office in Caracas (see page 91).

Boats can also be taken to the Orinoco Delta, and through the Bocas del Dragón to the miniscule settlement of **Patao** (3 hours), where you can hire a guide for a trek across the Peninsula or an ascent of Cerro Patas, climbing up from cacao and banana plantations into cool montane forest. Fishing boats can often be hired to take you to many small villages, making for a hot but relaxed trip in one of Venezuela's less-visited corners. For more information, contact Eduardo (see below).

● **Tours** A highly recommended guide for tours of the north coast is Eduardo, who lives in the old museum on Calle Bolívar, one block down from *Posada Beatriz* (a long, white house with a blue door). He is a splendid chap with an encyclopaedic knowledge of the immediate area and can advise on hiking in the National Park. Eduardo will take you on a day tour to 'Aricagua', a 6-hour walk passing mangroves and waterfalls. He also runs trips to Uquire and Don Pedro for US$10-15 per person per day. The trip includes a guided walk over the Sierra de Uquire, a day or two in Uquire and a boat trip back (which is not included in the price); US$60 per boat. Bring your own tent or hammock and food etc. Seeing the north of the peninsula this way involves roughing it. It's about 5 times cheaper than going with a tour agency, but definitely only for the adventurous. Another good trip run by Eduardo is to go fishing in the morning, and then to Cariaquito Bay in the afternoon to fry the freshly-caught fish, and then visit the mangrove swamps. It costs US$30 per person per day, minimum 4 persons.

SOUTH TO MATURIN

At the point 13 km east of **Cariaco** where the main coastal highway, Route 9, turns north to **Carúpano** (see page 255), another highway, Route 10, heads south, all the way to the north bank of the Orinoco river, with **Ciudad Guayana** standing on the opposite shore. On the way, Route 10 passes through the town of **Caripito** (77 km south of the junction with Route 9).

East of Caripito is the giant **Guanoco Asphalt Lake**, which contains the largest asphalt deposits in the world. This was the only known source of asphalt for many years after John MacAdam made yet another Scottish contribution to human progress with his major road building improvement in 1815. With the development of asphalt as a by-product of oil refining, the lake became redundant. Today, locals from the nearby town of **Guanoco** will guide you there. There is no access from Caripito to Guancoco; the only road heads south from **El Pilar** (see page 258).

A further 59 km south of Caripito on Route 10 is **Maturín**.

MATURIN

Maturín (*population* 268,650; *phone code* 091) is the capital of Monagas State – a thriving, up-and-coming oil town being hailed as the new Maracaibo. As a result, hotels and tourist facilities tend to be relatively expensive. Many of the places offered as tourist destinations – Cueva del Guácharo, Puertas de Miraflores, trips to the delta etc – can be reached more cheaply starting from Caripe (see below). Despite the oil boom, though, Maturín is a relaxed and pleasant place.

Excursions

Morichal Largo is a tourist complex on the shores of the Río Morichal. There are places to eat and canoe trips are available to the delta. A similar place is **Caño de Bujas**. Both are about one hour from Maturín, heading towards the delta. They are expensive places to visit, but have been recommended. One option is to take a taxi from the bus terminal in Maturín, which costs anything from US$60-100 there and back. This may seem expensive, but it's cheaper than taking a tour, especially if there are four of you. If you befriend the taxi driver and be nice to him, the price may come down, but bargain beforehand, and give him advance notice: T 518109, or go to the terminal to negotiate.

NB Laguna Grande has been partially closed down due to people drowning in the whirlpools. You are not advised to go there.

Local information
● **Accommodation**
NB Hotel prices are constantly increasing. The following rates may well be out of date by 1998. All rooms have private bathrooms, unless indicated otherwise.

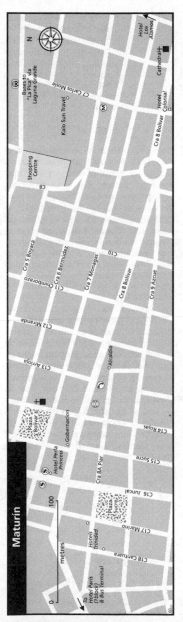

L1 *Morichal*, west of town on the road to Puerto La Cruz, T 514222, F 515444, 5-star luxury.

A1 *Stauffer*, on the road to Cumaná, T 430522, 4-star; **A3-B** *Colonial*, Cra 8 (Bolívar) with Calle 7, opposite the Cathedral, T 421183, air conditioning, TV, hot water, phone in room, restaurant, laundry service, travel agency and other small shops, accepts major credit cards.

B *Chaima Inn*, at the end of Avenida Raúl Leoni, near the 'Pedagocico de Maturín', T 416062, F 418881, air conditioning, hot water, TV, good restaurant with buffet lunch, accepts major credit cards, recommended; **B-C** *Friuli*, on Calle 30 with Cra 9 (Azcue), T 414162, air conditioning, hot water, TV, phone in room, restaurant, laundry service, major credit cards accepted.

C *Manolo*, Avenida Bicentenario with Calle 25, T/F 413341, air conditioning, hot water, TV (optional, cheaper without), good and reasonably-priced restaurant, major credit cards accepted, pleasant; **C** *París*, Cra 9 (Bolívar) 183, opposite Citilamp, T 4414028, air conditioning, hot water, TV, safe, recommended; **C** *Perla Princess*, Calle 16 (Juncal) y Cra 7 (Monagas), T 432754, F 432579, air conditioning, hot water, TV, good, but restaurant overpriced, accepts Visa and Mastercard.

D *Los Alamos*, Cra 3 (Rivas) with Calle 6, T 420466; **D-E** *Trinidad*, on Cra 8A (Piar) with Calle 17, just off Plaza Sucre, T 429356, air conditioning (cheaper with fan); there's another *Trinidad* at Calle Cantuara (Calle 18) with Piar, T 410626.

E *El Terminal*, at the bus terminal, just out of town on the road to Puerto La Cruz, very convenient, air conditioning, drinking water supplied, helpful owner, recommended.

● **Places to eat**

Yarúa (behind the Cathedral), expensive, seafood and grilled meat; *Parador Turístico Arauguay*, via La Cruz, Argentine barbecue speciality; *Mister Pasta*, Cra Juncal, three blocks from *Perla Princess*, good value, wide variety. There's a vegetarian restaurant on the road opposite *Hotel Paris*, one block down. *Heladería Rigoletto*, Avenida Bicentenario with Calle 28, excellent Italian ice cream, including yoghurt ice cream and specialities such as Brandy Alexander.

● **Banks & money changers**

Banco Consolidado (American Express), Avenida Raúl Leoni, Edificio D'Amico (take bus 1 or 5 along Cra Bolívar, heading away from bus terminal); **Banco Mercantil**, on Cra Monagas, near the central market, most likely to accept travellers' cheques. **Banco Unión** and **Banco Provincial**, are opposite one another on Calle Juncal with Cra Monagas.

● **Post & telecommunications**

CANTV/Ipostel offices are on Cra Bolívar with Calle 14, next to the *Alcaldía*.

● **Tour companies & travel agents**

Lilio Tours, on Calle 16 (Juncal) opposite Plaza Sucre, T 414177/411718. *Kalo Sun Travel*, Centro Comercial Fundemos on Calle 7, next to the *Mercado Viejo*, T 433852, F 411577, friendly, helpful and recommended, they run day tours to various places (minimum 6 persons); to Morichal Largo (US$86 per person), Caño de Bujas (US$56 per person), both tours include transport there and back, piranha fishing, lunch (piranha?), canoe trips and soft drinks. Also trips to Cueva del Guácharo (US$60) or Puertas de Miraflores (US$51), including a visit to the El Guamo reservoir and a city tour. Apart from tours, they offer taxis to and from all the sites mentioned above and arrange accommodation at Morichal Largo and Caño de Bujas.

Another jungle lodge is *Boca de Tigre*; they offer packages of 3 days/2 nights, with trips through the jungle on foot or by canoe, visits to indigenous communities and piranha fishing, US$85 per person per day fully inclusive: contact T/F (091) 626923, F 416566 (all prices are subject to change).

● **Transport**

Air Flights to Caracas (Aeropostal, Aserca and Servivensa), Ciudad Ordaz (Servivensa), Puerto Ordaz (Avensa), Barcelona and Maracaibo (Aeropostal); also to Aruba, Barbados, Curaçao, Manaus and Port of Spain with Aeropostal (T 425353, T/F 410346). **Car rental** at the airport (also on Cra 8 near the bus terminal). There's a good restaurant upstairs in the airport. To get to the airport from town, or vice versa, take a *por puesto* Nos 1,5,6 (US$0.25), or a bus from the main road outside the airport (US$0.10).

Buses The central bus terminal is at the end of Cra 8; take bus No 1 or 5 to get there. Buses leave for **Caracas** from the central bus terminal at 2030, 2200 and 2245, US$6.50, 8 hours (*por puesto* US$13). Buses for **Ciudad Guayana-San Félix** (at 0815, 3 hours, US$4, including ferry crossing) and **El Dorado** leave from the bus terminal near the airport. To **Puerto La Cruz** or **Barcelona**, take a *por puesto* to Cumaná and change, 2 hours, US$4.20. To **Ciudad Bolívar** (US$4.50), you have to change in Ciudad Guyana-San Félix (no *por puesto*). Bus to **Carúpano**, at 1000, US$3, 3 hour journey through beautiful landscape. To **Caripe**, 2½ hours, US$1.10, *por puesto*, 2-3 hours, US$4.50. To **Río Caribe**, US$3, 4 hours, at 1100 with Expresos Maturín (be quick to queue for the bus, a ticket does not guarantee a seat or even transport). Bus to **Tucupita** at 1100, US$3 with Expresos Guayanesa (poor standard), 3-4 hours. Bus to **Güiria**, US$3.50, 6 hours, with Expresos Maturín; also to **Irapa** at 1230, 4½ hours, US$4.

MATURIN TO CARIPE

40 km west of Maturín, on Route 13, is the oil camp at **Jusepín**, beyond which is the turn-off to **Santa Bárbara**, where they sell native *chinchorros*, hammocks of woven *moriche* palm leaves, decorated with coloured yarn (see map on page 304). These can also be found in Tucupita (see page 305). They 'give' when you lie on them, do not absorb moisture when used on the beach and are very good for camping.

ROUTES   From Santa Bárbara, the road continues southwest, through **Aguasay**, to **El Tigre** (see page 242), on Route 16, which runs south to **Ciudad Bolívar** and north to **Puerto La Cruz**. Beyond the turn-off to Santa Bárbara, Route 13 continues west for 107 km before it meets the main highway (Route 16) from Puerto La Cruz to Ciudad Bolívar at Km 52, **La Encrucijada** (see page 241).

From Jusepín two roads head north towards Cumaná: one runs northeast to join the main Maturín-Cumaná road, which is paved and twists its way through 212 km of beautiful tropical mountain scenery; the other divides just beyond Jusepín and then converges again before meeting the Maturín-Cumaná road at **Guanaguana**. A few kilometres further on, at **San Francisco**, is a branch road running 23 km northeast to **Caripe**.

From San Francisco it's a further 54 km to **Cumanacoa**, and then another 56 km to Cumaná (see also page 251).

CARIPE

The attractive and well-kept town of Caripe (*population* 23,880; *phone code* 092) is set in a mountain valley, surrounded by gorgeous scenery. Though the main attraction of the town is the nearby **Cueva del Guácharo**, Caripe is a great place to relax if you get tired of the beaches, and is especially good for walking and cycling.

To the west of the town is a Mirador, from which there are great views over the whole valley.

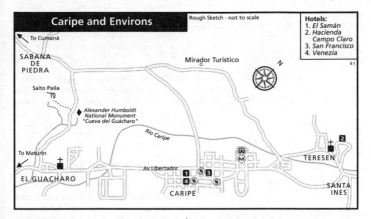

Caripe and Environs   Rough Sketch - not to scale

Hotels:
1. El Samán
2. Hacienda Campo Claro
3. San Francisco
4. Venezia

To Cumaná

SABANA DE PIEDRA

Mirador Turístico

Salto Paila

Alexander Humboldt National Monument "Cueva del Guácharo"

Río Caripe

To Maturín

TERESEN

Av Libertador

EL GUACHARO

CARIPE

SANTA INES

Excursions

20 minutes by car from Caripe on the road to Cumanacoa (see above) you reach the *Balneario de Miraflores*. From there it's an hour's walk along the river to **Las Puertas de Miraflores**, which are two huge walls of rock which form a canyon with the river running between them. When the river bends round a corner the walls of the canyon give the impression of closing off the river. You'll need a guide for this trip as the river has to be crossed seven times before you reach the Puertas, and it can be tricky getting across. This walk can only be done during the dry season, when the river level drops. There are several other walks around Caripe, through cloud forest to lakes and waterfalls.

There are several little villages around Caripe which specialize in various types of craftwork, such as wood, clay etc. **Guanoco** is recommended for its jams (including one made from rose petals) and fruit liquors. There are also loads of horticultural places to nose around and bird watching areas, which the agencies in town will take you to. Further afield are waterfalls and lakes. Some are a jeep ride away; others can only be reached on foot, eg El Salto Chorrerón. Frances Osborn, our correspondent in Cumaná, recommends hiring a bike and cycling round the various places of interest.

Local festivals
2-12 August, *Feria de las Flores*; **10-12 October**, *Nuestra Señora del Pilar*.

Local information
● **Accommodation**
D-C *Hacienda Campo Claro*, at Teresén (see map), T 551013, managed by Nery and Francisco Betancourt, cabins with fridge and cooking facilities, all with private bathroom, hot water, restaurant open to residents only, horseriding, the farm is run on an ecological basis (though planting pine trees is not ecologically sound), also coffee and orange plantations, all the produce is sold on the farm, mostly to tourists; **D-C** *Samán**, Enrique Chaumer 29, at the entrance to town, 5 minutes from the centre, T/F 51183, private bathroom, hot water, pool, restaurant, accepts Visa and Mastercard, owner Oscar Gregorio runs tours to the Cueva del Guácharo and other local sites; **D** *Venezia*, Avenida Enrique Chaumer 118, opposite *Hotel Samán*, T 51035, F 51875, private bathroom, hot water but not in every room – check first, no sheets on the beds only a blanket, excellent restaurant serving gourmet food at reasonable prices, accepts Visa and Mastercard, the owner speaks English.

E *San Francisco*, opposite the church on Plaza Bolívar, T 51018, private bathroom, hot water, pool room, restaurant (but closed in mid-1997), not very clean.

F *La Posada*, next to *Hotel San Francisco*, fans, restaurant closes at 2000, friendly; **F** *La Fogata*, opposite *Hotel San Francisco*, not well signposted, shared bathroom, large rooms, very noisy, women's shower is clean but the men's is a bit smelly, good value.

● **Places to eat**
Lonchería Arabe, recommended; *Tasca Restaurant Río Colorado*, cheap, good local food, try the *chipi-chipi* a consomme made with *guacuco*, a kind of baby clam, friendly service, recommended; *El Cafetín*, snack bar on main road, delicious food, recommended; *La Solana*, popular with locals, souvenir shop and very good food; *Heladería Nícola*, on Avenida Bolívar, good ice cream.

● **Banks & money changers**
Banco Unión, Avenida Guzmán Blanco, on the same block as Copi Center; Banco de Venezuela, on Avenida Enrique Chaumer.

● **Entertainment**
Cinema: *Teatro de Caripe*, next door to *La Fogata*, shows movies (dubbed) on Thursday and Sunday at 1930, US$0.50.

● **Tour companies & travel agents**
Ecoturismo Struppek, on Avenida Guzman Blanco next to Centro Humboldt, T 525-1364, open daily, English and German spoken, German/Venezuelan run with an emphasis on ecotourism, conservation and integration with the local community, they have made attempts to involve local people in tourism through handicrafts, local cuisine, etc. They offer several 1-day tours: city tour; trips around the valley to orchid gardens and handicraft villages; Cueva del Guácharo; Puerta de Miraflores and horseriding tours. Their speciality is a 'Rural life' tour, during which you find out about how local people live, visit their homes, make *arepas*, try different types of bananas etc; this helps to involve the locals in tourism. Day tours to local sites cost US$10-12 per person per day. They also run 1-3 day hikes which cost US$40-45 per person per day, including tents and food, with guides who are park guards of the Cueva del Guácharo National Park. They have their own *cabañas*, B *El Jardín Ecológico*, in the heart of the mountains near Caripe, price includes all meals.

Trekking Travel, Avenida Guzmán Blanco, two blocks from Centro Humboldt towards *Hotels Venezia* and *Samán*, T/F 51352, open Monday-Saturday, they run similar day tours around the valley for US$15 per person per day; also horseriding and biking tours, bikes rental, and 1-3 day hikes for US$25 per person per day, including tent/hammock, food and insurance. They also run tours to the Gran Sabana and 3-day tours to the Delta Amacuro for US$55 per person per day (sleeping in hammocks); the latter is reported as better than taking a delta tour from Tucupita as you hit the delta much further up and get to see the more remote parts. Alexander the owner is recommended and speaks German as well as Spanish; the other guides speak English and Dutch.

● **Transport**
Bus from Caripe to **Caracas** at 1800 (it stops in Cumaná), catch it at the San Remo Sur office, next to *Hotel San Francisco*. A bus direct to Caracas leaves at 2000. Bus to **Maturín**, direct at 0600, 2 hours, US$1.

ROUTES   A paved road runs 52 km north from Caripe, hitting the coast at **Villa Frontado**, on Route 9, the main Cumaná-Carúpano highway (see page 254). At **Santa María**, 15 km north on this road, another road branches northeast to meet the main Maturín-Carúpano highway (Route 10).

CUEVA DEL GUACHARO

12 km from Caripe is the remarkable **Cueva del Guácharo**, or **Alexander Humboldt National Monument**, in honour of the great German scientist who first explored and measured it in 1799, before revealing its existence to the outside world in his writings in 1816. The cave, the largest in the country, has since been penetrated to its full extent of $10^{1/2}$ km along a small, crystal-clear stream.

The cave takes its name from the *guácharos* (oil birds) which live here, about 18,000 of them, with an in-built radar system for sightless flight. Their presence supports a variety of wildlife in the cave: blind mice, fish and crabs in the stream, yellow-green plants, crickets, ants, etc. For 2 hours at dusk (about 1900) the birds pour out of the cave's mouth, continuously making the clicking sounds of their echo-location system, coming back at dawn with their crops full of the oily fruit of certain local palms.

Through a very narrow entrance is the *Cueva del Silencio* (Cave of Silence), where you can hear a pin drop. About 2 km in is the *Pozo del Viento* (Well of the Wind). The streams are bridged and the path is paved, but there is still quite a lot of water around. You should wear old clothes, sturdy shoes or hiking boots and be prepared to take off your shoes and socks. In the wet season it can be a bit slippery. Tours into the cave may be shortened or even closed in August-September because of rising water levels.

The whole area is protected as part of the 45,500 hectare **Cueva del Guácharo**

National Park. There is a caving museum with a good range of publications, including a leaflet about the cave in English, US$0.80, and a good cafetería. Opposite the road is a paved path to Salto Paila, a 25m waterfall, about 30 minutes' walk; guides are available. You'll see orange and other fruit trees along the way. Other routes are suggested at the cave. A beautiful path, built by Inparques, starts at the caving museum, with some nice shelters for picnics.

Local information
● **Access**
The cave is open 0830-1700; US$4 entry with compulsory guide. Alexander at *Trekking Travel* (see above) is recommended. A guided tour takes 2 hours. Leave backpacks at the ticket office. Tape recorders and cameras are allowed; the guides inform you when you can use a flash. To go further than 1½ km into the caves, permits from Inparques in Caracas and special equipment are needed.

● **Accommodation**
For a small tip you can stay the night at the museum, which is guarded. There's good bird-watching around here.

● **Transport**
There are frequent buses from Caripe to the caves. If staying in Caripe, take a *por puesto* (a jeep marked 'Santa María-Muelle'), at 0800 (US$3), see the caves and waterfall and then catch the Cumaná-Caripe bus which goes past the caves between 1200 and 1230. Taxis from Caripe cost US$5; hitching is difficult. A bus from Cumaná direct to the Cueva del Guácharo leaves at 0715, costs US$2.50, and stops right in front of the caves. A *por puesto* from Cumaná costs US$7.50 and takes 2 hours. Private tours can be organized from Cumaná for about US$10 per person, with guide.

ISLA DE MARGARITA

Margarita is the country's main Caribbean holiday destination and the nearest thing you'll find to a full-blown, Miami-style beach resort (if that's what you're after). But while some parts are very crowded and commercialized, there are still undeveloped beaches, attractive little villages, the colonial beauty of La Asunción and several national parks, including the fascinating Restinga lagoon.

Isla de Margarita and two close neighbours, Coche and Cubagua, form the state of Nueva Esparta (New Sparta). This rather curious name was given in recognition of the supreme heroism displayed by the inhabitants during the War of Independence; heroism that was compared to the ancient Spartans of Greece.

Isla de Margarita is in fact one island whose two sections are tenuously linked by the 18 km sandspit which separates the sea from the Restinga lagoon. At its largest, Margarita is about 32 km from north to south and 67 km from east to west. Most of its people live in the developed eastern part, which has some wooded areas and fertile valleys. The western part, the **Peninsula de Macanao**, is hotter and more barren, with scrub, sand dunes and marshes. Wild deer, goats and hares roam the interior, and 4WD vehicles are needed to penetrate it. The entrance to the Peninsula de Macanao is a pair of hills known as **Las Tetas de María Guevara Natural Monument**, covering 1,670 hectares.

BASICS The climate is exceptionally good, with very little rain. Water is piped from the mainland through pipes that are said to be rusty. However, potable water trucks can be seen delivering water to most major tourist resorts to keep up with demand, and avoid using piped water. Plans are rumoured to be underway to build a major desalination plant on the island. The roads on the island are good, but not well marked; it's not advisable to drive around after dark. A bridge connects the two parts. The total population of Nueva Esparta is over 200,000, of whom 68,000 live in the main city, Porlamar, which is not the capital (La Asunción is the capital).

The island has enjoyed a boom since 1983, largely as a result of the fall in the value of the bolívar and the consequent tendency of Venezuelans to spend their holidays at home. Margarita's status as a duty-free zone also helps. Venezuelan shoppers go in droves for clothing, electronic goods and other consumer items. Gold and gems are good value, but many things are not.

Great efforts are also being made to attract more foreign visitors and, to this end, large resorts are expanding on the northeastern corner of the island, with the major new beach development being Playa El Agua. The original resorts, such as Bella Vista, were built around Porlamar and along the east coast, known as Costa Azul, where the Hilton and Marina Bay resort are now found. But there has also been extensive building in Porlamar, with new shopping areas and Miami-style hotels going up.

This expansion has created a glut of hotel rooms and apartments. Some large resorts are packaging trips to the island, making it virtually impossible during the high season to get an independent flight without buying a package. August and September are the vacation months when

Humboldt

Alexander Von Humboldt was 29 years old when he set sail from the Spanish port of La Coruña in 1799 to begin a journey of scientific discovery in the New World. On 16 July he and his travelling companion, Aimé Bonpland, landed in Cumaná to begin their 5 year-long exploration of the Americas.

The successful completion of this expedition earned Humboldt an international scientific reputation. He and Bonpland had gathered on their journey a huge amount of information on climatology, geology, mineralogy, terrestrial magnetism, plant geography, zoology, political economy and ethnography as well as thousands of dried plant specimens. The rest of Humboldt's life would be dominated by the publication of the results of this expedition, a vast body of work extending to 30 volumes and not completed until 1834.

Born in 1769, Humboldt grew up in what has been called the "Second Great Age of Discovery". In the 18th century expedition was no longer just a matter of travelling to unknown locations. Where early explorers had only observed, the aim of the new scientific traveller was to record more accurately, measure more precisely and collect more comprehensively. One of Humboldt's greatest influences was the legendary Captain James Cook (1728-79) who navigated the southern oceans. But Humboldt took 18th-century exploration several steps further. He showed a wider variety of scientific interests and intellectual concerns than any other explorer before, or even since.

At this time the Spanish colonial territories were virtually closed to foreigners, but Humboldt's reputation as a mining geologist in Europe so impressed the Spanish government that they granted him permission to travel anywhere and guaranteed the assistance of colonial government officials. Almost no scientific work had been carried out in the South American interior since the expedition of the French mathematician and naturalist Charles-Marie de la Condamine over 60 years earlier. Given the considerable advances in science in the meantime, Humboldt was making the first real exploration of one of the earth's great land masses. His journey was described as "the scientific discovery of South America". He even used his astronomical skills to make the first reliable maps of the continent, most notably of the course of the Orinoco river.

Humboldt's sense of adventure came from his dissatisfaction with home life. In 1801, he wrote: "I was spurred on by an uncertain longing for what is distant and unknown, for whatever excited: danger at sea, the desire for adventures, to be transported from a boring daily life to a marvellous world". His yearning for travel was based on the premise that few scientists had made dangerous journeys into the interior of South America. Only by the risk of travelling could the scientist make flights and hotels are fully booked. However, the island's growing popularity means that many packages are on offer, sometimes at good value, especially off-season.

Aside from tourism, there are other local industries on the island; fishing and fibre work, such as hammocks and straw hats. Weaving, pottery and sweets are being pushed as handicraft items for the tourists. An exhibition centre has been opened at El Cercado, near Santa Ana, on Calle Principal, near the church.

Despite the property boom and frenetic building on much of the coast and in Porlamar, much of the island has been given over to natural parks. Of these the most striking is the 10,700 hectare **Laguna de La Restinga National Park**. Launches provide lengthy runs around the mangrove swamps, but they create a

observations and comparisons with his own eyes, ensuring that science advances beyond dogma and hypothesis.

It is virtually impossible to overestimate the importance and influence of Humboldt on the world of science. He was a major inspiration for a certain young Charles Darwin and Johann Wolfgang Goethe (1749-1832). However, his fame spread beyond the confines of science. In France, writers and painters like Balzac, Victor Hugo, Chateaubriand, Gerard and Flaubert admired his descriptive prose. The North American poet and philosopher, Ralph Waldo Emerson called Humboldt the "Encyclopaedia of Science", and Lord Byron satirized his precise empirical investigation in 'Don Juan' (1821) by referring to the cynometer – an instrument for measuring the blueness of the sky.

The recently independent Spanish American intellectuals and politicians especially revered Humboldt. The Liberator, Simón Bolívar, no less, spoke of his debts to his friend: "Baron Humboldt did more for the Americas than all the conquistadores". Humboldt's account of his journey, documented in his *Personal Narrative* is not only a scientific journal but also the first objective travel book on South America. (*Personal Narrative of a Journey to the Equinoctial Regions of the New Continent*, published by Penguin Books, 1995).

Scene from Humboldt and Bonpland's expedition

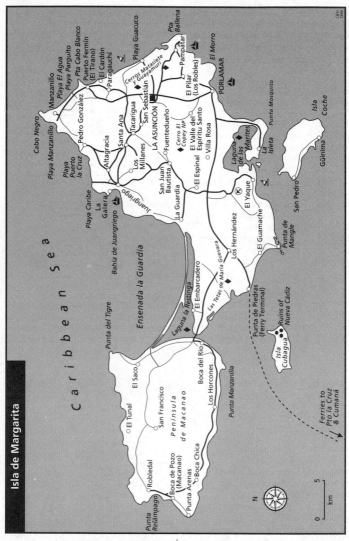

Isla de Margarita

lot of wash and noise. The mangroves are fascinating, with shellfish clinging to the roots. The launch will leave you on a shingle and shell beach (don't forget to arrange with your boatman to collect you), and you can rummage for shellfish in the shallows. Protection against the sun is essential – see below for prices, etc. Flamingos also live in the lagoon.

There are mangroves also in the **Laguna de las Marites Natural Monument**, west of Porlamar. Aside from Las

Tetas de María Guevara (see above), the other parks are **Cerro El Copey National Park** (7,130 hectares), and **Cerro Mata-siete y Guayamurí Natural Monument** (1,672 hectres). Both can be reached from La Asunción.

Festivals on Margarita

6-13 January at Altagracia; **20-27 January** at Tacarigua; **16-26 March** at Paraguachí (*Feria de San José*); **3-10 May** at Los Robles; **24-30 May** at La Guardia; **6 June** in Tacarigua; **25-26 July** at Santa Ana; **27 July** at Punta de Piedras; **31 July** (*Batalla de Matasiete*) and **14-15 August** (*Asunción de la Virgen*) at La Asunción; **30 August-8 September** at Villa Rosa; **8-15 September** at El Valle; **11-12 and 28 October** at Los Robles; **4-11 November** at Boca del Río, **4-30 November** at Boca del Pozo; **5-6 December** at Porlamar; **15 December** at San Francisco de Macanao; **27 December-3 January** at Juan Griego. See map for locations.

PORLAMAR

Most of the hotels are at **Porlamar** (*phone code* 095), 20 km from the airport and about 28 km from **Punta de Piedras**, where most of the ferries dock. At Igualdad y Díaz the Museo de Arte Francisco Narváez. The main, and most expensive, shopping area is Avenida Santiago Mariño, but better bargains and a wider range of shops are to be found on Gómez and Guevara. The centre of the city is crowded with cars and shoppers. To the east there is continuing, apparently chaotic development of big holiday hotels and condominiums, separated by vast areas of waste ground and construction sites. At night everything closes by 2300; women alone should avoid the centre after dark. Porlamar has many casinos, all of which lack legal status.

Excursions

By boat from Porlamar you can go to the Isla de los Pájaros, or Morro Blanco, for both bird-spotting and underwater fishing. You can also make trips to the nearby islands of **Coche** and **Cubagua** (see page 281).

Local information

● **Accommodation**

NB There is both a Calle Mariño and Avenida Santiago Mariño in the centre.

L3 *Hilton*, Calle Los Uveros, T 624111, F 620810, sailing dinghies for hire.

A2 *Dynasty*, T 621252, F 625101, opposite the *Hilton*, nice restaurant, pool; both are at Playa Moreno, to the east of the city on the Costa Azul, where there are several other top class hotels.

A1 *Bella Vista**, Avenida Santiago Mariño, T 617222, F 612557, swimming pool, beach; **A3** *Stauffer*, Avenida Santiago Mariño, T 612911, F 618708, large rooms, excellent service and restaurant, bar on roof, casino; **A3-B** *Marbella Mar*, Avenida Principal y Calle Chipichipi, T 624022, F 624488, clean rooms, friendly, especially with children, free bus service to the beach, highly recommended.

B *Aguila Inn*, Narváez, ½ km north of the centre, T 612311, F 616909, swimming pool, restaurant, recommended; **B** *Colibrí*, Avenida Santiago Mariño, T 616346, new rooms, **D** in older rooms, air conditioning, recommended; **B** *Imperial*, Avenida Raúl Leoni, Vía El Morro, T 616420, F 615056, best rooms are at the front with balcony, comfortable, safe, air conditioning, good showers, triple rooms available, English spoken, recommended; **B** *La Perla*, Calle Los Pinos, swimming pool, bar, restaurant, laundry service, shops in lobby including *Latsa* travel agency, recommended; **B** *Venus*, Milano y San Rafael, T 23722, air conditioning, safe.

C *Contemporáneo*, Calle Mariño entre Igualdad y Velásquez, modern, air conditioning, bar, restaurant; **C** *Italia*, San Nicolás, cold water, air conditioning, safe, recommended, but the district is a bit unsafe.

D *Porlamar*, Igualdad y Fajardo, good restaurant and video bar *La Punta*, air conditioning or fan, hot water; **D-E** *Boulevard*, Calle Marcano entre Boulevard Guevara y Gómez, clean, TV, restaurant.

E *Brasilia*, San Nicolás, quiet, nice new rooms at back; **E** *Domino*, La Libertad 7-40, with fan or air conditioning, basic; **E** *España*, Mariño 6-35, T 095-612479, cold shower, good breakfast, fan, highly recommended; **E** *La Viña*, La Marina, No 14-24, T 635723, bath, air conditioning, bar, restaurant, laundry; **E** *Malecón*, Marina y Arismendi, T 635723, seaview from front rooms, the Mexican owner, Luis and his wife are very helpful and generous, recommended; **E** *Palermo*, Calle Igualdad, opposite the cathedral, the best rooms are on the top floor with views of the plaza; **E** *Robaldar*, Igualdad, near Libertad, shower, air conditioning, recommended. **E** *Tamá*, next

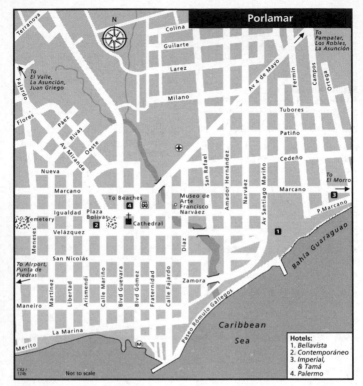

Porlamar

Hotels:
1. Bellavista
2. Contemporáneo
3. Imperial, & Tamá
4. Palermo

to *Hotel Imperial* (see above), very popular with foreign tourists, basic rooms, OK, excellent restaurant and atmosphere, bar is German-run, lots of languages spoken; **E** *Torino*, Mariño entre Zamora y Maneiro, T 610734, with private bathroom, air conditioning.

There are many other places around Plaza Bolívar; eg **F** *San Miguel*, which is good value.

● **Places to eat**

La Gran Pirámide, Calle Malave y JM Patiño, superb food, very good service, cocktails worth trying, very good value, highly recommended; *Doña Martha*, Velázquez near Hernández, Colombian food, good, inexpensive; *El Punto Criollo*, Igualdad near *Hotel Porlamar*, excellent value, good; *Rancho Grande*, Calle Guevara, near Playa El Agua bus stop, Colombian, good value, recommended; *El Pollo de Carlitos*, Marcano y Martínez, nice location, live music most nights, good food and value; *Bahía* bar-restaurant on Avenida Raúl Leoni y Vía El Morro,

excellent value, live music. Excellent pizzas at *París Croissant* on Boulevard Santiago Mariño; *Los 3 Delfines*, Cedeño 26-9, seafood, recommended; *La Isla*, Mariño y Cedeño, 8 fast food counters ranging from hamburgers to sausages from around the world; *Dino's Grill*, Igualdad y Martínez, T 642366, open 0700-1400, buffet lunch, indoor/outdoor seating, grill, homemade sausages, wood-fired pizza oven, cheap, good service, recommended.

● **Banks & money changers**

Banco Consolidado, Guevara y San Nicolás. *Casa de cambio* at Igualdad y Avenida Santiago Mariño; also *Cambio La Precisa*, Maneiro entre Mariño y Boulevard Guevara, good rates. The Amex office is opposite *Hotel Bella Vista*, they give the best rates for Amex travellers' cheques and charge no commission; open 0900-1200, 1400-1630, closed Mondays. Banks are open 0830-1130, 1400-1630; they are generally slow and give poor rates. Most shops accept credit cards and *Rattan* will change US dollars on any purchase in Venezuelan currency. **NB Do not** change money on the street, unless you have too much of it and really feel the need to give some away. The rates offered may seem attractive, but you will end up losing out as there are many skilled con-artists.

● **Entertainment**
Mosquito Coast Club, behind *Bella Vista Hotel*, a disco with a genuine Venezuelan feel, good merengue and rock music, bar outside, also does excellent Mexican meals (beware of overcharging on simple items like water); *Village Club*, Avenida Santiago Mariño, a bit of a meat market but recommended for good music with variety of styles, expensive drinks, cover charge. *Doce 34*, Avenida 4 de Mayo, two dance floors, highly recommended. The nightlife in Porlamar is generally good, but at European prices. Porlamar also has two sports bars, *Cheers* and *The Dugout*, which are both packed full of baseball fanatics during the season. Perhaps the most dangerous thing you could do on the island would be to ask to change TV channels during a match.

● **Post & telecommunications**
Post Office: Calle Arismendi.
Telephones: CANTV, Bolívar, entre Fajardo y Fraternidad.

● **Shopping**
Besides all the duty-free shops, *Del Bellorín*, Cedeño, near Santiago Mariño, is good for handicrafts. There's a good selection of jewellery at *Sonia Gems*, on Cedeño; *Ivan Joyería* and *Inter Gold*, both on 4 de Mayo (the latter is between *Ivan* and *Hotel Flamingo*). Many other places on the main street are overpriced. When purchasing jewellery, bargain hard, don't pay by credit card (surcharges are imposed), get a detailed guarantee on the item. Designer clothes are cheap in many places, especially on Boulevard Guevara, Boulevard Gómez, and Calles Igualdad and Velázquez. Cosmetics and perfumes also good value. **NB** There are plenty of bargains to be had, but be sure of the quality as there are many copies (*tipos*) of brand name merchandise. The shops in the old town are better value than those on 5 de Mayo.

● **Tour companies & travel agents**
Supertours, Calle Larez, Quinta Thaid, T 618781, F 617061, tours of the island and elsewhere; *Zuluoga Tours*, San Nicolás entre Arismendi y Mariño No 16-40, helpful. Ask travel agents about excursions on the sailing catamaran, *Catatumbo*, which is recommended. Many hotels offer island tours with multi-lingual guides: a typical tour includes a visit to the mangroves by boat, and perhaps also

to La Restinga beach, La Asunción, Juan Griego fort, a 2 hour stop at Playa el Agua, Virgen del Valle and the fort at Pampatar. For horseriding trips through the desert, mountains and on the deserted beaches of the Macanao Peninsula, T (016) 681-9348. *Linea Turística Aerotuy* (LTA) makes trips to many of Margarita's national parks, as well as arranging flights to various destinations on the mainland. They also have 3 large charter catamarans, and run day trips to Los Roques (see page 101) and the Isla La Blanquilla (see page 281); T (095) 632211/630367, F 617746 (Caracas 02-761-6231/6247, F 762-5254. For details on scuba diving on the island see **Adventure Tourism** section (page 22).

● **Tourist offices**
A tourist information booth on 4 de Mayo has a map, a coupon booklet, and a tourist magazine '*La Vista*'. Travel agencies can also provide a tourist guide to Margarita. An outspoken and well-informed English-language newspaper, *Mira*, is published on the island, and the editor/publisher acts also as an inexpensive tour guide. Their offices are at Avenida Santiago Mariño, Edificio Carcaleo Suites, Apartamento 2-A, Porlamar (T 613351). The best map is available from Corpoven.

● **Transport**
Local Car hire: this is an economical proposition for any number above one and a good way of getting around the island. There are several offices at the airport. **Ramcar**, at the airport and *Hotel Bella Vista*, they are recommended as cheap and reliable, non-deductible insurance (as do Avis and Hertz; others on Avenida Santiago Mariño). **Lizmar** is the cheapest, but watch insurance excess, and the cars are in poor condition. In all cases, check the brakes. Scooters can also be hired from, among others, **Maruba Motor Rentals**, La Mariña (English spoken, good maps, highly recommended, US$16 bikes for 2, US$13 bikes for one). Motor cycles may not be ridden between 2000 and 0500. **NB** Remember to keep an eye on the fuel gauge; there are service stations in towns, but air conditioning is heavy on fuel. Always check the gauge on the fuel pump carefully: overcharging is common.
Driving on Isla Margarita: the roads are generally good and most are paved. Signposts are often poorly-positioned (behind bushes, around corners), which adds to the night-time hazard of vehicles with badly-adjusted lights. It is best not to drive outside Porlamar after dark. Also beware of robbery of hired vehicles. Check conditions and terms of hire carefully.
Public transport: Por Puestos serve most of the island, leaving mainly from the corners of Plaza Bolívar in Porlamar. Fares: to **Punta de**

Piedras (leave from four blocks from Plaza Bolívar, towards the sea front), US$0.50, to the ferry terminal US$0.65; to **La Asunción**, US$0.25, from Calle Fajardo, half a block from Igualdad; to **Pampatar**, US$0.15; to **La Restinga** (from La Marina y Mariño), US$0.70; to **Playa El Agua**, leave from the corner of Guevara and Marcano, US$0.40; to **Juan Griego**, US$0.40. **Taxi**: fares are published by *Mira* but are not uniformly applied by drivers. If you want to hire a taxi for a day you will be charged US$7-10 per hour. Always fix the fare before you get in the car. There is a 30% surcharge after 2100.

Air General Santiago Mariño Airport lies between Porlamar and Punta de Piedras. It's comfortable and modern, and has the international and national terminals at either end. Bus from Plaza Bolívar, US$0.70, taxi US$7. There are up to 12 flights a day from **Caracas**, with Servivensa, Aeropostal, Laser and Aserca (50 minutes flight). Tickets are much cheaper if purchased in Venezuela in local currency. Reservations made from outside Venezuela are not always honoured. Aeropostal also flies daily to **Puerto Ordaz** and **Maracaibo**, daily except Saturday to **Barcelona**, **Valencia** and **San Antonio**, and also twice a week to **Barbados**. There are also flights from Canaima, Barquisimeto, Aruba, Curaçao, Port of Spain and Manaus. Contact Aeropostal at T (095) 631341, F 695840; airport T (095) 691240, F 691172. Avensa are on Calle Fajardo, Porlamar, T 617111; airport 691021.

Ferries For details on boats to and from Margarita see page 280.

Road Several bus companies in Caracas sell through tickets from Caracas to Porlamar, arriving about midday. Buses return from Porlamar from the terminal at Centro Comercial Bella Vista, at the bottom end of Calle San Rafael.

AROUND MARGARITA

LA ASUNCION

The capital of the island, La Asunción (*population* 16,660), is a few kilometres inland from Porlamar. It has several colonial buildings, a cathedral, and the fort of **Santa Rosa**, with a famous bottle dungeon. The fort is open Monday 0800-1500, other days 0800-1800. There is a museum in the Casa Capitular, and a local market, which good for handicrafts. On Plaza Bolívar, as well as the statue of Simón Bolívar, there is a statue of Luisa Cáceres de Arismendi, heroine of the Liberation and second wife of General Arismendi.

Santa Rosa Fort

Nearby are the **Cerro Matasiete** historical site, where the defeat of the Spanish on 31 July 1817 led to their evacuation of the island, and the Félix Gómez look-out in the **Sierra Copuy**.

• **Accommodation B-C** *Ciudad Colonial*, Calle La Margarita, upmarket, nice; **E** pp *Asunción*, Calle Unión, two blocks from Plaza Bolívar, with bath, air conditioning, fridge, rooms with a balcony cost more but face a noisy road, rooms without a window cost less. A frequent *por puesto* service stops in front of hotel.

EL VALLE DEL ESPIRITU SANTO

Between La Asunción and Porlamar are the Parque Francisco Fajardo, beside the Universidad de Oriente, and **El Valle del Espíritu Santo**. Here is the church of the Virgen del Valle, a picturesque building with twin towers, painted white and pink. The Madonna is richly dressed (one dress has pearls, the other diamonds). The adjoining museum opens at 1400, it displays costumes and presents for the Virgin, including the 'milagro de la pierna de perla', a leg-shaped pearl. A pilgrimage is held in early September. You should dress appropriately before entering the church.

Throughout the island, the churches are attractive: fairly small, with baroque towers and adornments and, in many cases, painted pink.

PAMPATAR

Northeast of Porlamar, **Pampatar** (*population* 10,590) has the island's largest fort, **San Carlos de Borromeo**, built in 1662 after the Dutch destroyed the original, and the smaller **La Caranta**. Also worth visiting is the church of Cristo del Buen Viaje, the Library/Museum and the customs house.

There is an amusement park to the southwest of Pampatar, called **Isla Aventura**, with a ferris wheel, roller coaster, water slide, dodgems, etc; it is open Friday and Saturday, 1800-2400, Sunday, 1700-2400, and more frequently in the peak holiday season. Entrance in peak season is US$5 adults, US$3.35 children, all rides included; in low season entrance is US$0.50 and each ride US$0.30-0.60. See also **Beaches**, below.

● **Accommodation & places to eat**
A1 *Lagunamar*, a few kilometres north of Pampatar, T (095) 620711, F 621445, occupies a vast spread of flat coastland, beach, 9 pools and 6 restaurants; **A2** pp *Flamingo Beach*, T (095) 624822, F 620271, 5-star, all-inclusive, food, drinks, entertainment, service, taxes, casino, good value; *Hippocampus Beach*, next door, T 623090, F 623510, 4-star, package holidays, gaudy; **D** *Residencial Don Juan*, with bath and fan. **F** pp guesthouse of David Hart (Windward Lines agent), Avenida Principal 12, T 623527, next to the supermarket, with private bathroom, fan, welcoming, dark rooms, lots of mosquitoes. Apartments sleeping 6 are also available. The beach restaurant *Antonio's*, is recommended; also *Trimar*, good value; *El Farallon*, beside the Castillo, excellent seafood.

BEACHES ON MARGARITA

Apart from the shopping, what attracts the holidaymakers from Venezuela and abroad are the many beaches, which are attractive, long white stretches of sand bordered by palms. Note that it can get very hot, and there's little shade, so sunscreen is essential.

There are so many varied beaches here that there must be one for everyone, and certainly more than even the most devout sun-worshipper could possibly visit in one outing. Some beaches are calm, some rough, some almost deserted and others complete with all tourist facilities. More development is still taking place around the island.

Note that many of these resorts and hotels are not located on the beach, so you'll need to confirm your location or transport available to the beach. Also note that nude sunbathing is forbidden; topless is not sanctioned and usually not found on beaches frequented by Venezuelans. However, as more European tourists visit Margarita, topless sunbathing can be found at resort pools and beaches. The *tanga* or *hila* (dental floss) bathing suit is common.

In Porlamar, the main beach suffers from its popularity. It has calm shallow water, pedalos for hire, and windsurfing classes. The **Bella Vista** beach, although crowded, is kept clean, and has lots of restaurants. **Playa Morena** is a long, barren strip of sand serving **Costa Azul**, the expanding hotel zone to the east of the city. **La Caracola** is a very much the 'in beach' with younger people, with kiosks and beach chairs.

For a more Venezuelan atmosphere than Porlamar go to **Pampatar**, whose picureque beach is circled with palm trees and kiosks serving fresh fish from the fleet anchored in the bay. It is favoured by yachtsmen as a summer anchorage.

Jet skis are for hire. A scale model of Columbus' *Santa María* is used for taking tourists on trips. A fishing boat can be hired for US$12 for 2½ hours, 4-6 passengers; shop around for the best price.

THE EAST COAST

The beaches on the eastern side are divided into ocean and calm beaches, according to their location in relation to the open sea. The former tend to be rougher and colder, but with good surfing and windsurfing, clear and unpolluted water. It is still possible, even in high season, to find practically deserted beaches. Restaurants, *churuatas* (bars built like Indian huts), sunshades and deckchairs are widespread; hire charges are about US$1.50 per item.

A popular beach on the eastern coast is **Playa Guacuco**, reached from La Asunción by a road through the Guayamurí reserve. There's a lot of surf, the water is fairly shallow, and there's shade from palm trees. There's also a restaurant and parking lot. From here, you can also make excellent horseriding trips up into the hills. These cost US$30 for 2 hours; contact Harry Padrón at the ranch in Agua de Vaca, or phone his travel agent on 611311.

● **Accommodation At Playa Guacuco**: *Hotel Guacuco Resort*, 1 km from beach, T/F (02) 242-9497, 10 apartments for 4, pool, bar, German-owned, recommended.

Another good beach on the east coast is **Paraguito**, which is the best for surfing, with strong waves. It also has full public services. **Puerto Fermín** (El Tirano) is where Lope de Aguirre, the infamous conquistador, landed in 1561 on his flight from Peru. The El Caserío handicrafts museum is nearby.

● **Accommodation In Puerto Fermín**: **C** *Casa Picaflor*, Calle Fraternidad 11, T (095) 48654, (014) 996-3561, in a lovely old colonial house, private bathroom, air conditioning, very clean and safe, English, German and French spoken, great breakfast, recommended.

El Cardón is an attractive limestone outcrop. A nice, isolated beach is **El Humo**, with deeper water and stronger currents than El Agua (see below), but the advantage of being more peaceful.

PLAYA EL AGUA

The 4 km of palm-ringed, stone-free white sand of Playa El Agua is the most popular beach on the island and at Venezuelan holiday times it is overcrowded. At other times it is ideal for sunbathing and walking. The fashionable part is at the southern end; the northern end is popular with younger people, is less touristy, has fewer facilities, and less shade. There are many restaurants and *kioskos*, which have palm-leaf shade areas. A couple of sun chairs under one of these cost US$2-3, umbrella US$1 extra. All kinds of watersports are possible here, as well as parasailing and bungee jumping.

It's also possible to see the island by Ultralight from here at weekends. Contact Omar Contreras, T 095-617632 or José-Antonio Fernández 095-623519, English spoken, US$35 per flight. (There's also an Ultralight airport at La Caracola, in Porlamar.)

Note that the sea is very rough for children, but fairly shallow. Beware the cross current when you are about waist deep, it gets very strong and can quickly carry you out to sea. El Agua is 45 minutes by bus from Porlamar (US$0.45).

● **Accommodation L2** *Playa El Agua Beach Resort*; **A3** *Miragua Club Resort*; **B** *Casa Trudel*, T/F 589-548735, 4 rooms, bed and breakfast, homely atmosphere (Dutch/Canadian owners), no young children allowed, evening food service, barbecue once a week, 5 minutes' walk from the beach; **B** *Trudel's Garden Vacation Homes*, Calle Miragua, T/F 095-48735, 6 large 2-bedroom houses set in a beautiful garden, 200m from the beach, fresh towels daily (fully equipped kitchens), for reservations by post write to Dan and Trudy O'Brien, Apartado 106, 6301, Porlamar, Venezuela; **B** *Pelican Village*, at the northern end of the beach, small group of bungalows, satellite TV, pool, restaurant, bar, German-run, quiet; **C** *Residencias Miramar*, Avenida 31 de Julio via Manzanillo, esquina Calle Miragua, 3 minutes from the beach, 1 minute from the supermarket, family-run, self-catering apartments, comfortable, barbecue, recommended; **E** *Hostería El Agua*, Avenida 31 de Julio vía Manzanillo, T 48935, contact Sarah Studer, English, French German and Italian spoken, clean bathroom, good beds, fan, fridge, laundry facilities, 4 minutes' walk from beach. There's an unnamed chalet park next to the *Miragua Club Resort*, self-catering, all facilities, very welcoming, highly recommended.

● **Places to eat** *El Paradiso*, at the southern end, also rents out cabins for US$12, small but comfortable; *Kiosko El Agua*, helpful, English spoken; *Posada Shangri-Lá*, recommended; *Casa Vieja*, for seafood; *La Dorada*, French-owned by Gérard and Hilda, with a good beach view, recommended as good value. Many beach restaurants stay open till 2200. Recommended are *Moisés* (Venezuelan-owned), *Sueño Tropical* (Italian-owned), as is *Jardín Tropical*, further down the beach, spacious, pasta, traditional seafood dishes, *Tinajón del Agua* (on main road near the beach entrance), small, popular, good.

JUANGRIEGO

On the north coast is **Juangriego** (*population* 8,300), a small, sleepy town whose picturesque bay is full of fishing boats and which is famous for its fantastic sunsets. The little fort of La Galera is on a promontory at the northern side, beyond which is a bay of the same name with a narrow strip of beach, more fishing boats and many seafront restaurants. Juangriego is a nice place to shop for bargains. It has the same choice as Porlamar, but is quieter and safer. Cash can be changed in most shops; the only place to change travellers' cheques is **Banco del Orinoco**

● **Accommodation B** *El Yare*, T 55835, one block from the beach, some suites with kitchen, owner speaks English, highly recommended; **C-D** *Nuevo Juan Griego*, right next to the beach, Dutch owners, fan, clean, English spoken, expensive restaurant, very popular, recommended; **D** *Gran Sol*, La Marina, entrance in shopping arcade, T 55736, air conditioning, TV; **D-E** *Aparthotel y Residencial El Apurano*, Calle La Marina y El Fuerte, T 530901, English-speaking manager, 2-bedroom apartments with private bath, hot water, air conditioning, but no utensils or towels (because of theft); **D-E** *Le Coral*, next to *Gran Sol*, similar standard but cheaper; **E** *Fortín*, air conditioning, cold water, opposite the beach, most rooms have good views, good restaurant and tables on the beach; **E** *La Posada de Clary*, Calle Los Mártires, T 530037, restaurant, recommended, also apartments for 4, **D**, air conditioning, kitchen, parking; **E** *Residencial Carmencita*, Calle Guevara 20, T 55561, air conditioning, private bath, recommended.

● **Places to eat** *Restaurant Mi Isla* is recommended, also the Lebanese restaurant on the beach; *Viña del Mar*, opposite *Hotel Fortín*, air conditioned, attractive, excellent food; *Juan Griego Steak House*, same building as *Hotel El Yare*, good value, recommended, as is *El Buho*, a nice French-owned pub, open till 0600; *Viejo Muelle*, next door, good restaurant, live music, outside beach bar.

NORTH COAST

North of Juangriego is **La Galera**, a good place to relax and enjoy the famous sunset.

● **Accommodation D** *Posada del Sol*, kitchen, sitting area, fan, fridge.

Northeast from La Galera is **Playa Caribe**, which has many beach restaurants, palm trees and some deserted caverns at its southern end. The water is usually rough here. The *Mosquito Coast Beach Club* is an outdoor disco, with live action all day and into the wee small hours. Aside from the weekends, Wednesday is a good night.

The next beach is the wide and windy **Playa Puerto la Cruz** which adjoins **Pedro González** (*population* 3,700), with a broad sweeping beach, running from a promontory (easy to climb) to scrub and brush that reach down almost to the water's edge. The next bay is accessible by scrambling over rocks. There's major building going on around here.

● **Accommodation A1** *Isla Bonita*, T (095) 657111, F 657211, at Playa Puerto Cruz, a monstrous edifice of reflective glass, 18-hole golf course, business centre and expensive restaurants; **A3** *Dunes*, Playa Puerto Cruz, T 631333, F 632910, a more modest option, all-inclusive resort of low rise, tiled buildings in pinks and creams, activities, sports, fun and games. Ask for Antonietta Luciani at *Restaurant Pedro González*, she has an apartment to rent, US$40 per day, sleeps 6, well-equipped, recommended, as is her restaurant.

The coast road between Pedro González and Manzanillo is interesting, with glimpses of the sea and beaches to one side. There are a number of clifftop lookout points and the road winds from one beach to the next.

Manzanillo (*population* 2,000) is a picturesque bay between the mountains on the most northeasterly point of the island. The water gets deep rather suddenly. There are fishing huts and fish is sold on the beach. There are holiday apartments and an expensive restaurant. Playa Escondida is at the far end.

● **Accommodation In Manzanillo**: **B** *Hotel Karibek*, overlooks the sea, wonderful view, quiet, balcony, fan, swimming pool, bar and restaurant adjacent, breakfast provided, evening meals not great but there are a couple of good restaurants down on the beach, easy taxi ride to other beaches, recommended; **C** *Pahayda Villas*, nice apartments, large rooms, 2 baths for 4 people, sign at main road. 100m further on towards Playa Azul is a beach house with rooms to let and German-owned restaurant, good food.

SOUTH FROM JUANGRIEGO

South of Juangriego, the road goes inland to **San Juan Bautista**, a pleasant colonial town ringed by hills. Rosa Hernández has apartments for rent, **E**, on Calle La Vega, on the left leaving town, past the cemetery, they are spacious, with fan, air conditioning and cold water. You can catch a *por puesto* to San Juan from Juan Griego.

Due south of San Juan is **El Yaque**, near the airport and the mouth of the Laguna de las Marites, where the hinterland is very bleak. This is said to be the best place on the island for windsurfing, and it has become a real international windsurfers' hangout. Surf boards can be hired at the *Club El Mistral*, good service, very helpful, ½-day costs US$30. It is being rapidly developed with small hotels, but it suffers from aircraft noise and lacks public transport. Accommodation here is expensive and generally run by foreigners. The only reasonably-priced restaurant is at *El Yaque Club*. A taxi from Porlamar is US$5. You can take boat from here to Isla Coche for US$12.

• **Accommodation In El Yaque**: **C** *California*, T (014) 951907, F 950908, 46 rooms, small pool; *Casarita*, T (016) 695-0290 (cellular number), resort, pleasant building in neo-colonial style, bed and breakfast, 400m from the beach.

PENINSULA DE MACANAO

The peninsula is connected to the other section of Margarita by La Restinga, a dyke of broken seashells which is part of the eponymous National Park. On the right is a spotlessly clean beach, on the left the lagoon. At the far end are many little restaurants and a cluster of fishermen's huts with landing stages from which the launches make trips into the mangroves. A boat trip costs US$14 per boat, taking 5 passengers. Take a bus from Porlamar harbour front (US$1), and ask the driver to drop you off.

The peninsula is quite underdeveloped, although it is hardly an untouched paradise. Some of the beaches, however, are very good, such as **Boca de Pozo**, **Macanao**, and **Manzanillo**. **Punta Arenas** is the home of many local fishermen; after watersports you can have a lunch of fresh fish. **La Pared** has one fish restaurant, with an excellent setting to watch the

magnificent sunset. **El Tunal** is a shadeless, isolated beach near a small fishing village. There is a harbour at **Chacachacare**. In **Boca del Río** there is a Museum of the Sea.

BOATS TO MARGARITA

The ferry terminal for the island is at **Punta de Piedras**, 31 km west of Porlamar on the island's only highway. Regular transport runs from Porlamar and there are also *por puestos* from Juangriego. The terminal gets very busy at weekends and on Monday.

From Puerto La Cruz

Ferries depart with Conferries from their Los Cocos terminal (see map on page 2 ·8), T 677221 (tickets can also be bought at the *Meliá Hotel*, T 653001). Four ferries a day, at 0800, 1300, 2000 and 0100 each way, with extras at 0400 and 1600 at busy times. Check times in advance as timetables can change. The journey takes 4½ hours; passengers pay US$10 one-way 1st class, US$5.10 2nd class (in enclosed middle deck with limited views), children and pensioners half price; cars pay US$16-17. A new fast ferry, *Margarita Express*, takes 2 hours and costs US$24. To get to the ferry terminal; take a *por puesto* marked 'Bello Monte' from Calle Libertad y Calle Anzoátegui, two blocks from Plaza Bolívar. **NB** Ferries are not always punctual. Don't believe taxi drivers at the bus terminal who may tell you there's a ferry about to leave.

From Cumaná

Ferries depart from the Conferry Terminal at Puerto Sucre (see map on page 249), T 311462; at 0700 and 1600 to Margarita, returning 1000 and 2000, US$5.75 one way for passengers.

To/from Trinidad

Windward Lines sails to Margarita every other week, on Tuesday, from Trinidad, St Vincent, Barbados and St Lucia. It sails from Pampatar to Trinidad on Wednesday at 1800, and on alternate weeks from Güiria to Trinidad (see page 262 for address and fares). Contact: David Hart, Windward Lines agent, Calle José María

Vargas, frente Monederos, Pampatar, T 623527; he is friendly and efficient, speaks English and ensures that immigration/customs goes smoothly.

OTHER ISLANDS

Many of Venezuela's other offshore islands can be visited with diving companies, including **Los Testigos, La Blanquilla, La Tortuga** and **Las Aves**. For details on **Los Roques** see page 101. The easiest islands to visit from Margarita are **Cubagua** and **Coche**, which form part of the state of **Nueva Esparta**.

Isla Cubagua

Cubagua's pearls helped initiate one of the first European settlements in the Americas. Christopher Columbus found natives wearing pearls when he landed near Macuro in 1498, and the Spanish returned to exploit this new-found source of wealth, using the local inhabitants as slaves and pearl divers. In 1541, an earthquake and tidal wave destroyed the island's town, and when the pearl beds were finally exhausted, divers moved to Coche and Cumaná. Today, the island is uninhabited, save for a research station and a few fishermen, and pearl fishing is now prohibited. You can visit the ruins of Nueva Cádiz, which have been excavated. There's good snorkelling and diving off the coast (see **Scuba diving section** on page 22).

Ferries go, on hire only, to Cubagua. The luxury motor yacht, *Viola*, also makes the trip, including drinks, lunch, snorkelling equipment and hotel transfer.

Isla Coche

Coche (*population* 4,500; 11 km by 6 km), has one of the richest salt mines in the country. It is a dry, but colourful desert-like island surrounded by beautiful turquoise water. Flocks of vultures inhabit the island and can be seen flying overhead as you hike through the hills.

Day charter catamarans bring visitors to Coche to snorkel and swim; *Amazonia* and *Catatumbo* leave from Margarita. Ferries

also go to Coche from **Punta de Piedras**: on Monday-Friday at 1600, returning at 1730; on Saturday and Sunday at 0800 and 1730, returning at 0530 and 1730.

● **Accommodation** At Playa La Punta is *Coche Speed Paradise*, T (014) 952-7226, 48 rooms with more under construction, offer windsurfing, sandsurfing and swimming, you can visit via the car ferry from Margarita (beach camping is permitted) or the small airstrip, on weekends they have a wonderful buffet for US$6.50. It is affiliated with *El Yaque Paradise* on Margarita, T (014) 942726. Also *Isla de Coche*, an older resort with pool and windsurfing, T 991431.

Isla Los Testigos

Los Testigos (The Witnesses) are in a protected area where spearfishing and scuba diving is forbidden. You can troll or fish using handline from a yacht or buy fish or lobster (in season) from fishermen, about 150 of whom live here all year round. There is no ferry or airport, but there is a vast colony of frigate birds.

Isla Blanquilla

Located 80 km north of Margarita, Blanquilla can be visited by air on a day trip with *Linea Turística Aerotuy* (see page 275), which includes lunch, drinks and snorkelling equipment. Americano Bay, north of Playa Yaque (where most yachts anchor) is a wonderful, secluded white sand beach with crystal clear blue water and excellent snorkelling. There are no palm trees but shade is at hand in caves along the shore. You can swim into underwater caverns and see all types of fish and coral. If that ain't enough, the sunsets are something else.

Isla La Tortuga

This low-lying, dry island has wonderful beaches, good snorkelling, gorgeous water and good anchorages for yachting types. You can visit Los Palaquemos, an offshore reef, by dinghy. There's a small airstrip which is used at weekends by light aircraft from Caracas.

Las Aves are visited mainly by yachts travelling to and from Bonaire and the Venezuelan mainland.

Guayana and the Orinoco

T HE REGION of Guayana accounts for a massive part of Venezuelan territory – almost half of the entire country's area. Everything south and east of the mighty Río Orinoco, in fact, can be  included in this province, which is politically divided into the State of Bolívar and the Federal Territory of Amazonas. At the eastern end of the region, the Orinoco disgorges into the Atlantic Ocean, creating a delta so vast in size that it, too, constitutes a separate political state; the Delta Amacuro.

For a region of such immensity, Guayana and the Orinoco Delta contain an incredibly small percentage of the country's population. A mere 5% of Venezuelans live here, mainly concentrated in the huge industrial city of Ciudad Guayana on the Río Orinoco. Further west, stands the historic city of Ciudad Bolívar, a good starting point from which to explore many of the country's greatest attractions: the table-top mountains and waterfalls in Canaima National Park, including the spectacular Angel Falls and the mysterious 'Lost World' of Roraima;

The Orinoco's flow

The mighty Orinoco is one of the world's great rivers. It rises in the Sierra Parima, at the very southeastern tip of Amazonas State and flows in a giant 'C' shape for 2,140 km totally within Venezuela. Amazingly, it is spanned by only one bridge along its entire length – the Angostura Bridge at Ciudad Bolívar.

This, the eighth largest river in the world, is fed by 2,000 other rivers. No less than 70% of Venezuelan territory drains totally or partially into the Orinoco, which then pours 1,110,000,000,000 cubic metres of water into the Atlantic Ocean each year at a rate of 18,000 cubic metres per second. This flow is braked by the strong Equatorial Current, causing it to dump sediment in such quantity that the 40,240 sq km delta is pushed out by about 40m a year. Between 1895 and 1980 more than 900 sq km of new land was created in the delta.

the indigenous peoples and varied wildlife of the remote Orinoco Delta; and in the southwest, on the banks of the Orinoco, Puerto Ayacucho is the gateway to the steaming jungles of Venezuelan Amazonia.

The area is Venezuela's largest gold and diamond source, a fact which inspired many fantastical tales of unimaginable riches and which led to countless ill-fated expeditions during the early colonial era in search of the mythical El Dorado. Ironically, though, the region's immense reserves of iron ore, manganese and bauxite are of far greater economic importance. The iron ore deposits are among the largest in the world. In order to exploit these resources, massive amounts of money have been invested in the development of this region into the fastest-growing industrial area in Venezuela.

ROUTES Ciudad Guayana can be reached easily by road south from **Maturín** (see page 305) to **Los Barrancos**, and then by ferry across the Orinoco (see page 305). Ciudad Bolívar can also be reached easily by road, southeast from **Caracas** and south

Toucan

from **Puerto La Cruz/Barcelona**, via **El Tigre**, on Route 16 (see page 241).

CAICARA DEL ORINOCO TO CIUDAD BOLIVAR

ROUTES Ciudad Bolívar can also be reached from the *llanos*. A road (Route 12) runs south from **Chaguaramas** (see page 224) to **Cabruta**, on the north bank of the Orinoco, opposite Caicara.

CAICARA DEL ORINOCO

The town of Caicara (*population* 28,600), on the south bank of the Orinoco, is 372 km west of Ciudad Bolívar by paved highway (Route 19). Its recent growth is due to the continuation of the road south to Puerto Ayacucho (Route 12) and the exploitation of bauxite at Los Pijiguaos.

● **Accommodation C** *Redoma*, near the airport, air conditioning, the best hotel in town; **D** *Venezuela*, Avenida Búlevar, air conditioning but regular power cuts leave the rooms feeling like furnaces; **E** *Bella Guayana*, Calle Merecey 3, with bathroom, hot water, fan, dirty, dark and depressing; **E** *El Diamante*, air conditioning (cheaper without), good value, English spoken, they run tours to the Gran Sabana and Amazonas; **E** *La Fortuna*, run by a blind family; **E** *Miami*, Antigua Calle Carabobo, with bathroom, no hot water; **E** *Tres Ríos*, air conditioning, parking.

● **Transport Air** Two LAV flights a week (Wednesday and Saturday) to **Puerto Ayacucho**; 2-3 weekly to **Ciudad Bolívar**; also to **Barinas**, **San Fernando de Apure** (weekdays), and **Puerto Páez**. **Buses** To **Ciudad Bolívar**, Transporte Orituco and Línea Bolívar, daily at 0700, 7-8 hours (including 2 ferry crossings), US$6.25; to **Puerto Ayacucho** 6 a day,

Red Macaw

6 hours (allow extra time for national guard searches), US$8. **River** Ferry from Cabruta, about 1 hour, 0500-2100, US$2 for car and passengers; a quicker way across is by *lancha* (*chalana*) which leave when full every 30 minutes or so, costing US$0.50 for the 25 minute journey.

Between Caicara and Ciudad Bolívar is the small town of **Maripa**, on the east bank of the Río Caura. There's basic accommodation at the *Hotel Maripa*; and several buses daily to and from Ciudad Bolívar (234 km, 3½ hours, US$3.50). Ask at Maripa gas station for a taxi to **Las Trincheras**, 1½ hours south (US$10-15). Carlos and Jonas have boat trips on the Río Caura from here for US$60 a day. Take your own hammock, food and drink (including enough for the guide), and cooking gear.

RIO CAURA

Maripa is the starting point for trips up the Río Caura, one of the least-visited parts of the country, and one which offers the more adventurous travellers the chance to indulge their wildest jungle fantasies.

The Caura, a tributary of the Orinoco, is a black-water river, which gets its colour from the tannic acid washed out of the forest. Because of this acid there are no mosquitoes. The Caura basin covers 30,000 sq km of Amazonian rainforest and extends uninterrupted into Brazil. It is one of Venezuela's cleanest rivers, since no mining, logging or any kind of industry which might pollute the water is permitted here.

Beyond **Las Trincheras** the indigenous communities of *Ye'kwana* and *Chirichano* (*Yanomami*) can only be reached by dugout canoe. On the way upriver are rapids and huge beaches where you can swim and fish. You'll see plenty of wildlife, including fresh water dolphin, caiman, turtles, monkeys and perhaps otters and tapirs, and lots of parrots, herons, cormorants, toucans and humming birds, among many other types of birds. You'll visit the local indigenous people and walk through the dense jungle to the mightily impressive and stunningly beautiful **Pará Falls**, which consists of a lagoon with five waterfalls up to 60m high.

Tours to the Río Caura can be arranged from Ciudad Bolívar with *Soana Travel* (see under **Tour companies** on page 288).

CIUDAD BOLIVAR

The old colonial city of **Ciudad Bolívar** (*population* 261,000; *phone code* 085), capital of Bolívar State, stands on the south bank of the Orinoco, by the Narrows which gave the town its old name of Angostura. Though the city has spread outwards from the old centre to the airport, its heart still remains along the elegantly wasted riverfront Paseo Orinoco, which harks back to the city's old days as a major river port. Today, the Paseo is a hive of bustling activity as residents go about their business and tour guides stalk the many hotels, cafés and restaurants, looking for unsuspecting tourists and waiting for the right moment to pounce.

A few blocks uphill from Paseo Orinoco the atmosphere is more sedate. There are few people or cars and you can enjoy a peaceful stroll around the shaded Plaza Bolívar, which is surrounded by brightly-coloured colonial houses in blue, yellow, green, ochre and pastel shades. The impressive cathedral takes up one side of the plaza and old colonial houses line the streets that run steeply down to the riverfront. There are nice views from the plaza across the Orinoco to the Angostura Bridge.

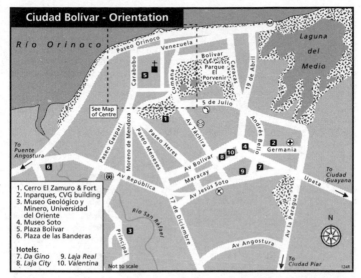

Ciudad Bolívar - Orientation

Río Orinoco · Paseo Orinoco · Venezuela · Laguna del Medio

Parque El Porvenir · Bolívar · 5 de Julio · 19 de Abril · Carabobo · Cumaná · Caracas · Andrés Bello · Germania

See Map of Centre

To Puente Angostura

Paseo Gaspari · Moreno de Mendoza · Paseo Meneses · Paseo Heres · Av Táchira · Av Bolívar · Maracay · Av Jesús Soto · Av República · 17 de Diciembre · Río San Rafael · Principal

Upata · To Ciudad Guayana

Av la Paragua

Av Angostura

To Ciudad Piar

N

Not to scale

124R

1. Cerro El Zamuro & Fort
2. Inparques, CVG building
3. Museo Geológico y Minero, Universidad del Oriente
4. Museo Soto
5. Plaza Bolívar
6. Plaza de las Banderas

Hotels:
7. *Da Gino*   9. *Laja Real*
8. *Laja City*   10. *Valentina*

Ciudad Bolívar is 400 km from the Orinoco Delta and 640 km by road from Caracas. Average temperature 29°C, but a cool and refreshing breeze usually springs up in the evening.

HISTORY

Founded in 1764 as Santo Tomás de la Guayana de Angostura, the town soon came to be known simply as Angostura. This name was also given to the famous concoction, made from the bark of a local tree, which was used as a successful remedy for fever. This remedy, which mixed honey with the tree bark, saved the life of Alexander Von Humboldt in June 1800, during his expedition. This tree bark was also the basic ingredient for Angostura Bitters, which were produced here until the Federal Wars forced a move to Trinidad.

Angostura had already risen to prominence as an important river port by the early 19th century, despite its isolation. The town was a patriot stronghold during the Wars of Independence and it was here that Bolívar came after defeat to reorganize his forces. He was joined, decisively, in his struggle for independence by British, Irish and German soldiers, veterans of the Napoleonic Wars in Europe.

On Bolívar's triumphant return from victory over the Spanish in Colombia, in 1819, he was declared President of his beloved Gran Colombia, the single republic comprising Venezuela, Nueva Granada (Colombia) and Quito, which he had yet to forge, and which was to fragment before his death (see also **History**, on page 44). Angostura was renamed Ciudad Bolívar on 3 May 1846, in honour of the great Liberator.

PLACES OF INTEREST

At the Congress of Angostura, 15 February 1819, the representatives of the present day Venezuela, Colombia and Ecuador met to proclaim Gran Colombia. The building, on **Plaza Bolívar**, houses a museum (guides in Spanish only), the **Casa del Congreso de Angostura**. It was built in 1766-76 by Manuel Centurión, the provincial governor.

Also on this historic plaza is the **Cathedral** (started 1764 and completed in 1840), the **Casa de Los Gobernadores de la Colonia**, which was also built by

Ciudad Bolívar

1. Archivo Histórico y Museo Etnográfico de Guayana, Carcel Viejo
2. Biblioteca Rómulo Gallegos
3. Casa del Congreso de Angostura
4. Casa de la Cultura
5. Casa de las Doce Ventanas
6. Casa de los Gobernadores de la Colonia
7. Casa del Correo del Orinoco
8. Hill Fort
9. Parque Miranda
10. Plaza Bolívar
11. Real Intendencia, Palacio de Gobierno
12. Teatro de Ciudad Bolívar

Hotels:
13. *Caracas*
14. *Colonial*
15. *Italia*
16. *Unión*

Places to eat:
17. Tasca La Playa
18. Arabe-Venezolano

Centurión in 1766, the **Real Intendencia**, and the **Casa de la Cultura**.

On the north side of the plaza, at Bolívar 33, is the house where General Manuel Piar, the Liberator of Guayana from the Spanish, was held prisoner before being executed by Bolívar on 16 October 1817. Piar refused to put himself under Bolívar's command.

A few blocks uphill from Plaza Bolívar is the restored **Parque Miranda**, on Calle Carabobo. It's a nice place to relax and escape the noise and bustle of the Paseo Orinoco. On one side of this little plaza is the old theatre, recently converted into an art centre. At one time the theatre was the Antigua Prefectura (1900-20) and then a military prison.

The present legislative assembly and **Consejo Municipal** are between Plaza Bolívar and Parque Miranda. When the town was still known as Angostura, a Prussian physician, Dr Siegert, invented the famous bitters there in 1824. The factory then moved to Port of Spain in 1875.

A walk along the river bank is enjoyable at dusk when the sun is setting and a cooling breeze begins to blow. Launches take passengers across the river (US$0.25), but there are no other passenger boat services.

The Paseo Orinoco leading west out of town goes to the **Angostura Bridge**, which can be seen from town. Opened in 1967, this is the only bridge across the Orinoco. It is 1,668m long (over a mile), and though cyclists and walkers are not allowed to cross, the military will flag down a car for you (toll US$0.80).

The **Zamuro hill fort** (1902), stands on another hill in the centre of town and dominates the city. The entrance to the fort is on Paseo Heres; closed 1200-1400. Just west of the centre is **Parque El Zanjón**, an area of vegetation typical of the region. To the east is **Parque El Porvenir**, with botanical gardens.

Outside the airport is the *Río Caroní* aeroplane, which Jimmy Angel landed on top of Auyán-Tepuy (see page 294).

MUSEUMS

The **Museo Soto** is on Avenida Germania, some distance from the centre, set in pleasant gardens. It shows works by Venezuela's Jesús Rafael Soto and other modern artists; open Tuesday-Sunday 1000-1700, guide in Spanish only, entry free, recommended. There's a museum at the **Casa del Correo del Orinoco**, Paseo Orinoco y Carabobo, with modern art and some exhibits of the history of the city, including the printing press of the newspaper which spread the cause of independence; the museum has a free town map (poor) and a booklet on Ciudad Bolívar.

Museo Geológico y Minero is at the School of Mines in the University of the East (UDO), on Avenida Principal, La Sabanita. The **Archivo Histórico y Museo Etnográfico de la Guayana** is housed in the former prison and governor's mansion, two blocks from the Cathedral, on Paseo Orinoco. It has a very interesting and original display of indigenous tools and artefacts.

There are many other museums in the city: the **Casa de los Doce Ventanas**, on Calle Venezuela entre Babilonia y Las Delicias, was the residence of President Soublette; the **Museo Casa San Isidro**, on Avenida Táchira, is a mansion where Simón Bolívar stayed; open Tuesday-Saturday 0900-1200, 1430-1700, Sunday 0900-1200.

LOCAL FESTIVALS

August, *Fiesta del Orinoco*; **5-8 September**, fair and exhibition.

LOCAL INFORMATION

● **Accommodation**

Hotel prices

L1	over US$200	**L2**	US$151-200
L3	US$101-150	**A1**	US$81-100
A2	US$61-80	**A3**	US$46-60
B	US$31-45	**C**	US$21-30
D	US$12-20	**E**	US$7-11
F	US$4-6	**G**	up to US$3

Those marked with an asterisk (*) are bookable through Fairmont International (see under Caracas).

Near the airport: **C** *Laja Real**, Avenida Andrés Bello y Jesús Soto, opposite the airport, T 27911/27955/27944, T/F 28778, pool open to non-residents for US$2 per day, air conditioning, TV, good restaurant, clean, very friendly, highly recommended.

D *Da Gino*, Avenida Jesús Soto, opposite the airport, T 20313/25621/25363/26634, F 25454, good service and restaurant, large rooms with balcony, friendly, recommended; **D** *Laja City*, Avenida Táchira y Avenida Bolívar, T 29910/29920/29919, with bathroom, quiet, air conditioning, hot water, TV, restaurant; **D** *Valentina*, Avenida Maracay 55, T 22145/27253/29311, F 27919, with bathroom, hot water, quiet, air conditioning, clean and comfortable, carpets, spacious rooms, very good restaurant (US$3-5 per main dish), recommended.

E *Táchira*, Avenida Táchira 40, near Briceño, T 27489/24607, with bathroom, air conditioning, TV, clean, parking, OK.

On Paseo Orinoco: **D** *Colonial*, T 24402, F 23080, has seen better days but still good value, with bathroom, air conditioning, has its own travel agency *Neckar Travel* in the lobby which offers all the usual tours at competitive prices, nice restaurant on balcony overlooking river, changes Amex travellers' cheques and cash, recommended.

E *Italia*, **F** without bath, noisy air conditioning, very basic rooms, veranda overlooking the Río Orinoco, mixed reports on security, store luggage, cheap restaurant, small portions, very popular with travellers, changes cash, travel agency in lobby (see below), all the guides hang around here so expect a hard sell on tours; **E** *Unión*, just off Paseo Orinoco at Calle Urica 11, T 23374, with bathroom, air conditioning, **F** with fan, good value, recommended; **E-F** *Caracas*, on the corner of Calle Roscio, T 26089, with bathroom, safe but very rundown, balcony overlooking river, noisy air conditioning.

F *Pensión Yocaima*, on Calle Zaraza, at the eastern end of the Paseo, T 28814, with bathroom and fan, laundry facilities, restaurant, basic.

On Avenida Moreno de Mendoza, near the bus terminal: **D** *Universo*, recommended; and **F** *Brasilia*, with shower and fan, basic, matrimonial rooms only.

● **Places to eat**
Savoy, Venezuela y Dalla Costa, good value breakfast and lunch; *Mi Casa*, Calle Venezuela, open air, good value; also on Venezuela is *Charly's*, *Fuente de Soda* serving good cheap lunches, fast service; *América*, Paseo Orinoco esquina Roscio, good food, dishes US$3-5, open late; *Arabe-Venezolano*, on Cumaná near Bolívar, clean, air conditioning, good Arabic food, friendly, not cheap; *Lonchería Ché*, next to *Hotel Colonial*, serves a good breakfast; *La Playa*, on Calle Urica entre Venezuela y Zea, good for fish, reasonable prices; *Lonchería Urica*, next to *Hotel Unión*, good lunch for US$1.25, get there early. You can find cheap food at the market at the east end of Paseo Orinoco.

● **Banks & money changers**
Banco Consolidado, Edificio Pinemar, Avenida Andrés Bello, Centro Comercial Canaima, near the airport, changes Amex travellers' cheques; **Banco de Venezuela**, near *Hotel Colonial*, cash advance on Visa, no travellers' cheques, efficient service, ATM outside; **Banco Mercantil**, at the east end of Paseo Orinoco, changes travellers' cheques and has ATM; **Banco Unión**, Calle Dalla Costa y Bolívar, ATM.

● **Embassies & consulates**
Danish Consulate, Avenida Táchira, Quinta Maninata 50, oficina 319, T 23490, open 0800-1200, 1500-1700.

● **Post & telecommunications**
Post Office: on Avenida Táchira, 15 minutes' walk from the centre.

Telephones: CANTV, Avenida 5 de Julio, 100m from Avenida Táchira; closed on Sunday. There are public pay phones on Paseo Orinoco, just to the left of the *Hotel Colonial* looking towards the river.

● **Shopping**
You can buy baskets and items made by the local indigenous peoples, and good hammocks. The gold orchid pin or earrings, or a gold nugget (known as *cochano*), are the best souvenirs of Venezuela. Worth seeking out, but now rare, is the handmade orchid of red, yellow and white gold. There are many jewellers on Pasaje Guayana, which runs off Paseo Orinoco near *Hotel Colonial*. Gold items of comparable price and quality can also be found on the Plaza Bolívar in Caracas and in Santa Elena de Uairén. A very good jewellery shop is *Van Buren*, Avenida Venezuela 27, behind Paseo Orinoco, they also speak fluent English. *La Carioca* is a new shopping centre at the end of Paseo Orinoco, with restaurants, which is nice to walk around. There's a large and well-stocked supermarket close to the Museo Soto on Avenida Germania.

Camping equipment: white gas (stove fuel) is available at Avenida República 16, near the bus terminal.

● **Tourist offices**
The staff are helpful at the office on Avenida Táchira entre Avenidas M Briceño y Maracay; they have a street map and information on the Gran Sabana. **Inparques**: at Avenida Germania, Casa de Gobernador.

● **Tour companies & travel agents**
Soana Travel SRL, Calle Bolívar 50, con Calle Della Costa, T 014-851056 (cellular), T/F 22030 (office), run by Martin Haars, tours to Canaima and Gran Sabana, and a highly recommended 5-day tour to Río Caura (see page 284), Martin also offers accommodation, speaks fluent English and Dutch and is generally very helpful; *Cunaguaro Tours*, T 22041, F 27810, (cellular,

SOANA TRAVEL S.R.L.

Martin Haars
Tel/fax: 085 22030

Apartado Postal N° 454 Ciudad Bolívar 8001-A

Calle Bolívar #50, con Calle Della Costa

Specialists for:
RIO CAURA
with Para Falls
Expeditions to
Sarisarinama.
CANAIMA
Gran Sabana
Roraima
Orinoco Delta
Stay on farms,
swimm & ride.

014-850344), in the *Hotel Italia* entrance, tours to Gran Sabana, Canaima and Salto Angel, driver Lenin Linares is very good, friendly, recommended; *Marina Río Orinoco*, at *Hotel Unión*, F 49868, run by Sean Starr, tours to Roraima, Canaima and Orinoco Delta, speaks fluent English; *Turi Express* at the airport, run by Guillermo Rodríguez, arranges tours to Canaima and the Guri dam, speaks good English, Julio is a recommended guide; *Expediciones Dearuna*, at *Hotel Caracas*, T 014-851360 (Cellular), T/F 26089, run by Javier Cubillos, recommended for Canaima, English, Dutch, German and French spoken. Miguel Gasca is recommended for tours to Roraima, Gran Sabana and Canaima, T 014-235210/016-629-4600 (Cellular) or look for him at *Hotel Italia*; *Agencia de Viajes Auyantepuy*, Calle Bolívar, Edificio Roque, Centro No 8, T 20748, very helpful for tickets to Canaima, English and French spoken.

For 3 days/2 nights tours to Canaima expect to pay around US$220-260 per person; 4 days/3 nights to Gran Sabana US$180-240 per person; Roraima (5 or 6 days) US$50 per day per person; 3 days/2 nights to the Orinoco Delta US$180 per person.

Unofficial touts swamp the bars and restaurants around Paseo Orinoco. It may be better to go to your destination and find a tour there; eg tours to Roraima and Gran Sabana can be done easily, and as economically, from Santa Elena or San Francisco de Yuruaní. One option is to hire a jeep (about US$120 per day) and do your own tour. Motorized canoe trips to the Angel Falls are best organized in Ciudad Bolívar. Before deciding to purchase a tour with anyone in Ciudad Bolívar ensure that the guide who sells the package is the guide who leads the tour, that all equipment is good and waterproof, that initial prices are not grossly inflated and that you agree on what is being offered. Check where tours start from as some fly from Ciudad Guyana (eg, Turi Tours), and charge passengers for taxi transfers.

NB We have received several reports of tours being subcontracted to unskilled guides by unreliable operators. In addition, tourists have been deceived, or worse, by unscrupulous guides. We suggest that you choose a company or guide from the list above, all of whom have received positive recommendations. Also be very wary of any 'new' agencies that have recently started up – they may be disreputable agencies that had to close owing to complaints. Above all, ask other travellers who have just returned from a tour.

● **Transport**

Local Taxis: US$1-1.25 to virtually anywhere in town. US$1.50-2 from the bus station to the town centre. To Puerto Ordaz costs at least US$30 and takes 1 hour.

Air Minibuses and buses (Ruta 2) marked 'Terminal' go to the town centre. A taxi from the airport to Paseo Orinoco costs US$1.50. A yellow bus marked 'Aeropuerto' runs east along Paseo Orinoco; you can catch it one block west of *Hotel Colonial*. Flights to **Caracas** daily with Servivensa, 1½ hours, via Maturín. Rutaca fly daily to **Santa Elena**, US$65 one way. For information on all flights and for trips to Canaima you should ask for Jorge at the Ciaca office at the airport; he also changes travellers' cheques and cash. For details on flights to Canaima, Angel Falls and Kavác, see page 294. Airport tax is US$0.45. There are international phones at the airport, a good restaurant and car hire.

Buses The terminal is at the junction of Avenida República and Avenida Sucre. To get there take a bus marked 'Terminal' going west along the Paseo Orinoco (US$0.15). Several buses daily and overnight to **Caracas**, 9 hours, US$12, student discount available, *por puesto* US$24. To **Puerto La Cruz**, US$5 (US$2.50 with student discount), *por puesto*, US$10, 5 hours; to **Cumaná**, US$6, 6 hours with Expresos Guayanesa (8 daily); to **Maracay**, US$8-9, 10 hours; **Valencia**, via Maracay, US$10. **Tumeremo** US$5.25, and through to **El Dorado**, US$5.75, 3 daily. To **Santa Elena de Uairén** direct with Línea Orinoco, Transportes Mundial (5 daily) or Expreso Rápidos de Güiria at 0500, 0800 and 1900, spectacular views of the Gran Sabana at sunset (book in advance), US$9-10, 12 hours. To **Boa Vista** with Transportes Mundial, Monday and Thursday at 2000 (sometimes once a week) US$25, 20 hours. To **Ciudad Guayana**, hourly from 0700 with Expresos Guayanesa, US$1.35, 1½ hours, *por puesto*, US$3.60, 1½ hours. Bus to **Caicara**, 7-8 hours (including 2 ferry crossings), US$6.25; to **Ciudad Piar**, US$1.40, 3 hours; to **Luepa** (Canaima National Park), US$9, 10-12 hours. *Por puesto* to **Puerto Ayacucho**, 3 daily, US$12, 10-12 hours, direct with Caicara Amazonas, US$11, 10 hours (take food).

LA ENCRUCIJADA

70 km east of Ciudad Bolívar is **La Encrucijada**, a glorified road junction and truck stop, which is home to a small community.

● **Accommodation** F *La Gran Parada*, bathroom, fan, good value, the owner, Tadeo Venarusso, speaks English and Italian and is very knowledgeable about the area. His family lives in Playa Blanca (see below).

From La Encrucijada junction you can head straight on to Upata, via Paso

Caruachi, across the Río Caroní. There is no ferry here but private boats can be hired for the 2 minute crossing. You can also head northeast from the junction to Ciudad Guayana (37 km).

SOUTH FROM CIUDAD BOLIVAR

Another option from La Encrucijada junction is to head south (right) to Ciudad Piar and La Paragua. After 8 km on this road, turn left past enormous black rocks, on to an almost hidden trail. After a further 2 km is the **Cueva del Elefante**, where precolumbian relics were found and rock paintings can be seen. Following the track (10 km) you reach **Playa Blanca** on the Río Caroní, where miners dive for gold and diamonds. Since the discovery of gold in 1991, the population of Playa Blanca has exploded. A visit is worthwhile, particularly to see the gold dredgers. Transport can be arranged with Tadeo Venarusso in La Encrucijada; his brother Gyani does boat trips. Tadeo also visits the rock paintings in the area; contact him at Apartado 186, Puerto Ordaz, Estado Bolívar, Código Postal 8015, or at *Hotel La Gran Parada* (see above).

CIUDAD PIAR

86 km south of La Ecrucijada is **Ciudad Piar** (*population* 21,100), near the iron ore mountain, Cerro Bolívar. It's cheaper to visit Cerro Bolívar from Ciudad Bolívar than from Ciudad Guayana. Ciudad Piar can also reached by a direct road (Route 16) south from Ciudad Bolívar (90 km).

• **Accommodation A** *Hato El Burro*, run by the the Ackerman family, English, German and Spanish spoken. Trips are arranged around their own extensive ranch, Guri dam, Angel Falls etc, first class service. Contact at Vía La Paragua, Km 434, Ciudad Piar, T 938148, or Caracas T/F 793-6515/6150, PO Box 60636, Este Caracas, 1060.

LA PARAGUA

Following Route 16 south for a further 111 km on a good paved road you reach this old, somewhat unfriendly port on the Río Paragua. This small town still has a frontier feel, and like all mining settlements it is largely made up of immigrants (Guyanese and Brazilians) and prostitutes. The local indigenous groups of Pemón and Ye'kwana have had to give up trying to protect their ancient tribal lands and instead joined the miners prospecting for precious minerals.

BY ROAD TO CANAIMA

A dry-weather (December-May) overland route to Canaima follows the miners' track from La Paragua through savannah and heavy bush to **San Salvador de Paúl**, a large shanty town set amid a pockmarked landscape of diggings near the Río Caroní, some 25 km south of Canaima. It is home to a shifting population of around 3,500 miners panning or dredging diamonds from local streams. It is a rough, but not unfriendly place with a Guardia Nacional post, numerous bars and several stores selling expensive supplies. Gasoline is sometimes available but always hideously expensive. Bush pilots fly from the airstrip over to Canaima any day except Monday (which is engine maintenance day throughout the region).

The track begins opposite La Paragua, where a seat in the occasional jeep heading for Paúl can be found by asking around. Those with their own heavy-duty vehicle can cross the Río Paragua on a *chalana* (car ferry), which operates during daylight hours for a small fee. The road is gravel for the 23 km to La Comunidad, crossing the Río Chiguao en route on a new bridge, then deteriorates (take plenty of food, fuel, a spade and heavy tow rope and be prepared for unmarked turn-offs, gullies and narrow bridges) on the 56 km south to the indigenous village of Las Bonitas, a 15 minute walk west of the Río Caroní (there's good camping and swimming, but don't underestimate the current). A further rough 14 km leads to wheel tracks heading east across a ridge to Caño Negro (little more than a hut), where the resident family may arrange a crossing of the swiftly-flowing river by *curiara* (dugout) to a small landing and hut on the east bank, grandly named Puerto Kukurital. From here, it's normally a 2½ to 3½ hour walk along the sandy jeep trail, first through forest and then across hot, open savannah to Canaima, with Auyán-Tepuy looming ahead.

The above is the shortest crossing to Canaima but a *curiara* cannot always be guaranteed here. Most visitors continue on the track from Las Bonitas to the Karamacoto indigenous village of **Taraipa** (28 km), where arrangements are made with the *capitán* of the village, or his son, for parking your vehicle and crossing the river (take plastic bags for protecting cameras, etc during the rough passage). It is a 30 minute walk to the Río Caroní – 'tannin-stained, powerful and absolutely beautiful' (Kevin Healey) – but if negotiating a return crossing try to fix a specified time or you could be stranded (the locals are not always reliable, nor can they see the river from their village). On the east bank a scenic path runs north between parallel ridges to Puerto Kukurital, approximately a 1½ hour walk.

The Guardia Nacional at San Salvador de Paúl will call Canaima by radio to check on the availability of jeeps for a pick-up; the service is charged by the hour. Paúl is at the end of the road, a further 1 hour and 14 km south from Taraipa (135 km from La Paragua, 7 hours of difficult driving at the best of times), but separated from the Caroní by a rugged escarpment which marks much of the river's western margin. The locals at Taraipa may sometimes take visitors in *curiaras* to the Yuri Falls, but may also have better things to do with their time and limited supply of oil and gasoline.

CANAIMA NATIONAL PARK

From Ciudad Bolívar you can fly into the heart of **Canaima National Park**, which covers 3 million hectares and is one of the six largest National Parks in the world. Canaima protects a part of Guayana known as the **Gran Sabana** (see page 311), a unique and beautiful region characterized by around 100 tabletop mountains (*tepuys*), which rise straight out of the surrounding savannah with vertical walls up to 1,000m high, and countless waterfalls, including Angel Falls, the highest waterfall in the world (see below).

The most popular destination in Canaima National Park is **Canaima**, a beautiful tannin-stained lagoon with soft beige beaches. Canaima is undoubtedly a

Canaima's tourism pioneers

Canaima's history as a tourist destination began when bushpilot Charlie Baughan came across the tannin-stained lagoon in 1954. In an attempt to reap financial reward from his discovery, he formed a company, 'Empresas Gran Sabana S.A.' and took a German painter, Heinz Dollacker, with him to Canaima to reproduce the beautiful landscape on canvas and put it on the tourist map. Returning to Caracas, they staged an exhibition of Dollacker's work and produced a brochure entitled 'Canaima – a little piece of heaven on earth'.

Today, Canaima could still be described as a little piece of heaven on earth, even with the huge daily influx of tourists, some of whom have come to visit one of Canaima's earliest pioneers.

The island in the lagoon, Isla Anatoly, was named after a Russian gold prospector, who settled on the island and became a local *brujo*, or witchdoctor. The Russian's house is still there but the island is now inhabited by Tomás Bernal, a Peruvian from Ayacucho who bought it from Anatoly for the princely sum of US$1,000. Tomás now makes his living from the tourists who seek him out on his island.

When Tomás first arrived at Canaima he lived for almost 10 years as a hermit in a cave next to the Sapo Falls. The only access to the cave is by a path which Tomás cut himself into the sheer rock face behind the curtain of water. The path has now become a standard feature in every tourist agency's itinerary.

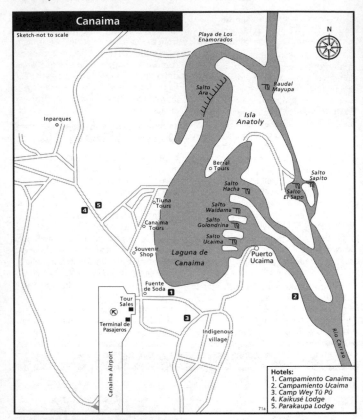

Canaima

Sketch-not to scale

Playa de Los Enamorados

N

Salto Ara

Raudal Mayupa

Isla Anatoly

Inparques

Berral Tours

Salto Sapito

Salto Hacha

Salto El Sapo

4 5

Tiuna Tours

Salto Waidama

Canaima Tours

Salto Golondrina

Souvenir Shop

Salto Ucaima

Laguna de Canaima

Puerto Ucaima

Fuente de Soda

1

Tour Sales

2

Terminal de Pasajeros

3

Indigenous village

Canaima Airport

Río Carrao

Hotels:
1. *Campamiento Canaima*
2. *Campamiento Ucaima*
3. *Camp Wey Tü Pü*
4. *Kaikusé Lodge*
5. *Parakaupa Lodge*

71a

Indian Mischief

You could say that the Pemón Indians settled around Canaima lagoon because it was the lesser of two evils. They chose not to live too close to Angel Falls (known to them as Churún Merú) as they believe the waterfall is inhabited by an evil spirit. This also explains the name of Auyán-Tepuy, which translates as 'Devil Mountain'. So, instead they opted for a place whose name means 'bad spirit', but more mischievous than evil.

stunningly beautiful place; the Río Carrao tumbles spectacularly over seven waterfalls into the lagoon below and the surrounding countryside complements the scene perfectly. Many package tours now visit on day trips, and Canaima can get very busy during the high season, when flights from Ciudad Bolívar and elsewhere take off and land every few minutes. Facilities, though, are very good, with several tourist lodges, and it's a convenient base from which to visit many of the highlights of the park. Note that, as one of the most popular destinations in the country, it can be quite expensive. There is an expensive snack bar at the

Laguna de Canaima

airport. Park entry US$6 per person; valid for 3 days.

Warning There are dangerous undercurrents in the lagoon; people have drowned while swimming near the falls. Tourists are not told of the possible dangers beforehand. Also look out for chiggers (*niguas*) in the sand.

TOURS AROUND CANAIMA

There are various short tours which can be made around Canaima; all are worthwhile (and usually crowded). You can make walking expeditions into the jungle to indigenous villages with a guide (but bargain hard on the price).

Other excursions are to the **Mayupa Falls**, including a canoe ride on the Río Carrao (US$45, half day); to **Yuri Falls** by jeep and boat (US$25, half day); to **Isla Orquídea** (US$65, full day, good boat ride, beach barbecue); and to **Saltos de Sapo** and **Sapito** (3 hours, US$20), where you can walk behind the waterfall, along the tunnel hewn by Tomás Bernal (see above).

C pp *Camp Wey Tü Pü*, T (086) 625955, rooms with fan and shower, bar.

D pp *Parakaupa Lodge*, 5 minutes from the airport, with bathroom, comfortable, hammocks outside rooms, restaurant; opposite is **D** pp *Kaikusé Lodge*, basic but clean, with bathroom, **F** pp in hammocks.

Some families in the village rent hammocks for US$5-10 per person. Travel agencies also rent hammocks for US$3-5 per person a night; ask at the airport.

Camping You can camp for free; fires are permitted and plenty of wood is available. You must first obtain a *permiso de excursionistas* from Inparques in Caracas (see page 91), in Ciudad Bolívar (see page 288), or at the CVG building in Canaima, US$1.50. No tents are available for hire.

● **Tour companies & guides**
There is fierce competition at the airport, but all the agencies pretty much offer the same thing at the same price. *Kamaracoto Tours*, *Tiuna Tours* and *Hermanos Jiménez* are recommended for trips to Salto Sapo, Kavác and Salto Angel. They will also help with finding accommodation.

Kamaracoto Tours, also have offices in Ciudad Bolívar, at Avenida Andres Bello con Germania, Centro Comercial El Diamante, Planta Alta, T/F (085) 27680, and in Caracas at Avenida Urdaneta, entre Veroes y Jesuitas, Edificio Cto. Imanta, 1st floor, oficina 17, T/F (02) 564-7355; *Tiuna Tours*, also at Ciudad Bolívar airport, T (085) 27072.

A recommended guide in Canaima is Tomás Bernal, who has his own camp on an island in the lagoon, with beds and hammocks, he is popular with travellers and very knowledgeable about flora and fauna; contact him in Canaima or through *Soana Tours* in Ciudad Bolívar (see page 288). Many agencies in Caracas, Ciudad Bolívar, etc, offer tours to Canaima, offering various accommodation, excursion and Angel Falls flight arrangements. Some are listed under Caracas and Ciudad Bolívar **Travel agents**. When booking a package beware of agents telling you that all the guides speak English: some do, but many don't.

● **Useful services**
It is advisable to take food, though the village near Canaima has a small store selling mainly canned foods. There's also a souvenir shop near the airport, and the *fuente de soda* overlooking the lagoon. Do not forget swimming costumes, insect repellent and sun cream; waterproof clothing may be advisable. Food is expensive at the Hoturvensa restaurant. A cheaper option is Simon's restaurant in the village which is used

by many of the agencies; breakfast is US$3 and lunch/dinner US$4-5 per person. **Warning** Necklaces of poisonous red and black seeds (rosary peas) are on sale here.

● **Transport**
The full air fare from Caracas is US$157. Servivensa flies to Canaima from Caracas, Porlamar or Puerto Ordaz for US$65 one way. Servivensa also has flights from Santa Elena de Uairén. A flight from Canaima to Porlamar and Caracas costs US$130. Note that Avensa flights to Canaima or Santa Elena depart from Puerto Ordaz. Do not rely on being able to change the return date on your flight and be even more wary of getting an open return. The airline is quite happy to change your ticket, but the next available seat could be in 5 days time and Canaima is a very expensive place to kill time. All arrangements are made through Avensa/Servivensa, direct (best in Caracas – address on page 190 – the Ciudad Bolívar Avensa office is closed for most of the weekend) or through travel agencies.

Aereotuy runs 1 day excursions by 19-seat Dornier aircraft out of Ciudad Bolívar, one landing at Canaima, the other at Kavác, giving good views of Angel Falls. There is a connecting Aereotuy flight from Isla Margarita (0900, returning 1600) and direct excursions from Barcelona and Margarita (0730 departure returning 1800). They have a new camp, which is recommended, near the foot of Nonon-Tepuy, bookable only through Aerotuy (T 02-761-6231, F 762-5254).

Various companies offer day excursions in 5-seater Cessnas to Canaima from Ciudad Bolívar; book early (0630-0700) at the airport, or preferably the day before. Expect to pay US$150-165 per person, including a flight over Angel Falls, a boat across Canaima lagoon, lunch and a trip to Salto Sapo; the flight only costs US$50 one way with Rutaca and Ciaca; to Santa Elena one way costs US$65. You can arrange your flight with Jorge Marinkovic at the airport; you'll find him in the Ciaca office opposite Avensa desk. He speaks English, and also arranges tours to the Gran Sabana and Los Roques. Reductions are available for parties. Note that you may not even see the falls from the air in the rainy season – and the additional cost of a trip to the Angel Falls may well bring the cost of your journey up to that of a package.

ANGEL FALLS

There are many unmissable sights in Venezuela, but right at the top of the list is the truly breathtaking Angel Falls, the highest waterfall in the world at 979m (its longest single drop is 807m). To fly over the falls on a clear day from Ciudad Bolívar is one of the greatest visual experiences anywhere in the world, only exceeded by seeing them from below, as part of a boat trip from Canaima, 70 km downriver from Canaima. **NB** Make sure you have plenty rolls of film; you'll need them!

The falls are named after Jimmy Angel, who first reported their existence in 1935, and later returned and crash-landed his plane, the *Río Caroní*, on top of Auyán-Tepuy (see *South American Explorer*, No 40, May 1995, pp 22-30). The site is now marked with a plaque. The sheer rock

The rise and falls of Jimmy Angel

Right up there with Hiram Bingham and Colonel Fawcett as one of the true greats of South American exploration is Jimmy Crawford Angel. Born in 1899 in the small mining town of Springfield, Missouri, he gave his name to the highest waterfall in the world.

This particular Angel gained his wings early on in life. Legend has it that he made his first proper flight at the age of 14. He then served in World War One, under age, in the Canadian Flying Corps, breaking records for the highest flight, highest landing and most loops. After the war he drifted in and out of various humdrum jobs: running the mail down through Mexico; training pilots in Shanghai; herding reindeer in Canada for the Hudson Bay Company. He even appeared as a stunt flyer in Howard Hughes' movie *Hell's Angels*. His real claim to fame would come later, though.

It all began in Panama City in 1921, and a chance meeting with a gold prospector who spoke of a river of gold in the Guayana Highlands and asked Jimmy to fly him there. On 12 May they flew out of Panama for Cartagena in Colombia, and from there onto Maracaibo, Caracas, San Fernando de Apure, south up the Río Caroní then westwards along the Río Carrao. They had no instruments and no map but eventually made it to the promised river, somewhere near Auyán-Tepuy. Angel described it as "a hell of a place to land a plane". The pair successfully panned the river for gold, limited only by the weight they could safely take on board.

For years afterwards, Jimmy Angel flew over the area, trying to relocate the 'river of gold'. Early in 1935, he set out on yet another expedition, this time with the backing of a New York company. He flew with his chief investor and a couple of prospectors. On 25 March 1935, he piloted his single-engined Cessna up a narrow canyon near Auyán-Tepuy and saw for the first time the monumental cascade of water that would later bear his name.

Angel's accounts of this historic sighting were dismissed as wild exaggeration back in Caracas, but he found the falls again 2 years later, this time crash-landing his plane, a Flamingo called El Río Caroní, on the summit of Auyán-Tepuy. The entire party, including his wife, Marie, had to walk for 12 days through the forest, finally arriving at the mission settlement of Kamarata.

However, it was not until 1949 that an overland expedition, led by the US journalist, Ruth Robertson, reached the base of the falls and established scientifically what Jimmy Angel had claimed all along – that he had discovered the highest waterfall in the world, 979m from summit to base.

In June 1956, back in Panama, Jimmy crashed a plane. Not an unusual occurrence for a man dedicated to flying, but one that proved fatal. He suffered a stroke and fell into a coma, later dying in hospital on 8 December 1956. The actual plane that Jimmy Angel crash-landed on top of Auyán-Tepuy is now proudly on display outside the terminal at Ciudad Bolívar airport.

Angel Falls

face of Auyán-Tepuy was climbed in 1971 by three Americans and an Englishman, David Nott, who recounted the 10-day adventure in his book *Angels Four* (Prentice-Hall). **NB** The falls face east, so they only receive the sun in the morning.

TRIPS TO THE FALLS

Trips by boat upriver to the **Angel Falls** only go from June to November, leaving usually in the afternoon. You stay the first night at Isla Orquídea, before continuing to the Falls the next day. 12 hour day trips cost around US$100. A 44 hour, '3 day', trip costs US$200; it is more relaxing, but shows nothing different. If you have a *permiso de excursionistas* (see page 294), you may be able to go on one tour and come back with another, giving yourself more time at the Falls (take all food and gear). Trips can be arranged with agencies in Cuidad Bolívar (see page 288), or at Canaima airport. All *curiaras* (dugouts) must have two motors, by law, and carry first aid, life jackets, etc. Take wet weather gear, swimwear, a mosquito net for your hammock and insect repellent.

● **Transport Air** The cheapest way to fly over the falls is as part of a scheduled flight from Ciudad Bolívar to Canaima with Rutaca or Ciaca (see **Canaima Transport** above). From Canaima a 45 minute flight costs US$45 per person and does some circuits over and alongside the falls. There are also 20 minute flights at 0930 for US$55-60 per person which return in time for the midday Servivensa flight out of Canaima. You can also go to the airstrip at Canaima and ask the pilots there if they will fly over the Falls for the same price as a tour.

EXCURSIONS FROM CANAIMA

Although not the highest or largest of the *tepuys*, **Auyán-Tepuy** (600 sq km) is one of the more accessible. **Kamarata** is a friendly indigenous settlement with a Capuchin mission on the plain at the eastern foot of the *tepuy*. It has a well-stocked shop but no real hotels; basic rooms can be found for about US$2.50 per person, camping is also possible at the mission (mosquito nets are necessary and anti-malarial pills advised). Take food, although there is one restaurant and locals may sell you dinner.

Aerotuy fly from Ciudad Bolívar (2 hours) on Thursday and from Santa Elena de Uairén on Monday. A co-operative of Pemón guides called *Macunaima Tours*, headed by Tito Abati, is based in Kamarata and can arrange *curiaras*, tents and porters for various excursions, but take your own food (guide Jorge Calcaño is very helpful). The whole area is within the Canaima National Park.

NB The local indigenous people have closed Auyán-Tepuy to climbers (since 1995). For details on the latest situation, contact *Alechiven*, run by Edith Rogge, which has a base and radio at Kamarata. T (014) 211828, F 217018.

Alechiven and *Macunaima Tours* run 6-day river trips from Kamarata to Angel Falls (May-December), descending the **Río Akanán** to the Carrao by motorized dugout then turning south up the 'Devil's Canyon' to the Falls; the tours continue downriver to Canaima. Tours cost about US$200 per person, and you need to supply your own food. River trips in this region are easier in the rainy season.

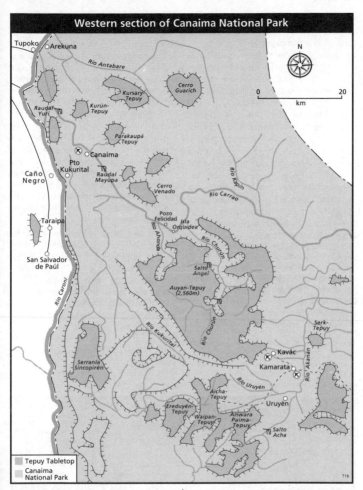

Western section of Canaima National Park

Tepuy Tabletop

Canaima National Park

KAVAC

Kavác, about a 2-hour walk northwest of Kamarata, is a new indigenous-run resort consisting of a dozen thatched huts (*churuatas*) for guests, a small shop, and an excitingly short airstrip serviced by Aerotuy prop-jets from Ciudad Bolívar and Isla Margarita (daily except Monday). These flights provide excellent views of Angel Falls and Auyán-Tepuy. There is a *carro* connection with Kamarata but it is expensive because all fuel has to be flown in.

The prime local excursion is to **Kavác Canyon** and its waterfall known as La Cueva, which can be reached by joining a group or by setting out early west up the Río Kavác, following the waterpipe installed by the fathers at Kamarata to provide the settlement with water from the falls. You come to a natural jacuzzi after a 30-minute wade/scramble along the sparkling stream, after which the gorge narrows dramatically until the falls are reached. It's best to go in the morning, to avoid groups of day trippers from Porlamar, and also because the sun's rays illuminate the vertical walls of the canyon only for a short time around 1100. Be prepared to get wet; bathing suits and shoes with good grip, plus a dry change of clothing are recommended, as is insect repellent, since there is a mosquito invasion around dusk. In the late afternoon winds off the savannah can make conditions chilly. Guide ropes have been installed where they are most needed along the river. There are pools and a further fall higher up the canyon but an Indian guide should be hired for this extension.

● **Tours to Kavác** A day excursion by light plane to Kavác from Canaima (45-minute flight) can be made with any of the tour operators at the airport; it costs around US$120 per person, depending on the number of passengers. Flight only from Ciudad Bolívar to Kavác or Kamarata costs US$65 per person one way. Trips from Ciudad Bolívar can be arranged with tour agencies in town (see page 288) or at the airport (see page 289). A 2 day/1 night tour to Kavác from Ciudad Bolívar costs around US$230 per person, including flight via Angel Falls, meals, and accommodation. A recommended Pemón guide in Kavác is Marino Sandoval, who works with *Excursiones Pemón* based in Kavác.

CIUDAD GUAYANA

In an area rich in natural resources, 105 km down-river from Ciudad Bolívar and 115 km east on an excellent paved highway, is **Ciudad Guayana** (*phone code* 086). This massive metropolis is a sprawl of factories, shopping malls, hastily-built housing, sports stadia and cement plants. Ciudad Guayana is really two separate towns; the old town of San Félix, beneath which lies the port, and the new town of Puerto Ordaz. Its population has already exceeded half of the planned million. The city straddles the mouth of the Río Caroní before it spills into the Orinoco. The mixing of the rivers' waters is like 'pouring cream into coffee'.

On the east bank of the Caroní is the commercial port of **San Félix**, where work is in progress to make a riverside walk and park, and the Palúa iron-ore terminal of the railway from El Pao. Across the Caroní by the 470m concrete bridge is **Puerto Ordaz**, which has an airport and the iron-ore loading port connected by rail with the famous Cerro Bolívar open-cast iron mine. Puerto Ordaz is reputed to be the richest place per square metre in Venezuela. Big cars cruise the wide boulevards, blasting out salsa music, and the streets are full of smart,

San Félix

Hotels:
1. *Aguila*
2. *Yolí*

determined revellers, while in the sleepy suburbs TV satellite dishes, iron window bars, padlocks and guard dogs are a feature of everyday life. Money is made and spent quickly and easily here. The precious assets of Guayana – gold, diamonds, topaz, jasper, bauxite, iron and water from the huge hydro-electric plants of the Caroní – are all turned into products which create the money to fill the many

The search for El Dorado

Sir Walter Raleigh will forever be associated with the introduction of tobacco to Elizabethan England in the early 1580s from the newly-settled province of Virginia in the United States. But Raleigh was also obsessed with the idea of finding the mythical golden city of El Dorado. By the time of his voyage to South America in 1595 he was already 40 years old, out of favour with Queen Elizabeth and deep in debt. His motivation for undertaking such a risky venture may have been to restore his damaged reputation but he was also determined to bring an end to the Spanish domination of the region.

Raleigh's interest in El Dorado had been fired by a certain Spanish gentleman, Don Pedro Sarmiento de Gamboa, an old American campaigner who had been captured by two pirate ships owned by Raleigh and brought to England, where he told Raleigh of El Dorado, which he claimed was an empire of Inca refugees from Peru.

Raleigh believed El Dorado to be in the Guayana Highlands, on the shores of a lake, at a point roughly 150 miles south of the confluence of the Caroní and Orinoco rivers. This belief was fostered by another Spaniard, Don Antonio de Berrio, who had been searching the area.

In May 1595, Raleigh reached the Venezuelan mainland on the Paría peninsula and found a suitable entrance into the great Orinoco delta at a place now called Boca Bagre, or Catfish Bay. The expedition progressed up the river, but lasted no more than a few months. It effectively ended at the confluence of the Orinoco and Caroní Rivers when an encounter with the chief of the local Pemón tribe led Raleigh to abandon his search. The chief told him of the occupation of Guayana by a strange and powerful tribe who had migrated into the region early in the 16th century. The chief warned Raleigh that they may have been Incas with an inpregnable outpost, defended by 3,000 troops, Raleigh withdrew, but at least it saved him the indignity of having his theory proved wrong.

His obsession was not over, however. Indeed, it could be said that Raleigh lost his head over El Dorado – literally. In 1617 he secured Royal permission for a second voyage to the New World, despite being imprisoned in the Tower of London for his alleged part in a conspiracy against King James I. The second expedition was a complete fiasco and Raleigh returned to England not only a broken man, but also facing certain death. He had broken his promise to the king of not engaging in battle with the Spanish during the expedition and was duly beheaded on 29 October 1618.

Sir Walter Raleigh

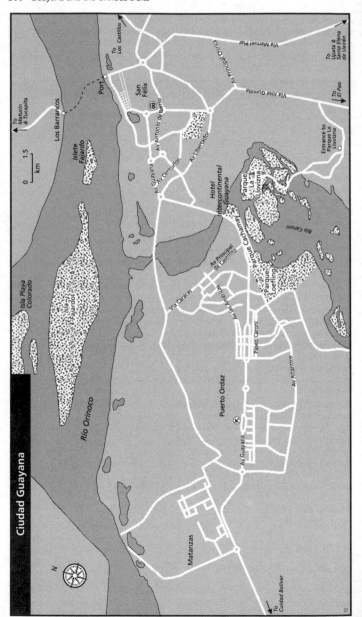

Ciudad Guayana

shiny, new shopping malls with every top brand name under the sun.

Ciudad Guayana may not be the most pleasant of places to spend time, but it's perfectly situated for trips south to the Gran Sabana, or east to the Orinoco Delta.

PLACES OF INTEREST

The iron-tinted waterfall in the pretty **Parque Cachamay** is worth a visit. The park is 20 minutes' walk from the centre, and closes at 1700. To the west are the government-owned *Siderúrgica del Orinoco* whose production is being raised to 4.8 million tonnes of steel a year, and an aluminium plant, *Venalum*. An excellent tour is offered by *Alcasa*, another aluminium producer, T 99343 (wear long trousers), they can be reached either from Ciudad Guayana or Ciudad Bolívar (US$1.40, bus from terminal, 1 hour).

EXCURSIONS

Just up the Caroní is the Macagua hydroelectric plant (with a second phase under construction). There are some truly beautiful cataracts called **Salto Llovizna** (*llovizna* means spray) as you enter the grounds of the plant, which is known as **Parque La Llovizna**. The park is reached by bus from San Félix most of the way, then hitch.

Higher up the river is the massive **Guri dam** and hydroelectric undertaking (see page 51). The trip to Guri takes 90 minutes by taxi; the plant is open daily 0900-1030 and 1415-1515. For a conducted tour (no pun intended), phone Edelca, Puerto Ordaz 20-80-66 (Relaciones Institucionales del Guri); there 4 daily tours of 1 hour. Note that the area gets very full during holidays, Easter or carnival. You can also visit the rest of the complex including the hotel (**C**, air conditioning, comfortable). Camping is also possible outside the entrance with permission. To get there, take a *por puesto* from Ciudad Bolívar, Route 70, US$12.50 one way; for the return trip, ask at Alcabala Río Claro (gatehouse) if they can get you a free lift. Excursion buses go from the main offices in the park

at 1300 and 1500 (take your passport). If there's no public transport, take a Ciudad Bolívar-Ciudad Guayana bus to Km 70 and take a taxi from there to Río Claro.

To **Cerro Bolívar** mine, take a *por puesto* (US$5.60) or hitchhike to Ciudad Piar (see page 290), or go with a guided tour organized by Ferrominera Orinoco at their headquarters building in Ciudad Guayana. Tours are free, and leave Ciudad Piar at 0900 and 1400. To visit other industries in the area, ask at the Corporación Venezolana de Guayana, Departmento de Relaciones Públicas, or Sidor, T 907534. Do not expect immediate permission and check if you need your own vehicle.

From San Félix or Puerto Ordaz you can go down the Orinoco to **Los Castillos** There are two old forts here: one is on a huge rock near the water, the other on top of a hill, and both are in good condition. A tiny village (*population* 500) lies at their feet. It is said to have been here that Sir Walter Raleigh's son was killed in battle while searching for El Dorado. You can get to Los Castillos either by *por puesto* (1 hour, US$1.50), or by bus to Aceiles (US$0.35), ask to be let off where the pick-up goes to Los Castillos (at 0700, 1130, 1530, returning at 0830, 1300 and 1700, US$1); it's difficult to get there by boat. It is possible to camp on the beach.

LOCAL INFORMATION

● **Accommodation**

Hotel prices

L1	over US$200	**L2**	US$151-200
L3	US$101-150	**A1**	US$81-100
A2	US$61-80	**A3**	US$46-60
B	US$31-45	**C**	US$21-30
D	US$12-20	**E**	US$7-11
F	US$4-6	**G**	up to US$3

Those marked with an asterisk (*) are bookable through Fairmont International (see under Caracas).

In Puerto Ordaz: **L2** *Intercontinental Guayana**, Parque Punta Vista, PO Box 293, T 222244, F 222253, next to Parque Cachamay, all facilities, lacks character, pool, they organize boat trips for US$32 per boat (12 passengers), or US$8.50 per person.

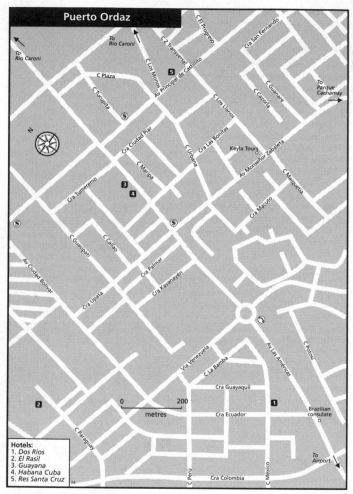

Puerto Ordaz

To Rio Caroni

To Rio Caroni

To Parque Cachamay

C El Progreso
Cra San Fernando
C2 Transversal
Av Principal de Castillito
C Los Monos
C Plaza
C Tucupita
5
C Guanare
C Los Llanos
C Cazoria
Cra Ciudad Piar
C Uhana
Cra Las Bonitas
Keyla Tours
C Maripa
3
4
Av Monsenor Zabaleta
Cra Maiquetia
Cra Tumeremo
C Guasipati
C Callao
Cra Macuto
C Upata
Cra Palmar
Cra Kavanayén
Av Ciudad Bolívar
Via Venezuela
C La Bamba
Av Las Américas
C Potoi
2
Cra Guayaquil
1
Brazilian consulate
C Paraguay
Cra Ecuador
To Airport
C Peru
C Mexico
Cra Colombia

0 — 200
metres

Hotels:
1. Dos Ríos
2. El Rasil
3. Guayana
4. Habana Cuba
5. Res Santa Cruz

B *El Rasil*, Centro Cívico, with all comforts, pool, intermittent hot water, car hire rep is helpful; **B** *Dos Ríos*, México esquina Ecuador, T 220679, shower, air conditioning, has seen better days, helpful.

E *Habana Cuba*, Avenida Las Américas, air conditioning, their tour agency organizes trips to the Orinoco delta; **E** *Guayana**, Avenida Las Américas, air conditioning, no hot water, unfriendly, OK value; **E** *Motel Los Faroles*, 1 km south on the 4-lane highway to Upata, air conditioning, immaculate rooms and grounds;

E *Turista*, Avenida Caracas, basic. Rolf and Rosa Kampen offer bed and breakfast at Calle Surinam 03-07, Villa Antillana, 3 km from central Pto Ordaz, T 220593, no buses, so take a taxi, **E**, breakfast US$1.30, restaurant serves Bavarian food, Rolf speaks English, German and Dutch, recommended.

F *Residencial Santa Cruz*, Avenida Principal de Castillito, opposite Gen Electric, fan, also short-stay.

In San Félix: only **D** *Aguila* and *Yoli* (no hot water, otherwise OK) have decent restaurants;

also **D-E** *Mucuchíes*, Avenida Moreno de Mendoza, by Cine Caroní, some rooms have TV and air conditioning, noisy but OK.

● **Places to eat**

There is a very good *churrascaría* restaurant 15 minutes' walk from *Hotel Guayana* towards the airport, in an old hacienda building on the left, next to a *cervecería*, very good food, recommended.

● **Banks & money changers**

Banco Consolidado (American Express), Calle Urbana, Edificio Don Andrés. **Banco Unión** for Visa. Banks will not exchange Brazilian currency.

● **Embassies & consulates**

Brazilian Consulate, Avenida Las Américas, near CANTV, T 227246, 0900-1700, friendly, helpful, visa issued in 1 hour, no onward ticket requested (some nationalities have to pay, eg Australians US$45), good information.

● **Shopping**

Bookshop: *Librería Orinoco*, Centro Cívico Puerto Ordaz, international magazines and English paperbacks. The Casa Machupicchu, Calle Guaspati, sells a city map.

● **Tour companies & travel agents**

Lobo Tours, Calle Zambia No 2, Villa Africana Manzana 39, Puerto Ordaz, T 616286, F 617708, Wolfgang Loffler organizes trips to Río Paragua, well-organized, excellent cooking, recommended for excursions south of the Orinoco; *Keyla Tours*, Avenida Monseñor Zabalete y Los Llanos, T 229195, F 226123, camping trips to the Gran Sabana, excellent guides, including Steve from the USA, strongly recommended (US$280 per person, 3 nights, 4 days, all inclusive). Also recommended are *Selva Tours*, T 225537/225044, for trips to the Gran Sabana; guides Carlos Quintero (T/F 622480) and Eleazer (T 612867) also act freelance. *Piranha Tours*, at *Hotel Intercontinental*, run good river trips, US$10 per person, to nearby falls and the meeting of Caroní and Orinoco, etc. A recommended guide is *Richard Brandt*, T/F 224370 (or in Santa Elena de Uairén, T 220078/226813), has his own car, speaks English and tailors trips to your requirements, including Roraima, from US$50-80 per person a day.

● **Transport**

Local Car hire: many different operators are based at the airport; Puma cars are recommended, and Hertz rents 4WD vehicles. A car is very useful in this area, especially for visiting the Cerro Bolívar mine and Guri dam. **Taxis**: San Félix-Puerto Ordaz US$1.50, Puerto Ordaz-airport US$2, airport-bus terminal US$7.50, San Félix bus terminal-Puerto Ordaz bus terminal US$3.50, bus terminal-town centre US$1.80, town centre-San Félix bus terminal US$2.50.

Air Daily flights depart from Puerto Ordaz to Caracas, Maracaibo and Barcelona; there are also flights to Porlamar, Valencia, Maturín, San Antonio, Santa Elena and Canaima. Aeropostal fly to Port of Spain and Barbados (T (086) 511147/51211, F 518737). From the airport, walk 600m to the gas station on the main road for buses to San Félix or Puerto Ordaz.

Buses The terminal is at San Félix. Minibuses are fast, frequent and cheap; San Félix-Puerto Ordaz, US$0.50; buses run until about 2100. Buses to **Santa Elena de Uairén** (via El Callao), at 0500, 0730, 0800 and 1900, US$9, 10 hours (or overnight bus, which misses the fine scenery, 9 hours). To **Tumeremo** (US$2.50) **El Dorado** (US$3.60) and **Km 88**, book a day in advance. *Por puesto* to **Ciudad Bolívar** US$3.60 (bus US$1.50); bus to **Maturín** US$4, 2½ hours; to **Caracas**, US$10, 10½ hours. To **Barcelona** and **Puerto La Cruz**, 8 a day; to **Cumaná**, 4 a day. To **Tucupita**, US$5 with Expresos Guayanesa at 0730 and 1400, 3 hours (including the 30 minute ferry crossing to Los Barrancos), the booking office opens 1 hour before departure, be there early. There's a passport check just before Tucupita.

River A free passenger ferry crosses to Los Barrancos. A taxi Puerto Ordaz-ferry costs US$3, or take a micro from the bus terminal (not very safe). The return trip takes about 1 hour.

ORINOCO DELTA

The Orinoco, which in the local *Warao* language means 'father of our land', has formed over time into one of the largest deltas in the world, covering an area of over 40,000 sq km (roughly the size of the Netherlands) in the far northeast of Venezuela. It is a region of wild forests, humid jungles and mangrove swamps, where the great Orinoco splits into a tangle of rivers, channels and estuaries carrying the waters of this great river to one or other of its more than 70 major mouths. The main part of the river continues east and pours out into the Atlantic at Boca Grande, near the Guayanan border. Northwards the river breaks into a mass of meandering channels which terminate in the bocas chicas, or little mouths. The delta, strangely enough, is named after the Amacuro River, which flows northwest from the mountains on the southern side of the Orinoco to merge with the great river.

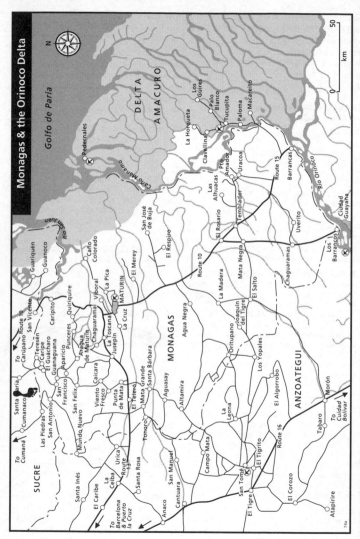

The Delta Amacuro, as it is officially known, is still inhabited by the *Warao* people, who have adapted so well to their particular environment that they are said to learn to swim and paddle a canoe before they can even walk. They have been preserved as an ethnic group thanks to the difficulties of travelling and living in the delta and by its lack of precious commodities. The *Warao* are famed as canoe-makers, or *curiara*, as they are called. In fact, *Warao* means 'people of the boat'. All others, outsiders, are called *Hotarao* – 'people of the land'. If you take a tour from Tucupita into the heart of the delta, you'll see the traditional *Warao* dwellings, called *palafitos*, which are open-sided buildings of wood and palm-thatch raised up on stilts.

TRAVEL TO THE DELTA

The main point of access to the delta is the town of **Tucupita**. From **Los Barrancos** on the north bank of the Orinoco opposite **San Félix**, head north on Route 10 for 68 km to the turn-off for **Temblador**, an expensive oil town with a few hotels and *posadas* which are all about double the price of the rest of the country. From Temblador, head south on Route 15 for 54 km to **Hato Flor del Orinoco**, just before **Barrancas** (see page 307). This is the turn-off for Tucupita, 53 km further on to the northeast. Tucupita can also be reached south from **Maturín** (see page 303).

Ciudad Guayana is ideally placed for a trip to the Orinoco Delta. From **Los Barrancos**, on the north bank of the Orinoco, opposite San Félix, *curiaras* and other boats can be taken to the delta. You should settle prices before setting out, also take a hammock, mosquito net and repellent, and canned food (in the rainy season, take a waterproof).

TUCUPITA

The main population centre on the delta, and the only notable town of any size, is **Tucupita** (*population* 81,820; *phone code* 087), standing on the banks of the Caño Manamo. Though capital of Delta Amacuro state and the main commercial centre of the delta, there's a one-horse feel about it. It's a fiercely hot and humid place, where the local pastime is to sit on a bench under the shade of a tree and watch the world go by. There's very little to do here, other than arrange a tour into the delta, and that's probably just as well, as it's far too hot to do anything anyway. It's the kind of place where you hang

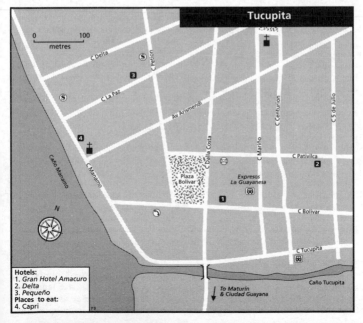

Tucupita

Hotels:
1. Gran Hotel Amacuro
2. Delta
3. Pequeño
Places to eat:
4. Capri

To Maturín & Ciudad Guayana

Caño Tucupita

around in banks just to enjoy the blast of air conditioning, and that's about all you can do in the banks here, as they won't change travellers' cheques.

Local information

● **Accommodation**

E *Gran Hotel Amacuro*, Calle Bolívar 23, air conditioning, big rooms, OK; **E** *Delta*, Calle Pativilca 28, air conditioning, basic; **E-F** *Pequeño*, Calle La Paz, fan, good value, safe, stores luggage, closes at 2200.

● **Places to eat**

Mi Tasca, Calle Dalla Costa, popular, varied menu, large portions, highly recommended. On Calle Manamo is *Refresquería La Cascada*, English spoken; and *Capri*, which is very good.

● **Tourist offices**

At Calle Dalla Costa beside Sonido Color 2000. Tourists should go here first for information on tours.

● **Transport**

Buses *Por puesto* from **Maturín** about US$6, 2-3 hours; bus to Maturín, US$3 with Expresos Guayanesa, 1100, 3-4 hours. To San Félix at 0730 with Expreso La Guayanesa, 3 hours, US$5. To **Caracas**, 10 hours, 2000, US$10; **Puerto La Cruz** at 0730 and 1400, US$6, 6 hours.

DELTA TRIPS

For a 3-4 day trip to see the delta, its fauna and the indigenous *Warao*, either arrange boats through the tourist office, or contact Juan Carrión. All the taxi drivers know him, but he is very expensive. Boats are not easy to come by and are expensive, except for large groups, but bargain hard and prices may drop considerably.

Recent favourable reports have been received for the following Romero Ildemaro (ask at *Bar Warauno*, or Calle Tucupita 19), he charges US$40 per person per day, in basic but watertight accommodation, with good food, hammocks and mosquito nets.

Raúl at the *Gran Hotel Amacuro* runs a 1-day trip for up to four persons, including food and drink and a visit to a *Warao* village.

Abelardo of *Delta Tours*, Calle Bolívar, is also recommended for trips deeper into the region, US$60 per person, the owner, Toni, is from the USA and has his own lodge in the delta, he charges US$85 per person per day (with reductions for backpackers).

Aventura Turística Delta SA, Calle Centurión, No 62, T (087) 211391, run 1-5 day trips to the delta, Nicolás and Vidalig are very helpful, they speak French and English, and charge US$85 per person per day, or US$65 per person per day for more than four.

Wakeriana Tours and Paradise Camp is 4 hours by boat from Tucupita; accommodation in private and shared rooms, shared bath, typical meals, tours to *Warao* settlements, general manager is Danielle Homsiova. Contact them at: Calle Pativilca 21, Tucupita, T/F 087-210224.

Viaje a la Naturaleza, Calle Mariño 23, run by Trinidadian Yance, he charges US$40 per person per day and is recommended.

Some boat owners visit hotels in the evenings looking for clients and may negotiate a price.

NB The quality of some guides is poor and trips are expensive. Some guides are reported to pester visitors as soon as they get off the bus; bargain hard and never pay up front. There are other guides from Ciudad Guayana whose boats are unsuitable and whose services are untrustworthy. For shorter excursions by boat, ask at the gas station (*bomba*) by the river, but you won't see much in a day. Excursions often only travel on the main river, not in the caños where wildlife can be seen.

LA HORQUETA

Instead of taking a tour from Tucupita, you can take a *por puesto* from Plaza Bolívar to the peaceful village of **La Horqueta** on the banks of the Orinoco (US$0.35, 45 minutes), where it is easier to get a boat. There are no hotels here, but there are shops selling drinks and dry foodstuffs. Be warned, if the river level rises after a downpour, arrangements may be cancelled. On all trips agree in advance exactly what is included, especially food and hammocks. Make sure there is enough food and water for you and your guide. Hammocks and mosquito repellents are essential. You can buy hammocks and local handicrafts.

Passports must be shown leaving La Horqueta. Ask permission before taking people's photos.

At the mouth of the Caño Manamo in the Boca Bagre (Catfish Bay) is **Pernales**, the only town on the delta coast. It's a small place, straggled along the bay, with only boats and bicycles for transport. The edge of town just sort of peters out into the surrounding swamps. There's an airport at Pedernales, but we have no information on flights, if indeed there are any.

BARRANCAS

10 km beyond the turn-off for Tucupita is **Barrancas** (*population* 13,000), on the banks of the Orinoco at the very apex of the delta. Founded in 1530, it is one of the oldest settlements in the Americas, and is an interesting and friendly place to visit. Barrancas has a large community of Guyanese people who speak English. It is possible to take a boat to the *Warao* village of **Curiapo** and **Amacuro** (near the Guyana border); check at the harbour.

It is also possible to go to Georgetown in Guyana from here. Ask for boats to Amacuro. The trip to Bellavista, Cangrejito or San José de Amacuro, all at the mouth of the Orinoco, takes 12 hours, then onto Mabaruma; but this is only for the adventurous. Check with the lady at the *librería* on the river at the bottom of the village; she is from Georgetown and travels there occasionally. The trip from Barrancas to Georgetown is likely to take 3-4 days.

Warning Avoid boats that are carrying suspicious goods, those that do not have adequate shelter from the rain and those that do not stop in Curiapo, as this is the only place to get an exit stamp out of Venezuela.

● **Accommodation F-G** *Hospedaje San Judas*, near the church, with shower, basic, small rooms but safe and good value; next door is a cheap restaurant, run by a helpful Guyanese woman.

● **Transport** Barrancas can be reached by road from Tucupita (63 km, US\$1); buses to Tucupita leave at 0945 and 1700. A bus leaves for Maturín daily at 0800 with Expresos Maturín.

SOUTH FROM CIUDAD GUAYANA

The main route south to the Gran Sabana and the border with Brazil, Route 10, leaves Ciudad Guayana as a 4-lane *autopista*.

UPATA

The 4-lane *autopista* ends 56 km south at **Upata** (*population* 51,500), the first major town. There's a good place to buy provisions opposite the petrol station.

● **Accommodation D** *Andrea**, Plaza Miranda, credit cards accepted, restaurant, safe parking, good; **E** *Adriático*, good; **E** *Comercio*, Calle Ayacucho, excellent, as is its restaurant. **NB** Water is rationed in Upata and hot water in hotels is rare south of Ciudad Guayana.

ROUTES From Upata to Km 88 the road is resurfaced and widened with broad hard shoulders. 104 km south of Upata is **Guasipati** (*population* 8,600), where there is accommodation at **C** *Hotel La Reina*, air conditioning, good; also **E** *Hotel Venezuela*.

EL CALLAO

18 km beyond Guasipati is **El Callao** on the south bank of the Río Yuruari, off the highway. It's a small, clean, bright town (*population* 7,400) whose Trinidadian inhabitants add a touch of calypso to its pre-Lenten carnival. A plant reprocesses the old gold mine tailings from El Perú, 8 km away, but the centre of gold mining has moved to Km 88 and Las Claritas (see below). The gold mine can be visited, the director will show you around. The town has many jewellery shops and several restaurants.

● **Accommodation D** *Isidora*, air conditioning, on the road to El Perú but still in town; **E** *Italia*, 10 rooms, in the centre of town; **E** *Ritz*, on same street as the post office, basic, serves cold beer; **F** *Callao*, Calle Bolívar, two blocks from the plaza, shared bath, laundry facilities, very welcoming owners, recommended. **NB** There is a chronic water shortage, check when it is available in your hotel.

● **Banks & money changers** You may be able to change cash dollars in Banco de Venezuela on the main plaza, but not travellers' cheques.

TUMEREMO

Another 41 km further on is **Tumeremo** (*population* 9,100), recommended as the best place to buy provisions and all grades

South from Ciudad Guayana to the Gran Sabana

1. Cueva del Elefante
2. Piedra de la Virgen
3. Danto Falls
4. Monumento al Soldado Pionero
5. Torón-Merú
6. Chinak-Merú
7. Karuari-Merú
8. Kama-Merú
9. Quebrada de Jaspe
10. Roraima

of gasoline are on sale at a normal price (better than El Dorado). 5 km from Tumeremo towards the Fuerte Tarabay is the beautiful artificial lake of San Pedro with free campsite.

● **Accommodation & places to eat** D *Cacique*, very good, noisy, excellent shower, recommended; D *Miranda*, OK, better than some of the others; E *Leocar*, next to the bus-stop, OK, with bathroom, fan or air conditioning, some rooms with fridges, restaurant recommended; **E** *Central*, near the plaza, fan, good, bakery and snackbar; **F** *Hospedaje Tumeremo*, on Calle El Dorado, fan, clean bathroom, good. *El Esturión*, Calle El Dorado, Edificio Bolívar, good, friendly restaurant; *Restaurante Turístico* expensive but OK, does not serve yucca with everything (is that a good or a bad thing?); *Restaurante Las Cuevas*, near the plaza, medium priced, very popular, food is average, service slow, check your bill.

● **Banks & money changers** Banco Unión, for Visa; *Banco de Orinoco*, for Amex, but only after 1500, US$5 commission.

● **Buses** To Santa Elena, US$8.75, 8-10 hours, Líneas Orinoco departs at 1100, two blocks from the plaza near *Hotel Leocar*; El Dorado, US$1.10, 1½ hours; Ciudad Bolívar, US$5.25, 6 buses a day, 6½ hours or *por puesto* (via San Félix and Puerto Ordaz); bus to San Félix (Ciudad Guayana), US$2.50, *por puesto* US$5; bus Tumeremo-**Caracas**, US$35. A direct bus to Caracas departs at 1600 and takes 14 hours.

FRONTIER WITH GUYANA

From Tumeremo you can go to the **Isla de Anacoco**, on the Río Venamo, which forms the border with Guyana. A paved road runs through the jungle to San Martín (one military and one police post en route), where you can arrange a visit to the island. Most people speak English in San Martín. The area around San Martín is a mining area and there are few tourists.

● **Immigration**

Get a Venezuelan exit stamp before reaching the border and a Guyanese entry stamp at the earliest opportunity.

● **River transport to Guyana**

From San Martín boats go to Nuevo Maico on the Río Cuyuní, US$0.12 for the fast boat (1½ hours), and US$0.07 for the slow boat (3 hours). Dugouts (*piragua*) go from Nuevo Maico to Puerto Dedos, or Soledad at 0400, 0900, 1300 and 1800, 1 hour, US$0.20, from where you can travel to Bartika, 4 hours, US$7 (boats leave at 0700 and 1200). In Bartika transport can be arranged to Georgetown (eg on horseback to Parika, US$4, then by road).

EL DORADO

278 km from Ciudad Guayana and 76 km from Tumeremo is **El Dorado** (*population* 4,000), 7 km off the road on the Río Cuyuní. It's a hot, dirty and very noisy miners' supply centre in dense forest. Owing to the government policy of leasing mining concessions to foreign consortia,

After the gold rush

The original El Dorado was not a place, but a person: the 'golden man' featured in a ritual of the Chibcha in the Andes of Colombia. Europeans transformed him into a golden king living in a golden palace at the centre of a kingdom of untold wealth. Not surprisingly, El Dorado proved elusive. Nevertheless, the rush to find the real stuff in the Guayana Highlands has brought real wealth to many. For centuries people have been panning for gold in them there hills.

European prospecting began somewhere around the end of the 16th century with prospectors using the already established missions in the region as a base. It was not until the middle of the 19th century, though, that the first major strike was recorded by a German prospector at Tupuquén, north of the Yuarari River, near present-day El Callao. Rumours that he immediately placed a huge beach towel over the site are unfounded, but he did christen it Nueva Providencia.

By the early 1880s there were over 8,000 settlers in the area. The richest mines, around El Callao, were producing over 15 tonnes of gold a year (about US$200 million at today's prices). Venezuela was, in fact, the largest gold producer in the world, until it was overtaken by South Africa at the end of the 19th century.

Gold prospecting still goes on across the uplands of southern Venezuela, with all its attendant ecological problems, and many of the mining towns still have a frontier feel. Others, though, have become little more than ghost towns. Successive governments have leased mining concessions to foreign consortia, thus forcing small-scale miners to look elsewhere in search of their own El Dorado.

most of the small-scale miners have been forced out, and El Dorado now relies for its existence mainly on its gas station (open 0800-1900, daily).

On an island in the river stands the infamous prison which once held the famous French jail-breaker, Henri Charriere, better known as 'Papillon', in 1945. The prison is in use again after renovation. It is possible to get police permission to cross the river (free) and land on the island. The accompanying officer is full of interesting information.

● **Accommodation** NB All hotels in El Dorado have problems with running water. **D** *San Antonio*, Edificio Ceferino, next to the bus stop, electricity intermittent, the owner prefers to let by the hour, fan; **E** *Hospedaje Portugal*, 6 rooms, the Portuguese owner also runs the store next door; **F** *Mirador*, basic, noisy at weekends but good; *Alfonso*, quite good, will take you to visit the mines; **F** *El Dorado*, with bath, very large rooms, fan; **F** *El Valle*, basic, safe, recommended.

● **Places to eat** *La Brasa*, on the left when entering the town, excellent food but small portions; *Archiven*, Plaza Bolívar, good, helpful owner. The restaurant beside the church serves delicious 'criolla vegetarian' food.

● **Banks & money changers** There is no bank, but exchange is possible with the gold buyer on the main street; cash only, poor rates.

● **Tour companies & travel agents** Contact Carlos at *Hotel San Antonio* for boat trips on the Río Cuyuní, US$25 per person per day, maximum 5 people, local guide. Boat trips can be taken 12 km up the Chicanán River to a gold camp for US$15, or other road excursions to miners' camps for US$7.

● **Buses** From Caracas, Expresos del Oriente, at 1830 daily, US$12, 14½ hours (925 km),

return at 1400. The Orinoco bus line connects with Ciudad Bolívar (6 hours) and Santa Elena, as does Transmundial; the latter has better buses, leaving at 1100, US$5.40 to Santa Elena, US$3.60 to San Félix, 4 hours. From El Dorado a bus runs to San Martín on the Guyanese border (see above). All buses stop on the main plaza.

SOUTH FROM EL DORADO

The turn-off to El Dorado is marked Km 0; distances south are measured from here by green signs 1 km apart. 6 km south of the turnoff to El Dorado, is the bridge over the Río Cuyuní. From here it is possible to take boat trips to the gold mines; eg Payapal, 1 hour 40 minutes each way, US$25 for boat, a beautiful trip. Payapal can also be visited by car, leaving from the plaza in El Dorado every hour or so; 30-minute journey, US$8 return. The people are friendly and will let you look into the 30m deep mines. South from here the roadside is dotted with tiny indigenous villages – San Miguel de Betania, Arai-matepuí – and subsistence level farms.

There's accommodation at Km 70; **E** *La Mentañita*, with cabins, and campsite (US$6), clean, good bathrooms, cold water, bar, restaurant, good.

LAS CLARITAS

At Km 85 is another gold-digging village, **Las Claritas**. This, and other settlements like it, is built out of oil cans and other rubbish, but comes complete with hotels, restaurants, small shops, hairdressers, brothels, etc. The miners guard their claims and diggings jealously, so in order to avoid suspicion, it's best to go with a

A zone of contention

↜ The Venezuelan gold rush of the 1880s attracted many British companies, some of which still have a stake in the area. At this time the British government, not surprisingly, renewed its claim to parts of Venezuela adjacent to British Guyana. The Venezuelan Boundary Commission searched for historical precedents to Britain's territorial claim and found in their favour in 1890. As a result, the frontier of British Guyana was extended to the west of the Essequibo River.

Venezuela, not surprisingly, does not recognize the boundary change and on modern maps of the region the addition to British Guyana is designated a 'Zona en Reclamación'. The people who live in this zone, which covers nearly 50,000 sq miles, may have Guyanese passports but are considered *de facto* Venezuelan citizens.

guide or friendly local. If you're visiting independent miners at work, ask permission to take photos, and take a small gift.

● **Accommodation & places to eat** C *Campamento Turístico Anaconda*, cabins with shower, toilet, fan, well-furnished, with bar, table football and snooker, includes breakfast and dinner, run by Larri Master, who speaks English, but it's reserved for tour groups. There's also a restaurant, a big market for food and gold and safe parking at the Las Hermanitas de las Pobres Convent, which can be better reached by the track from Km 88.

KM 88 (SAN ISIDRO)

At **Km 88** (also called **San Isidro**) there is gasoline (rarely 92 octane – the last before Santa Elena), a garage, the last telephone before Santa Elena and Banco Guayana. Everything here is expensive; there are better food shops at Km 85.

● **Accommodation & places to eat**: **D** *El Parador del Viajero*, restaurant, OK; **F** *La Pilonera*, opposite the Vargas store, with fan, safe parking, some rooms with bath, overpriced, restaurant with good fruit drinks; there's good food and a wide choice next door at the *Fuente de Soda*; *Restaurant Internacional*, grotty exterior but excellent and cheap. Rooms for rent, **F**, with bathroom, fan, clean, ask at the *farmacia*. Also at Km 88 is *Barquilla de Fresa*, owner Henry Cleeve speaks English and German, accommodation in bunk beds, good food, US$40 per day, nearby are trails for hiking and early morning bird-watching, car parking, safe.

● **Transport** Bus Km 88-Caracas, US$10.50; to Ciudad Bolívar wait at the gas station for buses from Las Claritas (depart at 0900, 1100, 1500 and 1800). Frequent *por puestos* run from El Dorado to Km 88, 1 hour, US$2. The only reliable public transport out of Km 88 is the bus from Ciudad Bolívar, which stops at 1400 daily; it's 6 hours to Santa Elena, US$4.50. The alternative is to get a ride with passing jeeps and trucks (very little passes after 1030).

THE GRAN SABANA

The road south to the Brazilian border at Santa Elena de Uairén passes over the beautiful Gran Sabana and is completely paved, with all bridges in place. Characteristic of this area are the large abrupt *tepuys*, hundreds of waterfalls, and the silence of one of the oldest plateaus on earth. The landscape is essentially savannah, with clusters of trees, moriche palms and bromeliads. This region is very sparsely populated and is protected as part of the **Canaima National Park**, which extends west across the Gran Sabana to the Río Caroní and includes Angel Falls and Canaima Lagoon (see **Canaima National Park**, page 291).

Camping is possible in the Gran Sabana but a tent with good waterproofing is essential (see also under **Canaima National Park**). There is plenty of firewood should you wish to spend a night under the stars, but nights are very cool. Insect repellent and long-sleeved/trousered clothes are needed against *puri-puri* – small, black, vicious biting insects, which you will come to hate more than anything else in the world, believe me – and mosquitoes (especially in El Dorado, at Km 88 and at Icabarú). Use baby oil mixed with vitamin B12. To camp in the park, a permit must be bought at Inparques in Ciudad Bolívar (see page 288); it costs US$1.30 per person per night.

Tours 5-day/4-night tours of the Gran Sabana can be arranged in Caracas (US$300, including hotel, food, excursions, eg *Passarini-Suárez*, Centro Comercial Los Altos, San Antonio de Los Altos, T 032-711327). But tours of the Gran Sabana are cheaper and easier from Ciudad Bolívar (see under **Tour companies** in Ciudad Bolívar, page 288).

Driving to the Brazilian Border

The road is in very good condition and presents no problem for conventional cars. 4WD is only necessary if you wander off the main road, particularly in the rainy season. It is highly recommended to take spare tanks of gasoline (spare tanks are available at Km 88, but better and cheaper to get one earlier). All petrol pumps have fuel, but not all octane levels. It is also advisable to carry extra water and plenty of food. There are police checks at the Río Cuyuní and at Km 126, and at a military check at San Ignacio de Yuruaní all driving permits, car registration papers, and identification must be shown. If hitchhiking note that if you're dropped away from a 'base' there will be no shade.

SOUTH FROM KM 88

The wall of the Gran Sabana looms above Km 88 and the highway climbs steeply in sharp curves for 40 km before reaching the top.

At Km 100 the huge **Piedra de la Virgen** (sandy coloured with black streaks) is passed before the steepest climb (La Escalera) enters the beautiful **Canaima National Park**, 30,000 sq km in size and one of the six largest parks in the world. There are good views, especially at sunrise, 100m west of the road at Km 102; note that the trail can be slippery.

At Km 119 (sign can only be seen going north) a short trail leads to the 40m **Danto ('Tapir') Falls**, a powerful fall wreathed in mosses and mist. If you are paying for your ride, try to persuade the driver to make a short stop. The falls are close to the road (about 5 minutes slippery walk down on the left hand side), but not visible from it. Buses cannot be flagged down here because of dangerous bends.

More fine views can be had at Km 135. The **Monumento al Soldado Pionero** (Km 137) commemorates the army engineers who built the road up from the lowlands, which was finally opened in 1973. There are barbecues, toilets and shelters.

Luepa is 4 km beyond. All travellers must stop at the *ciudadela* (military checkpoint) a little way south. There is a popular camping place at Luepa, on the right

Chinak-Merú Falls

going south, which belongs to a tour company. An informative guide on duty will rent you a tent or you can hang a hammock in an open-sided shelter (very cold at night, no water or facilities, possible to buy meal from tour group but expensive). There is a breakfast place, US$4.

KAVANAYEN

8 km beyond Luepa, a graded gravel road leads 70 km west to **Kavanayén**. There is little traffic on this road, so it's best to have your own vehicle with high clearance, especially during the wet season; and take plenty of snacks. The settlement is surrounded by *tepuys*. Bargain with pilots at the airstrip to fly you over the Gran Sabana. A tour of Auyán-Tepuy, Angel Falls, Canaima and back to Kavanayén is around US$200 for 5 passengers.

● **Accommodation & services** 18 km before Kavanayén is a rough road to the **E** *Hotel Chivaton*, good beds but icy water, no food, very isolated, recommended. There's also accommodation in Kavanayén at the Franciscan mission, **G**, very friendly, also in private homes. You can cash travellers' cheques here at a better rate than in Santa Elena. One of the 2 grocery stores will prepare food, or the restaurant opposite serves cheap breakfasts and dinners, order in advance. There's a medical post near the airstrip.

25 km down the road to Kavanayén, turn right down another side road for 17 km to the falls of **Torón-Merú**. The road is almost impassable for a normal car, is hell for cyclists, and at the end is a river, impassable even for 4WD. You must continue on foot, but the falls are hard to find.

Further on the same road is a left turn at Km 30 to the falls of **Chinak-Merú**, 110m high and very impressive. Take the trail to the Río Aponguao and the very friendly Pemón village of **Iboribó**; pay US$4 to cross the river and then walk 45 minutes to the falls, there is a trail descending to the bottom of the falls. This trip is reported not to be possible by normal car. Also take great care near the falls.

Beyond Kavanayén a beautiful but risky trail (18 km, 5 hours walk) leads along flat-topped mountains to the **Karuari-Merú** falls, with good swimming in the pool below.

TO SANTA ELENA DE UAIREN

For the remaining 180 km to Santa Elena de Uairén few people and only a handful of Pemón Indian villages are to be seen. The first village passed is **Kamoirán**, at Km 176. It has a restaurant which does a good breakfast, reasonable lunch, has rapids in the back garden, has rooms to let, **D**, and gasoline!

At Km 205 are the impressive 82m high Kawí falls at the **Kama** River. These should not be missed but note that the viewpoint is used as a public toilet. There's also a small lake, local handicrafts for sale, and canoe trips for US$1.50 per hour per person. There is a native hut to rent, **E**, or you can sling a hammock in a *cabaña*, **F**, or pitch your tent in the camping area, **G** (no facilities, take water purification tablets). There's also an overpriced restaurant and a small shop. Buses can be flagged down going south or north 3 times a day; check times in advance.

At Km 245 are the Río Sarapan falls, with a hotel and free campsite, immaculately kept, with toilets, canned drinks are sold but there's no restaurant, also small huts for rent for US$5-7.50 per night.

At Km 249, at the Río Yuruaní, is the **Quebrada Pacheco**, where there is a small Inparques office and cabins with hammocks for up to 12, **D**, cooking facilities. There are waterfalls and pools nearby where you can swim. Tour groups often stop here. A 15-minute hike to the Yuruaní waterfall leaves the main road 250m after the crossing, turn left. Next is **Balneario Suruape**, a good place for swimming and picnics, natural whirlpool, restaurant, and 10 minutes downriver is a natural waterslide.

Then comes the Pemón village of **San Francisco de Yuruaní** (see page 318), followed, 9 km of bends later, by the larger village of **San Ignacio de Yuruaní**, where there is military checkpoint, and also excellent regional food. As the highway crosses a wide plain, the impressive bulks of Kukenán and Roraima (the more southerly of the two) can be seen rising out of the savannah to the east on a clear day.

A trail at **Km 275** leads to the **Quebrada de Jaspe** where a river cuts through striated cliffs and pieces of jasper glitter on the banks (don't take them home to glitter on your shelf, don't walk on the jasper and don't add to the graffiti on the rocks). Visit at midday when the sun shines best on the jasper, or at 1500 when the colour changes from red to orange, which is very beautiful. There's a campsite beside the river, but it has no facilities, has bad drainage and is exposed; not recommended.

About 20 km from San Ignacio the highway begins to descend until, at the Río Kukenán, it leaves Canaima National Park and runs the last few kilometres to Santa Elena, 642 km from Ciudad Guayana.

SANTA ELENA DE UAIREN

This growing, pleasant frontier town (*population* 7,330; *phone code* 088; *altitude* 907m) was established by Capuchin monks in 1931. It's now a relaxed little place which is hot during the day, but thanks to its altitude, enjoys relatively cool nights. Coupled with a good supply of hotels at the cheaper end of the market, this makes Santa Elena a very attractive alternative to Ciudad Bolívar for arranging tours of the Gran Sabana or to Roraima. Gold is a better buy here than in Ciudad Bolívar.

Local festivals

9-19 August, featuring music, dance and handicrafts.

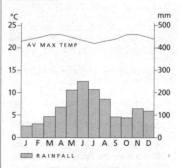

Climate: Santa Elena

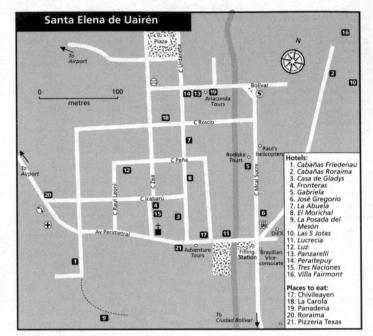

Santa Elena de Uairén

0 — 100 metres

To Airport

Plaza

C. Urdaneta

Bolívar

Anaconda Tours

C Roscio

To Airport

C Peña

Rodiske Tours

Raul's helicopters

C Zea

C Raul Leoni

C Icabarú

Av Perimetral

Adventure Tours

Filling Station

Brazilian Vice-consulate

DIEX

To Ciudad Bolívar

Hotels:
1. Cabañas Friedenau
2. Cabañas Roraima
3. Casa de Gladys
4. Fronteras
5. Gabriela
6. José Gregorio
7. La Abuela
8. El Morichal
9. La Posada del Mesón
10. Las 5 Jotas
11. Lucrecia
12. Luz
13. Panzarelli
14. Peraitepuy
15. Tres Naciones
16. Villa Fairmont

Places to eat:
17. Chivileayen
18. La Carola
19. Panaderia
20. Roraima
21. Pizzeria Texas

Local information

● Accommodation

Accommodation can be difficult to find because of visiting mine workers and Brazilian shoppers (particularly at weekends).

B *Cabañas Familiares Friedenau*, south of town, off Avenida Perimetral, T 951353, self-contained chalets, pleasant, also run trips to Roraima (see below), English and German spoken.

C *Villa Fairmont*, Urb Akurimá, T (02) 782-8433, at the northern edge of town, a few minutes' drive from the bus station, has an aviary (!); nearby is **C-D** *Cabañas Roraima*, fan, hot water, fridge, very comfortable, near a supermarket.

D *La Posada del Mesón*, Vía Penetración Sampai, T 951443, beautiful wooden bungalows, sanitary installations, modern and functioning, run by Margarita and José E Isurrualde, who are extremely helpful; **D-E** *La Abuela*, Calle Urdaneta, T 951422, hot water, fan, good, washing facilities.

E *Fronteras**, Calle Icabarú y Zea, T 951095, single or double, with bath, hot water, quiet, comfortable, fan, safe, good restaurant, recommended; **E** *Gabriela*, on Mariscal Sucre, 150m

from bus terminal on the opposite side, with bathroom, hot water, fan, modern, comfortable, free coffee, recommended, very good restaurant next door, US$4-5 per dish; **E** *Lucrecia*, Avenida Perimetral, near the bus terminal, with bathroom, fan, restaurant, nice rooms, arranges tours; **E** *Luz*, Calle Peña, with bath, cold water, fan, comfortable beds, good meeting point, *Tayukasen Tours* have their office here (see below), recommended, if the hotel's full, the owner will help to find a room in a private home; **E** *Panzarelli*, Calle Bolívar, near the plaza, T 951196, with room bath, hot water, fans, nice rooms, good value; **E-F** *José Gregorio*, next to the bus terminal, with bathroom and fan, cold water, basic, OK; **E-F** *Peraitepuy*, on Calle Bolívar, T 951127, with bathroom and fan, basic, small rooms, laundry facilities; **E-F** *Tres Naciones*, on Zea, next to *Hotel Fronteras*, T 951190, with bathroom, fan, hot water, parking.

F *Casa de Gladys*, Calle Urdaneta 187, T 951171, with bath, fan, cooking and washing facilities, tourist information, organizes day trips, recommended; **F** pp *Hospedaje El Morichal*, on Calle Urdaneta near Calle Lucas F Peña, set back from the road among some trees, with bathroom, fan, laundry facilities, basic and friendly; **F Las 5 Jotas**, near *Cabañas Roraima*, comfortable, good value.

● **Places to eat**
Roraima, Calle Icabarú, opposite the hospital and CANTV, at the west end of Calle Icabarú, not too expensive despite being tourist oriented, excellent steaks, highly recommended creole and international cooking; **Agua Miel**, same location, very good vegetarian dishes and takeaway snacks, owner speaks good English; **Pizzería Texas**, on Avenida Perimetral, at bottom of Calle Urdaneta, excellent; almost opposite is **Chivileayen**, expensive but tasty, great burgers; *La Carola*, around the corner from *Hotel Luz*, good lunches, popular, US$2-3 per dish, recommended; **Panadería Trigopán**, next to *Anaconda Tours* on Calle Bolívar, good breakfasts and coffee. There are several restaurants on Mariscal Sucre.

● **Banks & money changers**
Banco Orinoco, at Calle Bolívar and Mariscal Sucre, changes Amex travellers' cheques at 5% commission, in the morning only. Try the shops in the centre for dollars cash or travellers' cheques, eg *Casa de Los Cóchamos*, the gold shop south of main plaza, which changes cheques at a lower rate than the bank; **Inversiones Fortaleza**, Calle Urdaneta on the plaza, Sergio Rivera changes cash dollars, cheques or Brazilian currency; **La Boutique Zapatería** also changes travellers' cheques and cash at reasonable rates; also try the grocery store **El Gordito**, next to *La Abuela* on Urdaneta, for Brazilian currency (English and French spoken). Try at border with Brazilians entering Venezuela. Generally the rates are poor; check with travellers going in the opposite direction what rates should be. For better rates you must wait until Ciudad Guayana, or Boa Vista if going to Brazil (change some money into Brazilian currency before the bus leaves).

● **Post & telecommunications**
Post office: at Bolívar and Zea.

Telephone: CANTV office, on Avenida Perimetral, next to the hospital at the west end of Calle Icabarú, for international calls, but not all day.

● **Tour companies & travel agents**
Tayukasen Tours, at *Hotel Luz*, run by Roberto Fuenmayor Quintero, guides Pablo Vallenilla, Richard Mata, Andrés Emilio Pérez, Orlando Alder (El Gato) and Richard Prada, they offer 1-5 day tours of Gran Sabana, US$20 per person per day for guide and transport, US$45 per person day all inclusive, 6 day treks to Roraima cost US$230 per person all inclusive, they also run trips to El Pauji and the gold mines, Canaima, Angel Falls and Kavác; English spoken, highly recommended.

Adventure Tours, Avenida Perimetral at the end of Calle Urdaneta, T 951371, run by Frank Khasen and wife Arelis, tours of Gran Sabana or El Pauji, US$25 per person per day for guide and transport only, or US$50 per person per day all inclusive, group discounts, 6 days to Roraima US$450 per person all inclusive.
Rodiske Tours, Calle Mariscal Sucre, T/F 951467, tours to Gran Sabana, Canaima and Roraima; **Anaconda Tours**, Centro Comercial Augusto, Calle Bolívar, T 951016, tours of Gran Sabana/El Pauji, US$30-45 per person per day, not including accommodation and meals; *La Cosecha*, Calle Los Castañas near Avenida Icabarú, T 951756, recommended for tours to Roraima.

● **Useful addresses**
Mechanic: Antonio Mejías, good, cheap, 'a miracle-worker'. *Parks Auto Parts*, next to *Hotel Fronteras*, run by Floyd Park from Texas, USA, helpful.

● **Transport**
Air The airport is 10 km from town. Servivensa has daily flights to Canaima (US$75) and Puerto Ordaz (US$80); also flights to Ciudad Bolívar with Rutaca (US$65, but check prices as they may increase). Aereotuy has daily flights to Ciudad Bolívar, standby basis only on Sunday; they sometimes stop at indigenous villages. To fly to Icabarú and the villages of Uriman, Wonkin, and Kamarata you will have to charter an Airtaxi, which is quite expensive (eg Aerotécnica 6-seater, US$600 per day). Book a week in advance. Rutaca flies daily to El Pauji, depart when full, US$15 per person, last one at 1600.

Road Corpovén gas station open 0800-1900.
Buses The terminal is on Calle Mariscal Sucre. From **Caracas** it is best to go to Ciudad Bolívar and take a bus direct to Boa Vista, or Santa Elena. From Santa Elena to **Ciudad Bolívar** (10-12 hours), at 0700, 0930, 1330 and 1930 with Turgal (air conditioning, TV), US$9.50; at 1700 and 1900 with Línea Orinoco, US$9.30; at 0800 and 2000 with Travircan (some with air conditioning); with Ecuatur at 1130, US$11.60, 9 hours (air conditioniong, more comfortable). Alternatively take a daily bus to Tumeremo or El Dorado; Transmundial runs from **Tumeremo** to Santa Elena (US$8.75) and from **El Dorado** (US$5.40, 6 hours), returning from Santa Elena at 0830. Santa Elena-**Ciudad Guayana**, 0600, 1900, 2000 (US$10, 10-11 hours), or Expreso Maturín goes to Ciudad Guayana and Maturín daily. Transmundial go direct to San Félix daily, 1800, US$9, 10 hours, very few stops. Take warm clothing for overnight buses with air conditioning (the driver may even insist that the shades be closed throughout the journey, so as not to affect the air conditioning).

Hitchhiking North from Santa Elena is said to be easy. Stand at the roadside at the garage just opposite the terminal. Expect a small charge, up to US$5.

FRONTIER WITH BRAZIL

The 16 km road to the border is paved. The entire road links Caracas with Manaus in 4 days with hard driving. **NB** Border searches are thorough and frequent at this crossing.

● Venezuelan immigration
DIEX immigration office is uphill behind the bus terminal in Santa Elena. It opens at 0730-1130 and 1400-1700. All passports and car documents must be stamped here (not the border) on entry or exit.

Staff at the Ministry of Justice next to DIEX, and the Guardia Nacional headquarters have been recommended as helpful with entry/exit difficulties.

Entering Venezuela Everyone who crosses the border from Boa Vista, Brazil, must have a visa, regardless of nationality (passport must be valid for 1 year). Ask well in advance what health requirements are in force (yellow fever vaccination certificate, malaria test certificate and medical check-up may be required). Border officials may insist upon US$20 per day for your stay; regulations state that a visa is sufficient. Fresh fruit and vegetables may not be brought into Venezuela. There are frequent road checks. The Venezuelan consulate in Boa Vista is at Avenida Benjamin Constant 525E, T (095) 224-2182, open Monday-Friday 0830-1300, but may close earlier.

● Crossing by private vehicle
Allow 2 hours to undertake all formalities.

● Brazilian consulate
Near the bus terminal opposite the Corpoven gas station in Santa Elena; open 0800-1200 and 1400-1800. You can get a visa here.

● Transport
Buses To Boa Vista with Unión Cascavel at 0830, 1200, 1500 and 1600, 4 hours, US$13.70. There is no direct transport to Manaus.

● Entering Brazil
There is a basic hotel, *Pacaraima Palace*, on the Brazilian side of the border, also a guest house, camping possibilities and a bank. It is not easy trying to hitch a lift between the border and Boa Vista, but much easier from there to Manaus. Boa Vista has a good selection of hotels, restaurants and money changing facilities.

SANTA ELENA TO EL PAUJI

A road leaves the highway 8 km south of Santa Elena on the route to the border. It heads west (right) and after passing through a tunnel of jungle vegetation emerges onto rolling savannahs dotted with *tepuys*. The road is in terrible condition. At Km 58 is a Guardia Nacional checkpoint at Paraitepuy, with a waterfall nearby. At Km 68 is *Shailili-ko* camp, English, Italian and French spoken, recommended.

EL PAUJI

17 km further west is **El Paují**, an agricultural settlement which was founded by hippies from Caracas and abroad, and which now has a growing number of foreign residents. There are many nice places to stay and it's a very pleasant-looking, laid-back little town. Ask for Luigi, an Italian at El Cajón mine (he speaks English). A recommended guide is Marco, a friendly Swiss guy.

● Accommodation, places to eat & services
D *Hospedaje Maripak Tepuy*, in the village, near the airstrip and small store, T (02) 234-3661 (Caracas), (088) 951459, run by Mariella Gill, cabins for 2/3 with bath, English spoken, US$5 per meal, good food, organizes tours, camping US$3 per tent; **E** *Chimanta*, with bathroom, solar powered, restaurant, run by Louise Scott; **F** pp *El Caminante* tourist camp, just after the bridge, coming from Santa Elena, run by Danielle, helpful, camping, trips arranged, good restaurant; **F** *Alojamiento Weimore*, on the other side of the bridge from Danielle's camp, has owner-designed space-age accommodation, peaceful, good food, natural pool; **F** *Hospedaje Karaware*, run by Nelson and Elizabeth, helpful. Just before the bridge is *El Merendero* restaurant. At *La Bodega* general store, Victoriano has information on guides for tourists. 15 km from El Paují, at Solís, Arquimedes and Philippe have a tourist camp and organize tours. 25 km from the town is the *Canta Rana* tourist camp with basic accommodation, owners, Alfonso and Barbara Borrero, speak German, English and Spanish, there's waterfall in lovely surroundings, they also have a private plane that collects people from Puerto Ordaz (T 086-226851 or 220709, Sr Haissan Al Atrache).

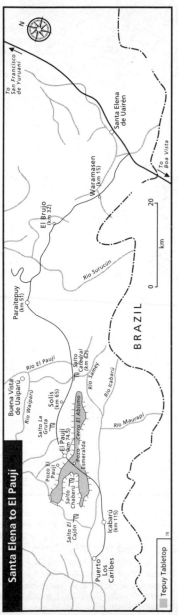

Santa Elena to El Pauji

Tepuy Tabletop

● **Transport Air** El Pauji to Ciudad Bolívar, US$60; also to Santa Elena (see above). **Road** Conventional cars and pick-ups can go no further than 30 km from Santa Elena on this road. 4WD can get to El Pauji. From Santa Elena, US$8-10 by jeep – if full, more if not, daily at 0600 and 1500-1600 from Plaza Bolívar, 3 hours; ask for Sr Manriques, or try hitching from the airport. Jeep hire in El Pauji, US$50 per day.

EXCURSIONS FROM EL PAUJI

El Pauji is located in a lovely area, with good walking. There are many excellent sights, including **Chirica-Tepuy**, a huge, beautiful, jet black mountain, surrounded by rolling savannah, and **Río Surucún**, where the largest diamond in Venezuela was found. **Salto Catedral**, is a lovely waterfall in a beautiful small hollow, with bright red water below due to the tree roots, which is excellent for swimming. **Salto La Gruta** are very impressive falls, but very slippery. **Pozo Esmeralda**, just outside El Pauji, are fine rapids and pools for swimming. It is 20 minutes to **Los Saltos de Pauji**, which are good for a bath.

A good walk is to the small hill, 2 km from El Pauji beyond the airfield. There are views from the crest on one side into **El Abismo**, a small tepuy, where the Brazilian jungle begins (2-3 hours from the village), and on the other side down to the Venezuelan savannah. It's a beautiful area and highly recommended walk.

120 km west of Santa Elena is **Icabarú**, a diamond-producing centre with few facilities, where prices are high.

MOUNT RORAIMA

One of the great treks of South America is to the summit of Mount Roraima (2,810m). It ranks right up there with Machu Picchu in Peru and Torres del Paine in Argentina as one of **the** essential destinations on this continent.

Roraima is a word in the Pemón language meaning 'The great, ever fruitful mother of streams'. Owing to the tough terrain and extreme weather conditions, this hike is only suitable for the fit. Supplies for a week or more should be bought in Santa Elena. If your food is

Santa Elena to Roraima

To Ciudad Guayana
Salto Kamá (km 201.5)
Kauchik-Merú
Route 10
Río Karaurín
Arapan Merú
Quebrada Pacheco (km 238)
Arapena-Merú (km 247)
Puente Río Yuruaní
San Francisco de Yuruaní (km 250)
Río Yuruaní
Río Kapuy
Wadaka Piapo-Tepuy
Salto Kunkuyita
Río Yuruaní
Yuruaní-Tepuy (2,400m)
ZONA EN RECLAMACIÓN
Kukenán-Tepuy (2,680m)
Monte Roraima (2,810m)
Salto Kukenán (610m)
Parai-Tepuy
La Base
San Ignacio de Yuruaní (km 259)
Río Yuruaní
Río Mapauri
Paraitepuy
Salto Chirimatá
Río Warari
Río Kukenán
Wei-tepuy (2,150m)
Salto Warari
Quebrada de Jaspe (km 273.5)
Salto Apa
Ma Tepuy
Abak Merú
Kay Merú
Salto Arabopó
Río Wari
Salto Rue
Salto Morok
Puente Río Kukenán (km 303)
Río Arabopó
BRAZIL
Río Kanaveuta
N
Santa Elena de Uairén (km 315)
Salto Seita
To Paraitepuy & El Pauji
To Boa Vista
(km 330)
Salto Arcoíris
0   20
km
Tepuy Tabletop

being supplied by a tour company, check what food you will be eating; often vegetarians go hungry.

SAN FRANCISCO DE YURUANI

The starting point is the Pemón village of **San Francisco de Yuruaní**, 60 km north of Santa Elena and 9 km north of the San Ignacio military checkpoint (at which you are required to register). There are three small shops selling basic goods but not enough for the Roraima hike. Meals are available and tents can be hired, US$3 per person per day, but the quality of tents and stoves is poor; try to get hold of good equipment.

● **Accommodation G** *Hospedaje Mínima*, shower, very basic; there's also **G** *hostal*, run by *Roraima Tours* (see below), which is usually full.

The Land that Time Forgot

Roraima is the most famous of all the *tepuys* in Guayana, and for a good reason. Arthur Conan Doyle's novel, '**The Lost World**' was based on the accounts of Everard Im Thurn, who was the first explorer ever to climb to the summit of Roraima, in 1884. On his return, he gave a series of lectures, which inspired Conan Doyle to write of a strange and mysterious land lost in time and inhabited by prehistoric creatures.

But Conan Doyle's imaginings may not be so far fetched. Scientists have called these *tepuys* ecological islands – or islands in time. These separated from the surrounding land 2 billion years ago and unique species of plants have been found on their wild, marshy summits. New sub species of fauna, too, have been discovered.

Indeed, one of the legendary old pioneers of Canaima, Alexander Laime, who lives in a hut below Auyán-Tepuy, claimed he had seen prehistoric creatures near the summit. He made a sketch, and it turned out that they looked uncannily like plesiosaurs, aquatic mammals of the Jurassic period, which were thought to have been extinct for nearly 100 million years.

It's true that when you reach the top of Roraima, you do experience a strange, eerie sensation – almost as if you had travelled far back in time. So, perhaps one of the questions you should be asking any potential guide is "how fast can dinosaurs run?"

● **Tour companies & guides** *Roraima Tours*, T (088) 951283, F 951339, are recommended, Ana Fernández is very helpful, their Roraima tour costs US$550 per person including food, or US$100 for a guide only (group rates can be arranged), they also hire tents (US$10 for 6 days) and stoves. Guides in San Francisco charge about US$20-25 a day, more if they carry your supplies: Basílio is highly recommended, as is Donald Mitchel, who speaks English; Carmelo is also good.

● **Transport** Buses from Santa Elena will let you off here and pick up passengers en route to Ciudad Bolívar at 1700 and 1900. A jeep to Paraitepuy is around US$40; the cheapest is Oscar Mejías Hernández, US$25 one way, ask for him in the village.

PARAITEPUY

The badly eroded track to Paraitepuy (sign-posted), the nearest village to the mountain, leaves the highway 1 km south of San Francisco. There's very little traffic and it's difficult to hitch. In the rain many vehicles get stuck on the last stretch and the authorities are tired of pulling them out; the full 25 km can be walked in 7 hours. Spanish-speaking guides are available here from US$12 a day and carriers for US$15 (see **NB also** below). Ask for El Capitán, he is in charge of the guides.

You can sleep for free in the village if you're hiring a guide, and camping is permitted. Few supplies are available; one small shop sells soft drinks and biscuits. The Ayuso brothers are the best-known guides. The villagers speak *Tauripen*, the local dialect, but now most of them also speak Spanish.

CLIMBING RORAIMA

The foot trail winds back and forth on a more direct line than the little-used jeep track; it is comparatively straightforward and adequately marked descending from the heights just past Paraitepuy across rolling hills and numerous clear streams. The goal, Roraima, is the mountain on the right, the other massive outcrop on the left is Mata Hui (known as Kukenán after the river which rises within it).

If you're leaving the village early enough in the day, you may reach the Río Kukenán crossing early in the afternoon. This river floods quickly after rain, the bottom is slippery and the current is swift; take a 50m rope if you're not going with a party and be prepared to get wet. There's good camping here and you can swim in the many pools, but there are lots of mosquitoes and *puri-puris* on the river bank.

A 3-hour walk brings you to a lovely bird-filled meadow below the foothills of the massif, another perfect camping spot known as *campamento base* (10 hours to base camp from Paraitepuy). The footpath now climbs steadily upwards through the cloud forest at the mountain's base and becomes an arduous scramble over tree trunks and damp rocks until the cliff is reached. From here it is possible to ascend to the plateau along the 'easy' rock ledge which is the only route to the top. It is quite broad and supports much vegetation. It manoeuvres around three spurs, drops sharply in places, and passes under an icy waterfall before heading steeply and directly to the summit. Walkers in good health should take about 4 hours from the meadow to the top. The vistas across the Gran Sabana are magnificent, and the summit is an eerie world of stone and water, where it is difficult to move around easily.

There are not many good spots to camp. The best is *El Hotel* – a sandy patch under an overhanging ledge – to which red painted arrows lead the way to the right after reaching the summit. From *El Hotel* a marked track leads to the survey pillar near the eastern cliff where Guyana, Brazil and Venezuela meet. Allow a day for this as the track is very rough.

Full camping equipment including stove is essential. An igloo-type tent is best for the summit. Wear thick socks and boots to protect legs from snakes. Also essential are warm clothes for the summit, where there's a lot of mist, rain squalls and lightning at night. You'll also need effective insect repellent – biting insects infest the grasslands.

The whole trip can take anywhere between 5 days and 2 weeks. If you don't wish to camp on the summit, a trip to the top and return can be done in a day, but keep an eye on weather conditions. A cloud belt usually wells up around the massif after dawn and often remains all day to blot out Roraima, even though the summit may remain clear. The water on the summit and around the foot of Roraima is very pure, but bring bottled water or a purifier for the Savannah. There is very little firewood on top, so it's better to bring gas or liquid fuel stoves. Litter is beginning to appear along the trail; please take care of the environment.

NB The dry season for trekking is November-May (with annual variations). During June-August Roraima is usually enveloped in cloud. **NB also** that the National Guard requires first-time visitors to have a guide beyond Paratepuy, otherwise you will be fined. It is not recommended to go alone; best to go with a guide from Santa Elena or San Francisco. Those hired in Paraitepuy have no accident insurance cover. A guide can be of great assistance for the hike's final stages (it is very easy to get lost) and for knowing the best places to camp. Thorough searches are now made on your return. Do not remove crystals from the mountain; on the spot fines up to US$100 may be charged.

AMAZONAS

In the southwest of Venezuela is the Federal Territory of Amazonas; 175,750 sq km (one fifth of the country) of largely unexplored and unspoiled tropical forests. It's an area of unrivalled biodiversity, thanks to the late arrival of 'the white man'. Not until the second half of the 18th century did the first European expeditions brave the impenetrable jungles. Another advantage of this has been the relative health of the indigenous population. Many different ethnic groups inhabit the forests and riverbanks of Amazonas; among them the *Ye'kwana, Piaroa, Yanomami, Guajibo* and *Piunæve*. Much of this territory is protected by a number of National Parks and Reserves: the **Yapacana, Duida-Marahuaca, Parima-Tapirapecó** and **Serranía de la Neblina National Parks**, the **Sipapo Forest Reserve** and the **Alto-Orinoco-Casiquiare Biosphere Reserve**.

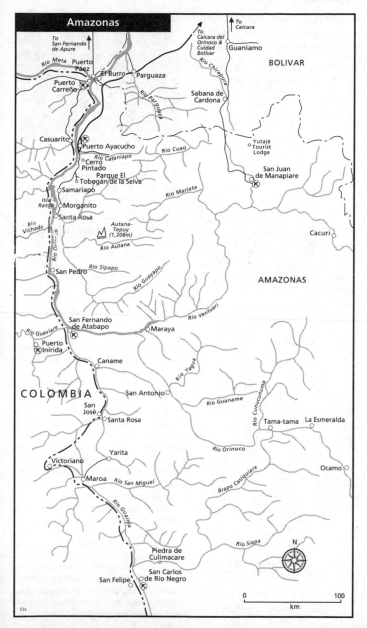

Amazonas

To San Fernando de Apure

Río Meta
Puerto Páez
El Burro
Parguaza
Puerto Carreño
Río Parguaza

To Caicara del Orinoco & Cuidad Bolívar
Guaniamo
Río Chirapure
BOLIVAR

Sabana de Cardona

To Caicara

Casuarito
Puerto Ayacucho
Río Cataniapo
Cerro Pintado
Río Cuao
Parque El Tobogán de la Selva
Samariapo
Río Marieta
Yutajé Tourist Lodge
San Juan de Manapiare

Isla Ratón
Morganito
Santa Rosa
Río Vichada
Río Orinoco
Autana-Tepuy (1,208m)
Río Autana
Cacuri

San Pedro
Río Sipapo
Río Guayapo

AMAZONAS

Río Ventuari

San Fernando de Atabapo
Maraya
Río Guaviare
Puerto Inírida
Caname
Río Yagua

COLOMBIA
San Antonio
Río Guaname
Río Cunucunuma
Tama-tama
La Esmeralda
San José
Santa Rosa
Yarita
Río Orinoco
Ocamo
Victoriano
Maroa
Río San Miguel
Brazo Casiquiare
Río Guainía
Río Siapa

N

Piedra de Culimacare
San Felipe
San Carlos de Río Negro

0   100
km

53a

BY ROAD TO PUERTO AYACUCHO

Amazonas can be reached from **San Fernando de Apure** in the *llanos*, via **Puerto Páez** and Puerto Ayacucho (see page 228). Puerto Ayacucho can also be reached from **Caicara del Orinoco** (see page 283). From Caicara a new paved road runs 370 km southwest to Puerto Ayacucho, passing scruffy settlements and bauxite-mining towns like Los Pijiguaos and Parguaza. The turn off to **El Burro**, where the boat crosses the Orinoco to Puerto Páez (ferry US$1, also to Puerto Carreño, Colombia), is 88 km north of Puerto Ayacucho. A *por puesto* El Burro-Puerto Ayacucho takes 1 hour.

NB On arrival in the Amazonas territory, it is necessary to register at a Guardia Nacional checkpoint about 20 km before Puerto Ayacucho. Around this area the national guard can be very strict and travellers are likely to be searched. **NB also:** Malaria is prevalent in this area; take precautions.

PUERTO AYACUCHO

Puerto Ayacucho (*phone code* 048) is the capital of the Federal Territory of Amazonas, which has a population of 80,000, 73,660 of whom live in Puerto Ayacucho. At the end of the dry season (April), it is very hot and sticky. It is 800 km up the Orinoco from Ciudad Bolívar, deep in the wilds of the jungle, but no direct boats do

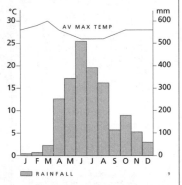

Climate: Puerto Ayacucho

Petroglyph in Amazonas

the 5 day journey up river. Prices in Puerto Ayacucho are generally higher than north of the Orinoco.

Places of interest

The **Museo Etnológico del Territorio Federal Amazonas**, on Monseñor Enzo Ceccarelli, opposite the church, has a library and collection of regional exhibits, and is worth a visit. It is open Tuesday-Saturday, and Sunday mornings; entry US$0.80. In front of the museum is a market, open every day, where local indigenous people sell handicrafts, eg wooden sculptures, musical instruments. One block away is the cathedral, which has colourful paintings, especially on the ceiling. The Salesian Mission House and boys' school on Plaza Bolívar may also be visited.

Excursions

Locals recommend October-December as the best time for trips, when the rivers are high but the worst of the rains have passed. In the low season, May-June, it may be difficult to organize tours for only a few days.

You can walk up **Cerro Perico** for good views of the town, or go to the Mirador, about 1 km from the town centre, which offers good views of the Ature rapids. A recommended trip is to the small village of Pintado (12 km south), where petroglyphs described by Humboldt can be seen on the huge rock called **Cerro Pintado**. This the most easily accessible petroglyph site of the hundreds scattered throughout Amazonas.

35 km south on the road to Samariapo is the **Parque Tobogán de la Selva**, a pleasant picnic area with tables and refreshments centred around a steeply inclined, smooth rock over which the Río Maripures cascades. This water-slide is great fun in the wet season, though it's crowded on Sunday. Take a swimsuit, bathing shoes, food and drink, and stick to the right to avoid crashing into barrier, there are some painful rocks to the left near the bottom; also beware of broken glass. A small trail leads up from the slide to a natural jacuzzi after about 20 minutes. A taxi to Cerro Pintado and Parque Tobogán will cost US$15-20 return; be sure to organize your return with the driver, otherwise you may face a lengthy hike. Agencies in town arrange tours to these places, which is easier but more expensive.

Nearby, also by paved road, is the **Coromoto colony**, founded by the Salesian Fathers to protect and evangelize the 'howling Guaharibos' (as early explorers called this nomadic tribe).

The well-paved road from Puerto Ayacucho to **Samariapo** (63 km) was built to bypass the powerful and very impressive Maripures Rapids, which here interrupt the Orinoco, dividing it

Traditional Piaroa house

into 'Upper' and 'Lower'. The road (gravel, but being paved) continues for 17 km to **Morganito**, from where smaller launches continue on up river. Boats run from Samariapo to Isla de Ratón and Santa Rosa.

Local information
● Accommodation
D *Apure*, Avenida Orinoco 28, less than 1 km from the centre, air conditioning, restaurant, recommended; **D** *Guacharo's Amazonas Resort Hotel**, at end of Avenida Evelio Roa, two blocks from Avenida Río Negro, T 210328, air conditioning, restaurant.

E *Residencial Internacional*, Avenida Aguerrevere 18, T 21242, air conditioning (cheaper without), comfortable, shower, safe, laundry, warmly recommended, a good place to find tour information and meet other travellers, if no rooms are available you can sling up your hammock, bus drivers also stay here and will drive you to the terminal for early morning journeys; **E** *Residencial La Cueva*, Avenida 23 de Enero, one block from the Redoma (traffic roundabout, Corpoven station), air conditioning, luggage stored, recommended; **E** *Residencial Río Siapa*, Avenida Orinoco, behind Banco de Venezuela, T 210138, air conditioning, modern, mixed reports, very crowded at weekends, some rooms without locks; **E** *Tobogán*, Avenida Orinoco con Avenida Evelio Roa, T 210320, popular, air conditioning, reasonable value.

F-G *Residencial Ayacucho*, Urb Pedro Camejo, two blocks off Calle Amazonas behind *Guacharo's Amazonas Hotel*, with bathroom, fan, the cheapest in town.

● Places to eat
Las Palmeras, Avenida 23 de Enero, two blocks from the Redoma, pizzas and fast food; *El Padrino*, in Urb Andrés Eloy Blanco on Avenida Belisio Pérez off Avenida 23 de Enero, good Italian; *Cherazad*, Calle Aguerrevere y Avenida Orinoco, Arabic food; *El Encuentro*, cheap, good, ideal place for meeting travellers. There's good food in the restaurant at *Hotel Apure*. *Capi Fuente de Soda*, on Avenida Evelio Roa behind *gobernación*, vegetarian and other dishes.

● Banks & money changers
Banco Unión and Banco de Venezuela, both on Avenida Orinoco near the roundabout in the town centre, gives cash on Visa and Mastercard. Changing dollars is difficult; try *Hotel Tobogán* or *Hotel Orinoco*. The *casa de cambio* opposite *Wayumi* charter flights on Avenida Evelio Roa gives appallingly low rates.

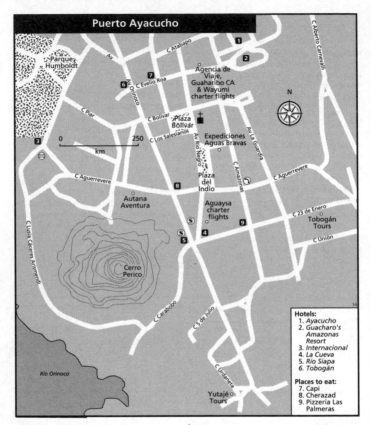

Puerto Ayacucho

Hotels:
1. *Ayacucho*
2. *Guacharo's Amazonas Resort*
3. *Internacional*
4. *La Cueva*
5. *Río Siapa*
6. *Tobogán*

Places to eat:
7. Capi
8. Cherazad
9. Pizzería Las Palmeras

● **Entertainment**

Cinema: *Galaxia 2000*, on Avenida Orinoco, T 210212.

● **Hospitals & medical services**

Centro de Salud José Gregorio Hernández, on Avenida 23 de Enero, T 210221.

● **Laundry**

Lavandería Automático Unión, Centro Unión on Avenida 23 de Enero. Dry cleaning at Avenida Aguerrevere with Avenida La Guardia.

● **Post & telecommunications**

Post office: Ipostel on Avenida Aguerrevere three blocks up from Avenida Orinoco.

Telephone: international calls from CANTV, on Avenida Orinoco next to *Hotel Apure*; also from *Las Churuwatas* on Avenida Aguerrevere with Calle Amazonas, one block from Plaza del Indio.

● **Shopping**

Good *artesanía* can be found in the Plaza del Indio; also in *Artes Amazonas* on Avenida Evelio Roa, next to *Wayumi*, and in *Topocho* just up from Plaza del Indio. Many tourist souvenirs are on offer and Vicente Barletta, of *Típico El Casique*, Avenida Principal 583, Urb Andrés Eloy Blanco, has a good collection of masks (free). He also works as a guide (T 21389), and is recommended but take your own food and equipment.

● **Transport**

Air The airport is 7 km southeast along Avenida Orinoco. Scheduled LAV flights go to Caracas. Scheduled LAV flights go to Caracas, 2 a day, one non-stop (1 hour), one via San Fernando de Apure and Calabozo (3-4 hours). LAV office is at Avenida 23 de Enero 27, T 21422. Avensa flies once daily to Caracas via

San Fernando. There are daily flights to San Fernando de Atabapo and San Juan de Manapiare, also flights once a week to Maroa, La Esmeralda and San Carlos de Río Negro, with Wayumi (at Avenida Evelio Roa, one block from Avenida Río Negro). No permits are needed for San Fernando de Atabapo or San Juan de Manapiare, otherwise permits must be obtained from recognized travel agents. Charter flights are also available with Wayuma (from US$500 per plane, 3-7 seater). Aguaysa (Avenida Río Negro, one block from the Redoma) also flies to San Fernando de Atabapo and San Juan de Manapiare, and they offer a flight over Autana-Tepuy for US$70 per person in a 5-seater plane; they also offer charters for the same price as Wayuma.

Road Vehicle hire: *Servicio Amazonas de Alquiler*, Avenida Aguerrevere, T 210762.
Buses: Expresos del Valle to Cuidad Bolívar (US$11, 10 hours; take something to eat, bus stops once for early lunch), Caicara, Pto Ordaz and San Felix (T 210840); Cooperativa Cacique to San Fernando de Apure, US$9, 8 hours (T 210091); both companies are based at the bus terminal. Expresos La Prosperidad to Caracas and Maracay (T 210682) from Urb Alto Parima. Bus from Caracas daily at 2030, 2230, US$12.50, 12 hours (but much longer in the wet season). *Por puesto* to Ciudad Bolívar, 3 daily, US$12, 10-12 hours, with Caicara Amazonas.

River Ferry across the Orinoco, US$0.50. Boat to Caicara, 1½ days, US$15 including food, but bargain; insect repellent and hammock required.

FRONTIER WITH COLOMBIA

88 km north of Puerto Ayacucho a paved branch road leads west to El Burro, from where a ferry-barge crosses to Puerto Páez. On the south bank of the Meta opposite (ferry, US$1) is Puerto Carreño in Colombia.

Bongos and ferries run regularly across the river from Puerto Ayacucho to Casuarito (Colombia), which has quite good shopping, locals make these excursions without formalities, and many travellers have experienced no problems or formalities crossing for a few hours (ferries leave from the Guardia Nacional post on the northern edge of town). On the other hand, some difficulty with the local authorities is not uncommon, both here and at Puerto Carreño. You may be asked

how much money you have and where you are going. Some travellers have had to obtain Colombian visas when only a passport and ticket out of the country were strictly necessary. From Puerto Ayacucho there is a cargo boat to Puerto Páez, 4 hours. Check with the Guardia Nacional and insist on an exit stamp if you're crossing to Colombia.

TOURS IN AMAZONAS

Much of Amazonas State is stunningly beautiful and untouched, but access is only by river. For starting out, the best base is Puerto Ayacucho. By ascending the Autana or Sipapo rivers, for example, you can see **Autana-Tepuy**, a 1,200m-high soaring mass of rock resembling a petrified tree trunk, riddled with massive caves. It was first explored in 1971 by Charles Brewer Carias, who descended by helicopter (an Anglo-American expedition parachuted onto the summit in 1986 – no-one has yet climbed from the base). There are other *tepuys* in the region, including the great mass of the Sierra de la Neblina on the Brazilian border.

South of Puerto Ayacucho on the Orinoco, the next largest settlement is **San Fernando de Atabapo**. There are daily flights from Puerto Ayaycucho (see above).

Further south, on the Río Negro, towards Brazil, is **San Carlos de Río Negro** (*population* 1,500). There's a hotel at the customs post. Flights leave from Puerto Ayacucho on Friday with Wayumi (see above). A permit is required to visit. San Carlos is situated just beyond the **Brazo Casiquiare**, the 320 km long canal which joins the Orinoco and Amazon basins. This link between the mighty Amazon and Orinoco rivers, via the Río Negro, was discovered by Alexander Von Humboldt, in 1801, during his epic expedition through the Venezuelan jungles (see also page 270).

San Juan de Manapiare (*population* 3,700) is the regional centre for the middle Ventuari. A beautiful track winds around the Cerro Guanay to get there. The road starts at Caicara and goes through Guaniamo and Sabana de Cardona.

Death, despair and diabolic deeds

👣 Of all the searches for the mythical lost city of El Dorado, the most infamous must be that of Lope de Aguirre, the Basque *conquistador* who left a trail of blood and mayhem during his year-long journey up the Amazon.

The expedition set out from Lima in September of 1560, led by a Spanish nobleman from Navarra, Pedro de Ursua, who was accompanied by his lover, Inez de Atienza, described as the loveliest woman in all Peru. Aguirre was soon up to his bloodthirsty ways, however. On 1 January 1561, Ursua, was stabbed to death by a mutinous band led by the Basque. Another leader, Don Fernando de Guzmán, was sworn in as Ursua's replacement with Aguirre as *maestro de campo*. A document was drawn up to that effect, which Aguirre signed, 'Lope de Aguirre, traitor'.

The journey then deteriorated into a bloodbath. Men were stabbed, hanged, garotted or drowned by Aguirre and his henchmen. Out of 370 Europeans on the expedition, about 150 were murdered or marooned, among them Guzmán and the beautiful Doña Inez.

By this time Aguirre's loyalty to the Spanish Crown had weakened to the point where he announced: "We must renounce our allegiance to Spain." As they drifted downriver through the depths of the jungle Aguirre's delusions of grandeur reached new heights. He styled himself 'Lope de Aguirre, Wrath of God, Prince of Freedom, King of Tierra Firme'. All thoughts of El Dorado were now obviously abandoned, judging by Aguirre's statement that "There is nothing on the river but despair".

The remainder of the party reached the Atlantic on 4 July 1561, having sailed down the mighty Amazon and Orinoco rivers. After a few months of ransacking the coast, Aguirre was killed near present-day Valencia, having just murdered his own daughter to prevent her falling into enemy hands.

Travel in the southern part of Amazonas is heavily restricted to protect the *Yanomami* and the Alto Orinoco – Casiquiare Biosphere Reserve, which covers most of the southeastern portion of Amazonas from the Neblina range to the Orinoco headwaters.

A permit is required from the Bureau of Indian Affairs (Orai), in Caracas or Puerto Ayacucho (several copies of photograph and description page in passport required). A permit is also required from Inparques in Puerto Ayacucho. To get there, go through the Mercadito and it's two blocks further down. Another permit is needed from the Catholic Vicariato, if you intend to visit the missions along the rivers. And yet another permit is required from *Servicio Autónomo para el Desarrollo Ambiental de Amazonas* (Sada), in the same building as Inparques in Caracas, T (02) 408-1822/1026, Dr W Frank. **NB** Travellers without a guide may be turned back by the Guardia Nacional in San Carlos de Río Negro.

● **Accommodation** There are a number of private river camps on the upper Orinoco but they do not welcome casual guests. The most welcoming is *Yutajé Camp*, located on a tributary of the Río Manapiare due east of Puerto Ayacucho. This can theoretically be reached from the track running south from Guaniamo to San Juan de Manapiare, but the passability of the track depends on how recently it was used and the season. The camp accommodates 30, with restaurant and bar, full board, fishing, canoes, horses, airboats, excursions to indigenous villages, and spectacular falls in the vicinity. There's a lot of wildlife around and tours are expensive but professional. Also in the area is the *Campamento Camani*, T (02) 284-9006, F (02) 285-7352 (Centro Plaza, Torre C, 19th floor, Caracas), in a forest clearing on the banks of the Río Alto Ventuari, 2 hours by launch from San Juan de Manapiare. A private aircraft leaves Caracas each Thursday and Sunday, 2 hours 20 minutes. From Puerto Ayacucho the daily aero-taxi takes 50 minutes. The camp takes a maximum of 26 guests at any one time, mosquito nets provided, bathroom, restaurant, bar, TV, handicraft shop, football and petanque courts, excursions available; a 3 day/2 nights costs

US$290 per person with lodging and meals, excluding air fare.

Near Puerto Ayacucho, in mixed jungle and dry forest setting, is *Jungle Camp Calypso*, run by *Calypso Tours*, T 210572 (or Caracas, T (02) 545-0024, F 541-3036), it costs US$150 per person for 2 days including food, basic cabin accommodation and excursions in canoes, highly recommendation.

B *Canturama Amazonas Resort*, T 210266 (or Caracas, T (02) 941-8813, F 9435160), is 20 minutes by vehicle south of Puerto Ayacucho, on the banks of the Orinoco amidst dry, open savannah, 40 km from the nearest jungle, highly recommended accommodation and food but very few animals and beware biting insects by the river; buffet meals cost US$4-7, full day tours cost US$10.

Dantos Adventure, is a very basic jungle refuge, accommodation and canoe tours cost around US$45 per person per day, and is probably the cheapest option available, there's also space for camping; run by Reni and Danitza Barrio (Reni is also a recommended guide, who speaks English), ask at *Aguas Bravas* (see below) or contact Juan Carlos Garcia, T 210478/ 211771.

● **Tour companies & travel agents** Tourists are strongly recommended to go on tours organized by tour agents or guides registered in the *Asocación de Guías*, in the Cámara de Turismo, Casa de la Piedra, on the Arteria Vial de la Avenida Orinoco with Avenida Principal (the house on top of the large rock). Permission is required to visit Amazonas and some independent guides may not have access to this. Tours generally cost US$50-120 per person per day, depending on the agency and trip. Those listed below will arrange permits and insurance, but shop around.

● **Recommended companies** *Tobogán Tours*, Avenida 23 de Enero near *Instituto del Menor*, T 214553, F 214865; *Autana Aventura*, Avenida Aguerrevere, one block from Avenida Orinoco, T 212821, F 210605, owned by Julián Jaramillo; *Guaharibo CA*, Calle Evelio Roa 39, in the same building as *Wayumi*, T 210635, or Caracas T 952-6996, F 953-0092, manager Levis Olivo; *Yutajé Tours*, in Urb Monte Bello, one block from Avenida Orinoco, past the Mercadito going out of town, T 210664, they give rides to doctors and nurses to remote parts; *Expediciones Aguas Bravas Venezuela*, Avenida Río Negro, No 32-2, in front of Plaza Rómulo Betancourt, T 210541, F 211529, whitewater rafting trips, 2 daily from 0900-1200 and 1500-1800, 3-13 people per boat, US$35 per person, they also offer a visit to Isla Ratón plus a set of rapids for US$100 per boat, reservations are required at peak times, take insect repellent, sun protector, light shoes and swimsuit (raincoat in rainy season).

Information for travellers

BEFORE TRAVELLING

ENTRY REQUIREMENTS

● Documents

Entry is by passport and visa (normally valid for 3 entries), or by passport and tourist card. Tourist cards (*tarjetas de ingreso*) are free and valid only for those entering by air and are issued by most airlines to visitors from: Andorra, Antigua and Barbuda, Argentina, Australia, Austria, Barbados, Belgium, Brazil, Canada, Chile, Costa Rica, Dominica, Denmark, Finland, France, Germany, Ireland, Italy, Iceland, Japan, Liechtenstein, Luxembourg, Lithuania, Malaysia, Mexico, Monaco, Norway, Netherlands, Netherlands Antilles, New Zealand, Paraguay, St Kitts/Nevis, St Lucia, San Marino, St Vincent, South Africa, Sweden, Switzerland, Taiwan, Trinidad and Tobago, UK, Uruguay, and USA. They are valid for 90 days with, theoretically, 2 extensions of 60 days each permissible, at a cost of US$25 each (alternatively leave the country and re-enter). Overstaying your 90 days without an extension can lead to arrest and a fine when you try to depart. DIEX offices in many cities do not offer extensions – it's best to go to DIEX, Avenida Baralt on Plaza Miranda in Caracas, T 483-2744; take passport, tourist card, photograph and return ticket. It opens at 0800; your passport, with the extension, is returned at the end of the day.

If you enter the country overland, it is safest to obtain a multiple entry visa in advance. In theory, this may not be necessary, but in practice you may well be asked for it. Apply to a Venezuelan consulate prior to arrival. For a Tourist Visa, you need 1 passport photo, passport valid for 6 months, references from bank and employer, onward or return ticket, completed and signed application form. The fee in the UK is £22 (costs vary from country to country). Transit visas, valid for 72 hours are also available, mostly the same requirements and cost (inward and onward tickets needed). DIEX in Caracas will not exchange a transit for a tourist visa.

It appears that you cannot get a visa in advance in the USA, although a 1 year, multiple-entry visa is available in advance from: 455 Market St, San Francisco, open Monday-Friday, 0900-1300 (with dollars cash and letters of reference from your bank and employer). This is also available in Canada.

To apply for an overland visa in Colombia or Brazil you need: passport, one photo and an onward ticket. In Manaus you also need a yellow fever inoculation certificate. A tourist card issued by Viasa in Bogotá is only valid for arriving in Caracas by air from Bogotá, not if you travel overland. To extend a visa for 1 month, in any city, costs about US$25 (passport photo needed). Consuls may give a 1-year visa if a valid reason can be given.

To change a tourist visa to a business visa, to obtain or to extend the latter, costs £42 in the UK. Visas to work in Venezuela also cost £42 and require authorization from the Dirección General Sectorial de Identificación y Control de Extranjeros in Caracas. Student visas require a letter of acceptance from the

Venezuelan institution, proof of means of support, medical certificate, passport photo, passport and £42. It generally takes 2 days to issue any visa. Tourist visas are multiple entry within their specified period.

If you are in full-time education you will be entitled to an International Student Identity Card, which is distributed by student travel offices and travel agencies in 77 countries. The ISIC gives you special prices on all forms of transport (air, sea, rail etc), and access to a variety of other concessions and services. If you need to find the location of your nearest ISIC office contact: The ISIC Association, Box 9048, 1000 Copenhagen, Denmark T (+45) 33 93 93 03. If you're planning to study in Latin America for a long period, make every effort to get a student visa in advance.

Membership cards of British, European and US motoring organizations can be useful for discounts off hotel charges, car rentals, maps, towing charges, etc. Student cards must carry a photograph if they are to be of any use in Latin America for discounts. Business people should carry a good supply of visiting cards, which are essential for good business relations in Latin America. Identity, membership or business cards in Spanish or Portuguese (or a translation) and an official letter of introduction in Spanish or Portuguese are also useful.

NB Carry your passport with you all the time you are in Venezuela as the police mount frequent spot checks and anyone found without identification is immediately detained (carrying a certified copy for greater safety is permissible, though not always accepted by officials). There are many military checkpoints, especially in border areas, at which all transport is stopped. Have your documents ready and make sure you know what entry permits you need; the soldiers may be unfamiliar with regulations for foreigners. It is your responsibility to ensure that your passport is stamped in and out when you cross frontiers. The absence of entry and exit stamps can cause serious difficulties: seek out the proper migration offices if the stamping process is not carried out as you cross. A press card as identification is reported to work wonders. Border searches are very thorough. Do not lose your entry card (replacing one causes a lot of trouble), nor the carbon copy of your visa as this has to be surrendered when leaving the country.

If you're staying for several weeks, it is worth while registering at your Embassy or Consulate. Then, if your passport is stolen, the process of replacing it is simplified and speeded up. Keeping photocopies of essential documents, including your flight ticket, and some additional passport-sized photographs, is recommended.

MONEY

● Cost of living
Venezuela is now one of the cheaper options for travelling in South America. Food and accommodation can be expensive in certain parts of the country – eg Isla de Margarita and south of the Orinoco – but in the rest of the country you can find a decent hotel and meal for a lot less money than in Europe or North America. Road transport, meanwhile, is very cheap. On the cheapest possible budget you can get by on around US$15 per person per day, depending on which part of the country you visit. A less basic budget would be about US$25 per day, rising to US$95 for first class travel.

● Currency
In March 1998 the exchange rate was Bs250 = US$1, though this will probably have changed by the time you travel. Always check the official rate. The unit of currency is the bolívar, which is divided into 100 céntimos. There are nickel alloy coins for 25 and 50 céntimos and 1, 2 and 5 bolívares, and notes for 5, 10, 20, 50, 100, 500, 1,000, 2,000 and 5,000 bolívares. There is a shortage of small coinage and small notes: many shops round up prices unless you have small change and bars may refuse to serve you unless you produce the correct change.

Popular names for coins are: Fuerte, Bs 5; Real, Bs 0.50; Medio, 0.25; Puya or Centavo, 0.05. The brown Bs 100 note is sometimes referred to as a marrón, or a *papel*, the Bs 500 note as an *orquidea*, because of its picture.

In response to the political and economic crisis of mid-1994, which saw the collapse of 10 banks, stringent exchange controls were introduced which, for the traveller, mean: to convert unused bolívares back into dollars upon leaving, you must present the original exchange receipt (up to 30% of original amount changed); only banks and authorized *casas de cambio* can legally sell bolívares. The three main ways of keeping in funds while travelling are with US dollars cash, US dollars travellers' cheques, or plastic. In 1997/98, though, it was becoming very difficult to change dollars cash or travellers' cheques in Venezuela. Visitors are strongly advised to use Visa or Mastercard. It is virtually impossible to change cash in banks; best to try *casas de cambio*. Details of which banks or *casas de cambio* will change cash or travellers' cheques are given under the relevant sections on the main text. If changing money in hotels, do not take sterling or any other European currencies. There are cash machines for Visa, Mastercard and Amex at Simón Bolívar airport.

● **Cash**
US dollar notes are only accepted if they are in excellent, if not perfect condition (likewise, do not accept local currency notes in poor condition). Low-value US dollar bills should be carried for changing into local currency if arriving when banks or *casas de cambio* are closed (US$5 or US$10 bills). They may be useful for shopping: shopkeepers and exchange shops (*casas de cambio*) tend to give better exchange rates than hotels or banks (but see below). The better hotels will normally change travellers' cheques for their guests (often at a poor rate), but if you are travelling on the cheap it is essential to keep in funds; watch weekends and public holidays carefully and never run out of local currency. Take plenty of local currency, in small denominations, when making trips to more remote areas.

● **Travellers' cheques**
These are convenient but they attract thieves (though refunds can of course be arranged) and you will find that they are more difficult than dollar bills to change in small towns (denominations of US$50 and US$100 are preferable, though you should also have a few of US$20). American Express, Visa or Thomas Cook US dollar travellers' cheques are recommended, but less commission is often charged on Citibank cheques, if they are cashed at branches of that bank.

It is a good idea to take two kinds of cheque: if large numbers of one kind have recently been forged or stolen, making people suspicious, it is unlikely to have happened simultaneously with the other kind.

Casas de cambio may be reluctant to change travellers' cheques; they always insist on seeing a passport and may also insist on proof of purchase. Ital Cambio seems to be the most fastidious; they may even take your photo.

● **Plastic**
It is straightforward to obtain a cash advance against a credit card and, in the text, we give the names of banks that do this.

There are two international **ATM** (automatic telling machine) acceptance systems, Plus and Cirrus. Many issuers of debit and credit cards are linked to one, or both (eg Visa is Plus, Mastercard is Cirrus). Look for the relevant symbol on an ATM and draw cash using your PIN. Frequently, the rates of exchange on ATM withdrawals are the best available. Find out before you leave what ATM coverage there is in the countries you will visit and what international 'functionality' your card has. Check if your bank or credit card company imposes handling charges. Obviously you must ensure that the account to which your debit card refers contains sufficient funds. With a credit card, obtain a credit limit sufficient for your needs, or pay money in to put the account in credit. If travelling for a long time, consider a direct debit to clear your account regularly. Do not rely on one card, in case of loss. If you do lose a card, immediately contact the 24-hour helpline of the issuer in your home country (keep this number in a safe place). (With thanks to Nigel Baker, Debit Card Manager, Natwest Bank plc, London.)

For purchases, credit cards of the Visa and Mastercard (Eurocard, Access) groups, American Express (Amex), Carte Blanche and Diners Club can be used. American Express is not as useful as Visa, or, to a lesser extent, Mastercard.

Make sure you know the correct procedure if they are lost or stolen. Credit card transactions are normally at an officially recognized rate of exchange; they are often subject to tax. Many establishments charge a fee of 5-10% on credit card transactions; although forbidden by credit card company rules there is not a lot you can do about this, except get the charge itemized on the receipt and complain to the card company. For credit card security, insist that imprints are made in your presence and that any imprints incorrectly completed should be torn into tiny pieces. Also destroy the carbon papers after the form is completed (signatures can be copied from them).

NB It is quite common for tour companies not to accept credit cards, other than for flights, so you will need cash or travellers' cheques for buying tours.

Visa and Mastercard transactions at banks offer good rates. Banco Consolidado is affiliated with American Express, they charge no commission, and some branches cash personal cheques from abroad on an Amex card. Banco Unión, Banco de Venezuela and Banco Mercantil (not all branches) handle Visa and ATM transactions, including cash advances, and Banco Mercantil handles Mastercard. For refunds on lost or stolen Thomas Cook Visa travellers' cheques, phone T 000811-784-0553, 24 hours a day, multilingual staff, for instructions.

Money can be transferred between banks. A recommended method is, before leaving, to find out which local bank is correspondent to your bank at home, then when you need funds, telex your own bank and ask them to telex the money to the local bank (confirming by fax). Give the exact information to your bank of the routing number of the receiving bank. Funds can be received within 48 banking hours. Do not have money sent to you by post, it can take weeks.

● **General tips**

Whenever you leave, sell any local currency before leaving, because the further away you get, the less the value of a country's money. **NB** If departing by air, do not leave yourself too little money to pay the airport departure tax, which is never waived.

North Americans should know that if they run out of funds they can usually expect no help from the US Embassy or Consul other than a referral to some welfare organization. Find out before you go precisely what services and assistance your embassy or consulate can provide if you find yourself in difficulties.

WHAT TO TAKE

Everybody has his/her own list. Those items most often mentioned include: air cushions for slatted seats; inflatable travel pillow for neck support; strong shoes (and remember that footwear over 9½ English size, or 42 European size, is difficult to obtain in Latin America except Argentina and Brazil); a small first-aid kit and handbook; fully waterproof top clothing, waterproof treatment for leather footwear; wax earplugs (which are almost impossible to find outside large cities)

and airline-type eye mask to help you sleep in noisy and poorly curtained hotel rooms; sandals (rubber-thong Japanese-type or other – can be worn in showers to avoid athlete's foot); a polyethylene sheet 2 x 1m to cover possibly infested beds and shelter your luggage, polyethylene bags of varying sizes (up to heavy duty rubbish bag size) with ties; a toilet bag you can tie round your waist; if you use an electric shaver, take a rechargeable type; a sheet sleeping-bag and pillow-case or separate pillow-case – in some countries they are not changed often in cheap hotels; a 1½-2m piece of 100% cotton can be used as a towel; a bedsheet, beach towel, makeshift curtain and wrap; a mosquito net (or a hammock with a fitted net); a straw hat which can be rolled or flattened and reconstituted after 15 minutes soaking in water; a clothes line; a nailbrush (useful for scrubbing dirt off clothes as well as off oneself); a vacuum flask, a water bottle; a small dual-voltage immersion heater, a small dual-voltage (or battery-driven) electric fan; a light nylon waterproof shopping bag; a universal bath- and basin-plug of the flanged type that will fit any waste-pipe (or improvise one from a sheet of thick rubber); string, velcro, electrical insulating tape; large penknife preferably with tin and bottle openers, scissors and corkscrew – the famous Swiss Army range has been repeatedly recommended (for knife sharpening, go to a butcher's shop); alarm clock or watch; candle, torch (flashlight) – especially one that will clip on to a pocket or belt; pocket mirror; pocket calculator; an adaptor and flex to enable you to take power from an electric-light socket (the Edison screw type is the most commonly used); a padlock (combination lock is best) for the doors of the cheapest and most casual hotels (or for tent zip if camping); spare chain-lengths and padlock for securing luggage to bed or bus/train seat. Remember not to throw away spent batteries containing mercury or cadmium; take them home to be disposed of, or recycled properly.

Useful medicaments are given at the end of the 'Health' section (page 361); to these might be added some lip salve with sun protection, and pre-moistened wipes (such as 'Wet Ones'). Always carry toilet paper. Natural fabric sticking plasters, as well as being long-lasting, are much appreciated as gifts. Dental floss can be used for backpack repairs, in addition to its original purpose.

Never carry firearms. Their possession could land you in serious trouble.

A note for **contact lens wearers**: most cities have a wide selection of products for the care of lenses, so you don't need to take litres of lotions. Ask for it in a chemist/pharmacy, rather than an optician's.

Be careful when asking directions. Women probably know more about the neighbourhood; men about more distant locations. Policemen are often helpful. However, many Latin Americans will give you the wrong answer rather than admit they do not know.

Lastly, a good principle is to take half the clothes, and twice the money, that you think you will need.

GETTING THERE

BY AIR
● **From Europe**
British Airways fly from London to Simón Bolívar twice a week direct. There are also services from Europe by Air France, KLM, Iberia, Alitalia and TAP.

● **From North America**
Direct flights with American Airlines (New York, Orlando, Miami, Chicago), United Airlines (New York, Miami, Los Angeles, Chicago), Servivensa (Miami, New York), LanChile (Miami).

● **Latin America and the Caribbean**
From Colombia (Bogotá-Caracas), there are direct flights with Avianca, Servivensa, Saeta and Ecuatoriana. Also Lacsa from Barranquilla. Lacsa flies from San José (Costa Rica) and Panama to Caracas. From Argentina, Brazil and Bolivia there are direct services by Aerolíneas Argentinas, Varig, LAB and Aeropostal. There is direct air service from Chile (LanChile twice weekly), Peru (Saeta, Ecuatoriana, AeroPerú, Servivensa, Avianca), Ecuador (Saeta, Servivensa, Avianca and Ecuatoriana – from Quito; from Guayaquil, Saeta, Ecuatoriana), Santo Domingo (Aeropostal), Puerto Rico (Lacsa), Curaçao (ALM, Servivensa, Aeropostal), Aruba (Air Aruba, Servivensa, ALM, Aserca, Aeropostal), Bonaire (Servivensa, Aeropostal). BWIA have services to Port of Spain (5 days a week from Caracas). Aeropostal also flies from Port of

Spain (to Caracas, Maracaibo and Porlamar), Barbados, St Maarten and from Curaçao. Air France flies to Guadeloupe once a week; Cubana 3 days a week to Havana.

Avensa/Servivensa operate an airpass, which must be bought outside Latin America or the Caribbean. It is valid for 45 days and passengers must buy a minimum of 4 coupons. No route may be flown twice in the same direction. Economy class only; children pay 66% and infants 10% of the adult fare. Prices are by Zone: Caracas to Aruba, Bonaire or Curaçao US$55; Caracas-Miami (but not Barquisimeto or Maracaibo-Miami), Caracas-Bogotá, Bogotá-Quito, or Quito-Lima US$80; Caracas-Lima US$180; Caracas-Quito US$160; Caracas-Mexico City US$200; any internal Venezuelan flight US$45.

● **General tips**

Airlines will only allow a certain weight of luggage without a surcharge; this is normally 30 kilos for first class and 20 kilos for business and economy classes, but these limits are often not strictly enforced when it is known that the plane is not going to be full. On some flights from the UK special outbound concessions are offered (by Iberia, Air France, Avianca) of a 2-piece allowance up to 32 kilos, but you may need to request this. Passengers seeking a larger baggage allowance can route via USA, but with certain exceptions, the fares are slightly higher using this route. On the other hand, weight limits for internal flights are often lower; it's best to enquire beforehand.

● **Prices and discounts**

1 It is generally cheaper to fly from London rather than a point in Europe to Latin American destinations. Fares vary from airline to airline, destination to destination and according to time of year. Check with an agency for the best deal for when you wish to travel.

2 Most airlines offer discounted fares of one sort or another on scheduled flights. These are not offered by the airlines direct to the public, but through agencies who specialize in this type of fare. For full dwetails of agencies specializing in Latin America, see **Useful addresses**, page 355.

The very busy seasons are 7 December – 15 January and 10 July – 10 September. If you intend travelling during those times, book as far ahead as possible. Between February-May and September-November special offers may be available.

3 Other fares fall into three groups, and are all on scheduled services:

● **A. Excursion (return) fares** with restricted validity eg 5-90 days. Carriers are introducing flexibility into these tickets, permitting a change of dates on payment of a fee.

● **B. Yearly fares**: these may be bought on a one-way or return basis. Some airlines require a specified return date, changeable upon payment of a fee. To leave the return completely open is possible for an extra fee. You must fix the route in advance (some of the cheapest flexible fares now have 6 months validity).

● **C. Student (or Under 26) fares** Some airlines are flexible on the age limit, others strict. One way and returns available, or 'Open Jaws' (see below). Do not assume that student tickets are the cheapest; though they are often very flexible, they are usually more expensive than A or B above. On the other hand, there is a wider range of cheap oneway student fares originating in Latin America than can be bought outside the continent. **NB** If you foresee returning home at a busy time (eg Christmas-beginning of January, August), a booking is advisable on any type of open-return ticket.

4 For people intending to travel a linear route and return from a different point from that which they entered, there are 'Open Jaws' fares, which are available on student, yearly, or excursion fares.

5 Many of these fares require a change of plane at an intermediate point, and a stopover may be permitted, or even obligatory, depending on schedules. Simply because a flight stops at a given airport does not mean you can break your journey there – the airline must have traffic rights to pick up or set down passengers between points A and B before it will be permitted. This is where dealing with a specialized agency (like Journey Latin America) will really pay dividends. On multistop itineraries, the specialized agencies can often save clients hundreds of pounds.

6 Although it's a little more complicated, it's possible to sell tickets in London for travel originating in Latin America at substantially cheaper fares than those available locally. This is useful for the traveller who doesn't know where he will end up, or who plans to travel for more than a year. Because of high local taxes a one-way ticket from Latin America is more expensive than a one-way in the other direction, so it's always best to buy a return. Taxes are calculated as a percentage of the full IATA fare; on a discounted fare the tax can therefore make up as much as 30-50% of the price.

7 If you buy discounted air tickets *always* check the reservation with the airline concerned to make sure the flight still exists. Also remember the IATA airlines' schedules change in March and October each year, so if you're going to be away a long time it's best to leave return flight coupons open.

In addition, check whether you are entitled to any refund or re-issued ticket if you lose, or have stolen, a discounted air ticket. Some airlines require the repurchase of a ticket before you can apply for a refund, which will not be given until after the validity of the original ticket has expired. The Iberia group and Air France, for example, operate this costly system. Travel insurance in some cases covers lost tickets.

8 Note that some South American carriers change departure times of short-haul or domestic flights at short notice and, in some instances, schedules shown in the computers of transatlantic carriers differ from those actually flown by smaller, local carriers. If you book, and reconfirm, both your transatlantic and onward sectors through your transatlantic carrier you may find that your travel plans have been based on out of date information. The surest solution is to reconfirm your outward flight in an office of the onward carrier itself.

SEA

● **Shipping**

Voyages on passenger-carrying cargo vessels between Venezuela and Europe, the USA, or elsewhere, are listed here: Projex Line's *EWL West Indies* sails Felixstowe, Paramaribo, Georgetown, Port of Spain, La Guaira, Puerto Cabello, Willemstad, Oranjestad, Cartagena, Santa Marta, Bremen, Rotterdam, Felixstowe, 44-day round trip, £2,600 per person.

From the USA, Ivaran Lines serve East Coast USA, Brazilian ports, Montevideo and Buenos Aires; the *Americana* container ship carries 80 passengers in luxury accommodation (New Orleans, Houston, Puerto Cabello, La Guaira, Rio, Santos, Buenos Aires, Montevideo, Rio Grande do Sul, Itajaí, Paranaguá,

Santos, Salvador, Fortaleza, Bridgetown, San Juan, Veracruz, Tampico, New Orleans, £6,645-11,340 per person per round trip, fares depend on season, one-way north or south possible). Ivaran also have the *San Antonio*, carrying 12 passengers on the route Port Elizabeth (New Jersey), Baltimore, Norfolk, Savannah, Miami, Puerto Cabello, La Guaira, Rio, Santos, Buenos Aires, Montevideo, Rio Grande do Sul, Itajaí, Santos, Rio (possibly Salvador and Fortaleza), Port Elizabeth; 44-day round trip £4,085-4,825 per person, one-way subject to availability. *Sven Ottmann*, 2-week round trip Fort Lauderdale, Oranjestad, Willemstad, Puerto Cabello, La Guaira, Fort Lauderdale £1,300 per person.

Enquiries regarding passages should be made through agencies in your own country, or through John Alton of Strand Cruise and Travel Centre, Charing Cross Shopping Concourse, The Strand, London WC2N 4HZ, T 0171-836 6363, F 0171-497 0078. In Europe, contact Wagner Frachtschiffreisen, Stadlerstrasse 48, CH-8404, Winterthur, Switzerland, T (052) 242-1442, F 242-1487. In the USA, contact Freighter World Cruises, 180 South Lake Ave, Pasadena, CA 91101, T (818) 449-3106, or Travltips Cruise and Freighter Travel Association, 163-07 Depot Road, PO Box 188, Flushing, NY 11358, T (800) 872-8584. Do not try to get a passage on a non-passenger carrying cargo ship to South America from a European port; it is not possible.

NB Shipping details for travel to Curaçao and Aruba can be found in the text under Coro.

● **Shipping a car from Europe**

Harms Hamburg of Bremerhaven ship a car in a container for US$4,100 plus port handling to Venezuela.

On arrival in Venezuela (La Guaira), you must get a letter from the shipping agent stating that the boat has arrived and go to the Tourism Department at Simón Bolívar airport where you must obtain a document identifying your car (take photocopies of driving licence, passport, tourist card, car documents and bill of lading). With this you can get your car out of the port: a shipping agent is not necessary, though knowledge of Spanish is useful. A freight forwarder can be useful; they charge US$40-45, agree price in advance. Go then to Aduanas Marítimas at the port with your bill of lading, ownership documents and passport, and 5 hours to spare. They stop for lunch 1200-1300 and close at weekends. You will have to pay US$100 to the docks company to get your car out. If you will be taking your car out of Venezuela overland, make sure that the freight forwarder gives you a sealed letter for Venezuelan customs at your point of exit.

● **Shipping a car from the USA**
Shipping a car from Miami to Maracaibo or La Guaira: Venezuelan Line (agent Oceanic Steamship Co – recommended, contact Gene Taylor) and Delta Line, fare is less Maracaibo-Miami; no passengers. From New Orleans: Delta Line, passengers carried, but very expensive. Alternatively, agent Hansen and Tiedemann charges same price as Delta for vehicle, but you can accompany it at much lower cost (5 days, including meals). Also recommended: Coordinadora del Caribe Transmodal CA (CCT), Calle Veracruz, Ed Torreón, 7th floor, Las Mercedes, Caracas, T 927133. Vencaribe (shipping) agent is Taurel y cía, Edificio Taurel, Calle Cuji a Romualdo No 69, Apartado 1592, Caracas; representative is Sonigar on 3rd floor, but Paul Paulheim on 1st floor is helpful. In the port of La Guaira Taurel is on the main street, just ask; Johnny Hilahl is the representative, but Wendy the receptionist and Bobby Momighan are also helpful, all speak English. Taurel's shipping department is called 'vapores'. A recommended agent for importing a vehicle is Sr Freddy Diz, T (031) 22028; for unpacking a containerized vehicle, Sr Gustavo Contreras V, Transporte Gusconval, T (Radio) 02-661-9222, or (031) 943901. At the shipping agent Transportadoras Marítimas Venezolanas, Centro Comercial Litoral, on the main street in Maiquetía, Carlos Hernández is very helpful.

● **Yacht**
Do not try and clear Customs and Immigration without an agent in a commercial port; it's well worth the fee. Get your tourist card at a Venezuelan embassy before arriving, although if you arrive during a major storm officials may make an exception. The time a yacht may stay in Venezuelan waters is to be increased from 6 to 18 months. During the busy hurricane season, **security** problems increase; thieves arrive by night in boats with bolt cutters and fast engines and steal dinghies, motors and other items left on deck. Best security is in marinas. Porlamar even has trouble with swimmers during the day. There are fewer problems in the outer islands of La Blanquilla, La Tortuga,

Los Roques, Los Aves and Los Testigos, but trouble has been reported in coastal anchorages, eg Cumaná, Mochima, Morrocoy, Puerto La Cruz. Take all precautions possible. Chris Doyle's *Guide to Trinidad and Tobago and Venezuela*, 1994 edition, has information on yachting. A new edition is expected for Venezuela and Bonaire.

CUSTOMS

● **Duty free allowance**
You may bring into Venezuela, free of duty, 25 cigars and 200 cigarettes, 2 litres of alcoholic drinks, 4 small bottles of perfume, and gifts at the inspector's discretion. New items to the value of US$1,000 may be brought in.

ON ARRIVAL

● **Clothing**
Tropical weight in normal city colours is best for business in Caracas, otherwise clothing is less formal, but smart jackets and ties are required in the most exclusive restaurants and clubs. In Maracaibo and the hot, humid coastal and low-lying areas, regular washable tropical clothing is best. Generally, people are less formal on the coast and shorts are acceptable at most times. The climate in the Andes is cooler, especially at night, so you'll need warmer clothing. For women: blouse and trousers (shorts quite acceptable on the coast); cotton dresses, with a wrap for cool evenings, and for air-conditioned restaurants and cinemas. Cinemas may not admit men in shorts or anyone in flip-flops.

Most Latin Americans, if they can afford it, devote great care to their clothes and appearance; it is appreciated if visitors do likewise. How you dress is mostly how people will judge you. Buying clothing locally can help you to look less like a tourist. It may be advantageous to carry a letter from someone in an official position testifying to one's good character, on official-looking notepaper. A medium weight shawl with some wool content is recommended for women: it can double as pillow, light blanket, bathrobe or sunscreen as required. For men, a smart jacket can be very useful.

● **Courtesy**
Remember that politeness – even a little ceremoniousness – is much appreciated. In this connection professional or business cards are useful. Men should always remove

any headgear and say "con permiso" when entering offices, and be prepared to shake hands (this is much commoner in Latin America than in Europe or North America). Always say "Buenos días" (until midday) or "Buenas tardes" and wait for a reply before proceeding further. Always remember that the traveller from abroad has enjoyed greater advantages in life than most Latin American minor officials, and should be friendly and courteous in consequence. Never be impatient; do not criticize situations in public: the officials may know more English than you think and they can certainly interpret gestures and facial expressions. Be judicious about discussing politics with strangers. Politeness can be a liability, however, in some situations; most Latin Americans are disorderly queuers. In commercial transactions (buying a meal, goods in a shop, etc) politeness should be accompanied by firmness, and always ask the price first.

Politeness should also be extended to street traders; saying "No, gracias" with a smile is better than an arrogant dismissal. Whether you give money to beggars is a personal matter, but your decision should be influenced by whether a person is begging out of need or trying to cash in on the tourist trail. In the former case, local people giving may provide an indication. Giving money to children is a separate issue, upon which most agree: don't do it. There are occasions where giving food in a restaurant may be appropriate, but first inform yourself of local practice.

● **Drugs**
Users of drugs, even of soft ones, without medical prescription should be particularly careful, as some countries impose heavy penalties – up to 10 years' imprisonment – for even the simple possession of such substances. In this connection, the planting of drugs on travellers, by traffickers or the police, is not unknown. If offered drugs on the street, make no response at all and keep walking. Note that people who roll their own cigarettes are often suspected of carrying drugs and subjected to intensive searches. It's advisable to stick to commercial brands of cigarettes.

● **Hours of business**
Banks are open from 0830 to 1130 and 1400 to 1630, Monday to Friday only. Government office hours vary, but 0800-1200 are usual morning hours. Government officials have fixed hours, usually 0900-1000 or 1500-1600, for receiving visitors. Business firms generally start work about 0800 and some continue until about 1800 with a midday break. Shops, 0900-1300, 1500-1900, Monday-Saturday. Generally speaking, Venezuelans start work early, and by 0700 in the morning everything is in full swing. Most firms and offices close on Saturday.

● **Official time**
4 hours behind GMT, 1 hour ahead of EST.

● **Photography**
Always ask permission before photographing people. Pre-paid Kodak slide film cannot be developed in Venezuela; it is also very hard to find. Kodachrome is almost impossible to buy. Some travellers (but not all) have advised against mailing exposed films home; either take them with you, or have them developed, but not printed, once you have checked the laboratory's quality. Note that postal authorities may use less sensitive equipment for X-ray screening than the airports do. Modern controlled X-ray machines are supposed to be safe for any speed of film, but it is worth trying to avoid X-ray as the doses are cumulative. Many airport officials will allow film to be passed outside X-ray arches; they may also hand-check a suitcase with a large quantity of film if asked politely.

Dan Buck and Anne Meadows write: "A note on developing film in South America. Black and white is a problem. Often it is shoddily machine-processed and the negatives are ruined. Ask the store if you can see an example of their laboratory's work and if they hand-develop."

Jeremy Till and Sarah Wigglesworth suggest that exposed film can be protected in humid areas by putting it in a balloon and tying a knot. Similarly keeping your camera in a plastic bag may reduce the effects of humidity.

● **Police**
Whereas in Europe and North America we are accustomed to law enforcement on a systematic basis, in general, enforcement in Latin America is achieved by periodic campaigns. The most typical is a round-up of criminals in the cities just before Christmas. In December, therefore, you may well be asked for identification at any time, and if you cannot produce it, you will be jailed. If a visitor is jailed his/her friends should provide food every day. This is especially important

for people on a diet, such as diabetics. In the event of a vehicle accident in which anyone is injured, all drivers involved are automatically detained until blame has been established, and this does not usually take less than 2 weeks.

Never offer a bribe unless you are fully conversant with the customs of the country. Wait until the official makes the suggestion, or offer money in some form which is apparently not bribery, eg "In our country we have a system of on-the-spot fines (*multas de inmediato*). Is there a similar system here?" Do not assume that an official who accepts a bribe is prepared to do anything else that is illegal. You bribe him to persuade him to do his job, or to persuade him not to do it, or to do it more quickly, or more slowly. You do not bribe him to do something which is against the law. The mere suggestion would make him very upset. If an official suggests that a bribe must be paid before you can proceed on your way, be patient (assuming you have the time) and he may relent.

● **Rape**
This can happen anywhere in the world. If you are the victim of a sexual assault, you are advised in the first instance to contact a doctor (this can be your home doctor if you prefer). You will need tests to determine whether you have contracted any sexually-transmitted diseases; you may also need advice on post-coital contraception. You should also contact your embassy, where consular staff are very willing to help in cases of assault.

● **Safety**
Venezuela is generally a safe place to visit and travel around, but in large cities, especially, Caracas, the threat of robbery or mugging is a very real one. Reports of assaults and mugging of tourists have also been received from Mérida. You need to take great care in Caracas, in daylight as well as at night. You need to take particular care in and around bus stations and in markets. More specific warnings are given in the relevant sections.

General tips Keep all documents secure and hide your main cash supply in different places or under your clothes. Extra pockets sewn inside shirts and trousers, pockets closed with a zip or safety pin, moneybelts (best worn below the waist rather than outside or at it or around the neck), neck or leg pouches, a thin chain for attaching a purse to your bag or under your clothes and elasticated support bandages for keeping money and cheques above the elbow or below the knee have been repeatedly recommended (the last by John Hatt in *The Tropical Traveller*). Keep cameras in bags (preferably with a chain or wire in the strap to defeat the slasher) or briefcases; take spare spectacles (eyeglasses); don't wear wrist-watches or jewellery. If you wear a shoulder-bag in a market, carry it in front of you. Backpacks are vulnerable to slashers: a good idea is to cover the pack with a sack (a plastic one will also keep out rain and dust) with maybe a layer of wire netting between, or make an inner frame of chicken wire. Use a pack which is lockable at its base.

Ignore mustard smearers and paint or shampoo sprayers, and strangers' remarks like "what's that on your shoulder?" or "have you seen that dirt on your shoe?" Furthermore, don't bend over to pick up money or other items in the street. These are all ruses intended to distract your attention and make you easy for an accomplice to steal from. If someone follows you when you're in the street, let him catch up with you and "give him the eye". While you should take local advice about being out at night, do not assume that daytime is safer than nighttime. If walking after dark, walk in the road, not on the pavement/sidewalk.

Be wary of 'plainclothes policemen'; insist on seeing identification and on going to the police station by main roads. Do not hand over your identification (or money – which he should not need to see anyway) until you are at the station. On no account take them directly back to your lodgings. Be even more suspicious if he seeks confirmation of his status from a passer-by. If someone tries to bribe you, insist on a receipt. If attacked, remember your assailants may well be armed, and try not to resist.

It is best, if you can trust your hotel, to leave any valuables you don't need in safe-deposit there, when sightseeing locally. Always keep an inventory of what you have deposited. If you don't trust the hotel, lock everything in your pack and secure that in your room (some people take eyelet-screws for padlocking cupboards or drawers). If you lose valuables, always report to the police and note details of the report – for insurance purposes.

When you have all your luggage with you at a bus or railway station, be especially careful: don't get into arguments with any locals if you can help it, and lock all the items together with a chain or cable if you are waiting for some time. Take a taxi between airport/bus station/railway station and hotel, if you can possibly afford it. Keep your bags with you in the taxi and pay only when you and your luggage are safely out of the vehicle. Make sure the taxi has inner door handles, in case a quick exit is needed. Avoid night buses; never arrive at night; and watch your belongings whether they are stowed inside or outside the cabin. Roof top luggage racks create extra problems, which are sometimes unavoidable – make sure your bag is waterproof. Major bus lines often issue a luggage ticket when bags are stored in the bus' hold. When getting on a bus, keep your ticket handy; someone sitting in your seat may be a distraction for an accomplice to rob you while you are sorting out the problem. Finally, never accept food, drink, sweets or cigarettes from unknown fellow-travellers on buses or trains. They may be drugged, and you would wake up hours later without your belongings. In this connection, never accept a bar drink from an opened bottle (unless you can see that that bottle is in general use): always have it uncapped in front of you.

● **Shopping**

Remember that souvenirs can almost invariably be bought more cheaply away from the capital, though the choice may be less wide. Bargaining seems to be the general rule in street markets, but don't make a fool of yourself by bargaining over what, to you, is a small amount of money.

If British travellers have no space in their luggage, they might like to remember Tumi, the Latin American Craft Centre, who specialize in Mexican and Andean products and who produce cultural and educational videos for schools: at 23/2A Chalk Farm Road, London NW1 8AG (F 0171-485 4152), 8/9 New Bond Street Place, Bath BA1 1BH (T 01225 462367, F 01225 444870), 1/2 Little Clarendon Street, Oxford OX1 2HJ (T/F 01865-512307), 82 Park Street, Bristol BS1 5LA (T/F 0117 929 0391). Tumi (Music) Ltd specializes in different rhythms of Latin America. See *Arts and Crafts of South America*, by Lucy Davies and Mo Fini, published by Tumi (1994), for a fine introduction to the subject. There are similar shops in the USA.

● **Tipping**

Taxi drivers are tipped if the taxi has a meter (hardly anywhere), but not if you have agreed the fare in advance. Usherettes are not tipped. Hotel porters, US$0.50; airport porters US$0.50 per piece of baggage. Restaurants, between 5 and 10% of bill.

● **Travelling alone**

Many points of security, dress and language have been covered already. First time exposure to countries where sections of the population live in extreme poverty or squalor and may even be starving can cause odd psychological reactions in visitors. So can the exceptional curiosity extended to visitors, especially women. Simply be prepared for this and try not to over-react. These additional hints have mainly been supplied by women, but most apply to any single traveller. When you set out, err on the side of caution until your instincts have adjusted to the customs of a new culture. If, as a single woman, you can befriend a local woman, you will learn much more about the country you are visiting. Unless actively avoiding foreigners like yourself, don't go too far from the beaten track; there is a very definite 'gringo trail' which you can join, or follow, if seeking company. This

---

Hotel prices

Our hotel price ranges, including taxes and service charges but without meals unless stated, are as follows:

L1	Over US$200	**L2**	US$151-200	**L3**	US$101-150
A1	US$81-100	**A2**	US$61-80	**A3**	US$46-60
B	US$31-45	**C**	US$21-30	**D**	US$12-20
E	US$7-11	**F**	US$4-6	**G**	Up to US$3

NB Prices are for double rooms, except in **F** and **G** ranges where the price is almost always per person.

can be helpful when looking for safe accommodation, especially if arriving after dark (which is best avoided). Remember that for a single woman a taxi at night can be as dangerous as wandering around on her own. At borders dress as smartly as possible. It is easier for men to take the friendliness of locals at face value; women may be subject to much unwanted attention. To help minimize this, do not wear suggestive clothing and, advises Alex Rossi of Jawa Timur, Indonesia, do not flirt. By wearing a wedding ring, carrying a photograph of your 'husband' and 'children', and saying that your "husband" is close at hand, you may dissuade an aspiring suitor. If politeness fails, do not feel bad about showing offence and departing. When accepting a social invitation, make sure that someone knows the address and the time you left. Ask if you can bring a friend (even if you do not intend to do so). A good rule is always to act with confidence, as though you know where you are going, even if you do not. Someone who looks lost is more likely to attract unwanted attention. Do not disclose to strangers where you are staying. (Much of this information was supplied by Alex Rossi, and by Deirdre Mortell of Carrigaline, Co Cork).

● **Voltage**
110 volts, 60 cycles, throughout the country.

● **Weights and measures**
Weights and measures are metric.

ON DEPARTURE

● **Airport information**
To avoid overbooking the Government obliges airlines to post a passenger list, but it is important to obtain clear instructions from the travel agent regarding confirmation of your flight and checking-in time. **NB** Passengers leaving Caracas on international flights must reconfirm their reservations not less than 72 hours in advance; it is safer to do so in person than by telephone; not less than 24 hours for national flights: if you fail to do this, you lose all rights to free accommodation, food, transport, etc if your flight is cancelled and may lose your seat if the plane is fully booked. Beware of counterfeit tickets; buy only from agencies. If told by an agent that a flight is fully booked, try at the airport anyway. International passengers must check in 2 hours before departure or

they may lose their seat to someone on a waiting list. Handling charge for your luggage US$0.50. When leaving Maiquetía airport, beware Gate 5. This is subdivided into gates A-D; hundreds of passengers with different destinations are crammed into a lounge where flights are not called and the monitor does not work. Keep asking the staff with the walkie-talkie if your flight is boarding. All flights are subject to delays or cancellation.

● **Airport and land departure taxes**
All tourists and diplomats leaving the country, except transit passengers, must pay US$25 at the airport, land border or port of embarkation (payable in bolívares or dollars). Minors under 12 years of age do not pay the exit tax. Venezuelans, resident foreigners or those with a visa *transeunte* have to pay US$2.50 on departure. There is also an airport tax of US$0.45 for those passengers on internal flights, payable at every change of plane. Exit stamps for overland travellers, US$2 (except US$5 Maracaibo-Maicao, Colombia).

WHERE TO STAY

● **Accommodation**
Price largely depends on which part of the country you are visiting. The major cities tend to be more expensive; Isla de Margarita, Guayana and Amazonas are also more expensive. In Caracas, for example, you'll pay at least US$10 per person for a reasonably clean and comfortable hotel room. Also note that prices for air conditioned rooms are generally about 10-15% higher. In the Andean region, prices are lower, especially in Mérida, where you can find a good place to stay for around US$5 per person, or even less.

For those on a really tight budget, it is a good idea to ask for a boarding house – *casa de huéspedes, hospedaje, pensión, casa familial* or *residencial*, according to country; they are normally to be found in abundance near bus and railway stations and markets. Good value hotels can also be found near truckers' stops/service stations; they are usually secure. There are often great seasonal variations in hotel prices in resorts.

Remember, cheaper hotels don't always supply soap, towels and toilet paper; in colder (higher) regions they may not supply enough blankets, so take your own or a sleeping bag.

In any class, hotel rooms facing the street may be noisy; always ask for the best, quietest room. To avoid price hikes for gringos, ask if there is a cheaper room.

NB The electric showers used in innumerable hotels should be checked for obvious flaws in the wiring; try not to touch the rose while it is producing hot water.

Fairmont International (see page 83) will book hotel rooms both in Caracas and in other towns, where they have 102 hotels on their books, not all of which are mentioned in these pages. Hotels marked with an asterisk (*) are bookable through Fairmont. Officially controlled prices exist for 1-star and 2-star hotels. Hotels of our B price category upwards are often heavily booked up, especially in Caracas; advance reservations are advisable. 3-star hotels start at about US$15-20 a night. Prices for singles are often not much less than doubles.

● **Cockroaches**
These are ubiquitous and unpleasant, but not dangerous. Take some insecticide powder if staying in cheap hotels; Baygon (Bayer) has been recommended. Stuff toilet paper in any holes in walls that you may suspect of being parts of cockroach runs.

● **Toilets**
Many hotels, restaurants and bars have inadequate water supplies. **Almost without exception used toilet paper should not be flushed down the pan, but placed in the receptacle provided**. This applies even in quite expensive hotels. Failing to observe this custom will block the pan or drain, a considerable health risk. It is quite common for people to stand on the toilet seat (facing the wall – easier to balance).

● **Camping**
Organized campsites are referred to in the text immediately below hotel lists, under each town. If there is no organized site in town, a football pitch or gravel pit might serve. Obey the following rules for 'wild' camping: (1) arrive in daylight and pitch your tent as it gets dark; (2) ask permission to camp from the parish priest, or the fire chief, or the police, or a farmer regarding his own property; (3) never ask a group of people – especially young people; (4) never camp on a beach (because of sandflies and thieves). If you can't get information from anyone, camp in a spot where you can't be seen from the nearest inhabited place, or road, and make sure no one saw you go there. As Béatrice Völkle of Gampelen, Switzerland, adds, camping wild may be preferable to those organized sites which are treated as discotheques, with only the afternoon reserved for sleeping.

If taking a cooker, the most frequent recommendation is a multifuel stove (eg MSR International, Coleman Peak 1), which will burn unleaded petrol or, if that is not available, kerosene, *benzina blanca*, etc. Alcohol-burning stoves are simple, reliable, but slow and you have to carry a lot of fuel: for a methylated spirit-burning stove, the following fuels apply, *alcohol desnaturalizado, alcohol metílico, alcohol puro (de caña)* or *alcohol para quemar*. Ask for 95%, but 70% will suffice. Fuel can usually be found in chemists/pharmacies. Gas cylinders and bottles are usually exchangeable, but if not can be recharged; specify whether you use butane or propane. Gas canisters are not always available.

Equipment, perhaps not of the highest standard, is available at sports-goods shops in Caracas. It is impossible, in fact illegal, to refill portable gas cylinders. Cylinders are sold at Deportes el Llanero, Caracas, T 545-1634. Those using gasoline stoves should note that even the higher octane fuels will cause blockages of fuel jets. Camping in Venezuela is a popular recreation, for spending a weekend at the beach, on the islands, in the *llanos* and in the mountains. (People pitch their tents on Monte Avila overlooking Caracas.) Camping, with or without a vehicle, is not possible at the roadside. If camping on the beach, for the sake of security, pitch your tent close to others, even though they play their radios loud. For information on hiking, climbing and relevant equipment, telephone Alexander on (02) 573-0056 (Spanish only). See page 311 on camping in the Canaima National Park.

GETTING AROUND

AIR TRANSPORT

Most places of importance are served by Avensa, Servivensa, Aeropostal and LAI. Aerotuy and Aserca (recommended for good service) fly to a variety of destinations. For flight details on specific destinations, see under that particular section. The most economical way to fly is with the Avensa/Servivensa airpass, see page 334. Internal airlines offer special family discounts and student discount but practice is variable, photocopies of ISIC card are useful as it allows officials to staple one to the ticket. Sometimes there is little difference between 1st class and tourist class fares. Beware of overbooking during holiday time, especially at Caracas airport; it is recommended that you check in 2 hours before departure, particularly at Easter.

LAND TRANSPORT

● Trains
The only passenger traffic of any importance is on the Barquisimeto to Puerto Cabello line. The 110 km Yaritagua-Acarigua-Turén electric railway line was opened at the beginning of 1983, intended mostly to transport agricultural products. Passengers are carried on the Acarigua-Yaritagua stretch.

● Road
Venezuela has an extensive road system for motor traffic, with frequent bus services. Buses are relatively cheap, but the quality of long-distance travel varies a lot. There are numerous services between the major cities. Buses stop frequently, but there may not always be a toilet at the stop. For night journeys in air conditioned buses take a sleeping bag or similar because the setting is set to freezing. Also take earplugs against the loud stereo systems.

The colectivo taxis and minibuses, known as *por puesto*, seem to monopolize transport to and from smaller towns and villages. For longer journeys they are normally twice as expensive as buses, but faster. They may be reluctant to take luggage and the ill-kempt. If first on board, wait for other passengers to arrive, and do not take a *por puesto* on your own unless you want to pay for the whole vehicle. Outside Caracas, town taxis are relatively expensive. At peak periods *revendedores* (touts) will try to sell tickets at 2-3 times face value. Note also that buses and *por puestos* leave when they're full, regardless of whether or not this is before the scheduled time.

Tall travellers are advised to take aisle rather than window seats on long journeys as this allows more leg room. When the journey takes more than 3 or 4 hours, meal stops at country inns or bars, good and bad, are the rule. Usually, no announcement is made on the duration of a stop: follow the driver, if he eats, eat. See what the locals are eating –

and buy likewise, or make sure you're stocked up well on food and drink at the start. For drinks, stick to bottled water or soft drinks or coffee (black). The food sold by vendors at bus stops may be all right: watch if locals are buying, though unpeeled fruit is of course reliable. (See also above under **Security**.)

● Motoring
All visitors to Venezuela can drive if they are over 18 and have a valid driving licence from their own country; an international driving licence is preferred. A tourist can bring in his/her car without paying duty. See above for **Shipping a car from the USA** or **Europe**. A visa is required for overland entry (this is necessary despite what Consulates may tell you). An entry permit for a car costs US$10 and requires one photograph (takes 24 hours); ask for a permit for 6 months, or unspecified time.

● **Documents** A great deal of conflicting information surrounds what documents are required in addition to the vehicle's registration. According to the RAC in the UK there are three recognized documents for taking a vehicle into South America: a *carnet de passages* issued by the Fedération Internationale de l'Automobile (FIA – Paris), a *carnet de passages* issued by the Alliance Internationale de Tourisme (AIT-Geneva), and the *Libreta de Pasos por Aduana* issued by the Federación Interamericana de Touring y Automóvil Clubs (FITAC).

Official requirements for Venezuela are: either *carnet* or the *libreta*. The consulate in London says a *Certificado de uso por turismo* must be completed at a Venezuelan embassy before arrival, no other documents required; in the USA the vehicle's title document must be legalized by a Venezuelan consul, US$100, this, plus title and a letter of intent from your shipper's agent must be taken to US customs at least 2 days before sailing, no *libreta* or *carnet* needed. Nevertheless, motorists in South America seem to fare better with a *libreta* or *carnet de passages* than without it.

The *libreta*, a 10-page book of three-part passes for customs, should be available from any South American automobile club member of FITAC, but in practice it is only available in Venezuela to non-residents (see pages 206 and 91 for addresses of the **Touring y Automóvil Club**). The cost is about US$350,

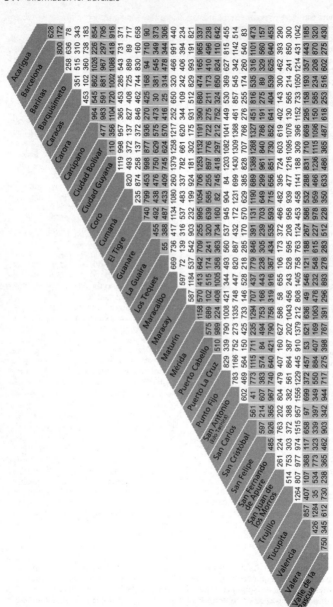

Distances between main cities (km)

but is more for those who are not members of automobile clubs; about a third of the cost is refundable.

It takes 24 hours and your vehicle must be presented to the Club. Before shipping your vehicle to Venezuela, go to a Venezuelan consul to obtain all necessary documentation, including visa, to allow you to enter the country prior to getting the *libreta*. You must also go to a Venezuelan consul in the country in which you land your car if other than Venezuela.

The *carnet de passages* is issued only in the country where the vehicle is registered (in the UK it costs £65 for 25 pages, £55 for 10 pages, valid 12 months, either bank indemnity or insurance indemnity, half of the premium refundable value of the vehicle and countries to be visited required), available from the RAC or the AA. In the USA the AAA does not issue the *carnet*, although the HQ in Washington DC may give advice. It is available from the Canadian Automobile Association (1775 Courtwood Crescent, Ottawa, K2C 3JZ, T 613-226-7631, F 613-225-7383) for Canadian and US citizens, cost C$400; full details obtainable from the CAA.

For vehicles with Venezuelan registration leaving Venezuela the following documents are required: an Automóvil passport book from the Touring y Automóvil Club de Venezuela; the original car papers; the registration document; a police *revisión* obtained from the Policía Técnica Judicial; and a temporary import/export licence for a vehicle obtainable from the Ministerio de Hacienda, Caracas, or from a customs agent in San Antonio de Táchira (border town) for about US$100. The export/import licence and the passport book must be signed and stamped by the Customs Administrator. In the border area with Colombia, police checks are frequent; make sure you have all your papers. If possible, check all details on bringing in/taking out a car in advance.

● **General motoring hints**

Do not drive at night if you can help it (if you do have to, don't drive fast). Carry insect spray if you do; if you stop and get out, the car will fill with biting insects.

Motoring restrictions in Caracas include a ban on parking in front of a bank; motorcycles may not be driven at night; pillion passengers may not be carried on motorcycles if of the same sex as the driver. You are more likely to be penalized for infringing these rules than for driving through a red light; they are designed to improve security for banks and pedestrians. In addition, motorcyclists are obliged to wear a crash helmet but it must not be of a type which obscures the face. Use private car-parks whenever possible as break-ins on streets are common in Caracas and all large cities.

There are five grades of gasoline: 'normal', 83 octane; 87, 89, 91 and 'alta', 95 octane (average cost US$0.10-0.12 a litre). Diesel (US$0.10 a litre) is used by most goods vehicles, available from many filling stations in Caracas. Fuel prices are due to rise, by an unknown amount. Oil costs US$0.60 a litre. Service stations are open 0500-2100, Monday-Saturday, except those on highways which are open longer hours. Only those designated to handle emergencies are open on Sunday. In the event of breakdown, Venezuelans are usually very helpful. There are many garages, even in rural areas; service charges are not high, nor are tyres, oil or accessories expensive, but being able to speak Spanish will greatly assist in sorting out problems. Carry spare battery water, fan belts, the obligatory breakdown triangle, a jack and spanners. **Warning** There is an automatic US$20 fine for running out of fuel. See also **Tourist Information** under Caracas, and Maps under Rounding Up.

● **Driving your own car**

What kind of motoring you do will depend on what kind of car you set out with. The roads in Venezuela are generally poor, except for the 4-lane autopistas. While a normal car will reach most places of interest, high ground clearance is useful for badly surfaced or unsurfaced roads and for fording rivers: 4-wheel drive is recommended for mountain terrain and unmade roads off the beaten track. In Amazonas, roads are frequently impassable. Consider fitting wire guards for headlamps, and for windscreens too, if you don't mind peering out through a grill like a caged chimpanzee. Wherever you travel you should expect from time to time to find roads that are badly maintained, damaged or closed during the wet season, and delays because of floods, landslides and huge potholes. Don't plan your schedules too tightly.

Diesel cars are much cheaper to run than petrol ones, and the fuel is easily available; in Venezuela you may have to look hard for it outside Caracas. Most towns can supply a mechanic of sorts, and probably parts for Bosch fuel injection equipment. Watch the mechanics like a hawk, since there's always a brisk market in spares, and some of yours may be highly desirable. That apart, they enjoy a challenge, and can fix most things, eventually.

For prolonged motoring over 3,000m, you may need to fit high altitude jets on your carburettors. Some fuel injection engines need adjusting too, and ignition settings may have to be changed: check the manufacturer's recommendations. The electronic ignition and fuel metering systems on modern emission controlled cars are allergic to humidity, heat and dust, and cannot be repaired by bush mechanics. Standard European and Japanese cars run on fuel with a higher octane rating than is commonly available. A high compression fuel injection engine will not like this. The most easily maintained petrol engined cars, then, are the types manufactured in Latin American countries, ie pre-emission control models such as the VW Kombi with carburettors and conventional (non-electronic) ignition, or the old type Toyota Landcruisers. Older model American cars, especially Ford or GM pickups, are easily maintained, but high fuel consumption offsets this advantage. Note that Venezuela does have a network for spares and repairs of VW.

● **Preparation**

Preparing the car for the journey is largely a matter of common sense: obviously any part that is not in first class condition should be replaced. It's well worth installing extra heavy-duty shock-absorbers (such as Spax or Koni) before starting out, because a long trip on rough roads in a heavily laden car will give heavy wear. Fit tubes on 'tubeless' tyres, since air plugs for tubeless tyres are hard to find, and if you bend the rim on a pothole, the tyre will not hold air. Take spare tubes, and an extra spare tyre. Also take spare plugs, fan-belts, radiator hoses and headlamp bulbs; even though local equivalents can easily be found in cities, it is wise to take spares for those occasions late at night or in remote areas when you might need them. You can also change the fanbelt after a stretch of long, hot driving to prevent wear (eg after 15,000 km/10,000 miles). If your vehicle has more than one fanbelt, always

replace them all at the same time (make sure you have the necessary tools if doing it yourself). If your car has sophisticated electrics, spare 'black boxes' for the ignition and fuel injection are advisable, plus a spare voltage regulator or the appropriate diodes for the alternator, and elements for the fuel, air and oil filters if these are not a common type. (Some drivers take a spare alternator of the correct amperage, especially if the regulator is incorporated into the alternator.) Dirty fuel is a frequent problem, so be prepared to change filters more often than you would at home: in a diesel car you will need to check the sediment bowl often, too. An extra in-line fuel filter is a good idea if feasible (although harder to find, metal canister type is preferable to plastic), and for travel on dusty roads an oil bath air filter is best for a diesel car. It is wise to carry a spade, jumper cables, tow rope and an air pump. Fit tow hooks to both sides of the vehicle frame. A 12 volt neon light for camping and repairs will be invaluable. Spare fuel containers should be steel and not plastic, and a siphon pipe is essential for those places where fuel is sold out of the drum. Take a 10 litre water container for self and vehicle. Note that in some areas gas stations are few and far between. Fill up when you see one: the next one may be out of fuel.

● **Security**

Apart from the mechanical aspects, spare no ingenuity in making your car secure. Your model should be the Brink's armoured van: anything less secure can be broken into by the determined and skilled thief. Use heavy chain and padlocks to chain doors shut, fit security catches on windows, remove interior window winders (so that a hand reaching in from a forced vent cannot open the window). All these will help, but none is foolproof. Anything on the outside – wing mirrors, spot lamps, motifs etc – is likely to be stolen too. So are wheels if not secured by locking nuts. Try never to leave the car unattended except in a locked garage or guarded parking space. Remove all belongings and leave the empty glove compartment open when the car is unattended. Also lock the clutch or accelerator to the steering wheel with a heavy, obvious chain or lock. Street children will generally protect your car fiercely in exchange for a tip. Be sure to note down key numbers and carry spares of the most important ones (but don't keep all spares inside the vehicle).

Insurance for the vehicle against accident, damage or theft is best arranged in the country of origin, but it is getting increasingly difficult to find agencies who offer this service. In Latin American countries it is very expensive to insure against accident and theft, especially as you should take into account the value of the car increased by duties calculated in real (ie non devaluing) terms. If the car is stolen or written off you will be required to pay very high import duty on its value. Venezuela insists on compulsory third party insurance, to be bought at the border; it is easy to obtain. Short term insurance policies are available with Seguros La Seguridad, offices all over the country. Get the legally required minimum cover, not expensive, as soon as you can, because if you should be involved in an accident and are uninsured, your car could be confiscated. If you do have an accident and someone is injured, you will be detained as a matter of routine, even if you are not at fault.

● **Car hire**

It is a good idea to hire a car; many of the best places are off the beaten track. Some companies such as National have a wide network of offices in towns and airports allowing a fly-drive approach to travel, using a number of different vehicles. You have to have a credit card to rent a vehicle. Car hire with insurance varies from company to company: basic rates for a car are from US$16-50 per day depending on make; government tax of 12.5% is also added. Rates tend to be the same in all cities, except on Margarita, which is more expensive. Hotels and tourist agencies will tell you where to find cheaper rates, but you will need to check that you have such basics as spare wheel, tool kit and functioning lights etc. If planning to hire a car for any length of time it is worth the trouble to obtain a *licencia temporal para conducir*; for this you require a medical certificate (eye examination, blood pressure, US$2, issued by an authorized medical centre, try Touring y Automóvil Club, Caracas), photocopy of your home driver's licence and two black-and-white passport photos which must be presented at the Ministerio de Transporte y Comunicaciones, Torre Este, Parque Central, Dep Licencias. If you plan to do a lot of driving and will have time at the end to dispose of it, investigate the possibility of buying a second hand car locally: since hiring is so expensive it

may well work out cheaper and will probably do you just as well.

Car Hire Insurance Check exactly what the hirer's insurance policy covers. In many cases it will only protect you against minor bumps and scrapes, not major accidents, nor 'natural' damage (eg flooding). Ask if extra cover is available. Also find out, if using a credit card, whether the card automatically includes insurance. Beware of being billed for scratches which were on the vehicle before you hired it.

● **Recommended reading** Two books containing much practical information on South American motoring conditions and requirements are *Driving to Heaven*, by Derek Stansfield (available from the author, Ropley, Broad Oak, Sturminster Newton, Dorset DT10 2HG, T/F 01258-472534, £8.85 plus postage, if outside the UK), and the more recent *Central and South America by Road*, Pam Ascanio (Bradt Publications 1996); see **Maps and Guide Books**, below.

● **Motorcycling**

People are generally very amicable to motorcyclists and you can make many friends by returning friendship to those who show an interest in you.

The Machine It should be off road capable: my choice would be the BMW R80/100/GS for its rugged and simple design and reliable shaft drive, but a Kawasaki KLR 650s, Honda Transalp/Dominator, or the ubiquitous Yamaha XT600 Tenere would also be suitable. A road bike can go most places an off road bike can go at the cost of greater effort.

Preparations Many roads in Venezuela are rough. Fit heavy duty front fork springs and the best quality rebuildable shock absorber you can afford (Ohlins, White Power). Fit lockable luggage such as Krausers (reinforce luggage frames) or make some detachable aluminium panniers. Fit a tank bag and tank panniers for better weight distribution. A large capacity fuel tank (Acerbis), +300 mile/480 km range is essential if going off the beaten track. A washable air filter is a good idea (K&N), also fuel filters, fueltap rubber seals and smaller jets for high altitude Andean motoring. A good set of trails-type tyres as well as a high mudguard are useful. Get to know the bike before you go, ask the dealers in your country what goes wrong with it and arrange a link whereby you can get parts flown out to you. If riding a chain driven bike, a fully enclosed chaincase is useful. A hefty bash plate/sump guard is invaluable.

Spares Reduce service intervals by half if driving in severe conditions. A spare rear tyre is useful but you can buy modern tyres in most cities. Take oil filters, fork and shock seals, tubes, a good manual, spare cables (taped into position), a plug cap and spare plug lead. A spare electronic ignition is a good idea, try and buy a second hand one and make arrangements to have parts sent out to you. A first class tool kit is a must and if riding a bike with a chain then a spare set of sprockets and an 'o' ring chain should be carried. Spare brake and clutch levers should also be taken as these break easily in a fall. Parts are few and far between, but mechanics are skilled at making do and can usually repair things. Castrol oil can be bought everywhere and relied upon.

Take a puncture repair kit and tyre levers. Find out about any weak spots on the bike and improve them. Get the book for international dealer coverage from your manufacturer, but don't rely on it. They frequently have few or no parts for modern, large machinery.

Clothes and equipment A tough waterproof jacket, comfortable strong boots, gloves and a helmet with which you can use glass goggles (Halycon) which will not scratch and wear out like a plastic visor. The best quality tent and camping gear that you can afford and a petrol stove which runs on bike fuel is helpful.

Security Not a problem: try not to leave a fully laden bike on its own. An Abus D or chain will keep the bike secure. A cheap alarm gives you peace of mind if you leave the bike outside a hotel at night. Most hotels will allow you to bring the bike inside. Look for hotels that have a courtyard or more secure parking and never leave luggage on the bike overnight or whilst unattended.

Documents Passport, International Driving Licence, bike registration document are necessary. Riders fare much better with a *carnet de passages* than without it.

● **Cycling**

Hallam Murray writes (with recent additions from other cyclists): since the early 1980s, bicycle technology has improved in leaps and bounds. With the advent of Kevlar tyres and puncture-resistant inner tubes it is now theoretically possible to cycle from Alaska to Tierra del Fuego without so much as a single puncture. For the traveller with a zest for adventure and a limited budget there is unlikely to be a finer way to explore. At first glance a bicycle may not appear to be the most obvious vehicle for a major journey, but given ample time and reasonable energy it most certainly is the best. It can be ridden, carried by almost every form of transport from an aeroplane to a canoe, and can even be lifted across one's shoulders over short distances. Cyclists can be the envy of travellers using more orthodox transport, since they can travel at their own pace, explore more remote regions, meet people who are not normally in contact with tourists.

Choosing a Bicycle The choice of bicycle depends on the type and length of expedition being undertaken and on the terrain and road surfaces likely to be encountered. Unless you are planning a journey almost exclusively on paved roads – when a high quality touring bike such as a Dawes Super Galaxy would probably suffice – a mountain bike is strongly recommended. The good quality ones (and the cast iron rule is **never** to skimp on quality) are incredibly tough and rugged, with low gear ratios for difficult terrain, wide tyres with plenty of tread for good road-holding, cantilever brakes, and a low centre of gravity for improved stability. Although touring bikes, and to a lesser extent mountain bikes, and spares are available in the larger cities, remember that in the developing world most indigenous manufactured goods are shoddy and rarely last. Where imported components can be found they tend to be extremely expensive. (Shimano parts are generally the easiest to find.) Buy everything you possibly can before you leave home.

Bicycle Equipment A small but comprehensive tool kit (to include chain rivet and crank removers, a spoke key and possibly a block remover), a spare tyre and inner tubes, a puncture repair kit with plenty of extra patches and glue, a set of brake blocks, brake and gear cables and all types of nuts and bolts, at least 12 spokes (best taped to the chain stay), a light oil for the chain (eg Finish-Line Teflon Dry-Lube), tube of waterproof grease, a pump secured by a pump lock, a Blackburn parking block (a most invaluable accessory, cheap and virtually weightless), a cyclometer, a loud bell, and a secure lock and chain. *Richard's Bicycle Book* makes useful reading for even the most mechanically minded.

Luggage and equipment Strong and waterproof front and back panniers are a must. When packed these are likely to be heavy and should be carried on the strongest racks available. Poor quality racks have ruined many a journey for they take incredible strain on unpaved roads. A top bag cum rucksack (eg Carradice) makes a good addition for use on and off the bike. A Cannondale front bag is good for maps, camera, compass, altimeter, notebook and small tape-recorder. (Other recommended panniers are Ortlieb – front and back – which is waterproof and almost 'sandproof', Mac-Pac, Madden and Karimoor.) 'Gaffa' tape is excellent for protecting vulnerable parts of panniers and for carrying out all manner of repairs. My most vital equipment included a light and waterproof tent, a 3 season sleeping bag, an Optimus petrol stove (recommended as it is light and efficient and petrol can be found almost everywhere, but see **Camping** above), elastic survival bag for storing luggage at night when camping, 4 elastic straps, 4 one-litre water bottles, Swiss Army knife, torch, candle, comprehensive medical kit, money belts, a hat and sunglasses to protect against hours of ferocious tropical sun and small presents such as postcards of home, balloons and plastic badges. A rubber mouse can do wonders for making contact with children in isolated villages.

All equipment and clothes should be packed in plastic bags to give extra protection against dust and rain. (Also protect all documents, etc carried close to the body from sweat.) Always take the minimum clothing. It's better to buy extra items en route when you find you need them. Naturally the choice will depend on whether you are planning a journey through tropical lowlands, deserts, high mountains or a combination, and whether rain is to be expected. Generally it is best to carry several layers of thin light clothes than fewer heavy, bulky ones. Always keep one set of dry clothes, including long trousers, to put on at the end of the day. The incredibly light, strong, waterproof and wind resistant goretex jacket and overtrousers are invaluable. Training shoes can be used for both cycling and walking.

Useful Tips Wind, not hills is the enemy of the cyclist. Try to make the best use of the times of day when there is little; mornings tend to be best but there is no steadfast rule. Take care to avoid dehydration, by drinking regularly. In hot, dry areas with limited supplies of water, be sure to carry an ample supply. For food, carry the staples (sugar, salt, dried milk, tea, coffee, porridge oats, raisins, dried soups, etc) and supplemented these with whatever local foods can be found in the markets. Give your bicycle a thorough daily check for loose nuts or bolts or bearings. See that all parts run smoothly. A good chain should last 2,000 miles, 3,200 km or more but be sure to keep it as clean as possible – an old toothbrush is good for this – and to oil it lightly from time to time. Always camp out of sight of a road. Remember that thieves are attracted to towns and cities, so when sight-seeing, try to leave your bicycle with someone such as a café owner or a priest. Country people tend to be more honest and are usually friendly and very inquisitive. However, don't take unnecessary risks; always see that your bicycle is secure (most hotels will allow bikes to be kept in rooms). In more remote regions dogs can be vicious; carry a stick or some small stones to frighten them off. Traffic on main roads can be a nightmare; it is usually far more rewarding to keep to the smaller roads or to paths if they exist. Most towns have a bicycle shop of some description, but it is best to do your own repairs and adjustments whenever possible. In an emergency it is amazing how one can improvise with wire, string, dental floss, nuts and bolts, odd pieces of tin or 'Gaffa' tape!

The Expedition Advisory Centre, administered by the Royal Geographical Society, 1, Kensington Gore, London SW7 2AR has published a useful monograph entitled *Bicycle Expeditions*, by Paul Vickers. Published in March 1990, it is available direct from the Centre, price £6.50 (postage extra if outside the UK). (In the UK there is also the Cyclist's Touring Club, CTC, Cotterell House, 69 Meadrow, Godalming, Surrey, GU7 3HS, T 01483-417217, e-mail: cycling@ctc.org.uk, for touring, and technical information.)

Most cyclists agree that the main danger comes from other traffic. A rearview mirror has been frequently recommended to forewarn you of vehicles which are too close behind. You also need to watch out for oncoming, overtaking vehicles, unstable loads on trucks, protruding loads etc. Make yourself conspicuous by wearing bright clothing and a helmet.

Ryan Flegal of Los Angeles, California,

says that, instead of taking your own expensive bicycle from home with the attendant need for specialized tools and high risks of loss, one can buy a bike in Latin America. "Affix a sturdy rear rack, improvise securing luggage to the bicycle, and go. Carry only a patch kit and wrench to remove the wheel, and rely on the many bike mechanics in the area to do the rest". A steel frame is more durable when heavily laden and can be welded if damaged, unlike aluminium. If undertaking your own maintenance, make sure you know how to do it, and research what tyres you will need, before you go.

● **Hitchhiking**

Hitchhiking (*Cola*) is not very easy and not very safe in coastal regions, but elsewhere the Venezuelans are usually friendly and helpful if you know some Spanish. The best places to try are Guardia Nacional posts outside cities (may get free bus rides from them). It is illegal on toll roads and, theoretically, for non-family members in the back of pick up trucks. Some drivers may ask for money for the lift, especially if on a bus route, common in the Gran Sabana.

● **Boat**

In Amazonia wait at the police posts where boats are obliged to report.

COMMUNICATIONS

● **Language**

The official language is Spanish. Without some knowledge of this you can become very frustrated and feel helpless in many situations. English, or any other language, is absolutely useless off the beaten track. Some initial study, to get you up to a basic Spanish vocabulary of 500 words or so, and a pocket dictionary and phrase-book, are most strongly recommended: your pleasure will be doubled if you can talk to the locals. See **Useful words and phrases** on page 357.

● **Newspapers**

Caracas: *El Universal*, *El Nacional* and *El Diario de Caracas*, *La Religión*, *Ultimas Noticias*. The *Daily Journal* (English), *El Mundo* and *2001* (evening), *Número* (weekly), *Resumen* (weekly), *Elite* (weekly), *Momento* (weekly), *Venezuela Gráfica* (weekly), *Páginas* (weekly), *Semana* (weekly), *Ve Venezuela*, tourist bi-monthly. Maracaibo: *Panorama*, *La Crítica*. Puerto La Cruz: *El Tiempo*. For economic news, *El Globo* (daily), *Economía Hoy* (daily) and *Reporte* (3 times a week). The Sunday edition of Hoy contains the *Guardian Weekly* from the UK.

● **Postal services**

The postal service can be extremely slow and unreliable. For a letter up to 20 grams to the Americas the cost is US$0.30; to the rest of the world US$0.36. A 10-kilo package is US$25 to Europe, airmail only. All boxes must be wrapped up and sewn up with cloth. Airmail letters to the USA or Europe can take from 1 to 4 weeks and registered mail is no quicker. Internal mail also travels slowly, especially if there is no PO Box number. As in other Latin countries removing stamps from letters occurs (Trish and Tony Wheeler suggest that you insist on seeing your letters franked because you are a collector). Avoid the mail boxes in pharmacies as some no longer have collections. A private parcel delivery company, such as DHL, will charge around US$60 for parcels of up to 500g to Europe.

● **Telephone services**

All international and long distance calls are operated by CANTV. Most major cities are now linked by direct dialling (*Discado Directo*), with a 3-figure prefix for each town in Venezuela. Otherwise CANTV offices deal with most long-distance and international calls in the cities outside Caracas. Collect calls are possible to some countries, at least from Caracas, though staff in offices may not be sure of this. Calls out of Venezuela are more expensive than calls into it and are subject to long delays. Local calls are troublesome and the connection is often cut in the middle of your conversation; calls are best made from hotels or CANTV offices, rather than from booths. Most public phones operate on pre-paid CANTV cards in denominations of 1,000 and 2,000 bolívares. Buy them from CANTV or numerous small shops bearing the CANTV logo, or a scrap of card reading '¡Sí! ¡hay tarjetas!' They are also sold by street vendors. Make sure they are still in their clear plastic wrapper with an unbroken red seal. Many small shops impose a 25% handling charge and tarjetas may be out of stock particularly outside Caracas or larger towns. International calls can be made with a tarjeta, minimum needed Bs 2,000, but you get little more than 1 minute to Europe. To make an international call, dial 00 plus country code etc. Canada direct: 800-11100. For UK, BT Direct, 800-11440 (BT chargecard works from any phone). International calls are charged by a series of bands, ranging from about US$1 per minute to USA and Canada, to US$2 to UK, to US$2.15. There are various reduced and economy rates according to band. Fax rates are as for phones.

Communicating by fax is a convenient way of sending messages home. Many places with public fax machines (post offices, telephone companies or shops) will receive messages as well as send. Fax machines are often switched off; you may have to phone to confirm receipt.

● **E-mail**

E-mail is becoming more common and public access to the Internet is fairly widespread with cybercafés opening in both large and small towns. There is usually a charge per page sent or received, which compares favourably with fax charges.

● **World Band Radio**

South America has more local and community radio stations than practically anywhere else in the world; a shortwave (world band) radio offers a practical means to brush up on the language, sample popular culture and absorb some of the richly varied regional music. International broadcasters such as the BBC World Service, the Voice of America, Boston (Mass)-based Monitor Radio International (operated by *Christian Science Monitor*) and the Quito-based Evangelical station, HCJB, keep the traveller abreast of news and events, in both English and Spanish.

Compact or miniature portables are recommended, with digital tuning and a full range of shortwave bands, as well as FM, long and medium wave. Detailed advice on radio models (£150 for a decent one) and wavelengths can be found in the annual publication, *Passport to World Band Radio* (Box 300, Penn's Park, PA 18943, USA). Details of local stations is listed in *World TV and Radio Handbook* (WTRH), PO Box 9027, 1006 AA Amsterdam, The Netherlands, US$19.95. Both of these, free wavelength guides and selected radio sets are available from the BBC World Service Bookshop, Bush House Arcade, Bush House, Strand, London WC2B 4PH, UK, T 0171-257 2576.

HOLIDAYS AND FESTIVALS

There are two sorts of holidays, those enjoyed by everybody and those taken by employees of banks and insurance companies. Holidays applying to all businesses including: 1 January, Carnival on the Monday and Tuesday before Ash Wednesday (everything shuts down Saturday-Tuesday; make sure accommodation is booked in advance), Thursday-Saturday of Holy Week, 19 April, 1 May, 24 June (24 June is the feast day of San Juan Bautista, a particularly popular festival celebrated along the central coast where there were once large concentrations of plantation slaves who considered San Juan their special Saint; some of the best-known events are in villages between Puerto Cabello, and Chuspa, to the east, such as Chuao, Cata and Ocumane de la Costa), 5, 24 July, 24 September, 12 October, 25 December. Holidays for banks and insurance companies only including all the above and also: 19 March and the nearest Monday to 6 January, Ascension Day, 29 June, 15 August, 1 November and 8 December. There are also holidays applying to certain occupations such as Doctor's Day or Traffic Policeman's Day. From 24 December-1 January, most restaurants are closed and there is no long-distance public transport. On New Year's Eve, everything closes and does not open for a least a day. Queues for tickets, and traffic jams, are long. Business travellers should not visit during Holy week or Carnival.

See under the relevant sections for details for local festivals and holidays.

Rounding up

ACKNOWLEDGEMENTS

For their help in the research and preparation of this Handbook and hospitality while in Venezuela, I would like to thank the following: Dr Frances Osborn, resident in Cumaná, for her many contributions and valuable assisitance. Thanks to Tom and Raquel Evenou and all at Bum Bum Tours in Mérida for their hospitality and help, and to Alan Highton for a great tour of the llanos. Thanks to José Luis Troconis at NatourA in Mérida for all his help. Thanks also to Martin Haars of Soana Tours in Ciudad Bolívar; Miguel Gasca of Ciudad Bolívar; the guides at Tayukasen Tours in Santa Elena; María Eugenia Olívar of Mérida; Gil, Mery and José Olívar in Trujillo for their generosity and kindness; Edward Paine and Steven Chew of Last Frontiers in Long Crendon, Oxon, UK; Geoffrey Groesbeck of Massachusetts; Kathy Irwin of Texas; and Steve Collins of Journey Latin America. Also thanks to all the specialist contributors mentioned at the start of the book. Thanks to Ben Box, editor of the South American Handbook, for the benefit of his knowledge and experience, and to Jane for her patience and understanding. Finally, a special thank you to all the Handbook family; the many travellers and correspondents who supply such valuable comments, updated information and encouragement.

FURTHER READING

There are many fine coffee-table books on the various regions of Venezuela, for example Charles Brewer-Carias' books on Roraima and Venezuela as a whole. Venezuela in Focus (Latin America Bureau, £5.99), is a guide to the history, politics, economy and culture of the country.

Many general books contain information on Venezuelan history: The Cambridge Encyclopedia of Latin America and the Caribbean, edited by Simon Collier, Thomas E Skidmore and Harold Blakemore (2nd edition, Cambridge University Press, 1985); The Cambridge History of Latin America, edited by Leslie Bethell; The Penguin History of Latin America, Edwin Williamson, 1992. For more detailed information see also A History of Venezuela, by Guillermo Morón (London, 1964); The Spanish American Revolutions 1808-1826 (2nd edition, New York, 1986).

Bird watchers should see: Birding in Venezuela, by Mary Lou Goodwin (Audobon Society of Venenzuela, Caracas, 1990); and Birds of Venezuela, by Rodolphe Meyer de Schauensee and William H Phelps Jr (Princeton University Press, New Jersey, 1978).

A more personal account of travelling in Venezuela is given in the excellent Personal Narrative of Travels to the Equinoctial Regions of America 1799-1801, by Alexander von Humboldt (London, 1852). See also The Lost World, by Sir Arthur Conan Doyle; Green Mansions, WH Hudson (London, 1990); and Papillon, by Henri Charriere (London, 1980). For a detailed account of Sir Walter Raleigh's attempts to find El Dorado, see The Creature in the Map by Charles Nicholl (London, 1995). The fictional town featured in Isabel Allende's Eva Luna is based on Colonia Tovar (see West of Caracas).

Interested readers are recommended to see Jason Wilson, Traveller's Literary Companion, South and Central America (Brighton, UK: In Print, 1993), which has extracts from works by Latin American writers and by non-Latin Americans about Venezuela and the other countries and has very useful bibliographies.

MAPS AND GUIDEBOOKS

The Guide to Venezuela (925 pages, updated and expanded in 1989), by Janice Bauman, Leni Young and others, in English (available in Caracas) is a mine of information and maps (US$11). For hiking in Venezuela see Bradt's Guide to Venezuela (2nd edition) by Hilary Dunsterville Branch. A good description and summary of Venezuela's National Parks and a detailed calendar of seasonal changes in flora and fauna is given in Guia Ecoturistica de Venezuela, edited by Miro Popic (Caracas, 1995), US$10. A very thorough guide to accommodation throughout the country is the Guide to Camps, Posadas & Cabins, by Elizabeth Kline (Caracas, 1995). A very useful book, highly recommended, aimed specifically at the budget traveller is The Tropical Traveller, by John Hatt (Penguin Books, 3rd edition, 1993).

Maps

The official mapping agency is the Ministerio del Ambiente y de los Recursos Naturales Renovables, Dirección de Cartografía Nacional, Edificio Camejo, 1st floor, Avenida Este 6, Colón, south side; the office is not in the same building as the Ministry's other departments (Centro Simón Bolívar). It has 1:50,000, 1:100,000, 1:200,000 and 1:250,000 sheets covering most of Venezuela north of the Orinoco, plus some state maps and a 1:500,000 series.

Apart from the Guide to Venezuela, there is

the Guía Progreso (published by Seguros Progreso SA, available at the company's offices and elsewhere), which is very detailed, but not very accurate south of the Orinoco. The best road map is published by Lagoven and a similar version by Corpoven but at twice the scale and with a very good street plan of Caracas on the back, available from most service stations (not just Lagoven's), latest edition 1995, US$2. The best country map is the late Kevin Healey's, published by International Travel Maps, Vancouver, BC, Canada; available at good travel agents (eg, in Mérida).

The South American Explorers' Club is at Avenida Portugal 146 (Casilla 3714), Lima, Peru (T 425-0142), Jorge Washington y Leonidas Plaza, Apartado 17-21-431, Eloy Alfaro, Quito, Ecuador (T 225-228), and 126 Indian Creek Road, Ithaca, NY 14850, USA T (607) 277-0488, e-mail: explorer@samexplo.org. Books, maps and travel planning services are available at the US office. It is represented in the UK by Bradt Publications.

The Latin American Travel Advisor is a quarterly news bulletin with up-to-date detailed and reliable information on countries throughout South and Central America. The publication focuses on public safety, health, weather and natural phenomena, travel costs, economics and politics in each country. Annual airmail subscriptions cost US$39, a single current issue US$15, electronically transmitted information (fax or e-mail), US$10 per country. Payment by US$ cheque, MasterCard or VISA (no money orders, credit card payments by mail or fax with card number, expiry date, cardholder's name and signature). Free sample available. Contact PO Box 17-17-908, Quito, Ecuador, international F 593-2-562-566, USA and Canada toll free F (888) 215-9511, e-mail: LATA@ pi.pro.ec, World Wide Web http://www. amerispan. com/latc/.

Information on travel and language schools is available from AmeriSpan Unlimited, one of several language school brokers in the USA, PO Box 40007, Philadelphia, PA 19106-0007, T (USA and Canada) 800-879-6640, worldwide 215-751-1100, F 215-751-1986, e-mail: info@amerispan.com, website: http://www.amerispan.com. See also the website http://www.planeta.com of Ron Mader's El Planeta Platica: Eco Travels in Latin America.

Useful addresses

EMBASSIES AND CONSULATES

Australia
210 Queen Street, 5th Floor, Penneys Building, Suite 517, Queensland.

Austria
Doblhoffgasse 316, A-1010 Vienna.

Belgium
Avenida Louse N 176 Boite 6, 1050 Brussels.

France
12 Avenue Du Presidente Kennedy, 75016 Paris 16.

Germany
Konstantinstrasse N 16, D-5300 Bonn-2.

Italy
Via Toscana 30 Int 28, 00187 Roma.

Netherlands
Hacquartraat 4, 1071 SH Amsterdam.

Sweden
Sveav General 31e TR 11134, Estocolmo.

Switzerland
2 Rue Du Lyon D'Or 2/do Piso Gusa, CH 1003 Lausanne.

USA
3014 Massachusetts Avenue NW, Washington DC.

TOURIST INFORMATION

Tourist information may be obtained from Corpoturismo, Apartado 50.200, Caracas; the main office for information is floors 35-7, Torre Oeste, Parque Central, T 507-8831. GAM, the monthly *Guía Aérea y Marítima de Venezuela*, gives details of all flights into and within the country, but also of hotels, travel agents, car hire, etc.

NB Business visitors on short visits are strongly advised to enter the country as tourists, otherwise they will have to obtain a tax clearance certificate (*solvencia*) before they can leave.

Tourist offices overseas

UK
56 Grafton Way, London W1P 5LB, T 0171 387-6727, F 0171 383-3253.

Germany
AM Burghof 11, Postfach 5019, D-66623, Nohfelden, T 49-6852-900599, F 49-6852-900555.

SPECIALIST TOUR COMPANIES

Journey Latin America
14-16 Devonshire Road, Chiswick, London, W4 2HD (T 0181-747 8315) and 28-30 Barton Arcade, 51-63 Deansgate, Manchester, M3 2BH (T 0161 832 1441).

Trailfinders
194 Kensington High Street, London, W8 7RG (T 0171-938 3939); South American Experience, 47 Causton Street, Pimlico, London, SW1P 4AT (T 0171-976 5511).

Last Frontiers
Swan House, High Street, Long Crendon, Buckinghamshire, HP18 9AF, T 01844 208405, e-mail: travelinfo@lastfrontiers.co.uk, web: http://www.lastfrontiers.co.uk.

Passage to South America
Fovant Mews, 12 Noyna Road, London, SW17 7PH (T 0181 767 8989).

STA Travel
Priory House, 6 Wrights Lane, London, W8 6TA (T 0171-361 6166).

Encounter Overland
267 Old Brompton Road, London, SW5 9JA (T 0171 370 6845).

Hayes & Jarvis
152 King Street, London, W6 0QU (T 0181 222 7844).

Cox & Kings Travel
St James Court, 45 Buckingham Gate, London (T 0171-873 5001).

South American Experience
47 Causton Street, Pimlico, London, SW1P 4AT, T 0171-976-5511, F 0171-976 6908.

Geodyssey
29 Harberton Road, London, N19 3JS, T 0171-281-7788, F 281-7878, e-mail: enquiries@geodyssey.co.uk.

eXito Latin American Travel Specialists
5699 Miles Avenue, Oakland, CA 94618, USA, T 1-800-655-4053, F (510) 655-4566, e-mail: exito@wonderlink.com.

Interchange
Interchange House, 27 Stafford Road, Croydon, Surrey, CR0 4NG, T 0181-681 3612, F 0181-760 0031, e-mail: interchange@interchange.uk.com.

Writing to us

Many people write to us - with corrections, new information, or simply comments. If you want to let us know something, we would be delighted to hear from you. Please give us as precise information as possible, quoting the edition and page number of the Handbook you are using and send as early in the year as you can. Your help will be greatly appreciated, especially by other travellers. In return we will send you details about our special guidebook offer.

For hotels and restaurants, please let us know:

- each establishment's name, address, phone and fax number
- number of rooms, whether a/c or air-cooled, attached (clean?) bathroom
- location - how far from the station or bus stand, or distance (walking time) from a prominent landmark
- if it's not already on one of our maps, can you place it?
- your comments - either good or bad - as to why it is distinctive
- tariff cards
- local transport used

For places of interest:

- location
- entry, camera charge
- access - by whatever means of transport is most approiate, eg time of main buses or trains to and from the site, journey time, fare
- facilities - nearby drinks stalls, restaurants, for the disabled
- any problems, eg steep climb, wildlife, unofficial guides
- opening hours
- site guides

Useful words and phrases

NO AMOUNT of dictionaries, phrase books or word lists will provide the same enjoyment as being able to communicate directly with the people of the country you are visiting. Learning Spanish is an important part of the preparation for any trip to Venezuela and you are encouraged to make an effort to grasp the basics before you go. As you travel you will pick up more of the language and the more you know, the more you will benefit from your stay. The following section is designed to be a simple point of departure.

General pronunciation

The stress in a Spanish word conforms to one of three rules: 1) if the word ends in a vowel, or in **n** or **s**, the accent falls on the penultimate syllable (*vent**a**na, vent**a**nas*); 2) if the word ends in a consonant other than **n** or **s**, the accent falls on the last syllable (*habl**ar***); 3) if the word is to be stressed on a syllable contrary to either of the above rules, the acute accent on the relevant vowel indicates where the stress is to be placed (*pantal**ó**n, met**á**fora*). Note that adverbs such as *cuando*, 'when', take an accent when used interrogatively: *¿cuándo?*, 'when?'

Vowels

a   not quite as short as in English 'cat'

e   as in English 'pay', but shorter in a syllable ending in a consonant

i   as in English 'seek'

o   as in English 'shop', but more like 'pope' when the vowel ends a syllable

u   as in English 'food'; after 'q' and in 'gue', 'gui', **u** is unpronounced; in 'güe' and 'güi' it is pronounced

y   when a vowel, pronounced like 'i'; when a semiconsonant or consonant, it is pronounced like English 'yes'

ai, ay   as in English 'ride'

ei, ey   as in English 'they'

oi, oy   as in English 'toy'

Unless listed below **consonants** can be pronounced in Spanish as they are in English.

b, v   their sound is interchangeable and is a cross between the English 'b' and 'v', except at the beginning of a word or after 'm' or 'n' when it is like English 'b'

c   like English 'k', except before 'e' or 'i' when it is as the 's' in English 'sip'

g   before 'e' and 'i' it is the same as **j**

h   when on its own, never pronounced

j   as the 'ch' in the Scottish 'loch'

ll   as the 'g' in English 'beige'; sometimes as the 'lli' in 'million'

ñ   as the 'ni' in English 'onion'

rr   trilled much more strongly than in English

x   depending on its location, pronounced as

in English 'fox', or 'sip', or like 'gs'
z as the 's' in English 'sip'

GREETINGS, COURTESIES
hello
  hola
good morning
  buenos días
good afternoon/evening/night
  buenas tardes/noches
goodbye
  adiós/chao
see you later
  hasta luego
how are you?
  ¿cómo está?/¿cómo estás?
pleased to meet you
  mucho gusto/encantado/encantada
please
  por favor
thank you (very much)
  (muchas) gracias
yes
  sí
no
  no
excuse me/I beg your pardon
  permiso
I do not understand
  no entiendo
please speak slowly
  hable despacio por favor
what is your name
  ¿cómo se llama?
Go away!
  ¡Váyase!

BASIC QUESTIONS
where is_?
  ¿dónde está_?
how much does it cost?
  ¿cuánto cuesta?
how much is it?
  ¿cuánto es?
when?
  ¿cuándo?
when does the bus leave?
  ¿a qué hora sale el autobús?
    – arrive?
    – llega –
why?
  ¿por qué?

what for?
  ¿para qué?
what time is it?
  ¿qué hora es?
how do I get to_?
  ¿cómo llegar a_?
is this the way to the church?
  ¿la iglesia está por aquí?

BASICS
bathroom/toilet
  el baño
police (policeman)
  la policía (el policía)
hotel
  el hotel (la pensión,el residencial,
  el alojamiento)
restaurant
  el restaurante
post office
  el correo
telephone office
  el centro de llamadas
supermarket
  el supermercado
bank
  el banco
exchange house
  la casa de cambio
exchange rate
  la tasa de cambio
notes/coins
  los billetes/las monedas
travellers' cheques
  los travelers/los cheques de viajero
cash
  el efectivo
breakfast
  el desayuno
lunch
  el almuerzo
dinner/supper
  la cena
meal
  la comida
drink
  la bebida
mineral water
  el agua mineral
soft fizzy drink
  la gaseosa/cola

beer
la cerveza
without sugar
sin azúcar
without meat
sin carne

GETTING AROUND

on the left/right
a la izquierda/derecha
straight on
derecho
second street on the left
la segunda calle a la izquierda
to walk
caminar
bus station
la terminal (terrestre)
train station
la estación (de tren/ferrocarril)
bus
el bus/el autobús/ la flota/el colectivo/ el micro etc
train
el tren
airport
el aeropuerto
aeroplane/airplane
el avión
first/second class
primera/segunda clase
ticket
el boleto
ticket office
la taquilla
bus stop
la parada

ACCOMMODATION

room
el cuarto/la habitación
single/double
sencillo/doble
with two beds
con dos camas
with private bathroom
con baño
hot/cold water
agua caliente/fría
noisy
ruidoso

to make up/clean
limpiar
sheets
las sábanas
blankets
las mantas
pillows
las almohadas
clean/dirty towels
toallas limpias/sucias
toilet paper
el papel higiénico

HEALTH

Chemist
farmacia
(for) pain
(para) dolor
stomach
el estómago
head
la cabeza
fever/sweat
la fiebre/el sudor
diarrhoea
la diarrea
blood
la sangre
altitude sickness
el soroche
doctor
el médico
condoms
los preservativos
contraceptive (pill)
anticonceptivo (la píldora anticonceptiva)
period/towels
la regla/las toallas
contact lenses
las lentes de contacto
aspirin
la aspirina

TIME

at one o'clock
a la una
at half past two/ two thirty
a las dos y media
at a quarter to three
a cuarto para las tres/
a las tres menos quince

it's one o'clock
es la una
it's seven o'clock
son las siete
it's twenty past six/
six twenty
son las seis y veinte
it's five to nine
son cinco para las nueve/
son las nueve menos cinco
in ten minutes
en diez minutos
five hours
cinco horas
does it take long?
¿tarda mucho?
Monday lunes
Tuesday martes
Wednesday miercoles
Thursday jueves
Friday viernes
Saturday sábado
Sunday domingo
January enero
February febrero
March marzo
April abril
May mayo
June junio
July julio
August agosto
September septiembre
October octubre
November noviembre
December diciembre

NUMBERS

one uno/una
two dos
three tres
four cuatro
five cinco
six seis
seven siete
eight ocho
nine nueve
ten diez
eleven once
twelve doce
thirteen trece

fourteen catorce
fifteen quince
sixteen dieciseis
seventeen diecisiete
eighteen dieciocho
nineteen diecinueve
twenty veinte
twenty one, two veintiuno, veintidos etc
thirty treinta
forty cuarenta
fifty cincuenta
sixty sesenta
seventy setenta
eighty ochenta
ninety noventa
hundred cien or ciento
thousand mil

KEY VERBS

To Go
ir
I go '*voy*'; you go (familiar singular) '*vas*'; he, she, it goes, you (unfamiliar singular) go '*va*'; we go '*vamos*'; they, you (plural) go '*van*'.

To Have (possess)
tener
tengo; tienes; tiene; tenemos; tienen (also used as To Be, as in 'I am hungry' '*tengo hambre*')
(**NB** haber also means to have, but is used with other verbs, as in 'he has gone' '*ha ido*'. he; has; ha; hemos; han.
'*Hay*' means 'there is'; perhaps more common is '*No hay*' meaning 'there isn't any')

To Be (in a permanent state)
ser
soy (profesor – I am a teacher); eres; es; somos; son
To Be (positional or temporary state)
estar
estoy (en Londres – I am in London); estás; está (contenta – she is happy); estamos; están.

This section has been compiled on the basis of glossaries compiled by André de Mendonça and David Gilmour of South American Experience, London, and the Latin American Travel Advisor, Number 9, March 1996.

Health in Latin America

WITH THE FOLLOWING advice and precautions you should keep as healthy as you do at home. Most visitors return home having experienced no problems at all apart from some travellers' diarrhoea. In Latin America the health risks, especially in the lowland tropical areas, are different from those encountered in Europe or the USA. It also depends on where and how you travel. There are clear health differences between the countries of Latin America and in risks for the business traveller, who stays in international class hotels in large cities, the backpacker trekking from country to country and the tourist who heads for the beach. There is huge variation in climate, vegetation and wildlife from the deserts of Chile to the rain forests of Amazonia and from the icy remoteness of Andean peaks, to the teeming capital cities. There are no hard and fast rules to follow; you will often have to make your own judgment on the healthiness or otherwise of your surroundings. There are English (or other foreign language) speaking doctors in most major cities who have particular experience in dealing with locally-occurring diseases. Your Embassy representative will often be able to give you the name of local reputable doctors and most of the better hotels have a doctor on standby. If you do fall ill and cannot find a recommended doctor, try the Outpatient Department of a hospital – private hospitals are usually less crowded and offer a more acceptable standard of care to foreigners.

BEFORE TRAVELLING

Take out medical insurance. Make sure it covers all eventualities especially evacuation to your home country by a medically equipped plane, if necessary. You should have a dental check up, obtain a spare glasses prescription, a spare oral contraceptive prescription (or enough pills to last) and, if you suffer from a chronic illness (such as diabetes, high blood pressure, ear or sinus troubles, cardio-pulmonary disease or nervous disorder) arrange for a check up with your doctor, who can at the same time provide you with a letter explaining the details of your disability in English and if possible Spanish and/or Portuguese. Check the current practice in countries you are visiting for malaria prophylaxis (prevention). If you are on regular medication, make sure you have enough to cover the period of your travel.

Children

More preparation is probably necessary for babies and children than for an adult and perhaps a little more care should be taken when travelling to remote areas where health services are primitive. This is because children can be become more rapidly ill than adults (on the other hand they often recover more quickly). Diarrhoea and vomiting are the most common problems, so take the usual precautions, but more intensively. Breastfeeding is best and most convenient for babies, but powdered milk is generally available and so are baby foods in most countries. Papaya, bananas and avocados are all nutritious and can be cleanly prepared. The treatment of diarrhoea is the same for adults, except that it should start earlier and be continued with more persistence. Children get dehydrated very quickly in hot countries and can become drowsy and uncooperative unless cajoled to drink water or juice plus salts. Upper respiratory infections, such as colds, catarrh and middle ear infections are also common and if your child suffers from these normally take some antibiotics against the possibility. Outer ear infections after swimming are also common and antibiotic eardrops will help. Wet wipes are always useful and sometimes difficult to find in South America, as, in some places are disposable nappies.

MEDICINES AND WHAT TO TAKE

There is very little control on the sale of drugs and medicines in South America. You can buy any and every drug in pharmacies without a prescription. Be wary of this because pharmacists can be poorly trained and might sell you drugs that are unsuitable, dangerous or old. Many drugs and medicines are manufactured under licence from American or European companies, so the trade names may be familiar to you. This means you do not have to carry a whole chest of medicines with you, but remember that the shelf life of some items, especially vaccines and antibiotics, is markedly reduced in hot conditions. Buy your supplies at the better outlets where there are refrigerators, even though they are more expensive and check the expiry date of all preparations you buy. Immigration officials occasionally confiscate scheduled drugs (Lomotil is an example) if they are not accompanied by a doctor's prescription.

Self-medication may be forced on you by circumstances so the following text contains the names of drugs and medicines which you may find useful in an emergency or in out-of-the-way places. You may like to take some of the following items with you from home:

Sunglasses
   ones designed for intense sunlight

Earplugs
   for sleeping on aeroplanes and in noisy hotels

Suntan cream
   with a high protection factor

Insect repellent
   containing DET for preference

Mosquito net
   lightweight, permethrin-impregnated for choice

Tablets
   for travel sickness

Tampons
   can be expensive in some countries in Latin America

Condoms

Contraceptives

Water sterilising tablets

Antimalarial tablets

Anti-infective ointment eg Cetrimide

Dusting powder for feet etc
  containing fungicide
Antacid tablets
  for indigestion
Sachets of rehydration salts
  plus anti-diarrhoea preparations
Painkillers
  such as Paracetamol or Aspirin
Antibiotics
  for diarrhoea etc
First Aid kit
  Small pack containing a few sterile syringes
and needles and disposable gloves. The risk
of catching hepatitis etc from a dirty needle
used for injection is now negligible in Latin
America, but some may be reassured by
carrying their own supplies – available from
camping shops and airport shops.

Vaccination and immunisation

Smallpox vaccination is no longer required
anywhere in the world. Neither is cholera
vaccination recognized as necessary for international travel by the World Health Organization – it is not very effective either.
Nevertheless, some immigration officials are
demanding proof of vaccination against
cholera in Latin America and in some countries outside Latin America, following the
outbreak of the disease which originated in
Peru in 1990-91 and subsequently affected
most surrounding countries. Although very
unlikely to affect visitors to Latin America, the
cholera epidemic continues making its greatest impact in poor areas where water supplies
are polluted and food hygiene practices are
insanitary.

Vaccination against the following diseases
are recommended:
Yellow Fever
This is a live vaccination not to be given to
children under 9 months of age or persons
allergic to eggs. Immunity lasts for 10 years,
an International Certificate of Yellow Fever
Vaccination will be given and should be kept
because it is sometimes asked for. Yellow
fever is very rare in Latin America, but the
vaccination is practically without side effects
and almost totally protective.
Typhoid
A disease spread by the insanitary preparation of food. A number of new vaccines

against this condition are now available; the
older TAB and monovalent typhoid vaccines
are being phased out. The newer, eg Typhim
Vi, cause less side effects, but are more
expensive. For those who do not like injections, there are now oral vaccines.
Poliomyelitis
Despite its decline in the world this remains
a serious disease if caught and is easy to
protect against. There are live oral vaccines
and in some countries injected vaccines.
Whichever one you choose it is a good idea
to have booster every 3-5 years if visiting
developing countries regularly.
Tetanus
One dose should be given with a booster at 6
weeks and another at 6 months and 10 yearly
boosters thereafter are recommended. Children should already be properly protected
against diphtheria, poliomyelitis and pertussis
(whooping cough), measles and HIB all of
which can be more serious infections in Latin
America than at home. Measles, mumps and
rubella vaccine is also given to children
throughout the world, but those teenage girls
who have not had rubella (german measles)
should be tested and vaccinated. Hepatitis B
vaccination for babies is now routine in some
countries. Consult your doctor for advice on
tuberculosis inoculation: the disease is still
widespread in Latin America.
Infectious Hepatitis
Is less of a problem for travellers than it used
to be because of the development of two
extremely effective vaccines against the A
and B form of the disease. It remains common, however, in Latin America. A combined
hepatitis A & B vaccine is now licensed and
will be available in 1997 – one jab covers both
diseases.
Other vaccinations:
Might be considered in the case of epidemics
eg meningitis. There is an effective vaccination
against rabies which should be considered by
all travellers, especially those going through
remote areas or if there is a particular occupational risk, eg for zoologists or veterinarians.

FURTHER INFORMATION
Further information on health risks abroad,
vaccinations etc may be available from a local
travel clinic. If you wish to take specific drugs

with you such as antibiotics these are best prescribed by your own doctor. Beware, however, that not all doctors can be experts on the health problems of remote countries. More detailed or more up-to-date information than local doctors can provide are available from various sources. In the UK there are hospital departments specialising in tropical diseases in London, Liverpool, Birmingham and Glasgow and the Malaria Reference Laboratory at the London School of Hygiene and Tropical Medicine provides free advice about malaria, T 0891 600350. In the USA the local Public Health Services can give such information and information is available centrally from the Centre for Disease Control (CDC) in Atlanta, T (404) 3324559.

There are additional computerized databases which can be assessed for destination-specific up-to-the-minute information. In the UK there is MASTA (Medical Advisory Service to Travellers Abroad), T 0171 631 4408, F 0171 436 5389, Tx 8953473 and Travax (Glasgow, T 0141 946 7120, ext 247). Other information on medical problems overseas can be obtained from the book by Dawood, Richard (Editor) (1992) *Travellers' Health: How to stay healthy abroad*, Oxford University Press 1992, £7.99. We strongly recommend this revised and updated edition, especially to the intrepid traveller heading for the more out of the way places. General advice is also available in the UK in *Health Information for Overseas Travel* published by the Department of Health and available from HMSO, and *International Travel and Health* published by WHO, Geneva.

STAYING HEALTHY

INTESTINAL UPSETS

The thought of catching a stomach bug worries visitors to Latin America but there have been great improvements in food hygiene and most such infections are preventable. Travellers' diarrhoea and vomiting is due, most of the time, to food poisoning, usually passed on by the insanitary habits of food handlers. As a general rule the cleaner your surroundings and the smarter the restaurant, the less likely you are to suffer.

Foods to avoid: uncooked, undercooked, partially cooked or reheated meat, fish, eggs, raw vegetables and salads, especially when they have been left out exposed to flies. Stick to fresh food that has been cooked from raw just before eating and make sure you peel fruit yourself. Wash and dry your hands before eating – disposable wet-wipe tissues are useful for this.

Shellfish eaten raw are risky and at certain times of the year some fish and shellfish concentrate toxins from their environment and cause various kinds of food poisoning. The local authorities notify the public not to eat these foods. Do not ignore the warning. **Heat treated milk** (UHT) pasteurized or sterilized is becoming more available in Latin America as is pasteurized cheese. On the whole matured or processed cheeses are safer than the fresh varieties and fresh unpasteurized milk from whatever animal can be a source of food poisoning germs, tuberculosis and brucellosis. This applies equally to icecream, yoghurt and cheese made from unpasteurized milk, so avoid these homemade products – the factory made ones are probably safer.

Tap water is rarely safe outside the major cities, especially in the rainy season. Stream water, if you are in the countryside, is often contaminated by communities living surprisingly high in the mountains. Filtered or bottled water is usually available and safe, although you must make sure that somebody is not filling bottles from the tap and hammering on a new crown cap. If your hotel has a central hot water supply this water is safe to drink after cooling. Ice for drinks should be made from boiled water, but rarely is so stand your glass on the ice cubes, rather than putting them in the drink. The better hotels have water purifying systems.

TRAVELLERS' DIARRHOEA

This is usually caused by eating food which has been contaminated by food poisoning germs. Drinking water is rarely the culprit. Sea water or river water is more likely to be contaminated by sewage and so swimming in such dilute effluent can also be a cause.

Infection with various organisms can give rise to travellers' diarrhoea. They may be viruses, bacteria, eg Escherichia coli (probably the most common cause worldwide), protozoal (such as amoebas and giardia), salmonella and cholera. The diarrhoea may come on suddenly or rather slowly. It may or may not be accompanied by vomiting or by severe abdominal pain and the passage of blood or mucus when it is called dysentery.

How do you know which type you have caught and how to treat it?

If you can time the onset of the diarrhoea to the minute ('acute') then it is probably due to a virus or a bacterium and/or the onset of dysentery. The treatment in addition to rehydration is Ciprofloxacin 500 mg every 12 hours; the drug is now widely available and there are many similar ones.

If the diarrhoea comes on slowly or intermittently ('sub-acute') then it is more likely to be protozoal, ie caused by an amoeba or giardia. Antibiotics such a Ciprofloxacin will have little effect. These cases are best treated by a doctor as is any outbreak of diarrhoea continuing for more than 3 days. Sometimes blood is passed in amoebic dysentery and for this you should certainly seek medical help. If this is not available then the best treatment is probably Tinidazole (Fasigyn) 1 tablet four times a day for 3 days. If there are severe stomach cramps, the following drugs may help but are not very useful in the management of acute diarrhoea: Loperamide (Imodium) and Diphenoxylate with Atropine (Lomotil) They should not be given to children.

Any kind of diarrhoea, whether or not accompanied by vomiting, responds well to the replacement of water and salts, taken as frequent small sips, of some kind of rehydration solution. There are proprietary preparations consisting of sachets of powder which you dissolve in boiled water or you can make your own by adding half a teaspoonful of salt (3.5 gms) and 4 tablespoonsful of sugar (40 gms) to a litre of boiled water.

Thus the lynch pins of treatment for diarrhoea are rest, fluid and salt replacement, antibiotics such as Ciprofloxacin for the bacterial types and special diagnostic tests and medical treatment for the amoeba and giardia infections. Salmonella infections and cholera, although rare, can be devastating diseases and it would be wise to get to a hospital as soon as possible if these were suspected.

Fasting, peculiar diets and the consumption of large quantities of yoghurt have not been found useful in calming travellers' diarrhoea or in rehabilitating inflamed bowels. Oral rehydration has on the other hand, especially in children, been a life saving technique and should always be practised, whatever other treatment you use. As there is some evidence that alcohol and milk might prolong diarrhoea they should be avoided during and immediately after an attack.

Diarrhoea occurring day after day for long periods of time (chronic diarrhoea) is notoriously resistent to amateur attempts at treatment and again warrants proper diagnostic tests (most towns with reasonable sized hospitals have laboratories for stool samples). There are ways of preventing travellers' diarrhoea for short periods of time by taking antibiotics, but this is not a foolproof technique and should not be used other than in exceptional circumstances. Doxycycline is possibly the best drug. Some preventatives such as Enterovioform can have serious side effects if taken for long periods.

Paradoxically **constipation** is also common, probably induced by dietary change, inadequate fluid intake in hot places and long bus journeys. Simple laxatives are useful in the short-term and bulky foods such as maize, beans and plenty of fruit are also useful.

HIGH ALTITUDE

Spending time at high altitude in South America, especially in the tropics, is usually a pleasure – it is not so hot, there are no insects and the air is clear and spring like. Travelling to high altitudes, however, can cause medical problems, all of which can be prevented if care is taken.

On reaching heights above about 3,000m, heart pounding and shortness of breath, especially on exertion are a normal response to the lack of oxygen in the air. A condition called acute mountain sickness (*Soroche* in South America) can also affect visitors. It is more likely to affect those who ascend rapidly, eg by plane and those who over-exert themselves (teenagers for example). Soroche takes a few hours or days to come on and presents with a bad headache, extreme tiredness, sometimes dizziness, loss of appetite and frequently nausea and vomiting. Insomnia is common and is often associated with a suffocating feeling when lying in bed. Keen observers may note their breathing tends to wax and wane at night and their face tends to be puffy in the mornings – this is all part of the syndrome. Anyone can get this condition and past experience is not always a good guide: the author, having spent years in Peru travelling constantly between sea level and very high altitude never suffered symptoms, then was severely affected whilst climbing Kilimanjaro in Tanzania.

The treatment of acute mountain sickness is simple – rest, painkillers, (preferably not aspirin based) for the headache and anti sickness pills for vomiting. Oxygen is actually not much help, except at very high altitude. Various local panaceas – Coramina glucosada, Effortil, Micoren are popular in Latin America and mate de coca (an infusion of coca leaves widely available and perfectly legal) will alleviate some of the symptoms.

To **prevent** the condition: on arrival at places over 3,000m have a few hours rest in a chair and avoid alcohol, cigarettes and heavy food. If the symptoms are severe and prolonged, it is best to descend to a lower altitude and to reascend slowly or in stages. If this is impossible because of shortage of time or if you are going so high that acute mountain sickness is very likely, then the drug Acetazolamide (Diamox) can be used as a preventative and continued during the ascent. There is good evidence of the value of this drug in the prevention of soroche, but some people do experience peculiar side effects. The usual dose is 500 mg of the slow release preparation each night, starting the night before ascending above 3,000m.

Watch out for **sunburn** at high altitude. The ultraviolet rays are extremely powerful. The air is also excessively dry at high altitude and you might find that your skin dries out and the inside of your nose becomes crusted. Use a moisturiser for the skin and some vaseline wiped into the nostrils. Some people find contact lenses irritate because of the dry air. It is unwise to ascend to high altitude if you are pregnant, especially in the first 3 months, or if you have a history of heart, lung or blood disease, including sickle cell.

A more unusual condition can affect mountaineers who ascend rapidly to high altitude – **acute pulmonary oedema**. Residents at altitude sometimes experience this when returning to the mountains from time spent at the coast. This condition is often preceded by acute mountain sickness and comes on quite rapidly with severe breathlessness, noisy breathing, cough, blueness of the lips and frothing at the mouth. Anybody who develops this must be brought down as soon as possible, given oxygen and taken to hospital.

A rapid descent from high places will make sinus problems and middle ear infections worse and might make your teeth ache. Lastly, don't fly to altitude within 24 hours of SCUBA diving. You might suffer from 'the bends'.

HEAT AND COLD

Full acclimatisation to high temperatures takes about 2 weeks. During this period it is normal to feel a bit apathetic, especially if the relative humidity is high. Drink plenty of water (up to 15 litres a day are required when working physically hard in the tropics), use salt on your food and avoid extreme exertion. Tepid showers are more cooling than hot or cold ones. Large hats do not cool you down, but do prevent sunburn. Remember that, especially in the highlands, there can be a large and sudden drop in temperature between sun and shade and between night and day, so dress accordingly. Warm jackets or woollens are essential after dark at high altitude. Loose cotton is still the best material when the weather is hot.

INSECTS

These are mostly more of a nuisance than a serious hazard and if you try, you can prevent yourself entirely from being bitten. Some, such as mosquitos are, of course, carriers of potentially serious diseases, so it is sensible to avoid being bitten as much as possible. Sleep off the ground and use a mosquito net or some kind of insecticide. Preparations containing Pyrethrum or synthetic pyrethroids are safe. They are available as aerosols or pumps and the best way to use these is to spray the room thoroughly in all areas (follow the instructions rather than the insects) and then shut the door for a while, re-entering when the smell has dispersed. Mosquito coils release insecticide as they burn slowly. They are widely available and useful out of doors. Tablets of insecticide which are placed on a heated mat plugged into a wall socket are probably the most effective. They fill the room with insecticidal fumes in the same way as aerosols or coils.

You can also use insect repellents, most of which are effective against a wide range of pests. The most common and effective is diethyl metatoluamide (DET). DET liquid is best for arms and face (care around eyes and with spectacles – DET dissolves plastic). Aerosol spray is good for clothes and ankles and liquid DET can be dissolved in water and used to impregnate cotton clothes and mosquito nets. Some repellents now contain DET and Permethrin, insecticide. Impregnated wrist and ankle bands can also be useful.

If you are bitten or stung, itching may be relieved by cool baths, antihistamine tablets (care with alcohol or driving) or mild corticosteroid creams, eg. hydrocortisone (great care: never use if any hint of infection). Careful scratching of all your bites once a day can be surprisingly effective. Calamine lotion and cream have limited effectiveness and antihistamine creams are not recommended – they can cause allergies themselves.

Bites which become infected should be treated with a local antiseptic or antibiotic cream such as Cetrimide, as should any infected sores or scratches.

When living rough, skin infestations with body lice (crabs) and scabies are easy to pick up. Use whatever local commercial preparation is recommended for lice and scabies.

Crotamiton cream (Eurax) alleviates itching and also kills a number of skin parasites. Malathion lotion 5% (Prioderm) kills lice effectively, but avoid the use of the toxic agricultural preparation of Malathion, more often used to commit suicide.

TICKS

They attach themselves usually to the lower parts of the body often after walking in areas where cattle have grazed. They take a while to attach themselves strongly, but swell up as they start to suck blood. The important thing is to remove them gently, so that they do not leave their head parts in your skin because this can cause a nasty allergic reaction some days later. Do not use petrol, vaseline, lighted cigarettes etc to remove the tick, but, with a pair of tweezers remove the beast gently by gripping it at the attached (head) end and rock it out in very much the same way that a tooth is extracted. Certain tropical flies which lay their eggs under the skin of sheep and cattle also occasionally do the same thing to humans with the unpleasant result that a maggot grows under the skin and pops up as a boil or pimple. The best way to remove the boil is to cover the boil with oil, vaseline or nail varnish so as to stop the maggot breathing, then to squeeze it out gently the next day.

SUNBURN

The burning power of the tropical sun, especially at high altitude, is phenomenal.

Always wear a wide brimmed hat and use some form of suncream lotion on untanned skin. Normal temperate zone suntan lotions (protection factor up to 7) are not much good; you need to use the types designed specifically for the tropics or for mountaineers or skiers with protection factors up to 15 or above. These are often not available in Latin America. Glare from the sun can cause conjunctivitis, so wear sunglasses especially on tropical beaches, where high protection factor sunscreen should also be used.

PRICKLY HEAT

A very common intensely itchy rash is avoided by frequent washing and by wearing loose clothing. Cured by allowing skin to dry off through use of powder and spending two nights in an airconditioned hotel!

ATHLETES FOOT

This and other fungal skin infections are best treated with Tolnaftate or Clotrimazole.

OTHER RISKS AND MORE SERIOUS DISEASES

Remember that rabies is endemic throughout Latin America, so avoid dogs that are behaving strangely and cover your toes at night from the vampire bats, which also carry the disease. If you are bitten by a domestic or wild animal, do not leave things to chance: scrub the wound with soap and water and/or disinfectant, try to have the animal captured (within limits) or at least determine its ownership, where possible, and seek medical assistance at once. The course of treatment depends on whether you have already been satisfactorily vaccinated against rabies. If you have (this is worthwhile if you are spending lengths of time in developing countries) then some further doses of vaccine are all that is required. Human diploid vaccine is the best, but expensive: other, older kinds of vaccine, such as that derived from duck embryos may be the only types available. These are effective, much cheaper and interchangeable generally with the human derived types. If not already vaccinated then anti rabies serum (immunoglobulin) may be required in addition. It is important to finish the course of treatment whether the animal survives or not.

AIDS

In South America AIDS is increasing but is not wholly confined to the well known high risk sections of the population, ie homosexual men, intravenous drug abusers and children of infected mothers. Heterosexual transmission is now the dominant mode and so the main risk to travellers is from casual sex. The same precautions should be taken as with any sexually transmitted disease. The Aids virus (HIV) can be passed by unsterilized needles which have been previously used to inject an HIV positive patient, but the risk of this is negligible. It would, however, be sensible to check that needles have been properly sterilized or disposable needles have been used. If you wish to take your own disposable needles, be prepared to explain what they are for. The risk of receiving a blood transfusion with blood infected with the HIV virus is greater than from dirty needles because of the amount of fluid exchanged. Supplies of blood for transfusion should now be screened for HIV in all reputable hospitals, so again the risk is very small indeed. Catching the AIDS virus does not always produce an illness in itself (although it may do). The only way to be sure if you feel you have been put at risk is to have a blood test for HIV antibodies on your return to a place where there are reliable laboratory facilities. The test does not become positive for some weeks.

MALARIA

In South America malaria is theoretically confined to coastal and jungle zones, but is now on the increase again. Mosquitos do not thrive above 2,500m, so you are safe at altitude. There are different varieties of malaria, some resistant to the normal drugs. Make local enquiries if you intend to visit possibly infected zones and use a prophylactic regime. Start taking the tablets a few days before exposure and continue to take them for 6 weeks after leaving the malarial zone. Remember to give the drugs to babies and children also. Opinion varies on the precise drugs and dosage to be used for protection.

All the drugs may have some side effects and it is important to balance the risk of catching the disease against the albeit rare side effects. The increasing complexity of the subject is such that as the malarial parasite becomes immune to the new generation of drugs it has made concentration on the physical prevention from being bitten by mosquitos more important. This involves the use of long sleeved shirts or blouses and long trousers, repellants and nets. Clothes are now available impregnated with the insecticide Permethrin or Deltamethrin or it is possible to impregnate the clothes yourself. Wide meshed nets impregnated with Permethrin are also available, are lighter to carry and less claustrophobic to sleep in.

Prophylaxis and treatment

If your itinerary takes you into a malarial area, seek expert advice before you go on a suitable prophylactic regime. This is especially true for pregnant women who are particularly prone to catch malaria. You can still catch the disease even when sticking to a proper regime, although it is unlikely. If you do develop symptoms (high fever, shivering, headache, sometimes diarrhoea), seek medical advice immediately. If this is not possible and there is a great likelihood of malaria, the treatment is:

Chloroquine, a single dose of 4 tablets (600 mg) followed by 2 tablets (300 mg) in 6 hours and 300 mg each day following.

Falciparum type of malaria or type in doubt: take local advice. Various combinations of drugs are being used such as Quinine, Tetracycline or Halofantrine. If falciparum type malaria is definitely diagnosed, it is wise to get to a good hospital as treatment can be complex and the illness very serious.

INFECTIOUS HEPATITIS (JAUNDICE)

The main symptoms are pains in the stomach, lack of appetite, lassitude and yellowness of the eyes and skin. Medically speaking there are two main types. The less serious, but more common is Hepatitis A for which the best protection os the careful preparation of food, the avoidance of contaminated drinking water and scrupulous attention to toilet hygiene. The other, more serious, version is Hepatitis B which is ac-

quired usually as a sexually transmitted disease or by blood transfusions. It can less commonly be transmitted by injections with unclean needles and possibly by insect bites. The symptoms are the same as for Hepatitis A. The incubation period is much longer (up to 6 months compared with 6 weeks) and there are more likely to be complications.

Hepatitis A can be protected against with gamma globulin. It should be obtained from a reputable source and is certainly useful for travellers who intende to live rough. You should have a shot before leaving and have it repeated every 6 months. The dose of gamma globulin depends on the concentration of the particular preparation used, so the manufacturer's advice should be taken. The injection should be given as close as possible to your departure and as the dose depends on the likely time you are to spend in potentially affected areas, the manufacturer's instructions should be followed. Gamma globulin has really been superceded now by a proper vaccination against Hepatitis A (Havrix) which gives immunity lasting up to 10 years. After that boosters are required. Havrix monodose is now widely available as is Junior Havrix. The vaccination has negligible side effects and is extremely effective. Gamma globulin injections can be a bit painful, but it is much cheaper than Havrix and may be more available in some places.

Hepatitis B can be effectively prevented by a specific vaccine (Engerix) – 3 shots over 6 months before travelling. If you have had jaundice in the past it would be worthwhile having a blood test to see if you are immune to either of these two types, because this might avoid the necessity and costs of vaccination or gamma globulin. There are other kinds of viral hepatitis (C, E etc) which are fairly similar to A and B, but vaccines are not available as yet.

TYPHUS

Can still occur carried by ticks. There is usually a reaction at the site of the bite and a fever. Seek medical advice.

INTESTINAL WORMS

These are common and the more serious ones such as hookworm can be contracted from walking barefoot on infested earth or beaches.

Various other tropical diseases can be caught in jungle areas, usually transmitted by biting insects. They are often related to African diseases and were probably introduced by the slave labour trade. Onchocerciasis (river blindness) carried by black flies is found in parts of Mexico and Venezuela. Leishmaniasis (Espundia) is carried by sandflies and causes a sore that will not heal or a severe nasal infection. Wearing long trousers and a long sleeved shirt in infected areas protects against these flies. DET is also effective. Epidemics of meningitis occur from time-to-time. Be careful about swimming in piranha or caribe infested rivers. It is a good idea not to swim naked: the Candiru fish can follow urine currents and become lodged in body orifices. Swimwear offers some protection.

LEPTOSPIROSIS

Various forms of leptospirosis occur throughout Latin America, transmitted by a bacterium which is excreted in rodent urine. Fresh water and moist soil harbour the organisms which enter the body through cuts and scratches. If you suffer from any form of prolonged fever consult a doctor.

SNAKE BITE

This is a very rare event indeed for travellers. If you are unlucky (or careless) enough to be bitten by a venomous snake, spider, scorpion or sea creature, try to identify the creature, but do not put yourself in further danger. Snake bites in particular are very frightening, but in fact rarely poisonous – even venomous snakes bite without injecting venom. What you might expect if bitten are: fright, swelling, pain and bruising around the bite and soreness of the regional lymph glands, perhaps nausea, vomiting and a fever. Signs of serious poisoning would be the following symptoms: numbness and tingling of the face, muscular spasms, convulsions, shortness of breath and bleeding. Victims should be got to a hospital or a doctor without delay. Commercial snake bite and scorpion kits are available, but usually only useful for the specific type of snake or scorpion for which they are designed. Most serum has to be given

intravenously so it is not much good equipping yourself with it unless you are used to making injections into veins. It is best to rely on local practice in these cases, because the particular creatures will be known about locally and appropriate treatment can be given.

Treatment of snake bite Reassure and comfort the victim frequently. Immobilize the limb by a bandage or a splint or by getting the person to lie still. Do not slash the bite area and try to suck out the poison because this sort of heroism does more harm than good. If you know how to use a tourniquet in these circumstances, you will not need this advice. If you are not experienced do not apply a tourniquet.

Precautions

Avoid walking in snake territory in bare feet or sandals – wear proper shoes or boots. If you encounter a snake stay put until it slithers away, and do not investigate a wounded snake. Spiders and scorpions may be found in the more basic hotels, especially in the Andean countries. If stung, rest and take plenty of fluids and call a doctor. The best precaution is to keep beds away from the walls and look inside your shoes and under the toilet seat every morning. Certain tropical sea fish when trodden upon inject venom into bathers' feet. This can be exceptionally painful. Wear plastic shoes when you go bathing if such creatures are reported. The pain can be relieved by immersing the foot in extremely hot water for as long as the pain persists.

DENGUE FEVER

This is increasing worldwide including in South and Central American countries and the Caribbean. It can be completely prevented by avoiding mosquito bites in the same way as malaria. No vaccine is available. Dengue is an unpleasant and painful disease, presenting with a high temperature and body pains, but at least visitors are spared the more serious forms (haemorrhagic types) which are more of a problem for local people who have been exposed to the disease more than once. There is no specific treatment for dengue – just pain killers and rest.

CHAGAS' DISEASE (SOUTH AMERICAN TRYPANOSOMIASIS)

This is a chronic disease, very rarely caught by travellers and difficult to treat. It is transmitted by the simultaneous biting and excreting of the Reduvid bug, also known as the Vinchuca or Barbeiro. Somewhat resembling a small cockroach, this nocturnal bug lives in poor adobe houses with dirt floors often frequented by opossums. If you cannot avoid such accommodation, sleep off the floor with a candle lit, use a mosquito net, keep as much of your skin covered as possible, use DET repellent or a spray insecticide. If you are bitten overnight (the bites are painless) do not scratch them, but wash thoroughly with soap and water.

DANGEROUS ANIMALS

Apart from mosquitos the most dangerous animals are men, be they bandits or behind steering wheels. Think carefully about violent confrontations and wear a seat belt if you are lucky enough to have one available to you.

WHEN YOU RETURN HOME

Remember to take your antimalarial tablets for 6 weeks after leaving the malarial area. If you have had attacks of diarrhoea it is worth having a stool specimen tested in case you have picked up amoebas. If you have been living rough, blood tests may be worthwhile to detect worms and other parasites. If you have been exposed to bilharzia (*schistosomiasis*) by swimming in lakes etc, check by means of a blood test when you get home, but leave it for 6 weeks because the test is slow to become positive. Report any untowards symptoms to your doctor and tell the doctor exactly where you have been and, if you know, what the likelihood of disease is to which you were exposed.

The above information has been compiled for us by Dr David Snashall, who is presently Senior Lecturer in Occupational Health at the United Medical Schools of Guy's and St Thomas' Hospitals in London and Chief Medical Adviser to the British Foreign and Commonwealth Office. He has travelled extensively in Central and South America, worked in Peru and in East Africa and keeps in close touch with developments in preventative and tropical medicine.

Travelling with children

PEOPLE CONTEMPLATING overland travel in South America with children should remember that a lot of time can be spent waiting for buses, trains, and especially for aeroplanes. On bus journeys, if the children are good at amusing themselves, or can readily sleep while travelling, the problems can be considerably lessened. If your child is of an early reading age, take reading material with you as it is difficult, and expensive to find. A bag of, say 30 pieces, of Duplo or Lego can keep young children occupied for hours. Travel on trains, while not as fast or at times as comfortable as buses, allows more scope for moving about. Some trains provide tables between seats, so that games can be played. Beware of doors left open for ventilation especially if air-conditioning is not working.

Food

Food can be a problem if the children are not adaptable. It is easier to take biscuits, drinks, bread etc with you on longer trips than to rely on meal stops where the food may not be to taste. Avocados are safe, easy to eat and nutritious; they can be fed to babies as young as 6 months and most older children like them. A small immersion heater and jug for making hot drinks is invaluable, but remember that electric current varies. Try and get a dual-voltage one (110v and 220v).

Fares

On all long-distance buses you pay for each seat, and there are no half-fares if the children occupy a seat each. For shorter trips it is cheaper, if less comfortable, to seat small children on your knee. Often there are spare seats which children can occupy after tickets have been collected. In city and local excursion buses, small children generally do not pay a fare, but are not entitled to a seat when paying customers are standing. On sightseeing tours you should *always* bargain for a family rate – often children can go free. (In trains, reductions for children are general, but not universal.)

All civil airlines charge half for children under 12, but some military services don't have half-fares, or have younger age limits. Children's fares on Lloyd Aéreo Boliviano are considerably more than half, and there is only a 7kg baggage allowance. (LAB also checks children's ages on passports.) Note that a child travelling free on a long excursion is not always covered by the operator's travel insurance; it is adviseable to pay a small premium to arrange cover.

Hotels

In all hotels, try to negotiate family rates. If charges are per person, always insist that two children will occupy one bed only, therefore counting as one tariff. If rates are per bed, the same applies. In either case you can almost always get a reduced rate at cheaper hotels. Occasionally when travelling with a child you will be refused a room in a hotel that is "unsuitable". On river boat trips, unless you have very large hammocks, it may be more comfortable and cost effective to hire a 2-berth cabin for 2 adults and a child. (In restaurants, you can normally buy children's helpings, or divide one full-size helping between two children.)

Travel with children can bring you into closer contact with Latin American families and, generally, presents no special problems – in fact the path is often smoother for family groups. Officials tend to be more amenable where children are concerned and they are pleased if your child knows a little Spanish or Portuguese. Moreover, even thieves and pickpockets seem to have some of the traditional respect for families, and may leave you alone because of it!

Tinted boxes

Illustrations

CLIMATE CHARTS

Advertisers

Insurance tips

Insurance companies have tightened up considerably over recent years and it is now almost impossible to claim successfully if you have not followed procedures closely. The problem is that these often involve dealing with the country's red tape which can lead to some inconvenience at best and to some quite long delays at worst. There is no substitute for suitable precautions against petty crime.

The level of insurance that you carry is often dictated by the sums of medical insurance which you carry. It is inevitably the highest if you go through the USA. Also don't forget to obtain sports extensions if you are going to go diving, rafting, climbing etc. Most policies do not cover very high levels of baggage/cash. Don't forget to check whether you can claim on your household insurance. They often have worldwide all risks extensions. Most policies exclude manual work whilst away although working in bars or restaurants is usually alright.

Here are our tips: they apply to most types of policies but always check the details of your own policy before you leave.

1. Take the policy with you (a photocopy will do but make sure it is a complete one).

2. Do not travel against medical advice. It will invalidate the medical insurance part of the cover.

3. There is a 24 hour medical emergency service helpline associated with your insurance. You need to contact them if you require in-patient hospital treatment or you need to return home early. The telephone number is printed on the policy. Make sure you note the time of the call, the person you were talking to and get a reference number. Even better get a receipt from the telephone company showing the number you called. Should you need to be airlifted home, this is always arranged through the insurance company's representative and the hospital authorities. Ironically this can lead to quite intense discussions which you will not be aware of: the local hospital is often quite keen to keep you!

4. If you have to cancel your trip for whatever reason, contact your travel agent, tour operator or airline without delay.

5. If your property is damage by an airline, report it immediately and always within 3 days and get a "property irregularity report" from them.

6. Claims for baggage left unattended are very rarely settled unless they were left in a securely locked hotel room, apartment etc; locked in the boot of a car and there is evidence of a forced entry; cash is carried on your person or is in a locked safe or security box.

7. All loss must be reported to the police and/or hotel authorities within 24 hours of discovery and a written report obtained.

8. If medical attention is received for injury or sickness, a medical certificate showing its nature must be obtained, although some companies waive this if only out-patient treatment is required. Keep all receipts in a safe place as they will be needed to substantiate the claim.

9. Check your policy carefully to see if there is a date before which claims must be submitted. This is often within 30 days of returning home. It is now usual for companies to want your policy document, proof that you actually travelled (airline ticket or travel agent's confirmation of booking), receipts and written reports (in the event of loss). **NB** photocopies are not accepted.

TEMPERATURE CONVERSION TABLE

°C	°F	°C	°F
1	34	26	79
2	36	27	81
3	38	28	82
4	39	29	84
5	41	30	86
6	43	31	88
7	45	32	90
8	46	33	92
9	48	34	93
10	50	35	95
11	52	36	97
12	54	37	99
13	56	38	100
14	57	39	102
15	59	40	104
16	61	41	106
17	63	42	108
18	64	43	109
19	66	44	111
20	68	45	113
21	70	46	115
22	72	47	117
23	74	48	118
24	75	49	120
25	77	50	122

The formula for converting °C to °F is:
$$(°C \times 9 \div 5) + 32 = °F$$

and for converting to °C is:
$$(°F - 32) \times 5 \div 9 = °C$$

WEIGHTS AND MEASURES

Metric

Weight
1 Kilogram (Kg) = 2.205 pounds
1 metric ton = 1.102 short tons

Length
1 millimetre (mm) = 0.03937 inch
1 metre = 3.281 feet
1 kilometre (km) = 0.621 mile

Area
1 heactare = 2.471 acres
1 square km = 0.386 sq mile

Capacity
1 litre = 0.220 imperial gallon
     = 0.264 US gallon

Volume
1 cubic metre (m^3) = 35.31 cubic feet
     = 1.31 cubic yards

British and US

Weight
1 pound (lb) = 454 grams
1 short ton (2,000lbs) = 0.907 m ton
1 long ton (2,240lbs) = 1.016 m tons

Length
1 inch = 25.417 millimetres
1 foot (ft) = 0.305 metre
1 mile = 1.609 kilometres

Area
1 acre = 0.405 hectare
1 sq mile = 2.590 sq kilometre

Capacity
1 imperial gallon = 4.546 litres
1 US gallon = 3.785 litres

Volume
1 cubic foot (cu ft) = 0.028 m^3
1 cubic yard (cu yd) = 0.765 m^3

NB 5 imperial gallons are approximately equal to 6 US gallons

Index

Maps

Map Symbols

Administration

International Border

State / Province Border

Cease Fire Line

Neighbouring country

Neighbouring state

State Capitals □

Other Towns ○

Roads and travel

Main Roads
(National Highways)

Other Roads

Jeepable Roads, Tracks

Railways with station

Water features

River *Amazon*

Lakes, Reservoirs, Tanks

Seasonal Marshlands

Sand Banks, Beaches

Ocean

Waterfall

Ferry

Topographical features

Contours (approx),
Rock Outcrops

Mountains

Mountain Pass

Gorge

Escarpment

Palm trees

Cities and towns

Built Up Areas

One Way Street

National Parks, Gardens, Stadiums

Fortified Walls

Airport ⊗

Banks ⑤

Bus Stations (named in key)

Hospitals ⊕

Market ⓜ

Police station ⓟ

Post Office ⊜

Telegraphic Office

Tourist Office ⓘ

Key Numbers ❶ ❷ ❸ ❹ ❺

Bridges

Cathedral, church ✝

Guided routes

National parks, trekking areas

National Parks and
Bird Sanctuaries ◆

Hide

Camp site ⚑

Refuge

Motorable track

Walking track

Other symbols

Archaeological Sites

Places of Interest ○

Viewing point

Footprint Handbooks

All of us at Footprint Handbooks hope you have enjoyed reading and travelling with this Handbook. As our story starts back in the early 1920s we thought it would be interesting to chronicle our development.

It all started 75 years ago in 1921, with the publication of the Anglo-South American Handbook. In 1924 the South American Handbook was created. This has been published each year for the last 74 years and is the longest running guidebook in the English language, immortalised by Graham Greene as "the best travel guide in existence." Celebrations, presumably, next year as we hit the 75th annual edition!

One of the key strengths of the South American Handbook over the years has been the extraordinary contact we have had with our readers through their hundreds of letters to us in Bath. From these letters we learnt that you wanted more Handbooks of the same quality to other parts of the world.

In 1989 my brother Patrick and I set about developing a series modelled on the South American Handbook. Our aim was to create the ultimate practical guidebook series for all travellers, providing expert knowledge of far flung

places, explaining culture, places and people in a balanced, lively and clear way. The whole idea hinged, of course, on finding writers who were in tune with our thinking. Serendipity stepped in at exactly the right moment: we were able to bring together a talented group of people who know the countries we cover inside out and whose enthusiasm for travelling in them needed to be communicated.

The series started to steadily grow as we brought out new guides to the Indian sub-continent, Southeast Asia, Africa and Europe. At this stage we were known as Trade & Travel Publications, or "the people who publish the Handbooks!" In 1995 we felt that the time was right to look again at the identity that had brought us all this way and one year later Footprint Handbooks hit the bookshelves.

There are now well over 30 Handbooks in the series and many more in the pipeline but central to all of this is to maintain contact with our readers. Do continue to write to us with all your news, comments and suggestions and in return we will keep you up to date with developments here in the West Country.